T5-BQA-192

HENRY HOWARD
THE POET EARL OF SURREY

The portrait of the Earl of Surrey at Arundel Castle; painter unknown. By courtesy of the National Portrait Gallery, London.

HENRY HOWARD
The Poet Earl of Surrey
A LIFE

W. A. SESSIONS

OXFORD
UNIVERSITY PRESS

OXFORD
UNIVERSITY PRESS

Great Clarendon Street, Oxford OX2 6DP

Oxford University Press is a department of the University of Oxford
and furthers the University's aim of excellence in research, scholarship,
and education by publishing worldwide in

Oxford New York

Athens Auckland Bangkok Bogotá Buenos Aires Calcutta
Cape Town Chennai Dar es Salaam Delhi Florence Hong Kong Istanbul
Karachi Kuala Lumpur Madrid Melbourne Mexico City Mumbai
Nairobi Paris São Paolo Singapore Taipei Tokyo Toronto Warsaw

and associated companies in Berlin Ibadan

Oxford is a registered trade mark of Oxford University Press
in the UK and in certain other countries

Published in the United States
by Oxford University Press Inc., New York

First published 1999

British Library Cataloguing Publication Data
Data available

Library of Congress Cataloging in Publication Data
Sessions, William A.
Henry Howard, the poet Earl of Surrey: a life / W. A. Sessions.
Includes bibliographical references and index.
1. Surrey, Henry Howard, Earl of, 1517?–1547. 2. Poets, English—Early
modern, 1500–1700—Biography. 3. Nobility—Great Britain—Biography.
4. Humanists—England—Biography. I. Title
PR2373.S475 1999 821'.2—dc21 [b] 98-37016

ISBN 0-19-818624-X

1 3 5 7 9 10 8 6 4 2

Typeset in Sabon
by Alliance Phototypesetters, Pondicherry, India
Printed in Great Britain
on acid-free paper by
Bookcraft Ltd, Midsomer Norton, Somerset

Contents

PART III 'Enough Survives'

List of Plates

COLOUR

BLACK AND WHITE

Preface

This book tells the life-story of Henry Howard (1516–1547) or, as he is identified in the chronology of the Dukes of Norfolk and the Howard family, the poet Earl of Surrey. As the story of both an innovative poet and an earl intimately involved in the political life of his time, the book builds on both poetry and history. It must deal, in fact, with considerably more, especially as there has been no standard edition of the poet's work or comprehensive biography in the 450 years since his beheading. Not only are new interpretations needed, but the reinterpreting and juxtaposing of materials from literature, rhetoric, history, art history, theology, and the whole wealth of learning the period of Henry VIII brought forth. If crossing boundaries defines the method of this book, the intent of such cross-pollination of disciplines is to concentrate for the reader the complex moment of Surrey's activity, the life out of which came the production of his lyrics, translations, and religious paraphrases, and the invention of innovative forms enduring for over 400 years, notably blank verse and the English sonnet. It will also reveal the role of a poet writing and creating new forms in the midst of violence induced by his world and by his own nature.

The image of the poet writing in the midst of violence interested me from the start. In my earlier book on Surrey, I analysed his verse in detail, showing Surrey's humanist training, his rhetorical power, and his technical genius. But to understand the act of his writing a poem and originating what became the most powerful poetic forms in the English language demanded, I realized, a series of concentric circles. Surrey's solipsism, his personal origination in a period of massive historical displacement, demanded the formation of what is now called a 'cultural' biography. Thus, in order to get at that central act of originating a poem in the midst of violence, I had to ask the question Quentin Skinner requires: what was the author—in my case, the poet—*doing* when he wrote the text? What was the cultural matrix, past, present, and future, that surrounded Surrey's moments of origination? In other words, to get at what J. G. A. Pocock calls 'sophisticated verbal performances that are certainly events', I had to reconstitute 'a context, or a series of contexts, in which the text as event may be rendered intelligible'—and in my case, not only to the historian but to the literary critic (and even the art historian, the psychologist, and the sociologist).[1]

Furthermore, as I discovered, Surrey's texts have extraordinary generational force, a context of genealogies that range from the bizarre (as in the Geraldine

[1] Quentin Skinner, *The Foundations of Modern Political Thought* (1978), vol. 1, p. xiii. J. G. A. Pocock, 'Texts as Events: Reflections on the History of Political Thought' in *Politics of Discourse: The Literature and History of Seventeenth-century England*, ed. Kevin Sharpe and Steven N. Zwicker (1987), 28–9, 31.

myth) to central texts of Marlowe, Shakespeare, Milton, Wordsworth, Browning, and, in this century, Stevens and Frost. 'A text,' says Pocock, 'is an actor in its own history, and a polyvalent text acts in a multiplicity of concurrent histories.' Thus, the poet who creates such a text or a polyvalent form like blank verse amid violent history may not be the Wordsworthian poet recollecting emotions in tranquillity. Yet in violence that poet may create liberating forms, having survived not death but history and produced, in Eliot's phrase, a 'still point of the turning world', at least a recurring form or text that can be recapitulated, as in Surrey's blank verse, for example, to tell other violent histories.

But what gave birth to this polyvalent form and text—at least as I tell this story—was Surrey's own history. Only in his life can the reader recognize the bloody dialectic between Surrey as poet and Surrey as earl, out of which rose his mimetic texts. Beheaded at 30, Surrey was heir to the greatest title in early Tudor England outside the royal family (a title with its own turbulence), as well as first cousin to the Queens Anne Boleyn and Catherine Howard. He was also a military hero praised two centuries later by David Hume and a progenitor of the highest nobility of the English Renaissance, including a saint officially canonized in 1970 and a 'collector earl' whose conception of visual art helped to define the modern collection and redefine classicism for his time. Recent discoveries, especially in poetry and art, have given a more complex figuration to this violent history than the 'foolish prowde boy' of readers who have understood Surrey, in the litany of attacks, only as a prisoner of his class, an arrogant neurotic defying hysterically the 'right' progression of history, a rebel of questionable sanity committing 'treasonable follies,' etc. The new complexity hardly denies Surrey's own self-entrapment, least of all his neurosis (both personal and cultural), but it does require a sensitivity to the idea of a poet as an artist (certainly a modern sensitivity) and to the idea of a civilizer, in Surrey's case, the poet earl who revolutionized in his own texts and in his own life concepts of honour and nobility. This transformation of honour and nobility his extensive cult in the late Renaissance understood.

Above all, the new complexity supports the image of the poet who writes and sings in the midst of violence into which he is born and from which he cannot escape. If the story is old—the poet's severed head still singing is an ancient image for Orpheus—it is, for Surrey, told *sub specie Henrici VIII*. As Bakhtin notes, the renewal of literature, form, genre, or text, can only be located in history itself. In this sense, interpretations of history make the difference that may lead to death, to oblivion, or to greater life. In Surrey's radically new interpretation of history that killed him, the poet earl demonstrated a learning and a vision that made him, now and then, a living figure, if ambiguous and mysterious.

To offer some clues for understanding this mystery, I have organized my biography into three parts that roughly correspond to the two main movements of Virgil's *Aeneid*. The Roman epic was obviously at the heart of Surrey's culture as it was at the centre of his greatest undertaking. He translated the *Aeneid* into blank verse, into the new English he intended for the nobility of Britain and for the making of a Renaissance in England. As Pocock notes, 'the most interesting acts of translation are anachronistic.' Thus, with his own kind of anachronism and double vision of history, Surrey's life reflects Aeneas' epic quest, at least in intention, if not achievement. The first chapters (describing the years 1516–37) reveal Surrey's equivalent of the burning city of Troy, the burden of his father and the Howards, and then the special case of his mother, his friendship with Henry Fitzroy, the Duke of Richmond, his sojourns with him in England and France, all to end in Richmond's death in 1536 (among so many others in that year), and in the composition of his first major poems, the Windsor sonnet and elegy, whose subjects are death and disappearance. The second group of chapters—the bulk of the book (1537–46)—focuses on Surrey's drive to build his own new city, his own Rome. These reveal his construction of Surrey House both as the centre of a new nobility and as the nucleus of a new literary language for a special group of friends and family. They also narrate his imprisonments in the period and his psychic conflicts as the two roles of poet and earl begin to pull him apart. These chapters then analyse Surrey's greatest literary achievements, his 1542 elegy on Wyatt and the invention of blank verse. They end with a narrative of his extensive military achievements and his one disaster. The third and final section of the book (1546–7) deals with Surrey's last days, in which the dream of Rome fails; first, the painting of his last portrait, one version of which is at Arundel Castle, then the actual events leading to his arrest, his imprisonment, his trial, and his beheading on 19 January 1547, the end of his quest.

Of course, any organization of Surrey's life, texts, and beheading will have little meaning unless these contexts of existence are rendered as 'intelligible' as possible, and that means for Surrey's life their being seen as *one*, from true beginning to true end. It also means that, although such a biography is detailed, what will be gained in the unity and sweep necessary to narrate the life will be matched, for some readers, by a need for more elaboration. There will be, in short, a need for further work, and this life-story points out, I hope, rich opportunities for new investigation by readers and scholars. For this reason this book should be seen as conjunctive, not definitive. It is an opening to material that has, by and large, been hidden, and I should like this text to extend to interested readers the same cooperation in investigation I have received. This cooperation from so many kind and generous people has been immense, and I hope readers will experience the same when they build their texts on this one.

I can name only a few of those who have supported this project. From the beginning I have been encouraged by David Starkey and Emrys Jones. Starkey understood from the beginning what I intended and patiently and bounteously directed me towards places to work, texts to read, and the stages of research I needed. Professor Jones also understood early what I wanted to do in this project and gave, in visit after visit, his time and interest with a courtesy Castiglione would have honoured. Patricia Thomson also graciously encouraged the writing of Surrey's life and her conversations and reading of drafts guided me. Professor

Robert Knecht has been consistently helpful, especially in the first stages of my work in England, where I was quite lost, directing me, among other places, to the Institute of Historical Research in London, where I found, as in all the British libraries I have used, a peaceful place to work. I thank His Grace the Duke of Norfolk for his early interest in this project and for his hospitality at Arundel Castle, where, thanks to the generous assistance of Mrs Ian Rodger, I found texts, portraits, and archival material that illuminate Surrey's life. Alasdair Hawkyard has provided me with resource after resource, not least those of his own perceptions; Margaret Aston has been a stalwart supporter and thoughtful listener; Greg Walker has nobly read through various versions of the manuscript. I am grateful to all the editors at Oxford University Press with whom I have worked, especially Jason Freeman. On this side of the Atlantic, I am grateful for grants from the Georgia State University Office of Research and Sponsored Programs and its director, Dr Cleon Arrington, and for travel grants from the National Endowment for the Humanities. I am especially thankful to Professor Arthur F. Kinney, who initially directed me to the study of Surrey and who has always shown an interest in my work, to Sally Fitzgerald, and to Patricia Graves for her continuous readings of this text. I have also appreciated the support of colleagues at Georgia State University, especially my Renaissance comrades, as well as Marion L. Kuntz, Virginia Spencer Carr, Robert Arrington, Patricia Bryan, Robert Sattelmeyer, Dean Ahmed Abdelal, and Provost Ron Henry. In the early stages of writing, I appreciated conversations with our family friend, Dr Walker Percy, especially on the concept of honour. Any sense of narrative writing or literary form I owe to my earliest teacher of writing, Caroline Gordon, who was the first to show me the depths not only of a literary text but of history itself. I have appreciated the interest in my work on Surrey shown by John Hollander, Geoffrey Hill, and Jon Stallworthy; if the idea of the poet behind this biography has any validity at all, their own texts have helped me to understand that idea. Of course, they and all the others who have helped me are not responsible for my own failures to understand enough. My sons, Dr Eric A. Sessions and Dr Andrew C. Sessions, have supported a project whose importance they could only understand by faith alone. As always, I owe gratitude to my mother, Lee Cooper Sessions, for first bringing me to the love of poetry and literature, and to my father, Augustus Carl Sessions, for showing me how history and legend lead to moral encounters. The greatest debt is to my wife, Zenobia Urania, who has given me the sense of beauty and hope that has been my greatest strength in conceiving and writing this book, a text that is finally, to transpose Milton, 'hers who brings it nightly to my ear'.

W. A. *Sessions*
March 1998

Abbreviations

AH	*The Arundel Harington Manuscript of Tudor Poetry*, ed. Ruth Hughey. 2 vols. Columbus, 1960.
APC	*Acts of the Privy Council of England*, ed. J. R. Dasent. 32 vols. London, 1890–1907.
CPR	*Calendar Patent Rolls 1548–1549*. London, 1914–16.
CSP	*Calendar State Papers, Foreign*. 23 vols. London, 1863–1950.
DNB	*Dictionary of National Biography*.
EHR	*English Historical Review*.
G	Manuscript of Ellis Gruffydd in the National Library of Wales, Mostyn MS, 158, as translated by M. Bryn Davies, 'Surrey at Boulogne', *Huntington Library Quarterly*, 23 (1960), 339–48.
HA	Edward Hall, *Chronicle Containing the History of England During the Reign of Henry the Eighth*, ed. J. Johnson et al. London, 1809; reprint, New York, 1965.
HB	Edward, Lord Herbert of Cherbury. *The History of England under Henry VIII*. London, 1870.
HJ	*Historical Journal* (formerly *Cambridge Historical Journal*).
HLQ	*Huntington Library Quarterly*.
HMC	*Historical Manuscripts Commission*.
LP	*Letters and Papers, Foreign and Domestic, of the Reign of Henry VIII, 1509–47*, ed. J. S. Brewer et al. 21 vols. and 2 vols. addenda. London, 1862–1932.
M	Kenneth Muir, *Life and Letters of Sir Thomas Wyatt*. Liverpool, 1963.
MT	*The Collected Poems of Sir Thomas Wyatt*, ed. Kenneth Muir and Patricia Thomson. Liverpool 1969.
N	*The Works of Henry Howard, Earl of Surrey, and of Sir Thomas Wyatt the Elder*, ed. G. F. Nott. 2 vols. London, 1815–16.
NRO	Norfolk Record Office, Norwich.
OED	*Oxford English Dictionary*.
RES	*Review of English Studies*.
SP	*State Papers published under the authority of His Majesty's Commission, King Henry VIII*. 11 vols. London, 1830–52.
W	Charles Wriothesley, *A Chronicle of England During the Reign of the Tudors from A.D. 1485–1559*, ed. William Douglas Hamilton, F.S.A. London, 1865; reprint, New York, 1965.

Genealogy of Henry Howard, Earl of Surrey

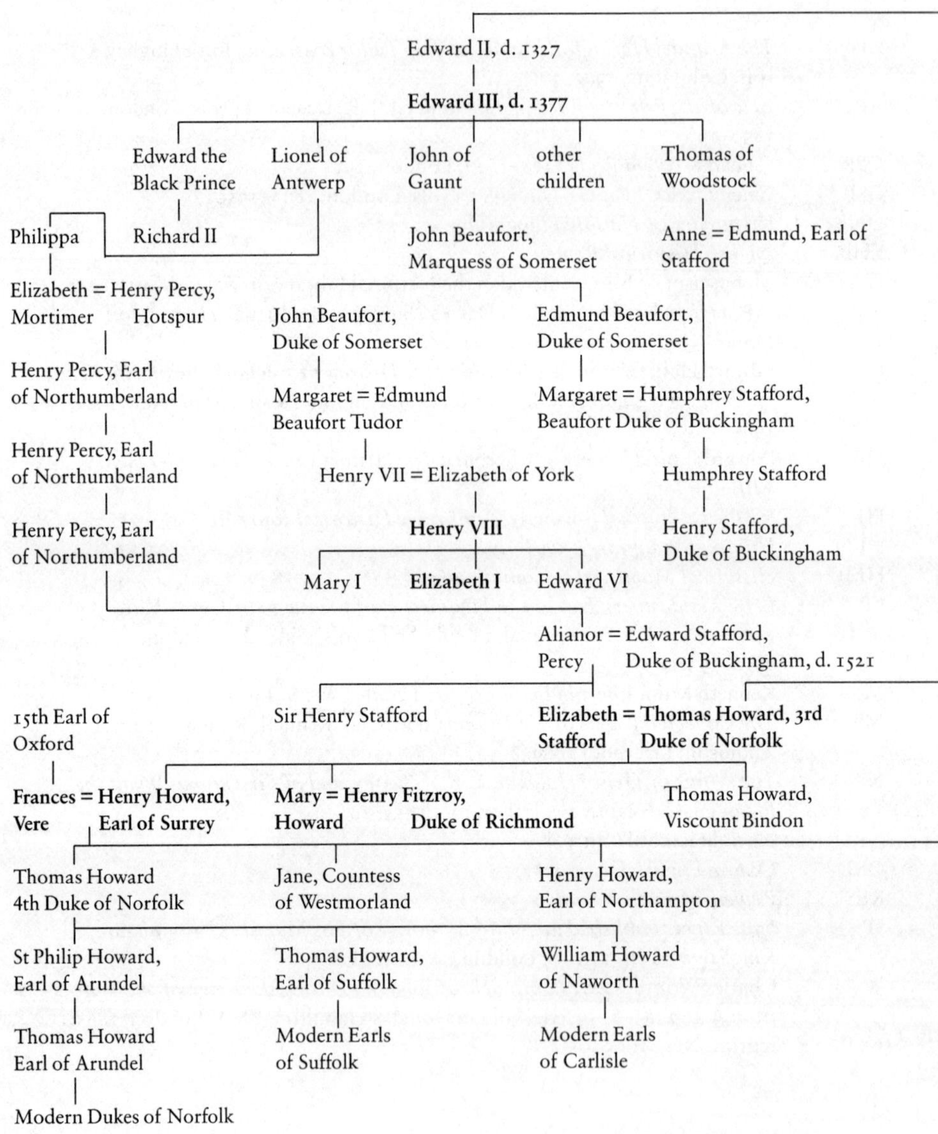

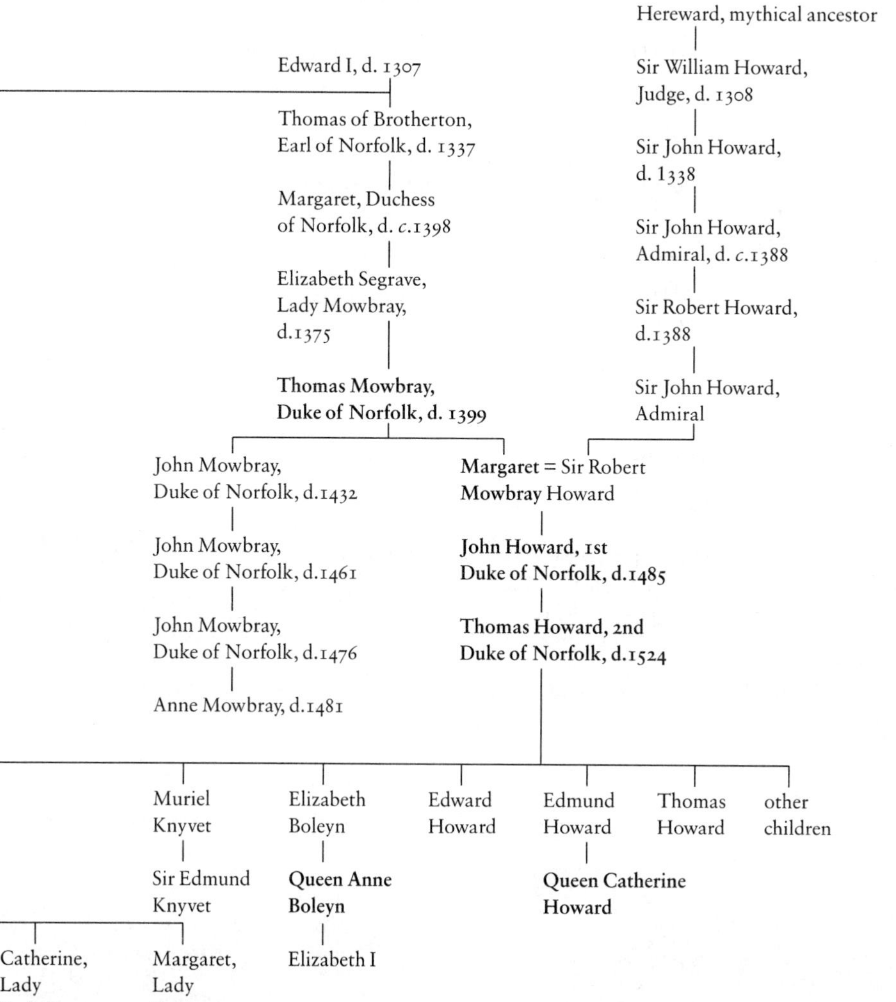

Hereward, mythical ancestor
Edward I, d. 1307
Sir William Howard, Judge, d. 1308
Thomas of Brotherton, Earl of Norfolk, d. 1337
Sir John Howard, d. 1338
Margaret, Duchess of Norfolk, d. c.1398
Sir John Howard, Admiral, d. c.1388
Elizabeth Segrave, Lady Mowbray, d.1375
Sir Robert Howard, d.1388
Thomas Mowbray, Duke of Norfolk, d. 1399
Sir John Howard, Admiral
John Mowbray, Duke of Norfolk, d.1432
Margaret Mowbray = Sir Robert Howard
John Mowbray, Duke of Norfolk, d.1461
John Howard, 1st Duke of Norfolk, d.1485
John Mowbray, Duke of Norfolk, d.1476
Thomas Howard, 2nd Duke of Norfolk, d.1524
Anne Mowbray, d.1481
Muriel Knyvet
Elizabeth Boleyn
Edward Howard
Edmund Howard
Thomas Howard
other children
Sir Edmund Knyvet
Queen Anne Boleyn
Queen Catherine Howard
Catherine, Lady Berkeley
Margaret, Lady Scrope
Elizabeth I

Descent of Henry Howard, Earl of Surrey, from the Anglo-Saxon Kings

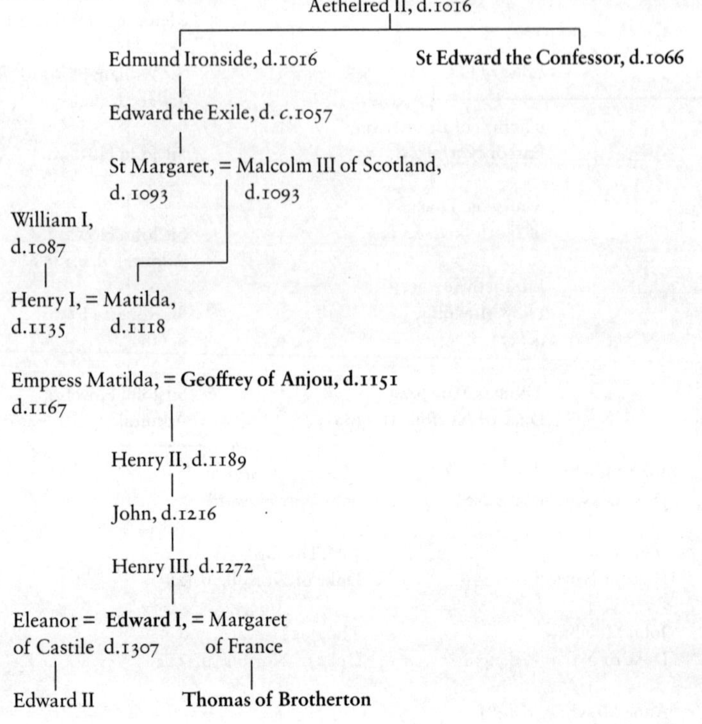

Prologue

On Wednesday, 19 January 1547, Henry Howard, the poet Earl of Surrey, was beheaded. His execution, the last in the reign of Henry VIII, took place on Tower Hill just north-west of the Tower of London. The young earl had walked up Tower Hill, ascended the nine steps of the scaffold, spoken, and then thrust his body forward, hands and arms outstretched and head across the block. After the executioner had raised his axe and brought it down, the poet's head, still bleeding, and his torso, cut loose and also bleeding, were thrown into a waiting wagon. The severed head and body were then taken to the nearby London church of All Hallows, Barking, where they were hastily entombed. Within weeks, the first elegy in a long line went straight to the shock of the event.

In his poem, Sir John Cheke is still stunned by Surrey's execution. The earl had embodied for him an identity so new it was almost a paradox: an originating poet—the greatest in England in 1547—who was also heir to the foremost dynasty outside the royal family and 'by upbringing and aspiration . . . a prince'. In his elegy, the reformed Christian humanist cannot control the flow of response in his English hexametres (themselves imitating Surrey's recent invention of the form in the Tower). As Steward of the University of Cambridge, the earl may have defended Cheke's pioneering Greek studies and, before his arrest, certainly represented for Cheke and many others the promise of a greater Renaissance in England, especially in promulgating the new diction Cheke had called for. Now friendship and admiration had turned to shock, and the ambiguity that always surrounded Surrey appears in this first elegy.

> What natures worke is this, in one wightes Corps to hyde
> so gaye gyftes and so badd, ill mixte without ameane
> The happie head of witt, the tongue well sett to speake
> the skilfull pen in hand to paynt the wittes device
> Vncerten is the rest whiche shame will not discrye
> nor rage with stroke of tongue that bittrest egg to byte

Cheke is fascinated by Surrey's body of contradictions, its severed 'head of witt', the silent tongue, and even the hand with 'skillful pen' now stilled on the mangled torso. Shame and dishonour have come upon this 'Corps', and Cheke as tutor to the new King Edward could only have been horrified at Surrey's indictment. Even for Cheke to inscribe an elegy on that 'Corps' took courage so soon in the regime that had branded the poet earl as a traitor threatening its stability and succession. Above all, the great scholar cannot fully express his 'rage' before 'that bittrest egg to byte', the bloody death of a body of such promise and the strange indeterminancy of history that allows such loss in nature.

Such was natures device, so fyne in sute to molde
and plentiful to make one kynd with shifted sorte
thie headd she made of witt, a paragon, of tongue
a subtill toole to fyle the rowghe hewen to the best,
of style a Streame to flowe, with conning to endyte
Whiche envie wyll denye moste perfectst grace to have
suche seldome thewes of kinde, is selde in one head fownd[1]

Yet, for Cheke, Surrey's 'Corps', despite its 'moste perfectst grace', remains ambivalent. On the one hand, Surrey's body—'the happie head of witt'—had sought to transfigure his own role as true 'prince' with the noble 'aspiration' of a special art—'of style a Streame to flowe'. Such texts the poet (with Cheke) had believed would bring about a new Rome, the Renaissance Surrey had seen in Fontainebleau, which his new translation of Virgil's entire *Aeneid* in his innovative English heroic line of blank verse could climax. With 'seldome thewes of kind . . . selde in one head fownd,' England's greatest living poet had sought a *Romanitas* that located itself for Surrey and Cheke, like Dante and all true classicists, in a new history, one's own special time and place. On the other hand, the young male body that attracted Cheke had projected itself as a clear threat to the dispensation of the realm of Henry VIII. This was now the realm of Edward VI and his uncle Edward Seymour, the new Duke of Somerset and Lord Protector. The earl had been condemned for misusing the signs of honour—a false coat of arms, a final portrait with prophetic emblems—to make himself appear the rightful Protector of the young king. This inexplicable defiance of the new state ahead—a state that, for Cheke, embodied superiority of doctrine and learning, control of the future, enlightenment for the next centuries—is a 'shame' Cheke cannot describe. All the indeterminancy of the 'Corps' and the event of its destruction is thus the 'bittrest egg to byte', even for one who was for Milton the hero of the early English Renaissance, the great 'soul of Sir John Cheke' whose age 'When thou taught'st Cambridge, and King Edward Greek' was, as Milton said in his divorce tract *Tetrachordon*, 'on record for the purest and sincerest that ever shone yet on the reformation of this Iland'.[2]

[1] The quotation describing Surrey is from Susan Brigden, 'Henry Howard, Earl of Surrey, and the "Conjured League" ', *Historical Journal*, 373 (1994), 509. The nine steps of the scaffold can be seen in van den Wyngaerde's 1549 drawing of Tower Hill in the collection of his drawings at the Ashmolean Museum, Oxford. As Steward of Cambridge, Surrey may have defended Cheke's innovations against the Bishop of Winchester, a Howard family friend; Cheke clearly had some powerful support in a linguistic debate of no major interest to the king or court but probably of importance for Surrey. See the episode in John Strype, *The Life of Sir John Cheke* (1881), 15–18. The Cheke elegy is in *The Arundel Harington Manuscript of Tudor Poetry*, ed. Ruth Hughey (1960), vol 1,332, cited hereafter in text.

[2] For a concept of *Romanitas* similar to Surrey's, see Frank Kermode, *The Classic* (1975), 15–16 and his view that the *Aeneid* can, as classic, 'be more or less immediately relevant and available, in a sense contemporaneous with the modern.' For The Milton references, see *The Poems of John Milton*, ed. John Carey and Alastair Fowler (1968), 306. Hereafter all reference to Milton's poetry will be to this text and listed by poem and line number if needed. The *Tetrachordon* line is in *Complete Prose Works of John Milton*, ed. Don M. Wolfe (1959), vol. 2 (1643–1648) 716. All reference to Milton's prose will be to the Yale edition and by page number in the text.

What Milton, writing his sonnet in the midst of the English Revolution, saw in Cheke is what Cheke himself had already found in Surrey's beheading: an authenticity of event that may have lacked the certainty of Milton's cultural ideal but did not lack its own powerful originating presence. If all such presence was framed by Surrey's act of treason, by his deliberate resistance, at least for Cheke, to a political and righteous inevitability, grandeur still remained in the new poetic texts. In original forms like the heroic quatrain, the English sonnet, and blank verse, Surrey had turned the older epic and lyric language into contemporary discourse for women and men at court, the ideological centre for all society in Early Modern Europe. Furthermore, grandeur still existed in the surviving portraits, the most striking of which Cheke may have seen unfinished, before the Privy Council took it away as evidence of treason. In its magnificence of emblem and colour, at least in its Arundel Castle version, Surrey's body as portrayed there promises a future that defies inevitability. Whatever the young earl's ambivalence, the presence in the portrait was enduring as the original body vanished.

In fact, as Cheke knew from the humanist motto on the portrait, Surrey intended to convince an audience of a surviving presence. The portrait was to represent the actual body of the poet himself, which body, for a renowned contemporary like the scholar Hadrianus Junius, projected an 'heroic figure', in the 1540s an heroic 'style' and presence ('Heroicum corporis filum'). Thus, in this last portrait, the heroic body of Surrey leans on a broken column, an ancient emblem of endurance. At the base of the fluted golden-red Ionian column, in the dark centre of its plinth, rises the Latin motto 'SAT SVPER EST.' As Cheke recognized, the motto had its own textual genealogy, linguistic wordplay beloved by Renaissance poets in Latin or English and here evoked with deadly serious political intent. The motto 'SAT SVPER EST' says to the Tudor audience that the poet Earl of Surrey survives. He exists, achieves, abounds. The portrait and the life revealed in it hold more than enough to justify the action of a noble earl to bring cultural order to his time and place, a Renaissance for which the unique self in the portrait is more than enough.

Cheke would have recognized the motto's authorization in two Latin sources, both marking endurance through time. The first, from Virgil, occurs in two special places with linguistic variants: at a crucial moment in Book II (567), Aeneas discovers he is the sole survivor fighting in burning Troy ('There was no more but I left of them all' in Surrey's translation, 743); and then in the ecstatic and prophetic climax of Virgil's fourth eclogue (53–55), the poet foresees his own death and cries out to the muse, 'O mihi tum longae maneat pars ultima vitae' ('O that the last part of a long life remain for me'), and then asks 'spiritus et quantum sat erit tua dicere facta' ('may there be breath enough to tell your story') because then 'non me carminibus vincat nec Thracius Orpheus' ('not even Thracian Orpheus can better my songs').

The second source, Seneca, had a major cultural as well as literary influence in Early Modern Europe. More than Virgil, Seneca uses a historicized version of the motto in his combined verb form: 'Medea superest.'[3] In Seneca's Stoic version of the Greek play, psychological realism before the horror of political and familial breakdown fortifies the will. Freedom may still emerge for Seneca in the processes of Nero's state (against which Juvenal, one of Surrey's masters, railed), but only through willed presentation, determined representation of the self as a free survivor controlling fortune. In fact, Surrey's last portrait and motto seem to be saying, a new community such as Sir Thomas More, Thomas Starkey, Sir Thomas Elyot, and Lord Berners had individually envisioned could be formed to survive—as did the generational community Aeneas set sail with to found Rome—if only the viewer will join that body of honour, for whom 'enough survives.' For Cheke, however, the sight and memory of that ambiguous 'Corps' offered, not survival, but pain and the loss of a noble earl who was a noble poet.

The dual genealogy became, in fact, the identifying mark for Surrey, not only in the elegies that followed but in the cult that flourished in the later Renaissance. As Thomas Nashe reiterated in his 1594 popular romance with Surrey as hero, *The Unfortunate Traveller*, the young earl embodied nobility itself: 'Oh, it was a right noble lord, liberality itself, if in this iron age, there were any such creature as liberality left on the earth, a prince in content because a poet without peer.' To reveal nobility of character had been, in fact, the point of the use of Surrey's motto almost four decades later by Surrey's long surviving son Henry Howard, the Jacobean Earl of Northampton. It was to impress a queen unsympathetic to him but one who had a clear memory of her mother's first cousin—'Wherefore, if the dew of my devotion may be drawn up by the beams of your remorse [pity], "SAT SVPEREST;" as once my father wrote on the breach of a distressed hope,' so wrote the son, rhetorically climaxing his dedication to Elizabeth I. After that inscription, William Camden noted Surrey's design of 'a broken piller with this word, *SAT SUPEREST*' and then used it to identify the poet in a stunning conjunction: 'This is that noble Earle of Surrey, who first among the Nobilitie of England, conjoyned the honour of learning to the honour of high Parentage.'

[3] The Hadrianus Junius description of Surrey was quoted by William Camden at the height of the Surrey cult for special Elizabethan and Jacobean audiences just after he had given his own crucial definition of Surrey's dual genealogy in *Remains Concerning Britain* (1984), 183 and added: 'Of whom the learned *Hadrianus Junius* giveth this testimonie in Latine, which I cannot so well express in English: "Heroicum corporis filum, ingenium velox, & expromptum memoria inexhausta, planeque Mythridatica, sermo ob ipsis Gratis effictus, linguarum multiplex cognitio, &c." ' For the most comprehensive account of the career of Hadrianus Junius and especially his activities within the Howard household and world, see Margaret Aston, *The King's Bedpost: Reformation and Iconography in a Tudor Group Portrait* (1993) especially pp. 176–84 and 190–9. *Medea* 166 (Seneca's plays are not designated by acts) but see also the crucial lines of 910 and 170, among others. Surrey thus makes his own variant on this Senecan phrase that Renaissance dramatists like Dolce and Cinthio later appropriated and that in England found its way into Elizabethan and Jacobean drama (written in Surrey's blank verse) as when, for example, John Webster's heroine proclaims: 'I am Duchesse of Malfy still' in *Duchess of Malfi*, IV. ii. 139. See also Massinger's *Duke of Milan* 'I would be Sforza still' in I. i. 190; Shakespeare's 'I am Anthony yet' in III. xiii. 93; and Richard II's 'You may my glories and my state depose / But not my griefs. Still am I king of those' in IV. i. 192–377.

Earlier, elegists following Cheke remarked on the death of the earl whom Cavendish called 'So noble a yong man / of wyt and excellence.' Within a year after his death, the reformer John Bale had described Surrey as 'vir ingeniossimus carminibus anglicis elucidauit' ('a man gifted with genius shone forth in English poetry'). Ironically, the spiral of elegies increasingly saw the initial perplexity of Cheke turn to a certainty that Surrey was a martyr for both genealogies. In fact, Turbeville's 1567 elegy said 'a thousand tongues at will' were needed 'to depaint at full / The flowing fountaine of [Surrey's] sacred Skull' and, in thundering fourteeners, Thomas Churchyard summed up in 1580 the image of the poet earl that followed for the rest of the Renaissance: this body was 'too worthy for the grave, his flesh no meat for worm,' and for this 'Earl of Birth; a god of sprite; a Tully [Cicero] for his tongue,' only 'crooked crafts that his own country wrought / [could] chop off such a chosen head as our time ne'er forth brought.' This sense of an exalted victim distinguished Surrey in one of the most ideologically powerful texts in English until the twentieth century, John Foxe's *Acts and Monuments*, first published in 1559 in Strasbourg during the Marian reign, then in an expanded form in 1563 in England and later called the *Book of Martyrs*. In his four references to the beheaded Surrey, Foxe, like Cheke, saw ambiguity in the events of Surrey's last days but was clear and elegaic about the nobility of this 'worthy and ingenuous gentleman'. He was even clearer about the causes of his destruction: the poet earl was one more example of what evil counsellors or 'makebates' can do to innocence (interestingly, in Surrey's case, Foxe sees no 'heinous purpose of any treason'); furthermore, the poet earl was the victim of Edward Seymour, the Duke of Somerset, a man otherwise greatly to be admired by right-thinking Protestant Englishmen in the new progression of history. Sadly, even Seymour committed two acts that 'distained his honour' and thus brought 'God's scourge and rod' on him; he agreed to the execution of his brother, Sir Thomas Seymour, and he arranged the killing of Surrey.

Over twenty years later, in 1586, Geoffrey Whitney identified Sir Philip Sidney as Surrey's heir in an emblem and poem on the immortality of poetry, noting how when 'The thred of noble SVRREYS life, made hast for to vntwine, / Apollo chang'd his cheare, and lay'd awaie his lute,' only to give it to Sidney. Earlier, in his *Defence of Poesy*, Sidney named Surrey's '*Lyrics*' as one of the four originating texts in all of English literature (along with Chaucer's *Troilus*, Spenser's recent *Shepheardes Calender*, and Sackville's *Mirror for Magistrates*). The only exemplary texts in a depressing dark age, they formed Sidney's new genealogy for the contemporary Renaissance poet. In Sidney's classic inscription, Surrey offers 'many things tasting of a noble birth, and worthy of a noble mind'—a dual genealogy.[4]

[1] Thomas Nashe, *The Unfortunate Traveller and Other Works*, ed. J. B. Steane (1972), 286–7, hereafter cited in text. For Northampton's letter, see Lambeth Palace Library, MS 711, f. 20. George Cavendish, *Metrical Visions*, ed. A. S. G. Edwards (1980), 78–82. This text would be the model in the next decade for the Chaucerian rhyme-royal stanzas of Thomas Sackville's 'Induction' (with its

What Sidney implicitly affirms in his inscription of 'noble' Surrey is the large sense of fluid time, the ease with which the present can move from a liberating past to a liberated future, implied in the concept of genealogy. A system of descents on all levels of society defines what the future might reveal and so promises, in Bloch's terms, a 'mental structure' by which to survive. In this sense, genealogy can be viewed as the cultural basis for all heroic action in the Renaissance. In fact, in that central literary text for all Renaissance genealogy, the *Aeneid* Book VI, Anchises in the underworld narrates a paradigm for Aeneas. It describes social, political, and historical identities, the son's destiny made possible only through the interplay of ancestors and future. But earlier than Book VI in the *Aeneid* came the mandate of genealogy—and the terms of this mandate better define Surrey's motto and the drive of his dual roots. The ghost of Hector brings to the sleeping Aeneas the mandate of generational survival: 'Flee, flee, O goddess' son, / And save thee from the fury of this flame!' in Surrey's translation (2: 367–8). Aeneas must preserve the genetic link for the new city because, as Foucault notes, 'the purpose of history, guided by genealogy, is not to discover the roots of our identity but to commit itself to its dissipation.'[5] Guided by the past, the present body liberates time, continues the line: 'SAT SVPER EST'. Enough survives.

No one understood this concept of genealogy better than Henry VIII. In fact, Surrey had to die because of the force of genealogy, not his own but the king's. Henry VIII had always recognized that his world turned on the proper representation of genealogy, both the oldest forms and the most avant-garde. The king's greatest portrait, Holbein's mural in the Privy Chamber at Whitehall, projected a body that 'resists', in Nietschze's definition of true genealogy, codified abstraction or *progressus* by defining in its own extended Latin motto the son's free

echoes of Surrey) to *Mirrour for Magistrates*. Cavendish's *Life and Death of Cardinal Wolsey* is structured on the rise and fall of the wheel of fortune, the medievel base of Surrey's lament in Cavendish. George Turbeville, *Epitaphes, epigrams, songs and sonnets* (1567), B8v—C1. For Churchyard, *The Works of Henry Howard, Earl of Surrey, and of Sit Thomas Wyatt the Elder*, ed. George Frederick Nott (1965), vol. 1, p. xlvii, hereafter cited as N in text. *The Acts and Monuments of John Foxe*, ed. S. R. Cattley and G. Townsend (1837–41), vol. 5, 399–400, 698; vol. 6, 297, 412. I am indebted for this information on Foxe and Surrey to Col. Peter Moore and his forthcoming essay ' "Gentlemen, of what have you found me guilty?": The Charges Against the Earl of Surrey'. Geoffrey Whitney, *A Choice of Emblemes*, ed. Henry Green, introd. Frank Fieler (1967), 196–7. For Sidney, *The Defense of Poesie* in Allan H. Gilbert, *Literary Criticism: Plato to Dryden* (1962) 448, cited hereafter in text. Raphael Falco, *Conceived Presences: Literary Genealogy in Renaissance England* (1994), 51. See also Falco's whole argument of poetic genealogy within the context of heraldic genealogy. Sidney knew Surrey in the edition of *Tottel's Miscellany* in the Sidney library catalogued *Epigrames &c by the Earle of Surrey, London Anno 1574, 8. [octavo]* as MS KAO U1475/2. I am grateful to Professor Germaine Warkentin for this information.

[5] For the place of genealogy in the period, R. Howard Bloch, *Etymologies and Genealogies: A Literary Anthropology of the French Middle Ages* (1983), 34: genealogy is 'a pervasive association operative at all levels of culture and as close as one may come to a "mental structure" of the age'. Michel Foucault, *Language, Counter-Memory, Practice* (1977), 163, 148. His latter quotation continues: genealogy's 'task is to expose a body totally imprinted by history and the process of history's destruction of the body' and 'genealogy, as an analysis of descent, is situated [in its] articulation of the [present] body and history' and nowhere else.

relationship to the father. Henry VIII's body, in its staging (surrounded by an updated holy family, his father, mother, and the wife who has produced his heir) and in its upright phallus, challenges time, Virgil's 'irreparabile tempus' ('time that cannot be recalled').[6] Not abstract progress, then, but the real presence of Holbein's enormous mural dominates and builds history, not Sidney's 'mouse-eaten records' (418) but myth and legend in art. Against that portrait, Surrey, in his last portrait, leans on a broken column with a Latin motto at its base. Henry VIII understood the total genealogical challenge of Surrey and, whatever the ambiguity of the earl's last portrait, the king was led to another false icon of genealogy. Here signs were official and legal. In the king's eyes, the display of a false coat of arms—the sole charge against Surrey in his bill of indictment—threatened the life of his only living son. Whatever the justice of the charge, the threat was quite real if the genealogy that grounded the culture was imperilled. In his sorrow, Cheke had been right. The death of Surrey—the severed 'head of witt'—was inevitable.

[6] Friedrich Nietzsche, *The Genealogy of Morals*, tr. Francis Golffing (1956), 209–11. '*Progressus*' refers to the idea of progress or an inevitable evolution of time that Nietzsche saw as a particularly English abstraction (embodied in Herbert Spencer). The Holbein portrait of Henry VIII referred to is now known only by the copies made by Remigius van Leemput in 1667 and 1669 now in the Royal Collection, and by the cartoon for the figures of Henry VII and Henry VIII, the crucial genealogical link described in the Latin motto, now in the National Portrait Gallery (4027). See the analysis of the portrait in Roy Strong, *Holbein and Henry VIII* (1967). For the importance of this portrait as a focus for the reign of Henry VIII, see Eric Ives, 'Henry VIII: The Political Perspective', 33–4 (and his excellent translation of the Latin motto) and Diarmaid MacCulloch, 'Introduction', in *The Reign of Henry VIII: Politics, Policy, and Piety*, ed. Diarmaid MacCulloch (1995) 10–11. Another portrait of Henry VIII that shows the force of genealogy came after his death. Cf. Aston, *The King's Bedpost:* for full analysis of this picture and also her *England's Iconoclasts: Vol. I. Laws Against Images* (1988), 210–11, 272; for another kind of genealogy, the archetype of the boy King Josaiah for Edward VI, 249. Also, see Roy C. Strong, 'Edward VI and the Pope', *Journal of the Warburg and Courtauld Institute*, 23 (1960), 311–13; and John King, *English Reformation Literature: The Tudor Origins of the Protestant Tradition* (1982), 294–5.

PART I

The Burning City

1

The Fathers: Two Battles

'It was merry in England afore the new learning came up,' said Surrey's father, Thomas Howard, the third Duke of Norfolk, in an uncontrolled aside. 'Yea,' he added, 'I would all thinges were as hath been in times past.' Such expressed bitterness was rare for this master of the English court who survived from the reign of Edward IV to that of Mary I, outliving six monarchs and watching the medieval world evolve into Early Modern Europe. The outburst came around the spring of 1540 in the tense months before the fall of Thomas Cromwell (Plate 16). The nearly 70-year-old father of the poet Earl of Surrey had found an Exchequer clerk's pious suggestions insolent and snapped at him: 'I have never read Scripture nor ever will read it.'[1] An older culture had vanished before his eyes. The abstract (at least for him) religion of the Word, with its origins in a humanism and 'new learning' he would never understand, had replaced the origin of God in complex liturgy, devotions, the communal experiences of saints and festivals, and the social principles that came from these, including a Dantesque devotion to system and master. For him, these phenomena had formed 'Merry England'.

The irony was that in 1540 his son Henry, Earl of Surrey, was using the very instruments of the despised humanism to express the father's sense, however momentary, of total loss. Whatever Norfolk's own manoeuvring and considerable profit from what, at an angry moment, he saw as a massive dislocation of English culture, Surrey's father had said what his son was expressing in a totally objective manner (unlike the father's outburst). The son was translating Virgil into a new English suited for new heroes, a redefined nobility. As ancient Rome had shown, poetry could serve political purposes as well as any prose text, especially at a turning-point. For the 24-year old, changes in his culture were coming both as a breakdown—what his only surviving translations of the *Aeneid* emphasize in the burning of Troy and the death of Dido—and as a breakthrough, transfiguration, the *renovatio* that defined, as Alsop remarks, the changes of the Tudor world: 'In the early sixteenth century reform was almost invariably conceived of in the sense of renewal, restoration, and regeneration' with 'subtle—and not so subtle—discrepancies in interpretation'.[2] Such a Renaissance as the young earl imagined out

[1] F. R. Grace, 'The Life and Career of Thomas Howard 3rd Duke of Norfolk 1473–1554,' unpublished MA thesis (University of Nottingham, 1961), 205. For a comprehensive view of the life and career of Surrey's father, see David M. Head, *The Ebbs and Flows of Fortune: The Life of Thomas Howard, Third Duke of Norfolk* (1995).

[2] J. D. Alsop, 'The Structure of Early Tudor Finance', in *Revolution Reassessed: Revisions in the History of Tudor Government and Administration*, ed. Christopher Coleman and David Starkey

of himself would thus transform the roots of Henry VIII's 'Britain'—a Roman word with a new Tudor meaning in Surrey's lyrics. For Britain, the poet Earl of Surrey was translating Virgil's *Aeneid* in an original metre to help make Henry VIII's language universal. Rome had understood such massive dislocation leading to an empire, and Norfolk's son sought a true language to express his own sense of breakdown and breakthrough, the Virgilian dialectic of history. What the father had cried out, the son now translated in utterly new English.

In an unrhyming heroic metre (pentametre modelled on the hexametres of classical Rome), but with innovative English uses of stress, caesura, *polyptoton*, *chiasmus*, *hyperbaton*, alliteration, assonance, and other devices of the humanist classroom, Surrey translated such a cry with a universality beyond the Howards. Thus, in his text, the Trojan priest Panthus calls out to the barely waking Aeneas, the two caught in the middle of the burning city.

> 'The later day and fate of Troy is come,
> The which no plaint or prayer may avail.
> Trojans we were, and Troy was sometime,
> And of great fame the Teucrian glory erst:
> Fierce Jove to Greece hath now transposed all.'[3]

If for Surrey the next stage in the Virgilian dialectic was the building of the new city, a Rome itself in England, then Aeneas in the old burning city represents the first stage. Recapitulating old Troy in England in 1540 meant recognizing that 'Fierce Jove' in the person of Henry VIII had indeed 'now transposed all'. Neither father nor son could doubt a reality confirmed by events of irreversible history. The past before Henry VIII could only be summed up in symbolic valediction, a gesture of inevitability such as Virgil had given to the death of the ancient king of Troy, old father Priam. No matter how much the events and doctrines of Henrician Britain had their roots and genealogy in the past and might have been expected, still the dramatic sense of irreversible history marked event after event and so text after text. In fact, by the time Surrey translated this passage, the poet's new prosodic dialectic of English syllables and stresses without rhyme could symbolize any beheading. It would recapitulate all the painful if inevitable changes and predict Surrey's own death.

(1986), 150. For the value of poetic discourse as a means of political control, see Robert Barrington, 'Philosophy and the Court in the Literature of the Early English Renaissance', unpublished Ph.D. thesis (European University Institute, Florence, 1993).

[3] Because there is no standard edition of Surrey's poems, I have used a variety of texts to form my own, notably that of Emrys Jones, ed. Henry Howard, Earl of Surrey, *Poems* (1964). I have also used an edition being completed for Oxford University Press that Professor William McGaw, its editor, has kindly allowed me to examine. Like him, I have modernized all spelling for the reason that Surrey's texts should be accessible to as wide an audience as possible. I have identified each poem by title (usually the first line as Surrey has no titles for his poems) and line number where relevant. Also, because of limited space, I have generally curtailed analyses of poems, for a more extended form of which students can refer to my previous book on Surrey, *Henry Howard, Earl of Surrey* (1986). In certain cases, because there is no standard edition, I have felt it necessary to give the entire text.

Of Priamus this was the fatal fine,
The woeful end that was allotted him.
When he had seen his palace all on flame,
With ruin of his Trojan turrets eke,
That royal prince of Asia, which of late
Reigned over so many peoples and realmes,
Like a great stock now lieth on the shore;
His head and shoulders parted been in twain,
A body now without renown and fame. (*Aeneid* 2: 721–9)

The severed head, the breakdown of kings (and with them, societies), always haunted old Norfolk, who had survived the Wars of the Roses. This was his real memory and not the 'Merry England' he had recalled in unguarded (but overheard and recorded) nostalgia. The histories of neither his father nor grandfather were particularly 'merry', and such a concept of 'merry' would have no meaning for his son, who never knew any monarch but Henry VIII. In fact, in that world of Howard father and grandfather, had the old duke not viewed, from Edward IV and Richard III on, body after body 'without renown and fame', as had his son by 1540? In his own time, had Surrey himself not seen in less than a decade what Scarisbrick calls the 'remarkable act of national amnesis' by which a civilization of over 1000 years, at least its monastic culture, virtually disappeared? History did not appear to change, supreme head or severed head.

Yet in his refusal to read Scripture, the old father was missing the essential transformation of his world. 'Teucrian glory', in Surrey's metonymy for Troy, had, in fact, vanished into Tudor realism and regeneration. In the year before Norfolk vowed never to read Scripture appeared a text whose title-page alone showed how much 'Fierce Jove' had 'now transposed all'. 'No move in the official Henrician Reformation,' comments Willen, 'was more profound than the appearance of the Great Bible' in 1539. Not only its publication but its 'mandated availability' as text in all parish churches throughout the entire realm defined irrecoverably the Henrician *renovatio* of Roman sacred emperor and the doctrine of the Supreme Head of that force in England—Christianity—Weber names as the central ideological support for all pre-modern European political life. Only religion in Tudor England—its ultimate 'structure of things'—could actualize the basis for 'the existence of a legitimate order' towards which 'conduct, especially social conduct, and quite particularly a social relationship, [could] be oriented on the part of the actors' of history.[4] As Nicholson has shown, the doctrine of Henry VIII as the Supreme Head of the Christian Church in England—the greatest transposition the Tudor king made in the deepest 'structure' of his society—had incrementally

[4] J. J. Scarisbrick, *Henry VIII* (1968), 241. Diane Willen, 'Women and Religion in Early Modern England', in *Women in Reformation and Counter-Reformation Europe: Public and Private Worlds*, ed. Sherrin Marshall (1989), 144. Max Weber, 'Social Psychology of the World Religions', in *From Max Weber*, ed. H. H. Gerth and C. Wright Mills (1958), 270, and *Theory of Social and Economic Organization*, trans. A. M. Henderson and Talcott Parsons (1947), 124.

but steadily unfolded in the decade before, reaching the point of irrecoverability expressed in the 1539 Great Bible.

From the time when 'the "Collectanea satis copiosa" [texts gathered to support the king's divorce that became the basis for a rediscovered *imperium*] had been assembled,' both king and court (and a retinue of philologists) had one 'clear idea', as Nicholson notes: finding 'texts that would uphold a high view of royal authority derived from God, that would associate the King's role on earth with Christ's'. In terms first spelled out in 1531, the king exists 'Ecclesiae et cleri Anglicani cuius protector et supremum caput is solus est' ('for the Church and English clergy whose protector and supreme head he alone is'). Into this position soon moved the whole conception of a new realm, the *imperium* modelled not only on Solomon's Jerusalem but on Constantine's Rome. The Supreme Head thus became, in Guy's image, 'a Trojan Horse' for the transformation of the whole period. Nobility was now to be redefined within the totality of newly discovered definitions of the Supreme Head in 'divers sundry old authentic histories and chronicles', in Cromwell's phrase. The symbolic value of the term grew beyond its origin as a catch-phrase from humanist linguistic research. Building on definitions of sovereignty from 1485 and Henry VII (and earlier English variations on the medieval debate of State and Church) and on research by St Germain and other common lawyers, the Supreme Head as a term finally acted as a metonymy for absolute power: 'Parliamentary statute became omnicompetent in the sense that the "king-in-parliament" could legislate for church and state alike' so that, as Guy emphasizes, 'treason, not heresy, became the penalty for denying the royal supremacy' and, conversely, impugning the honour of the king—through an improper coat of arms, for example—could be heretical. From the 1530s on, a conflict ensued between this definition and that of liberty in an England out of which the poet Earl of Surrey's beheading marked a stage as Henry VIII's last victim. The conflict was to end only in the Grand Remonstrance of the English Revolution that 'dismantled' the century-old concept of *imperium* and Supreme Head and, in Russell's phrase, 'the *damnosa hereditas* of Henry VIII'.[5]

What is remarkable about this Henrician process of discovery during Surrey's own lifetime is, as Nicholson shows, that 'arguments for the Henrician Reformation and the Royal Supremacy were not principally historical, but scriptural' and

[5] Graham Nicholson, 'The Nature and Function of Historical Argument in the Henrician Reformation', unpublished Ph.D. thesis (University of Cambridge, 1977), 49, 57, 78–81. For the textual and political significance of the *Collectanea satis copiosa*, see Virginia Murphy, 'Introduction', *The Divorce Tracts of Henry VIII*, ed. Virginia Murphy and Edward Surtz, SJ, with foreword by John Guy (1988) especially pp. xxxii–xxxvi. John Guy, 'The Henrician Age', in *The Varieties of British Political Thought 1500–1800*, ed. J. G. A. Pocock, Gordon J. Schochet, and Lois G. Schwoerer (1993), 27, 22. For the general background I have drawn upon for this brief analysis of complex material, see Guy's entire essay and also the relevant analyses in his comprehensive *Tudor England* (1988) and the relevant essays in his and Alastair Fox's *Reassessing the Henrician Age: Humanism, Politics, and Reform* (1986). C. Russell, *The Causes of the English Civil War* (1990), 61. Also cf. Public Record Office (hereafter PRO) *SP* 2/L ff. 78–80 (version of crucial draft bill) and British Library (hereafter BL) Cleopatra E.VI, f. 28v (key redefinition of the king's power).

part of the genealogical revolution in which Surrey himself would be a major player—a legacy of texts in 'pre-eminently an age of the proof-text' and 'an age of line-by-line confrontations and fierce partisan controversy'. Even the king proceeded to edit texts, restoring in 1533, in one revision of Cromwell's revision of the Act of Restraint of Appeals to Rome, 'the explicit statement of the derivation of spiritual jurisdiction from his imperial crown' and thereby affirming 'that all laws took their vigour from his highness "and of none other." ' In Cromwell's preamble to this Act, in which the allusion to old texts was crucial, Jerusalem and Rome became one in the actual body of Henry VIII: 'Where by divers sundry old authentic histories and chronicles it is manifestly declared and expressed that this realm of England is an empire, and so hath been accepted in the world, governed by one Supreme Head and King having the dignity and royal estate of the imperial crown of the same.' It is 'unto' this Supreme Head 'a body politic, compact of all sorts and degrees of people divided in terms and by names of Spiritualty and Temporalty, be bounden and owe to bear next to God a natural and humble obedience.' After such a definition, a Virgilian ' "translatio imperii," ' in Nicholson's phrase, 'had occurred. The political authority of the Roman Empire was shared now by sovereign kings and princes' and they can even call councils of the universal Church. So announced Thomas Cranmer, no longer the Cardinal-Archbishop of Canterbury (as Morton and Bourchier before him) but the head of the primatial see of the Church of England under the imperial Supreme Head.[6]

Thus, as early as 1529, Henry VIII began to revise his coronation oath, adding, in the final words of the oath, to the traditional 'his power' the new 'in that whych honour and equite do require'. With textual certainty, honour now sprang from the king himself (as King Henry soon informed the heralds). In a different Roman text that responded to these definitions, in Norfolk's half-brother's translation of Guevara's *The Golden Boke of Marcus Aurelius*, an ancient Roman emperor offers, in Lord Berners' stately English, the older Arthurian communion of 'divers

[6] Nicholson, 'Nature and Function', 113, 125. *Statutes of the Realm* (1817), vol. 3, 427. For the importance of this preamble, revised eight times by Cromwell, see Guy 'Henrician Age', 35: 'the classic conspectus of Henrician political thought'. For the laws resulting from the 'vigour', see *Statutes of the Realm*, vol. 3, 492. For a succinct analysis and chronology of the concept of the Tudor royal supremacy, see G. R. Elton, *The Tudor Constitution: Documents and Commentary* (1960; rev. ed., 1982), 338–45, where he calls 'the Henrician Reformation . . . a political and jurisdictional revolution'. For the Henrician distinction in the term 'empire', see J. R. Tanner, *Tudor Constitutional Documents A.D. 1485–1603, with an historical commentary* (1951), 40; for this term and the Henrician shift, see Elton, *England Under the Tudors* (1955), 165–75 and an updating in chapter 6 of his *Reform and Reformation* (1977). See also Walter Ullmann, 'This Realm of England is an Empire', *Journal of Ecclesiastical History* 30 (1979), 175–204; John Guy, 'Thomas Cromwell and the Intellectual Origins of the Henrician Revolution' in *Reassessing the Henrician Age*, ed. Alistair Fox and John Guy (1986), 151–78; Dale Hoak, 'The Iconography of the Crown Imperial' in *Tudor Political Culture* ed. Dale Hoak (1995), 54 103. For analysis of how reshaping texts (and textuality) can reshape history, see Nicholson's 'The Act of Appeals and the English Reformation', in *Law and Government Under the Tudors*, ed. Claire Cross, David Loades, and J. J. Scarisbrick (1988), 19–30. For perspective on Henry VIII and his Romanizing *imperium* and the language thereof, see the exchange between Elton and G. L. Harriss in *Past and Present*, 25 (1963); 29 (1964); 31 (1964); and 32 (1966). See also Scarisbrick, *Henry VIII*, 268–73. For Cranmer and a general council of the church, see Lambeth Palace Library MS 1107 and 1163.

men and one lord' as an ideal realm for Tudor readers: honour defined by the communion itself, not the king above it.[7] But in September 1530, Norfolk himself and the king's brother-in-law, Charles Brandon, Duke of Suffolk, the only other duke in the realm, told the papal nuncio the English king was both 'Emperor and Pope in his own kingdom'. By 1533, religious definition meant political definition—as never before so clearly expressed. By 1536, Cromwell could define, in his preamble to the Act against the Papal Authority, that the Bishop of Rome's jurisdiction is a textual lie, 'whereby he did not only rob the King's Majesty, being only the Supreme Head of this his realm of England immediately under God, of his honour, right, and preeminence due unto him by the law of God.' This is the true Roman mandate, and Cromwell's word 'immediately' is crucial. The English king has his power immediately of God. Cromwell's word not only operates to modify God's actions but conceptualizes urgent time as superior to tradition or historical continuity (but not necessarily destroying them). Immediate time is the true conduit for divine acts.[8]

The linguistic event of the publication of the Great Bible of 1539 thus confirmed a series of textual proofs. This time the proof was 'immedyatly' visual, a new synthesis of text and icon. On the title-page of the Great Bible (with a prologue by Cranmer), Holbein or a follower of his depicted, below the last human figure of God the Father in any English Church Bible, the much grander image of Henry VIII (Plate 15). The Tudor Supreme Head is now the Lord's Anointed, from whom all blessings flow, at least in this icon, onto all levels of society, moving here through

[7] For the revisions, see Pamela Tudor-Craig, 'Henry VIII and King David', in *Early Tudor England: Proceedings of the 1987 Harlaxton Symposium*, ed. Daniel Williams (1989), 187–8, 199. At the start of these revisions, Henry VIII is careful to limit what an English monarch is swearing to. The English king qualifies 'the lawfull right and libertees of old tyme' granted by earlier Christian kings to 'the holy chirche of ingland' by demanding that such preivileges be 'nott preiudyciall to hys [Henry VIII's] Jurysdiccion and dignite ryall'. In another instance, adding the crucial adjective 'approved', the king also qualifies all laws and customs of the realm by this same test of whether they infringe on his own power, a change no other previous monarch had ever made to the coronation oath. In two quite new additions, Henry VIII adds he shall 'Indevore hymself to kepe vnite in hys clergye and temporell subiec[ts]' and then 'according to hys consienc[e]' he shall administer 'equytee right Justice'. For Lord Berners' text, see Antonio de Guevara, *The Golden Boke of Marcus Aurelius* (1535), 28v. STC 12436.

[8] For the dukes' remark, *Calendar of State Papers, Spanish*, hereafter *CSP Span*, vol. 4, 734 (445). For Cromwell's language, *Statutes of the Realm*, vol. 3, 663. For Cromwell's linguistic prowess, see Skinner, *Political Thought*, vol. 1, 86 and Elton, 'The Evolution of a Reformation Statute', *English Historical Review*, 64 (1949), 174–97 (and see also here Henry VIII's close attention to textual shifts). For an example of the special linguistic settings of these arguments, see Hatfield MS 47, 'A Treatise concernynge generall Councilles, the Byshopps of Rome, and the Clergy'. Although Bernard may be right to emphasize that for the reign of Henry VIII continuities seem more significant than novelties (in his 'Introduction' to *The Tudor Nobility*, ed. G. W. Bernard (1992)), and certainly *renovatio* was the proper term, not revolution, as Alsop has shown, still, four years earlier than the Great Bible, Cromwell's Act of Supremacy (*Statutes of the Realm*, vol. 3, 492) can proclaim, with an almost social snobbery, *everyone* recognized the right of the English king to be styled 'the only Supreme Head in earth of the Church of England'—the aggressive tone of which Act implies its innovation. For the moderating force of Cromwell on Henry VIII in the definition of the doctrine of the Supreme Head, see Nicholson, 'Nature and Function', 159, 190, 195, 203. For Cranmer's own crucial use of 'immediately', see *Letters and Papers, Foreign and Domestic, of the Reign of Henry VIII*, ed. J. S. Brewer, J. Gairdner, and R. H. Brodie (London, 1862–1932), vol. 12, 2, hereafter referred to as *LP*.

clerical and lay figures (Cranmer and Cromwell) to the individual citizens of a new society. The restored Davidic king performs therefore as a social analogue to Luther's epistemology of Christ's own deep internal penetration of the individual redeemed self, a theology Cranmer personally affirmed. In a new kind of visual genealogy (modelled on the heraldic), royal power descends like a vine, crossing not only the page but all social barriers, even those on the margin. As the Supreme Head penetrates each individual self in the kingdom, the newly generated Christian cries out not the despair of the old Duke of Norfolk or Panthus in burning Troy but 'Vivat Rex,' the words springing from visibly open mouths, female and male (but for two boys at the bottom who look up from their books and cry out, perhaps for the first time in an English printed book, 'God save the King!').[9]

This carefully textured title-page had no meaning for Surrey's father. He could pronounce both 'Vivat Rex' and 'God save the King' but with no king, from Richard III to Mary I, would he ever be secure. All Norfolk could do in 1539 was play-act and remain loyal to the older languages and codes from deep in the 'merry' fifteenth century, interior images of honour from his childhood at Ashwellthorpe with his half-brother Berners who would also translate Froissart. Old images would transform with hope any chaotic struggle with Cromwell and the court, allowing the old duke to find arrangements of survival for his dynasty. But the son also had a past, both inherited and actual. Surrey wanted survival for the Howards as much as his father, for his own 'seed'—and where the son differed radically from the father was precisely in the matter of genealogy. The son's memories, from which he also could not escape, included those of poetic text as well as blood.

Thus, faced with representations from the most avant-garde artists in Europe, all increasingly in competition for the right images to encode new realities of dislocation all over Europe, Surrey sought what his father desired, survival in a new age. To that end, Surrey reshaped old codes with the 'new learning' and the languages that did dominate—the father was right—all discourse by 1539. This was the Howard heir's interpretation of history. Even the poet's translation of the *Aeneid* may have sprung from the hope of honouring the new Supreme Head as the first Roman Emperor Augustus had been honoured by Virgil. Ancient Rome had found the language in its poems and histories for its transformation into imperial power. In regenerated 'Britain', the poet earl translated—'transposed'—that ancient world and language into his own to give honour as never before in English. At least Surrey intended to. He knew true honour meant progression—the control of the future. Living memories or dynastic myths therefore operated only as frames for the future, not for 'tears'. For Surrey, this dialectic of past and future expressed the narrative his *Aeneid* was translating: out of fire and 'slaughter'

[9] For the textual significance of this title page and her reproduction of it from which I have drawn my analysis, see Tudor-Craig, 'Henry VIII', 193. For the influence of Luther's theology and social teaching on Cranmer, see Diarmaid MacCulloch, *Thomas Cranmer: A Life* (1996), especially chapter 6. One other source Holbein may have been using for the title-page was the Jesse tree as seen in cathedrals, especially Chartres.

came the building of new cities, new texts. For such building, Surrey had his own memories and a genealogy both of blood and text. His first memories could only come, of course, from the myths or actual experience of his family. Those memories of blood originated everything else.

The End of the Middle Ages

One such memory occurred in early summer 1524. Then the 8-year-old Henry Howard watched the death, last rites, and elaborate funeral of his grandfather, the first Thomas Howard, the 80-year-old second Duke of Norfolk. The narrative of Surrey's life begins here, for, with that death, the boy became the Earl of Surrey, the originating term for all the poet's search for the right language and representations. Thus the boy watched as, for over a month, from mid-May into June, family, households, retainers, and representatives of the nation, over 1000 people, performed a ceremony of the highest honour the nation could give to the 'Flodden Duke', so named because of his spectacular victory over the Scots at Flodden Hill on the border of Scotland a decade before. This ceremony and honour the boy Surrey remembered for his own life. Early on, he knew he too might close his life as a venerable and aged Duke of Norfolk. When in Alexander Barclay's elegy on the death of the second duke's heroic son Edward, the poet called Norfolk a 'worthy gouernour / A stock and fountayne of noble progeny' and 'the floure of chiualry' and a 'noble tree, / Whose braunches of honour shall neuer fade ne fall / While beast is on earth or fishes in the sea,' the early Tudor poet had been simply reflecting a social encoding which Surrey as heir to the heir could not escape.[10]

The death and funeral of the old duke displayed the highest ritualization of honour, outside those for the royal family. The new Earl of Surrey was at the centre of ceremonies that began with the duke's death on 21 May. Immediately after the sacrament of Extreme Unction for the old duke, witnessed by the immediate family flocking to Framlingham Castle in Suffolk, and then his death, the chamber of state in the massive castle and its great hall and chapel were draped in black cloth and the escutcheons of the Howard arms. In the chapel that 'his grace' the duke had 'kept prince like for he had great pleasure in the service of God', his body lay raised on an elaborate bier. For a month, daily around it, three high Masses were sung with nineteen mourners always kneeling before the corpse. Every night the body was watched by twelve gentlemen, twelve yeomen, and at least three gentlemen ushers. Exactly one day after the month of honouring, the funeral cortège began its 24-mile journey to Thetford Priory, the ancient place of burial for all the lords of Norfolk, whether Bigods, Mowbrays, or, after 1485, the Howards. Placed in a chariot drawn by three pairs of horses in black trappings and gold escutcheons,

[10] Alexander Barclay, *The Eclogues*, from the original edition by John Cawood, ed. Beatrice White (1960; reprint of Early English Text Society, Original Series, 175, 1928), 175, 170–1 (II. 847–54 and 1132–4).

the coffin of the Earl Marshal of the kingdom was followed by the Windsor Herald, who bore the duke's famous helmet and crest (today at Saint Michael's church at Framlingham), and by other heralds who carried hatchments of his arms. Of the 900 mourners who followed, including 400 torchmen in black gowns with hoods, friars and religious at all levels, marched the Howard family, foremost the new duke, then the little boy, now the heir to the new third Duke of Norfolk, followed by his sister Lady Mary, little brother Lord Thomas, his mother (the daughter of the once premier duke in the realm, Buckingham, beheaded only three years before); and then the boy's cousins including Anne Boleyn, already in her twenties and recently returned from the French court to the English court, her older sister Mary, their handsome younger brother George, Surrey's older cousin Edmund Knyvet, and possibly the baby Catherine Howard in her mother's arms. Behind them came the aristocracy of the nation, knights, esquires, and Howard clients and gentlemen of the duke's household led by his treasurer and comptroller, all representatives of the vast Howard 'affinity' or human beings directly dependent on the duke for their economic and social welfare.

The trek across Suffolk and Norfolk took two days. At the overnight break in Diss, its non-resident priest, John Skelton, may have sung a solemn dirge for the event. Alms were certainly distributed there as they had been at every church along the way, so that substantial crowds lined the roads, not merely for the spectacle so rarely seen but for the money distributed. At the priory itself, a short distance from the market-place, the funeral began at dawn in the northern European summer, around five, with the first of three Masses graduating in splendour to a pontifical High Requiem sung by the bishop of nearby Ely. Surrey's grandfather now lay on a tremendous catafalque in the middle of the black-festooned choir of the priory that represented a heraldic fantasia, its black and gold reflected in 700 candles that lit up 100 hatchments of the Howard arms and eight 'bannerols' detailing the genealogy of the duke and his illustrious family and the offspring of his two marriages. Before it, 100 wax effigies of black-dressed men holding rosaries prayed. An hour-long sermon followed the appearance of a knight on a horse with cloth of gold trappings, the man dressed in the dead duke's armour, his visor closed, the battle-axe down and presented to the bishop. The sermon stressed, with stylized oratory, the value of this hero to the nation, its subject 'Behold the lion of the Tribe of Judah triumphs.' The bishop then consecrated, with a sign of the cross, the new burial vault. As the duke's honoured body was lowered and the bishop cast a handful of earth and sprinkled the coffin with holy water in one of the last pontifical blessings in England, the main officers of the duke's household, like chivalric warriors, broke their staves of office. They threw them into their master's tomb. Then, as Thomas, now Duke of Norfolk and his small son Henry, now Earl of Surrey, stood near the tomb, they watched the body of the 'Flodden Duke' disappear into the vault.[11]

[11] John Martin Robinson, *The Dukes of Norfolk: A Quincentennial History* (1982), 21.

The work on the old duke's elaborate tomb in the priory at Thetford, once the capital of an ancient Anglo-Saxon kingdom, had begun almost ten years before his death. It cost the enormous sum of £133 and was suitable for a nobleman who spoke of himself as 'we' in his will signed four years earlier. The old duke left specific instructions for his tomb to bear a large brass tablet to chronicle his life, a life clearly as fascinating to him as he expected it to be instructive for future audiences, not least his offspring. In the years before the old duke's death, the language for this enormous self-honouring tablet on the tomb had been carefully dictated. In fact, the duke intended the engraved 'Table' to be displayed before a wide and continuous audience in a prominent religious and cultic centre such as Thetford Priory, where his father and all his prominent ancestors had been buried.[12] Reading over and over the biography encapsulated on that brass table, the grandson poet had thus seen from childhood on that this earlier life, an inescapable model for his own, turned on two historical events: the Battle of Bosworth Field in August 1485 and the Battle at Flodden Edge in September 1513, and the culmination of honour in the final victory after the disaster of the first.

The Meaning of the Victory at Flodden

On 9 September 1513, before Flodden Edge on the Scottish border, the most easterly spur of the Cheviots and more like a fortress than a field, the grandfather of the Earl of Surrey defeated the grandfather of Mary Stuart, James IV of Scotland, and his army, killing him and most of his nobility. In recognition of this victory, the young Henry VIII re-created the dukedom of Norfolk early in the next year for the older Howard. The king also allowed the Howards to carry the crown and crest of the Scottish king in their coat of arms. The result was a dynastic leverage for the heir to the Howards, born within the next three years, which lasted until his death. Flodden thus completed a remarkable reversal and recovery from the disaster of Bosworth Field on 22 August 1485.

During the reign of Richard III, the Howards had succeeded in a spectacular triumph before the total loss at Bosworth: the first Howard Duke of Norfolk was created by the last of the Yorkist monarchs. The creation was the highest point in the then 200-year recorded history of the Howard dynasty—all reversed when the

[12] For the sum, see Arundel MS A 1047. The actual bill for the completed tomb was £132.6s.8d. The tomb rose under the arch of the original apse of the ancient Cluniac abbey where the 'Flodden Duke's' grandmother's ancestors had lain for almost 500 years and where, in 1513, his heir's first wife, Anne Plantagenet, the sister of Henry VII's queen, had been laid to rest. There, in a special chapel, his own father's tomb had become a showpiece. Surrey's grandfather's tomb had detailed New Testament scenes and classical motifs similar in sophisticated blending to the surviving tombs at St Michael's in Framlingham today and probably made by similar Burgundian-French or native workshops. Cf. F. J. E. Raby et al., *Thetford Priory* (1984); also PRO PCC 23 Bodefeld. For the only record of this tablet, copied in the reign of Charles I and proving that the English Revolution destroyed what was left of the priory, see John Weever, *Ancient Funeral Monuments* (1979), 835.

duke led the Yorkist vanguard on Bosworth Field, for which, after his death, he was attainted and stripped of all honours. Under Henry VII, the Howard road to recovery had meandered but steadily prospered and so, after Flodden, the recovered dukedom consolidated the political and financial power that had been building since 1485 and continued until 1547. Afterwards, the Howard fortunes lost under Edward VI were recovered under Queen Mary I. Then the new heir, Surrey's older son, Thomas, the fourth Duke of Norfolk, continued to hold, at least at first, his rank and privilege under his cousin Elizabeth I. In fact, in those first years, before the débâcle of his proposed marriage with Mary Stuart and his own beheading, the young duke could exclaim on the tennis court at his palace in Norwich that he realized himself 'in a manner equal with some kings'.[13]

For Surrey, reinscribing his coat of arms in 1546, the Flodden victory just before his birth confirmed all grand illusions about his origins and verified the assurance of his motto on his final portrait 'SAT SVPER EST' and the truth of the Howard motto 'SOLA VIRTUS INVICTA' ('only unconquered virtue'). It offered a mark, as in the archery of his day, towards which he knew he must aim his own historical existence; in his world, as a modern theorist notes, 'temporal anteriority' and 'ontological priority' must be made equivalents before any 'historical consciousness' could be born. Given such urgency, therefore, as revealed in the texts, literary and visual, of his last days, Surrey could probably not accept that the victory of Flodden Field was, by and large, an accident. The main stage for an English victory in 1513 had been intended to be France, not an obscure hill and plain near Scotland. No one had calculated that the Scottish king would dare to make such an attack, at least on such a scale, when his Tudor brother-in-law was leading a royal army into France. In fact, when the elder Thomas Howard—a septuagenarian with gout—had accompanied the young Henry VIII to the port of embarkation for the Tournai campaign on 30 June 1513, he was trusted to assist Queen Catherine's rule in the king's absence, and Henry warned, 'My lord, I trust not the Scots; therefore I pray you be not negligent.' Never forgetting the codes of honour he had learned as much from the Burgundian world as from the English court, old Howard still had the élan of the fighter so that, when the young king sailed away, he was 'choking with rage and grief at missing the triumphs in France'.[14] He had just lost his beloved second son Edward, the Lord Admiral and a close friend of the new king. In a spectacular chivalric gesture of suicide, Surrey's uncle had thrown himself and his golden whistle (the emblem of his office) into the cold waters off Brest rather than be captured by the French.

France gave the young Henry VIII in 1513 another crusade to 'create', so recorded Polydore Vergil, 'such a fine opinion about his valor among all men that they could clearly understand that his ambition was not merely to equal but indeed to excel the glorious deeds of his ancestors' (particularly those of Henry V).

[13] Neville Williams, *Thomas Howard, the Fourth Duke of Norfolk* (1964), 159.

[14] Patricia Drechsel Tobin, *Time and the Novel* (1978), 8. Garret Mattingly, *Catherine of Aragon* (1941), 71.

Watching the young king leave, Thomas Howard had his own totemic remembrance of France that made him desire to return. Much earlier, in 1475, as the brass table on his tomb announced, Thomas Howard had followed into France his King Edward IV, the grandfather whom young Henry VIII most resembled, supposedly to help the English king's brother-in-law, the dazzling Duke of Burgundy, Charles the Bold. Edward IV had taken into France the greatest of English armies, consisting largely of horsemen, 'the best mounted and the best armed who had ever invaded France,' according to Philippe de Commynes, and the young Thomas Howard had waited beside him, at the signing of the peace, at the bridge at Picquigny. On this large swing-bridge or 'Barriars', the young Thomas Howard and another Englishman stood beside the French and English kings and their two chancellors and 'no mo men,' as the duke's grave tablet stated. When Edward IV promptly abandoned his invasion and left his brother-in-law isolated, no one was angrier than his younger brother, the future Richard III, at such a violation of honour. Four years later, when Duke Charles was killed in battle in January 1477, the corpse of the most gorgeously arrayed ruler in Christendom was found half-frozen, in the ice of a mud puddle near Nancy in Lorraine. As Jean Molinet describes the Burgundian Grand Duke's end, the corpse had been stripped of gilt armour and its fashionable sallet headgear (with steel or hardened leather also protecting the neck), and was so gnawed by wolves that he was identified only by his extravagant long fingernails.[15] Returning to France in 1513 would have offered the old Howard one more opportunity, his last, for *gloire*.

The First Howard Duke of Norfolk

The brass tablet also revealed for the young poet earl in 1524 (and the years afterwards) an even deeper relationship. By the time his grandfather had participated in his first campaign into France, he had become united, as the only surviving child, to his father in the closest of ties, a bond both Surrey's father and Surrey sought to imitate. The earlier bond ended in the death at Bosworth of the father, John, the first Howard Duke of Norfolk, a death interpreted even by the Tudor forces as a sacrifice of honour and loyalty. But such service to the realm and the king had always been a mark of all the Howards. William Howard, the first Howard to appear in the dynastic history in 1277, may have sprung from the heroic eleventh-century Hereward the Wake but, more probably, from a line of

[15] Polydore Vergil, *Anglica Historia*, ed. and trans. Denys Hay (Camden Society, 74, (1950), 107–99. For the persistent model of Henry V in Henry VIII's life, see S. J. Gunn, 'Henry VIII's Foreign Policy and the Tudor Cult of Chivalry', in *François ler et Henri VIII: Deux Princes de la Renaissance*, ed. C. Criny-Deloison (1996), 31–2. *The Memoirs of Philippe de Commynes*, ed. Samuel Kinser and trans. Isabelle Cazeaux (1969–73), vol. 1, 262. For this campaign, see also Francis Pierrepont Barnard, *Edward IV's French Expedition of 1475: The Leaders and Their Badges* (1925; reprint 1975). Jean Molinet, *Chroniques de Jean Molinet*, publiées par Georges Doutrepont (1935), vol. 1, 22.

humble Saxon or Scandinavian farmers living by the great cold Wash that sweeps in from the North Sea, his own parents merchants or even lower in class. There are no records for the elaborate Howard connections as depicted by Buck in the early seventeenth century or for Henry Lilly's grandiose genealogy for the Caroline Earl of Arundel, one still fabricated in various books of the peerage. These myths Surrey himself might have believed, such as that Hereward the Wake had defied the new Norman king in the name of a truer older Saxon culture represented by an oppressed blood nobility. William Howard purchased land in East Winch in 1277 near the medieval new town of King's Lynn. The grass-filled moat of his manor house still exists today in the small community, just off a busy highway with the heavily shaded elevated rise of the old chapel now, as then, the centre of that world. William's land purchase signalled the first stage of the Howard ascent and probably came from early profits of a law career that took him from counsel to the medieval borough into Parliament, then to the position of Chief Justice of the Common Pleas and a knighthood by 1297.[16] As the life of this first Howard showed, the real genealology lay in the thicket of facts and energies the Howards or Hawards had always been renowned for dealing with. Here was historicity more genuinely mythic than any legend or fantasy of Hereward the Wake.

Service to the realm eventually took the family from the windswept flat-lands and dykes of northern Norfolk, but it began locally, and, as Virgoe argues, when the Howards did desert East Anglia, their history took a dramatic downswing.[17] In the beginning, in their world, the family made shrewd investments and the good marriages that could determine financial success in any Early Modern dynasty. The Howards built that dynasty carefully, acre by acre in their world of Norfolk and East Anglia, not only through money and marriage but also through the practice of law, the perennial path of fortune-building, and then through that other path in the late Middle Ages, warfare. After almost two centuries of slow but steady wealth-gathering, and then the disaster of producing only a daughter (with the fortune passing to the de Veres, the family of the Earl of Oxford into which Surrey married in 1532), the Howards had their greatest success. Around 1420 Robert Howard married Lady Margaret Mowbray, a daughter of the Duke of Norfolk and Earl Marshal of England, who had died in Venice, exiled by his close friend Richard II. It was a marriage possibly arranged by Howard's patron and friend, the reigning King Henry V. A near contemporary of Prince Hal, this Robert Howard may have fought at Agincourt, did in fact command the English fleet ravaging the French coast south of Calais, and, although only an officer in the

[16] For more detailed accounts of the rise of the Howards and their history, see the first volume of Gerald Brenan and Edwards Phillips Statham, *The House of Howard* (1907) and the early chapters of Robinson. An interesting fact is that Lilly's 1637 drawing of the original medieval painted glass of the chapel smashed in the English Revolution shows the Howards from the beginning as cultic and heraldic.

[17] Roger Virgoe, 'The Recovery of the Howards in East Anglia 1485–1529', in *Wealth and Power in Tudor England: Essays Presented to S. T. Bindhoff*, ed. E. W. Ives, R. J. Knecht, and J. J. Scarisbrick (1978), 1–17.

Mowbray household, married the elder daughter of his duke. As a result, his son John Howard, Surrey's great-grandfather, may have lacked in land lost to the de Veres, but he entered life as a senior co-heir to the legacies of the Bigods, Warennes, and Mowbrays through his mother (after sixty years of no male heir for the Mowbray Dukes of Norfolk). This was a dynastic conquest undreamt of only two centuries before. As a direct result of this marriage, in 1483 the Howards reached their highest point: John Howard was made Duke of Norfolk.

In a lost original painting on glass once in the family chapel at Tendring Hall in Suffolk and now existing only in the antiquarian Weever's seventeenth-century drawing, the first Howard duke is depicted kneeling in prayer, with bright open face and dark focused eyes, his slight frame clad in armour with a tabard or surcoat bearing his coat of arms (the rampant Howard white lion especially vivid), an elegant sallet-helmet with plume beside him. This helmet would define his life. Surrey's great-grandfather had first fought, with the reality of Agincourt still fresh, in one of the last campaigns of the Hundred Years War, beside the 'mighty war-dog' John Talbot and against Joan of Arc. The same fierce energy (the Pastons thought him 'wode as a wilde bullok') led him, with Neville family connections, to his first battle for the Yorkists in a snowstorm at Towton on 29 March 1461, and then to knighthood. Edward IV brought a series of rewards to the new Sir John, recognizing at once the centurion-like faith and self-assertion of his new knight in East Anglia. Not surprisingly, the military and naval roles the king provided not only brought honour to Sir John and his family but increased the pace of his mercantile activity. He made investments in mineral mining, the wool trade, in fact, in all the range of ventures by which this prosperous era provided the best economic standards for English society, if not until the nineteenth century, certainly higher than the progressive disasters of the Tudor and Stuart reigns.[18] John Howard's household books and those of his son, 1481–90, provide a graphic picture of the full rewards of this steadily accumulating wealth. Thus, becoming the Duke of Norfolk in 1483 merely confirmed John Howard's personal achievement. When he became one of the four great magnates and supports of the kingdom by the time of Richard III, despite his relatively low birth in comparison to Buckingham, Northumberland, and Stanley, his sheer enterprise entitled him to higher rank. By ironic coincidence, three of these four magnates, two of whom led armies at Bosworth, would be great-grandfathers to Henry Howard, the poet Earl of Surrey.

In the critical period after the sudden death of the 40-year-old Edward IV, Lord Howard had been at his most cunning, as the abbreviated entries in his Household

[18] For the John Howard drawing, see Weever 775 and Charles Ross, *Richard III* (1981), 187. The figuration differs considerably, except for the same dark eyes, from the sallow features and fashionable moustache of John Howard's portrait now at Arundel Castle, probably painted in the early 1500s, long after his death, and found in the wreckage of Greenwich Palace during the Restoration. For the character of John Howard, see the judgements in *Paston Letters and Papers of the Fifteenth Century*, ed. Norman Davis (1971), vol. 3, 38–9; vol. 4, 33. For evidence about the prosperity of the period, see J. R. Lander, *Government and Community: England, 1450–1509* (1980), 32; also, A. R. Bridbury, *Economic Growth: England in the Later Middle Ages* (1962).

Book show. After Lord Howard had dashed up to London, in April and May after Edward IV's death, the great moment came when the Protector, Richard, Duke of Gloucester, seized the boy Edward V from another uncle, Anthony Woodville, Lord Scales (the brother of Surrey's great-grandmother), and within days killed the poet uncle. At that moment, the widowed Queen Elizabeth, a sister of Woodville's, fled into sanctuary at Westminster Abbey with her remaining son and her multitude of daughters, so despairing that, in Sir Thomas More's powerful image, she dropped to the Abbey floor, lamenting amid the rushes, trunk-bearers whirling about her. To get this second son out of sanctuary, the Howards sided with the Protector Richard against the powerful Chamberlain, Lord Hastings, because this son had married the child heiress Anne Mowbray (and thereby robbed the Howards of the hope of their dukedom). It is More, not the Household Book, who narrates how on that 13 June 1483, when Hastings was so precipitously beheaded, John Howard 'one of the priueyest of the lord protectours [Richard's] counsail and doyng' was 'sturryng that mornyng very earely'. What reveals the careful planning of the father and son is the deceptive courtesy of the son (Surrey's grandfather), 'a mean man at that time, and now of gret auctoritie,' wrote More cautiously around 1516. Not only did son Thomas try to hurry Hastings along from his chance meeting with a priest, laughing sardonically and saying, 'Ye haue no nede of a prist yet.' He actually hid in the next room as the Protector ranted, so that at a prearranged signal, Surrey's grandfather and others rushed in to seize Hastings, killing him in a few hours. For More, the ambiguity of these events may have kept him from finishing his narrative on Richard III, which was being written in the year Henry Howard was born.[19]

This same cunning and prudence had become such a hallmark of the new Duke of Norfolk that in the reign of Richard III even the mightiest turned to him. In a letter examined at Arundel House in the early seventeenth century by Sir George Buck (but now lost), Edward IV's daughter Elizabeth, the future mother of Henry VIII, wrote to the first Howard duke, beseeching his help in marriage and remarking how Howard was the 'one in whom she most' trusted, 'because she knew the king her father much loved him, and that he was a very faithful servant unto him and to the king his brother then reigning, and very loving and serviceable to King Edward's children.' In early 1485 Elizabeth, beautiful like all the daughters of Edward IV, was still unmarried; even her younger sister Anne had been engaged to John Howard's grandson, the second Thomas, by King Richard. At the previous Christmas, amid the continual festivities whose liveliness the pious Croyland Chronicler condemns, her dress and that of Queen Anne's (both probably chosen by the young King Richard) are depicted as 'vain changes of apparel of identical shape and colour'. Writing her letter possibly at the instigation of her Woodville mother or from her own desire, Elizabeth offered a remarkable proposition. Even though the dying Queen Anne was still alive, Henry VIII's mother wanted to be

[19] Sir Thomas More, *The History of King Richard III*, ed. Richard S. Sylvester (1963), 3, 21, 51, 274. Cf. Ross, *Richard III*, 84–5, and Polydore Vergil, 204–5.

very clear: far from rejecting a possible marriage proposal from her uncle Richard, she would be willing to honour such an proposal.[20]

John Howard's Choice

So, by the summer of 1485 and the invasion of the first Henry Tudor, John, Duke of Norfolk, held power less than only the king's. Why then did he gamble such power on Bosworth Field, threatening to destroy the Howard dynasty forever? At 63, he was already an old man by the standards of that age. The choice to fight appeared to run counter to the prudence of his whole life and that of his ancestors. To this one question must be posed the obvious: why not? Richard III had every likelihood of winning. After all, the Howard duke knew the numbers of Richard's forces and the quality of his own archers and his ordinance. According to a ballad written about the event, artillery linked together by chains was considered quite strong against the Tudor rebel penetration. Although Howard guessed at the betrayals of the Stanleys and Northumberland, the first Duke of Norfolk—small of stature like his son, grandson, and great-grandson—held on like the bulldog he had always been when it came to a fight for the Howards' best interests. To act otherwise was to betray, if nothing else, his long experience of life. His optimism and even his truculence had been born of an experience that combined in the fifteenth century a distinctive idealism and the most detailed self-interest. He had won a great many battles and always looked ahead, his acquisitive powers as alert at 63 as his body was ready to fight.

Yet at Bosworth, John Howard's fatal charge down the rather steep hill from Richard III's encampment threatened dynastic suicide. The other magnates had known this. In a century in which the inheritance or the 'lifelode' was held with the fervour of religious dogma among English landed families, such suicide was inexcusable. The life of a duke involved an 'affinity', no single self. What made the act even less practical was that the duke and his son Thomas, now the Earl of Surrey, had been approached by agents of the future Tudor king and offered full recompense if they switched sides, someone even writing on his tent the night before, in Shakespeare's lines, 'Jockey of Norfolk, be not too bold / For Dickon thy master is bought and sold.' It would appear that the first Howard Duke of Norfolk knowingly hazarded all.

The records of the battle show that he did this without hesitation. John Howard led the van of Richard III's army to the edge of Ambien Hill, his men stretched forth on the clear August morning like a crescent behind his standard and its fluttering rampant white lion of the Howards. His archers in the centre were his greatest personal contribution to Richard III's army. They were led by his son Thomas at

[20] Sir George Buck, *The History of Richard the Third*, ed. Arthur Noel Kincaid (1979), 191, 3, 113. Cf. Ross, *Richard III*, pp. xlix, xliv, 142; Alison Hanham, *Richard III and His Early Historians 1483–1535* (1975) 19.

the same time that the king's horsemen on the sides converged towards the forces of Henry Tudor near the stream and woods below the hill. Except for Richard III and his retinue, the Howards were virtually alone, Northumberland and his Percy retainers never leaving the rear and Lord Stanley, the stepfather of Henry Tudor, never moving at all. The Howard duke alone led a charge into the rebels, fighting directly against his cousin John de Vere, Earl of Oxford, who was leading the vanguard for the future Tudor king. In their hand-to-hand combat, Norfolk's visor was struck off. An arrow from nowhere pierced his eye and head. Soon it was clear Norfolk was mortally wounded. The son Surrey continued fighting around his dying father to the end of a battle that lasted barely two hours. To the end, both father and son refused to desert their young King Richard. Then, badly wounded himself, the son begged Sir Gilbert Talbot to despatch him lest someone of non-gentle blood kill him. After Norfolk's death, the 32-year-old Richard III himself charged towards the imposter Tudor on his white courser, his crown firmly set in a defiant gesture on top of his sallet-helmet. Leaping off his horse, Richard came within yards of Henry Tudor. He fought upright, his small but powerfully controlled body flailing the battle-axe before him until, all alone, he collapsed.

The Howard act of loyalty and sacrifice brought the greatest fame to the first Duke of Norfolk. The immediate result was that John Howard's body was unmutilated. His corpse was returned intact to East Anglia, to the Norman Cluniac priory at Thetford, the resting-place of his mother's ancestors. A vaulted chapel was built, still visible today in the fragments of the abbey. In contrast to the treatment of John Howard's body, Richard III's body was stripped after Bosworth, except for a halter about its neck, 'naked and despoyled to the skyne,' in Hall's description, 'and nothynge left aboue hym not so muche as a clowte to couer hys pryue members.' The naked body was then thrown over a horse to be taken to the Franciscans near Leicester, trussed 'lyke a hogge or a calfe, the hed and armes hangynge on the one syde of the horse, and the legges on the other syde, and all by spyncled with myre and bloude.' Although Henry VII grudgingly provided, a few years later, ten pounds and one shilling for a coffin for the last Plantagenet king, who had been praised by all chroniclers for his last-ditch fighting, his bones were finally thrown out and lost when the next Tudor king dissolved the Franciscans, the coffin sold for a horse-trough outside the local White Horse Inn.[21]

But for John Howard, death did bring lasting honour—at least it brought him into a printed book, Caxton's new method of myth-making. In the year after Surrey's death, Grafton published Hall's history, and the account there reified the legend about John Howard that had already stamped the whole dynasty: 'Yet all this notwithstandynge he regarded more his othe his honour and promyse made

[21] 'Ballad of Bosworth Field' (ll. 489–92) in *Bishop Percy's Folio Manuscript*, ed. J. W. Hales and F. J. Furnivall (1868), vol. 3, 233–59. Cf. W. Hutton, *The Battle of Bosworth Field*, ed. J. G. Nichols (1813). For 'lifelode', see Lander, *Government and Community*, 175. *Hall's Chronicle Containing the History of England During the Reign of Henry the Fourth and the Succeeding Monarchs, to the End of the Reign of Henry the Eighth* (1809; reprint 1965), 421, 515, hereafter cited in text, when necessary, as HA. For accounts of the battle, see Ross, *Richard III*, 226.

to king Richard [and] lyke a gentleman and a faythefull subiecte to his prince absented not him selfe from hys mayster, but as he faythefully lyued vnder hym, so he manfully dyed with hym to hys greate fame and lawde' (419). If the golden legend of John Howard's final act still remained by 1548, and may have been Hall's implicit commentary on Surrey himself and his own act of honour, so did the question of its inherent inconsistency, if not absurdity. Whatever his absolute belief that Richard III would win, the totality of John Howard's gesture, its *gloire* at 63, bespeaks another inscription or absolute imaging for his life. What motivated such an act of will to hazard everything, after a lifetime and several generations of Howard caution?

Honour: A Text from Bruges

If an answer to such a large question exists or if John Howard's death can be considered any kind of sacrifice for honour—at least as the Tudor historian Hall defined it—Howard himself would have sought a final meaning for his death in a more precise image of honour, one directly put before him, not contemplated. There were two such images of total honour, in fact, two bodies of honour he actually experienced. Of course, a choice to die for honour would have been made within the larger context of northern European culture in 1485 and Early Modern modes of self-transcendence, but no abstraction would have worked for John Howard. Seeing was believing. Thus, the first image came in a text he saw performed in Bruges and probably read. It derived from Burgundian culture, the power of which over Howard was shown in the only list of books existing from the Howards (fourteen texts the first duke carried with him on a military voyage to Scotland),[22] all Burgundian texts of chivalric romance. His son Thomas may also

[22] These books are catalogued in *The Household Books of John, Duke of Norfolk*, ed. J. Payne Collier (1844) pp. xxvii–xxviii, 277. See also *The Household Books of John Howard, Duke of Norfolk 1462–1471; 1481–1483*, introd. Anne Crawford (1992). Crawford's introduction is the best existing account of the life and career of John Howard. The books John Howard read are hardly military or business-oriented. In fact, the books, in French, reflect the tastes of the Burgundian and French courts and involve honour and *gloire*. Although the books were probably all in manuscript, several titles indicate books already published by 1482 (the date of the expedition to Scotland) by William Caxton in Bruges under the patronage of the Yorkist Duchess Margaret. One of these books, the second in fact, 'La Recuel des histories troianes', Caxton published both in French before 1470 and then in English in 1471 'in the holy cyte of Colen'. What is reflected further by both this text and the very first book in the list—'La destruco de troye'—is the continued European fascination not only with Virgil's second book of the *Aeneid* but with the whole Matter of Troy and its mythic centre. The cunning businessman and military strategist still looked to this text of nostalgia and loss that Virgil had placed before the winning of Rome and the building of an empire. For Howard, as for so many of his contemporaries, such texts of Troy explained a cultural origin comparable to the Bible's. The other books reflect French and Burgundian court tastes for romance and games and, as such, provide a background for Surrey's poetic and cultural experimentation. One text by Honoré Bonnor or Bonhor contains the tree–honour symbolism that haunted the early and late English Renaissance and another a

have seen this Burgundian performance of a text of honour. The first Thomas Howard had lived at the Burgundian court, as his 1524 grave tablet specifically announces, and knew first-hand how all the 'tendencies of the age found their fullest expression in the Court of Burgundy'. Protocol of ceremony abounded there as richly as intricate forms of nature, not only in physical display, as at meals, but in mental and aesthetic exercises as well. In fact, the master of ceremonies there, the greatest authority in Europe on courtly ceremony, Olivier de la Marche, wrote his *L'Etat de la Maison du Duc Charles de Bourgogne dict le Hardy* in 1473–4 in direct response to an English request for information about household management and the immensely complicated ritual of staging a banquet. Such a grand banquet occurred when Surrey's great-grandfather, John Howard, heard or saw performed a text of honour at 'the wedding of the century'.[23]

On Sunday, 3 July 1468, Margaret of York was married to the Grand Duke of the West, Charles the Bold, in the Church of Our Lady at Damme near Bruges. By late morning the newly-wed couple made their processional entry into Bruges, the crowded streets festooned with ribbons and bright banners, towards the decorated ducal palace and the ceremonies, pageants, and masques elaborately watched over (and later described) by La Marche. Young John Paston of Norwich with his brother had joined the English party accompanying the 22-year-old Margaret of York. Writing to his 'ryght reuerend and worchepfull modyr Margaret Paston', young John could barely restrain himself: after the wedding, Margaret of York had entered Bruges and 'was receyuyd as worchepfully as the world could deuyse, as wyth presessyon wyth ladys and lordys best beseyn of eny pepyll that euer I sye or heard of, *and* many pagentys wer pleyid in hyr wey in Bryggys to hyr welcomyng, the best that euer I sye.' In one of the tournaments, Anthony Woodville, Lord Scales, jousted with a nobleman of that Burgundian court from which had come

meditation on death by Olivier de la Marche himself. The penultimate title on the list (written oddly in another hand) is 'Les d dessages' and, says the Victorian editor of the *Household Book*, is 'unquestionably the original of Anthony Woodville's *Dictes and Sayings of Philosophres*, printed by Caxton in 1477'. If Howard did read this book, then the world of Christine de Pisan (whom Woodville was translating) entered directly into the mentality, the structure of choice, of this hero of Bosworth Field. Woodville's sense of glory and honour, from whom Howard borrowed and whose style he observed, certainly did. For further background, see Anne Crawford, 'The Career of John Howard, Duke of Norfolk, 1420–1485', unpublished M.Phil. thesis (University of London, 1975) and her 'The Mowbray Inheritance' and 'John Howard, Duke of Norfolk: A Possible Murderer of the Princes?' in *Richard III: Crown and People* (Richard III Society, 1985), 79–85, 90–4, the latter appearing first in *The Ricardian*, 5 (1980).

[23] A. R. Myers, *The Household of Edward IV: The Black Book and the Ordinance of 1475* (1959), 3. For young Thomas' sojourn in the Burgundian empire, see C. L. Scofield, *Life and Reign of Edward IV* (1923), 252; Brenan and Statham, *The House of Howard*, vol. 1, 29–30. For the description of 'the wedding of the century', see Christine Weightman, *Margaret of York: Duchess of Burgundy 1446–1503* (1989), ch. 2. For an intimate sense of Woodville, Lord Scales, who was the official presenter of the bride at this wedding, see the picture in Lambeth Palace Library MS 265. In his only surviving image he kneels, with Burgundian display, to Edward IV and his queen, Woodville's sister. This beloved uncle of Buckingham is presenting his book, in brilliant green, the first published book in English by Caxton (who also appears in the miniature along with the young future Edward V and, hovering by the prince, Richard, Duke of Gloucester).

earlier Woodville's own mother, Surrey's great-great grandmother, Jacquetta of Luxembourg, by her first marriage a sister-in-law of Henry V and a social arbiter of Paris in the late 1420s. Like all such knights at the 1468 marriage, Woodville was 'rychely beseyn' in 'clothe of gold *and* sylk *and* syluyr *and* goldsymthys werk' and with ornaments of 'gold *and* perle *and* stonys', reported young Paston breathlessly, for 'they of the Dwyks coort, neythyr gentylmen nor gentylwomen, they want non, for wyth-owt that they haue it by wyshys, by my trowth I herd neuyr of so gret plente as her is.' Indeed, so enthusiastic was young Paston about this 'goodlyest felawshep' at the Burgundian court that 'I herd neuer of non lyek to saue Kyng Artourys cort' at Camelot.

On that wedding day, at the high table in the middle of the court, Lord John Howard sat to the left of the bride. He was a major official sent forth from the court of his friend Edward IV, and both the Howard father and his son, the future 'Flodden Duke', participated in the activities of the long summer afternoon. Among the events viewed from that left side of the high table, Howard may have heard recited, as one manuscript suggests, or possibly seen performed as a masque, *Le Trosne d'honneur* (*The Throne of Honour*) by Jean Molinet, finished just the month before. It was one more diversion or *entremet* that La Marche saw as appropriate for the occasion and, more ingeniously, as a transcendent inscription for all nobility of the blood and, for the Burgundians, a kind of self-congratulation. Ostensibly written as an elegy for the recent death of the Grand Duke Philip the Good, *Le Trosne d'honneur* is an allegorical narrative modelled on the dream visions of Boethius, Macrobius, and Cicero, and centring on the new Grand Duke Charles. Its diction and elegaic recall of the old Duke of the West, Philip, gradually turn the work into a prophecy of Charles' own virtue and chivalry and the investing of the young duke by the male figure of Honour. In fact, in an early manuscript version of the work, the text has another title that stresses this generational subtext: 'La vigne d'honneur faitte au mariage de Charles le Hardy, duc de Bourgogne, avec la seur du roy d'Angleterre' ('The Vine of Honour performed at the marriage of Charles the Bold, Duke of Burgundy, with the sister of the King of England').[24]

The diction of this *entremet* reveals, in a description of Honour, a simile with a remarkable linguistic, political, and theological genealogy. In the words of the

[24] *Paston Letters*, vol. 1, 538–9. Howard's cousin's widow, the Dowager Duchess of Norfolk, who was also the Neville aunt of the bride, is recorded by Jean de Haynin as having sat to the bride's left, and it is likely that John Howard sat with her party. See R. Vaughan, *Charles the Bold* (1973), 52. For the manuscript title, see Gordon Kipling, *The Triumph of Honour: Burgundian Origins of the Elizabethan Renaissance* (1977), 75. In his own textual genealogy, Molinet derives his poem from the dream vision of Macrobius, a Latin genre descended from Cicero's *Somnium Scipionis* ('Scipio's Dream') in the *Tusculan Disputations*. Boethius had appropriated Cicero's genre for his *Consolation of Philosophy* where he melds prison imagery and dream vision in a text that became so universal for Europe that it was translated by the Howard offspring, Elizabeth I. The central figure of *The Throne of Honour*, Lady Virtue, is modelled on Boethius' Philosophia and performs her own consolation so that, in Molinet's allegory (not unrelated in its transcendent Platonism to the contemporary Ficino's academy in Florence), Charles the Bold ascends the throne of honour.

narrator, L'Acteur, 'the noble lady Vertue introduced him [the new duke] to Honour, whose face shone forth like the sun.' In the 1468 text, Molinet's description of Honour and his face reaches back to specific Christian texts. It points towards the feast of the Transfiguration of Christ, made universal for the Latin Church only ten years before, although the Orthodox feast called the Metamorphosis of Christ had been both ancient and major. The 6 August had been the Greek and Russian holy day of Transfiguration, and in 1457, one year to the day after the Christian victory over the Turks at Belgrade, the Latin Transfiguration was inscribed in the Church calendar for 6 August (although in England it had earlier been celebrated on 27 July). The background for this new Latin feast day in mid-fifteenth-century Europe centred on the West's dismay over the fall of Constantinople only a few years before (a sorrow not least demonstrated in the humanist Pope Pius II's ill-fated crusade to save Byzantium from the Turks). It was typical of Burgundian avant-garde style that Molinet could so immediately adapt to his own communal definition of honour the new voguish European religious feast and the recent political situation that gave rise to it (Molinet's first work had been entitled *The Lament of Constantinople*). In fact, Molinet's terms merely continued the pattern of the exaltation of the physical and the body that had been operating, particularly in northern Europe, since the inception of the famous Feast of Corpus Christi, the Body of Christ, 200 years earlier in Liège and the Burgundian world—the feast a development of the doctrine of the Real Presence of Christ on the altar after the consecration of the bread and wine of Mass.[25]

Molinet's simile has roots in Gospel narrative (in the Vulgate, Matthew 17: 1–9; Mark 9: 2–8; and Luke 9: 28–36) widely disseminated in the late Middle Ages and Renaissance. This related Christ's Transfiguration, the light-filled transformation of Jesus' body while still in the midst of his life and within the serial Gospel history. Molinet's simile derives from the Matthew description of the Transfguration (authorized in 1458 as the official Gospel reading for the newly inscribed Mass): 'Et resplenduit facies eius sicut sol' ('And his face shone like the sun'). Thus, for Molinet, the bright face of Honour reflects the shining face of the transfigured Jesus (and behind it, the shining face of Moses on Sinai in the Jewish text of Exodus). In Molinet, the face of Honour becomes for the courtly onlooker or

[25] *Les Faict et Dictz de Jean Molinet*, ed. Noël Dupine (1936), 56. The translations are my own. Molinet was sensitive to the political frame of his text. He had written his first text in 1464 on 'La coplainte de Constantinoble. . . .Et envoye aux nobles crestiens' responding to the most horrible international event of the day, the fall of Constantinople to the Turks (BL C. 107, c. 9). Corpus Christi was but one of the newly authorized devotions in an exceedingly religious and prosperous fifteenth century which were popular in England right up until 1530. They carried the same brilliant physical or personal imagery, such as the walking or Visitation of the Virgin Mary to her cousin Elizabeth, the mother of John the Baptist; the Holy Name of Jesus, a cult linguistic and English in origin; the Crown of Thorns; or the Precious Blood of Jesus, the latter one of Richard III's favourites. Kipling, *The Triumph of Honour*, 75–90 shows how Molinet's text on honour had enormous influence on the pageants for Catherine of Aragon and Prince Arthur over thirty years later when Surrey's father and mother (and his grandfathers and grandmothers) would have viewed the marriage processions and heard the text.

auditor the point of ultimate self-recognition as the face of Christ was for believers. In Molinet, Charles the Bold and his father are led by Honour's shining face towards destiny, as earlier Peter, James, and John saw eternity, their destiny, in a radiant face and body. Molinet's language describing the face of Honour thus points towards the narrative of the Transfiguration: 'Honneur, duquel la face resplendissoit comme le soleil. . . .' Of course, the Howards recognized the Gospel of the Transfiguration, with its simile read for centuries on every annual Lenten Ember Saturday and in the following Sunday Masses, and existing in popular consciousness on the level of mythology, if nothing else. Thus, for Dame Julian of Norwich, a neighbour of the Howards whose life and writings John Howard knew, the sixth of the Showings on her day of vision in Norwich (Sunday, 8 May 1371) is clear in its emphasis. In this Showing 'of the gratitude full of honour with which God rewards his servants,' the young East Anglian woman in her cell, up the hill from the dark River Wensum, sees the Lord taking 'no place in his own house' but leading his friends to 'fellowship' where, like the true Arthurian king, he 'himself endlessly gladdened and solaced his valued friends most modestly and courteously' with, above all, the sight of his shining human face. The 'glorious countenance of the godhead' so 'completely fills all heaven with joy and bliss' that the young woman sees 'the marvelous melody of endless love in [Christ's] own fair, blessed face'.[26]

Honour: An Anointed Body

If honour could hardly be exalted more than identifying it with the Transfigured Christ, John Howard, the first Duke of Norfolk, may have seen another exalted imaging of honour that meant more to his practical mind. A transcendence identified with honour also took place for him in the coronation of Richard III on Sunday, 6 July 1483. A vigorous male body had been transformed into a real presence in front of his eyes and those of his son. In that second summer ceremony fifteen years after Bruges, the most exalted body of honour in the kingdom, younger than John Howard's own son, was anointed as king by the Cardinal of Canterbury. Richard III's had always been a remarkably strong body, with the thick thighs and calves seen in an illumination to Jean de Waurin's *Chronicle* showing the author presenting his book to Edward IV. Richard's jutting chin is the same as that of his much taller brother in the illumination and as that of his sister the Duchess of Burgundy in her portraits. Not only does this figure gesticulating and arguing have the 'short and sour' countenance reported by Polydore Vergil but the vitality

[26] Dame Julian of Norwich, *Revelations of Divine Love*, trans. M. L. Del Mastro (1977), 106, 16. I am grateful to Anne Crawford for her affirmation that John Howard would have known of the life and writings of Dame Julian.

a German visitor to Richard III's court remarked on, during the magnificence of the music during Mass for King Richard and Queen Anne on 2 May 1484: his diminutive but noble stature and 'also his great heart'.[27]

The coronation of Richard III on a summer Sunday was the most elaborate in England in over a hundred years; nothing had been quite like it since Edward III's. In the procession the day before from the Tower, on either side of Surrey's grandfather Thomas, bearing the sword, rode the two leading nobles in the whole spectacle: John Howard on the right, the Earl Marshal of England, the newly invested Duke of Norfolk; on the left the Duke of Buckingham, the Lord Great Chamberlain, who dominated the whole ceremony in his greater rank as Constable and in his position as the new king's leading advisor (but whose wife, sister of the recently murdered Antony Woodville and aunt of the two young princes, refused to attend the coronation). One duke was the grandfather of Surrey's father, the other duke the grandfather of Surrey's mother.

At seven the next morning Richard entered Westminster Abbey 'bare foted into Saint Edwardes Shrine'. The great shrine of Edward the Confessor, the popular Anglo-Saxon saint whose physical touch had healing powers, was the spatial focus of the whole ceremony, with its occult floor mosaic like no other in the kingdom. Just ahead of King Richard walked 'the Erell of Surrey' Thomas Howard, with the 'swurde of *Estate* before the King in the skabarde, then came the Duke of Norfolk bearing the Kinges crowne be twine his handes and anone after him came Kinge Richard iiide in his robes of purpill velvet.' What followed was hardly a nostalgic drama but rather, as Schram has shown, a series of gestures that affirmed, once again, nothing less than the restitution of the nation in the very summer that Malory was completing *Morte D'Arthur*. Especially in the anointing of the royal bodies, the Howards and the entire audience of 1483 watched a moment of shining metamorphosis, as complete as that of the transubstantiation of the bread and wine on the altar. Performance (at least for this audience) now became reality. Separately, concealed by a canopy of double baldachin from the audience, with 'boeth pristes and clerkes singing *the Leten [Latin] and other* priksong [counterpoint melody] with greate realtie,' the 30-year-old king stripped his athletic body to the waist. In rituals from the Book of Samuel and then Davidic texts, the oil was poured on Richard's head and thick hair, on his balanced even shoulders, elbows and breast, and then over the slim young body and naked breasts of his queen, wearing her long hair loose and behind her ears. The two had 'departed from their robes and stode naked from the medle upwarde and anone the bishops anointed boethe the King and the Queene' and afterwards 'the King and the Queene changed their robes into clothe of golde,' and the 'Cardenall *of Caunterburye* and all the byshopes crowned boeth the King and the Queen with greate solempnitie.' Then

[27] For the illumination, see *Richard III* (London: National Portrait Gallery, exhibition catalogue, 1973), reprinted in Pamela Tudor-Craig, *Richard III* (1977), ch. 9, note 32; for images of the Grand Duchess, see Weightman, *Margaret of York*, 70, 73, 138, 121. The quotation is from Ross, *Richard III*, 141.

'anone they song *Te Deum* and the organes went and the Cardenall sensed [incensed the bodies of] the King and the Queene.'[28]

The Post-Bosworth Court

After the defeat at Bosworth, the disgraced Thomas Howard, the poet earl's grandfather, spent the next three years and five months in the Tower. He was stripped of everything. The moments of transcendent honour at Bruges and at Richard III's coronation had now disappeared into the memory of the nearly annihilated. His wife Elizabeth, whom Skelton later celebrated in *Garland of Laurel* as the highest female example of honour and nobility in Tudor England,[29] took refuge, in fact, on the treeless island of Sheppey in the mouth of the Medway, probably ready to take ship to Flanders and the Burgundian world of Richard III's sister. The Howard world had collapsed.

In the radically changed political conditions after Bosworth, all power depended on the young Tudor king, who ascended the throne at 27. Thus, performance at court by the 1490s took place not so much within a field of action centred loosely around a fluctuating and often dangerous court and monarchy, as with Richard III, but in a field of action centred on a monarch, with the precise difference of concentration that Elton pointed out. The difference could be seen in the first Tudor's household and chamber organization, where courtiers, as Hooker notes, 'administered because Henry authorized them to do so, and not by virtue of powers inherent in specific offices. So much depended upon personality and proximity to the throne that it is impossible to separate performer from performance.' Although personality and proximity had certainly counted before, as the life of John Howard illustrated, by the early 1490s courtiers knew the difference between the old and new courts. As Condon remarks, the small number of peerage creations in the reign of Henry VII resulted from 'a shift in the balance of power amongst the élites, from the use of the traditional noble councillors of the King, to councillors who held positions about the King only by the King's concurrence and whose authority was the delegated authority of the Crown and not

[28] For the unique occasion of the coronation, see Paul Murray Kendall, *Richard the Third* (1956), 557. All quotations are from *The Coronation of Richard III: The Extant Documents*, ed. Anne F. Sutton and P. W. Hammond (1983), 31–2, 277. Percy Ernst Schramm, *A History of the English Coronation* (1937), 10–11. The only representation of Queen Anne is from a sketch done that day (in BL Add. MS 48976, f. 62) and shows her hair in this style.

[29] For the plight of Surrey's grandmother, see Anne Crawford, 'Victims of Attainder: the Howard and de Vere Women in the Late Fifteenth Century', in *Medieval Women in Southern England*, Reading Medieval Studies (1989), 15. John Skelton, *The Complete English Poems*, ed. John Scattergood (1983), 336–7 (II. 877; 861–3). There is considerable literature on this poem and its subject; I have opted for the first Howard Countess of Surrey and not the poet earl's mother, Elizabeth Stafford Howard, because the evidence appears more convincing for the earlier countess (although it would strengthen my general argument if Skelton's subject were Surrey's mother).

derived from land or title'. Such a shift was paralleled by royal interference at the local level, breaking up ancient ties of nobility and gentry by 'active intervention by the central government'. If this were not a Tudor revolution, it was a Tudor reformation. As Gunn comments, Henry VIII's court was already adumbrated in his father's acts that renegotiated

> the relationship between crown and nobility . . . the centralization of justice in the royal prerogative courts, the tighter regulation of retaining, the continuing expansion of direct contact between the crown and the county élites of gentry, the exploitation of noblemen's debts to the crown as a tool of political control, the decline of the Great Council as a consultative body, and the exclusion of peers from automatic access to the restructured Privy Council.[30]

The dichotomous personality of the king appears to have determined the nature of his court. In the post-Bosworth court of the king who appears the most untheatrical of English monarchs, there were odd exaggerations on all levels, a new theatre (and logically, in this reign, the first Renaissance drama, *Fulgrens and Lucrece*, appeared in 1497). In the new political theatre, the pretenders that kept appearing and reappearing like Hydra heads, and the betrayals by English nobles like Stanley in 1495, could only mean that the king needed a greater real presence. There had to be the accumulation of the wealth noted by the Venetian ambassadors in 1497 (by the end of his reign, on jewellery and plate alone, Henry VII expended

[30] G. R. Elton, *The Tudor Revolution in Government: Administrative Changes in the Reign of Henry VIII* (1959), 36. J. R. Hooker, 'Some Cautionary Notes on Henry VII: Household and Chamber "System" ', *Speculum*, 33 (1958) 75. M. M. Condon, 'Ruling Elites in the Reign of Henry VII', in *Patronage, Pedigree and Power in Later Medieval England*, ed. Charles Ross (1979), 115. Gunn, 'Foreign Policy', 29. Henry VII had more attainders and fewer reversions than any monarch in 100 years; only one of his parliaments (1497) did not pass an Act of Attainder. Of the 62 noble (peerage) families in existence between 1485 and 1509, 46 were for some part of Henry VII's reign at his mercy legally and financially, especially through the method of recognizance that would oblige the nobility (as the king used the Star Chamber) to pay for acts chosen by the state as necessary for its survival. At the end of his reign, 'the point had almost been reached,' says K. B. McFarlane in 'Calender of Close Rolls, Henry VII', *English Historical Review*, 81 (1966), 150, 'when it could be said that Henry VII governed by recognizance,' a rule in which Henry was 'neither medieval nor modern, but *sui generis*.' Even the episcopate, the official protectors of that spiritual world that was not Caesar's, as Christ had said, was radically altered by these methods, which involved new uses of old texts and language (and more lawyers as bishops as opposed to Richard III's penchant for theologians). As a result of the first Henry Tudor's various pleasant agreements with the papacy, particularly with the Borgia Pope, Alexander VI, the king virtually eliminated the role of the cathedral chapters of priests in the selection of bishops for the dioceses of England and then made bishops also enter into recognizances or bond indebtedness. See Robert J. Knecht, 'The Episcopate and the War of the Roses,' *University of Birmingham Historical Journal*, 6 (1958); Condon, 'Ruling Elites', 110–11. See also the changes in the Star Chamber after 1487 in response to the first imposture of Lambert Simnell with their purpose of *quoad terrorem magnatum* (in regard to the magnates' fear) in which cases became almost entirely pleadings between party and party over questions of title, not simple criminal actions, as noted by Condon, 132. Such methods and those described by S. B. Chrimes, *Henry VII* (1972), 209 (most notoriously the political strategy called 'Morton's Fork' to gain benevolences and also Henry's reinterpretation of the rights of the overlord in the 13th-century *Statuta de praerogativa regis*) combined to accelerate that reserve towards the Crown on the part of the nobility from the time of Chaucer, as noted by K. B. McFarlane, *England in the Fifteenth Century: Collected Essays*, introd. G. L. Harriss (1981), 255–6.

between 1491 and 1509 the astronomical sum of £200,000 to £300,000). What this centring of power meant, above all, was that the ideal of the old dialectic of community and honour (Paston's 'goodlyst felawship' and Berners' 'divers men') had broken down except as it became, in trying to maintain the illusion, bad performance, melodramatic death (like Surrey's uncle Edward's), bizarre imposture (like Perkin Warbeck's), or quite elaborate spectacle, the latter more a cheering up of an audience in the midst of dread than a communal celebration. It was not that the Yorkist courts (much less the Burgundian) did not show the same exaggerations; it was simply that, after Bosworth, the universals the earlier exaggerations embodied could no longer be sustained as truth in the more realistic experience of history. Certainly Henry VII did not believe them. The death of such idealistic universals and the rise of empirical realism had been predicated in the 1300s by the English Franciscan Ockham (before he died of the universal plague). In this sense, Henry VII became the first Ockhamite king, endlessly reifying, endlessly reading and initialling the account books of his secretary John Heron, who once wrote on a page 'aboute certain persons which are not yet through with the king's grace. And his said grace hath a list of their names.' Nothing else but details and lists would or could authorize time, unless, as in Ockham's dialectic, it was a leap into faith. This latter was a subjective act utterly beyond the first Henry Tudor, as imaged in John Ford's 1634 play about the most powerful of the Yorkist pretenders to the Tudor throne. *The Chronicle History of Perkin Warbeck: A Strange Truth* (or its title in a possible version with Thomas Dekker, *Believe It Is So and It Is So*) was written within a decade before the English Revolution for Queen Henrietta Maria and her husband, the direct descendant of Henry VII, and for Caroline courtiers like Surrey's great-grandson, the Earl of Arundel. It begins with the first Tudor king's soliloquy: 'Still to be haunted, still to be pursued, / Still to be frightened with false apparitions . . . / As if we were a mockery-king in state' (1: 1–4).[31]

Such heightened pragmatism did not mean Henry VII was 'essentially an opportunist'. Rather, long before Bosworth Field, the young king knew history can suddenly open up like the ground in an earthquake. In his violent childhood, at the age of 2, he had fled on horseback holding his uncle Jasper tight, the pursuing nobles out to kill him. He had left behind his beloved 15-year-old mother,

[31] For the wealth, see Chrimes *Henry VII* 63, 215; see also Lander, *Government and Community*, 358. Heron's note is quoted in B. P. Wolffe, 'Henry VII's Land Revenues and Chamber Finance', *English Historical Review*, 79 (1964) 246. Cf. Bacon on Perkin Warbeck's 'stage-like greatness', his physical allure 'bewitching' with 'a kind of fascination and inchantment to those who saw him or heard him' in *The Works of Francis Bacon* ed. James Spedding, Douglas Denon Heath, and Robert Leslie Ellis (1857–74; reprint 1963), vol. 6, 133, 187. See also how this protégé of the Yorkist Duchess of Burgundy was also the object of a life-history Sir Thomas More intended to write (as later Mary Shelley tried) in which, as Sylvester remarks, More, the former page to Cardinal Morton at Henry VII's court 'seems to excuse Perkin himself' in a world of universal play-acting where appearance and reality could not be as easily sorted out as before. In fact, the player-king imagery of Shakespeare that Ford is building on More had set for the Renaissance, borrowing from Lucian for his *Richard III*, ed. Sylvester, 285, 80–1, 262.

Margaret Beaufort, the single parent who had schemed for his return and to whom he was bound more than, as he later wrote to her, 'any creature living for the great and singular motherly love and affection that it hath pleased you at all times to bear me'. In her only surviving letter to the son she outlived, this mother wrote to him from Calais on Saint Agnes' day, a cold 20 January, the day on which, she reminded him, echoing the Gospel, 'I did bring into this world my good and gracious prince, king, and only beloved son.'[32] In that lonely life of the exiled Henry Tudor, real presence could rise, if at all, from his own cultivated sense of terror and of readiness as a refugee in Brittany and France and everywhere an alien.

The Battle of Flodden

Because this king knew too well the drive of the Howards, he had sent the first Thomas Howard north to Scotland, away from his power base in East Anglia, when he freed him in 1489. He needed the surviving Howard to protect the border and control the northern kingdom in a time of terrible imposture, of threats to the king's throne and body, ranging from the handsome Perkin Warbeck to the king's own Stanley family. It was on the border and in the next decades that Surrey's grandfather developed that realism and patience marking his long life and winning him the Battle of Flodden. This loyalty and total service to the new king (stated on the old duke's brass tablet and then in the Jacobean Camden's cult story) had an ironic result: the disgraced earl began to amass a fortune and renew the old Howard power. By the end of the decade, the old warrior even knew well the Scottish King James IV, who had once challenged him to a chivalric hand-to-hand combat and to whom, in these same years, he brought a young wife, Margaret, the sister of Henry VIII. Thus, with a full memory of service and images of honour, the old Thomas Howard had stood at Dover in 1513, 'choking with rage' as Henry VIII and Wolsey sailed off to France. The task of guarding Scotland, another tedious labour after so many, only added to the heaviness he felt, not only in his gout-ridden foot (he often had to be carried in a litter during the Scottish campaign) but, most likely, within himself. Born seventy years before, probably at Tendring Hall at Stoke-by-Nayland, on the grand Howard promontory overlooking the bright valley of the River Stour, he had never reached the ducal honour his father had in 1483. What he could not know was that the accident ahead of him would result in a victory for the old Howard duke. It came not from any grand transcendent moment but from once more laboriously

[32] The first quotation is from Chrimes, *Henry VII*, 219; for both letters see 301–2. For a fuller discussion of the relationship of mother and son and the whole energizing character of Lady Margaret, see Michael K. Jones and Malcolm G. Underwood, *The King's Mother: Lady Margaret Beaufort, Countess of Richmond and Derby* (1974), ch. 6 and 8.

carrying out all the self-interest, service, and honour his father before him had followed through to Bosworth Field; only this time, the result was total success.

On Flodden Field in Northumberland, near the Scottish border, a stone today marks the place where, on 9 September 1513, Scotland not only lost her king to the cunning of the then Earl of Surrey but her own identity as a major political power. Fighting to the end for the mortally wounded king, the Scottish nobility was ruined. The carnage was terrible, exceptional for medieval and early Renaissance warfare, and the poet earl's father, the second Thomas, then Lord High Admiral, had fiercely announced for the Scots the policy of Henry V at Agincourt. He intended to give no quarter, as he instructed his Rouge Croix herald to tell the Scottish king: 'as hee looked for no mercy from his Enemies, so he would spare none, but the King only, if he came in his hands,' so Lord Herbert of Cherbury reported over a hundred years later.[33] In fact, the English took only two or three prisoners the entire day. Yet the Scots had all the advantages of numbers (according to Lord Herbert, 'some wrote one hundred thousand' but probably closer to 40,000 to the English force of about 20,000) as well as privileges of ground, artillery, provisions: all must have seemed a high moment of destiny for the Scottish army powerfully encamped on the security of Flodden Edge the night before the battle. The 39-year-old Scottish king, 'a Prince of Great Courage', had therefore a right to expect victory. The handsome James IV had reigned for twenty-four years and was recognized as one of the most attractive rulers in Europe, the last Scottish ruler so universally acclaimed. An unusually good linguist, he spoke seven languages from Flemish to Gaelic, and loved to read Suetonius and Tacitus as well as Froissart and the Holy Bible. He was abstemious and moderate in diet and in all relationships, even sexual ones. His decision to risk death on Flodden Field merely confirmed the texts of honour he had read and the performances in them he had lived by (and, in fact, the French queen had called on him to perform an act of chivalry in battle for her). Indeed, as his granddaughter Mary Queen of

[33] For the reputation of Surrey's grandfather, see Camden, 283. Edward Lord Herbert of Cherbury, *Autobiography* and *The History of England under Henry VIII* (1870), 42, hereafter referred to in text as HB where necessary. All remaining quotations in this chapter are from this text unless otherwise specified. Raphael Holinshed, *Holinshed's Chronicles of England, Scotland and Ireland* (1808), vol. 3, 595, hereafter cited in text as HO, where necessary. See also summaries of the battle in the following documents: (1) 'Surrey's Message', where the older Howard writes from the battlefield to the queen, the regent while Henry VIII is in France, that he is 'soo ferre weryed with labour and from being without mete and drynk and lak of slepe that I am right weke at this hour, but tomorough I trust to be freshe'; (2) 'Gazette', a report letter written by the poet earl's father, Lord Thomas Howard, to the master of the king's posts; (3) 'Articles of the Bataill', virtually the same as (2) except that it omits a list of the Scottish dead; (4) *Trewe Encountre*, with more detail than the others and probably by a Northumbrian soldier in the older Howard's division. These have all been analysed in the depiction of the battle by Susan Vokes, 'The Early Career of Thomas, Lord Howard, Earl of Surrey and Third Duke of Norfolk, 1474–*c.*1525', unpublished Ph.D. dissertation (University of Hull, 1988), 108–18. See also John McEwen, 'The Battle of Flodden, September 9th 1513', *History Today*, 8 (1958), 138–47 and Cadwallader John Bates, *Flodden Field: A Collection of Some of the Earliest Evidence Concerning the Battle of Branxton Moor, 9th September 1513* (1894).

Scots and her own grandson, Charles I of England, showed, whatever else they knew and did, the Stuarts knew how to die.

Under the rules that both sides had set up on the preceding Sunday, the Scots and English agreed to do battle on Friday, 9 September. The King of Scotland had crossed the border into England on 22 August, with a huge army supported by impressive artillery that the French had supplied (800 cannon-balls alone) as they had also drilled the Scottish divisions in the new German or Swiss manner. King James seized the initiative by bringing his powerful army to Flodden Edge, where he had two advantages. A steep incline of 600 feet made it suicidal for any English army to attack directly, particularly with a single field between a marsh and high rocky ground filled with the latest European artillery. Secondly, the border only six miles to his rear meant the Scottish king could make a safe retreat as he had done before, a strategy, in fact, that Surrey's grandfather wanted to frustrate. The Howards knew they had to move fast with a smaller force or to retreat; they had few supplies left of either food or ordnance. Indeed the only security for the commander and his men lay in the powerful relic they handled carefully, the 500-year-old banner of the Anglo-Saxon St Cuthbert given to them by the people and Bishop of Durham (which was to disappear by 1547).

For this reason of speed, the younger Thomas Howard proposed a daring strategy. He would move across the River Till north of Flodden Edge and thereby, as Holinshed noted, 'the Scottish king should either be inforced to come downe foorth of his strength and give batell, or else be stopped from receiving vittels or anie other thing out of Scotland.' There would be simultaneous but separate encounters, slowly closing on the Scots. The poet earl's father would in this sense be the vanguard, supported on the wings by Lord Thomas Dacre and Sir Edward Stanley, with the older Thomas Howard at the rear where he could survey the action and attack accordingly. The younger Thomas had roughly 10,000 soldiers and sailors, supported by his brother Edmund Howard. Recently married to a much younger second wife but with no living children, Surrey's father, like his own father, had little trust in fortune. If his men or the other parts of the English army were to work in a system of wedge and flank attacks, all had to hold not only to the meticulous coordination of a grand production but to strong trust and faith among the players. So, between four and five o'clock in the misty September afternoon, the driest part of the day, the younger Thomas edged his army to the foot of Branxton Hill while his brother Edmund—the future father of Queen Catherine Howard—pushed to the right, with a smaller force and baggage. Suddenly Thomas looked up. Descending on his brother in complete silence were Hume's Borderers, the most experienced fighters in the Scottish army, in four divisions and a reserve, strung out like a shot arrow, deep columns, wedge like, in classic pike formation. For all he knew, this was the whole Scottish army plummeting upon him and his brother. In a spectacular gesture, Surrey's father tore his votive jewel called *Agnus Dei* ('Lamb of God') from around his neck and gave it to a horseman to take to his father.

When the young Lord Howard looked up a second time, he saw the Borderers had descended on Edmund Howard, unhorsing him three times but not stopping him, and killing one of the few English knights lost that day. Then, after plundering the English baggage train, the Scots rode on, thinking they were winning. But when Lord Thomas looked up a third time, he saw descending on his own flank Scots arrayed 'in the Almayns manner', that is, with pikes or spears sixteen or eighteen feet long, Europe's latest weapon technology. The Scottish king was coming down from the Edge. Instead of despairing before streamlined weapons, the younger Thomas turned to the resources of the more obsolete English weapons. His prayers to the Lamb of God were soon answered. The long German pikes were superb against horsemen, but hopeless against the English yeomen's short sword or six-foot bill (a staff ending in a hook-shaped blade) that even penetrated body armour. The poet's father then rode forth, the banner of St Cuthbert clearly visible above the smoke of battle in the late autumn afternoon.

Soon the Scottish spearmen broke their close formations and turned to hand strokes for which their weapons were inadequate. Their horses became unmanageable. The result was a greater success than the younger Howard had dreamed: the English literally hacked the long pikes and then defenceless Scots to death. Within three hours, the battle was at a standstill, the Scots engaged, as the Howards had planned, section by section. Earlier, at a crucial moment, a rearguard of Highlanders, who had been waiting for English forces, came running over the hill, so restless that, when they first caught sight of English archers, they could not resist and raced out with Celtic cries. The wild yells alerted the English archers, who had been so unaware of a threat that their bows were still in their waterproof cases against the morning rain. But the distance between themselves and the yelling Highlanders gave them just enough time to prepare. With a single twang and then a roar through September twilight and fog, Stanley's archers shot their arrows into the sky onto the Scottish king's right flank and then into the whole army. 'Avoiding [the English] storme of Arrows, [the Scots] opened their Ranckes,' wrote Lord Herbert with a special nostalgia in the 1640s, 'and therein seemed to give one of the first overtures for Victory.'

The English pincer movement now snapped tight. The entire Scottish army lost more than 10,000 men, from bishops, abbots, and earls to Highland peat-digging peasants, coast fishermen, and Lowland hunters. But there was a last definition of honour. The young Scottish king, an epitome of Renaissance magnificence, was last seen, already wounded and dying, in the midst of the crowded fighting, within a spear's length of the older Howard. At that moment, there was nothing left for the Scottish nobles of 1513 to do but form a circle: 'They cast themselves into a Ring.' They would surround their bleeding young king and die themselves.

2

The Mother

Within three years after the victory at Flodden, Elizabeth Howard, then the Countess of Surrey, gave birth to her first son. To him her husband gave a Christian name that had no Howard precedent. He had given it to one of his dead sons by his first wife, and now, as then, probably intended the name to honour the young king who would act as godfather. Eighteen years later, the mother's relation to her first son ended abruptly on Tuesday in Easter Week of 1534. On that day her husband, Thomas, third Duke of Norfolk, came back suddenly to Kenninghall and told his duchess to get out. For the rest of Surrey's life there is no record of any meeting or reconciliation of the mother and son. The 18-year-old Surrey was probably at Windsor with the king's illegitimate son, Henry Fitzroy, the Duke of Richmond (both still judged too young to live with their wives), the two adolescents having returned only the autumn before from their year in France together. The father shipped the mother immediately to a minor Howard estate at Redbourn in Hertfordshire, where, until 1547 when the duke was sent to the Tower, she remained, an exile from the rich and powerful world she had once commanded as duchess. In the years between the duke tried to divorce his wife, but she refused to consent. In the end, she won, resisting, defying, and then remaining the Duchess of Norfolk to her death.

Of all the duchess' losses, the children may have been the hardest to bear, at least for her to come to terms with, as she wrote to Cromwell in one of her later letters in an almost illiterate script: 'but thozth [though] my chyldryn be [tear in manuscript, possibly 'untrue' or 'unkind'] to me I have all ways love unto them for I knew well my lorde my husbonde dyd but [tear—possibly 'try'] me to put me to schame.'[1] Exactly why the duke chose to exile his wife into 'schame' on that particular date is not clear, but the events of the previous eight years had given signal enough, particularly as the mother's bitterest enemy, her husband's niece, Anne Boleyn, became queen. This rupture in the life of Elizabeth Howard on Tuesday of Easter Week 1534 provides a narrative, a before and after that was the product of a woman's choice as deliberate as John Howard's at Bosworth Field.

The poet's mother was the daughter of Edward Stafford, Duke of Buckingham, intermittently the Lord High Constable of England (the last in England) 'eminent for his high blood, and large revenue' (HB 205). Of the father, a contemporary had coined two aphorisms: 'That which ruineth the world, ruineth him, his

[1] BL Cotton Titus B I, f. 889.

tongue' and 'Fate never undid a man without his own misdirection, and her first stroke is at the head.'[2] This father and the example of her mother, Eleanor Percy, daughter of the Earl of Northumberland, who had refused to help Richard III on Bosworth Field, remained the transfiguring forces of the duchess' life—certainly as she suffered the breakdown of two marriages, that of her beloved mistress Queen Catherine and then her own. Born in 1497, Elizabeth Stafford had entered the Tudor court at 12 as lady-in-waiting to the new Queen Catherine. This was a normal age for any young courtier, male or female, to begin what would become a lifelong series of encounters and service at the centre of the Tudor world. Two years before her birth, her future husband had married the Yorkist Princess Anne, sister of Queen Elizabeth and aunt of Henry VIII. Thomas Howard could have been young Elizabeth Stafford's father (Edward Stafford, Duke of Buckingham, was, in fact, five years younger). After an apparently happy marriage, the Princess Anne had died suddenly in 1512 having given her husband at least two sons, Henry and Thomas, who were buried with the Howards at Saint Mary Lambeth. The ambitious Lord Howard looked immediately for another wife. At his age (almost 40) he needed a male heir to survive, and he looked to the wealthiest and most powerful family in England, the Staffords, with their direct claim to the throne through Edward III. Thus, in the same year as his first wife's death, Thomas Howard, a little older than most bridegrooms, married Elizabeth Stafford, at 15 a little younger than most brides.[3] The young bride became a loving wife for almost fifteen years. By 1516, the probable year of Surrey's birth, she had already given birth to two infants who did not survive, Muriel, whose name may date the birth (Lady Muriel Knyvet, her husband's sister, having died in 1513) and another daughter with the name of the mother's beloved friend Catherine of Aragon. Elizabeth Howard bore, in all, five children to the younger Flodden hero. The records that survive from this period point towards a cohesive and affectionate couple at the centre of an increasingly complex social network.

The effects of the final breakdown in 1534, her separation from this network, and the abandonment of the mother and wife are narrated in a series of letters the duchess wrote, primarily to Thomas Cromwell, during the middle and late 1530s. As no small side effect, these erratic outbursts provide, in Harris' analysis, no better or 'more dramatic example of the reality of patriarchal power in the early sixteenth-century aristocratic family'. They also reveal, at the same time, another 'reality': the angry self that would not become 'historical', in Rackin's term, that is, allow the outside world to write her history in its terms only. Like Seneca's Medea, Surrey's mother would express her own history in spite of the social strictures of early Tudor England and the alienation, even isolation, she brought on herself. This history would not be focused on that primary source of female

[2] BL Sloane MS 34.

[3] Vokes, *Early career*, 19. For the age differential of marriages and the mean in this period of twenty years, see T. H. Hollingsworth, 'A Demographic Study of British Ducal Families', in *Population in History*, ed. D. V. Glass and D. E. C. Everseley, (1965), 365.

honour, chastity, although she would always be faithful to her husband, but on a woman's right to that transcendent value of human life centred, in Elizabeth Howard's time, in the concept of honour—a right she held as much her own as that of any male. It may appear a strange drive in a woman of her time, all the more difficult to understand in one barely literate who could not read the modern Latin of her husband's friend's *Utopia* and Hythloday's argument that the only way to transform the world was to challenge it, and certainly not what her son knew well, the ancient Latin poems of Juvenal, who had written in the midst of his own cultural breakdown what she would have affirmed: 'Consider it the greatest of crimes to prefer survival to honour and, out of love of physical life, to lose the very reason for living.'[4]

Yet, as shown by specific studies of honour in the English Renaissance by Council and James and the broader definitions by Stone and others, this ideology of honour dominated all political and social codes of the Tudor world, Tudor life demonstrating, in fact, as Council notes, an 'immediate relevance of the system to the day-by-day thoughts and actions of sixteenth-century Englishmen'—and women. In fact, in the same years when the Reformation Parliament was declaring him Supreme Head, Henry VIII began to reshape the whole basis for nobility in England, as Helen Miller's study details, but only by redefining honour in his own terms, not denying its transcendent meaning. Thus, there was no question in the 1530s for Elizabeth Howard or her son, the poet earl, of any other authentic relationship to society. As Weber makes clear, honour and the whole network of its quest that formed the systemic centre of Elizabeth Howard's culture 'also determined the life-chances of every individual in it'. Both mother and son learned what the consequences of challenge could do to their own 'life-chances'. As the poet-diplomat Sir Thomas Wyatt wrote to his only son: 'men punish with shame as the greatest punishment on earth, yea! greater than death' (N2: 268).

Thus, with a special violence, the biography of the mother of the poet Earl of Surrey illustrates the accuracy of Stone's placement of honour conceptualizations as one of the three foundation-stones for the early sixteenth-century family. Stone's metaphor of 'porosity' distinguishes this type of familial honour grouping from 'the more sealed off and private nuclear family type that was to develop in the seventeenth and eighteenth centuries,' so that the forms of this socially originating flood of honour 'poured', before 1530, inevitably into any self-dramatization. Honour must be held, in Stone's terms, with 'vigorous, even combative, self-assertion' and 'a scrupulous maintenance of good faith, backed by good lineage origins and good marriage connections'. This determination meant that no female

[4] Barbara Harris, *Edward Stafford, Third Duke of Buckingham, 1478–1521* (1986), 75. Phyllis Rackin, 'Anti-Historians: Women's Roles in Shakespeare's Histories', in *In Another Country: Feminist Perspectives on Renaissance Drama*, ed. Dorothea Kehler and Susan Baker (1991), 137. See her further development of these ideas in 'Engendering the Tragic Audience: The Case of Richard III', *Studies in the Literary Imagination*, 26/1 (1993), 47–66. For Juvenal, Satire 8, 83–4: 'Summa crede nefas, animam praeserre pudori / Et propter vitam vivendi perdere causas?' Translation mine.

at the heart of society, that is, at court, could escape the consequences of honour inscription, whether in outward social occasion or in self-reflection. As well as being personal, all inscriptions of honour needed to be collective, as Chaucer had shown, and they could include both male and female terms, what the Wyf of Bath had indicated in her ironic definition of 'gentillesse' for the male 'gentils of honour'. Above all, honour demanded that the individual, male or female, gain the respect or 'worship' that only a community could give. Honour could not be separated from what Jäger calls, in his definition of classical *paideia*, the 'public . . . conscience'.[5] This sense of honour as the virtue that upholds authentic community was, in fact, the strongest classical inscription Tudor culture received.

The humanists understood this inscription. In Aristotle's *Ethics* (4: 3), honour is 'the greatest of external goods because it is what we offer as a tribute to the gods': it 'is coveted by men of high station, and is the prize awarded for the noblest deeds'. Above all, in Roman society, there could be no subjective internalization of honour as its own reward. Cicero made quite clear in the *De officiis* (I, 19) that 'true and wise magnitude of soul' consists in real acts, not glory ('in factis positum, non in gloria') and in *De amicitia* (XXVII), he provided the actual model of Scipio Africanus using language Surrey paraphrased for his last poem and concluding: 'No one will ever take on, with courage and hope, the greater tasks without putting before self his memory and image.' Elizabeth Howard knew then, from her own models like Catherine of Aragon (daughter of Isabella of Spain), from her immense legacy of customs and experience, and from what few texts she could read (or have read to her) that such honour had to be maintained whatever the ambiguity of event, even by sacrifice. In fact, Chaucer's account of honour in his ballad 'Gentilesse' follows precisely the actualizing inscriptions he might have found in Virgil's *Georgics* or *Aeneid* or in Cicero: 'What man desireth gentil for to be / Must followe his trace, and alle his wittes dresse / Vertu to sewe, and vyces to flee' (654). In Chaucer's ballad, 'gentilesse' demands that a path be followed, an activity in the link Chaucer's 'Duke' Theseus calls 'successiouns' (3014). Elizabeth Howard understood such 'successiouns' of activity as a genealogy of honour, Cicero's 'memory and image', in fact, a living genealogy she may have recognized in Chaucer's own family, his de la Pole offspring, claimants to the throne against the Tudors. Chaucer's granddaughter Alice, Duchess of Suffolk (of recent memory) and matriarch of the defiant dynasty, had been one of the most self-assertive duchesses in English history.

[5] Norman Council, *When Honour's At the Stake* (1973), 24; and Mervyn James, *English Politics and the Concept of Honour 1485–1642, Past and Present Supplement 3* (1978). This latter work appears substantially reprinted in *Society, Politics and Culture: Studies in Early Modern England* (1986), ch. 8, 308–415. Helen Miller, *Henry VIII and the English Nobility* (1986). Lawrence Stone, *The Family, Sex, and Marriage in England 1500–1800* (1977), 90 (Stone sees honour as 'the third highly prized value' of this society); see also Lawrence Stone, *The Crisis of the Aristocracy, 1558–1641* (1965), 89–90. Weber is quoted on 90. *The Riverside Chaucer*, ed. Larry D. Benson, 3rd ed. (1987), III D, 1110–1220, hereafter all references in the text by line number or, where appropriate, by page number. Werner Jäger, *Paideia* (1945), vol. 1, 9–10.

'Desireth gentil' then is the key to honour in Chaucer's ballad. Honour cannot be a given but must be renewed and reclaimed, no matter what one's 'mytre, croune, or diademe'. Chaucer's definition therefore puts the question of honour squarely in the will of the hero. In such desire and choice of the self lies the power of internal fashioning so central to medieval romance and its questing knights, as Lee Patterson has shown. For Chaucer, there can be no external moving ('noght the revers') from a corporately defined rubric to the internal, except as the external facilitates inward choice. A dialectic of choice is set up in which not even a Supreme Head can create a questing knight. In Chaucer's terms, from choice, the seeker for honour will 'dresse' talents in order to follow 'vertu'. He or she will invent it anew in an indeterminate history no one can escape.[6]

Her Choice

For Elizabeth Howard in the years before and after 1530, self-historicizing had to begin and end as a transgendering of male formulae, rituals of honour that correspond, as Castiglione pointed out in his *Book of the Courtier*, to a woman's own 'love of true virtue and [her] desire for honour' but identified for her as sexual purity or chastity. What Castiglione saw as a transcendent desire in Renaissance woman could have social effects greater than chastity, as the very structure of his *Book* shows. Woman could become an 'anti-historian', in Rackin's term, a type who in Shakespeare's history plays 'challenges the logocentric, masculine historical record' with its exclusive certainties. If such challenges were often muted in Shakespeare, 'what was unusual in the duchess of Norfolk's case was the openness,' Harris argues, 'with which she protested against her husband's behavior, as well as her willingness to destroy her marriage rather than tolerate his infidelity.'[7] Defying society, then, as an 'anti-historian', in the name of a higher genealogy and transcendent honour (as had the Old Testament prophets and Christian saints she saw in all the stained-glass windows), Elizabeth Howard chose to resist her world in order to keep her honour as wife. In her choice, the duchess did not transcend her existence so much as give it total meaning. She refused to be divorced, as before she had deliberately chosen, to her husband's anger, the old queen over the new, and by this choice and by refusing her own divorce throwing the whole question of the king's choice into question, his own morality. Although Surrey's mother was probably relegated to the kind of inconsequence as had been the old queen's sister in Spain, Joanna the Mad (who was, it turned out, quite sane), her

[6] Lee Patterson, *Chaucer and the Subject of History* (1991), 96. For the meaning of the term *dialectic* used in interpretations throughout this entire book, see Hans-Georg Gadamer, 'The Hermeneutics of Suspicion', in *Hermeneutics: Question and Prospects*, ed. Gary Shapiro and Alan Siod (1984) especially 59.

[7] Baldesar Castiglione, *The Book of the Courtier*, transl. Charles S. Singleton (1959), 244. Rackin, 'Anti-Historians', 137, 151. Harris, *Edward Stafford* (1986), 64.

acts did remain, however marginalized. They questioned the whole male figuration of authority increasingly viewed in the magnificence of the Holbeins and the totalizing image they projected.

Quite naturally, such a grand resistance by an 'unhistorical self' carried the dangers of its absurdity and the mad sidelines of ambiguity, as Shakespeare's plays reveal. The self could easily be destroyed, at least sacrificed; the threat of the margin always remained as long as the defiance lasted. Thus, once at Redbourn, Elizabeth Howard could not leave her exile unless she wanted to starve. A consequence followed. In the years of ostracism, in financial and social isolation, the old duchess grew steadily eccentric, if not finally mad, becoming one more odd female relative in a special Tudor attic. Yet by the time she died on 30 November 1558, less than two weeks after the accession of Elizabeth I—the child of honour of her enemy, Anne Boleyn—Elizabeth Howard had outlived all of her immediate family, except her son Lord Thomas, whom the Howard queen Elizabeth I made Viscount Bindon. Through it all Surrey's mother had remained the legal Duchess of Norfolk.

In one of her last public acts before what was (for her) the disaster of Elizabeth I, she became godmother to her great-grandson Philip Howard, the heir to Surrey's son Thomas. This Howard was intended to be the fifth Duke of Norfolk. Standing in Whitehall chapel with the baby's godfather, King Philip of England and Spain, and his wife, Queen Mary, her own god-daughter and now the first female ruler of England since the Norman Conquest, the old woman offered the child, amid eighty burning torches,[8] as another text of herself. This new life was a promise for what seemed to her at that moment, before Elizabeth I, an inevitable progressing history of survival and at last the redemption of her near-madness and death, her father's and her son's beheadings, the old world of Catherine of Aragon and their religion. This child Philip might just redeem all lost honour for her, and indeed her will for the child did strangely survive. Canonized in 1970 by Pope Paul VI as a martyr of the universal Church, the child became part of a universal litany that would have had, at least for her, total reality. On those terms she did win.

The Birth of Henry Howard

Elizabeth Howard's own child of honour, the heir to her husband's title and her first son, was probably born in 1516. The superscription on the arch in the Arundel Castle portrait of Surrey is the only clue to his age, and the 29 years named there may date back from 1546 or 1545, when the portrait was being painted (assuming, of course, that the arch was not added later by Inigo Jones). In fact, 1516 is the more likely as Surrey's birth-date if a certain notation is correct in the 1519 household book of Surrey's father, the younger Thomas Howard, then the Earl of Surrey,

[8] J. Strype, *Ecclesiastical Memorials* (1822), vol. 3, 2, 9.

and his Countess Elizabeth. This Latin manuscript account-book of Howard's long-time comptroller Ralph Holditch reveals the whole panorama of life for the father and the young mother just before their sojourn in Ireland. It exists, like all such household books, as a concentrated negative to the positive of a many-layered community.[9] In it Surrey appears, from the 1519 records of gifts given and his place as first in the list, older than 2 years (1517 being the usually assumed date of Surrey's birth). The two younger children, Mary and Thomas, are also more than a year old and an infant simply because of the gifts they receive. Entries for the nursery and the three children appear in the Latin text (21; 34; 36; 38), significantly with none listed as an infant. In the first mention of Henry Howard, his mother or someone has brought the little boy a blue ribbon from nearby Norwich (36v). All three children receive sugar candy from nearby Diss (10Av); special gifts of silk and red roses and shoes are also recorded (37–37v); and all three children travelled to London on occasion (38).

Such details as these children's gifts define this Latin text and open up the early world surrounding the infant and child Henry Howard. In this text a whole network of the early Tudor world comes alive, not least in the detail of the travelling expenses between London and Kenninghall, one estate belonging in 1519 to the Howards, then an old Mowbray manor house on the border of the counties of Norfolk and Suffolk and conveniently set at a proper distance from the Lord Thomas' father's ducal castle of Framlingham in Suffolk and Lord Howard's other estate of Tendring Hall at Stoke-by-Nayland near Essex. Other references show all the life at Kenninghall in 1519: nearby Shelfanger farm (where later the tutor Hadrianus Junius lived) with its wheat and rye (6v; 7v); rabbits brought from one of the de la Pole manors returned to the crown and recently given to Charles Brandon, Lord Edward Howard's close friend and now the Duke of Suffolk married to the king's sister (19; 19v; 20; 37v); joint financial ventures for both the earl and for Holditch and other members of the household (1–2); and on Michaelmas, the 29 September feast day of the Holy Archangels and a traditional time for reviewing finances, eight gentlemen of the household, including a priest and lawyer, listed as meeting with twenty yeomen and nineteen grooms (35).

But no record of Surrey's birth or christening exists (only after 1538, in Cromwell's reshaping, were parish records organized or even kept) either at the old Howard church at Kenninghall, named for the Virgin Mary; or at parish churches by the same name at Stoke-by-Nayland near Tendring Hall and at Lambeth; or at Saint Michael the Archangel's in Framlingham. The absence meant little, of course, even if records were kept. The households of the Howards maintained not only private chapels and their own clergy but musicians, organs, strings, other musical instruments, and boy choristers for the ceremonies in their chapels. The heir to the Howard fortunes, finally arrived, would thus have been christened more naturally in any of the Howard mansions than in a church. But, if the king were

[9] Norfolk Record Office (hereafter NRO and cited in text) NRS 2378 11 Dr.

the poet's godfather, no record of the king's sojourns and progresses in the years 1516 and 1517 includes East Anglia. Proxies could act for the king, of course, but if the christening took place in London, Henry VIII might indeed have come to the Lambeth Howard mansion. In fact, between 1513 and 1522, whenever business took the royal couple to the capital, the king and queen resided at Lambeth Palace (Westminster Palace having been largely destroyed by fire in 1512 and Bridewell not finished until 1522)—exactly next door to Howard House. Although Henry was a Stafford name and would have pleased the powerful Duke of Buckingham, the gesture towards the king was paramount: Norfolk would want immediately to place his first son under the care of the Tudor monarch.[10]

In fact, in 1516 Elizabeth Howard had been one of the godparents with the Countess of Devonshire and Cardinal Wolsey to the first and only living child of Henry VIII's first queen, carrying the infant on its silk pillow. The friendship of the queen and the countess was so close, in fact, that Henry VIII's first queen made a personal visit just to see Elizabeth Howard at Kenninghall in 1519, after a pilgrimage to the great 'sea-shrine' (as Erasmus called it) of Our Lady of Walsingham, probably the most crowded Marian shrine in northern Europe.[11] On her way back to London, the queen spent two days visiting her friend and her three children in the home Elizabeth Howard had made on the plain of western Norfolk. Although a rare venture for the Spanish queen, who increasingly did not journey with the king or leave her growing contemplative routine, the visit may have been interpreted by both women according to a female cultural model of the time: the meeting of the Virgin Mary and her cousin Elizabeth, the future mother of John the Baptist, a meeting celebrated on 31 May as the Feast of the Visitation and in the second decade of the joyful mysteries of the Rosary that both women probably said daily (together or in a group of women). In 1516 both women were pregnant at the same time, as the holy women were in the joyful mystery. If Surrey were born in that winter of 1516 when the Thames was so frozen 'that men with horse and carts might passe betwixt Westminster and Lambeth', the 19-year-old mother and her female friends like the queen (residing next door) would have set up earlier, in the six weeks of retirement before delivery, decorations for the delivery room at Howard House: fetishes and ornaments of clothing, tapestry, revered icons, and even sculpture that women of this period gave to places of delivery for what was considered the most honourable function for a woman, outside of total devotion to God.[12]

[10] Stephen Greenblatt in 'Psychoanalysis and Renaissance Culture', in *Literary Theory/ Renaissance Texts* ed. Patricia Parker and David Quint (1986) notes that such church records are 'for demography what the Renaissance English theater is for literary history'. I am indebted to Dr Neil Samman for a copy of the king's itinerary in PRO OB8 1 1419. Also, see his 'Progresses of Henry VIII, 1509–1529', in *The Reign of Henry VIII*, ed. D. MacCulloch (1995), 70, for the Lambeth Palace sojourn of the king and queen.

[11] *Pilgrimages to Saint Mary of Walsingham and Saint Thomas of Canterbury*, trans. John Gough Nicols (1849), 11.

[12] John Stow, *Annales* (1631), 505. I am grateful to Dr Susan Vokes for information about the preparations for childbirth.

A Full and Happy Life

Building her own world and nourishing her children and family would continue until the late 1520s. In fact, in an early letter generally unnoticed, Elizabeth Howard disclosed how deeply she loved her husband and longed for his return. The separation of 1524 marked the only time the couple had ever been apart. In fact, earlier, in the tradition of the Howard women, she had even accompanied her husband to Ireland where Surrey's father ruled in the name of the English king. At the age of 3 or 4 (or older), the child Henry Lord Howard spent almost two years in Dublin, in the castle enclave of the English pale. In her later letters, the duchess recalled those times: on one occasion, she generously recommended to Cromwell one Arnold ('I have known him many years when I was with my lord my husband in Ireland; then he was brewer to my lord my husband'). In Ireland in 1520, the younger Thomas Howard was deeply concerned about his wife and children. Despite the Irish pollution, he wrote to London, 'I am fayne to kepe my wiff and chylderne here still, for I know no place in this contre, wher to send them in clene aire' but he asked 'leve to send my wiff and childerne in to Walys or Lancasshire, to remayne nere the see syde, unto the tyne it shall please God to sease this deth here'. Loathing the assignment in Ireland, Surrey's father may have surmised that Wolsey was attempting the same manoeuvre that Henry VII had used in the 1490s with his father in the north: to keep him away from court. In 1520 the preparations for the arrest, trial, and beheading of Elizabeth Howard's father, the Duke of Buckingham, were being carried out—a strategy many considered the king's and Wolsey's strongest attack thus far on the nobility.

On Lord Howard's return from Ireland, his next arena of military service lay on the border of Scotland. When his young wife wrote to Wolsey from her winter residence of Hunsdon on 4 November 1524, she was worried. After an elaborate and sycophantic opening gesture to this East Anglian butcher's son, the same age as her husband and the mastermind behind her own father's execution three years before, she announced how grateful she had been for his 'special good grace towards' her. She hoped it would continue by showing 'the same in my lord's return now out of the north parts, which by your gracious assistance and favor, I looked for this side Hallowmas [All Saints' Day, 1 November]; whereof, as yet, I hear no word.' To sweeten her request, she sent him deer, 'a couple of does . . . the most dainty in the world, whereof your grace should be well assured, if it lie in me to give.' Elizabeth Howard's husband had also been longing for her. He desired her to be with him on the border. Had he not written to Cardinal Wolsey just six weeks before, on 19 September 1524, wanting to come back home, but if not, 'if he is to remain,' he 'would like some other place to lie in, that he might send for his wife, and put his affairs in order'?[13] The love and affection between the couple appeared

[13] Mary Anne Everette Wood, *Letters of Royal and Illustrious Ladies of Great Britain* (1846), vol. 1, 358. For the duke's letter, *State Papers Published Under the Authority of His Majesty's Commission: Henry VIII* (London, 1830–52), hereafter SP, vol. 2:7, 4. *LP*, vol. 4, i, 672.

then in 1524 mutual and deep. In fact, in the year before, as another household book for her family in this period demonstrates, the family was cohesive and functioning at its most resilient just before the Whitsuntide death and burial of the 'Flodden Duke' and the successions of the Surreys themselves to the exalted rank of Duke and Duchess of Norfolk. The period of this second household book (in English) dates from approximately 18 April 1523 to 17 January 1524. Its lists of activities (and the little boy's own diet listed separately for 'Lord Howard') demonstrate a functioning family at the peak of an enormous social pyramid, and the position of the boy who was heir to it all.

The 'Catorers Book of the Household, and Expences in Provisions and Beer of Thomas Howard, Earl of Surrey, at his Halls of Stoke by Neyland in Suffolk, and Hundson in Hertfordshire, 1523–1524' records 'an exact daily account of every breakfast [after Mass at daybreak or earlier] or dinner [late morning] or supper [five in the afternoon],' with quantities of food and beer (the general substitute for water in northern Europe), all priced weekly. It also reveals an annual migration. In more than thirty carts and with at least a hundred servants, the Howards moved on 29 October from Tendring Hall in the colder East Anglia to the warmer Hunsdon, also nearer the court, a late medieval house of magnificence admired by Henry VIII and ceded to him by Surrey's father in 1525. The move took the boy Henry Howard from the beauty of Stoke and the view there from Tendring Hall across the Stour river valley, a place of exceptional freedom, to the more formal world of Hunsdon, which later functioned as the residence of the Princesses Mary and Elizabeth (and her lady-in-waiting, Geraldine) and of Prince Edward. In fact, all that remains of Hunsdon today is a view of it in a portrait of Edward VI, probably by Scrots: towers and surrounding buildings, including an old Norman church, shine almost dream-like in the distant Hertfordshire landscape.

At Hunsdon and throughout East Anglia, an extraordinary range of activities for the Howards reveals itself in this 1524 household book, as later it also does in a third household book for 1526–7, when Thomas Howard, now the Duke of Norfolk, was living at Framlingham, the ducal castle.[14] In the world of both these books, Elizabeth Howard, the Duchess of Norfolk, commands her residences as one of the foremost ladies of the realm. She participates in all the events allowed a woman, hunting with her husband on occasion and even once riding back from Lambeth and London, without her husband, with a retinue of forty she had lodged in Lambeth at the Saracen's Head Inn near the Howard mansion. In 1524, among many other visitors, a draper from Long Melford up the Stour valley came to her for a fitting or decoration; a merchant from Norwich who had been a naval officer

[14] The first manuscript can be found in the Bancroft Library, University of California, Berkeley, HF 5616 E5 N6 (formerly MS B 49). In this household book and the manuscript of the household book in Pembroke College library, Cambridge, MS 300, ff. 59–61 and 81, I have not indicated page numbers (the numbering is not altogether clear in either) but used the dates to indicate references to these household books; both are in English. For a description of such a move, see Mark Girouard, *Life in the English Country House: A Social and Architectural History* (1978), 14–16. For Hunsdon, see Simon Thurley, *The Royal Palaces of Tudor England: Architecture and Court Life 1460–1547* (1993), 79–80.

under Norfolk came for consultation with her. Although she was no longer a lady-in-waiting after 1524, Surrey's mother still served the queen during what was becoming the critical period for Queen Catherine's survival. She may have been required at court for a month to six weeks at a time and was, in fact, on a summer progress with the court in 1527.

Her husband was constantly moving, of course, and when not at war, off to London or Norwich during law terms or travelling with his riding household of thirty-two on duties for the king. At Christmas and New Year, when not called to court, the two were at home, where the duke gathered his family, 'affinity', and administrators for both business and pleasure. At Framlingham Castle during Christmas 1526, for example, the duke and duchess entertained their household and guests totaling 144 (not counting any of the lower servants); on that 30 December, they entertained 235 'strangers', 35 of them knights, gentry, priests and their servants, the 200 others simply 'persons of the country' or the lower gentry. But guests abounded on all occasions during 1523–4 and 1526–7, and the young duchess welcomed them all. A special visitor for the boy Henry was his half-uncle Lord Thomas, hardly ten years older, on 5 and 6 August 1523, at the height of summer. In the fields and river valley near Tendring (later painted in their magnificent light by Constable), the adolescent uncle may have given Surrey lessons in archery, horsemanship, and martial arts, including the tilt-horse, falconry, and other arts and fundamental skills a future Duke of Norfolk needed.

The household books also disclose the deeper world given to the boy Henry and his younger sister, for both of whom pages or younger servants are recorded. Although there is no record of tutors or lessons for the children, the famous humanist intellectual John Leland was, in fact, in residence with the Howards, acting as tutor to Surrey's younger brother Lord Thomas. Such fees for a tutor may have come directly from the duke's own personal expenses and were thus not recorded in household books. Certainly, as its privileged centre, the children had the resources of all the world around them. They could watch the comings and goings: for example, at Tendring, a painter stayed on 3–9 May 1523, who may have been a housepainter, stainer, or decorator, or perhaps the maker of Elizabeth Howard's portrait painted during this period; gypsies also appeared in the summer at Tendring on 2–8 August, one of their last recorded visits before Henry VIII banished them as a people after 1530; during 27 December to 2 January at Hunsdon, five players performed interludes, with scripture stories. On 6 January, the Feast of Christ's Epiphany, the Howards held a great banquet with entertainment, dancing, and music. The connections with Ireland had also continued, with two Irish priests on 30–31 August and other Irish visitors on 22 October. Two Franciscans, Friars Observant, came down from Greenwich on 16–22 September (possibly with messages from the queen, who was later to ask to be buried in their Greenwich friary). These may have been the same Franciscans who also visited Norfolk at Framlingham in 1526–7. In fact, in these last years before the suppression, the Howard households were filled with religious of all orders, East Anglian monks as well as a hermit from Coggeshall and various priests from London and Ireland. The Howard household illustrated in microcosm the immense religious activity in the kingdom just before 1530. The Duchess Elizabeth herself took retinues on pilgrimages to shrines in the region (the Rod of Grace at Kersey, with two gentlemen and six yeomen; Walsingham, with sixteen; to Our Lady of Ipswich, with twenty) and always fasted, in the ancient Greek and Roman Christian traditions, on Wednesdays and Fridays, and ate fish on Rogation Days. On those holy days, to consecrate the change of seasons, no breakfast or dinner was provided 'except for my Lord Howard in the nursery'.

If meals illustrated the elaborate ceremony inherited from the Burgundians, the level of complexity in response to the occasion, then, in the summer of 1525, when the duke was in residence at Kenninghall (Plate 12), the accounts kept for twenty-six days reveal a grand occasion for hardly fewer than 100 persons, including guests and household officials, and costing £202, an immense sum in early Tudor currency. Meat, fowl, and fish comprise the bulk of these menus, and in these days the Howards and their table consumed 12 oxen, 12 calves, 47 sheep, 3 bucks (Kenninghall park was over 700 acres and well stocked with deer), 44 suckling pigs, 263 rabbits, 18 swans, 403 chickens, 416 pigeons, ducks and pheasants, 1 crane, 2 porpoises, 840 small fish such as flounder, fresh herring, cod, and whiting, 1449 eels, 3200 oysters, 2370 eggs, 134 loaves of bread, and 58 barrels of beer, among other items. Duchess Elizabeth knew of greater feasts. In her childhood, on Epiphany of 1508, just before she left to begin her life at court, her father gave a dinner and then supper for 459 guests. On that day alone he served 12 sheep, 2 calves, 22 rabbits, 3 swans, 18 chickens, and 308 peacocks, herons, woodcock, ducks, among other items. Buckingham's guest-list at Thornbury also included those who saw the duke as their natural lord, including the Seymours, who were nearby gentry and tenants in Savernake Forest.

The household book of 1523–4 shows that the young Lord Howard did not leave the family during this period. He remained totally in the world of Tendring and Hunsdon, having his breakfast each morning with his mother and then eating later meals with other adults. He ate the same food heavy with protein and drank the same beer. His breakfast diet included, rather regularly, mutton, rack or breast, except on Fridays and Saturdays when he had milk, 'a dish of butter' (probably of a consistency like yogurt), sometimes eggs, and on occasion, a rabbit, or once a stewed capon. Thus, in his quiet world, every morning was begun in the presence of his mother, still in her twenties. His father, now in his mid-fifties, returned periodically, once, at Hunsdon in 1523, arriving on 7 December from the Scottish front for a brief stay, then back out again on 15 and 22 December, and then the Christmas obligation of himself and his wife at court before he returned to the war front just after Epiphany or January 6. In all these trips, he had probably brought along his private secretary, John Holland, the father of the young Elizabeth or Bess, because Norfolk often held a series of winter meetings for his own household at Hunsdon in order to keep the expenditures of his vast estate in order. But

Surrey's mother ruled those days, at least for the child, and during those crucial years, in her presence and conversation the Howard heir began each day of his life. It was a quiet beginning but, for the boy, the beginning of everything that mattered.[15]

Sacrifice: The 'Mirror of all Courtesy'

This world and plenitude Elizabeth Howard, Duchess of Norfolk, chose to give up. When the collapse of her marriage came in Easter week of 1534, she must have known she had begun to choose a path of exile over seven years before. At that earlier time, the crisis over Anne Boleyn had appeared, and the duchess had begun to separate, perhaps physically, certainly politically, from her husband, an outrage and an insult by the social codes of her time. On those mornings with her little son Henry in the early 1520s, the mother's was still a quiet presence, but she was no longer innocent. After the beheading of her father in May 1521 and the shift in the attitude of the king towards the royal marriage, her world had been transformed. The Howards and all their retinues and networks could not but be deeply affected by the redefining values of the court. Their wealth and power made them vulnerable in any new violent encoding of the realm, precisely because of their rank. Particularly after her own father's death when her older son was 5, Elizabeth Howard may have developed, in her anger, the same transcendence over time that Rilke saw in the mothers of heroes such as the mother of Samson: 'There, already inside you, didn't his commanding choice begin?' Earlier her own mother Eleanor, the Duchess of Buckingham, had written a poem to the Virgin Mary, and its second stanza also made absolute a mother and hero-son: 'Gawde virgine off all humylytie / [show] to us thy sonnes humanitie / whan he without paine borne was of the.'[16]

The poet earl probably resembled his mother in his reddish auburn hair and his light expressive face (the Howards tended to be darker and their features more saturnine, the father's hair remaining black until he was well into his sixties).[17] A strong will and self-assurance reveal themselves in the mother's two portraits, one showing Elizabeth Howard just as she looked when Surrey was a child. Today, in the archives of Arundel Castle, in a miniature dated 1528, Elizabeth,

[15] For the dinner ceremonies, see Girouard, *Life in the English Country House*, 46–51. For the finances, see Richard Howlett, 'The Household Accounts of Kenninghall Palace in the Year 1515', *Norfolk Archaeology*, 15 (1904) 51–60. The accounts as compared here to other prices being paid for the same items show that the Howards paid more in general. For Buckingham's expenses, see John Gage, 'Extracts from the Household Book of Edward Stafford, Duke of Buckingham', *Archaeologia*, 25 (1834), 321, 325. Howlett also records the Epiphany dinner and has some slightly different figures, although the point of largesse is the same. See also Melville Tucker, 'California MS. AC 523, Formerly Phillipps MS. 3841', *Notes and Queries*, 11 (Oct. 1964), 375–6.

[16] Rainer Maria Rilke, *Duineser Elegien* (1958), 33–4. Other citations for the elegies are in the text and in my own translations. For the duchess' poem, see BL Arundel MS 318, ff. 152–152v.

[17] *Calendar of State Papers Venetian*, hereafter CSPVen, vol. 4, 694.

Duchess of Norfolk, stares intently downward towards the viewer's left at some object she has focused on. The miniature was probably painted in the nineteenth century, possibly from a lost original, but its dress so resembles the portrait of the young Princess Mary around the time of Surrey's beheading that it may be more of a Victorian *mélange* than an accurate portrait. If there were an original, its full length, its backdrop of a grand green chair behind the tense figure (the chair a sign of rank and dignity when women at court often sat on cushions as men stood), and the realism of the petite young woman would be remarkable. The bone-structure of the duchess' face appears delicate, and the refinement of skin is matched by her reddish, almost blonde hair pulled back (with a parting in the middle) under a wide-framed French hood, such as Anne Boleyn wears in her only surviving portrait. Emerging from an elaborate dress with its pendant of blue sapphires and one white pearl, the young woman's small refined white hands with long fingers hold a bright red Missal with a large jewelled cross on it. Beneath eyes as sharp as her father's in his last portrait, now at Magdalene College, Cambridge, the young duchess also has a large but tightly held mouth and a somewhat recessive chin that completes, exactly as her father's does, an oval face. By 1546, in the duchess' second portrait (Plate 4), another miniature at Arundel, this face has filled out with jowls just like her father's in his 1515 portrait. In fact, the older duchess' whole frame in the half-body miniature appears bloated. The years (she was 49) have coarsened her physically, the bright red stole adding weight to a breast and bodice cut too low. The mouth also seems fuller, at least the chin more recessive. Light reddish hair peeks out beneath an elaborate gabled headdress of wood panels, an English hood such as Catherine of Aragon wears in her only surviving portrait, edged here by a billiment or band of jewels and peaking high in light red velvet, from which falls a long train of darker material. Beneath this artifice and in the whiteness of the face, the black piercing eyes above a strong Roman nose are the same as her father's.

In the years immediately after Buckingham's death, as Surrey and his mother spent their quiet mornings together, Elizabeth Howard could not but pass on the memory of her father to her first son. As that daughter knew, Buckingham had a series of cultural texts before him at all times, especially those in his own memory of the life and writings of his beloved uncle, Anthony Woodville, Lord Scales. What Woodville gave his nephew, as translated through the fierce memory of Buckingham's own mother Catherine Woodville, was a style the younger Edward Stafford incorporated to the end in 1521. Thus, in his 1506 meeting with the Burgundian Archduke Philip, he was remarkable in his 'soo large and so riche a gowne of clothe of golde, his courser richly trapped, and the trapper enramplished with littel prety belles of silver and gilt, of a very goodly fascyon'; at the wedding of Prince Arthur and Catherine of Aragon, he wore a gown 'wrowght of nedyll work and sett upon cloth of tyssu ffurrid wyth Sablys', a garment valued at £1500, a sum much greater than the combined yearly livelihood of hundreds of artisans; and at the Field of the Cloth of Gold in 1520, one of his last occasions, 'none,' wrote Lord Herbert, 'so gorgeous' (191). Anthony Woodville may also have given Buckingham a literary text the Duchess of Norfolk had doubtless viewed (her father's reputation for skill in tournaments and lists was matched only by his genuine 'love of letters'). This rare manuscript extract, the one surviving text from Buckingham's library, comes from an illuminated moral treatise *La Toison d'or*, written around 1470, in the reign of Charles the Bold and his Duchess Margaret of York, by the bishop of Tournai Guillaume Fillastre, the Chancellor of the Order of the Golden Fleece (the highest honour in the empire). As Kipling noted, in this work, for the first time, magnificence heads the princely virtues in the place of justice (and the text may have influenced Skelton's morality play in 1516 for Henry VIII, *Magnificence*).[18]

Such style and magnificence would characterize the memory of Surrey's grandfather in the late Renaissance. During the reign of James I, who venerated Buckingham, Shakespeare wrote his own inscription of the legendary figure in the part of *Henry VIII* attributed to him. Shakespeare's Buckingham is clad in black and resembles, in this drama, more his grandson Surrey or Prince Hamlet than the actual duke. His speech at the scaffold is one of Shakespeare's most vivid in *Henry VIII* precisely because it inscribes a sacrifice for honour. Speaking to his friends, who call him 'the mirrour of all courtesy,' Buckingham affirms the meaning of his beheading: 'Go with me, like good angels, to my end, / And as the long divorce of steel falls on me, / Make of your prayers one sweet sacrifice.' (I, i, 53; 75–8).

The grandest and most aggressive sign of Buckingham's magnificence had remained on the Jacobean English landscape as a relic, as it probably remained for the poet Earl of Surrey as a particular point of his mental geography, remembered from his first five years. Thornbury in Gloucestershire was 'a contemporary *tour-de-force*' and 'the last private castle to be built' completely new in England. It was also the last great house to be built in a castellated style but hardly for defensive purposes, as Hawkyard has shown, despite the quick-tempered Buckingham's unpopularity in the nearby Welsh marches he controlled. Thornbury had risen to evoke another culture and by that means to define a new social order beyond the Tudors', so that the antiquarian Leland, the friend and admirer of Surrey, looking at the unfinished monument, called Thornbury 'a noble piece of work purposed'. As Girouard notes, Thornbury demonstrated a social aggression with symbolism 'so lavish' in form that it inevitably left the house, like his grandson's Surrey House, unfinished and the owner beheaded. As Maurice Howard notes, 'in the case of both the Duke of Buckingham in 1521 and . . . of the Earl of Surrey at the

[18] *Chronicle of Calais*, ed. John Gough Nichols, Camden Society, 34 (1846) 50–1. A. H. Thomas and I. D. Thornley, eds., *The Great London Chronicle* (1938) 311 and 339; Richard Grafton, *Chronicle or History of England* (1809), vol. 2, 260. For Buckingham's love of literature, see Carole Rawcliffe, *The Staffords, Earls of Stafford and Dukes of Buckingham 1394–1521* (1978), 40. For the exact figures and fluctuations of the Stafford estates during Duke Edward's life, as well as the rise in the family fortune, see her ch. 6. For the manuscript, see BL MS Royal 19A vi, f. 1v; cf. Kipling, *The Triumph of Honour* (1977), 138. For the importance of this document in conceptualizing literary culture in early modern England, see Seth Lerer, *Courtly Letters in the Age of Henry VIII: Literary Culture and the Arts of Deceit* (1997), 17–18.

end of 1546, splendid houses were key points of accusation in the process of attainder.'[19]

In fact, although the whole style of Thornbury embodied clear nostalgia and 'romantic adjuncts of nobility', as McFarlane argues, and Buckingham remained for Stone the last of the great magnates, 'a man of towering strength, the like of which was never to be seen again,' nevertheless not nostalgia but the future of the English nobility concerned Buckingham. In the Tudor court of 1521 with a diminishing treasury because of a foreign policy that focused on France, the son of Henry VII did not miss this message of magnificence from a descendant of Edward III with his own large number of retainers. The king did not need the direction of Cardinal Wolsey, whose scarlet silk shoes had once had water poured on them, in full view of the court, by Duke Edward, who refused to hold the basin for Wolsey to wash his hands as Buckingham had just done for the king. Of course, the third Duke of Buckingham was hardly alone in his 'anger and rage', in Rawcliffe's terms, at Henry VIII's 'attempts to turn the nobility into satellites and courtiers whose function was to act as vehicles for royal propaganda rather than as ministers of state'. He was, however, at 43 the richest and the most stylish, genealogically the most assured of all the nobility, and even popular with the people. The Venetian ambassador believed that 'were the king to die without male heir'—a real possibility in 1519, except for the newborn bastard Henry Fitzroy—'the Duke might easily obtain the crown,' a contingency also discussed at the end of Henry VII's reign. The rising forms of Thornbury thus provided enough evidence for those who saw it as a base for insurrection.

Buckingham's trial of 13 May 1521 bears an uncanny resemblance to Surrey's own trial over twenty-five years later. Charles Knyvet of the East Anglian family had the most damaging evidence of all (detailing a knife drawn in a supposed threat to the king), and Buckingham spoke an hour in his defence, with rhetoric that moved the courtroom. He had known, Buckingham said, that the king willed him to die. Had he not heard that Henry VIII himself had written by hand a letter indicting himself, the king's mother's first cousin, and even underlining the charges against Buckingham, a remarkable act for the young king, who had confessed recently to Wolsey, 'writing is to me somewhat tedious and painful'? After Buckingham's defence (but, like Surrey's, with no confession) the 'Flodden Duke' condemned his daughter-in-law's father to death as a traitor, although he wept. Despite the urgent pleas of the queen, who may have interceded because of her close friend Elizabeth Howard, no pardon came to Surrey's grandfather. On 17 May 1521, when Surrey was 5 and in Ireland, Buckingham, surrounded by two

[19] For the reputation of Thornbury, see Girouard, *Life in the English Country House*, 73 and Stone, *Aristocracy*, 217. The text of the licence for building can be found in PRO C66/613, m.5. A. D. K. Hawkyard, 'Thornbury Castle', *Transactions of the Bristol and Gloucestershire Archaeological Society*, 95 (1978), 57–8. John Leland, *Itinerary*, ed. L. T. Smith (1964), vol. 5, 100. Girouard, *Life in the English Country House*, 69. Cf. Barbara Harris, *Edward Stafford*, 87. Maurice Howard, *The Early Tudor Country House: Architecture and Politics 1490–1550* (1987) 28.

sheriffs and a guard of 500 men, walked to Tower Hill. After reciting the Penitential Psalms, the duke took off his outer gown, asked for a swift execution and, being blindfolded, laid his head on the block, 'miserably', reported the Venetians, 'but with great courage'.[20]

Warfare

This death may have radicalized the young mother—or at the least taught her the violence of her culture. She could no longer depend for her freedom on the established forces of history as she had known them. If this radical lesson were one the son learned instinctively from his powerful mother, the duchess offered her own counter-blow, resistance, and challenge. The opportunity came soon. In the late 1520s and early 1530s, the battle had moved for the duchess to the Tudor court itself. The Imperial Ambassador was soon writing to his master, the nephew of the English queen, Charles V, about the intrigues of the Duchess of Norfolk in helping her friend, Queen Catherine. On 27 November 1530, after referring to a Tyndale book, he relayed information about the king's 'Great Matter' and the opinions of the various universities abroad and then tells of a new conspiracy for the queen: 'A few days ago the duchess of Norfolk sent the Queen a present of poultry and with it an orange.' Inside this orange the young duchess had enclosed a copy of a letter that the emissary from Rome, Gregory Casale, had written. The duchess' daring is serving the queen well, he reported. Except for such secret smuggling of information to her household, the queen had little knowledge of just how the talks between the papacy and her husband on the divorce were proceeding. Although Chapuys did not trust Norfolk and suspected the wife was his pawn, Queen Catherine herself 'imagines that the Duchess has sent her this present and letter of her own accord, and out of the love and affection she bears her'. Even the Imperial Ambassador had to admit to the emperor the value of the duchess' conspiracy: 'At all events this seems to open a way for the Queen to communicate more freely and disclose her plans to the Duchess, for which purpose it has been deemed expedient to dissemble better in future.' In any case, the duke himself, wrote the ambassador, was 'a bad dissembler' although now 'La Dame' (his codename for Anne Boleyn) was using her uncle in her plot to destroy Cardinal Wolsey completely (the cardinal's physician was even staying at the Howard mansion in Lambeth). Furthermore, this warfare was so consuming that Norfolk's niece wept and wailed, 'regretting her lost time and honour', and threatened to leave the king until he begged her not to, 'most affectionately, and even with tears in his eyes'.

[20] K. B. McFarlane, *The Nobility of Later Medieval England* (1973) 209, 211; Stone, *Aristocracy*, 253–4. Rawcliffe, *The Staffords*, 86, 185. See Kenneth Pickthorn, *Early Tudor Government* (1951), 2, 45, 48, for Buckingham's popularity (as a landlord, however, he was considered tyrannical). For Henry VIII's complaints, see Scarisbrick 120. For the Venetian responses, *CSPVen*, vol. 2, 1287; vol. 3, 213 (124).

Two months later Chapuys reported: 'Yesterday the duchess of Norfolk sent to tell the Queen that her opponents were trying to draw her over to their party, but that if all the world were to try she would remain faithful to her.' The duchess also 'desired the Queen to be of good courage, for her opponents were at their wits' end, being further off from their object than the day they began.' Three months later, in late April 1530, so Chapuys wrote, the duchess reported to the queen that 'the Lady' had been vituperative when the king had praised his daughter Princess Mary, whom 'the Lady' hated as much as she hated the queen. Indeed Norfolk's niece 'becomes more arrogant every day, using words and authority towards the King, of which he has several times complained to the duke of Norfolk, saying that she was not like the Queen, who had never in her life used ill words to him.' The duchess reported, so Chapuys heard, that in all this, her husband Norfolk 'was in marvellous sorrow and tribulation'. No doubt, the duke was suffering because of his wife's behaviour in choosing such a disastrous side in the battle. The duchess had even announced that she knew 'quite well she would be considered the ruin of all her family'—Chapuys' subjunctive mood here showing that, from the start, the young duchess had contemplated such 'ruin' as a consequence of her choice—but now, 'if God wished that she should continue in her fantasy, it would be a very good thing for the Queen.'

Two weeks later, Chapuys reported again to his imperial master that the young duchess had been secretly reading other correspondence at court (riffling through her husband's papers?) and had found a copy of a secret but crucial letter from the Scottish Duke of Albany (at the French court) to Henry VIII on better prospects for the divorce. Norfolk himself had just told the Imperial Ambassador that the queen's 'courage was supernatural' and 'It was the Devil, and nobody else, who was the inventor of this accursed dispute.' But Anne Boleyn was winning: the king was clearing a great park in front of Cardinal Wolsey's house at York Place and had built a 'very long gallery' across the busy street to it, and for all that, he had demolished 'a great many houses, to the great injury of those to whom they belonged, and there is no talk of compensation'. He was now building at this spot of Whitehall a new palace of honour for Anne Boleyn. At the same time, 'at the desire of the same lady the duchess of Norfolk has been sent home, because she spoke too freely and declared herself more than they [Anne Boleyn and the king] liked for the Queen.' Elizabeth Howard, the Duchess of Norfolk, had now been banished from court. She would not return for twenty years.[21]

Thus, by 1531 Norfolk must have realized that his wife could not remain at the commanding centre of a household and community so interwoven with the court. If the Howards were to rule their own world, much less to live at court, they needed unity. Almost 60, Norfolk had probably not sought physical comfort or feminine solace anywhere else except with his wife. Now she had estranged herself by her choice. He turned elsewhere, and, not surprisingly, he was as faithful to his young

[21] *CSP Span* vol. 4, i, 509 (818–19). *LP*, vol. 5, 70, 216, 238. For the Bouche of Court allowed the duke and duchess and her enormous expenses at court, see *LP*, vol. 1, 2, 1939; vol. 4, 2, 374.

mistress Bess Holland, the daughter of his private secretary, as he had been earlier to his wife (neither the grandfather John nor the father Thomas had ever been implicated as adulterers, unlike Edward IV and Henry VIII). Old Norfolk understood quite well that shame from a female arose not just from having been cuckolded and rearing bastards and false heirs but, more telling in the hierarchy of values, from losing one's property and thus one's honour as the rightful owner of a woman and commander of her life. Being shamed by a female was to surrender to a kind of chaos. The irony is that the duchess held this same attitude of control and property due to rank. It explains her grave sense of personal insult at being ejected from her house: her insistence on the adverb 'styll' in her letters makes this point. The house 'styll' belonged to her, the rightful Roman chaste wife, not to 'harlottes'. What made her attitude and action in this matter unusual, if not unique, at the court of Henry VIII was her defiance of an injustice that offended, at least for her, a larger moral order, not her disapproval of the social order itself. What added to Elizabeth Howard's particular shame in losing any possible right to property was that her husband, no longer a young man, sought a mistress, although it was probably his first and last time. The choice of someone else could only remind the duchess of just how deeply her choice had hurt Thomas Howard. What Norfolk was seeking, after Elizabeth's choice to seek a higher honour than her marriage and children, was order in marriage as elsewhere in his life. When his wife deserted him, in effect if not in actuality, he filled her space with Bess Holland—probably around 1527 because, writing in 1538, the brooding exiled wife had kept count of the years: '& ytt ys a xj yere syn my lorde my husbonde furst fell in love wyth hyr.'[22]

Just as the breakdown of Queen Catherine's marriage was caused by an upstart like Anne Boleyn, so the fury of Elizabeth Howard at her husband's adultery lay in his choice of a social inferior. Elevated to lady-in-waiting in Anne Boleyn's court, Bess Holland was allowed to become a quite vocal critic of the duchess, as Surrey's mother complained in a letter of 10 November 1537: 'I have so many Inimys: besse howland in the courtt for cheffe & the bawde & the harlott at Kennyngar [Kenninghall]' and she added: '& the men as sothwell one' (389), a prophetic inscription for her son about the family cousin Richard Southwell. But her chief enemy Bess Holland was not to be tolerated by the true wife. Writing to Cromwell earlier on 30 December 1536, Elizabeth Howard had noted that terrible as her exile was, 'yet I am content wt all for I am aute of daunger of my ennemyes and of the ille lyff that I had with my lord my husband syne he loved besse holand first which was butt washer of my Norcery [nursery] viij yeres and she hath been the cause of all my trouble' (392). The duchess raged at the friendship of her daughter and Bess Holland, who is not only 'that harlott weche hase putt me to al thys trobull' but is 'a churles darte [daughter] & off no gentyll blode'. Worst of all, her husband 'kepys hyr [Bess] styll in hys hous & hys chylder [the mature Surrey, her duchess daughter, and Thomas] mayntene the mater [situation].' It

[22] BL Cotton Titus B I, ff. 888–8v, all references hereafter in text.

was all a deliberate insult to herself and her property, and so 'therefore I wyll never cum att hym [and by implication, her children] duryng my lyff' (888v).

Her main attacks in her letters were on her husband. Thus, on 26 June 1537, she wrote from Redbourn in an 'imprisonment' she compared to confinement in the Tower and where she was forbidden a visit from any noble male and most gentlewomen (389; 391). She was angry that 'my lorde my husbande' has 'so meche welth & honoure' yet 'he nether regard god nor hys honoure.' Sadly, she remembered that in the beginning 'he chose me for love' and the marriage had lasted 'xxv yeres & [she] hath borne hym v chyldes' (390). Her Dido fury built on that first innocent love and its ultimate failure to last. On 24 October of the same year, remarking how Norfolk has kept all her jewels and apparel and her money, she recalled that the choice of marriage 'never came off me nor non off my fryndes' so that, when Norfolk came to Thornbury long ago at Easter 'tyde, he wold have non off my systers but only me.' Now she had been abused (at least in her memory) and she repeated the details in three letters to Cromwell: 'They [Bess Holland and other women in the household] bounde me & pynnaulled [pummelled] me & satt on my brest tyll I spytt blod wech [which] I have ben worse for ever syns & all for spekyng agayne ye woman in ye courtt besse holand' and 'therefore he put me out at ye dowrs & kepys ye bawde & ye harlotte styll in hys house' (390).

Finally Surrey's father wrote to Cromwell (Plate 00) one Friday morning before dawn. Norfolk had heard that his 'wilful wife' had 'come to London' and met with Cromwell with plans of meeting him. 'My Lord,' said the almost 70-year-old Norfolk, 'I assure you as long as I live I will never come in her company' until she had first written to him. As the cunning duke who had survived four kings knew, the duchess' letters had now became prima facie evidence that Cromwell was finding very valuable. She must apologize in writing, Norfolk continued, so there will be a legal record that 'she hath untruly slandered me in writing' in the absurd story that after her daughter Mary's birth, he had drawn her 'out of her bed by the hair of her head, about the house, and with my dagger give her a wound in her head.' What she writes is not true: he has witnesses, 'many honest persons,' that she had the scar in her head over a year before from the drawing of two teeth (N1: XXXII).

The violence of this language—from which neither Surrey nor his sister could escape—and the public display continued. The duchess refused to be divorced even though the duke sent her two 'chaplens' telling her 'yff I wolde be devorsed he wold gyffe me all my Joelles & all my aparell & a grett partt off hys platte & off hys stuffe off houshold' (389). But, although she even visited the king, who told her to go home to her husband, she said in her November 1537 letter that she would have none of the counsel coming from her husband (and by implication, from others), knowing 'yt schall not be for my profett nor yet for my honure' (389). In her last surviving letter in 1540, she stated flatly that Cromwell had done nothing for her, but beseeching him 'to have pytte uppon me & remember I am a gentyllwoman borne & hath bene browte up dentely & not to lyve so barly as I do' and now 'age cummyth on a pase wt me & besydes yt [that] her was nevar woman yt [that] bare so ungracyus a eldest sone & so ungracyus a dawter & unnaturall as I hawe done' (391).

The Last Years

By the next decade, one fact was becoming clear. She had won—at least the battle of the divorce. She remained legally the Duchess of Norfolk for the rest of her life. As legal duchess, she was allowed after 1547 to return to Lambeth and the Howard mansion there while her husband remained in the Tower during the Edwardian years. In fact, over two months after her son's beheading, on 28 March 1547, the duchess was still getting her annuity of £200 as though the duke were not imprisoned, and she soon had funds to pay for gifts for her brother's daughters. In her will eleven years later, she named her brother Stafford as residuary legatee and sole executor, not her surviving son Thomas. In the will, 'sick and diseased in body but sound in mind' and willing her 'soul to God, the Virgin Mary, and all the blessed company of heaven,' she left son Thomas a silver and gilt cup; then a velvet gown to the young wife of her grandson, the fourth Duke of Norfolk; to Surrey's youngest daughter, Margaret, not yet married, two taffeta gowns; and to her sister-in-law Ursula, affectionately referred to as 'suster Stafford' (and the sister of the new Archbishop of Canterbury, Reginald Pole), she left most of her clothes and jewellery, including her 'best French hode' (such as she wore in her last miniature) and 'best sadle, with cover of velvett, and all that belongith therto'. On her tomb in St Mary's Lambeth (before her grandson, the fourth Duke of Norfolk, transferred her body to the newly embellished Howard tombs at Framlingham), her brother wrote her epitaph: 'Thou wast to me, both far and near / A Mother, sister, a friend most dear.'[23]

At the end, in addition to the baptism of Philip Howard, there were two key moments of justification for the old duchess. Bess Holland, the imprisoned third duke's mistress, died within a year after Surrey's beheading. The new Protector of the realm had returned all her jewels and her grand manor house in Suffolk because of her cooperation. She was rich enough now to make a respectable marriage, the only hope for a spoiled woman near 40 whose aged lover had lost everything. Thus, after an interval of several months, she married an East Anglian,

[23] *Acts of the Privy Council of England*, ed. J. R. Dasent (London, 1890), hereafter APC, vol. 2, 77. For the brother's letter, *LP*, vol. 6, 475. *Wills from Doctors' Commons: A Selection from the Wills of Eminent Persons, 1495–1695*, ed. John Gough Nichols and John Bruce, Camden Society, Old Series, 83 (1863), 54–5. For the will see PRO Prob 11/42A, ff. 345–345v (PCC 31 Welles). It should be noted that she left 'my greater tablettes' to Surrey's son, the new fourth Duke of Norfolk, whatever these pictures were. The epitaph can be found in *Letters*, ed. Wood, vol. 3, 189. In the 1530s, Stafford had written to Cromwell about his older sister's 'sensual and wilful mind' and the 'jeopardy from her wild language' (*LP*, vol. 6, 475).

Henry Reppes. By summer 1547 she was pregnant and then, probably as a result of a botched Caesarean birth, dead by April 1548.[24] A greater justification occurred on 3 August 1553. The new Queen Mary 'came riding to London' to claim her city with its multitude of ruined churches and monasteries (noted by the ambassadors). She went first to the Tower, 'making her entrance at Aldgate' where streamers hung about the gate, and children sat on a stage singing 'with their masters and mistresses'. All the streets to the Tower were laid with gravel and all 'the crafts of London stood in a row,' with banners and streamers hanging over their heads. Before the 37-year-old queen walked 1000 footmen in 'velvet coats and cloaks in embroidery' and then the Lord Mayor of London with the mace and the Earl of Arundel with a sword, 'all trumpets blowing'. After the new queen came the Princess Elizabeth and 'next her the Duchess of Norfolk' and then the Marchioness of Exeter, the mother of Edward Courtenay (in the Tower with Surrey in 1546), and then, after the order of ladies and the aldermen and then guards with bows and javelins, 3000 horsemen with spears and javelins. On the next day, in a ceremony, the queen released the prisoners in the Tower, among these the young Courtenay and Stephen Gardiner, the Bishop of Winchester, who declared 'he was delivered out of prison as it were by miracle, and preserved of God to restore true religion, and to punish heresy.' Then the Duke of Norfolk was released and on Tower Green, in the presence of the queen, his wife received him into her freedom. She had won, and she took him to their Lambeth mansion, the couple united once more after twenty years.[25]

At Mary I's coronation ceremonies, the duchess who had never ceased to be a duchess played a greater role. The duke had been restored to his honour as Earl Marshal (and during the dinner, even at his advanced age, he rode up and down Westminster Hall as Buckingham had at the coronation of Henry VIII). The young Earl of Surrey, Thomas, the poet earl's first son, was 'doer' under his grandfather. In the Saturday coronation procession from the Tower, the old duke, who had seen the coronation of Richard III, marched before the queen, and after the queen, in the first chariot sat Princess Elizabeth and Anne of Cleves. 'Then rode on horseback four ladies of estate, appareled in crimson velvet, and their horses trapped with the same,' and the first of these in red velvet was Elizabeth Howard, the Duchess of Norfolk. The next day of the coronation, Sunday, 1 October 1553, the duchess singly bore the train of her god-daughter as she became queen of England.

[24] After Bess Holland's miserable death, there was the ignominy of a controversy over just how long her baby lived in order to determine who would get her land. For the record of the marriage, *Calendar Patent Rolls 1548–1549* (1914–16), hereafter CPR, vol. 2, 140, where the couple are pardoned, possibly for marrying without a licence. For the land controversy, *Historical Manuscripts Commission*, Crawdy, ed. Walter Rye (1885), 2 (11 and footnote) and also 3 (15); *CPR 1548–1549*, 92 and 1553, 244; NRO, NRS 27260, 361 v3f6v; and PRO C1/1379/24. For help here, I am indebted to Gary Hill.

[25] Charles Wriothesley, *A Chronicle of England During the Reign of the Tudors, from A.D. 1485 to 1559*, ed. William Douglas Hamilton, F.S.A. (rpt. 1965; London: The Camden Society, 1865), hereafter cited in text as W, 2:94.

When the old duke died in August 1554 at Kenninghall, after helping defeat his poet son's close friend, the younger Sir Thomas Wyatt, in his rebellion against the new queen, the duchess was with him. After the hurried and disgraceful end of her first son, the old duke was laid to rest in St Michael's at Framlingham in what became one of the famous Howard tombs, with 'a goodly herse of wax, with a dozen of bannerols of his progeny' and then 144 'pensils' and 144 escutcheons, with standards and three coats of arms and four heralds. After the burial, an enormous meal was served in the open countryside around the ancient castle of Framlingham for all the county, with 40 oxen, 100 sheep, and 60 calves roasted for the occasion. Three days later, elaborate obsequies at St Mary Overy's in London were followed by two days of bells ringing in dirge.[26] In his will the old duke, with memory 'full, hole, and perfitt' and trusting in Christ's Passion, made no mention of the duchess, whose jointure was managed by the Howard estate as a separate subsection but still might have been mentioned. Norfolk willed Tendring Hall to Surrey's second son Henry (the future Earl of Northampton) £1000 each to Surrey's three daughters on reaching 20 or being married, and almost everything else to his heir, the fourth Duke of Norfolk, Thomas, except £500 to his daughter Mary, the Duchess of Richmond, who incurred expenses, he noted, 'trying to free me from prison' and bringing up Surrey's children. As evidenced by Norfolk's own will, Surrey's sister must have remained on good terms with her father, whom she had visited in the Tower on 24 February 1549, 'with train convenient' (her brother Lord Thomas paid a similar visit on 8 April 1551).[27] On 9 December 1557, quite suddenly, it seems, Mary, the only daughter and sister, died. She was only 40, and there is no record of any reconciliation with her mother nor evidence of the Duchess of Norfolk, who spent lavishly on her nieces, giving anything to her daughter.

The Choices of the Duchess of Richmond

In her evidence against her brother at his trial in December 1546, the Duchess of Richmond reported that the poet earl told her of his fear that nothing would survive. He too might be lost. 'And that her brother,' she declared, said 'God long save my father's life; for if he [the father] were dead, they would shortly have my head.' And it was clear who 'they' were, as the duchess pointed out: 'Moreover, that the earl her brother should say, these new men loved no nobility' and 'that her brother was so much incens'd against the said earl [Edward Seymour, Earl of Hertford, and soon after Surrey's beheading, the Lord Protector of the realm, Duke of Somerset]' that 'as the duke her father said thereupon, his son would lose as much as he had gather'd together.' Once more, in that fatal December, Surrey's

[26] For the procession and the duke's funeral, see Strype, *Ecclesiastical Memorials*, vol. 3, 26–7, 318–19.

[27] PRO Prob 11/37/14; *APC*, vol. 2, 400; vol. 3, 254.

Ophelia-like sister was caught between her father and brother in two powerful loyalties, if not loves, as earlier she had found herself in a *ménage à trois* with her brother and his beloved friend Henry Fitzroy, the Duke of Richmond, her husband.

What became clear to the young woman quite early is that she could never compete with the hard absolutes of honour both Surrey's acts and her mother's defiance revealed. For her both may have offered signs without meaning, talk and more talk. What she wanted was, in fact, what the new Christianity offered: a realism with the hard and exact language of Holy Scripture that could offer sanity, not symbolism. Early at court, under the eager tutelage of her new friend Archbishop Cranmer, she had found it. Literalism and the internal realism of the new faith could transform her own painful, often confused subjectivity. With this holy empiricism, she could make a clear choice in 1546. She could directly condemn her brother and save her father and herself and the children. She would tell all. 'And if God call'd away the king,' the young duchess continued in her December evidence in her brother's voice (at least as reported by Lord Herbert), the Howards 'should smart for it. And that her brother hated them all [the new men] since his being in custody in Windsor-castle; but that his father seemed not to care for their ill will' but her brother (or the father—the reference is ambiguous here) had said: 'his truth should bear him out' (378).

This sense of a transcendent 'truth' was finally Surrey's sister's enemy. Oppressed by it, Mary Richmond sought her own more pragmatic 'truth'. As the only surviving daughter and doubtless cherished as a baby and child, she soon became, in defiance of her mother, a strong supporter of Anne Boleyn. She appeared as a major participant in four crucial ceremonies, her first cousin's investiture as Marchioness of Pembroke before the trip to France in 1532, the masque and ball in Calais when Francis I danced with Anne Boleyn, the new queen's coronation in May 1533, and then the christening of the Princess Elizabeth in September of that year. To the court of Anne Boleyn, the Howard daughter brought all the training of her family and their sophisticated codes of etiquette. She also brought a high sensitivity to language and literary ideas, as evidenced by her relationship to the Devonshire Manuscript of poetry, a major source for the texts of Wyatt and other early Tudor poets and, for Marotti, a crucial 'medium of socioliterary intercourse' in the English Renaissance. She also gave intellectual friendship and patronage to reformed Christian humanists such as John Foxe and John Bale and became, at her estate at Reigate in Surrey during the Edwardian years, one of the two greatest patronesses of reformed Christian writing in the Edwardian world, collecting numerous dedications. In fact, she wanted to be identified with the power of the new Christian humanists, and in this respect she had brought up the episode that further hurt her brother by accusing him of having erected an altar in the ruins of the Boulogne cathedral at the request of the populace during Christmas 1545.[28]

[28] Arthur F. Marotti, *Manuscript, Print, and the English Renaissance Lyric* (1995), 39. For questions about the Duchess of Richmond's exact role in the formulation of the Devonshire Manuscript, see Raymond Southall, 'Mary (Howard) Fitzroy's Hand in the Devonshire Manuscript', *RES*, 45

Her grandest gesture, by which she gained her title and a lifetime of virtual celibacy, was her first, however. She had entered the court at the same time as her brother to serve, like him, as a pawn in one of Norfolk's most vaunted strategies (one supported by Anne Boleyn), the assimilation of Henry VIII's illegitimate son Fitzroy into the Howard clan. Her marriage to Henry, Duke of Richmond, a year or two younger than she, held immense political promise in the early 1530s because, unless a son was born soon to Henry VIII, Norfolk and his daughter had good reason to think the Duchess of Richmond might just become the next queen of England.

During this halcyon period, Holbein drew her—a peculiarly effaced drawing on his pink paper, obviously unfinished, probably a sketch for a full painted portrait (Plate 9). In Holbein's drawing, the ceremonial motif is heightened by the fact that the colours for the dress and for the hat are precisely inscribed on the drawing as though for a portrait, in Holbein's German, *samet rot* (red velvet) and *schwarz felbet* (black velvet). Although the dress and its high lace collar are only sketched in black, white, and coloured chalks, the hat of black velvet is filled out with heavy ink applied with a brush. This hat dominates the drawing.

Beneath it, the duchess's long oval face is like her brother's in Holbein's drawing of him in the same early series. Her hair, even more red and auburn than her brother's, is pulled severely back, but beneath the hat, the face is almost blank. Her eyelids appear closed and the mouth tightly pursed. What focuses the blankness of the young woman's face is the large hat over it, its spreading trapezoidal design both bent and curved in the centre with a plume on it that flows to the right of the drawing. It is exactly the same sort of hat her brother is wearing in his early Holbein, although his hat stands at a more rakish angle to show his large uneven eyes and straight hair falling over his forehead in a fringe. Holbein obviously intended his completed oil portrait to do more with the duchess' hat (apparently adapted from a male fashion, possibly for hunting). Despite the two rough sketches on the bottom of the drawing that show Holbein working towards a finished portrait, the drawing remains her only image.

During this same period of the Holbein portrait, the latent tensions in the household of the third Duke of Norfolk broke out. In fact, Lord Herbert blames the events of the final Howard débâcle on this antagonism and 'intestine division' between male and female in the family (737). Thus, by the time of her December 1546 interrogation, it must have been clear to Mary Richmond that her brother

(1994), 318–35. John King, *English Reformation Literature*, 106 and his *Tudor Royal Iconography: Literature and Art in an Age of Religious Crisis* (1982), 85. For the Duchess of Richmond's total commitment to a reformed Christian position, see her letters (*Letters*, ed. Wood, vol. 3, 203–5) to the secretary of the Privy Council, interceding (in language similar to her brother's in France in 1545) for preachers. Her language is that of the true believer: she wants to help 'that thereby these poor men's preaching shall be of more authority among the people; whom, if I were not assured to be both honest and godly preachers, I would never [have] attempted this for them' and one 'is not only of godly conversation, but also with learning and eloquence able to edify his auditory'. His 'prayers to the Lord' will 'increase you in all godliness'.

was lost. She must save her father if she could. He was her only source of income and family stability and family name, even if her choice to condemn Surrey meant the beheading of the heir and main stem of dynastic survival. As her earlier frantic letters to the king demonstrate, she had already suffered more than humiliation from the king's constant refusal to give her income that she deserved as his daughter-in-law.[29] So in December 1546 it was her father that she needed most of all to survive. 'Some passionate words of her brother she likewise repeated,' says Lord Herbert, 'as also some circumstantial speeches, little for his advantage; yet so, as they seemed much to clear her father' (739).

It is entirely probable that the Duchess of Richmond loved her brother deeply—at the same time that she feared his rivalry and strength, which might destroy all she could love and needed for her own survival. In fact, the devotion shown by the Duchess of Richmond towards Surrey's fatherless children may suggest not expiation for her destruction of him but the strength of her love for him. Children were the most vulnerable targets in a court ideologically turned against the Howards and in a court where children like the Yorkist princes in the Tower or those of the White Rose had been exterminated, the latter as recently as 1541. Her sense of family and self-preservation, nurtured by her experience at court and as a humiliated royal daughter-in-law, left her with a clear understanding of the terror of the December 1546 crisis. In a historical irony, by 1547 the head of the Howard dynasty had reverted to a woman who, whatever intimidation she may have suffered, brought the Howard children through to the reign of Mary Tudor, all taught by John Foxe, whom she had rescued from despair, as his autobiography testified. If she herself slowly disappeared and died, the children would live on. She had acted out her own version of Howard honour, and her father rewarded her specifically for this in his will.

The most terrible moment of her life had come, however, in the trial and death of her brother. The most telling indictment she did not bring up against him but was forced into by the examiners. 'Mary Dutchess of Richmond being examin'd,' says Lord Herbert, 'confess'd that the duke her father wou'd have her marry Sir Thomas Seymour, brother to the Earl of Hertford, which her brother also desir'd, wishing her withal to endear her self so into the king's favour, as she might the better rule here as others had done; and that she had refused.' The duchess was lying if she told her inquisitors that Surrey approved of Thomas Seymour. Although Surrey's French biographer Bapst makes the duchess into a coquette,[30] the young woman, who had presumably never known physical love, may have been genuinely attracted to Sir Thomas Seymour, who later tried to seduce the Princess Elizabeth in her adolescence and who had already won Catherine Parr before Cranmer had decided she should marry Henry VIII (and then won her again, outliving her). Whether the widowed duchess expressed her feelings or not, she soon

[29] PRO SP 1/131, ff. 252–3; 111, ff. 221–2v.

[30] Edmond Bapst, *Deux gentilshommes-poètes de la cour de Henry VIII* (1891), 339. See also Edwin Casady, *Henry Howard, Earl of Surrey* (1938), 179–81.

became the target of Surrey's violence at what he saw as the betrayal of family honour and the violation of his (and he thought her) intimate memory of Richmond—a bitter recall of innocence for both surviving Howards in 1546. So, with his own sensitivity unleashed, Surrey cried out that instead of wife to Seymour, she 'should become the Royal Mistress and play the part in England played in France by the Duchess d'Etampes,' the mistress of Francis I, whom in 1533 Surrey had seen in action at the Louvre and Fontainebleau (HB 738). She should make a play for the decrepit Henry VIII. It was 10 June 1546, during Whitsuntide, and all may have been in the public view of the court, in an anteroom at Whitehall. Surrey had just learned of his father's humiliating proposals to marry the poet's children to Edward Seymour's. The outburst, heard by the court, amounted to a prelude to treason for many, a grand insult to the king.

According to the Imperial Ambassador, at his trial Surrey's final comment on his sister reveals what a once loving relationship had turned into. Presented with his sister's handwritten accusation against him and knowing it would kill him, Surrey cried out, 'Must I, then, be condemned on the word of a wretched woman?'[31] 'Wretched' she may have been in her terrible choices, but the Devonshire Manuscript, brilliant reformed Christian texts, and Surrey's children—the Howard line—all survived because of the effaced young woman under the large hat.

Death and After Death

Five months before her daughter's death at 39, the old Duchess of Norfolk had presided over the baptism of her grandson Philip with all its promise (and in the records there is no mention of the Duchess of Richmond attending). After that, the dowager duchess' last recorded presence shows how eccentric she had become: the duchess attended the funeral of the Countess of Sussex, her husband's stepsister, dressed oddly, appearing 'in coloured habilments [such as yellow], instead of the usual garb of sorrow [black].'[32] Then came the series of disasters culminating in Mary Tudor's sterility and finally the realization by the court of her tumour and approaching death with no heir. Slowly, for the old duchess, all the justice and revision of history that had appeared so certain began to fade. Indeed, for every Counter-Reformation dream Elizabeth Howard and her grandson, the future St Philip Howard, may have held, Anne Boleyn's child did finally succeed. She survived the duchess' god-child Mary I as Queen of England and even her saint cousin in the Tower. Triumphant ideology did not become inevitable history, even for the suffering duchess. She may have refused to attend the 1533 coronation of Anne Boleyn on the Feast of Pentecost (as her grandmother had refused to attend the 1483 coronation of Richard III), and then in September refused to attend, on the

[31] *CSP Span*, vol. 9, 4.
[32] College of Arms MS 1:16, f. 266.

Nativity of the Blessed Virgin on 8 September, the christening of Anne Boleyn's child. But when that child ascended the throne in November 1558, the old duchess could not last two weeks. She had learned, as did her son, that no guarantees exist in the unfolding of history.

But survival of a sort went beyond death. In 1841, when Surrey's father's elaborate tomb was opened at St Michael's Framlingham, the excavators found three bodies with miscellaneous bones and skulls, suggesting children buried there with parents. Of the three adult bodies, the first was a male skeleton in a wooden coffin, doubtless the third Duke of Norfolk, Surrey's father; the second, a skeleton with the crown of the head detached, a fact that indicated an earlier form of embalming such as that used for Norfolk's first wife, the Princess Anne; and the third skeleton, in a lead coffin, presumably that of Elizabeth Howard, the Duchess of Norfolk. Her hair and the skin on her face were still, after three centuries, amazingly well preserved.[33]

[33] BL Add. MS 19193, f. 8.

3

The Other Henry: Windsor and France

Surrey's friendship with the illegitimate son of Henry VIII, Henry Fitzroy, the Duke of Richmond and Somerset, took him from childhood to early manhood. In the years between 1529 and 1536, when English culture underwent fundamental changes, the relationship of the two young men provided Surrey with a level of freedom from his past, that of the fathers and the mother, he had never known before. At least he dramatized it so, imprisoned at Windsor Castle in 1537, in his elegiac poems on Richmond's early death in 1536 and his own loss: 'Thus I alone, where all my freedom grew.'

This next stage in the life of Henry Howard is, in many ways, the most compelling and, in others, the most problematic. However later centuries judged the two poetic texts that resulted from this experience of friendship and love, a reader can only conclude from their language that Surrey had found in Richmond the other self that every Petrarchan poet was seeking. Both his elegy in newly invented heroic quatrains and his sonnet in original English interlocking rhymes reveal an immense sorrow that could only have come from profound loss. But the 'personal' emotion or sincerity, as one Victorian described the effect of the elegy, proves nothing. It simply extends the question: did, in fact, the lyric experience of the two young men as one—the clear meaning of both linguistic icons—actually happen? Or is the legend that came from this quintessential friendship so 'rendered' in art, in Henry James' term, that it becomes a history of its own, blocking out any real judgement of a historical relationship? The mystery here is not so much an interpretation of the scattered facts of the lives of Richmond and Surrey that do exist as the problem of that moment when text does produce, in fact, what Pocock sees as 'events' with their own history—in this case, the poetic 'event' of a special love and presence whose special absence and death just about kills the remaining Other.[1]

In 1537, when Surrey invented both his radically new forms, the Howard heir had good reasons to dramatize his position. Fictionalizing, even lying, may have seemed the most natural procedure to 'render' his years with the king's son. The young earl had begun to realize his distinctive place in a nobility now threatened. In death his friend could symbolize, even metonymize, all nobility of blood itself.

[1] Henry James, 'The Art of Fiction', in *The Art of Criticism: Henry James on the Theory and the Practice of Fiction*, ed. William Veeder and Susan M. Griffin (1986), 173. For what James meant, see Caroline Gordon, 'Introduction', Gustave Flaubert, *Madame Bovary* (1950), p. x: 'It was the kind of style that Henry James was to speak of later as "written"—a style in which every detail is rendered and made active in terms of experience.'

Seeing signs of annihilation, Surrey might well have argued that what Richmond epitomized was increasingly threatened by less noble figures like the person (traditionally Edward Seymour) whom the poet had supposedly attacked at Hampton Court, and for which act he—the son of a duke—had been imprisoned at Windsor Castle. Surrey might even have figured that Richmond would have wanted him to 'lie' (as Sidney later said, poets never tell the truth) in order for the poet earl to gain favour, attention, and freedom from Richmond's father, Henry VIII. What was at stake was the whole question of the role of the older nobility, a question perhaps beyond the 17-year-old who died but who represented—at least in Surrey's contrived texts—the question. Had not the young Fitzroy suffered, in fact, not because of his bastardy but because of his nobility and proximity to the throne? Richmond, a duke, the son of a king, could thus form one more model for the young earl's developing conception of a renewed nobility and honour. Most of all, Surrey could write a text dramatizing such a model of honour and the loss of such nobility in contemporary England and so challenge, even resist, the prescriptive Cromwellian acts and texts around him. Indeed, in his innovative elegy, Surrey punned on the word 'freedom', with its meaning in the time of Henry VIII of blood nobility. Thus manipulated, the model of Richmond in 1537 could project Surrey. Surrey as Richmond could advance the future of a resurgent English nobility.

Given such motives, then, did the young earl write out of an actual experience of love and death or for political ambition or both? It is likely that no one can ever know. A reader may speculate that the relationship had provided the poet with a calm centre, a new awareness of self, in the midst of threatening storms both in his family and outside. The result of freedom or liberation growing, to use Surrey's imagery, in the literal and psychic embrace of the one in the other would have completed the poet earl's education. From that perspective, a special kind of love had moved the young Howard heir from the windy plains of Kenninghall and the dark Gothic corridors of Norwich, the pilgrimage world of East Anglia, to the actual heights of Windsor Castle and the English court, with the French influences of Surrey's first cousin Anne Boleyn and then to the actual experience of France itself: Calais, the Louvre, Paris, then the light-filled gallery rising at Fontainebleau.

But few facts appear to justify the extraordinary laments in Surrey's texts that mark the death of the young Richmond and the loss of his presence. Absence of a beloved and the breakdown of the speaker are generalized well beyond the simple record of the friendship of two adolescents. They appear to project a larger death than Richmond's. Indeed, almost no elegy in English before 1537 had begun with so personal a cry, a direct address, an anguished apostrophe to the place of love itself, not to the lost figure. 'So cruel prison, how could betide, alas,' begins Surrey, 'As proud Windsor,' the place where the poet 'in lust and joy / With a king's son my childish years did pass, / In greater feast than Priam's sons of Troy.' It is this transformation of the symbolic space that dominates: how could it happen ('betide') that Windsor, a metonymy for England, once a place of love and honour, has become 'so cruel prison' and mirrors the fall of Troy itself?

But if the Windsor elegy and sonnet are about death, they are also evidence of a special kind of birth. Breakdown becomes breakthrough. Surrey becomes, at 21, a poet with considerable mastery. If the elegy points to a greater subject than the loss of a beloved, this larger subject is so subsumed in the total figure of love that the larger subject can only be understood in the lost presence of the male friend and the pain of his absence. Love and its death are thus, in James' sense, 'rendered'. That is, Surrey's carefully structured analogy of breakdown in his elegiac text becomes, by the fact of its being so textualized, a breakthrough—a linguistic artefact, that is, for the humanist Surrey an 'event' of Aristotelian probability arising from a specific historical moment. It is also a moment of totally new poetic invention—the enduring forms of the heroic quatrain and the English sonnet, which both survived for centuries. So whatever the 'sincerity' of the cry in the Windsor poems, one fact is clear. From 1537 on Surrey became a poet. He now had the language and the mastery for the final stage of his life, the kind of counter-attack his father was seeking. As a Howard (out of a Stafford) and as a text-maker, moving in his texts from breakdown to breakthrough, Surrey turned himself into the most avant-garde figure in his culture in this sense of origination. So if these Windsor poems first reveal a figure who wanted to reinvent English nobility in an image of himself, and himself as a king's son, they are 'true', at least as a poetic event. The actual historical facts may be another matter, however.

In the next two chapters their historical 'truth' will be examined in the documents that do survive and reveal a chronology of four periods for the friendship that led to the 'event' of the Windsor poems: (1) the moment of origin at a supper party; (2) the first years together at court and the roles required of each young man, motifs dramatized in the Windsor elegy; (3) the crucial year in France, particularly in Paris and Fontainebleau; and (4) the last years in which Richmond married Surrey's sister and became the virtual pawn of his father-in-law, his royal father, and Cromwell, and in which Surrey began to live with his wife, begetting the first of his five children, and facing at 20 his own role in the historical turmoil of England. Finally the poems themselves will be examined as enduring lyrics surviving from the context of the four periods and the violence—what Wyatt called 'these blodye dayes'—both young men experienced.

A Supper Party

On 9 December 1529, the Imperial Ambassador in London wrote a long letter to Charles V. A seemingly pedestrian political affair was recounted in a rhetorically unpedestrian letter. Written in French, the Holy Roman Emperor's favourite language, the letter narrated Eustace Chapuys' recent evening with the Duke of

Norfolk, Lord Treasurer of England, into whose hands, so Chapuys had written in October, 'the whole government of this country was fast falling.'[2] The party that evening had been curious and rather different from Chapuys' other regular encounters with the duke, a difference Chapuys dramatized in the form of his narrative to the emperor. Chapuys composed here, more than in his usual dispatches, an indirect discourse, using monologues based on the evening. He wanted to clarify, as precisely as possible, the peculiar events of the supper party and the midnight meeting afterwards.

Of the speeches Chapuys attributed to Norfolk that evening, most disclose the almost 60-year-old duke's new strategy for power that now included his son and the child Duke of Richmond, as well as Norfolk's discovery, his 13-year-old son's linguistic talents. Whatever genuine surprise and even pride Thomas Howard may have held that evening, the experienced duke intended to use Surrey's gift. It had always been so at court, but now even more with the Tudors: all gifts, whatever the source, were to be manipulated. Why not that of the despised 'new learning' and its language? In Norfolk's eyes, his son Henry could use Latin and the humanist disciplines in ways that would bring more power to the dynasty. In Chapuys' narrative—the first appearance of Surrey in the court world of Henry VIII—Norfolk conveyed his plans to the stylish Chapuys with apparent frankness. Of course, as both conversants knew, Norfolk had a larger purpose: if anyone could be impressed by his son's talent, the sophisticated Imperial Ambassador might be, and he just might convey all this, in a quite natural way, to his master, the most powerful man in the Western world. In fact, Norfolk was carrying with him proof of this talent of the 13-year-old boy. A sample of Latin composition his heir had recently written might give the Howard father as well as the son an authenticity Charles V would understand and honour. There was always that chance: the political world of Europe still reeled from the capture of Francis I at Pavia by Charles V and from the Holy Roman Emperor's virtual destruction of papal Rome in 1527, and, in England, all had seen the impending fall of Wolsey and Norfolk's own niece's strange rise to an immense prerogative, if not authority. In such breaking up, there might be a breakthrough for the Howards with this equally strange new talent of Norfolk's son.

On last Tuesday morning, so Chapuys began his narrative to the emperor, on the vigil or eve (he noted carefully) of the Immaculate Conception of Our Lady, the ambassador received a message inviting him to attend a supper party with the Duke of Norfolk. It was to be at a house not too distant from his own ('une mayson non loingtaynne de mon lougis pour collationner avec le Duc de Norphole').[3] When the Imperial ambassador entered the duke's lodgings, he found his host and others playing a card-game popular at the English court. Norfolk had a reputation

[2] *CSP Span*, vol. 4, i, 292 (194).

[3] All references to this letter are from Hof-, Haus-, und Staatsarchiv, Wien, England Korrespondenz, Kart. 4, Berichte an Karl V, 1529. See also the transcription of this letter in Bapst, *Deux gentilshommes-poètes*, 164–5, and also the English transcription in *CSP Span.*, vol. 4, I, 228 (160–3).

as a good gambler, the king having recently paid him for playing at dice the considerable sum of £45. That evening Norfolk had the English and foreign guests playing 'la premiere' or primero, another of Catherine of Aragon's courtly importations. The Venetians in this period described the third duke as small and spare of stature, with probably the same shape and dark colouring as his father and grandfather; further, the older Howard carried himself with a flexibility of body that matched his wife's description of his social character ('he can speak fair to his enemy as to his friend').[4] This kind of open mercurial energy could command a room, so it was natural for the French ambassador and then other guests, some foreign merchants, to surround the duke, when, after the black-haired Norfolk had talked for a while, Chapuys attacked the oppressive trading measures. Norfolk was understanding if defensive, until du Bellay stepped in to argue and the atmosphere heated up ('ung peu chaudemant'). At that point Norfolk cut the matter short, asked the French bishop (a friend of his niece Anne Boleyn) to leave them, and turned towards Chapuys. The two crossed to a corner of the hall where they could lean on a buffet. There, as Chapuys related the narrative to the emperor, the duke built his conversation up to an intimacy. The King of England's scruples of conscience about his marriage to Catherine of Aragon were not abating but growing, and this because of the opinion of other men who thought as the king did, and 'there is nobody in this world capable of turning the current of [the king's] passion,' once it has begun. Indeed, suppose, said the duke, the king took another wife? This message had clearly been the main point of the evening.

But there had been another. After the first point had been made, the public duty done, the second followed in a more leisurely way and, if seemingly more personal, with its own political axis. From the buffet, Norfolk took Chapuys graciously by the hand, drawing him towards the supper table. Then 'estant à table, le Duc me monstra une lettre que son filz luy avoit escrit en très élégant latin, me demandant que m'en sembloit' ('as we sat at table, the Duke showed me a letter that his son had written to him in quite elegant Latin and asked me what I thought of it'). The Imperial Ambassador was impressed. Delighted at Chapuys' response to the letter, Norfolk went on to concede how pleased he was that his son had achieved ('proufite') so well in his studies ('en lettres'). Indeed, his son Surrey had come so very far 'qu'il fust en bon commencement de vertu' ('that he has made a good start in virtue'), and all this had been done, so Chapuys continued his indirect discourse, 'pour la cause qu'il me desclayreroit après' ('for a good reason that he would declare to me later'). Although there now came a break in the activities of the supper party, the strategy had been set, the first part launched.

[4] *LP*, vol. 5, 749. See the discussion of primero and its popularity at the Tudor court in A. Forbes Sieveking, 'Games', in *Shakespeare's England: An Account of the Life & Manners of His Age* (1916), vol. 2, 472–4. See also Shakespeare's allusion in *Henry VIII*, V, i, 7–8, where Bishop Gardiner announces he has just left Henry VIII playing 'primero' with the Duke of Suffolk. Cf. the very different reference 'pull for Prime' in George Herbert's 'Jordan (I)'. For the wife's comment, see *The Lisle Letters*, ed. Muriel St Clare Byrne (1981), vol. 1, 550.

In this supper-party strategy, Norfolk was casting a wide net, with the daring of his father and grandfather. His decision about his son had come within the last six months. As late as 1527 the boy Surrey had been served his meals in the nursery at Framlingham Castle, keeping, for example, on a winter Friday the traditional weekly fast in honour of the Crucifixion. There were, of course, earlier occasions on which the father introduced the son to his own grand household of around 300 servants and then to the outside world, particularly in East Anglia. In fact, one such visit is described in a Latin extract from a monastery in Suffolk then flourishing but soon to disappear, Butley Priory. On 23 July 1529, the Duke of Norfolk rode into the priory around ten o'clock at night and had supper. It appears to have been a favourite hunting stop. When that night Norfolk brought with him his own young son, the boy of 13 already had a retinue of twenty-four male servants who rode with him, as the Latin register noted—a sign of his graduation into manhood and the privileges of an earl. Father and son were there to sell Staveton Park to the priory; in those days the monasteries often acted as a sure source of either cash or land transactions.

The third Duke of Norfolk was never one to hesitate, as his action at Flodden had shown. So, after this July record of Surrey's growing up, the duke found the moment to take a bolder step. Chapuys (and just possibly the emperor himself) might do Norfolk's work for him. Indeed the old duke had already begun to see an authority operating in England such as Salutati's enemies had described at the beginning of humanism in Florence a hundred years before: an oration like Salutati's falls, it was said, onto the scales of political decision with the weight of a thousand horses. Language was now becoming the currency of power, however much the duke despised the 'new learning'. Norfolk was fluent in French, knew the Burgundian world of romance, and was quite literary in his way. He had certainly not missed the earlier signs of humanist power at the court of Henry VII. Indeed, as brother-in-law to the king, he had attended events like the court performance of the first modern English drama, Medwall's *Fulgrens and Lucrece*, out of Tiptoft's *Declamacion of Noblesse* (as then printed by Caxton), when the Spanish ambassadors had come to negotiate about the child Catherine of Aragon. He also remembered the bestowing of the Order of the Garter in 1505 on Guidobaldo, Duke of Urbino, 'of all the princes in our day the most versed in both Latin and Greek literature and the science of war'. This dual genealogy for the Duke of Urbino had been narrated by a fellow native of Urbino, Polydore Vergil, one of those new humanists attracted to England, the award accepted for the humanist duke by none other than his representative, Count Baldassare Castiglione.[5]

So Norfolk was hardly the anti-humanist nobleman invented in 1516 by Richard Pace. 'God's body,' says the old nobleman in Pace's treatise on education, 'I would rather see my son hanged than study letters, for it ought to be that sons of the nobility blow the horn well, hunt expertly, train and direct a hawk beautifully.

[5] For the Latin extract, N 1, p. xiv. For Salutati, see Garrett Mattingly, *Renaissance Diplomacy* (1955), 62–3. Polydore Vergil, 141.

By God, studies in letters should be left to country boys.' Alexander Barclay had been more specific: 'the understandyng of latyn [is] at this time almost contemned by gentylmen.' This had appeared in Barclay's 1519 dedication to Surrey's grandfather, the 'Flodden Duke', of his robust translation from the Latin of Sallust's *Jugurthine Wars*. So by 1529 Surrey's father knew the political winds had shifted. Had not his friend Sir Thomas More in his life of the Florentine Platonist Pico della Mirandola said that true nobility stems not from noble birth (which Pico had) and inherited possessions but that 'honour is the reward of virtue' and virtue is recognized nowhere else but earned honour? Then the recent appointment of More himself as Lord Chancellor and holder of the Great Seal meant that this high honour had devolved from clergy and even blood nobility to the lower gentry, to a lawyer known for his power of language. Norfolk had already seen the lessons of the grammar school enter the vocabulary of power. Had not the recently deposed Wolsey once written that Charles V 'doth play on both hands using the nature of a participle which taketh *partem a nomine et partem a verbo*' ('part from a noun and part from a verb')?[6] No courtier spoke like this before Bosworth. What might not lie ahead, then, for the Howards, particularly with Anne Boleyn on the throne, if his son could inscribe the future of England through authenticity of blood *and* power of language and syntax?

It was after midnight when the two men departed from the lodgings where the meal was held, deliberately being seen leaving together and leaving behind the wondering French bishop and the papal nuncio. Although there was a much shorter route to Norfolk's place, the duke insisted on going 'devant mon lougis' ('before my residence'), much more of a distance because, if Chapuys is accurate, they were probably dining in the Westminster area, only a short boat ride across the river from the Howard mansion at Lambeth but a longer trip otherwise. As they were travelling with their own entourage, the duke began to talk personally and directly to the ambassador (and in his letter to the emperor, Chapuys used a direct monologue for Norfolk): 'I've already told you how happy [joyeux] I was, and for a special reason, that my son had applied himself to virtue. Now, since one must communicate one's affairs with true friends, I want very much to tell you this.' The duke's sincerity was breathtaking. 'The King has turned over to me the training [gouvernement] of his bastard son the duke of Richmond, for whom my son can now be the preceptor and guide [incitateur]. In this way the King's son can succeed in knowledge and virtue, and the friendship thus begun in this way

[6] Richard Pace, *De fructu qui ex doctrina percipitur (The Benefit of a Liberal Education)*, ed. and trans. Frank Manley and Richard S. Sylvester (1967), 22. I have translated more directly from the Latin than the editors. Cf. Sir Thomas Elyot, *The boke named the gouernour*, ed. H. H. S. Croft (1880), vol. 1, 99. Alexander Barclay, *The famous cronycle of the warre which the romans had agaynst Jugurth usurper of the kyngdome of Numidy: which cronycle is compyled in latyn by the renowened romayn Salust. And translated into englysshe by Sir Alexander Barclay, Preest, at commandement of the righyt hye and mighty prince: Thomas duke of Norfolke* (1520), 2. *The English Works of Sir Thomas More*, ed. W. E. Campbell with introductions and notes by A. W. Reed (1931), vol. 1, 349. The Wolsey letter is transcribed from BL Galba B 6, f. 109v.

between them will become considerably closer and deeper [plus ferme et plus intrinseque].'

Norfolk had more to relate. The ambassador should also know, he continued, that this friendship of the two young men will be cemented by an alliance. The king wants his bastard son to marry Norfolk's daughter, Mary. Furthermore, the king has also allowed him to arrange for Thomas, his younger son (around 11), a marriage to the rich Marney heiress (Norfolk's own ward). Chapuys was still horrified at this English custom of buying a bride, he told the emperor. Furthermore, sensing that some such marriage might be tried between Surrey and the Princess Mary, the emperor's first cousin, the ambassador expounded to Norfolk the reproaches his son might get for what would appear as too purely a financial action. Before Norfolk could answer, the two had arrived at the gate of Chapuys' lodgings. Because it was late and the duke had more than a half a league (almost two miles) still to go, they parted for the night.

A King's Son

Revealing his plans to Chapuys had been part of Norfolk's strategy. If there were ever a battle over the succession, the Empire would support the Princess Mary but Norfolk had now announced that a future king might not only be his son's immediate companion but the son-in-law of a mighty duke sympathetic (at this time) to the Empire. So the strategy was set, and Surrey was to become a kind of bait, an *incitateur* who will revive an old chivalric custom that Norfolk could also use. The earl was now to become not merely a friend to the bastard son of Henry VIII but a teacher and guide in a service at court like that of a squire, a 'childe' or apprentice in a noble house, where, in the pattern of aristocrats (including his grandfather), Surrey will learn its levels of *courtoisie*. Furthermore, in this service male friendship, an ancient and pervasive classical topos, was expected to have its own code which, as Mervyn James notes, 'required faithfulness to friends as well as to one's lord,' so that a 'relationship of equals' often arose out of 'chamber companionship' or the sharing of the same quarters while in service at court or in the house of a magnate. In Froissart's world (and in Lord Berners' translation), heroic style would have been impossible to conceive, for example, without such noble male friendship, 'an admired feature of the world of honour idealism, celebrated in romance and story,' particularly in the northern epics.[7]

[7] As James, *English Politics* (1986) comments (18–22), friendship became more collective, ordinary, and political in the new societies. As a term, friendship would bear the highest form of political association and so transfigure an inscription from the old vocabulary of honour 'into the parliamentary jargon and parlance of another age'. What remained was the male intimacy that became once more collective but under a new political order and, in the revolution (on both sides), a powerful echo of an older honour. So, ironically, after 1530, male friendship as a primary mode of honour may have been increasingly emphasized in an aristocratic community redefining not only its own mode of

Thus, shortly after the supper party, the two young men probably met for the first time, when Richmond was brought down from Sheriff Hutton Castle in Yorkshire to the More, a major royal house in Hertfordshire, and from there to other royal residences. While Richmond's appearance after five years of isolation from the court would provide an insult to Queen Catherine and, in Richmond's manipulation by the Howards, increase Anne Boleyn's grip on the king, the bastard son was probably relieved to escape the tedium and intrigue that surrounded him in the bleak Yorkshire castle of Sheriff Hutton. Except for his mother and one particular nurse, Richmond had never known any sustained love, only scattered attention and ever-present danger. Yet Richmond himself was a love-child. 'One of the liberties which our king [at 26] took at his spare time was to love,' commented Lord Herbert, and the blonde Elizabeth Blount was 'thought for her rare ornaments of nature, and education, to be the beauty and mistress-piece of her time' and an 'intire affection past betwixt them, as at last she bore him a son.' This 'child, proving so equally like to both his parents, that he became the first emblem of their mutual affection, was called Henry Fitz-roy by the king, and so much avowed by him' that the child was knighted in a public ceremony by his father on 18 June 1525. Earlier in that January, when the 6-year-old was first taken from his mother and brought to court (from which his mother, no longer the king's mistress, was now excluded) Venetians reported back to the Doge and Signory: 'The King loves him [Richmond] like his own soul.'[8] Lord Herbert himself added: 'Howbeit, I find, [Richmond] was very personable and of great expectation, insomuch that he was thought, not only for hability of body but mind, to be one of the rarest of his time; for which reason also he was much cherished by our king' (270).

In fact, the gestures marking this entrance of the little boy into court occurred in spring and summer of 1525. Their ostentation demonstrated both Henry VIII's extreme affection and the urgency of a political crisis. The king made the little boy not only Knight of the Garter 'at the feast of Seynt George att Wyndesore,' the 6-year-old in his 'gown, black satin with botons and aglettes of gold, on his sleves furred with sables' but also, on the following 25 June, amid elaborate

honour but honour itself and seeing it in terms of intimate male friendship. By Lord Herbert's time and text (published in the middle of the English Revolution) and the Surrey–Richmond friendship dramatized, such male friendship was typified in the cavalier poets and the Van Dyck portraits of young men modelled on Surrey and Richmond and soon to die for the king. For the argument that the friendship of Surrey and Richmond was sexual, see Stephen Guy-Bray, ' "We Two Boys Together Clinging": the Earl of Surrey and the Duke of Richmond', *English Studies in Canada*, 21 (1995), 138–50. For incisive homoerotic readings of the Windsor elegy and other Surrey lyrics, see Jonathan Crewe, *Trials of Authorship: Anterior Forms and Poetic Reconstructions from Wyatt to Shakespeare* (1990), 48–78. For a fuller placement of Surrey in the context of the homosocial and homoerotic in early modern England, see Jonathan Goldberg, *Sodometries: Renaissance Texts, Modern Sexualities* (1992), 39–40 (where his theory of the conjunction of sexuality and 'the formations of courtly literariness' in general directly relates to my interpretation of Surrey's Windsor poems about Richmond in particular); 53; and 59–60; and also his 'Introduction' to *Queering the Renaissance*, ed. Jonathan Goldberg (1994), 1–14. For the interesting conjunction in the period of humanism and male same-sex love, see Alan Stewart, *Close Reader: Humanism and Sodomy in Early Modern England* (1997).

[8] Quoted in W. S. Childe-Pemberton, *Elizabeth Blount and Henry the Eighth* (1913), 129.

banquets and expensive masques or 'disguisings', named him Lord Admiral of the realm, Lieutenant-General beyond Trent, Warden General of the borders of Scotland, then Earl of Nottingham, and finally Duke of Richmond and Somerset, the latter title being most associated with the Tudors and their claim through Lady Margaret Beaufort to royal blood. Did the king intend, as Pollard suggests, to make the natural son his legal heir? Was some such legitimation in the mind of the king when, in the same June ceremony in which he invested his bastard, he made his own step-uncle Arthur Plantagenet, Viscount Lisle, the Vice-Admiral to the little boy, the greatest title this bastard of Edward IV ever held? By 1524 Henry VIII had become estranged from his Spanish queen and, with her hostility and the upsurge in power of her nephew in Europe with his overwhelming victory at Pavia and in it the death of the last Yorkist pretender, the 35-year-old king of England had to show the 25-year-old emperor (and behind him, defeated France) his own power. Here was no pretender. His own seed *had* produced a male heir. The whole strategy was rather hollow from the start, and, as Elton notes, a 'policy which could hope to put a Tudor bastard on the English throne, indicates how desperate the position looked to the King.'[9]

At this moment of failure for his French policy and Imperial indifference, Henry VIII began to cultivate Richmond for a higher role, sending him north to Sheriff Hutton, where the child lived a constricted life with eminent humanist tutors like Richard Croke, who had succeeded Erasmus as Reader in Greek at Cambridge, and John Palsgrave, who had compiled a famous French grammar for Henry VIII's sister when she became Queen of France and who was also tutor to Surrey's younger brother. The little duke was hardly more than a puppet, if his rote letters are any evidence with their constant appealing in the name of guardians for money or influence from the king or Wolsey. These tutors were quite successful, however, in training Richmond's vigorous body (if one judges by his equestrian accomplishments alone) and his intellect. Surrey's friendship built on this education of body and mind and so, when the poet introduced the other Henry to figures like John Leland, as Holinshed was to report almost fifty years later, the young Richmond responded and particularly 'loved John Leland the reverend antiquarie'. Holinshed also noted that 'this duke was verie forward in the knowledge of toongs, and also in knightlie activitie,' a catalogue of which the Elizabethan historian then listed for his queen, the dead Richmond's little sister (3: 37). At 8, the boy had already mastered Caesar's *Gallic Wars* and could express himself well in Latin. In two English letters of January 1527, written in a beautiful italic hand from the northern castle, the young duke demonstrated to both his father and Wolsey his education in, and penchant for, riding and the martial skills as well as the classics. In fact, in one letter, he asked for 'on harnes for my exercise yn armys accordyng to my lernyng yn Julius Caesar'. The desperation surrounding

[9] 'Biographical Memoir of Henry Fitzroy, Duke of Richmond', in *Camden Miscellany*, ed. J. G. Nichols (1855), p. lxxxix. A. F. Pollard, *Henry VIII* (1968), 183. G. Relton, *England Under the Tudors* (1955), 100.

Richmond surfaced, however, in his coat of arms, which his guardian Page devised for him. These arms are, as the *Complete Peerage* comments (in a rare aside), 'somewhat remarkable'. In fact, they illustrated, in contrast to the simplicity of the royal arms, a complexity that not only emphasized the boy's bastardy but a kind of heraldic fantasizing that, as in his own last days, Surrey was accused of having indulged in for the same purpose, greater political identity.[10]

There was an exceptional figure living with Richmond in the north during those years: Sir Edward Seymour. In 1525, only in his twenties, Seymour must have witnessed the investiture of Richmond as Duke of Richmond and Somerset and then moved north as Master of the Horse in the young duke's household. There he became one more of those agents who drew their power and influence from Richmond, quietly serving the little boy who held immense honour and the wealth of a dukedom. In accounts for the young duke's household for the last 'half a year and seventeen days' of 1525, a particular item shows the sum collected for himself by the future Duke of Somerset in the service of the present Duke of Somerset: 'Expenses for Sir Edward Seymour, master of the horses, for horses bought, provender, and other expenses of the stable' total £91. 9s. and 10d.[11] This future duke and virtual ruler of England twenty-five years later would also accompany both young men to France in 1532.

Seymour was only a small part of an immense world that now surrounded the king's son. It increased as Richmond returned south, joined Surrey, and went on progresses and to one court function after another. Here appearance and dress were decisive. The series of inventories that followed Richmond's death record not only his clothes but his household possessions and reify the imagined world of Surrey's Windsor and its images of nobility. The vast inventory of Richmond's clothes reveals, in fact, how much the father may have been grooming the bastard son for the throne: 'Item, a Gowne of blak velvet, embroudered with a border of Venice golde, the same lyned with a blak velwet and a satten of Bridges [Bruges]'; 'Item, a Ryding Cote of grene satten, with a fringe of sylver'; 'Item, a pair of Hose of blak velwett, embrodered with fringe of Venice golde'; and 'Item, a hole furre of sables.' Richmond's head-dress was equally elaborate, even involving jewellery on one hat with Renaissance motifs of Roman goddesses, and another carrying a small portrait. In addition to decorative swords, daggers, and knives, his jewels were most elaborate: 'a Coller of xxj garters, and xxj knottes of crowne golde, with a George set with dyamondes'; 'a Garter of clene golde, set with ij. diamountes (one pointed and the other plaine)'; 'two Garters of Damask golde, the bokles and pendentes of golde'; and, as the emblem of his office as Lord Admiral, 'a Whistelle of golde'.

[10] For Richmond's letters (both are essentially the same) see PRO, SP 1/46 95424. *The Complete Peerage, or a History of the House of Lords and all its Members from the Earliest Times*, ed. George E. Cokayne (1910–40), 830. The descriptions and illustrations of Richmond's coat of arms may be found in 'Memoir', pp. lxxxvii–lxxxix.

[11] 'Memoir', p. xxvi.

Richmond's household possessions showed the same level of public display, with icons such as 'an Image of Saint George standing upon a dragon on a bace, with hys swyrde, spere, and shilde, and an ostrige fether on his hed,' all weighing 40 ounces. Amid the vast array of gold and silver chandeliers, basins, ewers, pots, flagons, dishes, spoons, and bowls, certain tapestries revealed cultural inscriptions that were the basis for gesture and ceremony in that society. Tapestry subjects ranged from Moses and Balaam to 'Lady Plesaunce' to the saint King Louis to 'a faire pece of rich Arras of the Image of Man and of Jessey', the Jesse tree of Christ's genealogy so popular in the Middle Ages. The largest of all the tapestries (and clearly Burgundian in motif as the actual tapestries were all probably woven in Flanders) is 'a fair pece of Arras of the Coronation of Honnour, with divers grete images therin, aswelle of the olde Testament as also of the newe,' 24 yards in length and 5 yards in depth, and obviously related to Molinet's *Trosne d'honneur*. This tapestry of 'Honnour' greeted and informed the young duke and the poet Earl of Surrey every day in Richmond's apartments.[12]

Until recently, only one portrait of Richmond was known. This miniature may have survived fortuitously; there appears to have been a deliberate attempt to suppress all images of him (strangely, none by Holbein survives). The miniature may have been painted in 1535 or 1536, when Richmond was already dying of what may have been a form of tuberculosis. In this *tour de force* attributed by Strong to Lucas Hornebolte (Plate 8), the young man hardly resembles the athletic friend described in Surrey's elegy or the robust figure described by Lord Herbert. In it, Fitzroy's head is covered in what appears to be an elegant satin or silkish nightcap. Then, down the half-body, a shirt opens and plunges to the bottom of the picture, showing a white neck, a hairless chest, and a well-developed, if lithe, torso. A long and aquiline face shows the tight lips and prominent nose and eyes that are narrowed as in pain or illness. A recent identification shows the young Duke of Richmond in two illuminations for the manuscript, 'The Black Book of the Garter', begun in 1534, the probable date of these scenes. In the illumination showing the procession of the Order of the Garter (Plate III), Richmond is readily identifiable by his heraldic robe (as is the hovering presence of his new father-in-law, the Duke of Norfolk). Even in this group scene his bearing is vigorous and strong. In the illumination above it, in the picture of Henry VIII surrounded by the companions of the Order, the young Duke of 15 stands to the left of the king, identified by the same red cap worn in the illumination below and by his blonde hair and light features, inherited from his mother.[13]

[12] See *Inventories of the Wardrobes, Plate, Chapel Stuff, etc., of Henry Fitzroy, Duke of Richmond and of the Wardrobe Stuff at Baynard's Castle of Katherine, Princess Dowager*, ed. J. G. Nichols. Camden Society, 61 (1855), p. xv. The long lists present the fullest context of the material world surrounding Surrey's elegy on Richmond, only a part of which sumptuousness I can indicate here.

[13] Roy Strong, *The English Renaissance Miniature* (1984), 36. 'The Black Book of the Garter', MS G 1, Windsor Aerary, St George's Chapel, Windsor Castle. I am indebted to Colonel Peter R. Moore for the identification of Richmond and Norfolk in the Garter Procession.

Surrey as a Prince's Guide

Surrey's own portrait by Holbein in this period shows more accurately how both young men might have appeared to the Tudor court and to France. Surrey's picture and that of his wife in the same series of Holbein drawings may have been wedding portraits, as Roberts suggests,[14] or at least sketches, like his sister's drawing, for oil portraits now lost. In February of 1532, the Duke of Norfolk had contracted his eldest son to the Lady Frances de Vere, daughter of John, Earl of Oxford. This appears to have been a sudden decision by Norfolk and may have had a political origin. Earlier Norfolk may have been angling for his son to marry none other than the Princess Mary herself (after all, had he not married a princess once?). If so, Anne Boleyn would not tolerate this threat of Catherine of Aragon's daughter being legitimized by a marriage with the highest English genealogy—her own blood. Even if the princess were bastardized, the children of Surrey and Mary Tudor would always threaten her children. At least this is the interpretation Chapuys offered Charles V on 16 April 1532. As Chapuys had assured the Emperor two years before, Norfolk had confirmed that he will marry Surrey 'pour oster la sospicion du monde qu'il ne voulsist tascher à la Princesse' ('in order to avoid the suspicion of the world that he would stain the Princess'). 'La dame Anne' has now compelled her uncle to do this. It must have been for some such 'urgente cause' because the match is not very good, says the ambassador. The son will not be 'habile a marriage de troys ans et la fille n'est de grands biens ne grands alliance' ('capable of marriage for three more years and the young woman is neither of great wealth nor of important alliance').[15] Chapuys was misinformed on both counts. Of ancient Essex nobility, Oxford settled lands on Surrey that yielded a yearly rent of £300. The formal marriage then took place in the following spring, with the Earl of Oxford giving his daughter a fortune of 4000 marks (around £2664 in Tudor currency), 200 paid on the day of marriage (N1: xxiii–iv). Immediately after the

[14] *Drawings by Holbein from the Court of Henry VIII*, catalogue by Jane Roberts (1987), 21.

[15] *LP*, vol. 4, iii, 6452 (2899). These rumours of Surrey's possible marriages (including to Anne Boleyn in 1530) would last until 1535. Bapst, *Deux gentilshommes-poètes*, 191–3, 195. For the original French of Chapuys, see Hof-, Haus-, und Staatsarchiv, Wien, England Korrespondenz, Kart. 5, Berichte an Karl V, 1532. Bapst makes an even stronger indictment of Frances Surrey based not only on Chapuys but on a mistranslation (178 and 209). He concludes that the Countess of Surrey was not very bright, 'timide, nonchalante, et en somme ne répondait nullement aux aspirations du duc de Norfolk qui desirait que ses belles-filles aidassent leurs maris dans la vie' ('timid, nonchalant, and in sum did not correspond at all to the aspirations of the Duke of Norfolk who wanted his daughters-in-law to help their husbands in life'). He bases this generalization on a passage from a Latin letter in January 1546 (already cited) from Hadrianus Junius, complaining about life at Kenninghall. The physician and tutor remarks on the 'headlong acts of insolent young boys', presumably sons, and then remarks in a parenthesis 'loquor de istius albae gallinae filiis' which could be translated 'I speak of those sons of the white hen,' or as Bapst develops the inference in the French of a *dinde* or 'turkey', a stupid woman. This is a mistranslation. In Latin, the phrase 'son of a white hen' was proverbial for a person blessed with good luck (as in Juvenal's 'fortune's favourite'). Here Hadrianus may have been ironic or merely factual: Surrey's sons were at this moment in their history quite blessed by fortune. The Flemish tutor was not referring in any negative sense to the Countess of Surrey.

wedding, the groom and bride returned to their previous worlds, hers at Castle Hedingham in Essex and his at Windsor or wherever Richmond led him.

Around this marriage date of 1532, Holbein drew quite realistic portraits of the couple (Plates I, 2, 3; in fact, two of Surrey with the kind of sober demeanour he and Richmond probably shared). In the two drawings of Surrey on Holbein's pink paper, one frontal and the other in profile, the poet's dress—the puffed shoulders, the lace collar, the pull of his coat around his neck, the elegant wide hat with the sweeping plume—sets the frame for his totally serious gaze from a long face like his father's. His thick straight hair combed in an auburn fringe over his forehead and ears emphasizes his face with tightly held lips and slightly flared nose. The eyes mark, even in profile, Holbein's most perceptive rendering, and give evidence, at least in Surrey's only frontal view, of what may have been a congenital physical condition of exotropia, a cast in Surrey's right eye. Obviously the condition lasted during Surrey's entire lifetime for, in a final portrait now in the National Portrait Gallery in London (Plate VI), probably taken from the Scrots portrait of 1546, Surrey also has an eye miscast but this time it is the left eye. Unless this is an inaccuracy of the painter, such an alternating condition meant that Surrey had no single ambyopic eye but a lesser degree of stereopsis in which the cast condition could shift from one eye to the other. Needless to say, the psychological effect of this shifting could be unsettling for an audience of any kind, though the owner of the eyes might not have been conscious of their effect. A condition now curable in early childhood, a cast or wandering eye may have been disturbing enough in the early sixteenth century for the heir to the greatest title outside the royal family. Certainly in common folklore, whereas the eye turned inward was thought to show a person inferior or stupid, the eye turned outward showed wiliness, deceit, even treachery. The attempt to disguise the defect can be traced in almost all other portraits of Surrey. Because in the Windsor Castle drawings, Holbein's precision gives characteristically, as Ganz notes about the artist, 'the moisture and mobility of the eye,'[16] any misalignment can be assumed to be accurate.

If this 'wall-eyed' effect were there from birth, without treatment, the poet would early have had to choose one eye as dominant over the other. The whole field of perception would then be unusually solipsistic, making the dependence on the

[16] For most of Surrey's portraits, see Roy Strong, *Elizabethan and Jacobean Portraits*, (1969) 307–8. All four versions of the Arundel portrait are here listed as one; the painting of the eyes is similar in all (the Knole portrait more obvious in misalignment than the Parham Park one). Of the four, misalignment appears most pronounced in the Arundel portrait. Although it is true that eyes are often difficult for artists to paint, it is not likely that in 1532 or 1541 Holbein made a mistake. Cf. his drawing of Sir John Russell, later the first Earl of Bedford, whose eye is missing, and the miniature of the daughter of Sir Thomas More, Margaret Roper, whose eyes are also misaligned and one quite turned out. It is also unlikely that a master of Mannerist detail like Scrots would make such a mistake. Paul Ganz, 'A Portrait by Hans Holbein the Younger', *Burlington Magazine*, 38 (1921), 215. For an interesting analysis of the distortions in the frontal drawing of Surrey (which may explain something of the shock of Surrey's eye), see Lorne Campbell, *Renaissance Portraits: European Portrait-Painting in the 14th, 15th and 16th Centuries* (1990), 13–14. For Holbein's graphic technique in general, see John Rowlands, *Holbein: The Paintings of Hans Holbein the Younger* (1985).

one-eyed self even more demanding and, at least in one aspect, Surrey's body more vulnerable than that of any stable boy with two strong eyes.[17] Thus, however much the centre of his world, the boy would have to adapt himself in order to compete anywhere. Whether in the tilting yard at Kenninghall, where he would practise vaulting on wooden horses, running the barriers, swordsmanship, or the arts of the lance, the dagger, and the shield, or in the fields near the Stour valley or on the flat fields of Kenninghall, where he raced and followed the falconry rituals so beloved by the Howards and where he practiced archery with his one good eye, he would need a sense of athletic form as demanding as any court form or ceremony or poetic prosody. With his young half-uncles or the many sons of his uncle Edmund, the poet earl obviously learned to be a good hunter because his father complained in the mid-1530s about his deer being excessively hunted by Surrey. In such hunts through the flat or gently rolling Norfolk and Suffolk landscapes or in eel-fishing in the slow dark rivers of East Anglia, taught perhaps by his older cousin Southwell, he practised the same adaptation of the good eye to the scene, constantly adjusting.

This adaptation of the lonely eye to its world became a poetic theme in one of Surrey's 'translations' of Petrarch, a sonnet, 'The soote [sweet] season, that bud and bloom forth brings'. Written in the older English rhyming scheme of *equivocatio* derived from the medieval Latin rhyming treatises, *abab* rhymes run throughout until the couplet and frame a psychological density as detailed as a Hopkins sonnet (a density Alastair Fowler has analysed). In the couplet, the insistent rhyme (*aa*) echoes the loneliness of the eye before such a profusion of new spring life: 'And thus I see among these pleasant things / Each care decays, and yet my sorrow springs.' The same adaptation of the lonely eye can be found in the young earl's elegy on Richmond, in the only passages that hint at what Surrey had to learn to control his body under stress to excel and in physical activity. One passage

[17] I am grateful to Dr Hugh Klotz for interpretation here. Cf. Keith L. Moore, *Clinically Oriented Anatomy*, 2nd ed. (1985), 886. This consciousness of a blemish could, of course, turn a negative into a positive. In a text Surrey certainly read in his formative years after his uncle Berners' translations appeared in 1523 and 1525, Froissart tells a story of a group of young bachelor English knights who made themselves deliberately one-eyed for honour. Edward III had sent these young men 'of great estate and port' to Burgundy with the Bishop of Lincoln to exert or 'show off' to the court there, and they 'dyd gette great renowme and prayse' as 'yonge bachelars, who had eche of them one of their eyen closedde with a piece of sylke . . . . They had made a vow among the ladyes of their contrey, that they wolde nat se but with one eye, tyll they had done some dedes of armes in Fraunce but the time and place of that deed they did not know.' Inner readiness was all they needed. *The Chronicle of Froissart*, translated out of French by Sir John Bourchier, Lord Berners, introd. William Paton Ker (1967), vol. 1, 93. For arguments that little necessary correlation exists between achievement in bodily sports and binocular vision, see Arthur Seiderman and Steven Schneider, *The Athletic Eye* (1983), 196–7. It should be noted that, if this displacement of eyes did occur, there is no evidence that any special tutor directed his intellectual development, no record in fact of any tutor. The tutor's expense probably came not from household expenditure, where no tutor is listed, but from the main ducal coffers, where no name is indicated either. Cf. Sergio Baldi, 'The Secretary of the Duke of Norfolk and the First Italian Grammar in England', in *Studies in English Language and Literature Presented to Professor Dr Karl Brunner on the Occasion of His Seventieth Birthday*, ed. Siegfried Korninger. Weiner Beiträger zur Englische Philologie, 35 (1957). There is thus no evidence for any crucial Alexander–Aristotle relationship to account for Surrey as a poet, although many possible tutors have been named (Clerke, Barclay, Skelton, Leland, Winchester, and Palsgrave).

describes the two young men around Windsor Castle and its yards, the two in a game of outdoor handball beneath the walls and 'leads' of the castle. Although Surrey emphasizes the effect of 'the dame' on his skill, the lapse shows the constant pressure of 'The palm play' in which 'With dazed eyes oft we by gleams of love / Have missed the ball and got sight [above] of our dame.' Another passage reveals Surrey's adaptation to the one art every male aristocrat had to master in Tudor England: fine horsemanship. To walk in the streets without a horse was an act of shame ('chivalry' and horsemanship are synoymous). In his will, Richmond's only bequest for the poet earl was a horse, a jennet (a small saddle horse): 'And the same jennet delyvered to the erlle of Surrey, with saddell and harnes of blak velwet.' The fact that Surrey proved later such a powerful military figure meant that the one-eyed young man had mastered the art of riding in which a good rider always keeps the head and mane of his horse as a focus, his lateral vision often deliberately limited. As one Tudor rider's manual put it,[18] the face of the rider needs always to be set obliquely, guiding himself with his right eye (in Surrey's case, with his left). Particularly in tournaments, with helmet on, as Richmond had learned early in the north, a good rider must maintain, even with binocular sight, only the vision of the opponent with his weapon and a charging frontal line of action, hardly the ambiguities of the periphery.

But what counted most to ensure dexterity of performance in riding was what Surrey had developed from his earliest moment of choice: an act of will. From the beginning, Surrey must have had an intensity of narrow vision in such an act of moving rapidly forward and leaping. Such will led to pleasure in moments of tense alignment and the unity of body and horse that led the ancient world to invent the myth of the centaur. At some length in the Windsor elegy, with its deliberate recall to chivalric diction, Surrey depicts his two young riders becoming one in a chase, a 'secret' world recollected with increased alienation in 1537 in the prison of Windsor. Then Surrey's language gave the relics of a lost life.

> The graveled ground, with sleeves tied on the helm,
> On foaming horse, with swords and friendly hearts,
> With cheer as though the one should overwhelm,
> Where we have fought and chased oft with darts.
> With silver drops the meads yet spread for ruth,
> In active games of nimbleness and strength
> Where we did strain, trailed by swarms of youth,
> Our tender limbs, that yet shot up in length.
> The secret groves, which oft we made resound
> Of pleasant plaint and of our ladies praise,
> Recording soft what grace each one had found,
> What hope of speed, what dread of long delays.

[18] Thomas Blundeville, *The Arte of Ryding and Breakinge Greate Horses* (1560; reprint 1969), Bk I, ch. 5, Bii–iii. I owe much of this discussion of Surrey's riding to Dr Alan Rogers, both Tudor historian and professional horseman. For a vivid description of the centaur effect of good riding, see *Hamlet* IV, ii, 84–90.

The wild forest, the clothed holts [woods] with green,
With reins avaled [slackened], and swift ybreathed horse,
With cry of hounds, and merry blasts between,
Where we did chase the fearful hart [deer] aforce. . . .

Calais

Buried in the poetic landscape of Surrey's Windsor elegy and sonnet are the actual landscapes of France. These landscapes formed the next stage in the relationship of the two young men, and although France is not mentioned in either poem, its experience probably defined, more than England, the friendship, certainly its textualization as art in 1537. France taught Surrey new shapes of beauty and the Renaissance sense of form, a new recovery of the ancient, as it was originating in Italy and appearing in Paris and Fontainebleau. The first of these actual landscapes was at Calais, in 1532 the last English territory on the northern coast of France. There both young men had roles to play in a kind of theatre. In October 1532 the poet Earl of Surrey and the Duke of Richmond sailed to Calais with Anne Boleyn, Henry VIII, and most of the court, with thousands of retainers and servants. King Henry demanded that the English nobility accompany him (although, according to Chapuys, few wanted to go). In fact, for this occasion and the introduction of Anne Boleyn to her first real display of honour, Calais would have its last great display before its fall twenty-five years later and the disappearance forever of the old Angevin empire and the presence of England on the Continent. As Miller remarks, Calais was a Cromwell production and not a Wolsey spectacle as the previous Field of the Cloth of Gold had been, and therefore more subdued and efficient. The ostensible point of signing a treaty against the Turks encroaching on European civilization fronted for the real purpose of the trip. Henry VIII was to win Francis I over as mediator for his divorce from Queen Catherine. The English king had been aware since the summer that, at some time in 1533, the French king and the Pope would meet at Marseilles. Given such high stakes, the energy to ignite elaborate preparations for such a production could only have come from one real stage-manager, whom even the genius of Cromwell could only assist: Henry's 'mistress and friend', his 'darling', his 'own sweetheart', as he wrote in his French love-letters to Anne Boleyn, surviving from their seven years of chaste courtship.[19]

[19] P. A. Hamy, SJ, *Entrevue de François Premier avec Henry VIII à Boulogne-sur-Mer, en 1532* (1898), p. XV. *LP*, vol. 5, 1373. The plans may also have been such that the number of attendants was to be kept comparatively low. Miller, *Henry VIII*, 96. *The Letters of King Henry VIII: A Selection, with a few other documents*, ed. M. St Clare Byrne (1936), vol. 2, 55, 57, 82, 59 (these are references to the letters throughout, the editor's references to Henry VIII's idealism on 53; 57; 61). The idealism of Henry VIII in a different context but in the same period is perceptively traced by Virginia Murphy in 'The Literature and Propaganda of Henry VIII's First Divorce', in *The Reign of Henry VIII*, ed. D. MacCulloch, 135–58. As noted in *The House of Commons 1509–1558*, ed. S. T. Bindoff (1982), vol. 3, 86–8, the record of another illegitimate son, Sir John Perrot, belies any theory of Henry VIII's unlimited chastity (different, of course, from his idealism).

Surrey's first cousin differed from almost all other young women brought up in English halls and manor houses such as her own Blickling in East Anglia, a difference soon to be emphasized by the plainer and more uncultivated Jane Seymour or by Surrey's other first regal cousin Catherine, functioning more for the king as daughter-lover than as companion and wife. Of course, Anne Boleyn needed her supporting players, including the Howards and her future step-son Richmond. In the last months of his life, her own uncle Lord Berners as Deputy of Calais welcomed the king and his 'sweetheart' to France, but this translator of Froissart had already given his niece, in fact, the language for her deepest desire, for the personal honour and *gloire* looming inside herself as large as that of any male jouster at the barriers. Small-boned and dark like her Howard kin (if her one surviving portrait is accurate), with the falcon as her totem, this great-granddaughter of John Howard would have found in her uncle's recently translated *Huon of Bordeaux*, one of the most chivalric of medieval romances, a definition of honour no daring knight, male or female, and particularly this translator's niece, could fail to absorb: 'The foundation of all true fame and repute . . . consisteth in bold, honourable, and heroycall resolution which enflames the soule with a continuall thirsting desire.'[20]

Such 'heroycall resolution' demanded patient cunning. Thus, the degrees of manipulation that led to Calais had begun early, and Anne Boleyn's love-letters

[20] N. F. Blake, 'Lord Berners: A Survey', *Medievalia et Humanistica*, NS 2 (1971), 123. The whole quotation is important for understanding the motivation of Anne Boleyn, who may have accepted the terms of Molinet's *Trosne* as an essential definition of her own existence: 'The foundation of all true fame and repute which in this world is most to be reckoned of and esteemed (according to the opinion of all writers both ancient & moderne) consisteth in bold, honourable, and heroycall resolution which enflames the soule with a continuall thirsting desire of pursuing braue and generous purposes, perfourming of high and aduenturous actions, which, when their bodies are mantled vp in the obscure moulde of the earth, leaueth their names canonized in fame's aeternall calender and renownes them as rare presidents to all following posterities.' The character of Anne Boleyn has been one of the most investigated in Tudor historiography and 'something of the atmosphere of trench warfare' that Gunn sees pervading the study of early Tudor politics does appear in many studies of the character of Surrey's first cousin, whose violent life is referred to in his later poems. Gunn's own 'The Structures of Politics in Early Tudor England' in *Transactions of the Royal Historical Society*, Series 6, 5 (1995), 59–90, analyses some of the problematics of the Anne Boleyn debate. In addition, E. W. Ives, *Anne Boleyn* (1986) summed up several previous generations of scholarship; see for a recent spectrum Maria Dowling in *Humanism in the Age of Henry VIII* (1986); 'Anne Boleyn and Reform', *Journal of Ecclesiastical History*, 35/1 (1984); ed., "William Latymer's Chronickille of Anne Bulleyne" *Camden Miscellany*, 30 (1990); and 'A Woman's Place? Learning and the Wives of Henry VIII', *History Today*, 41 (June 1991); also, Retha M. Warnicke, *The Rise and Fall of Anne Boleyn: Family Politics at the Court of Henry VIII* (1989); G. W. Bernard, 'The Fall of Anne Boleyn', *EHR*, 106 (1991) 584–610; Ives, 'The Fall of Anne Boleyn Reconsidered', *EHR*, 107 (1992), 651–64; Bernard, 'The Fall of Anne Boleyn: Rejoinder', Ibid. 665–74; Warnicke, 'The Fall of Anne Boleyn Revisited', ibid. 108 (1993), 653–65. Also, for a debate on Anne Boleyn's religion, see Bernard, 'Anne Boleyn's Religion', *Historical Journal*, 36 (1993), 1–20; and Ives, 'Anne Boleyn and the Early Reformation in England: The Contemporary Evidence', ibid. 37 (1994), 389–400. See also Appendix II in MacCulloch, *Cranmer*, for a new dating of Anne Boleyn's marriage to Henry VIII and the 'full sexual intercourse leading to the pregnancy'. If Anne Boleyn's life has become a tapestry conjoining thread after thread from various narratives (with different subjects), they centre on her character and its ambiguity, including the idealism reflected in her uncle's texts which was clearly hers. Here honour is a transcendental value as real as any of those of religion.

from Henry VIII (and her control over their inscription in French) have survived as one of several strategems that show the brilliant transformation of the Tudor king. Henry's own 'thirsting desire' for this long-necked woman (a source of her attraction, according to the Venetians) revealed his own strange vagaries; he ended one letter with a foreshadowing of the final charge against his beloved: 'Written with the hand of your servant, who oft and again wisheth you in your brother's room.' Thus, although for seven years he could not enter her body (as he had so easily her sister's), the 40-year-old Henry VIII entered, at her beckoning, a solipsistic vision of honour that included and subsumed his own. By deliberate strategy, by introducing new texts, English and French, to him and the court,[21] through a metamorphosis apparently connected directly with the honour of her presence and body, she turned one level of desire in Henry VIII into another. Her transfiguration of honour soon became his. Thus, in his final French love-letter, Henry praises their friendship that will produce another real presence when they are finally joined: 'Nevertheless, the perfect accomplishing thereof cannot be until the two persons are together met, the which meeting is on my part the more desired than any earthly thing; for what joy in this world can be greater than to have the company of her who is the most dearly beloved.'

In her cunning, Calais was to mark a climax for the seven years of schooling Anne Boleyn gave the king as preceptor or *incitateur* and guide. To Europe, she may have appeared sensational, at least in the strange transcendent terms she and her lover were using for what was, after all, something as trivial as adultery. But this king's chaste lover demanded that, before she was represented to Francis I, she be given a male title. Only such an investiture would allow Francis I to receive her as something more than the 'mule' the French king's own mistress, Madame d'Etampes, was calling her. Such nuances of investiture a woman trained in three courts knew well. Thus, to cap her forthcoming display of honour, Anne Boleyn received, a month before she left, the unusual creation from Henry VIII of a nobleman's title. On 1 September 1532, the great-granddaughter of the first Howard Duke of Norfolk was invested by her patient lover, in an elaborate ceremony, as the Marchioness of Pembroke, whose title only a male heir could inherit. The investiture had to precede the trip to France.[22]

For that trip to Calais in 1532, Anne Boleyn literally launched from Dover, if not a thousand ships, thousands of people, with thousands of preparations. The extent of just such a voyage is indicated in the painting called *The Embarkation*

[21] Ives, *Anne Boleyn*, 411. For a recent discovery about Anne Boleyn and her interests in new texts, see James Carley '"Her moost lovyng and fryndely brother sendeth gretyng": Anne Boleyn's Manuscripts and Their Sources', in *Illuminating the Book: Makers and Interpreters Essays in Honour of Janet Backhouse*, ed. Michelle P Brown and Scot McKendrick (1998), 261–80.

[22] I take Helen Miller's term here (24) because the Latin document of creation (PRO C 82/660) uses the female. For more details of this event, see BL Add. MS 6113, f. 70; E. Hall, *Chronicle*, 790; *LP*, vol. 5, 1274 (3) and 1499 g. 23; Miller, *Henry VIII*, 223; and Ives, *Anne Boleyn*, 198–9. For the maleness of Anne Boleyn's appeal to Henry VIII, see Lerer, *Courtly Letters*, 91. I am arguing that her sense of honour was as strong as that of any male in that time.

for Boulogne, with its enormous canvas displaying (in the late medieval style of narrative painting) nine large ships and numerous rowing-boats filled with men, and hundreds of other males at work on the quay at Dover or in the turrets preparing for this triumph, a visual display just right to be hung in the newly erected Orchard Gallery at Anne Boleyn's palace of honour at Whitehall. As Sir Edward Seymour himself recorded carefully, Henry VIII took most of his court for this occasion of honour, a total of 590, and to this must be added 2139 servants—a ratio of almost four to one—and these did not include Anne Boleyn's personal entourage of around eighty nor the uncounted servants with them, nor the transporters and port authorities and shipmen. At least two poets were among the hurrying thousands, one of them, Sir Thomas Wyatt, possibly writing (and later revising in pale brown ink) a lyric about the event and the woman at its centre: 'Some tyme I fled the fyre that me brent / By see, by land, by water and by wynd' but now he is following the 'coles' of this fire, 'From Dovor to Calais against my mynde.' It is all one more example of 'how desire is boeth sprong and spent!'[23]

Leaving at five in the morning, Surrey and Richmond were part of this huge flotilla that landed at Calais before ten. With the royal party, the two attended Mass at once (it was the vigil of St Ethelburga and St Wilfrid, two popular English saints, and in two days would be the Feast of St Edward the Confessor). Then the young men went on to their lodgings, possibly at the Exchequer with the king himself. The Duke of Richmond had forty men in his entourage, as did the other two dukes, Norfolk and Suffolk. Surrey himself is the first named of the earls, with twenty-four attendants for him, the same as for his recently acquired father-in-law, John de Vere, Earl of Oxford.[24] In his first appearance for such an occasion, Sir John Dudley, the virtual ruler of England twenty years later, had only eight attendants and so did Sir Edward Seymour, now advanced from master of the horse for Richmond to one of four riding masters of the royal household. Wyatt had only four attendants, almost the smallest retinue.

[23] For the picture, see Strong, *Holbein and Henry VIII*, 26. The painting was the product of over fifty artists with a presiding painter, possibly the Flemish Joannes Corvus. Because in it there are no visible military preparations, it can be dated to Henry VIII's only state visit to Boulogne and Calais in 1532. For the most detailed summary of just how many persons on both side of the Channel were involved and just how much preparation and money it took for the less than a month visit, see Hamy, *Entrevue*, esp. ch. 7 and 8. If the events were not as spectacular as those of the Field of the Cloth of Gold, they were nevertheless expensive and labour-intensive, even in an age where labour was cheap. For Seymour, see *Report on the Manuscripts of the Most Honourable the Marquis of Bath Preserved at Longleat*. Vol. 4. *Seymour Papers 1532–1686*, ed. Marjorie Blatcher (1968) 3. The text of Wyatt can be found in *The Poetry of Sir Thomas Wyatt*, ed. Kenneth Muir and Patricia Thomson (1969), XIV, hereafter in the text as MT. For Wyatt's revisions, see Richard Harrier, *The Canon of Sir Thomas Wyatt's Poetry* (1975), 152, 204–5; MT VII, and R. A. Rebholz, *Sir Thomas Wyatt: The Complete Poems* (1975), 374: 'The speaker comments on the irony that he is now thrown into intimacy with the person whom he once loved but no longer loves, and whom he sought, while in love, to flee, because a relationship with her was so dangerous and painful.'

[24] Oxford was making the trip, it would appear, for a particular purpose: although with Wolsey's help, he had regained the ancient office of Great Chamberlain for the de Veres in 1532, he wanted other 'offyceys of myn inherytauns' that he feared would be given to newly enobled courtiers (as happened before his death in 1540). Cf. Miller, *Henry VIII*, 29.

The first meeting of the kings was to be at Boulogne, where Francis I was the host. Although Henry VIII had pressed for the occasion of Calais alone and Anne Boleyn's presence, no women attended the French nobility. Except possibly for her first cousin Lady Mary Howard, no English noblewoman of high rank accompanied Anne Boleyn to France, most conspiciously absent being Henry VIII's own sister Mary, the Dowager Queen of France, who loathed her brother's 'concubine' and his whole 'Great Matter'. The king's son Richmond remained at Calais with Anne Boleyn. The Boulogne meeting of the two kings, each surrounded by 600 persons (including the young Earl of Surrey), 'was the lovyngest metyng that ever was seen: for the one embraced ye other V or VI tymes on horsebacke and so dyd the lords on eyther party eche to other and so dyd ryde, hande in hande, with greate love, the space of a myle.'[25] The kings immediately went to the high part of the city to hear Mass at the ancient votive shrine of Our Lady of Boulogne and there the royal singers sang motets, polyphonic hymns in the Burgundian mode developed from Gregorian chant, which the Council of Trent would soon discourage for its lack of verbal clarity. In the five days during which the kings conferred in Boulogne, Henry VIII dined, with a precise visual and aural ritual, servants bareheaded and on their knees, in the refectory of the abbey where both kings resided. There Surrey saw tapestries Francis I had delivered to Boulogne, one representing the victories of Scipio Africanus, and another the fables of Ovid's *Metamorphoses* (with its legend of Orpheus). Surrey was also to hear in Boulogne, according to Wynkyn de Worde, 'syngyng and playenge of all kyndes of musyke', which included trumpets, hautboys, and cornets, chiefly during meals, with song-forms like the Italian *frottola* Surrey later used for his lyrics. A high moment occurred on the final day in Boulogne when, with solemn ritual, Surrey's father and the Duke of Suffolk were elected into, and then invested with, the Order of Saint Michel, France's highest chivalric honour.

That same day, Friday, 25 October, the whole entourage departed from Boulogne for Calais for the second phase of the meeting. In the French contingent were 1200 horsemen, and 'without Calice twoo mile, met with them the Duke of Richemond, the Kynges bastard sonne of Englande, a goodly young Prince, and full of fauoure and beautie, with a greate compaignie of noble men' (HA 790). The zenith of English hospitality came at the English king's supper party on the last night, witnessed by Surrey. Over his robe of violet cloth of gold, Henry VIII wore a spectacular collar for the occasion. Its ostentation signified how seriously he took this moment of the meeting of Francis I and the woman who had originated it and had doubtless planned his attire of honour. This collar across the king's broad chest and shoulders had three tiers, the first of forty rubies as large as eggs, a second with brilliant pearls, and the last with forty diamonds. From the collar dangled

[25] Hamy, *Entrevue*, 57. The report from Wynken de Worde is reprinted in Hamy XXXVIII–XLV. All references to this Tudor document are to these pages. For references to this event and others as cited and quoted from in the text below, see both Hall 792–4 and Hamy CXXXVII; 50; XXXIII; LXVI and as cited below.

heavily his famous carbuncle (a deep-red garnet) that weighed as much as a goose egg. The French king wore a doublet embroidered with diamonds. Then, in the dining chamber, from a cupboard with seven levels holding only gold plate, the French and English kings and their guests were served three courses, a first course of forty dishes, a second of sixty, and a third of seventy, above them ten candelabra of silver and gold, each hanging by a silver chain and each holding five candles.

Immediately after the supper came the masque, the most elaborate of all the entertainments at the 1532 meeting of the monarchs. It was the only one to involve women. The dozen or so women who had come with Anne Boleyn now displayed themselves with Surrey's first cousin as their centre-piece, all 'gorgyousley apparayled, with visers on theyr faces' until Anne Boleyn 'came and toke the frensshe kynge by the hande and other lordes of France and daunced a daunce or two' after which Henry VIII 'toke of theyr visers and they daunced with gentylmen of Fraunce, an houre after'.[26] In that hour or more, the French King added an extra honour to the immense diamond he had already dispatched to Anne Boleyn on her arrival in Calais. The French King asked her to dance 'and after they had daunsed a while they ceased, and the French Kyng talked with the Marchiones of Penbroke a space' (HA 791). The French King led Anne to the embrasure of a window where, as the whole gathering watched carefully, including Surrey and Richmond and Wyatt and, not least, Henry VIII, the King of France and Anne Boleyn chatted for an hour, their presence and unheard conversation filling the room.

The next day, Monday, 28 October, the Most Christian Kings signed the treaty of alliance against the Turks, the reason announced for the trip. Shortly thereafter, the King of England invested the Grand Master and the Lord Admiral of France into the Order of the Garter with the French King participating, wearing his own blue mantle of the Order. Only one other item of business remained. The king's son Richmond was to ride forth with the French King and remain in the entourage of Francis I's son, the Dauphin, for a year, ostensibly as a guarantee for the treaty just signed. For this singular honour, Richmond was to take with him as his chief companion, the 16-year-old Henry, Earl of Surrey, who had his own retinue of sixty men. The next day, at the edge of the Calais Pale, before leaving with the French King and his sons, the two young men paused 'in a faire grene place, where was a table set' with wine, hippocras (a wine cordial sprinkled with spices), fruits, and condiments. Then, after talking, the parties mounted and came to the border where each embraced the other with 'hartie wordes'. The English King said farewell for almost a year to two of the most aristocratic young men in Europe.

The events at Calais now became the talk of three kingdoms and most courts of Italy, but the return home for the English was almost disastrous. Autumn storms swept the Channel and, after waiting into November, parties from the multitude

[26] Hamy, *Entrevue*, CLXXXII ff. and XLIII; also see XLIV. 'The Lady Mary' could not have referred to Mary Boleyn, an obvious embarrassment on this trip as elsewhere, and in this report, she would have been in the wrong order of precedence, as Ives, *Anne Boleyn*, 201 notes.

that had flocked over were still being turned back into Calais or into Flanders, as heavy tides flooded the lowlands and the north and north-western winds increased with thunder and lightning. By Sunday, 12 November, the weather turned fair, and the king shipped his great bed and other valuables. But he and Anne Boleyn were delayed by a very thick fog in which 'no master could guide a ship' (HA 794). On the next Tuesday at midnight, the King of England and his newly honoured companion sailed, landing at Dover the next morning. The following Saturday, before Sir Thomas More, the Lord Keeper of the Great Seal, and the Mayor of London and others, a great *Te Deum* was sung in Saint Paul's Cathedral.

It was, more than they knew, a time for thanksgiving for Henry VIII. At some point on that return trip, whether in Calais as the Channel storms whipped and threatened or in the great silent fog or on the ship itself, Anne Boleyn surrendered her chastity. The surrender was on her own terms. After seven years of patience and schooling for the idealistic man now in middle age, in which years a new kind of honour and supreme self-justification had revealed itself, surrender came with her own enormous hope of genealogy—her own child of honour to transfigure history.

Paris

Surrey became ill in Calais before he and Richmond left. It was one more in a persistent series of physical collapses that marked his life at moments of stress. He was suffering from an 'ague' or fever that had begun in late October or early November and had already lasted until the middle of December, as the informant Richard Tate wrote to the watchful Cromwell. The illness was serious enough to draw attention: 'My Lorde of Surrey which had a spece of an agews before hys departing from Calleys, his seid seckness somewhat has put him in remembrance sith comyng fourth, but as I verry well trust, the worste is past.' For Surrey, the sudden freedom of France may have proved a shock. The more vigorous Richmond enjoyed good health. He found the country, so Cromwell also learned, 'very naturall unto him'. Surrey recovered, as the young men turned with the French court from Saint-Hvert where Henry VIII had bidden farewell to them, to Boulogne-sur-Mer, then to Etaples, and then to Amiens, where the court stayed seven days, and then on to Compiègne, where the court waited five more days, and then at Chantilly, they were 'very welcome met in all places' with gifts of wine and 'other gentelle offres'. Here Surrey may have seen in the Grand Master Montmorency's collection Leonardo da Vinci's cartoon of his *Monna Vanna* and Michelangelo's sculpture *The Fugitives*. In the welcome here the French King embraced Richmond 'saing that he thought hymselve nowe to have IIII sonnes and extimed hym no lesse'. His sons embraced Henry VIII's son as well and, possibly with Surrey, the king took all the young men into his privy chamber, where Francis I assured

Richmond that he would always be one of the king's chamber. The Grand Master had already notified the French ambassador in Rome of the visit and the plans for the young men: 'The king of England has sent hither his bastard son and the son of the Duke of Norfolk, who are being brought up with the King's children.'[27]

The Dauphin was less than a year younger than Surrey, but he was already distinguished for being more of a sportsman than an affected courtier, as the reformed Christian poet Marot noted. He was quite handsome, 'le plus beau des plus beaulx' ('the most handsome of all the handsome'), according to the poet Mellin de Saint Gelais, who had recently introduced the Petrarchan sonnet to France (at least he vies with Marot for the honour).[28] In fact, the young Dauphin's death three years later came from overexertion in playing tennis, the same kind of physical drive that had characterized his father in battle and in the chase. The Dauphin's two younger brothers made up the rest of this close-knit circle that fully included Surrey, as the surviving sons of Francis I indicated to the English ambassador seven years later. The second son Henry, named for his godfather Henry VIII, was exactly the same age as Richmond and became the successor to his father as Henry II, the husband of Catherine de Medici, the Pope's niece, whose betrothal would result from the Pope's visit to the south of France in the autumn of 1533. Francis I's youngest son Charles, also quite enthusiastic about Surrey, was only 11, and he completed the active male household in which Surrey was the oldest. Charles would die fighting Surrey outside Boulogne in the autumn of 1545.

Francis I had reason, of course, to be generous. After all, at Calais, as one more sign of the seriousness of the occasion of introducing Anne Boleyn, Henry VIII had forgiven, in a dramatic gesture, the considerable sum outstanding from the loan made to redeem the French King's middle and younger sons after Francis I's capture at Pavia, when they were substituted for him. Francis I owed the English King for the lives of his sons. The English young men thus formed part of an implicit political gesture, and their place with the French court made them hostages in the best sense. If the two most exalted young men of the English court were treated as equals in the suite of the Dauphin, it was not really necessary to secure the treaties just signed in Calais about the Turks or whatever, but only to insure the terms by which the debt had been cancelled. Equally, the English King expected help with the Pope about his proposed divorce. Above all, he wanted Francis I universally to acknowledge the justice and honour of his new consort, as he had done in the masque at Calais.

After Chantilly, Paris awaited the young men, who arrived there on 3 December 1532. The winter had set in and the Christmas festivities had begun in this city of

[27] The itinerary for Francis I in this year can be found in *Catalogue des Actes de Francois ler* (1905), vol. 8, 480. For the art at Chantilly, see Anthony Blunt, *Art and Architecture in France 1500 to 1700* (1953), 65. For the Grand Master's letter, see *LP*, vol. 5, 1627.

[28] Dora and Erwin Panofsky, 'The Iconography of the Galerie Francois ler at Fontainebleau', *Gazette des Beaux-Arts*, 42 (1958), 172.

10,000 houses with streets often ankle-deep in mud and other filth.[29] Although it is not certain that Surrey, Richmond, the Dauphin, and his brothers followed the exact itinerary of the king, they did spend at least the next four months in Paris in the apartments of the Dauphin in the Louvre. In the typically cold Paris winter, both Surrey and Richmond could rest indoors in the vast palace and there assimilate the language, the customs, and, above all, the art and books surrounding them. They could also enjoy recreation like an indoor game of *jeu de paume* or handball. That winter the grand hall of the Louvre palace may have contained, as later for a state visit of Charles V, tapestries with scenes from Homer's *Iliad* and from narratives in St Luke's *Acts of the Apostles*, and, in the great courtyard, a gigantic statue of Vulcan. The young men now lived, surrounded by servants on every level, in a world of splendour and beauty few European princes could see. As Tate wrote to Cromwell, 'so that nowe, syns the King's commyng to Parys, my Lorde hath lodging for hymselfe in the Daulphin's owne lodging and dineth and souppeth daily with the Daulphin and his brethen.'

What the two friends absorbed was more than a daily routine of luxury. The two read together as well as exercised. In fact, that winter of 1532–3 in Paris brought out many new texts, not least Luigi Alamanni's *Opere toscane*, actually published in Lyons in November 1532 (in the same month and place as Rabelais' *Pantagruel*) but only now beginning to circulate at court. The appearance of these texts was emblematic of the literary ferment everywhere around Surrey. At the Louvre (or more likely at Fontainebleau) Surrey may also have heard this Italian poet reading aloud Dante's *Commedia* to the French king, and it was probably not the only Italian text Surrey may have heard read aloud (a miniature at Chantilly shows Francis I listening to a reader). Surrey may have listened to Castiglione's *Il libro di Cortegiano*, in which the French king himself figured. As he and his court ate, Francis I wanted texts read aloud, in the custom of monasteries, and in Surrey's time the post of reader, *lecteur de roi*, was held by the Abbot of the Monastery of Saint Ambrose, Jacques Colin, who was finishing his translation of Castiglione. As Clough notes, the court of Urbino as it had existed at the date—1507—that Castiglione gave his narrative of conversations in the *Book of the Courtier* had become, within a decade, partially regrouped around Francis I as patron.[30] Also in 1533 a new edition of the old romance *Lancelot du Lac* appeared in Paris; this may have been the copy that the Duchess of Richmond directly accused her brother of using to devise one more roll for his coat of arms in 1546.

[29] N. M. Sutherland, 'Parisian Life in the Sixteenth Century', in *French Humanism 1470–1600*, ed. Werner L. Gundersheimer (1969), 52.

[30] BL MS Caligula E II, 192 (old I, 42). Henri Hauvette, *Luigi Alamanni, un exile florentin à la cour de France au XVIe siècle (1495–1556): sa vie et son oeuvre* (1903), 446–7, n. 2. See also Ernest Hatch Wilkins, *A History of Italian Literature*, rev. Thomas G. Bergin (1954; reprint 1974), 248. For Castiglione, see V.-L. Bourrilly, *Jacques Colin, abbé de Saint-Ambroise* (1905; reprint 1970), 36–41. For the influence of Castiglione's text at the French court, see Cecil H. Clough, 'Francis I and the Courtiers of Castiglione's *Courtier*', *European Studies Review*, 8/1 (January 1978) 23–70, 38, 40.

Luigi Alamanni (1495–1556) is important enough to have given the 16-year-old Surrey a unique strategy as a poet. Whatever connections did or did not exist between an adolescent English aristocrat and a much older Italian poet in a court of careful protocol, Alamanni was still the one living European poet whose work Wyatt and Surrey may have discussed in later years at the English court, Wyatt taking his satiric form of *terza rima* from the *Opere Tuscane*. In his republican youth, Alamanni had been part of a circle, strongly neoclassical, which included Machiavelli, Trissino, and the Rucellai brothers; and in the Oricellai gardens in Florence he had heard read aloud Trissino's *Sophonisba* and Rucellai's *Rosmunda*, both in unrhymed verse or *versi sciolti*—all models for Surrey's blank verse. In fact, Surrey could have read in 1533 Alamanni's own dedicatory preface to Francis I of the *Opere*, with its defence of using an unrhymed poetic line, a defence like Milton's: classical poets did not use rhyme and offered no sanction for it; modern poetry needs only 'sua maiesta' ('its own majesty').[31]

The republican Alamanni's new mixed forms of verse merely confirmed the ferment that ran throughout Paris. France was teaching Surrey that style could never be aesthetic without being communal and political. The young English noblemen thus turned to more visible civic forms of new beauty: sculpture, paintings, and, most apparent, rising palaces whose technology conjured up whole prophecies of possible new shapes for human communities. Being built in the Bois de Boulogne, for example, a good horse-ride from the Louvre, was Francis I's château referred to as Madrid. It combined an ambiguous façade of a high-pitched Gothic roof with the purest example of external galleries and Italian *logge* to be found north of the Alps. Inside the Madrid, Surrey could also have seen the actual execution of new shapes, the terracotta decoration being personally directed by Girolamo della Robbia himself, on a scale whose effect may have been, so Blunt suggests, quite 'startling and somewhat barbarous'.

Such new forms sprang not only from architecture. Other currents of new life moved as inevitably as the Seine's swift and swollen winter tides below the young men in their apartments at the Louvre. In fact, across the same river in the Sorbonne quarter of 30,000 students, Francis I had only recently created four royal professorships for Greek and Hebrew and then later two more, including one for Arabic (Guillaume Postel was lecturing as royal professor in the winter of 1533). Humanists throughout Europe praised the French King, and Erasmus urged the Louvain faculty to recognize the new competition from France and the French King's immensely civilizing acts.[32] In 1533, in that same quarter across the winter Seine from Surrey, a Spanish ex-military knight laboured at theology in the Collège des Lombards. Already over 40, Ignatius Loyola struggled for the coveted MA from the Sorbonne and had already begun the first steps towards founding

[31] Hauvette, *Luigi Alamanni*, 399.

[32] Blunt, *Art and Architecture*, 24–5. For the intellectual ferment in Paris, see Robert Knecht, *Francis I* (1982), 238 and the considerably enlarged version of this text in *Renaissance Warrior and Patron: The Reign of Francis I* (1994).

the Society of Jesus, which was born in Francis I's Paris. In the same spot the 24-year-old lawyer Jean Calvin had published, only the spring before, his Latin commentary on Seneca's *De Clementia* and, in this same Paris, was now slowly textualizing within himself a new form of Christianity before he fled to Geneva the next year.

In this Paris, three French Renaissance poets influenced Surrey, all of whom exhibited the same mixture of linguistic forms, poetic ideals, and ideological purposes. Mellin de Saint-Gelais (1491–1558) distributed alms for the Dauphin and taught him music, particularly lute-playing. The nephew (or perhaps illegitimate son) of the French bishop and poet Octavien de Saint-Gelais (who had himself recently translated the *Aeneid* into French rhyming couplets), the younger Saint-Gelais wrote some of the dozen or so sonnets existing in French in this early period. He encouraged the king himself to write poems, even correcting some. Wyatt may have made his acquaintance when he first visited France in 1526; he imitated him. Saint-Gelais' poetic forms sprang out of Italy, or at least the Italy that Francis I was engendering in France for good political reasons. The poet also appeared as Italianate in dress and manner as Surrey would later be accused of being. In his verse, Saint-Gelais was France's greatest exponent of the kind of *improvvisatore* mode made famous by the Petrarchan Seraphino's extravagant texts. Contrasted with the more serious *petrarchismo* of Cardinal Bembo's, Saint-Gelais' ostentatious conceits and their sharp amorous tone frequently used the short Italian musical stanzas. Thus, in Saint-Gelais, in both flamboyant style and affective texts, the young English poet could find a model.[33]

In fact, Surrey wrote one rather pure example of Saint-Gelais' favourite form of the *strambotto*. In what may be an early poem, if not an exercise, Surrey displayed the classical allusions typical of Seraphino and the Cariteo school of Petrarchism and its sexual puns. As the only secular poem of Surrey's that Tottel did not publish in 1557, the lyric has a theme derived from the erotic verse of the reformed Christian Clément Marot (1496–1544). In 1532–3 Marot was *valet de chambre* to Francis I and very much in the court scene. Imprisoned only a few years before for his strong reformed ideas about Christianity, he had sought the patronage of Marguerite, Queen of Navarre, the king's sister, and had landed a post at court. He too may have given readings to the French King that winter in Paris. In any case, in August 1532 he had published a collection of poems that would have appealed to Surrey, with their careful imitation of ancient genres and the evocation of the classical world, *L'Adolescence clémentine*. Then, just after Surrey and Richmond left, Marot published poems he had written during the time of their visit, *La Suite de l'adolescence clémentine*. In the rondeau that Surrey imitated, Marot transforms a blatant example of Seraphino's type of Petrarchism, adding

33 Sidney Lee, *The French Renaissance in England* (1910), 115 ff. Patricia Thomson, *Sir Thomas Wyatt and His Background* (1964), ch. VII. For an analysis of how the sharp musical phrasing of Saint-Gelais and Seraphino suited the English poets' newer psychological realism, see Sergio Baldi, *Sir Thomas Wyatt* (1961) 35.

his own touches as Surrey did in his imitation. Surrey writes in the popular epic metre of *ottava rima*, a rhyme scheme of *abababcc* which is difficult in English. The lyric epitomizes, in fact, Surrey's whole French experience—formal brilliance, visual art, and a fluid sexuality.

> If he [Apelles] that erst the form so lively drew
> Of Venus' face, triumphed in painter's art:
> Thy father then what glory did ensue,
> By whose pencil a goddess made thou art!
> Touched with flame, that figure made some rue,
> And with her love surprised many a heart.

Opening with the rhetorical figure of *antonomasia* (the Greek painter Apelles is only circuitously named), Surrey's innovative power of diction is soon evident: neither the idea of 'pencil', the central phallic pun, nor a French equivalent of the word exists in Marot, but 'pencil' centres Surrey's epigrammatic structure in this very early example of English *vers de société*. It also prepares for the final witty thrust and unexpected sting of the ending couplet, in which the male's sexual performance is evoked: 'There lacked yet that should cure their hot desire: / Thow canst inflame and quench the kindled fire.'[34]

Francis I

The third French poet who influenced Surrey was none other than the king himself. His verse set a model for the English earl because the king's updated *Romanitas*

[34] With English brevity, Surrey compresses Marot's conceit into this couplet, using reductive structure later typical of all his lyrics to give 'a greater urgency of movement towards a sharply delineated conclusion' than in the French originals, as noted by Anne Lake Prescott, *French Poets and the English Renaissance: Studies in Fame and Transformation* (1978), 9. For the sexuality, it should be noted that Francis I's household budget included a yearly gift to *filles de joie suivant la court*. For a vivid instance of sexuality and idealism, see *LP*, vol. 6, 692. Known for her protection and encouragement of reformed Christians, Francis I's sister Marguerite of Navarre showed in her devotions, poems, narratives, and not least conversation, a full sense of the erotic that does not appear to have added guilt to her Christian idealization of self. After a conversation in the following summer of 1533 with Surrey's father, Norfolk called Marguerite 'one of the most wisest frank women, and best setter forth of her purpose, that I have spoken with'. In that conversation, after making her main point of securing the help of the English for her second husband Navarre, the king's sister relates the narrative of the Dauphin's frustrated love that smacks of one of her own *Heptameron* tales, with the young heir near suicide, a *cercle d'amour* that may have occurred when Surrey and Richmond were traveling with the royal princes. More than this Petrarchan text made alive, the king's sister had a juicier morsel for Norfolk: the animosity of the King of France towards his new wife, the sister of the Holy Roman Emperor. Francis I has not slept with his wife for seven months, Marguerite reports breezily, and when Norfolk asks why, she replies 'Parce quil ne le trouve plesaunt à son apetyde' ('because he does not find her pleasant enough for his appetite'). When he does lie with her, he cannot sleep. Why? asks Surrey's father again. 'She is very hot in bed, and desireth to be too much embraced,' says the king's sister, roaring with laughter and adding: 'I would not for all the good in Paris that the king of Navarre were no better pleased to be in my bed than my brother is in hers.' If this conversation hardly fits the saintly image (for some) of the reformed Christian Marguerite of Navarre, a religious text of hers can show the same complexity as her gossip. Her *Miroir de l'âme pécheresse* ('Mirror of a sinful soul') has erotic imagery combining with religious.

could sanction royal poetic experiments that were, in fact, far more wide-ranging than any other Renaissance monarch's. In this, as in everything else, Francis I contrasted for Surrey the difference of Henry VIII. In the French King was a synthesis of stylistic nobilities as nowhere else in Europe, a kingship exactly defined by Cellini's famous medallion: Francis I on one side as a laurel-wreathed Roman emperor and, on the other side, as a Roman warrior (like St George) on a charging horse, defeating a fallen full-breasted figure representing Fortune herself. Even though Surrey would be admired by Charles V—and Henry VIII dominated his life (and death)—Francis I gave the young poet earl his most profound royal model. That model with its survival totem of the salamander in flames and the half-Latin, half-Italian motto 'nutrisco et extinguo' strengthened Surrey's image of a living Rome in contemporary France. In fact, Surrey found the king's greatest expression of *Romanitas* in Fontainebleau—what Vasari already called 'quasi nuova Roma' ('as if a new Rome')—the centre of a France centrifugal for a new Europe, so Francis I intended, and prophetic, so its art intended, of a new civilizing force.[35]

That force was embodied in the French king. Francis I was six feet tall, with an oval face and well-kept smooth chestnut hair that reached to the unusually wide nape of his neck. His long nose and gentle sensual mouth were accented by the reddish wiry hairs of a thin moustache and full beard, a watery-milk complexion, and hazel, almond-shaped eyes (Plate 7). According to a Welsh soldier in the service of Henry VIII, the French King was animated in conversation, even to the point of rolling his eyes upward, always speaking with an agreeable voice. In the famous portrait by the Flemish Clouet, what authenticates the king's face is the same engagement with a viewer, what the Welshman described and what Wyatt also found in his conversations. As Rearick notes, Clouet painted the king's lips 'parted as if to speak'. In fact, it was to Wyatt that Francis I spoke privately on one occasion and defined his court as one marked by honour. In late 1538 Henry VIII had sent Surrey's older friend on a mission with Edmund Bonner, the Bishop of London. They were to make the English position known in France's coming *rapprochement* with the emperor. Bonner was belligerent and awkward amid the deft courtesy of the French King, at least as Wyatt's dispatch narrates the scene. The occasion of their interview with the king made Wyatt's task as diplomat difficult, but throughout their interview, the French king delighted in conversation, once his initial shyness disappeared, revealing a candour about the events of the day. After the Guise Cardinal of Lorraine had greeted Bonner and Wyatt, 'affter a litill heryng' of the king's music, the two Englishmen entered 'the quens vtter chamber'

[35] For Vasari, see Knecht, *Francis I*, 268. Studies of Fontainebleau and especially of the gallery have emphasized the innovations there and their influence in their own time and in subsequent centuries. Among many are especially Panofsky, 'Iconography', 113–77; Sylvie Béguin, Oreste Binenbaum, André Chastel, W. McAllister Johnson, Sylvia Pressouyre, and Henri Zerner, *La Galerie François Ier au Château de Fontainebleau*, préface par André Malraux, Numéro spécial de la *Revue de l'Art* (1972); Janet Cox-Rearick, *The Collection of Francis I: Royal Treasures* (1996). Cf. *The School of Fontainebleau: An Exhibition of Paintings, Drawings, Engravings, Etchings, and Sculpture 1530–1619* (1965); *Fontainebleau: Art in France, 1528–1610* (National Gallery of Canada, 1973).

and here, following the exchange of communiqués, Francis I 'herd me very gentilly and notyngly', reported Surrey's older friend, 'and puttyng agayne off his bonett [a remarkable gesture of honour], thankyd the kyng [Henry VIII] his good brother ffor his good visitation and the frendly office that he doth with hym.' Turning from some gauche flattery by Bonner, who appears to have misunderstood the king's remarks on his health, Francis I was led by Wyatt to discuss the forthcoming trip of Charles V, his former enemy, through the realm of France. 'He was very joyfull off it, not only ffor that he myght have occasion therby to make hym [Charles V] good chere, but also for that the sayd emperour doth hym the gretest honour that can be, shewthe therby to take hym for an honest man.' Wyatt then interjected to the French King 'that th'emperour knew well with whom he delt as with a prynce off honour and Christian.' Francis I responded to Wyatt's compliment with what appears delicate joking and irony—a kind of Castiglione *sprezzatura*—that expresses, in fact, a serious conviction: ' "Oh," quod he [the king], "we have among vs all nothing but our honour." ' Later, 'laying his hand on his brest' in the ancient Roman gesture of affirmation, Francis I said he would not, whatever his own desire to confer with Charles V, 'move one word off eny such thing for that it were not honest'. When the French King finally left the two, after some tedious requests from Bonner, Francis I made once more the gesture of carrying 'his bonet in his hand' and assuring them he held their King Henry 'by hallff to be had as dere as the ball of his iye'.[36]

Later in England, probably after 1537, Nicholas Bellin da Modena, then in the service of Henry VIII, painted an emblematic bisexual representation of the French king whose distorted pregnant body and weird costume appear first as a parody and then a vicious joke. For Surrey, the French king offered more than this crude parody of sexuality Henry VIII loved. Two other key factors of Francis I's biography made any such English mocking irrelevant to Surrey: the king's library and, not least, his poems. Not only did Francis I have a travelling library in two chests that accompanied him on all his progresses, with romance texts, *Destruction de Troie la Grant* and *Roman de la Rose*, also Roman histories, and even a bound manuscript of Petrarch,[37] but the King of France as a practising poet wrote more than the few songs or lyric texts of a Henry VIII. Although the number of poems written by the French King cannot be determined precisely (none after 1535), he may have written 205 poems in a variety of forms, and some probably during the same months that Surrey was in his presence. If these poems are any

[36] Knecht, *Francis I*, 83; Cox-Rearick, *Collection of Francis I*, 11; Kenneth Muir, *Letters and Life* (1963), 97–9.

[37] Raymond B. Waddington, 'The Bisexual Portrait of Francis I: Fontainebleau, Castiglione, and the Tone of Courtly Mythology', in *Playing With Gender: A Renaissance Pursuit*, ed. Jean R. Brink, Maryanne C. Horowitz, and Allison P. Coudert (1991) esp. 126–7, 131. Cf. also Edgar Wind, *Pagan Mysteries in the Renaissance* (1968), 213–14; André Chastel, *The Age of Humanism: Europe 1480–1530*, trans. Katherine M. Delavenay and E. M. Gwyer (1963), 204. For the library, see Ernest Quentin-Bauchart, *La Bibliothèque de Fontainebleau et les livres des derniers Valois à la Bibliothèque Nationale (1515–1589)* (1971), 4–5, 8–9.

evidence, then Petrarchan language, certainly metaphor, provided a source for Francis I's own acts of self-reflection.

In fact, in one such sonnet, the French King invents his own metaphor for the power of the erotic to ennoble. With a Petrarchan frame, the French King shows how sexual attraction can define the gods themselves. Whatever its technical limitations or its hackneyed conceit, the poem specifically spells out such a transformation of sexuality. At dawn, probably over the forest of Fontainebleau, a young blonde woman, probably the Duchesse d'Etampes, collects all historical reality into herself because of her transcendent beauty. As dawn is breaking over the forest, 'auprès d'une fénestre' ('before a window'), the lover sees Aurora signalling the way for Phoebus ('Qui à Phoebus le chemin enseignoit'). Then the male looks at his female lover combing her long golden hair, and from her shining eyes ('ses luisans yeux') the beloved throws him such a gracious beam ('un traict si gracieux') that he is compelled to cry out in a loud voice: 'Immortal gods, take back your heavens! Her beauty weakens yours' ('Dieux immortels, rentrez dedans vos cieulx; / Car la beauté de ceste vous empire').[38]

Fontainebleau

The power of human beauty to outdo the power of the gods had a special history in France. In these years of the king's poems and Surrey's visit, Fontainebleau was the greatest centre of such beauty and its power. In the spring of 1533, Henry, Duke of Richmond and Henry, Earl of Surrey, and their entourage travelled the thirty miles south-east from Paris to Fontainebleau. They arrived probably a month or so before the king, who had left Paris at the beginning of March, heading, in one more phase of his 'grand voyage de France', for Soissons, Guise, Reims, Chateau-Thierry, Meaux, and points in between before arriving at Fontainebleau on 19 April. Although 5000 people could stay, as in this visit of April 1533, for three days or so at the château and then move on, there was still no village at Fontainebleau, only various mansions and an *auberge* amid the vast forest and the nearby ancient russet-coloured river. With the Dauphin and his brothers, Surrey and Richmond greeted Francis I, who then remained there five days until the celebration of the Order of the Garter on St George's Day, with the English duke as his honoured guest. During this period Alamanni returned from his usual wintering place in Provence, joining the court in spring.

The Venetian ambassador Giustiniani, travelling with the French court, noted on 23 April 1533 the importance at Fontainebleau of the English ceremony of the

[38] The most complete edition of the poetry of Francis I is his *Oeuvres poetiques: Edition critique*, ed. J. E. Kane (1984). I am grateful for her correspondence and help. I have taken this text, however, from Hamy, *Entrevue*, CCXLVIII and have borrowed his supposition that the poem is enacted at Fontainebleau. For more details on the texts and background of these poems, see Knecht, *Francis I*, 84.

Order of the Garter. Because the two young Englishmen were the key players, 'un araldo di Anglia' ('a herald of England') had arrived earlier in Fontainebleau to set up the ceremony, carrying 'li habiti del ordine' ('the dress and accoutrements of the order') for Richmond and the others. King Francis, wrote Giustiniani, celebrated the event with great ceremony, and the Duke of Richmond gave a speech himself (with Surrey probably writing or developing the language of his friend's great moment at the French court). The interlude at Fontainebleau had been timed to honour the English guests, and exactly on St George's Day, the Grand Master wrote from Fontainebleau to Jean de Dinteville (posing in this period for Holbein's *Ambassadors*) in London the plans of the French king and, more significantly, discussed the forthcoming visit of 'Monsieur de Norfolke' and the exact entourage of honour he will need.[39]

In April 1533 Fontainebleau was beginning to fulfil its historical destiny as a centre for the transformation of European society. The Renaissance conception of beauty was finding a new incarnation, from Italy to France, as Francis I sought to increase his power. Richmond and Surrey entered this historical moment, marked a decade before by the death of Leonardo da Vinci at Amboise in the Loire valley. As Renaudet has shown, France stood at a particularly sensitive crossroads once the English Franciscan Ockham had sliced the Thomistic synthesis of grace and nature, faith and reason, for all of Europe. If God could no longer be known by reason or by the things of this world but by leaps of faith only, then not only new forms of contemplation but mysticism itself offered truer forms of knowledge, even a Platonic ecstasy such as Nicholas of Cusa had experienced, sailing back from Byzantinium in the 1430s. In fact, under the influence of Ficino and Pico della Mirandola, both of whom Jacques Lefèvre d'Etaples had met in Italy, Guillaume Fichet had printed in Paris the Greek texts of Plato that led new humanists directly to the Greek world and a consciousness of an intuition beyond logic. God and the deepest reality could now be reached and encountered through forms of beauty (and in the ensuing centuries, such beauty offered encounters with reality purer for most Europeans than the war-weary dogmas of Protestants and Catholics). For the French, these transcendent, even mystic shapes included those of the human body and sexuality, as well as human art. As Knecht has summarized the new European consciousness now focused in France, 'beauty served to bridge the gulf between faith and reason which Occam's remorseless logic had created.'[40]

[39] *I Diarii di Marino Sanuto* (1879–1903), vol. 58, 62; Hamy, *Entrevue*, 172 and CCCVI. I am grateful to M. Doine of Fontainebleau for his general introduction to the château and the area and his walking tour there and by the Seine, especially the visit to Mallarmé's summer house.

[40] A. Renaudet, *Humanisme et Renaissance* (1958), esp. ch. 8 but see also the chapters on Erasmus, Lefèvre d'Etaples, and Marguérite de Navarre. For the ensuing discussion, see also E. F. Rice, 'The Humanist Idea of Christian Antiquity: Lefèvre d'Etaples and his Circle', in *French Humanism 1470–1600*, ed. W. L. Gundersheimer (1969), 163–80; and his 'Humanist Aristotelianism in France', in *Humanism in France at the End of the Middle Ages and in the Early Renaissance*, ed. A. H. T. Levi (1970), 143. For Cusa's experience in 1437, see Ernst Cassirer, *The Individual and the Cosmos in Renaissance Philosophy*, trans. Mario Domandi (1963), 9 and Cassirer's entire crucial first chapter. Knecht, *Francis* I, 133–4.

But this new beauty had its own remorseless logic, as André Malraux recognized when he wrote at the end of his life in the 1960s on the recently restored gallery at Fontainebleau. For Malraux, in that rather narrow corridor at Fontainebleau, with its fourteen paintings, seven on either side, surrounded by stucco figures, decorations, and dark northern wood (instead of marble) above and below the paintings, beauty had its own absolute presence. By the time Surrey arrived in 1533, Il Rosso and Primaticcio had arrived from Rome and Mantua, Rosso already inventing that mixed style of decoration for the gallery that combined painting and sculpture to focus on the body of Francis I in a series of representations. As the Panofskys have shown, this series operates in a system of 'allusive correlatives', in which correlations from classical history and mythology became contemporary in the representative body of the French King. The art makes his body symbolic in a real presence; the historical and contemporary thus become probable though artistic form, a special method of allusive immanence, and so transcendent for the audience.

This total presence and honour that only mixed beauty—historical and symbolic—could bestow was what Francis I intended when after an April 'chasse des bêtes rousses et noires' ('hunt for the red and black beasts') in the rock-filled crevices and pine forests by the nearby Seine, the French King decided to transform his hunting lodge. What Malraux found in the twentieth century Francis I imagined from the start: the formal and inevitable real presence of art in the gallery, a total presence out of ambiguity of time and probability, a new kind of transubstantiation on a new altar, history transfigured, in analogy to the Real Presence Francis I would affirm for his kingdom in a famous procession through Paris, holding the Host. This presence at Fontainebleau not only turned its intensity into a style of Mannerism as international and universal as the earlier Gothic style but proclaimed, on its own terms, a freedom—human, historical, and absolute—at least for Malraux: 'La résurrection de cette Sixtine Chapelle du maniérisme nous révèle la première présence de l'arbitraire en art qui ne serait soumis ni à la spiritualisation, ni à l'illusion, ni à l'idéalisation' ('The resurrection of that Sistine Chapel of Mannerism reveals to us the first presence of the absolute in art that would submit neither to spiritualization, nor to illusion, nor to idealization').[41]

In Malraux's 'étrange dialogue' ('strange dialogue') at Fontainebleau, 'the constant reappearance of Achilles, Hercules, and Diana reminds us,' remarks another

[41] See the analysis in Panofsky, 'Iconography' of each section of the Gallery—even what Surrey did not see but whose method of 'allusive correlative' he saw in what was begun. It should be noted that, although Le Breton had been contracted to begin the Gallery in April 1528, the first record of any painters working there is in August 1533 and of carpenters in the next year. If anything, Surrey saw the first stages and possibly some plans, although any communication between even a Primaticcio or Rosso and a foreign member of the Dauphin's entourage (age 16) would seem highly unlikely. For a new dating of the Gallery, made possible by recent restoration, see Knecht, *Renaissance Warrior*. For Francis' choice, see L. Dimier, *Fontainebleau* (1925), 10. For the Real Presence and the political significance of the French king's adoration of the Host in a special procession, see Donald R. Kelley, *The Beginning of Ideology: Consciousness and Society in the French Reformation* (1981), 13–20. For Malraux, *La Galerie Francois ler*, 'Préface', 9.

critic, 'that the art of Fontainebleau exists to define the image of the living hero' who exists in history, in 1533 Francis I. In such affective visual discourse, forms themselves could become historical life. Their structures of probability—at this period, a concept derived from Aristotle—provided their own real presence, representative art that was alive in its individuality of form. This level of formal probability is what Malraux means by 'the first presence of the absolute in art'. By concentrating earlier signs and rituals into a living text, forms of art (as in religion) could extend pragmatic directions for greater communal participation, as well as for individual transfiguration within that community. If such art was also absolute for Surrey, it was also concrete, realistic, and socially redemptive. This mingling among innovative forms of continuous myth and continuous history was what Ronsard saw as a boy (living with his bureaucrat father at Fontainebleau when Surrey visited) and Surrey had seen (at least, in its beginning), both poets wandering from bright windows (on both sides in 1533) to panels to bright windows of light.

In Norwich Cathedral Surrey had also viewed such mythic formal projections in the stained-glass windows, the enormous rood, and the statues of the saints from his own world, even including an image and quotation of Chaucer's Franklin in one side aisle. That art had existed in a total mythic community for Surrey, founded in a specific history, and Fontainebleau was now trying, at least as Richmond and Surrey must have seen it, to re-invent out of political and religious chaos its own arbitrary terms for the future of total presence and a new political mythology behind it. In all this, Francis I never doubted the consecrated nature of his gallery. In 1540 the English ambassador, Sir John Wallop, an old Howard friend, reported back to Henry VIII from Fontainebleau that the French King had personally pointed out to him features of the gallery, unlocking the gallery with a key he always carried with him and even standing on a chair to identify parts of the ceiling. Henry VIII should imitate the new forms, Francis I told Wallop, pointing out that he did not have to gild wood as the English king did but bought the best Brazilian wood with its own scents and native beauties.[42] From their own history they shaped this gallery of symbol and probability.

A single painted cartouche under the last panel on the north side of Francis I's gallery—the explicitly erotic Venus panel—reveals how the Porte Dorée looked in 1536, the gate by which Richmond and Surrey entered Fontainebleau in March 1533. The panel shows a quite active Cour de la Fontaine as well, with figures hurrying across as the young men might have seen it that first day; in the background is the gallery with its high windows and then the baths on the floor below, and then, on the third floor, between the huge brick chimneys, the dormer windows of Francis I's library watched over by Guillaume Budé himself. There thirteen encased windows brought light during the day, and twelve 'tablettes' filled

[42] Henri Zerner, *The School of Fontainebleau: Etchings and Engravings* (1969), 11. For Chaucer in Norwich Cathedral, I am indebted to Professor Brad Fletcher. For Wallop (and following quotations) see *SP*, vol. 8, 479–86.

the space between them, where Richmond and Surrey may have sat and read or looked at a whole spectrum of scientific objects; the two young Englishmen might have viewed, globes, spheres, mathematical instruments, and a 'cabinet of curiosities'.

Of the wonders that confronted the two young men strolling through the palace, two combined ennobling forms of eroticism and idealized art. The Pavilion of Pomona in the garden and orangery area just north of the gallery had its Ovidian story of androgyny and seduction and languorous male shapes, both clothed and naked. The statue of *La Nature* was created by Le Tribolo at Fontainebleau in 1527, before Francis had decided to embellish his palace. The statue was adapted from the Greek original of the goddess Artemis of Ephesus to the style of Fontainebleau, exhibiting that style of syncretism Yates sees as marking Renaissance France.[43] The upper part of the statue anticipates the whole erotic premise of the gallery as the figure of Nature reaches up to support the antique granite basin it was originally designed to hold. The reaching gesture adumbrates later art like Rodin's and the early Picasso and Matisse: with four full breasts, the woman raises fleshy arms and hands to hold a towel against thick hair and looks out with half-open mouth. Nothing in the sensuous mixed style of the pavilion or statue could be found in England, either in the fleshy gargoyles that sprang out of Norwich Cathedral or the Gothic interweaving of incense-filled chapels in London's Saint Paul's, whose great tower of a thousand feet rose over the city and the culture that before had represented all of Surrey's horizons.

The baths and sweat-rooms beneath the gallery literalized this presence of the human body at Fontainebleau. In fact, Francis I kept his personal art gallery next to his baths. Writing back to Henry VIII in 1540, Sir John Wallop found the baths not very agreeable, 'being warm and reeked so much, like it had been a mist, that the king went before to guide me'. In fact, the whole area was like a modern swimming club, the largest such area for any residence north of the Alps (and as an indoor pool perhaps south of the Alps as well). With its sweating-rooms and refreshment alcoves, the area was clearly designed to reproduce the famous Roman baths Francis I had read about. Set squarely in this bottom area beneath the light-filled gallery, the actual bath measured about 5 feet deep by probably 20 across. Reached by a flight of upward wooden stairs, the pool had spouts for both hot and cold water. Then, in another Roman imitation, a wooden balustrade surrounded the bathing area. Painted to look like bronze and designed as a promenade for two, the balustrade allowed courtiers not only to stare at the bathers' almost naked bodies and chat with them, but to gaze at the frescos in the lunettes of the bathing area before they walked on to see the art collection in gilded frames and stucco that hung on the walls of the vestibule leading to the baths.

[43] *La Galerie Francois Ier*, 18, 40–1. For the library, see Quentin-Bauchart. Frances A. Yates, *The French Academies in the 16th Century* (1947). For the first artists at Fontainebleau, see Blunt, *Art and Architecture*, 27.

Against a background of official readers or language games in French, Italian, and English, or social banter from lightly clothed male and female courtiers, the young men could lie in the warm bath-water together, side by side, and then rise, dry themselves, dress, and see, in the vestibule just outside, the greatest collection of art in northern Europe and one of the most spectacular in the world: Leonardo da Vinci's *Mona Lisa*; his *Leda and the Swan* with four infants; possibly his *Saint John the Baptist*; then da Vinci's enigmatic *Virgin of the Rocks*, unlike any other religious painting Surrey had seen before, St Anne's reaching light-filled body so different from the famous statue of Our Lady of Walsingham that sat stiffly in its dark cloister in East Anglia, lit only by hundreds of candles. Here both Surrey and Richmond may also have seen Raphael's *Portrait of the Artist* with a friend, the mysterious male companion looking back at the artist, and Bronzino's *Venus et l'Amour*, perhaps Pontormo's *Resurrection of Lazarus* and Rosso's *Judith*, and the original of Andrea Del Sarto's *Charity* in one of the refreshment alcoves, with her full open breasts ready to be sucked.[44]

Departure

On the day after the ceremonies for the Order of the Garter, Francis I left for the Loire valley with his entire suite, including the young Englishmen and their servants. For both, the climax of their trip had passed. The king headed south to Lyons where Surrey and Richmond were separated from their three royal friends, whom they had known intimately for almost eight months. The royal sons were to accompany their step-mother, Charles V's sister, into the Midi and to Nîmes, where she was to have a triumphal entry, and Richmond and Surrey travelled with the king, who now turned towards the Auvergne. They were to meet Surrey's father there.

Over a month before, at Anne Boleyn's Pentecost coronation, Henry VIII had told Norfolk to return to attend the papal interview with Francis I and keep the English divorce alive or at least to influence the French king to set up a general council of the Church. Just before he left, Henry VIII also made Norfolk Earl Marshal of the kingdom. The office of Earl Marshal had been granted to John Howard under Richard III and had belonged to Surrey's grandfather, but it had then been given to the Duke of Suffolk. Under pressure (Henry VIII did not appreciate the public snub of Suffolk and his wife, the king's sister Mary, towards his Howard queen) Suffolk had surrendered the title. Now Norfolk had to

[44] *SP* 8: 485. For the place of Francis I's collection, see C. Eschenfelder, 'Les bains de Fontainebleau; nouveaux documents sur le decors du Primatice', *Revue de l'Art*, 100 (1993), 45–52. For the paintings, see Jean Adhémar, 'The Collection of Paintings of Francis I', *Gazette des Beaux-Arts*, sér. 6, 30 (1946), the discussion in Cox-Rearick, and Knecht, *Francis I*, 261, 264–70. Francis I had a predilection for Flemish art and the Burgundian artists as well as the Italians.

compensate for this great honour by persuading the French king to intercede with the Pope. Henry VIII had given Norfolk the petulant command to 'consult by what ways and means we can best annoy the Pope.' The English king smelled treachery everywhere, and he wanted Norfolk to warn Francis I of those who 'play and dally with kings and princes', a replay of his vow to Chapuys earlier in 1533 when the English king walked up and down in his garden at Greenwich, promising to revenge the insults by the papacy to the English Kings John and Henry II (the latter of whom had had to deal with the tiresome Becket). With his new Queen Anne ready to deliver what he was certain was a son, and now believing all his new texts of supremacy and honour, Henry VIII wanted Norfolk to make Francis I 'conceive in his stomach' that the Pope threatened 'the greatest dishonour that ever might be imagined or compassed towards the honour and liberties of princes'.[45]

In the Auvergne, Surrey met his father again, after nine months (his longest separation ever from his family). At Riom, on 10 July 1533, hearing of his father's approach at seven in the morning, Surrey with Richmond raced on their horses to about a mile and a half from the city, where the young man greeted his father with enthusiasm. This enthusiasm was needed. Within days Norfolk learned the news Francis I had tried to conceal, the Pope's decision to excommunicate Henry VIII. The shock made Norfolk almost faint. He knew he had to return to England. Rather than risk a complete collapse of the new-found *rapprochement* at Calais, Francis I had already arranged that Surrey and Richmond would accompany the French King further south in the 'eccessivi caldi' ('excessively hot') Provence summer.[46] The red-headed English poet with the pale complexion and the vigorous Richmond were now hostages of another kind. At Montpellier, after Richmond and Surrey had visited the legendary Toulouse and Carcassonne, Norfolk came once more to visit Francis I, whatever the heat, begging him to cancel the promised interview with the Pope. Norfolk also requested the return of Richmond and Surrey on the grounds that Richmond was now to marry his daughter Mary, by the king's command. Then Norfolk headed north, arriving in Moulins on 24 August and in Amiens on the afternoon of 28 August (where he wrote to Lord Lisle at Calais requesting warships ready to take him home at once). Norfolk arrived at the English court two days later. His entire travelling expenses for the fruitless months in France had been enormous, over £333 (exactly the amount the French king would now give him in annual pension), but he had done everything with characteristic efficiency—all in devotion to his king. In fact, in his haste to report to his master and to be on hand as his niece delivered her child, he had averaged, starting from the south of France, more than 60 miles per day by post horse and carriage for nine days straight, the Channel crossing his only break, and all of this at the age of 60. As always, there was a particular political reason: he must now

45 *SP*, vol. 6, 473–93 (8 Aug. 1533).

46 Quoted in Bapst, *Deux gentilshommes-poètes*, 189. For Norfolk's activities, see *LP*, vol. 811, 831, 846.

get to court and act out the particular role of the first ten days of September 1533, when Anne Boleyn's child of honour would be born.

The turmoil of England thus awaited both young men. The liberty of France was leaving them as they lingered where they could, one place in particular, Avignon, the holy city of Petrarch. The poet earl may have accompanied the French King when he visited the tomb of Petrarch's Laura. There the French King read aloud his eight verses written in honour of this September 1533 visit.[47] If he did, Avignon signalled a fitting end to Surrey's first sojourn in France. When he returned again, he was to be an enemy to this court, in fact, the English 'Lieutenant General of the King' who would defend Boulogne against the forces of Francis I. But he had also been remembered at that court, and the French memory of Surrey contradicts strongly the later Edwardian descriptions of his character as frivolous and arrogant. Writing to Henry VIII in 1540, Sir John Wallop recorded his conversation with the 21-year-old Dauphin Henry (the Dauphin Francis having died in 1536) and his younger brother Charles, now Duc d' Orléans, 'two goodly Princes, and full of actyvitie, specially the Dolphin'. The conversation took place at an evening 'banckett' where 'I dyd sett with Monsr. Dolphin and Monsr. dOrleance,' who spoke of the English King, 'preasing of Your Majestie in dyvers and sundry things with grete affection,' even asking if Wallop knew Henry VIII was the Dauphin's godfather. When the English ambassador said he 'knewe it very wel', the future Henry II then 'beganne to speke of my Lord of Richemounte, lamenting his dethe gretely'. After a pause, both the royal princes immediately asked about 'my Lord of Surrey, geving grete prease unto hym, aswel for his wisedome and sobrenes, as also good learning'.[48]

Avignon had also provided a clear route towards Paris and then to Calais, and so arrived on 'the XXV of Septembar the duke of Richemond, bastard sone to king Henry the Eighth, and the erle of Surrey [at] Caleys owt of Fraunce, where they hade bene almost xij monthes.' Lady Lisle entertained the two young men of such importance with her own interests at work, as the 'thank you' messages from Surrey and Richmond revealed, her agent in London writing less than three weeks after 29 September 1533, the day the young men crossed the Channel and arrived back at the English court: 'My lord of Surrey saith that the Earl of Oxford [Surrey's father-in-law] is not yet comen to the Court, but as soon as he commeth he will remember his promise to your ladyship, as our Lord God knoweth, who long continue your ladyship in honour, and to attain your noble heart's desire.' Richmond wrote in February of the next year, greeting his father's bastard uncle, Lord Lisle, the son of Edward IV, and offering 'most hearty thanks for the great cheer and kindness the which you and my good Lady your wife made unto me at my last being at Calais' and noting that he would be glad to prefer one of their servants.[49]

[47] For Norfolk's trip, *Lisle Letters*, vol. 1, 550–2. For Francis I's poem, Clough, 'Francis I', 33.

[48] *SP*, vol. 8, 649 (500).

[49] *Chronicle of Calais*, 44; *Lisle Letters*, vol. 1, 587; vol. 2, 42.

By February of that year Richmond was already a married man, Surrey reunited with his young wife.

They had come back to an England that was moving into another series of upheavals that would engulf them both. The child of honour had been born, a girl, Elizabeth, from whose christening in the Franciscan friary church at Greenwich, the king had absented himself in chagrin. Now, with France behind them, in another year the young men would separate forever. Then, in three years Richmond would be dead, and just over a decade later, Surrey himself. All that exists of this friendship would be in two poetic texts, and there, at least in Surrey's representation of those years, recollected not in tranquillity but in misery, what pervades is the rendering of an exalted union, one of both a physical intimacy and an idealism they had seen depicted in the life and art of France.

The sweet accord, such sleeps as yet delight,
The pleasant dreams, the quiet bed of rest,
The secret thoughts imparted with such trust,
The wanton talk, the diverse change of play,
The friendship sworn, each promise kept so just,
Wherewith we passed the winter nights away.

4

The Deaths of 1536

After the late November 1533 wedding of the Duke of Richmond to Mary Howard, performed by her new friend, Thomas Cranmer, the Archbishop of Canterbury, Norfolk functioned as the virtual protector of the adolescent son of the king. The Howards, father, son, and daughter, now controlled a key link to the royal family. They would need this special link and the strength it brought them to survive not only Surrey's estranged mother's continuing defiance and eccentricity but the imminent collapse of Henry VIII's second marriage. By the time of that collapse, as almost every document of the last two years of Richmond's life shows, the young duke had moved as a puppet dangling between father and father-in-law, performing a series of obediences and little more. Even in the one surviving letter in which he is personal, defiantly rejecting a client (one of Cromwell's friends), his father rebuked him.

Thus, after returning from France in 1533, Richmond attended Parliament for thirty-two sittings of the important 1534 session, which defined the Act of Succession and the role of the Supreme Head, missing only a few times. Just as conscientiously he observed, in place of the absent king, the executions of Sir Thomas More, Bishop John Fisher, and the Charterhouse monks (the ones who were not starved to death). To most of these events, the young duke was accompanied by his father-in-law, the older duke, with whom he often entertained as well. Indeed, the spectacular occasion in which Anne Boleyn burst into hysterical laughter, while dancing with the French admiral and after seeing Henry VIII turn to another woman, was an entertainment given by Richmond and Norfolk. On consecutive evenings in November 1534, on the vigil and feast of St Andrew, the two dukes gave a spectacular farewell entertainment for the French Admiral, Philippe de Chabot, and it was he who reported to Francis I on the English queen's odd behaviour.[1] Surrey also had to perform his acts of obedience. After 1535, the poet earl was expected to produce an heir for the Howards. For this, the two men were forced to separate, returning to their wives. Richmond's apparent failure to consummate his marriage, a fact muted for the court but noted by all, appeared rather strange by 1535. In March 1536, Surrey's first child was born, and the young couple remained physically intimate until the end, the countess pregnant with their fifth child at Surrey's arrest and execution.

[1] *Lisle Letters*, vol. 2, 159, 603 and for more of the activities *LP*, vol. 7, 684 (the dismissal letter), 1316; vol. 8, 168, 259, 981; vol. 9, 779. See the illumination of the Garter Procession cited above for a view of Norfolk and Richmond together.

Thus the distance between the two young men grew by the sheer demand of new roles, particularly Surrey's. The earl and his countess were learning, for example, that however satisfactory their private lives, their public roles were costly. No sooner were the young husband and wife ensconced in the new mansion his father had built for himself at Kenninghall than Surrey found they needed money. Surrey's first recorded letter shows a financial stress, which may have resulted from his own mismanagement but more likely from the problems of cash-flow from the vast Howard estates and revenues, and from Norfolk's extreme caution with money. In 1535, Surrey could still turn to the one institution that offered credit to the nobility (at least to the Howards), the monasteries. This time Surrey wrote to the prior of nearby Bury St Edmund, a friend of his absent father. Norfolk had returned to France and was now negotiating a possible marriage between Surrey's friend Charles, the youngest son of Francis I, and Anne Boleyn's Elizabeth, not quite 2 years old, the first of many engagements for Elizabeth and clearly the work of her mother. Writing on 29 June 1535, the Feast of Sts Peter and Paul, the young husband had discovered new expenses he did not suspect: 'by very ned & extreme necessyte I am agayne constrayned, my nown good Lord, at this present affectuowsly to desyre yow to shew yoore self so mych my cordiall frend as to lend some over & above XX pound, in syche haste as I may have it here to-morrow by VIII of the clock for syche is my present nede and thowght.' Although the letter opened in the tone of a pampered teenager applying to a rich uncle, the rest of the letter revealed the warm naïveté of a young man asking for his first loan. For such kindness, said the earnest 19-year-old husband, he could never 'offer the lyke recompense, yet my lord ye shall so bynd [me] to be your inward & affectual frend while I lyve & your money first & last to be honestly repayd to yow agayne wt hartye thanks.' In fact, 'iff I wer so ingrat (whch god defend) to deny' payment, the abbot will find his father 'will not see your harty kyndnes vncontenid' when 'My Lord' returns from 'beynge owt off the cowntree' and Surrey had 'rather attempt to assay yoow his anycent frend than other farther off'. He is writing 'from Kenngale this St. Peters' and signed it 'yowrs assuredly duryng his liff', adding on the front 'To his very good lord & frend, my lord abbott Birry gyve these. In hast hast hast.' Wisely the accounting abbot marked on the letter 'My lord of Surre XX and, besydes that, XXX.'[2]

What Surrey was now learning was that the young couple had courtly roles—already the king had sent them on New Year's days a silver bowl and platter—and that these roles required more funds than either expected. In the following winter, for example, the teenaged Countess of Surrey was named the third official mourner of Catherine of Aragon at her burial on 27 January 1536, and, uncompensated, she went from Kenninghall, in the last months of her first pregnancy, to

[2] BL Add. MS 24493, f. 234. For an example of the further expenses Surrey would have, cf. Society of Antiquaries MS 129, Inventory of Henry VIII, f. 71r: 'Item three gilt bolles with a Couer hauing therupon a Doble Rose the shankes of the bolles chased vpright and the Feet grauen in one payne geuen by Therle of Surrey on Newyeres daye Anno XXIX weyeng lxix oz.'

Peterborough. On the vigil of the funeral she was the chief mourner and presided over the whole ceremony for a queen she barely knew, except as a woman completely defeated.

The Destruction of Anne Boleyn

1536 was to be a year of deaths and near-deaths in the world of the young Howards. After the January death of his first wife, the new Supreme Head announced to the Imperial Ambassador Chapuys that he had finally seen, in all their absurdity, the lies of the papacy, as had the Greek Christians earlier (the king had recently ordered his goldsmith to make a heavily jewelled two-headed eagle for himself like that of Byzantium) and as the German and Scandinavian princes had done in his own time. After all, had he not always been sensitive to religion and the call of God? His crisis of conscience over the proper reading of Leviticus in the late 1520s had deep roots. From childhood on, when his brother Arthur was still alive, Henry VIII had been destined, at least as Lord Herbert reported it, by his grandmother Lady Margaret Beaufort and her beloved friend Bishop John Fisher for a religious vocation, nothing less than Archbishop of Canterbury (109). As a young man, he had been pious and unusually chaste (if the Spanish ambassador is correct), seeing himself, long before the Pope gave him the title, as 'Defender of the Faith' and even planning a crusade in 1513. Thus it was natural for the king in 1529, even without the tutelage of his chaste mistress, to be attracted to a subject like Tyndale's *The Obedience of the Christian Man* when confronted with a crisis of faith over his exhilarating love and the wickedness of his first incestuous marriage. He appears to have read Tyndale's magnificent prose immediately when handed the book, soon announcing 'This book is for me and all kings to read.'

In exile in the Low Countries, Tyndale had written: 'The king is, in this world, without law and may at his lust [will] do right and wrong and shall give accounts but to God only.' By 1536, when the New Treason Act left no doubt about the king's 'lust' in the realm, the transformation of the Tudor rosebush under the 'touch' of Anne Boleyn, in Ives' imagery, had become complete. Her device of a silver falcon standing poised on a golden trunk that sprouted roses was bearing fruit, as was her motto 'Mihi et mea'. 'Your Majesty' came quite naturally during the years of Anne Boleyn to replace the 'Your Grace' Wolsey had habitually used to address the king. And a new majesty was everywhere: in 1535, the king had almost attended the gala execution (at least Chapuys reports on the masks and dress of spectators like Richmond and Norfolk) of the Carthusian monks, the order to which had once belonged Sir Thomas More, himself executed a few weeks later, after Fisher. Anne Boleyn herself had Latimer preach against the visitation and annihilation of lesser monasteries; and indeed for More and Fisher, Cranmer suggested that these traitors merely swear allegiance to the new succession, not disown Rome.[3] The new Supreme Head, now assured of his own role, acceded to neither intercession.

On 21 January 1536, six days before Catherine of Aragon's funeral, there came a near-death. England almost lost the Supreme Head. It is a genuine question if that head were ever right again. Although Henry VIII continued the same patterns of magnificent self-embodiment as before, physical changes became more evident. Deterioration followed in the metamorphosis of the golden-red-headed young man with the long torso and 34-inch waist admired by the Venetians into a caricature with a 55-inch waist by the age of 55. On that January day, running the lists at Greenwich and trying once more to prove at a corpulent 44 that he could compete, Henry VIII was suddenly unhorsed by his opponent and thrown to the ground in his heavy armour put on for the display. His horse, equally mailed and decorated, landed on top of him. Those watching thought he had died instantly (as Surrey's friend, the French Henry II, died two decades later in similar circumstance). But the English King lay unconscious for two hours before recovering. He never ran in the lists again nor rode to hounds, although he did hunt. In fact, from this point on, the ulcer on one leg, probably generated from an earlier jousting injury, now developed into a condition of osteomyelitis in both legs, a condition he later used as an excuse to Norfolk for not visiting the north of England, as promised, after the destruction of the Pilgrimage of Grace.[4]

For Anne Boleyn, whom the Imperial Ambassador Chapuys called during these years 'braver than a lion,'[5] the news of near-death brought near-hysteria. Now vanished was the joy with which, earlier in January, she had put her swollen pregnant body into a yellow costume to dance with her husband, also dressed in yellow, to celebrate the death of Catherine of Aragon. She immediately began to miscarry. Within a week she had delivered a dead child, a boy. The accident and then the dead child confirmed the religious king's growing suspicion: his life with the woman was an offence to God. By Lent of 1536, Henry VIII was ignoring his queen, when before he suffered if he did not see his confessor-lover every day. Although the Howard offspring refused to surrender in her last months, she now had two formidable enemies: the forces of Catherine of Aragon's daughter Princess Mary, largely orchestrated by Anne's step-cousin's husband, Sir Nicholas Carew, an early favourite of the king's (who had been painted by Holbein as a Burgundian

[3] Ives, *Anne Boleyn*, 161–3. William Tyndale, 'The Obedience of a Christian Man', in *Doctrinal Treatises and Introductions to Different Portions of the Holy Scriptures, by William Tyndale, Martyr, 1536*, ed. H. Walter, Parker Society [32] (1848), 178. For the device see Carley, 'Her moost lovyng and fryndely brother', 275 n. 24: 'This was Anne's device: a silver falcon crowned gold, holding a gold sceptre in its right talon, standing on a golden trunk out of which sprouted both red and white roses and the words "Mihi et mea".' Cf. R. V. Pinches, *The Royal Heraldry of England* (1974), 146. For the monastery reference, see William Latymer, *A Brief Treatise or Chronicle of the Most Virtuous Lady Anne Boleyn Late Quene of Englande*, Bodleian Library MS Don C. 42 26r–33r. For Cranmer, see Scarisbrick, *Henry VIII*, 337; and *LP*, vol. 11, 860, 1250; vol. 7, 499.

[4] Sir Arthur S. MacNalty, *Henry VIII: A Difficult Patient* (1952), 159 ff., and Scarisbrick, *Henry VIII*, 485–6.

[5] *LP*, vol. 5, 10.

knight in armour); and the forces of a new woman, Jane Seymour, lady-in-waiting to both Queen Catherine (whom Jane appears to have admired) and then Queen Anne.

The power of this latter woman was orchestrated by her brother, Sir Edward Seymour. His first step had been to make his sister deny the king easy access to her; she told him 'she had no greater treasure in the world than her honour which she would rather die a thousand times than tarnish.'[6] To respect these wishes of his new beloved and see her only in company of relatives, the king forced Cromwell to vacate his lodging, with its private passage to the royal apartments, in favour of Seymour and his ambitious second wife Anne. Then in March 1536 he appointed Seymour to the Privy Chamber. The turning-point for the annihilation of Surrey's first cousin may have come, in fact, under Seymour's direction. On 18 April 1536, the Tuesday after Easter, in a routine visit to Greenwich, Chapuys was deliberately engaged by Seymour in conversation after the king had harshly indicated that plans for a new alliance with the Empire were not working out. As Seymour talked, the Imperial Ambassador witnessed what he described as the extraordinary scene of Henry VIII and Cromwell arguing. Chapuys then saw the visibly disturbed Cromwell go out for a drink and then, out of the king's sight, sit on a chest to control himself. Chapuys was right about the crucial nature of what he saw. Cromwell went to his bed and arrived at the conclusion that the woman for whose honour he had managed to dislocate a kingdom had to be annihilated.

Now, as Cromwell had built her honour, he would destroy it. It did not matter that no English queen had been accused of adultery for centuries. He built a text of shame that could destroy any knight, especially this new androgynous figure. Adultery and incest with her brother would reverse any imaging of honour and mirror, through shame, the king's ordeal of seven years of chastity.[7] The queen's 'sweet brother', the handsome poet cousin of Surrey, was soon arrested as he emerged from dinner, and taken to the Tower the same afternoon. His trial over two weeks later revealed his wit and sense of language. Not even Sir Thomas More, so one French observer noted, replied better to the accusations, and, in fact, the conversation between brother and sister became the focus of the trial. Handed a paper with a charge he was to read silently but under no circumstances aloud, the Howard offspring saw that he was accused of discussing Henry VIII's sexual power of erection. Rochford's own wife had told Cromwell that her sister-in-law, the queen, had said the English King 'nestoit habile en cas de soy copuler avec femme, et quil navoit ne vertu ne puissance' ('is not capable of copulating with a woman because he lacks both strength and staying power'). At once, with considerable wit, the young Rochford replied that to discuss the king's sexual prowess with his sister would impugn the royal issue (and, he knew, defy the Succession Act of 1534). He would not be so discourteous. The more direct second question—was

[6] Ives, *Anne Boleyn*, 348.

[7] For Chapuys' observation of Cromwell, see *CSP Span* vol. 5, 2, 43A (94–5). Cf. *LP*, vol. 10, 1069. For the whole development of Cromwell's plot, see Ives, *Anne Boleyn*, ch. 15–17.

Elizabeth the real child of Henry?—he answered with the courtesy and discretion of silence. It was a silence into which he vanished.[8]

The Earl of Surrey was directly involved in the trials of both first cousins, Queen Anne and Viscount Rochford. The 20-year-old poet held the golden staff of the Earl Marshal of the realm and deputized for his father, the Earl Marshal now presiding as High Steward at the trials. The Duke of Norfolk sat under the cloth of estate, holding a long white staff in his hand, with the Lord Chancellor Audley at his right and the Duke of Suffolk on his left, and down from him 'other marqueses, earles, lordes, everie one after their degrees' (W 37). At his feet sat Surrey to witness the first state trial he had ever attended and to listen to his cousins' language, their wit and control. Anne Boleyn was unusually eloquent. For the Windsor Herald Wriothesley, generally unsympathetic, 'She made so wise and discreet answers to all things laid against her, excusing herself with her words as clearly as though she had never been faulty to the same' (1: 37–8). After the jury of twenty-six peers all voted 'guilty', despite the evidence that convinced even Chapuys of Anne Boleyn's innocence, Norfolk gave the sentence on his sister's child. For his niece, 'the water ronne in his eyes,'[9] as it had for his father condemning the Duke of Buckingham. Norfolk had good reason to weep this time. This beheading was one more Howard loss and signified the rise of another dynasty, the Seymours.

The queen may have kept the same level of eloquence at her execution. The 17-year-old Richmond had watched the May beheading of his stepmother Queen Anne on Tower Green in his last public act before his own death in July 1536. Once more, he took the place of the absent king. Sir Thomas Wyatt may also have been present, at least watching behind the bars of his cell in the Tower. Using a Senecan choral ode with its theme of the power of *fortuna*, he translated what he saw: 'these blodye dayes,' Wyatt wrote, 'haue brokyn my hart' (MT 176). A Venetian, probably the ambassador (not particularly sympathetic), wrote back to the Signoria in Italy to describe the queen's execution by the stylish French sword she had requested. Translating from the spoken English of Surrey's first cousin into the obvious Venetian dialect of his dispatch, he reported her last words: 'Estimate l'honor vostro piu che la vita e pregate Iddio per l'anima mia' ('Esteem your honour more than life and pray to God for my soul'). After that, in a contemporary account, with one swift blow, the head of Anne Boleyn 'fell to the ground with her lips moving and her eyes moving'.[10]

But no performance of language or death could match the intricate structure of shame Cromwell had wonderfully erected. Henry VIII found Cromwell's unfolding

[8] *LP*, vol. 10, 1036; 908.

[9] *Archaeologia*, 23 (1831) 66.

[10] The Italian report is written in a Venetian dialect and ends with the phrase 'your most observant [servant]' and the name 'P. A.', probably the Venetian ambassador in London. Dated 1 June 1536, the report can be found transcribed in Hamy, *Entrevue*, pp. CCCCXXXI-XXXVI. The dispatch also reveals intimate details of the eloquent scaffold speech from Anne Boleyn's brother, whom the writer considers the true father of the Princess Elizabeth. The contemporary account is in *The Reports of John Spelman*, ed. J. H. Baker, Selden Society, 93 (1977), 59.

strategy particularly gratifying. The Tudor king could bring at last a revenge of almost cosmic shame on Anne Boleyn, who had failed him so miserably after seven years of deceptive idealism. To incest, Henry VIII added charges of witchcraft and poisoning. In fact, on the night of the queen's arrest, the Duke of Richmond had come to his father to ask for his blessing before he went to sleep. This was an English custom, Chapuys noted, and on this occasion, after making the sign of the cross over him, Henry VIII particularly embraced his son and began 'to weep and say that he and his sister [Mary] owed God a great debt for having escaped the hands of that cursed and poisoning whore who had planned to poison them.' Of course, as the king told the Bishop of Carlisle, he had long since expected such a tragedy from his second queen and, in fact, drawing from his bosom a little book written in his own hand, Henry VIII announced to the bishop that he had himself composed a formal five-act tragedy on the event.[11] The day after Queen Anne's execution, the king cheered himself up by betrothing himself to Jane Seymour and, within ten days, marrying her privately in her own new apartment in Anne Boleyn's palace of honour at Whitehall. A week later, the new queen's brother Sir Edward was ennobled as Viscount Beauchamp and then elevated in the peerage as Earl of Hertford, and another brother, Sir Thomas, succeeded him as a groom of the privy chamber.

Star-crossed Lovers

But the Howards had reason for dynastic joy in 1536, and Surrey provided it. On 12 March, the Countess of Surrey gave birth to her first child, his name Thomas. The teenaged countess had no difficulty, and Surrey had performed the first of his duties as the Howard scion: he had produced a male, a living heir. At 20 he had begun the task of building his own family for dynastic survival in a time of deaths and destruction. Two other events occurred that showed the tight dynastic network and more Howard joy. On Sts Peter and Paul's (29 June) in the same year, the month after the queen's execution, Surrey's young uncle Lord William Howard, the oldest son of the second marriage of the 'Flodden Duke', was married in the Chapel Royal at Whitehall. His younger brother Thomas, from the same second marriage of the second duke, with the 10-year-old heir to the Earl of Rutland led the bride to the church. After the wedding, around two o'clock in the afternoon, a grand mock-naval battle on the Thames followed, with the shooting of ordnance that actually wounded some passing sailors.

The other wedding was a highlight of the London season. Near the Rutland London mansion at Holywell in Shoreditch, on 3 July 1536, a triple marriage took place. The event reflected the kind of social network that dominated Surrey's life. Such an occasion became for him, as for everyone, a form of musical chairs, the kind of family and genealogical setting of Tudor England that determined, in fact,

[11] *CSP Span*, vol. 5, 2, 55 (124–7). Cf. *LP*, vol. 10, 908.

its economic structure. In this case, on that day the 10-year-old Rutland heir married the daughter of the Neville Earl of Westmorland; Rutland's sister married Lord Neville, the son and heir of the Earl of Westmorland; and an older daughter of the Earl of Westmorland married the Countess of Surrey's brother, Lord Bulbeck, the de Vere son and heir of the Earl of Oxford. To add to this clan density, the mother of the Westmorland children was the sister of Surrey's mother, the ostracized Duchess of Norfolk. The elder Neville daughter, Dorothy, who was being married, had become a particular favourite of the duchess. The herald Wriothesley described the packed church: 'at which maryage was present all the greate estates of the realme, both lordes and ladyes'.

In fact, the event took on political overtones. In this wedding, less than six weeks after the execution of Anne Boleyn, the old blood nobility had asserted itself in a joyous display only they could muster against the Seymour queen's relatives or Cromwell and his new men, like the herald Wriothesley's cousin. Furthermore, the wedding had taken place at the Benedictine convent church of St John the Baptist, and that place itself may have made a statement just before the Pilgrimage of Grace polarized the court with more religious divisions. So did the recessional from the church. No one less than the Lords Audley and Norfolk led Dorothy Neville home from the church; the Lords Suffolk and Dorset led Lord Neville's wife; and the Lords Derby and Surrey the other Neville daughter, also Surrey's first cousin. This kinship could be matched by few in the realm. The dinner that followed displayed largesse, with 'diverse greate dishes and delicate meates with sotteltes, and diverse manner of instruments playinge at the same, where were to longe to expresse', at least for the admiring herald Wriothesley. The real coup came after dinner: 'The kinges grace came theder in a maske,' riding from nearby Whitehall. Henry VIII had eleven courtiers with him, and of these, seven wore, like the king, masks and Turkish turbans of black velvet with white feathers, while four wore purple sarcenet (a form of silk) as though Turkish pages to the others. After these had all danced with the ladies for a while, the king took off his mask and 'shewyd himselfe'. Then he himself summoned a great banquet of forty dishes, 'diverse sotteltes and meates, which was a goodlye sight to behold' as was, no doubt, the sight of the king and his courtiers riding back 'in their maskinge garmentes as they came thether' (W: 50–1).

But there had been another Howard marriage in these same days, a secret wedding that became the quintessential (and probably major) 'star-crossed' love story at the Tudor court and resulted in one more painful death for the young poet earl. On 18 July 1536, Lord Thomas Howard, the step-brother of the Duke of Norfolk and Surrey's beloved uncle, was thrown into the Tower, where he died on All Hallows Eve 1537. The sorrow of his passion and the rigours and punishments he received in the Tower killed him—at least, Surrey believed this. As Lord Thomas's new wife, Lady Margaret Douglas, wrote in her lyric: 'With thretnyng great he hath been payd / Of payne and yke of punnysment' but as she knew, 'to loue me best was hys yntent.' In his own poetry, Thomas had declared to his wife, 'My loue truly shall not decay,' whatever the terrors and tortures in the Tower, 'for let them thynke and let them say, / Toward yow alone I am full bent.'[12] The story was simple: at some point either before or during the June weddings, Surrey's beloved uncle, himself only 24, had decided to marry, and he had been accepted in love by Lady Margaret, the close friend of Surrey's sister and the daughter of Henry VIII's sister, the widowed Queen of Scotland (now separated from Lady Margaret's father, the Earl of Angus). Lady Margaret was now living, after her princess cousins had been bastardized, with the Howards. Her importance was signalled by the fact that Henry VIII had even offered his niece in marriage to the heirs of Francis I. Because of the young woman's proximity to the English throne (only her half-brother the King of Scotland stood before her in July 1536, with both princesses disgraced, and Richmond himself near death), the whole love affair had to be clandestine.

Involved with the highest level of nobility, the affair, in the eyes of the lovers and their friends, soon took on elements of the romances, a living out of the *gloire* of love only to be found in a world like that of *Lancelot du Lac*. The lovers not only found the right texts to read in Chaucer (in Thynne's elegant 1532 edition) but began to write imitations, inscribing themselves as characters in *Troilus* or the Knight's Tale. Their poems were actually secret love-letters carried back and forth, probably by the agency of another friend of the Howard circle, Mary Shelton, and her brother,[13] and so Lord Thomas could write to 'my none [mine own] swete wyfe': 'To yowr gentyll letters an answere to resyte, / Both I and my penne there to wyll aply' and even though 'I can not your goodness aquyte / In ryme and myter elegantly' Lord Thomas could 'meane as faythfully' as any lover that ever lived and this God can 'record whych knowyth my hart' (13). The literally imprisoned lover can use sophisticated tropes of *ploce* (same word with different meanings), *chiasmus* (balanced crisscrossing of words, phrases, clauses), and *polyptoton* (repetition of the root word in different grammatical forms) with patterns of caesura and alliteration straight out of the fourteenth-century Chaucerians included in Thynne's edition. 'Some tak no care wher they haue cure,' wrote Lord Thomas, 'Some haue no cure and yett tak care,' and he is of the latter kind, 'swett hart, be sure: / My love must care for your welfare' for 'I love youe more than I declare' and so, 'as for hap happyng this yll, / Hap shall I hate, hape what hap will' (23). In her only verse-letter to Lord Thomas, Lady Margaret called her young husband 'The faythfullyst louer that euer was born' and vowed to compensate for that love for the rest of her life: she will 'loue hym best vnto my graue' (12). However they derived their language of Petrarchan love from Chaucer, for the young Surrey the lines between art, romance, and living history had become blurred.

[12] Kenneth Muir, 'Unpublished Poems in the Devonshire Manuscript,' *Proceedings of the Leeds Philosophical and Literary Society*, 6/4 (1947) 253–82, poems 12 and 9; other citations by poem number in text.

[13] Paul Remley, 'Mary Shelton and Her Tudor Literary Milieu', in *Rethinking the Henrician Era: Essays on Early Tudor Texts and Contexts*, ed. Peter C. Herman (1994), 54. Remley also demonstrates how much diction from Chaucer and the Chaucerians is borrowed by the lovers.

It was hardly a surprise that the secret marriage or 'ragyng love', in Lord Thomas's phrase (22), did not elude Cromwell's network. Chapuys heard about the reinscribed Pyramus and Thisbe and understood the wife's case. What could one expect from this court, he wrote, 'seeing the number of domestic examples [of immorality] she [Lady Margaret] has seen and sees daily, and that at 22 she has been for eight years of age and capacity of marry'?[14] However informed, Cromwell had the two lovers examined at once by one of his new henchmen, Thomas Wriothesley, the herald's cousin, who with Ralph Sadler began a career with this case. In Wriothesley's hand, the examination revealed that Lord Thomas had loved the Lady Margaret for 'about a twelvemonth' but they had exchanged only a 'cramp-ring' and a diamond and her 'phisnamye' or portrait. They had met clandestinely, if discreetly, in the presence of 'my lady of Richmond', Lord Thomas watching 'till my lady Boleyn was gone, and then steal into her [Margaret's] chamber' (W1: 50–1).

All of this was, of course, a kind of theatre spun out of the fall of Anne Boleyn. In fact, the Scottish Queen Margaret, writing in bewilderment at her daughter's arrest, gave the whole plot away. She cannot understand why her brother is upset. After all, he knew about their plans for the wedding; they were acting 'by Your Grace avys' and the older sister cannot understand her brother's displeasure 'yat [that] sche suld promes or dissyr syk thynge.'[15] What Cromwell had done in his distrust of the Howards was to use the king's fear over the succession to push home an attack. The king obviously responded in a rage against the young lovers. The result was that unwittingly the young Lord Thomas, the composite image of Surrey's lover (as a later poetic text shows), instigated the origin of the very Act that led to Surrey's own arrest and beheading eleven years later.

The bill of the Act of Attainder was introduced in Parliament on the morning of 18 July 1536, the day of the lovers' arrest, and before noon had made its way from the Lords to the Commons. As Lehmberg notes, it carried against the young Lord Thomas 'a stream of invective not paralleled in bitterness'. The language of the preamble was clear: Lord Thomas 'beyng ledde and seduced by the Devyll not havying God afore his eyes' and certainly not regarding his duty of allegiance to the king, 'oure and his most dread Sovereign Lorde', now 'is vehemently suspected and presumed malicyously and trayterously myndyng and imagynyng to putt dyvisyon in this Realme' and break a lawful succession. Edward III's statute of 1352 had established the early Tudor definition of treason; and, as Elton and John G. Bellamy have shown, this basis continued into the Tudor reign so that before 1536, enemies, fallen ministers, rebels and potential rebels were annihilated by judicial means.[16]

[14] *LP*, vol. 10, 147, 48.

[15] *Letters of Royal Ladies*, ed. M. A. E. Wood, (1846), vol. 2, 287–8.

[16] *Journal of the House of Lords, Beginning Anno Primo Henrici Octavi, I, 1509–1577* (1808), 101; Stanford E. Lehmberg, *The Later Parliaments of Henry VIII, 1536–1547* (1977), 101. The text of the Act of Attainder is in *Statutes of the Realm*, vol. 3, 680. For a discussion of how the historical context led to the Act of Attainder, see David M. Head, ' "Beyng Ledde and Seduced by the Devyll": The

By 1536, however, a more specific means of signifying treason was needed because of a growing reluctance by judges to construe as treason whatever the king (or a minister like Cromwell) defined as treason. After the bill rushed through on that July day, the victims of it, in the years ahead, would be, not only the last remnants of the White Rose or Queen Catherine Howard or both Surrey and Norfolk, but Cromwell himself. What had passed was thus more than an Act that made it a treasonable offence to marry or espouse any of the king's children, sisters or aunts, or nieces and nephews, without the royal licence and seal first obtained. It was now treason to threaten in any way the lawful succession. In fact, two days later, on 20 July, as though to assert that absolute presence of the king even more, Cromwell, now the king's 'Highe Vycar over the Spiritualtye under the Kinge', broke up a convocation of bishops, abbots, and all other clergy. He forced them to subscribe to a new document that now totalized all power in the kingdom in the royal body of Henry VIII himself, 'the King heere and our emperour being the onelie supream heade of the Holie Catholike Church of Englande next ymediatlie under God.'

Under such power it was hopeless to think of the lovers surviving as one, no matter what hackneyed Chaucerian texts they produced. In October 1537, Lord Thomas Howard died 'of an ague' in the Tower. Only the most profound Greek myth (one the young lord took from Chaucer) would interpret his life for the young husband in his final poem to his wife: 'But ende I wyl as Edyppe [Oedipus] in derkeness / My sorowful lyfe and so dy in dystresse.' His only hope was for a continuing textuality from new lovers: 'O ye louers that hygh vpon the whele, God grawnte that ye fynden aye loue of stele' and 'whan ye comen by my sepulture / Remembre that yowr felowe resteth there' (14). In the following November his widow reappeared at court riding in the first 'chair' at the funeral procession of Queen Jane Seymour. Lady Margaret Douglas' restoration was completed with her appointment as maid of honour to Queen Anne of Cleves and then to Queen Catherine Howard. After the execution of the second Howard queen, Lady Margaret was to 'go to Kenengale, in Norfolk, with my lady of Richmond, if my lord her father and she be content.' But before she left in 1543, she was reprimanded for being frivolous with a Howard again. The king had Cranmer 'to call Lady Margaret Douglas apart and show her how indiscreetly she has acted, first with Lord Thomas and then with Charles Howard,' the dead Catherine's brother. She must 'beware the third time.'[17] After the reception for the Spanish Duke of Najera in 1544, where she danced with Surrey, Lady Margaret was swiftly married to Matthew Stuart, Earl of Lennox, an older Scottish nobleman whom Henry VIII was using against the regency government of the infant Mary, Queen of Scots. She

Attainder of Lord Thomas Howard and the Tudor Law of Treason', *Sixteenth Century Journal*, 13/4 (Winter, 1982), 8; G. R. Elton, 'Treason in the Early Reformation', *Historical Journal*, 11 (1968), 211–36, and John G. Bellamy, *The Tudor Law of Treason: An Introduction* (1979) and his earlier *The Law of Treason in England in the Later Middle Ages* (1970), esp. 102–39.

[17] *Statutes of the Realm* 3:663–6. LP 14, i:1331;1333.

left for Scotland, probably with copies of all the poems of those years in England, if not the Devonshire Manuscript itself. Within a year Lady Margaret had produced her son Darnley, who married that infant queen and fathered James I of England. That grandson finally succeeded Anne Boleyn's child of honour on the throne of England, so Margaret Douglas became the originating mother of the entire Stuart line. In her last years at the Elizabethan court, in her determination to make her grandson the successor to the last Tudor, she bore insults and hardships hardly conceivable four decades earlier, but today her tomb in Westminster Abbey identifies her just as she wanted: the grandmother of a king and the matrix of a royal dynasty she survived to found.

As his uncle had called out in his Oedipus cry to future generations never to forget, so Surrey did not. The figure of love alienation central to Petrarch assumed, in Surrey's poetic texts, a particular trenchancy, the realism of experience. Thus, a few years later, in the middle of a bitter satire he was writing after being snubbed on the dance floor, Surrey inserted the tragedy of his uncle Thomas. In the long almost epic metre of Poulter's Measure, he defined the uncle as an archetype of Howard honour and superior nobility. Lord Thomas died for true love like the Chaucerian Prince Troilus of Troy.

> And, for my vaunt, I dare well say my blood is not untrue.
>   For you your self doth know it is not long ago,
> Since that, for love, one of the race did end his life in woe.
>   In tower both strong and high, for his assured truth,
> Whereas in tears he spent his breath, alas, the more the ruth.
>   This gentle beast likewise, who nothing could remove,
> But willingly to seek his death for loss of his true love.

The Death of Richmond and the Howard Tombs at Framlingham

In that same July of 1536, Surrey suffered a more terrible loss. Two days after Cromwell's definition of the King of England as emperor and Supreme Head, his bastard son died. On 22 July 1536, Henry Fitzroy, Duke of Somerset and Richmond, 'departed out of this transitorie lief at the Kinges place in Sainct James, within the Kinges Parke at Westminster'. Wriothesley added: 'it was thought that he was privelie poysoned by the meanes of Queene Anne and her brother Lord Rotchford, for he pined inwardlie in his bodie long before he died' (W1: 53). This was not altogether true, for physically his natural vigour had held on (in one story he refused in his last days to be transported by litter but insisted on riding to his residence at Colleweston). The Duchess of Richmond was with her husband at the end. In Richmond's will, the 18-year-old widow received six geldings, with bridles, saddles, and 'alle other thinges belonging to them'; the same second hand that marked Surrey's gift also added 'such stuffe as it ys. Whereof iiij. delyvered unto the Duches of Richemonde, to convey her into Norfolk.' Not only was his young wife with Richmond at his death, but the grieving widow also accompanied the dead body of her husband in its tightly sealed lead coffin back to the Howard tombs at the Cluniac priory at Thetford in East Anglia. The death and its peculiar secrecy, with the arrest of her close friend Lady Margaret Douglas, must have made the month of July quite painful for the sister of Surrey.

But it raised a greater dilemma for the realm: the question of succession. It was to be a year before Queen Jane Seymour gave birth to Edward VI. If Henry VIII should die, or have another accident, the continuance of the dynasty was threatened. Indeed, the Act of Succession itself suggested that Richmond was considered healthy enough until quite late, and his death considered premature and untimely. John Husee, writing to Lisle on 18 July, appeared surprised: 'My Lord of Richmond [is] very sick, Jesu be his comfort.' This threat caused by a sudden demise may have genuinely terrified the king who lived in fear when it came to his children, both born (or born dead) and unborn. They represented an indeterminancy even his supreme will could not rein in. Almost immediately, Henry VIII turned on Norfolk for not according his only son full honour. In the next month, Norfolk even heard rumours that he might go to the Tower for such an offence. From Kenninghall, at eight o'clock on a Saturday night, 5 August 1536, Norfolk fired off a letter to Cromwell after hearing from friends and servants in London, 'all agreeing in one tale'. Defending himself, Norfolk said he had adhered to the king's instructions for burial (they were executed poorly by Richmond's servants). Furthermore, when the 63-year-old loyal hero of Flodden shall deserve to be in the Tower, 'Totynham [a village outside London] shall turn French. I would he that began first that tale of mine, he being a gentleman, and I, were only together on Shoter's Hill, to see who should prove himself the more honest man.'[18]

Beneath the role-playing, however, after the Yorkists and Henry VII, Norfolk had never lost a genuine sense of terror at where history might turn. The attack by the king had a consequence. The duke saw now that he must build his own set of secure funerary monuments, with the intention first of developing Thetford itself, where the young duke had been buried. Already, in 1532, Norfolk had petitioned successfully the Signoria at Venice for the removal from St Mark's to England of the bones of his ancestor Thomas Mowbray, the Duke of Norfolk whom Richard II had banished with Bolingbroke. Yet, gradually, Surrey's father began to dread what Henry VIII and his Vicar Cromwell might do. Indeed, as early as 1536, Lord de la Warr had petitioned that the priory of Boxgrove, where all his ancestors had been buried, be preserved or turned into a college rather than be totally destroyed as priories throughout the kingdom had been. By 1539, even Thetford and its ancient mausoleum of the Mowbray family, where Norfolk's ancestors and his own

[18] 'Biographical Memoir of Henry Fitzroy', *Camden Miscellany*, p. c; *Lisle Letters*, vol. 2, 458. For Norfolk's letter, *LP*, vol. 11, 233, 236.

first wife, 'the Lady Anne awnte to his highnes', had all been buried, was threatened. In his petition of 1539 to the king and Cromwell to turn the priory church into 'a parisshe Churche of the same', Norfolk could cleverly announce that he had already begun two tombs there, for Richmond and himself, and it will be a considerable cost ('iiij c li at the least') if left unfinished. The king denied him, and, even though the building was still standing in 1547 when the commissioners found it maintained well and richly decorated, the duke had decided by 1545, the year of the dissolution of all religious colleges, to move the tombs at Thetford to the parish church of St Michael's in Framlingham.[19]

In fact, at the end of 1545, with the disastrous French war at its height and his son a general commanding the defence of Boulogne, Norfolk could not but see the end of one world and prepare for another. It was not merely the violent destruction, for example, of the shrine of St Thomas à Becket at Canterbury in 1538, with the relics and bones of the saint either burned or thrown into garbage and utterly lost (HB 620) and the magnificent ruby given by St Louis, the King of France, to the popular shrine turned into a ring for Henry VIII. It was not even Wriothesley's demolishing of the tomb of Alfred the Great nor Cromwell's burning in public at Walsingham the ancient seated Virgin with Child, the wooden statue that had inherited the old Marian reinscription of the classical Roman Isis, a shape whose myth-making had centred constant pilgrimages from all of northern Europe to the 'sea-shrine'. It was more terrible for the old duke: now no family, much less dynasty, could be allowed to have what the previous Dukes of Norfolk had bestowed on Thetford and survive. The new supremacy encouraged no such display, even if the third Howard duke did own the priory himself. The idea of a chantry chapel where prayers for the dead were said was becoming by 1545 more and more absurd, if not illegal, and considered a genuine waste of money. One more part of 'Merry England' was disappearing. As Aston notes, iconoclasm in England 'destroyed more objects in more places than in any previous iconoclasm, including the Byzantine eight centuries earlier'.

For a new type of cultic centre, then, Norfolk chose St Michael's, the parish church less than 200 yards away from the main gate (at least today) of Framlingham Castle in Suffolk, the ancient seat of the Dukes of Norfolk. Until December 1546 Norfolk was actively involved in building the cultic centre, for in November

[19] For the situation of Norfolk and the king's clear refusal, see *Counties and Communities: Essays on East Anglian History presented to Hassel Smith*, ed. Carole Rawcliffe, Roger Virgoe, and Richard Wilson (1996), 105–6. Cf. *LP*, vol. 9, 530; vol. 10, 552; vol. 11, 1468; vol. 15, 211, 942. For the petition, PRO, SP 1/156,f.115. Three years earlier Norfolk's stepmother had also taken no chances. She promptly moved the body of her husband, the 'Flodden Duke', from Thetford Priory to her own parish church of St Mary's, Lambeth. In a special chapel her husband had built she put his body, with what remains she could save from the elaborate tomb at Thetford. Then the dowager duchess prepared her own tomb (originally the great tomb had been for her as well) with orders in 1542 to bury her in Lambeth as she promptly was in 1545, having just survived the humiliation of her step-granddaughter Queen Catherine. Like his stepmother, Norfolk knew he could no longer turn to the old Howard burial church of St Mary's in Stoke-by-Nayland, its lovely dimensions (later painted by Constable) much too small and identified with an earlier stage in the Howard evolution.

1547 the churchwardens of St Michael's complained to the Privy Council that Norfolk had torn down 'the isles' of the chancel but had not enlarged or rebuilt them before his imprisonment and, in Framlingham Castle itself, there still lay glass, boards, and framed timber ready for use in this new construction. Yet in 1554, when Norfolk had been out of the Tower a year and regained some of his wealth, nothing had been finished. In his will, the third duke merely asked that his body be buried in the order and place 'thought most convenient to my executours'.[20]

Thus, after Norfolk's death, the Lord Chancellor of the Marian kingdom, the Bishop of Winchester, probably continued the building of the tombs, with the fourth duke, the new young Thomas Howard, named for his grandfather. It was one final tribute from Winchester as executor of his will, his old friend Stephen Gardiner, whose effigy and tomb in the Cathedral at Winchester (today visibly mutilated and disfigured) showed the same Anglo-French influences. If Winchester aided by Queen Mary, who had chosen the Howard fortress of Framlingham as her point of resistance to Dudley and Lady Jane Grey, did renew the building of the tombs, the process led to their final form. As both Whinney and Marks have shown, the final shapes of the Howard tombs in Framlingham are masterpieces that developed piecemeal and probably because of such political currents. Thus today, across from the elaborate tomb of Surrey's son, the fourth duke, and the effigies on it, and across from the more distant Jacobean tomb of Surrey and his countess (Plate 23) lie the two marble tombs Norfolk began in the 1540s, probably from designs by Surrey himself. The surface of the third duke's tomb has two effigies, Surrey's father and mother, but the surface of Richmond's tomb (Plate 6), the same size as Norfolk's (9 feet long, 5 wide, and almost 5 feet high), is strangely bare. On the sides of the two tombs are sculptures that show a contrast between them, scenes of the Old Law and the New: Richmond's with Old Testament prophets, kings, and scenes; Norfolk's with the Apostles and episodes from the New Testament. As Stone and Colvin note, both tombs represent a zenith in Renaissance English art, reminding viewers today, together 'with the number of empty niches in church after church,' how spectacular and prolific English sculpture must have been in the last Marian years. Particularly the design 'in the apostle figures [Norfolk's tomb] represents the last major display of religious imagery in England before the full weight of reformation theology made such things impossible.'[21]

[20] Aston, *Iconoclasts*, 5. PRO Prob 11/37/14.

[21] Lawrence Stone and Howard Colvin, 'The Howard Tombs at Framlingham, Suffolk', *Archaeological Journal*, 82 (1965), 170–1. Their indictment of English iconoclasm is severe: 'This series of tombs of the late 1550s and early 1560s are the last, and perhaps the most distinguished, examples of the abortive sculptural Renaissance of the early 16th century before contacts were destroyed and England entered on the long years of provincialism and insularity under Elizabeth.' Cf. Margaret Whinney, *Sculpture in Britain, 1530–1830* (1964), 7; and Richard Marks, 'The Howard Tombs at Thetford and Framlingham: New Discoveries', *Archaeological Journal*, 141 (1984) 262 and *passim*. See also Anthony Blunt, 'L'influence française sur l'architecture et la sculpture décorative en Angleterre pendant la première moitié du XVIe siècle', *Revue de l'Art*, 4 (1969), 23.

Excavations have also shown the beginnings of another tomb at Thetford never moved to Framlingham, with a New Testament panel that may have been a complement to Richmond's Old Testament panels and similar angels, but holding the nails and thorns of Christ's Passion, with an elaborate baluster shafting such as that on the tomb of Surrey's son. Stone and Colvin conjecture that this tomb was designed for the Earl of Surrey and they date it in the decade after the poet's death, when his fame rose with the publication of his texts.[22] It may be more logical to assume, however, that before 1540, or shortly thereafter, Surrey designed his own tomb at Thetford Priory to complement Richmond's. The two tombs then would exist in a loving counterpoint that his father's tomb (in his son's designs) later took on with Richmond's. If this is so, then quite possibly Surrey had a strong hand in originating the initial designs of the tombs at Framlingham. As with his Windsor elegy and sonnet, Surrey's designs for Richmond's tomb (and his own) remained one more lasting inscription of the Other Henry and their relationship, which survives even in a counterpoint of tombs.

The Pilgrimage of Grace

Less than three months after Richmond's death, when the kingdom stood without an heir, the rebellion in the north known as the Pilgrimage of Grace broke out. It was the first widely popular outbreak in Henry VIII's reign—'the largest rebellion to occur in England between the peasants' revolt of 1381 and the civil war of the 1640s', as Bush notes—with a scale immense ('10,000–12,000 spears with 30,000 others') when compared to the apprentice revolt in 1517 that the Howards had quelled. This people's insurrection had been supported by gentry and higher nobility with a variety of causes and backgrounds. But all levels of society agreed on hatred of Cromwell and certain central goals, as Aske said: 'he [Aske] and his company would go to London, of pilgrimage to the king's highness, and there to have all vile blood of his council put from him, and all noble blood set up again; and also the faith of Christ and his laws to be kept and full restitution of Christ's church of all wrongs done unto it, and also the commonty to be used as they should be.' Whatever the essential nature of this rebellion as religious, the political attacks were foremost. Specifically the ballads of the pilgrims lashed out at Cromwell, Cranmer, and the king's new men who were radically transforming, at least for these singers, all of English culture: 'Crom, Cram, and Riche . . . / As some men teach, / God them amend.' Thus the outbreak saw itself as a political *renovatio*, not a rebellion, advocating precisely a series of returns: to monasteries that had literally enriched their lives and fed their poor and cared for their sick, the emergency centres of the time; to the Princess Mary as the sole heir to the throne;

[22] Stone and Colvin, 'Howard Tombs', 163–4, 168.

to the Pope as the true head of the English Church because it was universal, not provincial; to certain nobility as the true rulers of the realm and not Henrician 'new men'. The banner of the Five Wounds of Christ carried by thousands across Lincolnshire, Yorkshire, and the northern counties from October 1536 through the spring of 1537 focused on the eucharistic Real Presence centred in the Exposed Host at the heart of the banner.[23]

Although certain gentry and common people could thus express their simple desires, Norfolk could not. The old duke had recognized the choices before him: to take up the sympathetic cause of the Pilgrims and their recall to 'Merry England' or to follow the higher service of his master in the moral code Dante had defined for his world, which Norfolk saw as the essence of honour. It was a choice more terrible than anything at Flodden Edge. If he chose the latter role of total service, he must lie and deceive innocent men who based their lives on Norfolk's integrity and reputation of honour; if the former, he could die in the challenge and his son and family with him, or, if he succeeded, he might bring civil war to his beloved country. This ambiguity of torn allegiance, a fault-line in his character, Cromwell may have set out to exploit. Having been hurt and humiliated by Norfolk from the time of his intercessions for his own beloved master, Cardinal Wolsey, Cromwell could now crack the old Howard's deepest image of himself as a loyal servant for the king. The crack would serve as leverage to keep Norfolk from siding with his natural conservative allies, the Pilgrims of Grace, who themselves looked to the Duke of Norfolk as a natural leader.

For the Supreme Head, for whom Thomas Cromwell acted at all times, directing him where he could, the Pilgrimage held no ambiguity at all. As Henry VIII told the people of Lincolnshire, they came from 'one of the most brute and beastly shires of the whole realm' and they had dared, 'contrary to God's law and to man's law, to rule your prince, whom ye are bound to obey and serve, and for no worldly cause to withstand'. Indeed, Henry fumed, 'I have never heard, read nor known that princes' councillors and prelates should be appointed by rude, ignorant and common people.' He promised 'the utter destruction of them, their wives and children' and, in King Henry's name, Norfolk did hang some seventy peasants in Cumberland on trees in their gardens because of their love and support of the monasteries. Furthermore, the killing of the monks of one religious house that the Pilgrimage had dared to reopen actualized the king's immense power: the whole countryside could see the hanged bodies of what they called holy men

[23] Michael Bush, *The Pilgrimage of Grace: A Study of the Rebel Armies of October 1536* (1996), esp. 7, 14, 18. *SP*, vol. 5, 486–7. For the religious context, see David Knowles, *Religious Orders in England* (1959), vol. 3, 322, 168. See the negative responses to Knowles in A. G. Dickens *The English Reformation* (1964) and Joyce Youings, *The Dissolution of the Monasteries* (1971). For defence of Cromwell, see G. R. Elton, 'Politics and the Pilgrimage of Grace', in *After the Reformation*, ed. B. Malament (1980), 25–56. For counter-attacks, see C. S. L. Davies, 'The Pilgrimage of Grace Reconsidered', *Past and Present*, 41 (1968), 54–75, and 'Popular Religion and the Pilgrimage of Grace', in *Order and Disorder in Early Modern England*, ed. A. Fletcher and J. Stephenson (1975), 58–91; and Christopher Haigh, *Reformation and Resistance in Tudor Lancashire* (1975) and *English Reformation* (1993). For the chant, see Robinson, *Dukes of Norfolk*, 30.

swaying from church steeples in all directions. Of the 222 to 250 finally executed (including one woman burned alive), the abbots of four ancient monasteries, the roots of the rebellion, were hanged outright by Norfolk, the buildings looted and finally torn down. Once destroyed, Jervaulx and Bridlington, both over 500 years old, had lead worth almost £4000, reported Norfolk eagerly when the mopping up had begun in May. Bridlington was so close to the sea, he wrote, that the lead could easily be dismantled and shipped to the Office of Works for immediate use in the royal building projects.[24]

This dispatch from the northern war front was written by Norfolk in May of 1537, but in the previous October he had been more ambivalent in his letters. The Earl of Surrey made the difference. In the previous March, Norfolk's son and son-in-law Richmond had been designated as hostages to the Scots when Henry VIII and James V were to meet (they never did). Thus, on Sunday, 8 October 1536, still in the south with the Duke of Suffolk and Surrey's father-in-law Oxford, Norfolk received a letter from the king, the most 'discomfortable' of his royal nephew's that ever came into his hands. Whatever he had heard of the pilgrims in the north, Norfolk had not sought any warrant to organize his men into a force to suppress them, and certainly he had not volunteered any force, as had other noblemen like the Earl of Shrewsbury with patriotic fervour. The letter had shocked him into a new kind of fear, however. Norfolk answered directly, coming to the point: how could he send his son ahead to battle with all the horses he can furnish while Norfolk has yet to return home, and once there, still lack full preparation? Norfolk would not sit still while other noblemen served the king, he wrote. Service to the king had defined his entire life. Thus, on that Sunday afternoon, he announced that he would send to court his son 'in post as pledge for his truth' and his preparation, no matter what others think. Norfolk thus set up his own counter-strategy. By no means should his 20-year-old son be sent to lead a huge army, standing every chance of being killed and the whole dynasty threatened.

It is probable that Cromwell had no intention of letting someone so inexperienced as Surrey lead an army. He simply wanted to force Norfolk's hand. His gamble was working. Norfolk asked only that Surrey eventually accompany him, leaving his other son, Lord Thomas, then 18, at Kenninghall in command of 300 or 400 'tall fellows' under the guidance of his steward Robert Holditch and other Howard clients. Norfolk then wrote on October 12 that his son will remain in the south with his men while Norfolk visited the king and sought more bows and arrows. On Sunday, 15 October 1536, Surrey himself responded to all the furore about him. Recently made a father, the poet wrote to his own father from Cambridge, the first of his letters in the midst of military service. It is a remarkably clear and decisive letter.

The 20-year-old poet earl was writing around midnight, having received letters from Windsor from Cromwell and, '(as was your pleasure) I unclosed' the

[24] M. H. and Ruth Dodds, *The Pilgrimage of Grace 1536–7, and the Exeter Conspiracy, 1539* (1915), vol. 1, 100. *LP*, vol. 12, i, 1172.

dispatches. Cromwell had devised a strategy for the 'traitors' that Norfolk was to follow. For the moment Surrey was to stay with his company of soldiers, to which Surrey enthusiastically added in parenthesis 'which is judged by those here who have seen many musters the finest ever raised on such short warning'. Surrey now devised his own strategy in the light of this information and the dire financial situation of Norfolk's army: 'I have consulted here with my friend Mr. Sowthwell and the treasurer of your house alone' because if the command to stay were known 'the companies might withdraw without the King's command.' He would hold musters in Cambridge the next day, as his father had previously suggested, and then Surrey would inform his father of what happened at the musters in order to take action: 'so that you may give orders for the payment of the soldiers and appoint me a council, for otherwise they give their advice with diffidence.' The numbers of men had doubled and trebled, and the livery lacked 1500 buff jackets, for which Surrey had sent into Suffolk and to the supply houses of the Howards. The soldiers had already received payment on the march through Thetford, Bury, and Newmarket, wrote the concerned Surrey, but they needed more because of 'the great price of victuals' on the road, and Surrey, signing his letter, 'your humble son', was seeking to relieve their distress.[25] The practising young poet who had returned from Fontainebleau only four years before was already displaying a remarkable level of military competence and, above all, concern for his men, acting as their protector.

Norfolk's Choice

In the end, Norfolk succeeded in deceiving the pilgrims—and the deception succeeded precisely because he had embodied for them the image of honour, theirs and his own. They were not the same. As one of the Pilgrimage leaders, Sir Robert Aske, said later at his trial before his execution in May 1537, 'the Duke was beloved in the North and it was thought he would not dishonour himself.' Thus, on Doncaster Abbey bridge on 27 October 1536, the Pilgrims agreed to surrender because he told them the king would meet their terms. When it became clear in the hard winter of 1537 (for weeks the Thames was frozen solid from London to Greenwich) that the king would not, rebellion broke out again. This time Cromwell arranged that the court should blame Norfolk for initial laziness and his cowardice in not destroying the rebellion in the autumn. Behind it all, to Cromwell's delight, Norfolk was more and more viewed as a real friend of the rebels. Surrey's father recognized this when he wrote, in the middle of a new campaign of terror, that those who had accused him of lack of proper conduct at Doncaster 'shall now be proved false liars'.[26] Norfolk would show them all.

[25] For the duke's activities and Surrey's letter, see *LP*, vol. 11, 659, 671, 727.

[26] *LP*, vol. 12, 1175. Also, PRO SP 1/115, ff. 244–5.

But the country was clearly as divided as its leading nobleman. In fact, during that cold winter, an old minstrel, John Hogan, with his 'crowde' or fiddle, went around East Anglia and, particularly in John Skelton's old parish of Diss, sang a political ballad to the tune of one of the most popular of English folksongs, 'The Hunt is Up.' The old man composed, in time-honoured fashion, his own words to the tune and referred to the renewed rebellion, with the verse 'The masters of art and doctors of divinity / Have brought this realm out of good unity.' When told not to sing that song in neighbouring Suffolk, the fiddler answered that he had twice sung it 'before my lord of Surrey' at Cambridge and Thetford Priory. He probably did. A poet with Surrey's originating ear, whose Petrarchan lyrics became popular tunes themselves, would have sought out the native music that later fascinated Sidney. But it was dangerous if Surrey did listen. In fact, the old crowder in 1537 was told that if he had sung it before the Earl of Surrey, 'he [Surrey] would have set him by the feet for slandering him' about his service to the king. It was obvious that Surrey's listening to the ballad might be passed on to Cromwell's network.[27]

Once Norfolk's decision had been made, and his choice was made for the entire dynasty, there were no limits to Norfolk's destruction of those who had trusted him. Neither his royal master nor Cromwell would have tolerated less, as he knew. Writing from Pontefract and then at York a few weeks later, Norfolk recounted his retribution, hanging a man for speaking ill of Cromwell and remarking how 'almost all the gentlemen and substantial yeomen of the shire will bear him witness that he [Norfolk] is neither Papist nor favourer of traitors.' He detailed how he had resorted to martial law for his executions, because if he proceeded by jury, not one in five would have been killed. Even though the fear and threat of Cromwell in 1537 could drive this hero of Flodden to one of the fiercest reprisals in English history—a clear foretaste of the forthcoming persecutions of Recusants and the Irish—Surrey's father was not rewarded by Cromwell.

By May, in the mopping-up phase, Norfolk was still in the north, and rumours about his son circulated again. Had not the father sent for him to come north to be trained and then made deputy, as the elder Howard left the king's service or even joined the rebels to become their dictator and then ruler of England? Never such a thought, Norfolk denied angrily in a letter, but he did not *want* to stay until next Michaelmas because the northern cold will bring on his old disease of diarrhoea which may cost him his life. He wanted his son to come north. Surrey's lively presence would help him keep his servants up here because of the son's natural affability; 'and then in truth I love him better than all my children, and would have gladly had him here to hunt, shoot, play cards, and entertain my servants, so

[27] *LP*, vol. 12, i, 424. Cf. Bruce Pattison, *Music and Poetry of the English Renaissance* (1948), 170–1. Surrey's nephew, the Earl of Oxford's "In peascod time" is set to this tune. Cf. Sidney's *Defense of Poesie*, 433: 'I never heard the old song of Percy and Douglas that I found not my heart moved more than with a trumpet; and yet is it sung but by some blind crowder, with no rougher voice than rude style.'

that they should be less desirous of leave to go home to their wives.' Surrey's ability to establish a social milieu, to blend with a circle of friends, demonstrated later when he sought an audience for his Petrarchan and Virgilian poems and then at the war front in France, had appeared early. The warm, witty, and intelligent presence of the young man was what the father (and all his company) desired, and 'if I intended any other thing in sending for him, let me die.' Of course, he did want him to come up to escape a bad debt, and there were some other private reasons, but Norfolk concluded by appealing to the king, 'if he thinks me a true man,' to support him.

To this letter, in a rare moment, Henry VIII himself answered. His former nephew assured Norfolk 'of our confidence in your experience and devotion' and would his king not tell him otherwise if there were a problem? 'You know,' said the monarch, 'our nature is too frank to retain any such thing from him that we love and trust.' The father had erred about Surrey's debt of £500 pounds, however; it was the king's own treasurer who was owed the money (now resolved), but 'we beg you henceforth to believe no light tales.' Norfolk did not believe any more in 'light tales'. He had been thoroughly terrorized. At the end of spring, he could boast to the king and Cromwell of total suppression and complete order: 'These counties thanked be God be in such order that I trust never in our life no new commotions shall be attempted. And surely I see nothing here but too much fear.'[28]

But the Pilgrims did not die silently. Interrogated before his beheading on 30 June 1537, at Tower Hill, Lord Darcy, the elder noble leader of the rebellion, a former Privy Councillor, a knight of the Order of the Garter, who had fought at Flodden, appeared to have suggested the sympathy of the Earl of Surrey for the cause of the Banner of the Five Wounds of Christ. Although the exact circumstances are unknown, fictionalizing about Surrey's imprisonment at Windsor springs directly from this ambiguous historical moment. So do the two originating Renaissance lyrics that rose explicitly from the death of Henry, Duke of Richmond, and implicitly from all the other deaths and losses of 'these blodye dayes'.

The Windsor Sonnet

Early in 1537, Surrey appeared near death. At least, he had another of his chronic physical collapses under the stress of events. Turning 21 in the year after Richmond's death, the new parent stayed in a deeply depressed condition for most of the year. His father explained the illness and its duration to Cromwell in the summer of 1537 as the result of Richmond's death. Writing on 12 July from the north, Norfolk added, at the end of a detailed report on the insurrection, a note on his son. His servant Richard Fulmerston had just arrived from Kenninghall and brought the news that 'his son of Surrey is very weak, his nature running from him

[28] *LP* 11:1138 and 12,i:252;336:337:381:498;777;1162;1192, but see all the dispatches in this period as well as the introduction to vol. 12 of *Letters and Papers*. See also PRO SP 1/118, ff. 216–17.

abundantly.' In fact, wrote the father, Surrey 'was in that case a great part of the last year, and as he showed me [the weakness] came to him for thought of my lord of Richmond, and now I think is come again by some other thought.'

It was probably an accurate description, but by mid-July 1537 Norfolk needed to write a special script for his son. So, with his next sentence, the old father told the Lord Privy Seal Cromwell that he believed his son would do better in the north with him. The earl was isolated in East Anglia with his wife, 'an ill medicine for that purpose,' and furthermore, 'his being there doth not only cause many to resort to the' young head of the household 'to my charge but also doth cause my deer not to be spared.' There was a background for this letter and its casual asides. In an earlier letter to Cromwell on 3 July 1537, Norfolk had written thanking the most powerful man (after the king) in the kingdom for his 'kind handling' of Howard causes, specifically in the affair of the 'false surmise' that one of the rebellion leaders—Darcy—just executed had made against Surrey. Norfolk was overtly disturbed about this accusation, and by 8 August the results of it had worsened. Writing to Cromwell again, the calculating Norfolk followed his ploy of making discourse personal: 'If I shold reherse unto you the multitude of prickes of agonye that ar in my hert, I shold molest you with too tediouse and long a letter; but for a fewe of them: what chawnces of informations hath [been] of my sonne falsely ymagined, no man knoweth better than ye. And now to amende the same in my hert, by chawnce of lightlihode [for Surrey?] to be maymed of his right arme.'[29]

In a few weeks, something near a catastrophe had happened. If the clue in the letter's last line is correct, the Earl of Surrey had been arrested. He had been accused of committing violence within the precincts of the court, for which the Howard heir stood to lose his right hand, the violent punishment a sign of the shame of such an act. Once more, the actual facts of the case are blurred, but the event in Surrey's life—or some event like it—emerges in the dynamics of a myth-like narrative or, as it turned out, of a cult memory between an actual event and the legend of it. In this case, a letter from Surrey's father about a maimed right hand leads to the historicized story that the 21-year-old poet earl at Hampton Court, sensitive to slights to his family and himself, committed the crime of an act of violence, striking an accuser, within the precincts of the king's presence. At Wolsey's former palace, in this cult narrative, none other than Edward Seymour himself made some remark questioning Surrey's loyalty and impugning the honour of the Howards in the late insurrection of the Pilgrimage of Grace, or Surrey heard that he had done so. In any event, a quarrel ensued between these two. The dramatized heroic Surrey, driven by such insults to family and character, struck the older Seymour, brother to the pregnant queen.

The supposed attack occurred when the king was in residence. As a result, the younger Howard was arrested and 'not onlie judged to lose his hand, but also his

[29] *LP*, vol. 12, ii, 248 and vol. 11, 21. *SP*, vol. 5, 325.

bodie to remaine in prison, and his lands and goods at the kings pleasure,' as the penalty for such a crime reads. This punishment had its own ritual. The sergeant of the woodyard was to have his mallet and block ready, the master-cook his distinctive knife, the sergeant of the larder to lay the knife straight on the joint to be cut, the sergeant-'ferrer' to have searing irons to seal the bleeding veins, and so on, with the sergeant of the cellar ready with some wine, ale, and beer to cheer both the spectator and the victim, and the yeoman of the ewery ready with basin and towels for the blood pouring from the poet's hand (HA 801). For the first time the body of the young poet earl was threatened by imprisonment and physical harm. Of course, because no nobleman in the reign of Henry VIII had ever suffered such a punishment as the severing of a right hand,[30] not even Cromwell would dare to begin now by maiming the probable godson of the king and incurring the wrath of the Howards. Cromwell also knew that, to save his son, Norfolk would risk a great deal, most of all, by implicitly acknowledging who now had the greater power.

Therefore, as his sister herself reported at Surrey's trial, Surrey was sent that summer to live at Windsor Castle in restricted custody. No worse punishment occurred, but the event, so the Duchess of Richmond told her December 1546 inquisitors, had been traumatic and had radicalized her brother's loathing of Seymour and the newly risen men at court. Interestingly, she named the fact of her brother's place of imprisonment—the only source for the episode—in the context of Seymour and others (HB 378). Thus, in summer isolation at Windsor, with the court gone, the tapestries down (a significant detail in the elegy), Surrey may have written his long poem on the loss of Henry Fitzroy, the Duke of Somerset and Richmond, and, with it, a sonnet that rose from the same memory of the friend's death the year before. However tenuous this conjectured narrative, the relationship of the poems to the episode is less clear. Both elegy and sonnet name Windsor Castle as the site for their dramatizations, but neither gives a specific date. The sonnet appears to describe spring and not late summer, as Norfolk's letter said. Yet all later retelling, however incredible, of the Windsor episode from Nashe, Drayton, Lord Herbert, and the modern biographers Bapst and Casady (after Windsor, in summer 1537, Surrey never visited Italy, as Casady claims)[31] have an obvious source: the power of the poems themselves. The lyrics lead the entranced or entrapped reader to demand a greater context, a narrative or greater fiction beyond the fiction of the text. It had been so in saints' legends or even in lives like Plutarch's that demand greater life than the ordinary (or cultic expansion of the initial act of the extraordinary). Only a fiction can fully explain the extraordinary 'truth' of the hero.

[30] T. B. Howell, *Complete Collection of State Trials* (1816), vol. 1, 443.

[31] Bapst, *Deux gentilshommes-poètes* 227–32 and Casady, *Henry Howard*, 60–3. Where Lord Herbert mentions Windsor and Surrey, it is *only* with Richmond. The Elizabeth cult-makers like Nash and Drayton do not mention at all this episode or the circumstances for the writing of the elegy and the sonnet.

Thus, the elegy, 'So cruel prison, how could betide, alas' and the sonnet 'When Windsor walls sustained my wearied arm' prove once more what Sidney later argued in his *Defense of Poesie*: poetic language—the poet's necessary apparent lie ('he nothing affirmeth' and so 'never lieth' [439])—is transformed by history and transforms history. The probable life in a text may be greater than actual life, as Aristotle defined such life in his *Poetics*, a new definitive text of which had just appeared in Paris, for Surrey's generation.[32] The poem, the poetic text, has its own realized history equivalent to any other living phenomenon, as Pocock has noted, and may have enormous social influence. Its 'event' may be strong enough to demand an act of fiction on the part of an audience beyond the 'event'—at least for Aristotle—with its pity and fear. As Surrey had seen at Fontainebleau, in a method of interlocking 'allusive correlatives', art can reform life and history by setting up its own history, a 'polyvalent' history in Pocock's terms. So it was natural that, even if Surrey invented his English sonnet form just for his lament over Richmond, it soon became continuous in a series of texts in actual societies. After Daniel chose Surrey's form for his sonnet sequence in 1590 and Shakespeare followed, the form changed history or at least what makes history, its sense and sensibilities. The English sonnet has survived as a form until the late twentieth century in varying cultures and with varying concepts of love and history, yet never varied from the original flexibility and dialectical structure of formal intimacy set by Surrey.

But for a critic like Bapst, true to his 'scientific' nineteenth-century premises, both Windsor poems are lies: 'il faut admettre que Surrey a tracé de leur existence un tableau tout imaginaire' ('one must admit that Surrey has traced in their existence a picture entirely imaginary').[33] Surrey did not tell the truth about his relationship with Richmond. Both the elegy and the sonnet may be rooted in a place, Windsor Castle, the space inscription all Greek and Latin art demanded and at which Surrey was a master, but finally, for Bapst, Surrey's poetic texts are lies. For the empirical Bapst, the poems are located only in representative form, perhaps building out of historical contingency but only, with their inaccurate or incomplete facts, 'tout imaginaire'. But for Surrey this was his aim, to create probability, a probable, not a factual history, for the simple reason that, as Aristotle had argued almost two millennia before, possibility can never be as inclusive of life as probability (the existence of a centaur unifies and strengthens life, does not separate it into unnatural singularity). Remembering Fontainebleau, the lessons of its

[32] For the way that Surrey came to Aristotle, see Bernard Weinberg, *A History of Literary Criticism in the Italian Renaissance* (1961), vol. 1, ch. 9–12. Weinberg details the history and analysis of a major literary event in Surrey's own life-time, the rediscovery of the *Poetics*. The earliest 'extensive exploitation' of the *Poetics* in Italian came first through a source Surrey probably read early, Trissino, in the Italian's first definitions of his experiments in blank verse or the unrhymed hendecasyllabic line in his 1524 preface to his tragedy *Sophonisba*. See also Wolfgang Clemen, *English Tragedy Before Shakespeare: The Development of Dramatic Speech* (1961), 39, and Max J. Wolff, 'Die Theorie der italienischen Tragödie im 16 Jahrhundert', *Archiv*, 66 (1912), 351 ff. For Aristotle's conception of probability, see Gerald Else, *Aristotle's Poetics: The Argument* (1967), 305–8, 468, 551, 630.

[33] Bapst, *Deux gentilshommes-poètes*, 169.

dialectical art between actual history and representation, Surrey knew something else the empirical Bapst could not conceive: to set up the representative and mimetic probability of all true art (for Bapst, to tell a lie), he must first tell the truth for the purpose of his more unifying lie. That is, the poet must make his form as 'true', as realized as much as possible by the audience, so that the act of audience belief in a probable history can occur. Probable realism was needed for greater representative form, 'tout imaginaire'.

So, with purpose, Surrey's sonnet 'When Windsor walls sustained my wearied arm' announces from the beginning its realistic setting. It is as precisely rendered as any Chekhov short story. The realism will form the basis to set up an objective structure of probability (its final intimacy and subjective outcry the result of that objective rational structure). With considerable technical skill, Surrey thus invents in his sonnet not only a new conversational and intimate rhyme scheme but, at the same time, a historical (non-allegorical) setting. Calculation of scene leads to spontaneity and intimacy. Wyatt's lyric about crossing to Calais in 1532 had marked such calculated realism of place and isolation, a 'lie' to render intimacy and heartbreak. Surrey's sonnet exploits such a scene, an actual parapet visible to anyone at the English court (or to any tourist who has ever visited Windsor Castle). Such structural realism had been encouraged by northern humanists like Erasmus, More, and Luther. Thus, when Daniel's sonnet sequence *Delia* in 1590 marked the first deliberate turn to Surrey's form as ideal, and Shakespeare's would soon follow, these poets found powerful the realism associated with prose in Surrey's varied rhyme scheme *ababcdcdefefgg*, his sharp conversational formation of octet and sestet, the distinct *volta* or turn, and with that, the more realistic enjambement, one line overflowing into another to render natural speech, and, most of all, his declarative final couplet. The couplet dramatized the English difference in the sonnet: the moral frame, the summary, most Tudor audiences demanded of their speech arts.

Although there is no hard evidence that Surrey's Windsor sonnet was written in 1537 (or indeed that it was his first sonnet), the immense sorrow and abandonment it enacts do appear to date it after the death of Richmond in July 1536. But in it, Surrey drew on a literary genealogy he would use many times in his Petrarchan lyrics. In Book IV of the *Aeneid*, Dido's famous night lament has the same two fold structure as Surrey's sonnet. If Surrey's own translation of the passage in Virgil became an originating text for others in the later Renaissance, its experience of a female self severed from nature—the classic misfit of Western history—gives Surrey a voice speaking from the centre of a probable disastrous history.

> It was then night; the sound and quiet sleep
> Had through the earth the wearied bodies caught;
> The woods, the raging seas were fallen to rest;
> When that the stars had half their course declined;
> The fields whist; beast, and fowls of diverse hue,

And whatso that in the broad lakes remained,
Or yet among the bushy thicks of briar,
Laid down to sleep by silence of the night,
Gan 'suage their cares, mindless of travails past.
Not so the spirit of this Phoenician:
Unhappy she, that on no sleep could chance,
Nor yet night's rest enter in eye or breast.

Virgil's 'infelix Dido'—'Unhappy she'—contrasts her love sorrow with the placid order of nature in Virgil's use of a famous Greek text. Sappho, waking at night, had earlier looked out over the Greek sea, noted the place of the Pleiades in the sky, the force of time, and then cried out: 'I lie alone.' This classic basis for Western poetry of alienation, Surrey's genealogy from the ancient world, Petrarch's in his sonnet sequences and Chaucer's in *Troilus*, had one remarkable inversion: in the modern poets the female had become male. The 21-year-old Surrey now gives his own remarkable inversion. He becomes a male Dido, ready like her for suicide in his sonnet. The lament that in Sappho had been of female over female, in Dido female over male lover, and in Petrarch and Chaucer male over female beloved, becomes in Surrey that of a male lover lamenting the death of a male beloved. In that love and loss, the poem becomes representative form, a history 'tout imaginaire'.

When Windsor walls sustained my wearied arm,
My hand my chin, to ease my restless head,
Each pleasant plot revested green with warm,
The blossomed boughs with lusty Ver [spring] yspread,
The flowered meads, the wedded birds so late
Mine eyes discovered. Then did to mind resort
The jolly woes, the hateless short debate,
The rakehell life that 'longs to love's disport.
Wherewith, alas, mine heavy charge of care
Heaped in my breast, broke forth against my will,
And smoky sighs that overcast the air.
My vapoured eyes such dreary tears distill,
  The tender spring to quicken where they fall,
  And I half bent to throw me down withal.

The 'restless head' emphasizes the poem's solipsism and its suicidal base. An image also in the longer elegy for Richmond, this metaphorically severed head, emphasized by the initial gesture of hand cupping chin, cannot rid itself of sorrow in this tale. For relief, it looks down from the castle walls on the panorama of a Windsor spring that the Elizabethan Drayton described for Surrey and Geraldine (his socially correct substitute for Richmond). A pleasant landscape turns green and warm; trees blossom with spreading green leaves amid flowering meadows and birds mating. Deliberate Chaucerian archaisms from the opening of *The Canterbury Tales*, Palamon's lament in the Knight's Tale, and Troilus' outcry at the palace of his lost Criseyde, as well as Latin neologisms, play linguistic artificiality against the 'sincere' disharmony of the isolated lover. The difference from Chaucer is that what was for Surrey and Richmond fiction in the texts of Petrarch and the French Petrarchans and the Thynne edition of Chaucer, all of which the young men probably read together, has now become actual loss, real history. Furthermore, transvestism, male as Dido, comes full circle as probable history. Here is an actual English setting, as real as the Greek, not as artificial as Chaucer's Trojan or Athenian castle.

Thus, in Surrey's historicizing drama, the male figure leans in an originating melancholy pose to be imitated not only by Romeo and Hamlet but by the Romantics and their modern descendants. His arm on the castle parapet is already wearied of life and no longer ready for use, his chin in his hand (a gesture Wyatt borrows for his melancholy David),[34] both arm and chin set in this gesture to rest the conflicts raging in the speaker's head. Here the severed head or isolated consciousness leans over, as in a ritual *epicedium*, staring at an imagined beloved body with whom it once held a living relationship of oxymoronic 'jolly woes, the hateless short debate'. The syntax renders this leaning gesture of the head and body, keeping the reader in suspense until the sixth line. Only then, after an elaborately inverted *hirmus*, the Greek and Ciceronian sentence Puttenham called the 'long loose' and particularly admired in Wyatt,[35] does the speaker break in a stated subject and verb.

At that moment in the sonnet, in a brilliantly placed caesura, one of the first so powerfully set in English lyric or elegiac verse, the 'restless head' turns inward from the leaning gesture of vision. Nature, the outward spring—the major premise of Surrey's syllogism—can only be contrasted, as with Dido, to the love within and the speaker's memory of a free 'rakehell [unconsidered] life'. The controlled syntax that follows here is a technical breakthrough in 1537 for English poetry and the English language: enjambement leads fluidly into the *asyndeton* (words or phrases in a series usually joined by conjunctions) and *oxymora* (words in grammatical relationship whose meanings contradict each other) of short phrases. They dramatize the turn inward, the subjective cry in the minor premise that climaxes in the last line with the conclusion of Surrey's syllogism. Their logical conclusion appears as bitter breakdown. The imprisonment within the speaker with 'heavy charge of care' reveals the alienation of a death—physical, erotic, and, at Windsor, cultural. The sighs that break forth, Surrey's historicizing of a

[34] The Wyatt borrowing can be found in his *Penitential Psalms*, Prologue to Psalm 130, 30–1. I am assuming that Wyatt wrote his Penitential Psalms in the years immediately following 1537 and, as many Wyatt scholars (especially H. A. Mason) do not, that Wyatt would have imitated Surrey. Wyatt's poem CCXXVIII (MT) from the Arundel Manuscript (in which Wyatt's poem to Surrey may also be found) reflects Surrey's new rhyme scheme. The motifs in this poem, so similar to Surrey's Petrarchan motifs, particularly in a poem like Surrey's famous 'The sun hath twice', show that either Wyatt borrowed from Surrey—a real possibility after 1537 (Wyatt probably took imagery from the Windsor sonnet for his later Penitential Psalms)—or Surrey found a basis in Wyatt for his invention but not the invention.

[35] George Puttenham, *The Arte of English Poesie*, ed. G. D. Willcock and A. Walker (1970), 176.

Petrarchan cliché, are the outward sign of inward horror before death and return the speaker to the spring before him. The moisture coming from the breath of sighs fills the cool English spring air like smoke, and the tears pouring from that 'restless head' now produce their own spring and life. In Surrey's syllogism, the inescapable logic of nature has revealed the speaker's alienation from that living world, driving him 'half-bent' to the edge of the parapet. He can leap to his death and escape not only too solid flesh, the pain of his feeling, but the terrible demands of his history that never seem to end.

Yet all of this is within the probability of Surrey's art. Although such an abrupt closure may fit the epigrammatic nature of the English sonnet the poet is inventing, closure acts here to dramatize, in a kind of fear and pity, the loneliness of the speaker, the point of the representative form. This lover is a sole survivor who can now count on very little except his own gifts—on little transcendence other than that of writing, in fact, the poem itself. Certainly no religious or national or natural solace exists in the poem. Remarkably modern, Surrey's is a lyric without ideology. This lover can order and build his own life only with the enough that is surviving within him, the memory of his friend. In his mimetic text, Surrey has taken Troilus' lament for his lost Crysede a step forward into greater subjectivity and the modern consciousness. Like Aeneas in burning Troy, the poet, after the deaths of 1536, finally does not choose the option of suicide but writes a poem out of lost Windsor; even more, a text originating for other centuries lyrics of loss.

The Windsor Elegy

In the early Renaissance there was nothing like Surrey's elegy. It revolutionized the style of the English elegy, light-years away from Alexander Barclay's 1514 elegy on Surrey's extravagantly heroic uncle Edward or Skelton's on Surrey's great-grandfather Percy, the Earl of Northumberland. A Victorian critic spotted the difference in the poem: 'I know of few verses in the whole range of human poetry in which the voice of nature utters the accents of grief with more simplicity and truth; it seems to me to be the most pathetic personal elegy in English poetry.'[36] This sense of representative personal pathos in the Windsor elegy introduces a genre that will lead not only to Surrey's own great elegy on Wyatt but to Spenser's *Astrophel* and then to Milton's *Lycidas* and beyond. But, as these later elegies reveal, the effect of personal pathos and 'simplicity' is arrived at through a calculated method of composition, the Aristotelian probability and history within what Bapst names correctly as 'un tableau tout imaginaire'.

In this sense, then, Surrey's Windsor elegy, 'So cruel prison, how could betide, alas,' eventuates not so much from Richmond's death—the subject of the elegy—but from all the deaths and imprisonments and losses of 1536. To these contingent

[36] W. J. Courthope, *A History of English Poetry* (1897), vol. 2, 185.

phenomena, Surrey writes a personal response (however historically accurate). Through its language, it becomes a public collective text, a representative form. The larger subject of England, its nobility of blood, the erosion and loss of that blood, becomes the implicit focus of the elegy (the topos of Windsor, the Garter matrix, metonymically directing this level of meaning). Beyond England, the elegy points to the nature of all honourable existence and its disappearance. From that disappearance, the elegy moves to the question of time itself, the mutability themes of later poets like Spenser, Shakespeare, and Milton introduced in 1537 (and after 1557, in a major social text). In Surrey's originating form, then, dramatized grief is played against the larger indeterminacy of history and time. Absence of subject is played against presence of text. The dialectic of the two shows that, in the poem, nothing cultural or even human is guaranteed, except the representative language that expresses the grief to an audience that reads or hears or enacts it in centuries ahead.

For this reason, Surrey knew his language must be as original as possible, even startling. For such a public text—the only major poem written directly about the death of any member of the Tudor royal family (virtually nothing exists on the untimely death of Edward VI) and designed to influence a court—Surrey (and no one else) invented heroic quatrains. These vary both Petrarch's majestic *capitolo* and Dante's *terza rima* and then take their concision into a mastery of classical reductive syntax. In these vigorous stanzas rhyming *abab*, the dramatized sole survivor of the elegy speaks in three calculated dialogues. The dialogues are bracketed, in an extended figure of *partitio*, by a catalogue of places. The system of dialogues starts in the poem's initial dichotomizing topos, the historical Windsor, 'Where each sweet place returns a taste full sour.' Thus, the first dialogue is between two places, the 'sweet' Windsor only a few years past (but by 1537, like another world) and the 'sour' Windsor of his imprisonment. This dialogue dramatizes cultural and personal entrapment, the 'cruel prison' of its first line. A second dialogue follows: Surrey in the space of 1537 speaks to the earlier Surrey who lived in the innocence of the old world before its destruction. A third dialogue enacts an outside social world imprisoning the speaker, in contrast to the deeply intimate world of 'friendship sworn' and memory. Three dialogues progress, therefore, from the initially unspoken classical topos *ubi sunt* (where are they now?) to the ironic reversal of the 'sweet' and 'sour' motifs at the end and to Surrey's closure with its resolve for the future.

One powerful tool of this tight linguistic construction is a controlled use of syntax learned from Virgil and Horace (and awakened by Wyatt): special use of the old classical formulae for universalizing, the ancient Latin and Greek rhetorical devices. They are characteristic of Surrey's objective art. They fit his method of active reality. The poem's sole survivor recalling his loss could not be an early Romantic, as Sir Walter Scott and the Victorians thought. Surrey's lover speaks, not a nostalgic Romantic discourse based on a contrast of symbols or resonant description, but a discourse of logical topics. In fact, in figures of *hypotaxis* (subordination of clauses with key connectives) and *parison* (grammatical serial balance of clauses), the simple naming of places or events is amplified by other phrases and subordinate clauses, as in the naming of athletic feats and love play: 'What hope of speed, what dread of long delays' (28). Such focused control pinpoints, as if in a 1530s avant-garde Mannerist painting, event and emotion through examples of *symploce* (repetition of first and last words or phrases in successive clauses and sentences), *hyperbaton* (normal word order changed for emphasis), and especially *chiasmus* (as in lines 9 and 10: dances were short but the reading of long romances brought 'great delight'). All the ancient figures of speech thus work to render the density of the young men's life together. They become probable history themselves. With a special irony, the poem develops the representation—the probability—of utter subjectivity through the most precise kind of objective structure.

Thus, as a composite form, the poem gives a believable view of court life, even, remarkably for C. S. Lewis,[37] a happy one in spite of the 'sour' counterpoint. A probable history rises from such logistically controlled form—nowhere more than in the uncontrolled emotional outburst seemingly so spontaneous in stanza 12, the climax of the elegy. The most self-consciously emotional stanza in the poem, stanza 11, precedes this calculated climax. The first-person voice has been restrained for the previous ten stanzas of the poem, only remembering, but now, recalling the winter nights and their most intimate moments together, a dramatized (and logically enumerated) subjectivity comes centre-stage. In an objectively rendered single voice, the speaker can now ask the prison walls what Troilus in his empty castle asks, that is, the first line of the speaker's outburst in Surrey's stanza 12: 'O place of bliss, renewer of my woes,' where is the Other Henry, my other Self?

In this logical dénouement for all three dialogues, intimacy can now be revealed because of the poem's modulated counterpoint and technical interplay. The three units have led to the self-recognition at the heart of all classical art: the lover realizes all the previous stanzas have been only memory. He is abandoned, alone, at the mercy of an alien culture, of his own death. The stanza thus shifts all three dialogic contrasts from themselves as vehicles to a single tenor, a single theme: where is the other Henry now? More terribly, where is the world both Henrys knew and loved as one? In the silence and literal echoes around him, the answer is devastating. He is nowhere.

> And with this thought the blood forsakes my face,
> The tears berain my cheek of deadly hue;
> The which, as soon as sobbing sighs, alas,
> Upsupped have, thus I my plaint renew;
> 'O place of bliss, renewer of my woes,
> Give me accompt where is my noble fere [mate],
> Whom in thy walls thou didst each night enclose,
> To other lief [loved] but unto me most dear.'

[37] C. S. Lewis, *English Literature in the Sixteenth Century Excluding Drama* (1962), 232.

In a poem with no consolation beyond its own terms (certainly no Christian consolation), the only answer forthcoming to the apostrophe (direct address) and *erotesis* (rhetorical questioning) is the senseless echo on stones—the 'hollow sound' of his 'plaint' on walls empty of their winter tapestries.

The 'plaint', the lyric within the lyric, ties all three dialogues together in a closure. Any closure for Surrey would probably be derived from Stoic models, as in Seneca's translation of Aristotelian catharsis, models sixteenth-century England had received only in Roman drama, the Senecan Latin, for example, that Wyatt quotes as a refrain in his lyric on Anne Boleyn's death. Now, for the first time in England, Surrey transfers the ancient Senecan method to the lyric and its mode of self-resolution. The lines 'Thus I alone, where all my freedom grew, / In prison pine with bondage and restraint' identify the ironic self-recognition of ancient drama that begins the act of catharsis and healing. The final lines reverse the 'sweet' and 'sour' split of existence (the 'sweet' memory is now too 'sour'; the 'sour' prison is 'sweet' in comparison), adding one more ambiguity to the coping self.

But the recognition of nothingness in representative form is itself a sign of survival. What the progression and therapy of the poem have taught its speaker is clear. Like Stoic drama, the lyric has made its structure therapeutic: seeing the 'nowhere' of existence in objective form, the surviving lover may bear a world no longer free (with the old Chaucerian meaning of 'freedom' as a condition belonging to the blood nobility), at least as the speaker remembers that earlier world. 'Endure and keep yourself for better days!' says Aeneas to his men after the shipwreck that begins Virgil's epic. Freedom now exists in the ironic recognition of a sole survivor. The speaker begins in the indeterminate nature of all burning history and the deaths it brings. As Spearing notes, in these final lines the Petrarchan metaphor of the lover on fire has been reified. The text enters time: in Surrey's elegy, 'as in so many of Wyatt's [poems], courtly metaphor is reliteralized: the metaphorical prison of hopeless love has become a literal prison, and the beloved friend is really dead.'[38]

Death and constant change now constitute all human existence, including conceptions of honour. All human beings live like Priam's doomed sons. With that recognition, the poem ends as it began. The next stage, the journey of Aeneas out of the burning city, must now begin. If there is any act of faith possible in the total absence that burning history encodes, it is in a new text written in a progressing genealogy. Surrey's last lines (with their modulated assonance) could not be clearer: 'And with remembrance of the greater grief, / To banish the less I find my chief relief.' The honour Richmond and Windsor epitomized has been redefined as a process of endurance, a function of Surrey's progressing history, 'remembrance' but not nostalgia. The speaker has survived through the language of memory to work again, as does Milton's Lycidas. He writes a poem 'tout imaginaire'. The

[38] A. C. Spearing, *Medieval to Renaissance in English Poetry* (1985) 320.

closure and the linguistic structure of the poem Surrey has written thus embody an early version of his later motto: 'SAT SVPER EST.'

In the last decade of Surrey's short life, the poet earl would try to build urgent new texts for what he thinks will be a new history, a dynasty of both blood and poetry, his own new Rome. The next section of this book will explore just what these texts of architecture, politics, and poetry would involve. Immediately Surrey would build a house as a space to exhibit his new texts and, most of all, himself. It too would be one more proof that 'Enough Survives.'

PART II

Building a New Rome

5

Mount Surrey

Mount Surrey as a legend lingered into the later Renaissance. In prose Thomas Nashe had fully textualized the poet's life by the early 1590s and, as with many cult narratives, by giving false historical facts but getting the essential interpretation right. In poetry, Drayton added to the momentum developed from Turbeville, Whitney, and Sidney in previous decades with more inaccurate but revealing details. Drayton's Geraldine, in fact, wrote a tribute to Mount Surrey in her epistle to her chivalric Surrey. She chastises her lover for going off to Italy 'When thou shouldst reare an Ilion to thy name.' He should be re-creating, in England's time and place, the classical world: 'Why art thou slacke, whilst no man puts his hand / To raise the mount where Surrey's towers must stand?' By the 1590s in Drayton's England, re-creating the classical world or Jerusalem in England's green and pleasant land had energized generations, but the process of actually making the English landscape classical, as found later in Spenser and Milton, was new in 1542. It took an originating force to see so medieval and commercial a city as Norwich as an Urbino or Florence or even, as Geraldine's allusions intimate, Greece itself, the landscape of the muses.

> When shall the Muses by faire Norwich dwell,
> To be the citie of the learned well?
> Or Phoebus altars there with incense heap'd,
> As once in Cyrrha, or in Thebe kept?
> Or when shall that faire hoofe-plow'd spring distill
> From great Mount-Surrey, out of Leonards hill?

In his 1599 footnote to these lines, Drayton archaizes the magnificence of the house Surrey had erected on his rechristened mount: 'Alluding to the sumptuous house which was afterward builded by him upon Leonards Hill, right against Norwich; which, in the rebellion of Norfolke, under Ket, in King Edward the sixts time, was much defaced by that impure rabble.'[1] Drayton's reference to Surrey House and its defacement alludes to a long-standing tradition. Already by 1575, the earliest written reference to Mount Surrey and its grand house on fourteen acres overlooking the River Wensum and the city of Norwich shows nostalgia The Latin diction conveys the sense of a thing of immense and pure beauty ('magnificentissimam') lost because of new barbarians. Alexander Neville alludes to Surrey House in a dedicatory letter to Elizabeth I's Archbishop of Canterbury,

[1] Michael Drayton, *Poems*, ed. E. J. M. Buxton (London, 1953), vol. 1, 482, 715.

Matthew Parker, himself an East Anglian admirer of Surrey's poems. Neville's text is a history that analyses (and revises) the rebellion in East Anglia. In the summer of 1548, Kett's rebellion of lower gentry and common people had centred on Norwich, the second largest city in the kingdom. The rebels had converged on the old Roman road from Yarmouth and specifically on the high promontory overlooking the city 'quo in loco Comes Surreius, praeclaram aedificaverat et plenam dignitatis domum' ('in which place the Earl of Surrey had built a house very beautiful and full of dignity'). On this commanding spot the rebels took over Surrey House as their headquarters while they besieged the city below during that summer. They kept prisoners 'in aedes Comitis Surraei instar furii conclusi' ('in the house of the Earl of Surrey like confined thieves'), hanging one Italian mercenary from its walls. What the ransacking of Surrey House in December 1546 by Gates and Southwell had not done, Kett and his rebels completed in 1548, as Nevylle noted, 'Quinetiam domum illam magnificentissimam homines impurissimi inuaserunt: atque omnibus in locis scelerum suorum impressa vestigia reliquerunt' ('Moreover, these most impure men have invaded that most magnificent house; and in all places they have left behind remains marked with their crimes').

Three years after Neville published his account, the grandeur of the house may not have been lost entirely. Apparently it was at Surrey House on Wednesday afternoon, 20 August 1578, that Surrey's grandson, the sexually promiscuous playboy Philip Howard, entertained his cousin, Elizabeth I, at 'a most rare and delicate dinner and banquette' in her progress through her mother's homeland. A witness to the future saint's banquet was none other than the poet Thomas Churchyard, who may have known the house when Surrey was alive and he was his servant. Churchyard had devised a masque (most of it written in his master's Poulters Measure) to be presented as a spontaneous outburst for Queen Elizabeth when she emerged from Surrey House and processed down the hill: 'At whiche season I dyd watch with a shewe (called Manhode and Dezarte) at my Lord of Surreys backe dore, going to the Queenes barge' but then, as now, the narrow Wensum River, near the old Bishopsgate (the ancient Roman entry to the city), could accommodate 'neyther the shotte, the armed men, nor the players' and so, going upstream near a landing place (probably Pull's Ferry), they waited. Finally, after three hours, the party at Surrey House, with the French ambassadors and Leicester lingering into the darkness, Churchyard and his players had to depart, needing more than candlelight for his masque.[2]

But is there any real evidence that Surrey was building, in fact, some remarkable structure in Norwich when he was arrested and beheaded? Was the Revd George Frederick Nott, the Romantic editor of Surrey's works, correct when,

[2] *Alexandrii Nevylli Angli, De Furioribus Norfulciensium Ketto Duce, Liber Unus, Eiusdem Norvicus* (1575), 29, 49. *The joyfull Receyving of the Queenes most Excellent Majestie into hir Highnesse Citie of Norwich: the Things done in the Time of hir abode there: and the Dolor of the Citie at hir Departure* (1578). *A Discourse of The Queenes Majesties Entertainement in Suffolk and Norfolk: With a Description of many Things then presently Seene. Devised by Thomas Churchyarde, Gent. with divers shewes of his own invention, sette out at Norwich* (1578).

following hints in Drayton or with evidence no longer available, he described the architecture of Surrey House as 'purely Grecian' and 'the first specimen of a building formed correctly on ancient models, seen in this kingdom' (lx–lxi)? For Nott, the Earl of Surrey was the first to introduce the Renaissance style that the poet's contemporary Palladio was developing in Italy or, at the least, exhibiting more of the classical styling already to be found, for example, in the pediments and pilasters at Whitehall, in the Ionic columns and mouldings in the courtyards, chimneystacks, and Doric fireplace at Lacock Abbey, and in the lost humanist sculptures in the designs of Nonsuch that Surrey himself knew. In 1562, when his first son, Thomas, the fourth Duke of Norfolk, built in Norwich his 'capitol mansion' with playhouse, bowling green, tennis courts, between the Wensum River and the city's Charing Cross, his new Norfolk House had classical columns, as the abandoned Surrey House high on the promontory above the river may also have had.[3]

But could Surrey have been so original as to introduce a style that would serve, for example, as pivotal model for a residence of Seymour or his steward Thynne? The drawing of the façade of the first Somerset House on the Strand is all that remains of one of the earliest classical houses built in England, one modelled on the Ecouen palace outside Paris, which Surrey had viewed in 1533; the centrally placed gateway of Somerset House with its triumphal arch, brick pavilions extending on either side, was a design that could have been copied from Surrey's own new gateway on Mount Surrey, as may have been the Romanizing effects (Corinthian columns 'standing on pedestals, having cornices or friezes finely wrought' and seats shaped like scallop shells) of Berry Pomeroy in Devon, where, as Pevsner notes, the new Protector Somerset intended to establish 'his major seat of power in the South West' (like Surrey's in East Anglia).[4] It is probable that many of Somerset House's fittings and furnishings, particularly the tapestries, came directly from Kenninghall and Surrey House. Could the Earl of Surrey's architectural text on Mount Surrey have even pointed towards the later consistent building of classical orders on all four sides of the residence of Seymour's steward, John Thynne, at Longleat? Answers may be found in five documents that indicate the size and display of Surrey House.

Views of Surrey House

The first two of these five documents show that apparently Surrey did not build such a house. The evidence from drawings on two contemporary maps reveals

[3] *The History of the King's Works*, ed. H. M. Colvin (1975), vol. 3, 1485–1660 (Part I), 42. Ernest A. Kent, 'The Houses of the Dukes of Norfolk in Norwich', *Norfolk Archaelogy*, 24/2 (1930) 80–2. The spot of the fourth duke's palace is now occupied by a rather large car park.

[4] Bridget Cherry and Nikolaus Pevsner, *Buildings of England: Devon* (London, 1989), 168.

(under magnification) Surrey House as a traditionally English Gothic structure with military battlements, an Arthurian statement like his grandfather Buckingham's abandoned masterpiece, Thornbury. If, at best, the evidence of these drawings is tenuous, what is not is the fact that Surrey could manage, before he was beheaded at 30, little more than a rudimentary conversion of an old priory to a grand mansion (such as Henry VIII was doing at Rochester and Dartford and Wriothesley at Tichfield). The Dutch humanist Hadrianus Junius wrote, for example, about the atmosphere at Kenninghall but never mentioned Surrey House.[5] The actuality is that then Surrey House was in process, hardly different from the mansions Surrey knew first-hand being built all over England and France.

But what proves that Surrey House was being lived in, and quite luxuriously, with the house being the centre for audiences of all kinds, is the inventory made after Surrey's beheading, the last of the five documents. The inventory reveals its vast array of furnishings, much of it mortgaged. Surrey's last preserved letter before his arrest illustrated his financial state in his last years. On 19 October 1546, the young earl wrote to Paget, the secretary to the king, with one more anxious request: 'I have viewed the clocher [bell-tower] and dorter [sleeping quarters] of Christ Church in Norwich, which is in all things (as I informed you) unserviceable to their church—saving for a memory of the old superstition.' Surrey wanted to dismantle both and sell what he could strip, specifically the lead, in order 'to discharge me out of the misery of my debt'. Furthermore, 'if it were his most excellent Ma[jesty's] pleasure to give it me, I will faithfully promise never to trouble his Ma[jesty] with any suit of profit to myself hereafter. And [I will] spend that and the rest in his Ma[jesty's] service with the old zeal that I have served with always.'

The 'old zeal' referred to Surrey's enthusiastic defence of Boulogne only the year before, when Thomas Hussey, his father's steward, had written to the young heir reminding him that the old duke was impervious to his son's demands for money and that the merchants of Norwich were demanding payment: 'As concerning the provisions [furnishings] of the house, the same are not to be obtained at my lord's [Norfolk's] hand. We shall practice how to come by them, as such shift as may be made upon my credit in this town.'[6] Whatever his financial stresses, especially after the French wars in which Surrey had paid for most supplies and wages out of his own pocket, he would not abandon the project of Surrey House. The young earl had already heavily mortgaged its furnishings to a John Spencer of Norwich, probably in order to raise money for the Boulogne campaign, which he had correctly calculated as the grand opportunity for himself as a *vir armatus*.

[5] Hadrianus Junius, *Epistolae, Quibus accedit Eiusdem Vita et Oratio De Artium liberalium dignitate: nunquam antea edita. Cum Indice* (1570). This is a letter directed to the Marquis of Dorset on 2 January 1546, when Surrey had been out of the country in France for almost a year and a half. The whole atmosphere at Kenninghall in the middle of the flat plain and probably dominated by Bess Holland, the Dutch humanist found stifling and the children difficult to manage. Cf. Bapst, *Deux gentilshommmes-poètes*, 178 for his misinterpretation of this letter.

[6] Both letters are in *LP* vol. 21, ii, 287; vol. 20, ii, 658.

Thus, where he had intended splendid display, he offered, in the autumn of 1546, a floundering disarray; expenses of his house and his role of general in France had drained him. This was exactly the picture Surrey's enemies wanted of him, of course: a bad manager and an illusionary wastrel. Although Surrey was not the first nobleman to have financial problems, a failure in 1546 on his part had to be nothing if not spectacular for the simple reason that Surrey House had been part of a calculated strategy. From the early 1540s on, Surrey had been consciously setting up a political frame for all his representations, which were to lead to the one aim of securing the Protectorate for his father or himself. Surrey House had been an integral part of this drive towards power.

For such ambition, it is easy to see why Surrey chose fourteen acres on the edge of a promontory. Still today the spot commands an eagle-eye view of Norwich. In Dr William Cunyngham's 'Cosmographical Glass, 1559' folio, a map of Norwich 'Nordovicum, Angliae civitas, anno 1558, I. B. F.' captures some of the ferment felt in the city only eleven years after Surrey's beheading in London. But already by the 1540s, the export trade in woollen cloth had reached 'boom proportions' in Norwich, with its proximity to the Netherlands. With a population of around 15,000, Surrey's city was bustling in a fluctuating cycle of trade and prosperity, a cycle closed to many but quite open to the Howards, who had immense landholdings in the whole of Norfolk. Indeed Norwich was fast becoming 'a centre of conspicuous consumption' with nearly 70 per cent of the city's freemen connected to the sale of clothing but in non-textile trades. So in the year of the accession of Elizabeth I, the first map shows two male figures, one obviously an aristocrat (wearing a flowing gown and a cap with a feather) and the other more simply dressed, a professional, leaning over a sundial with the motto 'Praeterit tempus' ('time disappears'). The aristocrat points to a new area of the city and the professional also points, looking there with considerable excitement. Just to the right of the windmills at which they are pointing is the ancient wasteland of Mousehold Heath; to its right, across the old Roman road is Mount Surrey, on another of the high ridges on this side of Norwich, where the Romans had built a series of mounted forts as protection. Formerly the site of St Leonard's priory, Surrey House can be seen on the 1558 map with a large tower, either the old monastic bell-tower or a new structure in a Gothic military shape, then two rectangular structures with high windows, possibly part of the old cloister or newer more classical wings, and then behind these, larger more undefined structures with what appears a roof portico or turret. Together, all these structures form Surrey House, with the thick forest and park of Thorpe just behind it. Just in front of the large building a grand lawn stretches, broken in the map by trees and possibly some pavilions. The trees mark the start of a steep declivity to the Wensum River that winds underneath, flowing downstream here from the abandoned Benedictine abbey of Carrow (once inhabited by Skelton's heroine of 'Philip Sparrow') and the ruined cell of Dame Julian, and veering at the Cow Tower back around the city of over 500 churches.

A second document compiled by Richard Taylor in his *Index Monasticus* in 1821 from both Cunyngham's map and Braun's *Urbium Praecipuarum Totius Mundi* of 1577 and showing precisely Surrey's quadrant of Norwich reveals that little had changed on Mount Surrey just before Queen Elizabeth's progress (and indeed had not in John Speed's Tudor atlas of 1610). In these, the tower and the other two front buildings still exist. The windows are more clearly drawn than in the earlier drawing (on one side, placed lower); the tower and wall and the military crenellations of the buildings are more exact. But there is nothing else in this map, no buildings behind the other structures, and no pavilions or anything else in the grounds. If most of the structures of Surrey House were built, like almost all early Tudor houses in Norwich, of framed wood filled in with plaster, then rebellion and neglect may have already begun the destruction of Surrey's dream estate.[7]

All these documents reveal a grand size and proportion. They show the lengths to which Surrey may have gone to fulfil a political ambition that was increasingly after 1540 a necessity. The building of Surrey House was, in fact, 'a public art . . . determined not so much by Renaissance aesthetics as by the social and political needs that [the courtiers'] position as creatures of the state imposed on them.'[8] By the 1540s, Surrey had a particular purpose. He could now move slowly out of the margins where, as the son of Norfolk, he was naturally relegated (two Howards in a Privy Council would not be tolerated). From his own house, the young poet earl could assert his potential authority as the rightful leader, if not ruler, of the second largest city in the kingdom. At least his residence rose in a commanding position. As Surrey knew well, textualization of self in a powerful local setting increased his power in London (as châteaux on the Loire did in Paris), whatever personal freedom Surrey House might also give the poet in Norwich. Thus, hardly by accident, the young earl designed for himself at his residence in Norwich a chair of purple velvet and satin, embroidered with *passement* silver and gold lace, and 'pomelles' or knobs of silver (as well as another 'ioyned' chair of crimson velvet). He also had a foot-cushion of the same expensive materials with handiwork like the chair's, and two other foot-cushions of silver and crimson velvet. Above his chair, Surrey placed a canopy of blue and red sarcenet or soft silk. This was his chair of state.

[7] These maps are available, under citations as given, in the Norfolk County Room of the Norwich Public Library. These maps are discussed in George Stephens, *Descriptive List of Norwich Plans 1541–1914* (1917), 219–20. See also John Speed, *The Counties of Britain: A Tudor Atlas [1610]*, introduction by Nigel Nicolson, county commentaries by Alasdair Hawkyard (1988), 131 (and also the picture of the strange coat of arms of the Duke of Richmond on p. 143). See also Thomas Cleer, *A True and Exact Map of the Ancient and Famous City of Norwich* (1696) for evidence that Surrey House had disappeared after the Revolution but that the area was still known as Mount Surrey. I am indebted to Clive Wilkins-Jones for his generous help with these maps. For references to Norwich, see Lander, *Government* 362; Walter Rye, 'Surrey House and St. Leonard's Priory, Norwich', *Norfolk Archaeology*, 15 (1904), 194; James Campbell, *Norwich* (1975), 18, 20; *The Victoria History of the Counties of England: Norfolk*, vol. 2, 494–5.

[8] Eric Mercer, *English Art, 1553–1625*, vol. 7 of the Oxford History of English Art, ed. T. S. R. Boase (1962), 5. Cf. his definitions of honour and his discussion of the Arundel portrait of the Earl of Surrey on 163, 166.

The 1546 inventory of Surrey House also names a pair of 'vestimentes of white bawdekyn embrodred with a white lyon with thappurtenaunces' which were high ceremonial robes. These Surrey probably wore for public occasions in Norwich. Because the gowns with the Howard white lion are in Norwich and not at Kenninghall, they may have been vestments suited (as was his chair of state) for the personal display of Surrey's eminence on ceremonial occasions, either at Norwich Castle or at certain Masses in the cathedral or in any other public forum, such as receptions at Surrey House itself. After all, in May 1542, when he signed the lease for Mount Surrey, the young earl had been named to the bench for the county of Norfolk, with headquarters for such a position at Norwich Castle. And interestingly, in this inventory of Surrey House are also two banners of soft silk, both for displaying the Earl of Surrey's arms, one red, blue, and yellow, and the other yellow, purple, and black.[9] These banners, and the trumpets accompanying them, would be used for the military Surrey in Scotland or France, but in Norwich they would announce his presence. With trumpets blaring to announce this presence, the young earl and his men and horses would gallop over the cobblestones of narrow streets in Norwich, the bright outlines of the Howard silver lion and Surrey's own coat of arms in fluttering multicoloured banners. They would race past the Gothic cathedral, then through Bishopsgate, across the bridge and the river up the hill, finally through the gateway to Mount Surrey and the rising structures of Surrey's high mansion. Here, from the great tower Drayton describes, on the highest spot of the city, the poet earl could display himself and his estate—the absolute opposite of his father's palace on the flat plains of Kenninghall or at Lambeth by the noisy traffic of the Thames. Surrey could view the city and its life in contemplative silence, at the centre of his own certain power.

Roman Roles

Why did the Howard heir want all this display? Was it simply arrogance and pride, as his enemies said, posturing, in the words of a reformed new dean, by 'the most folish prowde boye that ys in Englande'? What was the 26-year-old planning when he signed the lease in 1542 for the land and old priory? For one thing, after the beheading of Queen Catherine Howard earlier in that year, Surrey must have known with certainty that he would counter-attack as his father and conservatives had done earlier with their first major offensive in the Act of Precedence of 1539. In fact, as David Starkey has remarked, the period after 1540 in England showed a 'marked politicization of the peerage'.[10] In 1542 Surrey stood at the

[9] All the references to the inventory of Surrey House are from PRO LR 2/115, ff. 71v to 74v.

[10] David Starkey, *The Reign of Henry VIII; Personalities and Politics* (1985), 132. For a special analysis of how these transformed conservative forces in this period led to the events in 1546, see A. J. Slavin, *Politics and Profit: A Study of Sir Ralph Sadler 1507–1547* (1966).

centre of such activity. He needed to appropriate more of the Roman roles of nobility and power recently redefined and invested with new meaning.

Hardly by accident, in this same period Surrey sat for his most Roman portrait, a sketch by Holbein or his school. The sketch of the poet earl is about as near a formal icon as any Tudor portrait could be (Plate 20). Now at the Pierpont Morgan Library in New York, this ink drawing of Surrey against Holbein's pink paper may have been prescribed by the sitter. It looks exactly like a bust of a Roman emperor, in profile looking right, the only portrait of Surrey as bare-headed as Wyatt in his final portrait. In his clear ideological pose, the English court would have recognized the image of Surrey's royal namesake, Henry V. Surrey's is, in fact, a reverse side of the well-known image of the hero of Agincourt (who had himself adopted a Roman imperial profile). The hairstyle, even to the point of being combed forward and covering the single ear, is similarly Roman. Surrey's sharp nose in profile, the focused eye, the tightly held mouth, and elongated light beard, all keep the same Roman purity of sculptured line. Even the garment beneath the long neck shows, as far as the incomplete sketch can, a wide opening like a toga, gathered in the lower right, on Surrey's shoulder, with a brooch, such as a Roman garment had.

After the early 1542 beheading of Queen Catherine Howard, which Surrey had been forced to witness as sole representative of the Howards, the dynasty was under threat. As both father and son knew, their 'livelode' was threatened in the new factionalism under the new queen, Henry's third Catherine. The battle lines had begun to be drawn in the fight for an England after the king's death and in the Protectorate of his son. Because of this urgency, the young man could not remain in the doorways of power and never enter its corridors, even if his father dominated any Howard offensive. Although no freer than Richmond had been, needing his father's direction and approval for every court action he attempted, the poet earl would not and could not remain always on the margins of political life. Annihilation threatened in a gathering storm. Thus, the daring in constructing his house in Norwich sprang primarily from Surrey and, judging by his debts, with little encouragement from his father. Surrey House was to be one more image of a new nobility centred on himself and springing from the court's new interpretations of ancient Roman nobility and its roles of power—all Roman roles now transferred to modern Britain. New monuments must be built and honoured in a landscape where old monuments like Thetford Priory were disappearing.

The crucial period in Surrey's public life occurred, therefore, in the years before and after his twenty-fifth birthday. At some point in those years of 1541–2, following the instinct of his father but radicalized by his Windsor imprisonment and then by transformations (and executions) at the English court, Surrey attacked. It was not for himself he would now make the fullest self-aggrandizement possible. It was for his sons, his new daughters, his sister, and all the estates that depended on him as heir. In fact, George Constantine had answered Cromwell's new Christian Dean of Westbury in 1539, who had scorned the 'boye' Surrey, by replying,

'What, man, he hath a wife and a child, and ye call him boy!' To this the dean answered: 'By God's mercy, he exceadeth,' to which Constantine gave a full rejoinder: 'What then? he ys wise for all that, as I heare. And as for pride, experience will correcte well inough. Not mervell though a yonge man [who is] so noble a mans sonne and heyre apparante be prowde, for we be to prowde ourselves withowt those qualities.'[11] Yet in 1542 neither pampered life nor wealth nor position but simple reality focused Surrey's choices. The 'heyre apparante' knew the Howards were too high not to have a majestic fall if he did not attack in some way. Death could come not only for him as heir but for the hundreds who stood behind the Howards in the social structure of Tudor culture.

Death from his enemies was exactly what the poet earl predicted in this same period. In Surrey's trial four years later, an unidentified witness (the testimony is not signed) reported a conversation between himself and the earl ('the place and time now being out of remembrance'). The earl was reported to have said: 'Note [how] these men which are made by the Kings Maiesty of vile birth hath been the distraction of all the Nobilitie of the Realme.' Surrey 'further said that the Cardinall [Wolsey] and the Lord Cromwell by diverse means sought the death of his ffather' and then his own. In these dislocations of the realm, the poet's older friend Sir Thomas Wyatt, in a Psalm paraphrase (just before his poem dedicated to Surrey), has his own name of 'owtragius' for the new kind of social climber and gives his ethical warning: 'Altho thow se th'owtragius clime aloft / Envie not thowe his blind prosperitye' (MT 94). More destructive, however, was the trial evidence of Surrey's first cousin, Sir Edmund Knyvet, the child of Lady Muriel Howard, whose beauty Skelton had praised in *The Garland of Honor* and who had died young on hearing of her husband's death in the October 1512 naval battle off the French coast. Although taken as an orphan into the large Howard household, Knyvet betrayed Surrey. In his evidence he reported that, after the death of Cromwell, Surrey said: 'Nowe is that ffowle churle dedd so ambityus of other bludd, nowe is he stricken with his owne staffe' and then added: 'These new erectyd men wowlde by their willes leave no noble men on lyff.' Surrey had identified his enemies, given them a name and a purpose: his death. For him, 'the Kinges Majesty' had given, in Cromwell's term, 'immediately' totalizing inscriptions of honour to men 'of vile birth'. Surrey's phrase, 'new erectyd men,' built on the Latin etymology of *erigo*, their being 'erectus' or 'raised' to honour they did not deserve by any genealogy.[12]

The name of the enemy was now clear. So was its goal, in Surrey's eyes. The enemy wanted the end of the nobility as the poet earl knew it, and his own death in particular. What remained then for any survivor after the deaths of 1536 (particularly with the memory of Richmond) was a strategy of survival, nothing more or less. And the poet earl had already learned, as he would demonstrate on the battlefield in France, that, for surviving, the best defence is offence. Being offensive

[11] *Archaeologia*, 23, (1831), 62.

[12] For the two depositions, see PRO, *SP* 1/227, ff. 97, 105–105v.

meant for the Tudor court showing, in essence, that enough survived. It was the nature of the Tudor court that the courtier—and the higher in rank, the more so—could only function as a defining self, however offensive, in 'a sign-producing organism' that might be, as Bloch comments, '*around* the notion of dynasty or lineage' but will work '*through* the mediatory semiotic fields of heraldry, patronymics, the plastic arts, and historical narrative'. Indeed 'above all, the organization of family lines coincides' in this courtly tradition 'with the appropriation' —and in rare cases, invention—'of vernacular literary forms'[13] so that ironically Surrey's blank-verse invention and his coat of arms would be related. A new heroic poetic line, brilliant new Petrarchan inventions, a new conception of the English poet could come out of the same desire to produce new heraldic signs—all for survival.

Approximately 80 per cent of Surrey's texts that can be dated with any certainty in or after his twenty-fifth year are public. They respond to social events or court situations or perform as communal translations of Virgil or the Bible. The Petrarchan texts may continue their themes (especially of alienation) in other guises, but Surrey's *vers de société* appears generally to have ceased by 1542. With such experimentation of public discourse on the edges of court, Surrey could launch an even more aggressive insurgency and conservative offensive. His problem now was remaining in the margins, at the doorways. Locked out of any political role by his father's dominance in the realm, he was left to himself in relative freedom. There, ironically, he could produce new and original texts. But in that fertile political exile, urgency ruled the day. Time was against him. By 1542, the question of the king's death and the future of the realm began to dominate the court. Surrey saw himself alone in seeking an answer to that question. Not only could (or would) any Howard not help him, but none, with the possible exception of his sister, had the least conception of what he was doing in the production of his texts, in his synthesizing of two genealogies.

'*Nobul hartys*'

In fact, to implement new Roman roles for himself and his family, Surrey may already have translated a text, using his humanist power of language. As early as 1536, Norfolk had cited the old Latin 'Treatise' on the rights of the Earl Marshal as reason for him to command the attack against the Pilgrimage of Grace. By 1540, when Surrey was beginning his own translation of Virgil's *Aeneid*, the poet earl may have translated for his father this 'treatise' on the role of the Earl Marshal as well as another medieval 'baronial' document, the 'Modus Tenendi

[13] Bloch 75, 217 (his italics); cf. *Boutell's Heraldry*, revised by John Brooke-Little, Richmond Herald of Arms (1970), 205–6.

Parliamentorum' ('The Manner of the Keeping/Holding of the Parliaments'). In them, the Earl Marshal is viewed as 'always next to the King at his coronation [as one who] ought to hold his crown in his hand'. In addition to this royal proximity, he is to have 'the forward of the host'. Fitting humanist modes, the document blends fiction and fact (e.g., Gilbert de Strogell was a Marshal of England but under Henry I, not Henry II) in order for its discourse to actualize a model for the day. The effect of the texts would be clear to Cromwell and the later factions, not only as a political theory that attacked them but as a new political fact; humanist language could be used by the conservative nobility as well as by any 'owtragius' or 'new erectyd men'.[14] Surrey could show that the future did not inevitably belong to any faction, however reformed.

In fact, during the last decade of his short life, Surrey recognized, more and more, that the role of Earl Marshal might form part of his inheritance, with its direct control over the College of Arms. He would thus be the head of what still existed in Tudor England: the High Court of Chivalry. In theory, Surrey would be arbiter (with the heralds under him) to determine whose coat of arms could be granted and whose not, an enormous power that could signify the social structure of the kingdom. This ranking by honour and its whole systemic functioning would be under his legal jurisdiction. The meaning of this position was emphasized for Surrey in a contemporary 1529 manuscript (revised as late as 1536 and probably circulating at the Tudor court in 1542 after the destruction of Cromwell): Thomas Starkey's *Dialogue between Thomas Lupset and Reginald Pole*. Here Roman roles were specifically analysed for a new English court. Starkey's call for an oligarchical constitution in his utopia was formed on a political model from classical Rome. Surrey would have made the connections: as Cicero's *cursus senatorum* had existed outside Caesar's *imperium* or, at the least, in dialectic with Caesar's greater power, so the College of Arms could keep the nobility independent. Starkey had even called for a leader from the blood nobility, redefining the role of the Constable (a high dignity Surrey's grandfather Buckingham held but never assumed as an office) but precisely a figure who also had a humanist command of texts and languages (and specifically of Roman law).

In this unpublished text of 1529, Starkey saw salvation for the current 'frencey in our commyn wele' in a system by which the nobility of the blood formed councils of natural leadership in the state. They then created a leader of such councils who combined both the blood-line and humanist education (his model was the exceptional White Rose survivor Reginald Pole, grand-nephew of two Yorkist kings and the last Cardinal-Archbishop of Canterbury).[15] This leader must have that desire to serve, in fact, as Lupset ends his part of the *Dialogue*, that drive to

[14] Cf. *Rivals in Power*, ed. David Starkey (1990) 70.

[15] Thomas Starkey, *Dialogue between Thomas Lupset and Reginald Pole*, ed. T. F. Mayer, Camden Fourth Series, 37 (1989), 142, hereafter cited in text. Also, for the interweaving of text (English and Italian), event, and intrigue, see Mayer, 'Nursery of Resistance: Reginald Pole and His Friends', in *Political Thought and the Tudor Commonwealth: Deep Structure, Discourse and Disguise*, ed. Paul A. Fideler and T. F. Mayer (1992), 50–74.

serve (and, for Surrey, to use instruments of service like self-representation and language) 'ys a certayn argument of true nobylyte, for sluggysch myndys lyve in cornarys & content themselfys wyth pryvate lyfe, wheras veray nobul hartys ever desyre to governe & rule, to the commyn wele of the whole multytude' (142–3). The role of the Constable in Starkey's utopia (itself a response to More's) represents such activity, a Virgilian georgic labour serving the state and suited to the Roman conception at its roots. As Surrey knew, the role of Earl Marshal had originally been defined as deputy to such a Constable of the kingdom.

Constable is precisely the office that Starkey in his Platonic dialogue had the fictional Lupset desire Reginald Pole to assume. In order to avoid '<any dangerouse> sedycyon betwyx the pryncys of our reame <& hys nobylyte>', and so that 'the authoryte of the prynce' be 'temperyd & brought to ordur' and 'thys same tyranny' avoided, 'our old aunceturys the instytutarys of our lawys & ordur of our reame . . . ordeyned a comustabul of englond to conturpayse the authoryte of the prynce & tempur the same.' These ancestors had even given the Constable the right to call a Parliament if the king should be a tyrant. The Constable also had the authority specifically to curb, if not control, the prerogative of the king in the name of the greater freedom of the state or commonweal. The Constable's authority was, of course, 'dyverse', shared with his council, 'even lyke as the authoryte of the prynce may not rest in hym alone, but in hym as the hede joynyd to hys counsel as to the body'. The Constable heads his council which represents 'the hole <body of the pepul wythout> parlyament & commyn counseyl' of the realm. In sum, all this authority of the Constable has 'one poynt chefely, that ys <to say> to see <un> to the lyberty of the hole body of the reame' (120–2). Surrey sought the same in his attempts to survive. Greater 'lyberty' was what he was seeking in his own representation, in his own new definitions of old roles. For Starkey, this liberty might even include, under the right circumstances, the election of a new king. Above all, in Surrey's eyes, it was the greater liberty of England—his new Roman word, 'Britain'—he was seeking, the 'freedom' that his own body, with its range of Renaissance styling, personified and, by its styling, could pass 'freedom' on.

Of course, by 1540 a certain predestination may have crept into the political concept of nobility held by Surrey (and others) and of the Court of Honour that sustained it. Whatever these forms of nobility may have been before, now that they had been radicalized by the violence of recent history, they too may have assumed the rituals and ideology of the new Christian reformed cults, the signs of the chosen and elected (as revealed later in the more dogmatic conceptions of honour and nobility in, for example, Michael Segar's paradigm of English nobility in 1602).[16] At such a critical moment of destiny, Thomas Howard, son of the 'Flodden Duke' and the third Duke of Norfolk, had his portrait painted (Plate II).

[16] *Honor Military, and Civill* (1602), liber 2, cap. 1, 51. For the nature of political certitude in English Protestants, see Michael Walzer, *The Revolution of the Saints: A Study in the Origins of Radical Politics* (1965).

Norfolk's slight figure, with a long, sallow face and heavy aquiline nose, lifts itself in the Holbein portrait with an erect posture under the weight of silk and satin robes and heavy white ermine. His gold collar of Tudor roses with the precisely carved figure of St George as a medieval knight dangling from it spreads out over the duke's shoulders and chest. This George identifies Surrey's father as one of the princes named in the first of the three ranks of those receiving the Garter. The totally white staff in his left hand identifies him as Lord Treasurer, the second of his Roman roles. The glistening gold baton in his right hand, with its black tip lifted high, identifies him as Earl Marshal of the kingdom, the first Roman role, the Custodian of Honour and the Court of Honour. Holbein's extraordinary fusion of robes and colours here confirms the implicit ideology that authorizes the Howards in all their great roles of honour in the kingdom.

Thus, in Surrey's eyes, organization of all noble life turned around two rubrics or poles of power essentially Roman and evolving from the old imperial *amici principis* (friends of the prince). These had been unspoken premises for Thomas Starkey's reorganization of the nobility because Roman roles had origins deep in English culture. More than in the Renaissance, the *vir togatus* and the *vir armatus* had elaborated forms in the medieval world in its memory of Rome, the *comes princeps* (or *principis*) and the *dux bellorum*. The exact leverage between the two poles of power could not always be determined. King Arthur was more the latter at times (as Nennius had signified him from the start), more the 'man in arms' and 'leader of wars' than the 'man in a toga' or 'the first courtier [or comrade or protector].' But in Surrey's world, real power and not just marginal influence meant identifying with and transforming both Roman roles. It also meant producing in oneself what Sir Thomas Elyot calls the 'fourme' of 'authoritie in a publike weale', a living personal style that came from being a man of both arms and the toga, Surrey's style or bold representation named by Hadrianus Junius and later quoted by Camden. In his praise of Surrey in the 1545 letter he composed for Surrey's children to send him at the war front in France, the famous Dutch humanist noted that the young earl possessed a 'filum', a heroic style in all that he did and commanded (N1: 171).[17]

For Elyot, 'nobul hartys' should go a step further, beyond the necessary personal style described by Castiglione in his book of courtesy that Surrey knew well. 'Nobul hartys' should form a system of *amici principis*. As Conrad explains, 'the educational programme outlined in Book One of the *Governour* was designed to produce contemporary English counterparts to the *philoi* of Hellenistic monarchs and the *amici principis* of imperial Rome.' What Elyot was doing in his educational theories, so Surrey would do with poetry: strengthen the language

[17] 'Comes' may be translated in 1542 as 'courtier', a designation found in the Roman historian Suetonius; or as 'comrade' or 'associate', its earliest meaning, as in Lucretius and Cicero; or as 'protector', a rarer usage but in Virgil. In late Latin, the term indicates a holder of a state office. Among recent studies that deal with these terms and their inscription in England, see Geoffrey Ashe, *The Discovery of King Arthur* (1985) and his earlier *From Caesar to Arthur* (1960). Elyot, *Boke*, vol. 1, 28.

and training of the *amici* so that no 'good' or noble counsellor 'be omitted or passed over', in Elyot's teaching. Although Elyot believed with Starkey (as did Sir Philip Sidney later) that a monarchy limited by a strong nobility would give more liberty to the state, the classical 'governors' or counsellors had learned to deal with tyrants; in fact, they knew little else. Governing in such a broken world as ancient Rome would be the basis, in fact, for their system of healing the nation. Had not Homullus said, in a passage Elyot translated from the *Scriptores Historiae Augustae*, '[The Emperor] Domitian was a most evil man but he had *boni amici*'? And did Surrey not recall that the official Protector of the young Nero was no one less than Seneca himself, the Stoic text-maker who wrote 'Medea superest'? Dealing with Henry VIII might be a far more reasonable task. Was there not always the hope of a good prince such as Elyot offered in his 1541 life of the Emperor Alexander Severus in his *Image of Governance* and, earlier, Surrey's step-uncle Lord Berners had offered in his 1535 *Golden Boke of Marcus Aurelius*? Surrey had studied such a figure of the true governor in a source both Starkey and Elyot were using, Cicero's *De officiis*, which described the act of ruling not as absolute but as contingent: 'si cum admiratione quadam honoure dignos putat' ('if, with definite admiration, [the people] think you worthy of honour').[18]

In Surrey's legacy of Roman texts and their new Tudor interpretations, however, none was more crucial than Elyot's life of a Roman emperor, *The Image of Governance*. It was remarkably different in its textualizing of imperial power from that, for example, seen everywhere in Holbein's portraits of Henry VIII. A new definition of the old nobility of blood as the *cursus senatorum* thus appeared in that *annus mirabilis* for Surrey, 1541. Catherine Howard was queen, and Elyot's work is dedicated to none other than the Duke of Norfolk, the Earl Marshal of the realm. Elyot's *Image* is one more Tudor 'courtesy book' describing the roles of honour and obviously influenced by Lord Berners' translation of *The Golden Boke of Marcus Aurelius*. Its full title, as Surrey first read it in 1541, is significant: *The Image of Governance Compiled of the Actes and Sentences Notable, of the moste noble Emperour Alexander Seuerus, late translated out of Greke into Englyshe, by syr Thomas Eliot Knight, in favour of the Nobylitie*. Elyot's metonymizing *Image* is, as the author himself says in his preface to the work, 'the fourme of good gouernance' promised in his programmatic *Book of the Governour*. Instead of precepts and theories, the Emperor Alexander's actual life represents, as the final sentence of the book states, not only an 'example to iudges' but a 'beautifull ymage to all thym that are lyke to be governours'.

[18] Frederick William Conrad, 'A Preservative Against Tyranny: The Political Theology of Sir Thomas Elyot', unpublished Ph.D. dissertation (Johns Hopkins University, 1988), 42, 37. See also Conrad's 'The Problem of Counsel Reconsidered: The Case of Sir Thomas Elyot', in *Political Thought*, ed. Fideler and Mayer, 75–101. For the role of the *amici*, see *Boke Named the Governor*, 15–94, 238–40; Fox and Guy, *Reassessing the Henrician Age*, 138–40; J. A. Crook, *Consilium Principis: Imperial Councils and Counsellors from Augustus to Diocletian* (1955), 21–30; and Guy, 'The Rhetoric of Counsel in Early Modern England', in *Tudor Political Culture*, ed. Dale Hoak, (1995), esp. 55–60.

By no accident, the Roman emperor hero of this text authorizes blood nobility as the source of the best political power. Also, by no accident, in this year 1541, Surrey was inventing for his translation of Virgil his heroic line of blank verse, the language of the 'beautifull' images of nobility that the friends of the ideal prince could speak as their own. In a long oration, speaking to the Roman 'multitudo', the Emperor Alexander praises the quasi-divine ordering of Roman society, how the founder of Rome, Romulus, 'ordeyned and stablyshed a counsayle, wherby the affaires of the citie, and appendaunces thereof shuld be ruled and minystred'. Out of this 'state' and only in political continuity with the nobility 'shoulde be a maiestie, which of all other men shulde be had in a syngular honour and reuerence'; thus did the Roman senate elect Romulus 'out of resydue' of the warring classes of the young *equites* on horseback and the *quirites* 'signified Speare men'.[19]

It was lucky for Sir Thomas Elyot that the Tudor king was so totally infatuated with the young body of Catherine Howard and that Cromwell had already been dead a year. Neither read this bold inscription. Both Elyot's text and Holbein's portrait of Norfolk confirmed a successful conservative coup after the Act of Precedence that toppled Cromwell and set in motion, among other new Acts, the Act of the Six Articles that would influence centuries of English-speaking religious life, permanently limiting the effects of the Reformation. *The Image of Governance* also pointed to the establishment of what Elyot had proleptically described in his imagined oration by his imagined emperor: an actual new council. On 10 August 1540, twelve days after Cromwell had been beheaded, and with Henry VIII safely bedded on his honeymoon with Catherine Howard, a Privy Council was formed such as the one Romulus had 'ordeyned and stablyshed', to be dominated, at least for a time, by England's Roman 'senators'. Earlier in 1529, after the downfall of Cardinal Wolsey, Norfolk as Treasurer and Suffolk as Earl Marshal (and therefore president designate) had sat 'with assent of other lords' to hear cases in Wolsey's Star Chamber, the nucleus of his power. In 1540, however, as Pollard has shown,[20] there was a genuine difference from all earlier councils, and that difference was the organization of the Privy Council itself. In fact, William Paget, its first appointed clerk and always sniffing shifts in power, had moved from attending Anne of Cleves in the spring to becoming secretary to Catherine Howard in July 1540 and then, in August, to assume this role.

Wearing the Toga in 1542

The Roman view of the nobility as *boni amici*, inheritors of the nobility of Alexander's *philoi*, could only be realized for Surrey in two places at the Tudor

[19] Sir Thomas Elyot, *Four Political Treatises: The Doctrinal of Princes (1533): Pasquil the Playne (1533): The Banquette of Sapience (1534): and The Image of Governance (1541)*, ed. Lillian Gottesman (1967), 206, 422, 337–8.

[20] A. F. Pollard, 'Council, Star Chamber, and Privy Council under the Tudors', *EHR*, 37 (1922), 342, 351.

court: the position of Earl Marshal and in the Privy Council, both newly defined. There would be only one other political goal for the poet earl beyond these. It subsumed both roles: the Protectorate for the future king Edward VI. Until his father died, and the old man was now at a precarious age for the Tudor world, the poet earl could not expect to assume any of these renewed Roman roles. He could only prepare himself as heir to such roles and therefore make himself worthy of them. The level of this preparation marked every activity for the rest of his short life. Building Surrey House was part of that projection of himself as heir to such roles. But he had other activities that were equivalent to his wearing of the toga in 1542. These specific social roles were routine but increasingly demanding, for in addition to socially compulsory appearances at christenings, weddings, executions, and burials, from the late 1530s on, Surrey was initiated into county and regional management: in 1538, he became Commissioner of Sewers (for the all-important maintenance of watercourses and sea defences in Norfolk); in 1539 he became steward for the Duchy of Lancaster's lands in Norfolk, Suffolk, and Cambridgeshire (for which he received £20 per annum), and a year later—reflecting his local importance as much as his intellectual stature—steward to the University of Cambridge; also in 1540, he acted as a commissioner of the coastal defence of Norfolk, in which, with his father-in-law, the Earl of Oxford, he inspected, built, and repaired beacons and coastal fortresses, as far as Essex, notably the elegant beacon castle of Orford, and also, on his own, made an inventory of all ships, sailors, and defenders in East Anglia ports, particularly the most accessible to Imperial invaders at Yarmouth; in 1542, he became Commissioner of the Peace for Norfolk (suited for his new residence in Norwich); at court in February 1544, he was designated by Henry VIII to host the Duke of Najera, and in May 1544, the Duke of Alburquerque, and in August 1546, to honour the French Admiral, his last official court function; by 1545 he was chief cup-bearer to the king (receiving £50), being helped by his brother Lord Thomas Howard and their cousin Sir Francis Bryan.

But all such wearing of the toga had one goal only: preparation for the larger Roman roles the poet earl must assume. Athough Surrey could not inherit the role of Earl Marshal, he could prepare himself for what had first been a Howard function under Richard III. Further, the redefined terms of the Privy Council may have given the poet earl even greater hope. The young earl might enter his role there sooner if his elderly father resigned or died. Although precedence in 1542 was still determined by 'ancienty', that is, the age of the creation of the noble title, and rank still determined seating in Parliament, the 1539 Act implemented precedence, whether of old or new nobility, by tying it to specific centres of power that in the hands of older nobility could make all the difference. Henceforth the four great officers of the state, the Lord Chancellor, the Lord Treasurer, the Lord President of the Council, and the Lord Privy Seal sat above all peers, except the royal dukes. The next seven officers, headed by the Great Chamberlain and Earl Marshal, took precedence above all other nobles of their rank, no matter what their 'ancienty'. Such rank (the real reason for Norfolk's portrait display of self) was also declared true for all meetings of the Privy Council, and the Council itself had to be composed only of great office-holders. Of course, new nobility (or civil servants) could and did hold such offices, but so could the old nobility. There was now a battlefield. In fact, the Household Ordinances of Christmas 1539 implemented the Act of Precedence by making the topos of the Council the actual Court dwelling: the nobles in charge had to eat, sleep, and meet at the centre of political power. The English peerage could now be headed by an older nobility decidedly active, at the literal heart of government, with no White Rose survivors in their castles dreaming of chivalric challenges. Following his father, the poet earl could aim towards the heart of government, himself the centre of the *boni amici*, 'nobul hartys', their power renewed, perhaps sooner than expected.

Holbein

But there was another kind of Romanizing, another reading of classical Rome firmly established by 1542 that did not include the Roman roles of an updated mediating nobility. Beyond this image of Rome Surrey could not go, and increasingly he knew that the power of this role could annihilate him and his dynasty. It could certainly obliterate, at least in its theory and ideology, any role of the nobility, renewed or otherwise. Before that obliterating Roman role, even the newfound power of the Privy Council was fatally limited. The authority of Surrey's probable godfather now became absolute.

Ironically, the Pilgrims of Grace had helped to extend the supreme authority of the English King. Wearing their badges of the Five Wounds of Christ, the Pilgrims brought up as part of their agenda, as Guy notes, the 'fifteenth-century debate about the Council membership that focused on the supposed duty of the monarch to share political power with the old aristocracy and others born to traditional status (*consiliarii nati*)'. After all, had not the opening of Edward IV's *Black Book*—'the new house of the houses principal of England'—reflected a more Arthurian Round-Table conception of monarchy, whatever the actualities? If the English King in 1536 gave in response to the Pilgrims one of his few public defences of his monarchy, entering for the first and last time into a public political debate, it was clear that the king understood the dimensions of his new Roman role. In Guy's argument, 'it was Henry VIII himself who directed government strategy after 1529' and, although the Privy Council reappeared as an institution after Cromwell's beheading, partially in response to the Pilgrims of Grace, King Henry was never eclipsed by a 'ministerial *alter rex*'.[21]

[21] J. A. Guy, 'The Privy Council: Revolution or Evolution?' in *Revolution Reassessed*, ed. Coleman and Starkey, 80, 69.

In fact, he was eclipsed by little else. On 20 October 1529, Henry VIII, without the deposed Wolsey, had applied the great seal to documents with his own hand. The action merely confirmed what the crucial Eltham Ordinances had announced three years before (e.g., 'Have a vigilant and reverent respect and eye to his Grace so that by his look or countenance [you] may know what lacketh or is his pleasure to be done'). Even before the later definitions of the Supreme Head, the courts of honour and equity were reflecting what this applying of the great seal by the king's own hand symbolized. In fact, as Mervyn James has demonstrated, the quarrel among the heralds (including the Wriothesleys) in 1530 directly concerned who had the authority to extend (and therefore define) honour itself—the conception of rank in the kingdom—and in what mode. Henry VIII settled the dispute by reminding the heralds of just where the origination of all honour lay, in terms quite different from Richard III's when the White Rose King had authorized the roles of the heralds. As shown by the later 1539 Bible title-page by Holbein (or his school), so the real presence of the king in 1530 gave and determined honour from himself alone. Furthermore, in James' terms, the honour that radiated from his royal person had also to be 'internalized' by each citizen, who was to see honour 'as the agent of a law that was not merely natural and human, but divine'.[22]

But after the October Act of 1529 not only courts of honour changed. The shape of Parliament itself had also changed, as two drawings by heralds reveal. In the first, drawn in 1523 for the herald father of the Lord Chancellor who would help condemn Surrey to death, a 32-year-old Henry VIII opens Parliament, closely surrounded by three seated lords spiritual and two secular figures and, before him, on his right, twenty-six seated bishops and abbots and, on his left, fewer lords secular, while further left, standing in the distance outside the bar but still close by, the seeming multitude of the Commons. In a drawing of 1551 by Sir Gilbert Dethick, Garter Herald 1550–84 and in 1546 the Richmond Herald who helped condemn Surrey, the 14-year-old Edward VI, the new Supreme Head, sits before the lords under his canopy almost alone, except for one secular lord on either side and further to the left five standing figures, and only seven bishops before him to his right. As Powell and Wallis comment on the events of 1529: 'Within the space of a few months the aspect of the parliament chamber had been drastically altered. The medieval face of the House of Lords had gone . . . the preponderance shifted from the spiritual to the temporal, the Crown withdrawn into isolation, and power and prestige derived from Crown appointment.'[23]

The result was, as Slavin notes, a period of ever greater 'patrimonial kingship' when Henry VIII became 'the sole appropriate object of a subject's political allegiance'. But already, a year before Surrey entered court, those who saw themselves as new Christians were reading Tyndale's English version of Martin Luther's

[22] Transcribed from Bodleian Library MS Laud Misc. 597, especially 33r. James, *English Politics*, 12.

[23] J. Enoch Powell and Keith Wallis, *The House of Lords in the Middle Ages: A History of the English House of Lords to 1540* (1968), 582. The first drawing can be found in this text as illustration XX and the second as XXIV.

I. Hans Holbein the Younger, *Henry Howard, Earl of Surrey*, Windsor Castle. The Royal Collection © Her Majesty the Queen.

II. Hans Holbein the Younger, *Thomas Howard, third Duke of Norfolk*, Windsor Castle. The Royal Collection © Her Majesty the Queen.

III. The Black Book of the Order of the Garter, showing Henry VIII and the twenty-five Knights Companion in 1534/5 and part of the procession of the knights. Reproduced by permission of the Dean and Canons of Windsor.

IV. Hans Holbein the Younger, *Henry Howard, Earl of Surrey*, Museu de Arte de São Paulo. Photographed by Luiz Hossaka, by courtesy of the Museu de Arte de São Paulo, Brazil.

V. English School, sixteenth century, *The Fair Geraldine* (Elizabeth, Countess of Lincoln), National Gallery of Ireland. By courtesy of the National Gallery of Ireland, Dublin.

VI. William Scrots, *Henry Howard, Earl of Surrey*, National Portrait Gallery. By courtesy of the National Portrait Gallery, London.

redefinition of the state. Luther derived his theory of kingship from a classic Pauline text—a Roman text, in fact, the Apostle's letter to the Romans, chapter 13—about the total allegiance of new Christians to the Roman emperor.[24] William Tyndale had translated those terms into his majestic English: the subject who resists such a Supreme Head as the king resists God, for such monarchs 'are in the room of God, and they that resist shall receive damnation.' In fact, 'God hath made the king in every realm judge over all, and over him is there no judge.' And a lesson for the blood nobility: 'He that judgeth the king judgeth God; and he that layeth hands on the king layeth hand on God.' In a later reply to Sir Thomas More, Tyndale could not be clearer about this political truth: 'No person, neither any degree, must be exempt from this ordinance of God. . . . all souls must obey'—not only in bodies but spirits. With this sense of assurance that his image of the political weal held the power of the future, Tyndale could even spell out to More the kind of state the reformer had in mind: 'We may remove them [saint's bones] whither we will, yea and break all images thereto, and make new, or if they be abused, put them out of the way for ever, as was the brazen serpent; so that we be lords over all things, and they our servants.' Thus, after the defection of Reginald Pole to Rome and the Pope's excommunication of Henry VIII following the full desecration of the sanctuary and shrine of Thomas à Becket, the terms for submission and the outcries by the state against disorder and rebellion of any kind became, in Skinner's phrase, 'increasingly hysterical'. Any failure to submit to the Supreme Head could now become an attack on the community of England itself. In 1540 the ideology at the heart of the state to which Surrey hoped to bring a new nobility came most clearly from Robert Barnes, the English Lutheran, whose burning by Henry VIII followed by two days Cromwell's beheading (and, for Barnes' death, Martin Luther never forgave the English King). If the Christian king turns out to be a tyrant, says Barnes, then 'let the king exercise his tyranny.' Never, 'under any circumstances', should the divinely ordained king be opposed 'with violence', no matter what he imposes 'on bodies [of the subjects] and their property'.[25]

[24] A. J. Slavin, 'The Tudor State, Reformation, and understanding change: through the looking glass', in *Political Thought*, ed. Fideler and Mayer, 228. Cf. Skinner, *Political Thought*, vol. 1, 89. For Luther's theory of kingship from which Tyndale derived his own doctrine, see, among many studies, Heinrich Bornkamm, *Luther's Doctrine of the Two Kingdoms in the Context of his Theology*, trans. Karl H. Hertz (1966), esp. ch. 2–4, 6; W. D. J. Cargil Thompson, *The Political Thought of Martin Luther* (1984), esp. ch. 3–6, 8; also the chapter on Luther in Rupert E. Davies, *The Problem of Authority in the Continental Reformers* (1946), 15–61. For the relationship of Luther to English thought and a philosophical background for Tyndale, see 'Luther: The Dialectic of Supersession and the Politics of Righteousness', in Joshua Mitchell, *Not By Reason Alone: Religion, History, and Identity in Early Modern Political Thought* (1993), 19–45. For a background to Luther, Melanchthon, and their texts—Tyndale's *métier*—see 'The Glad Tidings of Dr. Luther' in George Henri Tavard, *Holy Writ or Holy Church: The Crisis of the Protestant Reformation* (1959), 80–97.

[25] William Tyndale, 'The Obedience of a Christian Man', in *Doctrinal Treatises and Introductions to Different Portions of the Holy Scriptures, by William Tyndale, Martyr, 1536*, ed. H. Walter (Parker Society [32], 1848), 175. Tyndale, *An Answer to Sir Thomas More's Dialogue*, ed. Henry Walter (Parker Society, 1850), 178, 88. For the context of Tyndale's development of Luther's theory, see

Thus, by 1542, in Henry VIII's 'calculated drama'—with its developing Roman ideology of an anointed emperor—the great seal, 'the most formal and public instrument of government', depended on the personal will of the monarch. This seal was applied in the Privy Chamber of Whitehall Palace in the presence only of private servants and within sight of Holbein's great mural of the Supreme Head (Plate 1). The place, the topos of honour, was decisive, for nothing could have centred the new authority of the English realm more gloriously than the massive Holbein painting on a wall without doors or windows. The figure and the mural dominated the entire Privy Chamber, overwhelming anyone in it. From 1537 on, its ideological effect could not be missed by any audience, not least when the great seal was applied. In this concentrated space, Holbein drew on all his resources and techniques for a serial fantasy of the king's new-found supreme power. He included Jane Seymour, Henry VIII's father and mother, all within a Bramante architectural design of scallops, columns, niches, and serially decorated sculptures behind the three figures determined to be most intimate with that royal body of the Supreme Head. Holbein's 'seeming natural inevitability' in all his art now dramatized the immediate salvation of a nation, the unity of a kingdom in turmoil. In such 'inevitability', Holbein would certainly have agreed with his Basel compatriot of the nineteenth century, Nietschze, who asserted: 'All truly noble morality grows out of triumphant self-affirmation.' This Holbein proved: in his Whitehall Henry VIII, grace—both as Vasari defined it in Renaissance art and as Luther defined it as the liberating power of God—centres the royal body as body, a real presence whose sheer size, if nothing else, no spectator could deny.[26]

With totalization as his aim, Holbein painted Henry VIII out of proportion to the other figures: 5 feet, 10 inches tall, 3 feet across his shoulders, and the rest of the royal body in a corresponding sequence, except for the codpiece that was larger, in keeping with its symbolic function. The result is that, in its time and as seen by Surrey constantly in the last decade of his life, Henry VIII appeared 'to bend the wall with his weight'. This mural may have increasingly focused for the poet the single power that steadily controlled every aspect of his life, the young man knowing at all times that he could survive only in terms of that body and its centralizing codpiece. Holbein's distortion added, of course, to the effect of soaring power in the royal body and, with it, the artist made the point of his Lutheran theology. As Campbell points out about the mural's emblematic structure, 'the ingeniously distorted perspective . . . forced the figures forward so that Henry VIII confronted the spectator with frightening directness.' Adding to this 'directness' were the splayed legs of the Supreme Head, curiously like the Colossus of Rhodes, a breach of etiquette for the humanist Jodocus Willich in a 1540 rhetoric text, who noted

Skinner, *Political Thought*, vol. 1, 105–7. Robert Barnes, 'That Men's Constitutions, which are not grounded in Scripture, bind not the conscience of Man', in *The Reformation Essays of Dr. Robert Barnes*, ed. N. S. Tjernagel (1963), 85.

26 David Starkey, 'Court and Government', in *Revolution Reassessed*, ed. Coleman and Starkey, 30. Nietzsche, *Genealogy*, 170. John Rowlands, *Holbein*: (1985), 121; Paul Ganz, *The Paintings of Hans Holbein* (1950), 289.

'an excessive separation of feet is blameworthy.' Here the breach and vulgar posture—the distortion as deliberate as that in Holbein's symbolic *Ambassadors* only four years earlier—project an implicit male energy to sum up the central meaning of the mural. The English King makes possible the redemptive work of Christ in his realm. He is identified with that redemption and new divine life. In this sense, the codpiece of Henry VIII so portrayed is the source of all new life in the kingdom (in 1537 he had, in fact, just produced a male heir who would be another Supreme Head). Thus, in portraits based on the lost painting (such as the cartoon with a three-quarters face), Henry VIII balances, in the middle of his incarnational body, the upright and righteous force that literally carries seeds of salvation for the kingdom in the power of his scrotum, as Aristotle had defined such power.[27] This new Holy Father, not the false father of Rome but the Father of the true Christian Kingdom, is ready to seize his audience in an embrace. He can generate, as in his vine-force depicted on the title-page of the 1539 Bible (Plate 15), a solution to history, England's and Europe's.

In such a theological painting, there could be no mediation between this Father, this Supreme Head, and his collective people depicted in the frontispiece of the 1539 Bible. Nothing like the mediation of a nobility could be tolerated, nor could any other graduated force in the kingdom be tolerated, not least Virgilian poets with their own freedom to create symbols. Henry VIII was rather clear about his gift from on high of total interpretation. In the 1540s the king told Winchester that indeed he 'had been directed in the mean [middle] way of truth, and therefore was meet to be arbiter between the others to reduce them to truth.'[28] The reducing meant, among other things, a system of honour that moved directly from absolute human monarch to internal self, without mediation or any emblems but the monarch's. For Luther, Christ was the absolute Saviour penetrating the self of the sinner and needed no mediation, only the sinner's recognition of 'Sola Fides' in the phrase Luther made central (even adding his own adjective to the original Bible phrase in Romans). Why then would the English living representative of Christ in his God-given scrotum-power, Holbein's clearly superior model to any German arrangement, need any mediation at all? Here was a transcendence and real presence far greater than anything Anne Boleyn could have dreamed of or earlier English kings embody.

[27] The description of the mural is from Lacey Baldwin Smith, *Henry VIII: The Mask of Royalty* (1971), 26. Lorne Campbell, *Renaissance Portraits* (1990), 84, 95–6. Aristotle, *Generation of Animals*, trans. H. A. L. Peck (1953), 716a1, 718a1, 726b1, 730a1, 730b1, 766b1. Male superiority stemmed not necessarily from intelligence (nor spirituality) nor even from bodily strength but from physiological fact. Cf. Helen Gardner, *A Reading of Paradise Lost* (1965), 82–3. For Henry VIII's power of erection and sexuality in general (not relevant, of course, to Holbein's symbolizing), see the rather specific if dated analysis by J. C. Flügel, 'On the Character and Married Life of Henry VIII', in *Psychoanalysis and History*, ed. Bruce Mazlish (1971), 124–49. For the Holbein mural as holy altar under which the living king, as Eucharistic incarnation, sat, and the continuation of the force of this painting, see Louis Montrose, 'The Elizabethan Subject and the Spenserian Text' *Literary Theory / Renaissance Texts*, ed. Patricia Parker and David Quint (1985), pp. 312–314.

[28] Stephen Gardiner, Bishop of Winchester, *Letters*, ed. J. A. Muller (1933), 124, 308.

Thus, to assert Henry VIII's absolute new Christian dialectic—the Supreme Head and the separate self in a society in which rank held meaning only in relationship to that Head—nothing could be more noble and representative, more truly Romanizing, than Holbein's encapsulations in art, beginning in 1537 at Whitehall Palace, of this Supreme Head. Holbein's art evidenced this new Roman role with a particularly English incarnation of one side of the king's 'two bodies', the English stress on the term *body* rather than *person* posing, at least for Kantorowicz, 'a terminological peculiarity'. Holbein's art of building on this English difference revealed what Kantorowicz calls the 'head of the mystical body of the *Ecclesia Anglicana*', the king's body's presence as real in Holbein as any evoked by magic rites on an altar. Holbein was now the new priest of a new eucharistic reality, an art that reveals real presence on canvas and thereby becomes real presence itself. In no other image of Henry VIII does the priestly wizardry of Holbein match the impact of the Whitehall mural, neither in his cultic oversized Henry VIII painted in 1541 for the livery company of Barber Surgeons (the huge figure surrounded by almost twenty small physicians like patrons in a Nativity scene) nor in Holbein's second Whitehall mural with Henry VIII as Solomon. This king watches a line of adoring women and courtiers, Queen Sheba focused on him in wonder, and a Latin verbal text above Henry-Solomon's head from the Vulgate (2 Paralipomenon or Chronicles 9: 8: 'Let the Lord your God be happy / Who found pleasure in placing you / On His throne so that you would be a king / Established for the Lord your God') suggesting, as King notes, 'both Henry and Solomon are responsible to God alone and to no other worldly power.'[29] In sheer physical size, then, the Whitehall mural soared through the entire reigns of Edward VI, Mary I, Elizabeth I, James I, and Charles I, and was seen by all courtiers from Sidney and Surrey's sons and his nephew, the Earl of Oxford, to Bacon and Herbert and court visitors like Shakespeare, Jonson, and Donne. In the English Revolution, not surprisingly, Oliver Cromwell whitewashed the idolatrous body for its blasphemy and offence against God.

Against such a totalizing Roman role on the Privy Chamber wall, the heart of all power in his world, Surrey was to direct the energies of his last years of life. The mural and the figure in it had terrorized many spectators, and it took a particular courage, if not madness, to think it could be resisted, much less challenged, in the name of a higher genealogy. More absurdly, resistance was in the name of a new nobility yet to be realized and only viewed in Surrey's own body of honour. Given this seemingly irrational challenge, what exactly was Surrey resisting? To whom or what did Surrey offer his chivalric challenge? First and most important, it was a challenge not necessarily to the king himself nor to his personal incarnation of the new Roman role, certainly not to the glory that Holbein's art embodied. In fact, no evidence at all exists that at any time Henry, Earl of Surrey, did not believe

[29] Ernst H. Kantorowicz, *The King's Two Bodies: A Study in Medieval Political Theology* (1957), 447–8. King, *Tudor Royal Iconography* (1982), 83. The translation from the Vulgate is mine. See Roy Strong, *Holbein and Henry VIII* (1967) for discussion of the other Holbein portraits.

that a strong king and even the Supreme Head of the Church in England served, as roles, to bring the order and stability to his world that not just England but all Renaissance culture wanted more of, not less. In fact, as the actual phrasing of his later translations of the Psalms and Ecclesiastes—the last phase of his poetic career—shows,[30] Surrey had profound sympathy for reformed Christianity. Furthermore, had not More's Utopus himself had such total power and founded Utopia on his beneficent tyranny? Surrey might even have considered a new role for his king, in the years after 1536, after his sojourn in France at the court of the authoritarian Francis I. Henry VIII could serve as a model hero in his poetry, as the Roman emperor had for Virgil and Horace—the new Augustus as Supreme Head, the image in Holbein's Whitehall mural.

What turned admiration and honour to challenge lay in the redefinition of that new Henrician order, not so much by Thomas Cromwell or any other agent as by the ideology Henry VIII chose for this new definition of himself. Despite the godson's evident awe at the transcendence of the royal figure himself, he could not accept the consequences of his godfather's choices. It was not merely the slow eradication in the kingdom of all levels of symbolic representation except those of the king, but the choice of the king himself to alter the nature of nobility. Seeing the consequences multiply through the years led Surrey to break with the Henrician state, contemplating, if not enacting, treason, at least as treason was now defined by Holbein's supreme figure. Quietly, within himself, Surrey realized that such increasingly total authority was passing from the king himself, a rightful object of reverence, to a lesser group of nobility, honour 'made by the kinges majesty of vile birth', the 'new erected men'.

The Task Ahead

Long before any question of Henry VIII's will ennobling and enriching key courtiers, a number 'of vile birth', (and the will's possible forgery by them), the shift of power had come. The 'inevitable' nature of the power revealed on the wall of the Privy Chamber at Whitehall preordained the death of the nobility Surrey envisioned. Once Henry VIII had realized his own true dimensions, the question of transfer of authority to any more or less figure of nobility was relatively meaningless. As in the title-page of the 1539 Bible, below the Supreme Head everyone was relatively equal in the same dispensation that Holbein (or his school) drew so flawlessly down the page, passing from body to body. Increasingly there was no room for the nobility, and prophetically Stephen Gardiner, the Bishop of Winchester, wrote in July 1547: 'For the destruction of images conteineth an enterprise to subvert religion and the state of the worlde with it; and specially the

[30] Cf. Sessions, *Henry Howard, Earl of Surrey* (1986) 104.

nobilitie, who, by images, set forth and spread abrode, to be red of all people, their linage and parentage, with remembrance of their state and acts.' To his old acquaintance Thomas Cranmer, just before his own imprisonment, he prophesied: 'civil tumults and commotions here within this realm' in which 'the vehemence of noveltie' with its own power 'wyl floo further thenne your Grace wold admitte'.[31] By the 1540s, Henry VIII had authorized, directly and indirectly, nobility in his realm springing from a system not determined by the offices of the heralds and the Earl Marshal and graduated nobility, but from the royal person alone, separate and above all others.

What Surrey failed to realize—and what his father recognized when he tried to arrange marriages in 1546 between his grandchildren, including Surrey's own children, and the Seymours—was the ironic nature of history, its tendency to be more comprehensive and freer than its makers. Faced with the death he now saw hurtling towards him if he did not act, the poet Earl of Surrey did not have the experience or the time to gamble on the tendency of history to turn on itself, as in either Virgil's 'ruere in peius' ('to collapse into the worse') or St Ambrose's 'felix culpa' ('blessed fault'). What he could not see was the irony that, while the old nobility were excluded from the central corridors of power, except as they controlled offices, the 'new erectyd men' who did wander in those corridors desired the signs of the old nobility as never before. In a not uncommon historical paradox (in fact, one happening at the same time all over Europe in 1547, as Duby and Braudel have shown), never had the social tokens of Romanizing honour and nobility been sought so fervently as in this period, precisely as 'new erectyd men' began to take over. As David Starkey notes: 'The formal institution of the Privy Council in 1540 inaugurated a series of regimes more narrowly aristocratic than any England had known since the first half of the fifteenth century.'[32]

Surrey's enemies had noble desires for themselves and their offspring as great as any desire of Surrey's. Sir Thomas Wriothesley (grandfather of the young man most often identified as the beloved of Shakespeare's sonnets) would appear in public only with his 'family of gentlemen' before him and his yeomen dressed in velvet and chains of gold after him. From their higher social ancestry and royal descent, Seymour retained, when he became Lord Protector, 167 such 'family', and

[31] Gardiner, *Letters*, 273–4. For the question of Henry VIII's will, see Helen Miller, 'Henry VIII's Unwritten Will: Grants of Lands and Honours in 1547', in *Wealth and Power in Tudor England: Essays Presented to S. T. Bindoff*, ed. E. W. Ives, R. J. Knecht, and J. J. Scarisbrick (1978); and E. W. Ives, 'Henry VIII's Will: A Forensic Conundrum', *HJ*, 35 (1992), 770–804; then R. A. Houlbrooke, 'Henry VIII's Wills: A Comment', *HJ*, 37 (1994), 891–900, and Ives, 'Henry VIII's Will: The Protectorate Provisions of 1546–7', Ibid. 901–13.

[32] For this cultural transference among classes in European society in general, always with the ideals of nobility directing the transference, see, among many studies, Fernand Braudel, *The Mediterranean and the Mediterranean World in the Age of Phillip II*, trans. Sian Reynolds (1973), vol. 2, 725–33. Also, for the same phenomenon in another context, see Georges Duby, *The Chivalrous Society*, trans. Cynthia Postan (1977). David Starkey 'After the "Revolution" ', in *Revolution Reassessed*, ed. Coleman and Starkey, 207. See also Starkey, preface in *The English Court: From the Wars of the Roses to the Civil War*, ed. David Starkey (1987), 24.

Dudley (the father of Leicester and the future grandfather of Sidney), as Duke of Northumberland, had 171. Indeed, as a group, what Surrey called 'new erectyd men' had moved to virtual political parity with the Howards, certainly after the 1543 marriage of Henry VIII and Catherine Parr. If such men could not control Henry VIII except through their superior service, then, in the reign of the boy Edward VI, they had total power, with which a Dudley could annihilate a Seymour and become virtual dictator of England, exactly the breakdown Surrey had dreaded and foreseen.

Most devastating of all, as Surrey had, in fact, recognized, the new nobility were to inherit the same totalizing authority as Henry VIII's. They would control the Christian realm that linked history, in the new ideology, to eternity itself—God's own will. This new authority of God's future will be passed from the figure in Holbein's mural, not to Surrey or his renewed nobility but to 'new erected men', two new self-appointed dukes first of all. Indeed, as a later picture depicts, the king on his deathbed points a Michelangelo finger towards his young son sitting beside the bed in state, and to the boy's right, as though in a Roman bas-relief, Seymour, Dudley, Cranmer, and the new establishment. Had Surrey lived, he would have found it no surprise to learn that the new Protector, the Duke of Somerset, with Dudley had made the young King Edward VI decree in 1550 that the words 'by the advice of the council' should be left out of all official documents and expunged from anything 'as shall pass in the king's majesty's name'.[33] The English Roman senate of the Privy Council had now moved to the idea of a Roman triumvirate and then finally to a Caesar—as though it were a recapitulation of Roman history itself. This was the chaos Surrey had dreaded for his England in the 1540s, on the brink, at least in his eyes, of its own special Renaissance.

All the poet could do was resist. He could offer a series of texts in which enough of the old *and* of the radically new and stylish would survive and in far greater proportions, as his rising mansion of Surrey House revealed. In his new texts, the new civilization of the Renaissance he had seen at Fontainebleau could be transferred to England's landscape of the Muses (or even be strengthened by a greater nobility)—but only if he acted, quite alone, as the leading young nobleman in the realm and attacked the other factions coalescing to destroy him and his family and any renewal of nobility. This illusion of himself as sole survivor made it all the more urgent to build Surrey House. There was very little time left. Thus, when in 1542 he leased the dissolved Benedictine priory of St Leonard's on a high promontory just off the ancient Roman road going out from Norwich Cathedral, a height overlooking the entire city and river, Surrey rechristened it Mount Surrey. He proceeded to build one more text by which he could distinguish himself from all other courtiers, either blood nobility or 'new erectyd men'.

[33] For the retinues, see Smith, *Henry VIII*, 77. For a full discussion of this picture, not least with its connections to the story of the poet Earl of Surrey (and the role of Hadrianus Junius), see Aston, *The King's Bedpost*. A. F. Pollard, 'Council, Star Chamber, and Privy Council under the Tudors', *EHR*, 37 (1922), 342, 351.

A Third Document: The Lease for Surrey House

On 10 May 1542, the Dean and Chapter of Norwich leased (but did not sell) to Surrey the priory of St Leonard's, all the buildings with their orchards, grounds, and woods for 99 years from the next Lady Day (the Feast of the Annunciation of the Virgin Mary on 25 March) at 20 shillings a year. At its dissolution, St Leonard's had reverted to the Dean and Chapter of Norwich Cathedral, the priory up the hill across the river originally having been constructed to accommodate monks while the Cathedral and its priory were being erected in the eleventh century. Surrey's tenancy thus began on 25 March 1543, and on that day he was to start the construction of Surrey House, based on the principles of renovation and transformation described in the building lease: Surrey could sell the lead and 'redify or otherwise transpose at his will and pleasure' all other buildings, but he must maintain the old Roman wall that defined the property.[34] This wall remained from the old Roman fortress on the promontory, 10 feet high and 8 underground, built with the native black-flecked stone. Also Roman and surviving today is a huge well, almost 8 feet across and 203 feet deep, now concrete-capped, too large for a small priory to build, but demonstrating the size of a Roman defence garrison on their road from the Roman outpost of Norwich to the North Sea port of Yarmouth and thence to Rome itself. A hundred years after Surrey, Sir Thomas Browne excavated Roman urns in Norwich and wrote his magnificent prose meditation *Hydriotaphia* about them. Until the nineteenth century, in this spot, coins, Roman (one showing the wife of Emperor Septimus Severus) and Alexandrian, were discovered.[35] As with his invention of blank verse, on the remains of old Rome Surrey would build a new Rome.

How much of this landscape Surrey transformed in his few years is not certain.[36] In fact, in this period, 'the greater the man, the more . . . monastic fabric' he kept to build his house. If the drawings on the maps are at all accurate, Surrey

[34] NRO DCN 115/9 (3), 1542, 1544; DCN 47/1, ff. 18–20, 1544–5. Cf. *LP*, vol. 21(ii), 287 and *Norwich Cathedral, Church, City and Diocese 1096–1996*, ed. I. Atherton, E. Fernie, C. Harper-Bill, and Hassel Smith (1996), 526. Casady, *Henry Howard*, 106, dates the acquisition in the general land sale and exchange with the Crown on 14 January 1544, when Norfolk, Surrey and the 'Lady Frances, wife of the said earl' received Castle Rising, manor and chase, and manors belonging to the vast estates of the Bishop of Norwich (one of the richest clerics in England), including the area of Thorpe just beyond the Wensum River.

[35] I am indebted to Ted and Rosemary Hare, the owners of the present Mount Surrey, for their hospitality and information.

[36] Until 1530, just twelve years before, the church had remained the place of a popular cult of St Leonard, the French nobleman who was patron saint of prisoners and also protected ducks. The Paston family who lived nearby had noted its pilgrimages, especially to the cult statue of St Leonard with ten rings on its fingers (the statue of the Blessed Virgin there had a sapphire on its middle finger) and a special statue or icon of Henry VI, whom Henry VII wanted to canonize. Another pilgrimage spot just at the bottom of the hill had also accrued its cults, the pit into which Lollards had been thrown after they were burned and executed. Beginning with the time of Chaucer and Dame Julian in her cell down the river, the executions of these Wycliff Christians at this spot on the riverbank just east of the cathedral continued into the next century after Chaucer and then into the persecution of the Henrician new Christians, Little Bilney (later identified by the Anglican Bishop Fuller as the chosen

appears to have adapted the conventual buildings with the fortress-like structure of the old bell-tower and outer buildings to a military appearance. Surrey may even have added crenellations to monastic walls to complete the image of the once and future *vir armatus*. Today, an old fortress-like gateway remains as probably all that originated with Surrey. Inside the monastic frame Surrey made considerable changes, as shown by the inventories and in the one remaining relic from the interior: an elegantly carved fragment of a stone mantelpiece, with acanthus leaves, the original leaf decoration probably of framed wood filled in with plaster, a possible indication of the decoration throughout.[37] In the same new Renaissance fashion, if the drawings on the maps are evidence, Surrey may have added large windows, like those Leicester later added to Kenilworth, lighting up the countryside for miles around. On several of these windows, Surrey may have emblazoned his coat of arms, as he did on his silver. The trial records mention specifically a glazier of Norwich making such arms for windows at Surrey House. What is most significant is that, from these lavishly displayed windows, particularly those from the rising tower, Surrey would look out, across the cliff edge, at one of the most splendid prospects of any nobleman's house in England, the absolute opposite of the plain of Kenninghall.

Even today, the view from the patio and sliding glass doors of the California split-level house on Mount Surrey is spectacular. Then as now, it looks across the spire of Norwich Cathedral to the landscape and clouds that reflect the clear light of a Constable landscape and the nearby North Sea. It was this view, with its command over the city, that doubtless attracted Surrey from the start. The novelty of such topography for a noble house in the 1540s made the whole project unique, not only in all East Anglia (although the view from the remains of Tendring Hall across the Stour valley is still remarkable), but elsewhere—at least for such an exalted member of the nobility. In that general public disdain for heights until the Romantics, Surrey's choice reveals a daring aesthetic dimension. Indeed, the Romantic East Anglian painter John Sell Cotman painted in his *From My Father's House at Thorpe* exactly what Surrey saw when he looked from the height of Thorpe woods down the Wensum towards the bend at Cow Tower, the river in 1542 running over a hard clear chalk bottom, full of fish, and covered with top-sail barges. The later Romantic use of perspective would hardly have been new to the young poet earl of the 1540s, who had visited Fontainebleau less than ten years before. The grand perspective from Surrey House alone attracted Surrey to the spot, certainly its command over the city, as it had the Romans centuries before.[38]

martyr of God) being killed there as late as 1531. Cf. W. T. Bensly, 'St. Leonard's Priory, Norwich', *Norfolk Archaeology*, 12 (1901), 190. Eamon Duffy, *The Stripping of the Altars: Traditional Religion in England 1400–1580* (1992), 179. Walter Rye, 'Some Ancient Parts of Norwich', *Eastern Daily Press* (28 November 1902).

[37] Howard, *The Early Tudor Country House* 148. *Hamlets of Norwich*, ed. E. A. Tilletts (typescript in Norwich Public Library [survived the fire of 1994], n.d.), 14, 97.

[38] For the shift in taste, see Marjorie Hope Nicholson, *Mountain Gloom and Mountain Glory: The Development of the Aesthetics of the Infinite* (1963).

Three Pavilions and an Inventory

A fourth document that describes Surrey House occurs in a report from his trial. The Jacobean William Camden gave as one reason for Surrey's beheading his layout of the gardens and grounds of Surrey House (Plate 14). On those grounds, in the long sweep from the crenellated walls to the edge of the cliff, Surrey built three 'Banquetting houses' or pavilions or belvederes for outdoor summer entertainments and for observation points over the city. Adhering to current Tudor architectural convention, they were tower-like, situated on mounds like turrets, but unusually they were surrounded by cannons as decoration. The design may have dramatized Surrey as a *vir armatus*, adding to the Arthurian (synonymous with Roman in 1542) and military leitmotifs in Surrey House, the kind of inscription to be expected of the future owner of Framlingham Castle, the seat of the Dukes of Norfolk, and the grandson of the builder of Thornbury. Two of these artificial mounds still exist today, just in front of the edge of the promontory. It was precisely these 'Bastilions' that were believed to have been constructed 'so as to overawe the city'. At least Wriothesley interpreted it so in his document of charges to which Henry VIII added accusing annotations. Citing a law established under Edward IV for any such embattlement of a private estate, Wriothesley wrote: 'If a man presume to use [liberties] in his lordship, or to keep pleas, [or to make] himself free warrent in his ground[s without] license, what it importeth?' Was Mount Surrey to be the centre of a insurrection? Did the young earl really want to become king? Surrey House made an important statement to the whole court. All were watching.[39]

The cannons and 'Banquetting Houses' thus demonstrate how emblematically Surrey planned the design of Mount Surrey, and a later Surrey poem, his second paraphrase from Ecclesiastes, describes the design of a garden possibly on Mount Surrey. Alluding to an irrigation system possibly from the Roman well (there was also a famous spring at the bottom of the hill) and to the general ferment of erecting a house and grounds, Surrey describes, in essence, the pain of building in all his texts in his last years. These lines neither in the Vulgate nor in the Lutheran paraphrases of Campensis, Surrey's sources for these translations, express what may have been the effects of his last years, the anxiety and sleeplessness.

> But, Lord, what care of mind, what sudden storms or ire,
> With broken sleeps endured I, to compass my desire!
> To build my house fair then set I all my cure:
> By princely acts thus strove I still to make my fame endure.
> Delicious gardens eke I made to please my sight,
> And graft therein all kinds of fruits that might my mouth delight.
> Conduits, by lively springs, from their old course I drew
> For to refresh the fruitful trees that in my garden grew. (ll. 12–16)

[39] Camden, *Remains*, 183. Such a garden pavilion, built not many years later, survives at Long Melford in East Anglia.

Like the final portrait seized for evidence, Surrey House with its artificial mounds and garden became one more text to destroy the poet earl.

The fifth document that identifies Surrey House shows the grandeur of Mount Surrey in 1547: an inventory of the furnishings at 'St. Leonardes by Norwiche'. If English Renaissance architecture is first a matter of interiors, as Maurice Howard notes, then the list of furnishings at Surrey House made by the agents of the Crown in 1546 is full proof that a grand house did indeed stand on Mount Surrey. Such an exterior structure in proportion to the luxurious items in the inventory would have cost, when completed, considerably more than other noble estates in East Anglia. The inventory of Surrey House was compiled by Sir John Gates, brother-in-law to the powerful Sir Anthony Denny of the Privy Chamber, Henry VIII's close personal attendant. Gates was keeper of the 'little coffer of black leather' that kept the stamp of the king's signature and was decisive in the manoeuvres of the last days of Henry VIII and the first weeks of Edward VI, when Seymour, Dudley, and 'new erectyd men' took over the kingdom and Gates became a Knight of the Bath. Gates later proved to be quite a devastating hatchet-man for Dudley, the newly raised Duke of Northumberland.[40]

The most elaborate of the interior furnishings were twenty tapestries, some as large as six or seven yards across, bought by Surrey specifically for his new house in addition to five more tapestries from his military headquarters at Boulogne, two 'wrought with beastes and a Conduicte in the myddes', another 'with Cocombere and grapes with great roses beastes and buildenges'. In addition, huge 'Turkey' carpets with extravagant designs such as 'verdures wrought with buildenges beastes and burdes' or 'conyes birdes and thre Garlondes with Skutcheons' were noted, as well as a smaller carpet from Boulogne with 'red Skutcheon' and two more green cloth carpets. An idea of the grandeur Surrey wanted for the main rooms of his house can be found in three chimney coverings, two of tapestry design; a pair of carved and gilt bellows; room curtains of yellow and purple sarcenet; and a purple velvet and satin canopy over his bed, embroidered with the Howard white lions of silver and passement lace fringe of gold and silver. Surrey House also had the housekeeping essentials that show, by proportion, the grand dimensions of the whole building: ten feather-beds with ten bolsters, four new Flanders bedsteads, and many quilts and blankets of materials ranging from red wool to white linen (of Spanish making) to purple and yellow soft silk to plain white and brown canvas. Indeed, Surrey's bedstead 'made for the warres with murrey clothe' and decorated with 'therle of Surrey his armes and garters' Gates had delivered to the new Duke of Somerset. All other items of furnishing were to be Gates', however, at least until his own beheading after Queen

[40] As for other noble estates, see Maurice Howard, *The Early Tudor Country House* (1989), 117; cf. 41, 45. Hengrave Hall in East Anglia was built just four years before Surrey started his place and contained a special courtyard plan and service court, the whole inlaid with manufactured yellow brick and stone dressings. Its cost was £3500. For Gates, see Starkey, *Reign*, 136, 157. In the following I have used primarily the inventories as given in PRO LR 2/116 for Surrey House and 115 for Kenninghall and in Nott, Appendices XXXIX to XLVII, where spellings are modernized.

Mary I's successful bid for the throne in 1553. No evidence of Surrey's treason was found, it should be noted, in any 'Skutcheon' or in any other decoration.

The remaining items of the 1547 inventory disclose the extraordinarily full life that once existed in Surrey House. At one end of the reification of that life, a religious picture, 'a table of the maundye of our lorde', that is, the representation of Christ washing his disciples' feet at the Last Supper (Holy Thursday in Easter week), shows the central cultural matrix at work; at the other, a 'Gyttorne' or gittern or cithern, a type of primitive guitar with a pear-shaped body, with a different range from the lute but used for some of the same social occasions. The presence of this musical instrument points towards the kind of social audience before which Surrey read or played and sang his own poems or heard them sung. Gates also listed two 'mases [maces]' of some authority, perhaps for governance in Norwich, one white and gilt and the other black and gilt, and a gilt 'pomel hiltes and chape' for Surrey's sword, with a pair of gilt spurs and an elegant saddle of purple velvet with broad passement lace of gold, the plate of the saddle also gilt. The earl also kept at Surrey House six other 'arming saddels with plates' and twenty-four 'partisanes' or long-shafted blades for fighting (and general protection). Following the item of the Maundy painting, two other paintings were listed: 'Item the lord of Surreys armes' and 'Item the lord of Surreys Pictour' (probably the Holbein portrait of 1541).

The more valuable furnishings, as well as clothes, jewels, and accoutrements belonging to Surrey (either from Surrey House or Kenninghall), went to his rival, Edward Seymour, by the time of the inventory the Duke of Somerset. The new Protector Somerset took, as expected, the magnificent state gown, Surrey's parliament robe of purple velvet with a sign of the Garter upon the shoulder (even though his title was by courtesy only, Surrey as the son of a Duke and cup-bearer to the king could attend the opening of Parliament). Seymour also took items possibly connected with the costume of Surrey's last portrait by Guillim Scrots (William Stretes): a black velvet cap set with pearls and goldsmith's work; a hat of crimson satin and crimson velvet with a white feather; two gilt rapiers with graven antique designs (such as the heads of Roman emperors); a gilt dagger with a sheath of black velvet. From Surrey's bedchamber, in addition to the bed, the Lord Protector took coverings of white satin, orange tawny velvet, and yellow satin, and several long and short cushions of satin and velvet. Having already received most of the Duke of Norfolk's jewellery and clothes, the new Somerset could afford to be generous with Surrey's other accoutrements. He required for himself only minor items like Surrey's scarf of crimson gold sarcenet; two pairs of knit hose; Surrey's knit small jacket or 'petycote'; a horse harness of black velvet with copper and gilt studs; a foot-cloth of black velvet fringed with Venice gold; another horse harness of crimson velvet fringed with Venice gold; two more of Surrey's daggers gilt and graven all over and 'appendaunte to two Girdelles'; two dozen arming points; and numerous pairs of gilded stirrups and spurs. Somerset did not need Surrey's insignia of the Garter as it would have duplicated his acquisition of Norfolk's resplendent collar of the Order of the Garter. Appearing in Surrey's last portrait, the poet's gold Garter collar, with its fifty-four knots and flowers, weighing thirty-six ounces, and with its pendant of St George with ten diamonds, passed instead to William Paulet, Lord St John, almost certainly acting on Henry VIII's behalf for the Crown, and accordingly it is listed among the king's possessions at his death and then transmitted to his son and successor late in 1547.[41] Several items taken by Somerset appear, in fact, to share a link with the actual painting of his last portrait: the new duke received twenty-one aglets, five buttons of gold, and a parcel of a gown of purple satin that he then delivered over to a 'Mr. Strete', presumably the painter of Surrey's seized portrait.

Surrey's Romantic editor Nott sees this collapse of the Howards in epic terms and gave the Latin from the *Aeneid* in which the murdering Pyrrhus breaks, in Surrey's translation, 'through the timber pierc'd' of the Trojan palace into the 'secret chamber eke / Of Priamus and ancient kings of Troy' to behead him and his son. The new Pyrrhus in the person of Sir John Gates did not need force of arms. He had the total power of the state. With that authority, he took the furnishings of Surrey House and evidently used his official position to buy them back on terms favourable to himself. Sir Richard Sackville and Sir Walter Mildmay signed the inventory of Surrey House at Westminster on 6 November 1551, when Dudley was at his zenith of power. As attested by these two Court of Augmentation officials, all these 'goodes and Catalles' of the late earl had by 1546 been mortgaged to John Spencer for the sum of £157.23s. Now in 1551 Spencer rightly demanded all the furnishings as his by law. Gates had another idea. Sir John will pay Spencer the mortaged price and no more: 'Whiche saide somme of moneye and everie peny therof sithence the deathe of the saide Erle hath ben Well and trulie contented and payde to the said John Spencer by our trustie and Welbeloved Counsaillour Sir John Gate knight vicechamberlain of our householde and Capitayn of our Garde,' and so 'the said Sir John Gate [had] received and had into his handes and possession of the said John Spencer the said goodes and Chattels . . . forasmuche as the said goodes and Chattels ar of litell better value then the saide somme of moneye payde by the saide Sir John Gate.' Sir John had a second even better idea: he 'hath forborn his said moneye by the space of foure yeares or theraboughtes.' Gates will hold off payment for four years until which time Spencer might dare to ask for his money or, as it did indeed turn out under a new regime, write the whole venture off as a total loss. So the young King Edward VI declares in the inventory with his signature: 'Knowe you therfore we of our certayn knowleadge and mere mocion to have given graunted and released and by these patentes do give graunte and release to the said Sir John Gate all the said

[41] BL Harleian MS 1419A, *Inventory of Henry VIII*, Item 2529, f. 170v: 'Item a coller of gold with knottes and flowers of the garter poids xxxvj oz di with a George in a shelde with x small Diamountes garnished poids ij oz quarter di which collor was the late Erle of Surreys containing liiij knottes and garters. / deliuered the xxijth of decembre anno primo Regis Edwardi vji to william Fitzwilliams esquyer for the kinges wearing as appereth by his bill.'

goodes and Chattels and all other right interest and possession in [Surrey House] to have and to holde . . . forever.' In this 'forever', Sir John got everything free.

But no one in the new regime could control the texts that had once issued from this house and the other Howard centres. If the genealogy of blood could be ended, the genealogy of poetry could not. By 1542 Surrey recognized his advantage in being able not only to reveal a new nobility in himself but to write poetic texts. With his immense wealth and prestige, he could also act as patron, in this case, the poet as patron. He would create audiences for Surrey House and the other Howard mansions, and in that creation add to the revolution in language already underway. His name and honour, his patronage, not least his own innovative poems and the actual space of their production, ironically an aristocrat's house high on a mount, would enfranchise poets and makers of English in the next centuries on all levels of society. This was a revolution as powerful as any in English culture and would last longer than any newly erected Pyrrhus.

6

The Audience at Surrey House: Lyrics and Lives

The creation of an audience at Surrey House or at any of the other Howard mansions took shape as the historical lives of the poet earl and his friends at court intertwined. By 1542, lyrics and lives as one had already begun to identify the Surrey world, particularly in the self-dramatized love story of Lady Margaret Douglas and Surrey's young uncle Thomas. Special circles of friends not only read and recited but sang (and in at least one case, danced) poetic texts. The nature of their turbulent worlds could only be understood, so they felt, in the symbolic and intertextual language of poetry, and this circle which sought such language for its own violent histories became increasingly concentric with Surrey himself, as three sets of evidence demonstrate.

The first is the fact of the circle itself. By 1541 Surrey had widened his circle from family and intimates like Richmond and Lady Margaret Douglas to include practising poets like Wyatt, Challoner, Blagge, the young Thomas Churchyard, and numerous other poets represented in Tottel's 1557 *Miscellany*. Scholars like Leland, Cheke, and Hadrianus Junius joined, however irregularly, Surrey's circle in addition to a host of devoted readers and courtier dilettantes, including readers in the 1540s from circles around Queen Catherine Parr and her religious humanists. The ease and speed with which the next generation of poets like Thomas Sackville turned to Surrey as a model—a fact that Tottel could canonize—indicates the breadth of these Henrician circles. But such a circle centring, one way or another, on Surrey soon attracted intellectuals like the literary secretary to the Duke of Norfolk, John Clerke, who wrote an early piece of literary criticism on Surrey and illustrates, argues Baldi, 'another trace, beside that which we have from Churchyard, of the literary awareness of the Earl of Surrey and of his desire to see his literary practice spread at least among his circle'. This desire meant, above all, that the noble lord and patron himself must, as both French and English kings had done before 1542, not only sing and recite but invent new poems. Surrey became lord, poet, and patron like Francis I. Surrey House could imitate Fontainebleau.

Surrey's 'desire' probably led to the most remarkable product of his audiences in the 1530s and 1540s, the creation of the so-called Devonshire Manuscript, the second set of evidence. Its 160 lyrics express primarily, as Boffey notes, 'love among courtiers expressed in a refined and formal way' but their texts were inserted informally like notes and signatures 'in an autograph album'. Three women appear to have dominated the compilation of these poems, each having a tragic love story and each intimately associated with the poet Earl of Surrey: his sister Mary Richmond, Lady Margaret Douglas, and Mary Shelton, 'who acted as a kind of overseer,' with her scrawl found throughout the whole text. In fact, Mary Shelton, with whom Surrey had a special relationship in his last years, used the manuscript, as its inscription reveals, in ways that indicate possible activities at Surrey House or any of the other Howard centres. 'She went through it,' comments Harrier, 'marking certain poems for copy, memorization, or musical performance' and using the script 'as an album of courtly games, verbal and musical.' The fact that the manuscript is for her less like a book and 'more like a sequence of letters' with 'piquant personal relevance' for a 'closely-knit group of readers and contributors' supports the argument that Surrey's audience 'lived' their texts and performed them as in live theatre or concert (Surrey's first cousin, Anne Boleyn, was known, for example, for singing poetic texts and accompanying herself on the lute).[1] Surrey himself alludes to such performances. Writing his paraphrase of Ecclesiastes, chapter 2, probably after his return in disgrace from France in 1546, Surrey transformed a single line from the Vulgate original into a specific gender statement: 'To hear fair women sing sometime I did rejoice; / Ravished with their pleasant tunes and sweetness of their voice' (21–2).

These performances provided one more crucial function for a practising poet. Such loving audiences could be like sounding-boards for poetic experimentation. The Devonshire Manuscript was clearly a poet's book, one in which readers could participate directly and even insert notes, in a sense rewriting the love lyrics. The generous presence of Wyatt in the text could only point to that member of the circle who loved and admired him most and who saw the radical innovation of his lyrics, Surrey himself. His 1542 elegy on Wyatt would become one of his greatest poems. For this reason, it was probably Surrey, not the Duke of Richmond (as Harrier suggests), who bought the original blank volume (the manuscript still has its first binding) in London in 1533 and gave it immediately to his sister in a happy period for all three, husband friend, brother, sister. The fact that no holograph text of Surrey or Wyatt exists in the manuscript indicates simply that the book only originated with Surrey. Into her brother's gift the duchess could put, in addition to

[1] Baldi, 'Secretary', 13. Julia Boffey, *Manuscripts of English Courtly Love Lyrics in the Later Middle Ages* (1985), 8–9. Harrier, *Canon*, 28–9. See also R. Southall, 'The Devonshire Manuscript Collection of Early Tudor Poetry, 1532–1541', *RES*, NS 15 (1964), 142–50, and *The Courtly Maker: An Essay on the Poetry of Wyatt and his Contemporaries* (1964), 15–25. Cf. A. K. Foxwell, *A Study of Sir Thomas Wyatt's Poetry* (1911), 125 ff. It is not probable that Surrey at 9 received the manuscript from Wyatt and later presented it to his sister and Lady Margaret Douglas and their circle. For perceptive analysis of both the provenance of the Devonshire Manuscript and the women in Surrey's audience, see Elizabeth Heale, 'Women and the Courtly Love Lyric: The Devonshire MS (BL Additional 17492)', *Modern Language Review*, 90/2 (1995), 296–313 and especially her *Wyatt, Surrey, and Early Tudor Poetry* (1998), ch. 2. Lerer notes (159): 'For Devonshire, the romance of reading is a family romance'. Note also his argument (145) that 'the logic of the Chaucerian centos does imply [for the formation of the Devonshire manuscript], if not a male hand, at least a male literary agency behind them'. This agency, whether his handwriting or not, originates, I am arguing, in Surrey himself. The idea for originating the manuscript was Surrey's and he watched over its development.

her own choices, the poems he suggested she would enjoy, his own favourites, increasingly the poems of Wyatt after 1537. In this sense the Devonshire Manuscript may be a record of the earl's own taste but was certainly not a correspondence with Wyatt (N1: 161, 251; 2: vii–ix, 590–1). Rather, it was to be a record shared with an audience in the transcribing hands of three women with whom he held special relationships. For that reason the earl did not use it as a volume for his own poems. His lyrics would have been accessible from himself, there in person and directing the tastes of his friends, acting as *incitateur* for the group as he had for Richmond. Wyatt would be the master for all of them, in Surrey's guidance, and Surrey need not write in a script that belonged to his audience, specifically the three women and then the others to whom they passed the book on for the next six decades (in one legend, Mary Queen of Scots brought the book back to England after her mother-in-law, Lady Margaret Douglas, had taken it to Scotland). The script thus held the symbolic record of all their existences, greater than any mere history. And the presiding force behind this poetic record, as behind the circles, could only have been the poet with his dual genealogy commanding all such reading or writing and providing, in his wealth, places for their performance.

Surrey was, in this sense of originating texts and then the literal places for their production (the equivalent of theatres), a model patron for the Tudor court. His identity as a master of humanist power, the making of a new language out of his special genealogies, meant that Surrey was fulfilling, on his own terms, his father's plans as suggested to Chapuys in 1529. He would embody another Roman role, a Maecenas patron, but with his own originating elegance as a poet like a Horace or even a Virgil (his own lyrics, as C. S. Lewis notes, giving a sense of theatre and 'intensity' new to the English lyric). Following his father's instinct for power, yet in ways the old man could not imagine, Surrey would thus invent and encourage a new type of English discourse in which poetic language could quickly become the basis for public expression and social sensibilities. Thus, the third set of evidence came for Surrey's audience in the 1557 publication of *Tottel's Miscellany*, the appearance of which was as revolutionary as that of the *Lyrical Ballads* in 1798. After it, English poetry and court and university discourse would never be the same. As in ancient Rome, the language of private aristocratic audiences soon became public discourse.[2]

'When raging love with extreme pain'

A lyric with the concerns of Surrey's audience takes its title from its first line, 'When raging love with extreme pain.' It epitomizes the young earl's translation of

[2] C. S. Lewis, *English Literature*, 230. For the uses of poetry for purposes of prose, see Barrington 1–10. For the key significance of Tottel, see Marotti, *Manuscript, Print* (1995) xv, 216–18, and for the crucial place of coterie audiences in the later Renaissance, see Marotti, *John Donne, Coterie Poet* (1983). For a discussion of Surrey's handwriting, see Jonathan Goldberg, *Writing Matter: From the Hands of the Renaissance* (1990), 235.

Petrarch as both song and history. Probably addressed (and dedicated) to Wyatt (the initial letters of its five stanzas spell out his name), the lyric, popular in the Elizabethan world, ends with a resolution and hope seldom found in Wyatt but suited to Surrey's conception of history. In this extended *frottola*, the Italian song form Giustiniani had requested from Venice in 1515 at English noblemen's request, Surrey experiments with the human voice. The whole Erasmian call for clarity (as Erasmus had argued, words were 'pronounced plainly' in St Paul's time) was not neglected in Surrey's humanist re-creation of the lyric. 'Lyric' itself was a term (perhaps unknown to Wyatt and Surrey) that the Italian humanists had developed from the Greek 'lyre' (to which they compared the lute) and a form that French poets in Paris and Fontainebleau had refined through linguistic experiment. Earlier Castiglione had stressed how the line between sonnets and songs could become blurred in a new simplicity. More's Hythloday had also found simplicity in Utopian music where 'the fassion of the melodye dothe so represente the meaning of the thing' and the technical making of the music 'dothe so resemble and expresse naturall affections.'[3]

The result of the experimentation of Wyatt and Surrey at places like Surrey House was that the language of song became more like the English spoken at the court of Henry VIII, like human conversation. In fact, with the musical emphasis as in France, moving from the old Burgundian melismatic polyphony to the new Italian syllabic homophony and the more classically conceived *monodia*, 'song could be,' as Stevens notes, 'merely a superior kind of ornamented speech, a more distinguished delivery, heightened recitation.'[4] This closer connection of the new continental syllabic song and English verse thus accounts for a major difference of performance in Surrey's audience from the earlier more rhetorical performances of older English court audiences such as Skelton's or Barclay's or Hawes'. 'When raging love' builds on such a theory of realistic representation. The lover exists in a conflicting moment of history he cannot escape. In fact, through objectified 'feeling'—the result of extraordinary technique—the reader joins a real (as opposed to a merely rhetorical) lover who speaks as she or he does. The technical control that establishes this level of probable intimacy in the reader is thus as revolutionary and different for the Tudor court as the argument of the song itself.

[3] *Four Years at the Court of Henry VIII*, trans. Rawdon Brown (1854), vol. 1, 81. If the *frottola* is understood as generic (and as a form requiring a musical text with it), over 50% of Surrey's poems may be considered *frottole* whose chief motif is love 'understood in a very definite sphere', so Alfred Einstein argues in *The Italian Madrigal* (1949), vol. 1, 34 ff. For the musical setting of Petrarch's *canzone* 'Si e debile il filo' that greatly influenced Surrey and Wyatt, see 104. For Erasmus, see P. A. Scholes, *The Puritans and Music* (1934), 216; for Castiglione, see 94, 104–5; for More, see *Utopia*, ed. Edward Surtz, SJ, and J. H. Hexter, in the Yale Edition, vol. 2, 182–3.

[4] John Stevens, *Music and Poetry in the Early Tudor Court* (1961), 215; see also 54, 29, 131, 30–1. For Sidney's use of song and audiences that performed his work at Wilton House, see Katherine Duncan-Jones, *Sir Philip Sidney, Courtier Poet* (1991), 139, 171–2.

When raging love with extreme pain
Most cruelly distrains my heart,
When that my tears, as floods of rain,
Bear witness of my woeful smart,
When sighs have wasted so my breath,
That I lie at the point of death,
  I call to mind the navy great
That the Greeks brought to Troy town;
And how the boisterous winds did beat
Their ships and rent their sails adown,
Till Agamemnon's daughter's blood
Appeased the gods that them withstood;
  And how that in those ten years' war
Full many a bloody deed was done,
And many a lord, that came full far,
There caught his bane, alas, too soon,
And many a good knight overrun,
Before the Greeks had Helen won.
  Then think I thus: since such repair,
So long time war of valiant men,
Was all to win a lady fair,
Shall I not learn to suffer then,
And think my life well spent to be
Serving worthier wight than she?
  Therefore I never will repent,
But pains contented still endure;
For like as when, rough winter spent,
The pleasant spring straight draweth in ure,
So after raging storms of care
Joyful at length may be my fare.

Surrey's first stanza reduces a whole erotic tradition of *petrarchismo* to a few clichés. They exist only to lead immediately to the first step of the poet earl's real subject, the lover in 'extreme pain' and 'at the point of death'. Although it may be assumed that the lover is male and the beloved female, nowhere is gender specified, nor is the beloved significant as a person, only as a producer of alienation. Once more, the tradition of a near-suicidal Petrarchan lover and his love complaint will be retextualized, as in the Windsor sonnet. In a far more extended inscription than in his other lyrics (or in Wyatt's), history and myth in 'When raging love' will build a true Renaissance self-fashioning, a system of *peripeteia* in which, as Davis notes, 'so vivid has been [Surrey's] sense of the past that it has changed his lament into a firm resolution.'[5] Once more, as with Surrey's elegy on Richmond, the crucial myth for defining subjectivity and eros is the originating myth of the classical world: the fall of 'Troye town' (with the Chaucerian double syllable).

[5] Walter R. Davis, 'Contexts in Surrey's Poetry', *English Literary Renaissance*, 4 (1974), 47.

That historical and cultural collapse is an analogy, in Surrey's musical text, for the contemporary and personal disaster of the lover. The earl's argument, based on this analogy—collapse of the erotic self and of history—leads to broad social statement, a native English voice, and, surprisingly, an ideology of work.

In 1589 Puttenham authorized the popularity of the poem as song (it had become the equivalent of a fashionable show-tune) by using Surrey's lyric three times in *The Arte of English Poesie* to illustrate the best practice in contemporary poetry. In a long section 'Of Proportion', 'this ditty of th'Erle of Surries,' as Puttenham noted, is 'passing sweete and harmonicall' in its rhythm, caesura, and diction, particularly its resolution.[6] Its urbanity and a popular final stance of harmonious resolution—Tottel even entitled the poem 'The louer comforteth himself with the worthinesse of his loue'—rises, however, from an ambiguous structure set in the first stanza. The Petrarchan lover is effectively reduced to the 'point of death' and an act of reflection: 'I call to mind' (a frequent Surrey gesture) a parallel death. This second death or disaster has two stages, both actualized in a woman, one with a name, the other without. In Surrey's favourite figure of *antonomasia*, the myth of the innocent Iphigenia is reduced to 'Agamemnon's daughter's blood' and, with this figuration, an incisive epigrammatic couplet ends the stanza and the first stage of historical disaster with the Anglo-Saxon verb 'withstood'.

The verb highlights a compositional technique throughout the poem. Surrey uses a rhythmic undercurrent of the native Anglo-Saxon line, also with four stresses, frequent (if varying) caesurae, and strong alliteration and assonance at crucial places ('Agamemnon's'/'Appeased'; the same guttural vowel sounds as Surrey heard them in 'daughter's'/'blood'/'gods'). Condensation and correlation of events in figures of *metonymy* (blood for murder and war itself) and *anaphora* (the opening repetition of 'And how' unites the two stanzas, chronological reduction in 'many a') are all compressed into parallel phrasal units. These brush-stroking techniques lead to the climax of the first part of the lyric. If Helen is the erotic cause of historical disaster, then the worst effect of all 'those ten years' war' is named just before Helen herself: 'many a good knight overrun.' The chivalric system itself is collapsing because of the failure of eros and history.

The poet earl prepares for this climax by placing Helen of Troy at the closure of a long syntactic sequence. The Ciceronian *hirmus*, the long periodic sentence,

[6] Three times in the 16th century 'When raging love' was registered for publication as a ballad, with three other registrations of it as moralization, imitation, and parody ('When raging louts, with feble braines'). In a popular miscellany of 1584, *A Handful of Pleasant Delights*, a piece 'The complaint of a woman Louer' had in its margins 'To the tune of, Raging loue.' For Puttenham's analysis, see *The Art of English Poesie*, 132 but also xlv, 72, 123. Puttenham even contrasts Surrey's iambics with the trochaics of Wyatt whose 'wordes do best shape to that foote by their naturall accent'. 'With raging love' thus confirmed the public Surrey, Alexander Pope's 'noble Surrey', who 'felt the sacred rage' in his harmonious lines ('Windsor Forest', 291). Over 400 years after Surrey, critics could still find the art in this poem never pretending 'to more feeling than the occasion deserves' and its diction 'occasional, classical, and urbane' with 'nothing comparable until Ben Jonson' as in Maurice Evans, *English Poetry in the Sixteenth Century* (1967), 81–2.

moves to Helen, as a bold visual line is carried across a fresco at Fontainebleau. Surrey turns the sentence's introductory subordinate clause and then an independent clause into further subordination. The grammar thus dramatizes the inverting act of reflection in the main subject and verb. Two larger structures further textualize Surrey's theatre of eros and history. The *hirmus* of the first three stanzas provides the equivalent of a sonnet octet where the act of locating eros in history leads to the Petrarchan *volta* or turn. Then the sestet of the last two stanzas moves through two stages, each introduced by conjunctive adverbs: 'Then think I thus' and 'Therefore I never will repent.' These stages operate as two complete sentences with their own subordination. Yet here the sonnet frame that drives the reductive wit and concentrated music of the whole is itself subsumed by the second predominant structure of the whole poem: its syllogistic logic.

Thus, Surrey's major premise identifies the death that always rises from Petrarchan eros, the lover *in extremis*. The minor premise identifies such 'raging love' with the raging war for Helen. As a result, the point of the *volta* of the whole poem turns on a logical category or topic of comparison implicit from the start. Similitude or *homoeosis* frames the question that is the conclusion: 'Shall I not learn to suffer then, / And think my life well spent to be / Serving worthier wight than she?' The *hyperbole* (exaggeration) in the poem rises from the logical comparison of situational personal eros, the non-gendered 'worthier wight' (hardly a Petrarchan Laura!), to that of the greater historical eros causing the Trojan War (Helen). Thus, the conclusion to the syllogism comes with the two-phased question and answer signalled by conjunctive adverbs: 'Then think I thus' and 'Therefore I never will.' Through schoolroom grammar (and Surrey's mastery of it), the lover (or reader) now has the logic of history. Moreover, the lover/reader has received it in the universal form of the Aristotelian syllogism. One's own personal erotic disaster can be reinscribed as a larger cultural disaster, a failure of social eros. As in all rituals, so in the language of this poem: the specific has become universal.

Moreover, the language of the lyric has been concise. It builds on the psychological realism that in *Troilus* had freed the English narrative from medieval allegorizing, appealing to both Wyatt and Surrey. Conversation defines the poetic mode, not large symbolic frames or even grand discourses like Chaucer's Knight's. A new kind of succinct dramatic speech has entered the language, and only the focused dialectic of a realized self in history could render the harmony of song, subjectivity rising out of Surrey's precise musical control. In this new kind of drama of self, located in such metamorphosis and dislocation of time as Tudor England had revealed, learning how to survive meant the realizing in the self of work or labour—a dialectic between subjective eros and progressing history. Under the exigency of time—the Virgilian motto of 'Tempus praeterit' popular in the Renaissance—this labour had to be reductive and without delay. It also had to be collective to save time, waking up, as Aeneas does in Virgil's epic, from sleep and passivity to work, in Marcuse's image, within the terror of one's own cave. If the breakdown of community had first surrounded the 'raging' lover, then the labour of building the future community dominates the closure. The 'fare'—the last word of the text—or journey continues only after the lyric's rendered choice to act in history. In that journey through brief time, so argues the poem, neither death nor eros can be escaped. The dead girl—'Agamemnon's daughter'—represents the lover's own potential murder (or suicide) and exists even in the closure, in natural imagery of a 'pleasant spring' after 'rough winter spent' and even on a 'joyful. . . fare'. Any lover's Aeneas pilgrimage must be conditional, set by the last verb 'may be'. Even the final figure of *chiasmus* describing the natural seasons ('rough . . . spent'/'pleasant . . . ure [use]') and the entire rhyme scheme of the final stanza textualize the conditional dialectic of an ongoing history. Rage moves into action: 'repent' into 'spent'; 'endure' into 'ure'; and 'care' into 'fare' or the dangerous journey ahead.[7]

'Courtyers in princes and noblemens house'

A revolution took place in early Tudor England in the residences of nobility of the blood, one inspired by Petrarch but soon marked throughout the whole of society by new types of individuality, difference, even alienation of person. Indeed, in the early 1540s, Roger Ascham idealized as the 'home of the Muses' the London house of Charles Blount, the fifth Lord Mountjoy, Surrey's friend and a son of Erasmus' close friend. Blount himself may have visited Mount Surrey as well, and it has been conjectured that his house and certain great Tudor houses like Surrey's performed as the academies had in Italy and France, in their display of music, painting, and poetry, as centres for a new civilization. In these English academies, circles of aristocrats came in from the turmoil of the outside world to gather around the family 'minstrels' or musicians or to play themselves the cittern or clavichord (a generic term for instruments like the virginals) or lute (Richmond's favourite instrument), or possibly the recorder or the organ (John Howard's household books record the presence of two), or occasionally the harp or even more occasionally the sackbut or shawm. In these same years, in fact, specific compositions of music for solo voice and instrument were beginning to grow in

[7] For the influence of *Troilus*, see Thomson, *Wyatt* 154. Herbert Marcuse, *Eros and Civilization: A Philosophical Inquiry into Freud* (1966), ch. 4, and *Negations: Essays in Critical Theory*, tr. Jeremy J. Shapiro (1968), 257, 253. For an analysis of how Nashe's Surrey has a deep 'understanding of Surrey's censored meaning' and so reveals an eroticism that 'when desublimated and made self-conscious, promises to redeem' poetic language 'from its destructive antagonism and negativity' and so creates a public Surrey out of self-consciousness, 'full of freedom, magnanimity and bountihood' (287), see Jonathan Crewe, *Unredeemed Rhetoric: Thomas Nashe and the Scandal of Authorship* (1982), 84. Also, the closure in this poem rewrites even Virgil, the source in Surrey's poem for all its other subtexts, Petrarchan, Augustinian, and Chaucerian. Surrey's line 'But pains contented still endure' echoes Aeneas' advice to his men (1, 207) after Juno's raging storm has driven them to the coast of Carthage: 'Endure,' says Aeneas, 'and keep yourself for better days!'

England. In such a world, 'With raging love' was probably recited or sung (or even danced) by audiences themselves in either the long hall on the second floor of the 1542 Kenninghall overlooking the front court, or in the large chamber at the front of the Howard mansion at Lambeth looking towards the Thames and also looking back down formal gardens in 1545 to a deep rural vista, or in the front hall of Surrey House overlooking the cathedral spire and the sweep of Norwich and the River Wensum, and the majestic East Anglian sky. Although the exact nature of such courtly entertainment can never be ascertained, in 1549 there was a response that could not be missed. 'Would God,' said a reformed Christian writer at the time of Edward VI, 'that suche songes [as Solomon's] myght once drive out of office the baudy balades of lecherous love that commonly are indited and song [sung] of idle courtyers in princes and noblemens houses.'[8]

A letter from a marginal figure in the Howard circle shows the kind of courtier such a poem as 'When raging love' may have reached. It also reveals the extent of the friendship in the Howard circles amid war and violence. From the war front in northern France, 'towards Flanders', in September of 1543, Sir Ralph Vane wrote to Sir Henry Knyvet. After noting that 'half the Emperor's force will invade France by Arras, and the rest join us here,' Vane added a postscript, repeating in it a persistent motif from Surrey's work of the 'mens quieta' (developed in Wyatt's 1529 translation of Plutarch and perhaps a code term in the circle). The young Vane himself would need this 'quiet mind' in the years ahead. After distinguishing himself at Boulogne in 1544, where he was knighted by Henry VIII, and in Scotland, where he was made a knight banneret in 1547 by the new Duke of Somerset, he was falsely accused of conspiring to kill Dudley and was hanged on Tower Hill in 1552, his estate of Penshurst (originally owned by Surrey's grandfather Buckingham) given to Dudley's brother-in-law Sidney, for whose son Robert (brother to Philip) Ben Jonson wrote his famous eulogy of the estate. All the rest of Vane's considerable wealth was given by Dudley to the brother-in-law of Denny, Sir John Gates. 'Commend me,' wrote Vane in his 1543 postscript, 'to Mr. Barklay, Mr. Philip Hoby, and Mr. George Blage, otherwise called Tom Trubbe.' The first of the three young men was Surrey's cousin, and the second was in the circle of Queen Catherine Parr and a supporter of Anne Askew and probably an admirer of Surrey's religious paraphrases (Hoby's brother was the first translator in English of Castiglione). Blagge was Wyatt's close friend who would be used to betray him and is here called Tom Thumb because of his square shape (to Henry VIII, who found him great company, he was the 'pig'). Blagge also preserved poems from this circle and from Surrey, who dedicated one of his last

[8] Sir Roger Ascham, *The Whole Works*, ed. Dr Giles (1865), 19, 20; Leland, *Collectanea*, ed. Thomas Hearn (1770), vol. 5, 109; for the provenance of the personal manuscript BL Harleian 78, see Charles W. Eckert, 'The Poetry of Henry Howard, Earl of Surrey' unpublished Ph.D. dissertation (Washington University, 1960) 83–4. Cf. *The Renaissance: From the 1470s to the End of the Sixteenth Century* (1989), 41. For the musical background, Stevens, *Music and Poetry*, 102, 118–19, 301, 278, 280. For the attack, see William Baldwin, *The Canticles or Balades of Salomon phraselyke declared in Englysh Metres* (1549).

poems in the Tower to him. Then to this first postscript Vane added: 'I wish honour, long life, and quiet minds unto my lady Margaret's [Douglas] grace, and my lady Richemont, and no less to my lord of Surrey.'[9]

Evidence of Surrey's audience may also be seen in the textual history of a lyric. In Poulter's Measure (alternating twelve- and fourteen-syllable lines) 'Such wayward ways hath love that most part in discord' was probably written around 1540 under the direct influence of Wyatt, who had in fact, invented, Poulter's Measure for two poems of his own, one 'In Spayne' as meditative as 'Such wayward ways'. Surrey's lyric appears in the Blagge manuscript and is, in fact, initialed 'H S', that is, Henry Surrey, the poet's official signature. Copied into Blagge's text by Sir John Harington, the poem shows what may have been editing by Surrey himself (AH 2: 93–5). In this popular text, Surrey may also have been responding to Wyatt's attempt to translate a long poem of Petrarch's into English. In any case, for the last 35 of the 50 lines of the long lyric, Surrey makes his own translation of Petrarch's disquisition on the severity of the Love god's law in *Trionfo d'Amore*. The earl's grand opening maxim carries a generalization popular with Tudor audiences, the almost neoclassical epigram with heavy medial caesura showing the ballad base of the line: 'Such wayward ways hath love that most part in discord; / Our wills do stand whereby our hearts but seldom do accord.' In this long conversational poem, more experimental in its music than others, the initial pessimism never changes. Eros has finally given a condition of alienation from which there is no release. Surrey's closure, however, summarizes more than the Petrarchan lover's alienation: 'The slipper state I know, those sudden turns from wealth, / That doubtful hope, that certain woe, and sure despair of health.'

By the 1540s, what could no longer be in doubt was that these audiences and their production of texts extended the poet earl's unique style as courtier, whatever 'the slipper state' of Tudor England. Neither a Seymour nor a Dudley, much less a Paget, not even the king, could produce such originating art in 1542. In fact, Surrey could dominate in his Norwich world without the tensions and interference of the royal court, and in this respect of stylish lordship, Surrey House was known to house stylish guests and foreigners. At the earl's trial his cousin Edmund Knevet accused him, in fact, of this. As the brother-in-law of Mary Shelton, Knyvet may have known Surrey House and Kenninghall and their audiences; he accused his first cousin of keeping 'one Pasquil an Italian as a jester but more likely as a spy' and of entertaining 'one Peregrine an Italian', and 'adding that he [Surrey] lov'd to converse with strangers, and to conform his behaviour to them' (HB 739). Surrey's quarrelsome cousin may appear xenophobic and too much the reformed Christian, but at the other end of the political spectrum, the Imperial Ambassador Chapuys not only accused Surrey in these years of having modern Lutheran tendencies ('strongly infected') but exhibiting French manners and way of life ('French in his living').[10]

[9] *LP*, vol. 18, ii, 190. On the Blagge manuscript, with its texts (including one to the former Queen Catherine), see Harrier, *Canon*, 55–75.

[10] *CSPSpan*, vol. 6, ii, 127.

The Surrey presiding over all these events can be seen in both the 1541 Holbein portrait and the last portrait by Scrots (Plates IV, VI). But Surrey as poet can best be viewed in a drawing by either Holbein or his school from this period (Plate 10). In this most informal of the earl's portraits, a figure of alienation and sensitivity, even melancholy, looks out from Holbein's pink paper. In this portrait of the artist as a vigorous informal young man, Surrey appears as the poet-hero-artist who will predominate in the centuries ahead. The new temperament is focused in his eyes, unusually alert, even though the face is turned sharply to the left to hide the wandering right eye. The poet's lips are pursed, held tight, as if in anticipation or listening, adding even more intimacy to his look. With the sharp lines of the sketched nose, the ragged red hairs over his upper lip, and his slight beard beneath a recessive chin emphasizing informality, the naked ear has been worked over several times, probably to give directness of feature. The unfinished sketch of an elegant Italian cloth cap, with fashionable curves and a circular brim, repeats this looseness in the jaunty angle of the cap perched at the top of his small head. If the artist wanted to show a young courtier without any power poses or signs of rank, a figure whose strength and honour lay only in that riveting gaze and turn of head, he succeeded.

'The sun hath twice brought forth the tender green'

A lyric that has the tone of musical intimacy typical of Tudor house poetry was 'The sun hath twice brought forth the tender green' which opens *Tottel's Miscellany*, its editor in 1557 identifying all the Howard grandeur and Marian nostalgia with such a poem (and, of course, with Tottel's own book). Neither specifically male nor even gendered, the alienated lover in this most developed of Surrey's variants on both Petrarch and Troilus gives a succinct introspective music never heard before in England.

> The sun hath twice brought forth the tender green,
>   And clad the earth in lively lustiness;
>   Once have the winds the trees despoiled clean,
> And now again begins their cruelness,
>   Since I have hid under my breast the harm
>   That never shall recover healthfulness.

The first lines set the cyclical landscape of spring. Surrey echoes the opening of the last book of *Troilus* and adds what may have been his translated lines from Boccaccio's epistle 'Ad Pinum' or 'Pino de Rossi' (a translation by Surrey listed by Bale but evidently lost). Figures of *merismus* (the whole distributed into parts) and *amplificatio* in the first line set up the argument in a demonstrative oration that develops paradoxically more social isolation: 'So doth each place my comfort clean refuse.' Because a section of this poem directly imitates Petrarch's *Trionfi d'Amore*, the whole poem is the first English *capitolo* of love, the *terza rima* rhyme scheme *ababcbcdc*, etc. out of Dante, then Petrarch and Chaucer ('A Complaint to His Lady'), then Alamanni and Wyatt in the Renaissance for their satires. With that genealogy, Surrey's *capitolo* sets up a dramatic monologue that reflects contemporary Italian musical forms. Set in the epistolary tradition, the *capitolo* is more aristocratic than the *frottola* and was associated on the continent with the pathetic song or dramatic Virgilian eclogue. Its spoken Petrarchan language had become the intense song Surrey and Richmond may have heard performed in Paris and Fontainebleau. Francis I wrote in both the *capitolo* and the *frottola* forms.

But Surrey's real subject in the poem is mutability, the dissolution of all things in time. This subject transforms the form and shows the result of the continuous repression of one's subjectivity as Renaissance medicine detailed such a result: a literal heart disease brought on by melancholy at such suppression. Social repression thus leads to Surrey's real subject. The alienated lover speaks to himself in the midst of his own dissolution: 'Yet time my harm increaseth more and more, / And seems to have my cure always in scorn' and so it is 'Strange kind of death in life that I do try.' Surrey then describes this new death-in-life as an actual journey, a pilgrimage altogether subjective, as Jones notes, and not through an allegorical but a realistic and psychological landscape.[11] In fact, Surrey revalues the older erotic landscape. His is the confessional Augustinian landscape of total subjectivity—'my mind'—that originally served both Dante and Petrarch: 'And with my mind I measure pace by pace / To seek that place where I myself had lost' and to search for 'That day that I was tangled in that lace, / In seeming slack that knitteth ever most.' For this condition of being trapped by history, Surrey introduces an inherited image for the *Aeneid*. He probably identifies his male speaker/lover with Dido and her 'venom'd shaft' of love, a figuration for which Surrey gave the classic English Renaissance statement in his translation of Virgil's epic:

Unhappy Dido burns, and in her rage
Throughout the town she wandereth up and down,
Like to the stricken hind with shaft, in Crete
Throughout the woods which chasing with his darts
Aloof, the shepherd smiteth at un'wares
And leaves unwist in her the thirling head,
That through the groves and lands glides in her flight;
Amid whose side the mortal arrow sticks.

Like the bold colouring in a Fontainebleau fresco, Surrey's carefully modulated anguish reveals the lover's dilemma, most succinctly rendered in another of Virgil's lines: 'Improbe amor, quid non mortalia pectora cogis?' (4: 412) and translated by Surrey in a rare heroic couplet: 'O witless love, what thing is that to do / A mortal mind thou canst not force thereto!' Thus the lover's struggle, as

[11] Emrys Jones, *Surrey*, 111.

revealed in Surrey's genealogical image of Dido and a deer, leads to another level of interpretation: 'And if I flee, I carry with me still / The venomed shaft, which doth his [its] force restore / By haste of flight.'[12] The indeterminacy of history, like a 'shaft', can never be escaped. The more the lover tries to run away, the sooner it overwhelms the Dido self.

Surrey's Laura

There was one member of Surrey's audience who was probably quite marginal in the 1540s circle but became, through a paradox of English literary and cultural history, its central figure. Lady Elizabeth Fitzgerald was a young woman of 14 or 15 when she figured in two poems by Surrey (and perhaps two others). She became Surrey's Geraldine (she was the daughter of the attainted and dead Earl of Kildare, Gerald Fitzgerald). Cultural and literary myth made her Surrey's equivalent of Petrarch's Laura, lasting in that figuration for 400 years. Although Surrey's greatest translation of Petrarch was his Anglicizing of a figure of alienation, from the beginning his admirers insisted on a figuration of Petrarch's Laura in the poet earl's life. From Thomas Sackville in the 1560s on, both poets and critics insisted on the equivalence of a love figure for their native Petrarch (as they never insisted on for Wyatt).

Why? The answer probably lay in the initial power of the Windsor poems, where a beloved *was* named, and then in the mysterious melancholy and suffering in the later love poems, where only Geraldine is named (but in poems of no melancholy). Of course, the overwhelming irony lay in the fact that the most idealized beloved in Surrey's texts was the least socially acceptable for the English Renaissance. The young Duke of Richmond does fulfil the conditions of the Petrarchan archetype—at least as, two centuries before, the Italian poet had invented a woman whose death and unattainability authorized a moment of transformation for Europe. Yet, in Early Modern England, as Petrarchan lover, Henry Fitzroy lacked, among other things, the glamour of adultery required for courtly love. He also posed a graver transgression, not so much because this lover expressed the homosocial (even homoerotic) world of male friendship, but because he represented the

[12] Among many uses of Surrey's image in the Renaissance, Hamlet's song (taken from a song in *Tottel's Miscellany*) turns 'the stricken deer' image to mark the collapse of the Danish court. For his closure, Surrey transcribes lines from a Petrarchan ballad by Sir Thomas More he obviously knew well (N1, 240). Although the lover may complain 'my fill / Unto myself, unless this careful song / Print in your heart some parcel of my will,' the language of self is not enough: 'For I, alas, in silence all too long, / Of mine old hurt yet feel the wound but green.' The poem thus recycles one of Surrey's motifs: the limits of language. Can *anything* express the speaker's terrible alienation—the evergreen 'wound'—from society, history, and even self? Thus, the need for community and for an audience in which the limits of language can be endured together, Wyatt's solution in his lyric to Surrey, as discussed in ch. 9.

bad taste of spiritual transcendence other than through the Tudor God or the idealized monarch. In the Tudor world, even transcendence through a female had its problems, as revealed in the representations and responses to Surrey's cousin Elizabeth I and the Petrarchan sequences of Sidney, Spenser, and Shakespeare (a transcendence finally impossible for Elizabeth Drury in John Donne's 1612 *Anniversary* poems).

But, in fact, such transcendence of love is never paramount in Surrey. Rather, with more historical estrangement than Wyatt, Surrey textualizes anew Petrarch's alienated lover as in *Sparse rime 129*, who sits down, like a dead stone on the living rock of himself, 'in guisa d'uom che pensi et pianga et scriva' ('in the guise of a man who thinks and weeps and writes'). And this emphasis on the active self, not the beloved, an Elizabethan maker of the Surrey cult saw at once. In Thomas Nashe's 1594 *Unfortunate Traveller*, the cunning lower-class Jack Wilton immediately spots ambiguity when he hears his honoured master Surrey woo the morally obtuse Diamante as though she were Geraldine. 'I persuade myself,' Jack says cynically, 'he was more in love with his own curious-forming fancy than her face; and truth it is, many become passionate lovers only to win praise to their wits' so that 'who loveth resolutely will include everything under the name of his love' (307).

By Nashe and the 1590s, the early Tudor period had become a seed-bed of transference for the later English Renaissance. Surrey's life could and did actualize a *passio* greater than Petrarch's, a martyrdom for dreams of honour and nobility, all glowing with the erotic. Such dreams (especially held by the new rich, the bourgeois, and the Jack Wiltons of England) could not include actual love, either homoerotic or marital (especially not the happily married). That would contradict the communal and commercial dreams. What was demanded was not just correct political statements but the new social transcendence refigured in Petrarchan texts everywhere pouring forth after the 1557 *Tottel's Miscellany*, the turning-point in English Petrarchism. That text had become, through the sleight of hand of the title-page, Surrey's. In the *Miscellany*, the old *passio* of a Petrarchan lover, alienated through love of a woman, transformed Surrey's actual historical image, unspoken but ever-present: the betrayed earl annihilated by the Tudor state and by a monarch—Henry VIII—increasingly disliked in the English Renaissance. In the acceptable narrative of a male lover rejected by an inaccessible female beloved, the mirror-world, the mythic transference based on the power of Surrey's language, could begin. Geraldine was the fitting abstraction for the *passio* of Surrey.[13] Popular culture thus demanded and received the universal narrative of Surrey's Laura that was to last for almost 400 years as a rather strange Anglo-Saxon ideal.

[13] For this process of *passio* building, see Peter Brown, *The Cult of the Saints: Its Rise and Function in Latin Christianity* (1982), esp. ch. 2 and 5. For the Petrarchan figuration, contrast Surrey's solipsistic more Hamlet-like figure with the more socialized and less historically conscious melancholy figure in, for example, Charles of Orléans' texts or those in highly ritualized traditions from the *Romance of the Rose* or even in contemporary early Tudor *Court of Love* texts as in Stevens, *Music and Poetry*, 180–1, 190–1.

The Legend of Geraldine

With true hagiographical vigour, the mid-century transfer of historical fact into myth worked. In this age of John Foxe, revision of old editions and new historians like Holinshed controlled the public imagination. The myth of Surrey soon originated a workable love narrative and a new personality, Geraldine. Surrey's Laura—the true one for most subsequent readers—was born, although from the beginning the actual texts, if they were read at all, showed cracks in the myth. They appeared primarily as underlying fantasies, usually of sex. Quite naturally, in this determined cultural will to Geraldinize reality, the character of the dead Surrey himself was swept up into greater sexuality. If sexual ideologizing could bring appropriate closure to the legend of Surrey and transmute him into a hope (and money-maker) of transcendence for countless generations, then raw sexuality is exactly what Nashe had in mind in 1594. Eroticism identifies Nashe's best-selling setting for the legend of Geraldine in *The Unfortunate Traveller*, conveniently written just after the 1590 death of the real Geraldine, Elizabeth Clinton, the powerful Countess of Lincoln.

Hagiography as sex had been implicit from the first edition of Surrey's poems. Richard Tottel had given titles to the original texts that 'explained' them in terms of a prevailing love ideology: thus the opening Petrarchan *capitolo*, 'The sun hath twice', has the title, 'Descripcion of the restlesse state of a louer, with sute to his ladie, to rue on his dying hart'; for the sonnet 'Love that liveth and reigneth', the title 'Complaint of a louer rebuked'; for the sonnet 'Alas, all things', the title 'A complaint by night of the louer not beloued'; and for the famous originating sonnet about Geraldine, 'From Tuscany came my lady's worthy race,' a title pedantic if prophetic 'Description and praise of his loue Geraldine.' These titles signal for Marotti 'the recording of social verse as primarily *literary* texts in the print medium' and so abstracted all the more the legend and hagiography. Here was a literary subject that would sell.[14] Within six years, Thomas Sackville, whose *Gorbuduc*, written with the Calvinist Norton, would transform Surrey's blank verse into a medium for theatre, characterized Surrey in such a Petrarchan mode. Sackville praised Surrey not only as a cultural hero and a proud poet but as an alienated lover. Writing verses on the difficulty of any poet, whether Virgil, Chaucer, Wyatt, or Surrey, the youthful Sackville (to become the powerful Earl of Dorset in James I's Privy Council) described his pain in expressing the 'houge dolours' of Richard III's victim, Surrey's great-grandfather Buckingham, Sackville's subject in *The Mirror for Magistrates*. Cataloguing language-makers, Sackville gave the first full literary inscription of the poet Earl of Surrey. He prefigured the cult for the rest of the Renaissance by taking the three directions by

[14] *Tottel's Miscellany (1557–1587)*, ed. Hyder Edward Rollins (1929–30) 1:3,8,9, hereafter in text. Marotti, *Manuscript, Print*, 218. For this process of 'desemiotization' see Maria Corti, *An Introduction to Literary Semiotics*, trans. Margherita Bogat and Allen Mandelbaum (1978), 19.

which Surrey will be known for the next centuries: noble earl, noble poet, and noble suffering lover.

> Not surrea he that hiest sittes in chair
> of glistering fame for ay to live and raighn
> not his proud ryme that thunders in the aier
> nor al the plaintes wherin he wrote his pain
> when he lay fetterd in the fyry chain
> of cruell love. they cold no whit suffyse
> tepresse thes plaints in ful suffys my wyse[15]

When in the next decade Sir Richard Stanyhurst actually located Surrey's Geraldine texts within Ireland (repeated in Holinshed), the legend was reified. After 1590 and the death of the real Geraldine, Nashe could thus turn a historical *fait accompli* with its seeds for textualized sexuality into a best-seller based on both betrayed and sexually attractive nobility (with hints of support for Essex and his coterie—Nashe dedicated his romance of the heroic Surrey to the Earl of Southampton). In fact, to reify his narrative, Nashe radicalized Surrey's own love lyrics by writing his own. Because no text of Surrey could be found erotic enough for an Elizabethan narrative about archetypes from the time of Henry VIII, Nashe invented his own and called them Surrey's.

This cultic confusion of real and invented Surrey mesmerized later generations of readers. The erotic poet earl in Nashe's work allowed such readers to Geraldinize history in context with Surrey's dramatized personal extravagance and violence, Nashe's aristocrat with the freedoms many middle-class readers so desperately desired. Each reader could become, in fact, an aristocratic Surrey and enjoy freely sexual violence, if nothing else. Because the distance of a golden age framed the myth of the grand poet earl, readers could participate in Surrey's supposed wild adventures, his erotic texts and actual political defiance, and yet keep the Geraldine female immaculate. Thus, in Nashe's invented Surrey sonnet, Geraldine does all the work of sex: she will 'suck out' the lover's soul, her breasts acting as 'crystal balls' that will 'embalm' the lover's breath, which Geraldine is to 'dole all out in sighs when I [Surrey] am laid.'[16] Although this sexual violence is usually discounted as Nashe's brilliant parody of excessive Petrarchanism, and

[15] *The Mirror for Magistrates*, ed. Lily B. Campbell (1938), 545.

[16] As in such fantasies where the male dreams of being raped rather than raping, the aggressive Geraldine will 'clasp' her lips on his with the suction of 'cupping-glasses'. Their 'tongues' will 'meet and strive as they would sting'. Nashe's Surrey commands his Geraldine further to 'Crush out my wind with one straight girting grasp,' and then, completing the octet, Nashe describes the male stroking in intercourse as Geraldine's. Nashe's male lover joyously receives these violent strokes: 'Stabs on my heart keep time whilst thou dost sing.' The sestet of Nashe's invented sonnet heightens Surrey's violent seduction as Geraldine's eyes 'like searing irons burn out mine' and in delight he begs: 'In thy fair tresses stifle me outright' and even 'Like Circe's, change me to a loathsome swine.' And what is the purpose of all this violent taking and transformation? 'So I may live for ever in thy sight,' says Nashe's Surrey in an orgasm of transcendence, in the beatific vision of Geraldine. She alone can admit a lover to such transfiguration of the body, as the ending epigrammatic couplet shows: 'Into heaven's joys none can profoundly see, / Except that first they meditate on thee' (307–8). This was written in the

therefore not to be taken seriously, it cannot be so easily dismissed in a narrative where Nashe lovingly details his figures of idealism, precisely Surrey, and explicitly never parodies Surrey. From the beginning of his textualization of Surrey, Nashe has made Henry Howard both the poet *par excellence* and the essence of honour and nobility: 'Jesu, I was persuaded I should not be more glad to see heaven than I was to see him. . . a prince in content because a poet without peer' (286–7).

Given the bold dialectic of Nashe's piece, it was perhaps inevitable that later audiences seized on the obvious. They felt comfortable with the idealism but still savoured the latent sexuality that revealed the energy of a male drive towards consummation as transcendence, particularly in Nashe's made-up sonnet passing as Surrey's. At least on one level, the suppressed pornographic dialectic energized the Geraldine legend.[17] A few years after the last major gasp of the Surrey legend—the noble eroticism of Sir Walter Scott rendered in poetic imagery Keats borrowed for his 'Eve of St Agnes'—George Frederick Nott brought out his definitive edition of Surrey. For that edition, although not officially accepting the Nashe or Scott fictions, Nott took the sexual ideology of Geraldine into a purer story form than any other. Following Tottel, he entitled Surrey poems as stages in an elaborate love narrative, a kind of hagiographic novel. This text sealed Surrey's modern reputation. Indeed, the technical brilliance of Nott's research and commentary appeared to depend on this urge to tell the 'truth' about Surrey. This mode of legend-making continued, if less obviously, in the early twentieth-century editing of Surrey's poems by Padelford. The fictionalizing of episodes in Surrey's life has continued, in fact, in all modern biographies, even in the criticism of the best editors, and has led obversely, of course, to deconstructive texts. By the time of

same decade as Donne began his *Elegies*. Nashe's other two texts that he wrote as Surrey's keep the same dichotomy of utter ecstasy at both ends of body and soul, but in a more subdued manner (and it is no surprise that these poems are included in *England's Parnassus* whereas this sonnet is not).

[17] When a few years later Drayton misreads Nashe and the original Surrey, repressing the prosaic base and alienation but reifying the Geraldine story, he localizes the legend at Windsor Castle in detailed 'heroicall' verse epistles. He gives it, in short, a cult history. Drayton's prose preface even literalizes Nashe's fiction as short chivalric biography, the kind of Essex figure that the new Stuart king would admire. Lord Herbert of Cherbury could later represent the friendship of the two Henrys to Stuart cavaliers and to the world of Lady Margaret Douglas' doomed Stuart offspring like Prince Rupert (taken from his battlefield martyrdom in the English Revolution and buried inside the Westminster Abbey tomb of his great-grandmother Mary because of her 'saintly' defiant acts and the radiating relic of her body). In the Restoration, citing Drayton with nostalgia, Winstanley's *Lives* authorizes the Geraldine legend for the time of the Glorious Revolution, going well beyond the brief mention of Wyatt and Surrey by Milton's nephew Phillips, and from his *Lives* of honoured poets, Surrey's golden legend mushrooms in the neoclassical world. From texts like *Athenae Oxoniensis* to Colly Cibber's *Lives of the Poets* to Alexander Pope's canonization of Surrey ('Matchless his pen, victorious his lance / Bold in the lists, and graceful in the dance)' and Geraldine ('bright object of his vow'), the legend builds to Horace Walpole's succinct definition in his reverential analysis of Surrey: 'In imitation of Laura, our Earl had his Geraldine.' By the time of Sir Walter Scott's 1805 *Lay of the Last Minstrel*, life and texts are completely blurred (as Surrey's life in *Collin's Peerage* printed at this time also shows), and Scott's pre-Keatsian transcription lasted well into the early twentieth century in the popular imagination: 'Who has not heard of Surrey's fame? / His was the hero's soul of fire, / And the bard's immortal name, / And his was love, exalted high / By all the glow of chivalry.'

Bapst, Geraldine was thought to be a girl of 10 in 1537, a date arbitrarily set by Bapst for Surrey's famous sonnet to her, so Surrey was mocked by detractors as a paedophile. To debunk this debunking, Hughey demonstrated the accurate textual and historical context for the relationship (she was 14) and then dates a Geraldine text on a purely fictional biographical reading of her own! (AH 2: 77–84). In all this, although Bapst understood little beyond his own nineteenth-century need to debunk, the French biographer perceived the problem: in the composition of poetic texts, language generalizes experience so that 'lies' inevitably entrap all poetry whose probability may yet have 'pour point de départ une donnée précise' ('for point of departure an exact source').[18]

The Real Geraldine

There was 'une donnée precise' in the story of Surrey's Geraldine. The real Geraldine, Surrey's official Laura, was the youngest daughter of Gerald Fitzgerald, ninth Earl of Kildare, who died in the Tower in 1534, attainted for his complicity in his son's rebellion against Henry VIII. Beginning her long life (1527–90) quite destitute, Elizabeth Fitzgerald had little help except a noble Irish lineage, her father's good looks, and a poetic patronymic. Her famous great-grandmother provided her Christian name and an identity to make her marketable at court: 'Her sire an earl, her dame of prince's blood,' as Surrey wrote about her in his most anthologized sonnet. The daughter of the Marquess of Dorset, the mother could claim royal connection through her grandmother, Edward IV's queen, Elizabeth Woodville, Henry VIII's grandmother and also the sister of the Earl of Surrey's great-grandmother. Whatever else the poet earl intended in the poems he wrote about Geraldine, he was writing for a cousin, with the same great-great-grandmother, Jacquetta of Luxembourg, whose first husband had been brother to Henry V.[19]

Thus, when disaster struck in Ireland seven years after Surrey's Geraldine had been born at Maynooth, her mother could rush back to her brother Lord Grey in England and, as soon as Elizabeth had reached 10, put her in the court of her royal female cousins, at Hunsdon, the old Howard palace: 'From tender years in Britain she doth rest / With a king's child, where she tastes ghostly food,' the Eucharist or Holy Communion acting as *synecdoche* (the part for the whole) for religious instruction and proof of the young woman's careful education. To Hunsdon, Henry VIII had sent his daughter Princess Mary in 1534 and dispatched a few years later his second daughter Princess Elizabeth as, from the years 1536 to 1539,

[18] See the textual comments and editorial notes in *The Poems of Henry Howard Earl of Surrey*, ed. Frederick Morgan Padelford, University of Washington Publications in Language and Literature, 5 (1920). Bapst, 367, 368–9.

[19] James Graves, *A Brief Memoir of the Lady Elizabeth Fitzgerald* (1874), 5.

their households were one, having a single treasurer, whose household record does reveal for these years, under the list of attendants for 'the Lady Elizabeths grace', the name 'The lady garet'. Such a name, Garret or some version thereof, was a corrupt diminutive (from the Irish pronunciation of Gerald) frequently used by the Earl of Kildare's family and by Elizabeth Fitzgerald herself, whose 1580s will refers thus to her sister. This attendance at Hunsdon was further confirmed in 1539 by Henry VIII's refusal to allow any one else in the entourage of his daughter Elizabeth, as Lady Lisle heard, 'for my lady Garrett's daughter was lately admitted.'[20] To Hunsdon and the other royal residences, then, the penniless mother, herself living with relatives, with one daughter a deaf mute and her only son in exile in Venice, could send her youngest daughter to live with cousins, also the great-grandaughters of Edward IV's queen.

At Hunsdon Palace, Surrey first saw Geraldine: 'Hunsdon did first present her to mine eyes.' It was a natural meeting-place for the young earl, only ten years older. Experience of life had probably matured Elizabeth Fitzgerald early (even at 12, according to the laws of courtly love, a young woman was 'amenable to the service of love').[21] The beauty of the young woman drew attention at court, as Surrey's line makes clear and as the grandeur of her only surviving portrait reveals. She was also of considerable height, if her tomb effigy at Windsor Castle is accurate. With the simplicity of early teenage charm in a highly mannered court, she soon developed her own quick wit as a survival technique, as Surrey's texts also show. Whatever his physical attraction to her ('Hampton [Court] me taught to wish her first for mine'), this female cousin had a greater attraction for Surrey: she needed protection, a chivalric knight. It was obvious to all that her only solution for survival was to marry just as soon as possible. This had been the mother's whole point of putting her forward at 10. Thus, from the vantage point of Geraldine and her mother, Surrey as heir to the greatest peerage in the realm could help cousin Elizabeth to a marriage that might save her whole family from the disgrace of treason and poverty. Here Surrey could play the noble protector, a role begun with Richmond and continuing to his last days.

It was altogether natural, therefore, that Surrey should father texts about this new relationship—and his role as Geraldine's protector. Like St George before the dragon, he will save his young cousin from the beast in the palace hall and court chamber. As instruments for such a rescue, three texts dramatize Surrey's Geraldine and their relationship. They all reveal, incidentally but vividly, the social and political networking required for the existence of young men and women in the arenas of Tudor palaces and courts. In those spaces, marriage was almost the most serious game to be played, and where Surrey could help as protector matchmaker, he would. Particularly during the short reign of Queen Catherine Howard, Surrey could exert tremendous power. Precisely in that period, just before Elizabeth Fitzgerald's first marriage, the two cousins probably made their

[20] BL Cotton MS Vespasian C.XIV, part 1, f. 274v. *The Lisle Letters*, vol. 5, 543–4.

[21] Courthrope, *History*, vol. 2, 78–9.

fullest contact and Surrey may, in fact, have helped the future Geraldine to a good marriage that saved her.

Two Sonnets and a Dialogue

Written for the specific arena of the Henrician court, the sonnet 'From Tuscany came my lady's worthy race' builds on a series of subtle strategies designed, like all good advertisement, to sell a product. A punch-line as a mnemonic epigram closes the deal of the poem: 'Happy is he that may obtain her love.' The flexible rhyme scheme of Surrey's new English sonnet suits the fluctuating conversational idiom and polite verse needed to actualize Surrey's advertisement at court. For reasons of function, not idealization, Surrey fictionalizes the young woman by using neither the metaphysical raptures of Petrarch nor the bitter astringency of Wyatt, but the logical naming and placement the social occasion required in carefully modulated frames. Surrey uses, as Peterson accurately notes, 'rhetorical instructions to the letter'[22] using Aphthonian 'places' that structure the whole text in a method of periphrastic geography, the method of landscape cataloguing that informs so many of Surrey's texts. Here topology is angled towards certain considerations.

The first is to hide the ugly fact of Geraldine's bloody family history. Her 'worthy race' originally came from Tuscany and Florence (or so the Fitzgeralds claimed), not Ireland. The second is to deal with the bad reputation of her birthplace. Surrey uses *antonomasia*, the place is never named, and even Wales is made 'wild': 'The western isle, whose pleasant shore doth face / Wild Cambria's cliffs, did give her lively heat.' Only the slightest hint of origin is given in the time-honoured ritual of the wet-nurse for noble families: 'Foster'd she was with milk of Irish breast.' Diction also operates here as clever disguise: with no mention of Kildare or Fitzgerald, merely the patronymic 'Geraldine', the poet looks from a terrible past to the future in the term 'Britain' for England, Surrey's new coinage suitably patriotic. Then adding to the English glamour (and disguising the distasteful) is the aureate diction of the first lines 'worthy' and 'ancient seat' and the more archaic 'sire' and 'dame' from a ceremonial past. Thus the names, pulling back and forward at the same time, enact the epideitic strategy: this young woman is *au courant* but has the power of the past behind her. With the right genealogy (and topography) she is both ready to engage the history of her place and time and contemporary enough as to become an instrument for any dynastic future. The final mark for this public Geraldine completes the octet, her residence with the royal family. In careful positioning, then, Geraldine is objectified in terms of exalted place.

[22] Douglas L. Peterson, *The English Lyric from Wyatt to Donne* (1967), 53.

At this moment of establishing his almost legal case and starting the sestet, Surrey brings his intimate inscription of the young woman, suitably bold, just right for advertisement. The young earl met her at Hunsdon, and 'Bright is her hue, and Geraldine she hight.' The poem now enters into an accepted Petrarchan fiction. Although the speaker has desired her at Hampton Court, such personal desire is, in a suppressed syllogism, made typical. At Windsor he cannot see her enough or at all (was the reason her popularity, or Surrey as alien lover?). In any case, as in 'Of raging love', Surrey assumes the convenience and clichés of the Petrarchan admirer in order to frame his real intention, the point of the final couplet: Geraldine is ready to be married. The text has established her as quite a desirable commodity. The light Neoplatonic charade of the penultimate line, 'Beauty her made, her virtues from above,' is merely a concentrated quickstep before the finale. This finale moves from playful *hyperbole* (and an announcement once more of her good looks now made cosmic) to a wry *litotes* (understatement). Thus, after mannered topology and positioning of angles, the final blunt understatement makes its gesture all the more effective for public consumption. At the court of Henry VIII and for his audiences who will read the earl's poem (or sing it), Geraldine, the poet announces, will make a good wife for the right person. 'Happy is he that may obtain her love.'

Surrey's advertising strategy worked, or something did, quite spectacularly. On 12 December 1542, Elizabeth Fitzgerald married Sir Anthony Browne, Master of the Horse and Captain of the Gentlemen Pensioners (a crucial post), one of the wealthiest and most powerful men at court and, in general, an ally of the Howards, someone who might have heard the poem, in fact. There was a considerable discrepancy in age: she was 15 and he 60. Browne was a descendant of the Nevilles, and his father had been Constable of Calais. From 1524, when he became esquire to the body of Henry VIII, and to the end, he remained one of the king's closest associates, acting for him with Francis I in 1533 in Nice at the papal conference and then acting as proxy for the king in his marriage with Anne of Cleves. At the monastic dissolutions, he had received the king's favours, including a priory at Southwark that became the London house of his descendants, the Viscounts Montague. A few months after his marriage, his elder half-brother, William Fitzwilliam, Earl of Southampton, died, leaving him greater monastic spoils, not least the magnificent house at Cowdray that Browne and his young wife embellished and decorated with remarkable wall paintings of the period. In 1542 Browne also served with Surrey and Norfolk in the Scottish marches and then in 1544 with Henry VIII at the fall of Boulogne. After Surrey's beheading, he was given as 'knight Master of the kinges horses' four magnificent swift 'Coursers of the late Erle of Surrey'.[23] In January 1547, Browne shared with Denny the responsibility of telling the king, his old friend, of approaching death, and under the king's will, he was named guardian to Prince Edward and Princess Elizabeth.

23 *The Inventory of King Henry VIII*, BL Harleian MS 1419A, item 8481, f. 444r.

As guardian, Browne thus went to Hatfield to inform Edward VI of his accession and to bring him back to London; in the following month, he rode in the coronation procession from the Tower, the depiction of which covered walls at Cowdray House. As one close to Henry VIII, Browne was honoured at his wedding by the attendance of the king with the Princess Mary, the court preacher Nicholas Ridley giving the sermon. Surrey was probably at that moment fighting in Scotland, but his poetic strategy had succeeded.

Less than six years later, in April 1548, Browne died, leaving a young widow who had lost two sons in infancy and was never to bear another child. At 21 Lady Elizabeth Browne was enormously wealthy in her own right and stunning in her good looks. This time, she needed no advertisement. The one surviving portrait of her (Plate V), probably painted after she became Countess of Lincoln in 1552, reveals a powerful, almost exotic beauty radiating not least from her almond-shaped dark eyes in a boyish face. The auburn hair with its jewelled diadem sets off the ornately jewelled neck-ruff and both the delicate white complexion and the wide expansive forehead. Her high cheekbones, pointed chin, arched eyebrows, and fixed mouth (traits visible also in her Windsor effigy) give her direct riveting stare a natural arrogance. The slight turn in the oval face towards her viewers sharpens the determined eyes. If the tight mouth were to open below those eyes, one may conjecture, it could turn Irish wit into caustic repartee, the sophisticated speech of Surrey's court, the mastery of which could help, but not insure, survival for a woman.

Indeed, the theme of a woman surviving at the Tudor court marks Surrey's other poems to Geraldine. The only poem Surrey wrote directly to her, 'The golden gift' deals exactly with this question of surviving with honour. A unique text for Surrey, with no known source and free from *petrarchismo*, the poem may indeed have been sent directly, as a verse letter, to Elizabeth Fitzgerald. The Calvinist rhymes of dichotomy, 'elect' and 'infect', suggest the date of this sonnet as probably in the same 1542 autumn and early winter before Elizabeth Fitzgerald's first marriage, when Surrey's positive response to reformed Christianity can be seen in his elegy on Wyatt. The possibility is further strengthened by her being addressed as 'Garret', the title 'Lady' being correct after her marriage; in the second July 1557 edition of *Tottel's Miscellany* the text substitutes 'Garret' for 'lady'.

This second sonnet is about courtly manners. The serious Platonic codifying in the octet (as close to a serious Petrarchan like Cardinal Bembo as Surrey ever comes) sustains the argumentative logic that leads to the sestet, with its commanding conclusion and stern advice. In this way, the whole poem rises from an underlying syllogism, with a crucial shift in verb moods. The octet comprises major and minor premises: if the 'golden gift' of nature to the young girl 'in form and favor' has taught her to display herself, and since 'other graces' will follow that gift and that 'beauty [which] her perfect seed hath sown,' there are dangers. These are spelled out in the imperative sentence of the sestet with its volta ('Now certes, Garret'): 'gifts . . . thus elect' should not be defaced 'with fancies new, /

Nor change of minds let not thy mind infect' but rather, in conclusion, 'mercy him thy friend that doth thee serve, / Who seeks alway thine honour to preserve' (16).

One other poem, part of a dialogue, may rise out of the Geraldine matrix. It deals (more ironically) with this same role of Surrey as adviser and protector. The uncertainty of this lyric's provenance is reflected in an odd textual history.[24] Its structure is not, however, uncertain. The poem in the woman's voice answers explicitly Surrey's monologue 'Wrapped in my careless cloak'. The first line of 'Girt in my guiltless gown' directly imitates 'Wrapped', and lines 14–16 allude to it with full clarity: 'But I can bear right well in mind the song now sung and past, / The author whereof came wrapped in a crafty cloak, / In will to force a flaming fire where he could raise no smoke.' If both poems are Surrey's, they reveal the Howard poet's growing power to dramatize and transform, even ventriloquize, his inherent solipsism, the Petrarchan alienation. The earl has assumed here the voice of a woman, as he will (without any question) in poems for his wife. A different kind of Petrarchan ethos or voice thus emerges from Surrey's dialogic structure, and not only for the first poem, 'Wrapped in my careless cloak,' but for the second, 'Girt in my guiltless gown, as I do sit here and sew.' The voice is no longer solipsistic. Alienation has not disappeared; it is now plural, male and female.

Possibly read in the Renaissance as reciprocating soliloquies, a popular musical form, these dual texts (both quite popular in the later Renaissance) entertain and give the woman's text and its concluding Susanna myth (one frequently used in late medieval and Renaissance English culture) a special twist for the audience. Surrey's alternating lines of Poulter's Measure act as a kind of verse letter, and the woman speaker begins her logical counter-attack to the male with utter authenticity: she sits 'here' sewing in proper feminine role-playing. Her humble reality is played against appearances at court: 'I see that things are not indeed as to the outward show' and 'where playness seems to haunt, nothing but craft appear.' Her ambiguous world 'with indifferent eyes my self can well discern.' In a good humanist manner, the female speaker sets up her own narrative and language as a defence against these false realities. Retelling a popular Bible story (later transferred to the Protestant Apocrypha), she follows the pattern of the male's lyric. Like

[24] Although these two poems in Poulter's Measure, 'Wrapped in my careless cloak, as I walk to and fro' and 'Girt in my guiltless gown, as I sit here and sew', have traditionally been placed together, they were not so in the beginning. In the first edition of his *Miscellany* on 5 June 1557, Tottel had put the latter poem in the female's voice under 'Vncertain Auctours' and with the title 'Of the dissembling louer'. In the second edition, which appeared quickly on 31 July, the poem was moved to just after Surrey's 'Wrapped in my careless cloak', but its title still exhibits a refusal to announce the poem's provenance, 'An answer in the behalfe of a woman of an vncertain aucthor.' In the interim of these few weeks the immense popularity of the *Miscellany* that had brought Tottel surprising profits had also flushed out another manuscript, which Tottel judged as authoritative, possibly from Surrey's own family. It included four more poems by Surrey and six by Wyatt, which Tottel had printed originally as appendices. Yet, even in this second edition of the *Miscellany*, which became the standard for all later editions, the poem may have been balanced with the male's, but the Susanna episode of the second poem in the woman's voice was left out. Who this 'vnertain aucthor' was, if it were not Surrey, may never be known. It may have been a woman, perhaps Elizabeth Fitzgerald herself, but its dialogic inversion suggests Surrey.

him, she puts her narrative within her own monologue and, like the male, distances herself in order to tell her story within a story. In fact, like a good lawyer, the speaker takes her defensive case to the highest canon of communal myth, Susanna and the Elders, in the Vulgate Bible a classic instance of shame and vindication. When Susanna was ready to be killed because of the false accusations of adultery by the elders (who themselves desire her), 'he that doth defend all those that in him trust / Did raise a childe [young knight] for her defence to shield her from th'unjust.' This is the Biblical Daniel, who like St George now fights, with the weapon of language, the beast of calumny who will aggressively make use of, and even devour, the woman of 'tender years'. At the end, language, its power in a protector like the prophet Daniel and its power of continuous myth-making for defence, provides hope. Geraldine will survive at court: 'And he that her preserved, and let them of their lust, / Hath me defended hitherto,' she says, 'and will do still I trust.'

It may be coincidence, but the real Geraldine did learn lessons of survival. In fact, by 1561 the Archbishop of Canterbury, Matthew Parker, wrote to Cecil and noted, with no other explanation, that in his opinion, Surrey's cousin should be 'chastised in Bridewell' prison. By then the aggressive Elizabeth was too powerful. Four years after Browne's death, she had married Edward, Lord Clinton, fifteen years older and already an authoritative figure at the Tudor court. Clinton himself became one of the great survivors of the Tudors, as a seventeenth-century historian perceptively noted: 'as boysterously active as King Henry could expect, as piously meek as King Edward could wish, as warily zealous as Queen Mary's times required, and as piercingly observant as Queen Elizabeth's perplexed occasions demanded.'[25] Holbein's mid-1530s drawing of him shows—in a sensuous mouth, blondish moustache, sharp Roman nose—the young man ripe to be picked. The same age as Surrey, Clinton was first a husband for Henry VIII's former mistress, Lady Tallboys, the former Elizabeth Blount, ten years his senior, so that Surrey first knew Clinton as Richmond's stepfather, who accompanied Henry VIII and Anne Boleyn to France. After another marriage, Clinton had become by 1550 an ideal match for Geraldine and continued so, his life a reminder of what Surrey himself might have achieved, had he lived to be 73 and neither poet nor Howard earl. By the time Edward Clinton died in 1585, he had been created the Earl of Lincoln; this was in 1572 after he had attended the Paris wedding of the King of Navarre, observing the massacre on St Bartholomew's Eve with Philip Sidney. He then acted as peer in the trial of Surrey's son, the fourth Duke of Norfolk. At the end, he was buried in a tomb of alabaster and porphyry at St George's Windsor, where he had been Lieutenant of the Order of the Garter and Lord Steward. There, in the last chapel before the present exit, his effigy with its full head of hair, pointed beard, and handlebar moustache still resides with a

[25] *SP* 1547–1580, 183. *Complete Peerage*, 692–3 and the *DNB* entry that is more succinct: he possessed 'remarkable tact'.

greyhound at his feet, next to Geraldine's, hers always the first to be seen (particularly by children) with its monkey, the totem of her Irish family.

The story of Geraldine illustrates, then, the intertwining of poetic text and actual history that marks the origination of Surrey's audiences at Surrey House and elsewhere. Although her story is the most spectacular, another figure, more marginalized, was, in fact, the most important member of this audience, certainly the most loving of the young poet earl at its centre.

7
The Countess of Surrey

In an unexpected turn to his life, the poet Earl of Surrey had a happy marriage at the court of Henry VIII. The aristocratic child he had first met at 13 and married before he left for France turned out to be the woman who not only bore him five children but also helped to engender his texts, as specific poems reveal. In fact, there is no more living a portrayal or image of the countess than in Surrey's texts that describe a faithful relationship between a young woman and a young man. His inherent solipsism, for once, was transformed in texts of love to the countess. This deep affinity of a young woman and man performs, as the poems reveal, Surrey's ultimate solution to the Petrarchan dilemma of Laura and alienation. Surrey's wife is the third Laura through an ironic inversion of Petrarch. In fact, for her, Surrey dramatizes codes of fidelity that anticipate, in their minor key, Spenser's *Epithalamion* and Milton's 'Hail, Wedded Love'. He also makes remarkable gender reversals—himself as woman and wife (roles that seldom occur in the strongly male Renaissance lyric).

Nowhere is this sense of unity of wife and husband clearer than in Surrey's sonnet 'Set me whereas the sun doth parch the green.' Although it may not be quite correct to call the earl's sonnet form a 'fourteen-line strambotto', Surrey's English transformation of the originally Sicilian sonnet form (sung to lutes) allows a musical flexibility with his more frequent rhymes. In this sonnet, through formal flexibility, Surrey takes a Petrarchan landscape poem and turns it into both intimate conversation and *strambotto* song, the original epigrammatic drive of the sonnet becoming ceremonious language. A single boast from a faithful lover in three quatrains beginning 'Set me' finishes as a cry of faith in a mnemonic epigram equal to a vow.

Set me whereas the sun doth parch the green,
Or where his beams may not dissolve the ice,
In temperate heat, where he is felt and seen,
With proud people, in presence sad and wise;
Set me in base, or yet in high degree,
In the long night, or in the shortest day,
In clear weather, or where mists thickest be,
In lusty youth, or when my hairs be grey;
Set me in earth, in heav'n, or yet in hell,
In hill, in dale, or in the foaming flood,
Thrall, or at large, alive whereso I dwell,

Sick, or in health, in ill fame, or in good:
Yours will I be, and with that only thought
Comfort myself when that my hap is nought.

Transforming the original Petrarchan text of fidelity, Surrey enacts an objective and historically liturgical performance. A great deal of the text appears, in fact, to be a reinscription of the exchange of wedding vows, pronounced in 1532, the year of Surrey's wedding, in English in the middle of a Latin ceremony, beginning 'I *N.* take the *N.* to my weded wyfe [husband] to haue and to hold from this day forwarde.' Even the Latin questions of the priest who is witnessing the English marriage (the Catholic sacrament, unlike the Orthodox, is given by the couple to each other, not by the priest) contain in 1532 the chiastic injunctions Surrey adapts from the original Petrarch closure and its roots in Propertius.[1] The later Renaissance understood Surrey's popular sonnet in this formulaic mode, as it was transcribed into the lyrics of Gascoigne and Turberville and analysed in Puttenham, who sees this marriage poem (which he attributes to Wyatt) as a Renaissance model of *merismus, or the distributer* or *amplificatio* that 'Orators or eloquent perswaders' (such as lawyers) use and that moves 'peecemeale and by distribution of euery part for amplification sake'. Reinforced by such logical 'props of phrasing',[2] the *anaphora* (initial repetition of words) of 'Set me' introduces the three quatrains in a series of trochees and thereby sets the ceremonial mnemonic nature of Surrey's lyric. Supported by alliteration and strong caesurae as in 'With proud people, in presence sad and wise,' Surrey's units can perform as *periphrasis* (many words for a single word or phrase): 'where mists thickest be' for autumn; 'where his beams may not dissolve the ice' for the cold. They also use internal rhyme—slant or actual ('hell'; 'hill'; 'Thrall'; 'dwell'; and 'ill'), all such effects in a hovering rhythm between a ten-syllable line and the old Anglo-Saxon accentual four-stressed line.

Unlike Petrarch's lyrics and Surrey's other two direct imitations of Petrarchan landscape poems, 'The soote season' and 'Alas, so all things now,' landscape here

[1] H. B. Lathrop, 'The Sonnet Forms of Wyatt and Surrey', *Modern Philology*, 2 (1905), 469. For other sources for Surrey's invention out of the French and Italian, see Thomson, *Wyatt*, 212; and the general studies of Joseph Vianey, *Le Petrarquisme en France au XVIe siècle* (1909) and of Henri Gambier, *Italie et Renaissance poetique en France* (1936). Both the English and Latin marriage service may be found in *Manuale ad Vsum Perecelebris Ecclesiae Sarisburiensis*, ed. A. Jeffries Collins, Henry Bradshaw Society, 91 (1860), 47–8. In the Latin marriage service, these questions follow logically the initial act of choice ('Vis habere hanc mulierem in sponsam et eam diligere?'); and the first question is whether each desires 'honourare' ('to honour') and then 'tenere' ('to hold') and then 'et custodiri sanam et infirmam' ('and to keep, whether healthy or sick'), all ending with 'quam diu vita vtriusque vestrum durauerit?' ('as long as the life of either of you will last?'). Cf. Stephen Merriam Foley, 'The Honorable Style of Henry Howard, Earl of Surrey: A Critical Reading of Surrey's Poetry', unpublished Ph.D. dissertation (Yale University, 1979), 47. Petrarch's original closure borrows from the Roman legal formula of Propertius 2, 15: 36: 'huius ero vivus, mortuus huius ero' or 'Living I shall be yours; dead, I shall be yours' (the exchange in Roman law is a reminder of where the Catholic marriage liturgy originates).

[2] Puttenham, *English Poesie*, 222–3; Patricia Thomson, 'Wyatt and Surrey', in *English Poetry and Prose, 1540 to 1674*, ed. Christopher Ricks (1975), 176.

does not produce alienation but union. In fact, landscape is finally irrelevant to the central act of fidelity that marks the integrity of the lover/speaker. Surrey even renders a dialogic relationship stronger than that in Petrarch or in the Latin text serving both poems, Horace's ode (I, 23) beginning 'Integer vitae scelerisque purus' ('Unchanged in life and pure from evil deeds'). For all three poets, Roman, Italian, English, fidelity to another human being, whatever the landscape, signifies finally fidelity to self. This deeper fidelity was missed by Tottel, who did recognize the crucial place of the declaration—the epigrammatic couplet with chivalric oath and mnemonic 'all for love' motif. He changed 'Yours' to 'Hers', although, in this poem critically acclaimed as technically Surrey's most successful sonnet experiment, Surrey's series of imperatives does not allow for the change. Logically and grammatically, the epigram springs from the series of contraries announced as imperatives by the lover to his beloved. Each is dialectically set and balanced in landscapes of nature and society that define history as well as the lover's choice. In this balance and counterpoint, ambiguity in the genitive of the phrase 'Yours will I be' means not only the lover's fidelity but the beloved's as well—two as one. As Silvester notes, 'When Surrey does look in his heart and write, he seeks not so much to analyse himself as to portray relationships with others.'[3]

Frances de Vere Howard

The human being to whom the poet earl gave this fidelity and thereby transformed his own history had a special history herself. Frances de Vere was the daughter of John, the fifteenth Earl of Oxford, by his second wife, Elizabeth Trussell, herself from minor gentry in Staffordshire, the mother dying before her second (of three) daughters was married in 1532. The mother and father are both buried in the chancel of the church next to the Norman Castle Hedingham (still seen for miles across the Essex countryside), where, after 1526, the girl Frances de Vere lived in the imposing keep (or in the brick house built in the sixteenth century at the base of the keep). In the chancel, Surrey's wife is one of four daughters kneeling before a book at one end of the tomb, with its de Vere shield and heraldic totem, the Oxford boar at the top of the slab. She is praying with folded hands for her

[3] For the acclaim, see J. W. Lever, *The Elizabethan Love Sonnet* (1956), 46. See also Maurice Evans' *English Poetry* comparison (78) of its structure—'a perfect correspondence of form to content'—to Shakespeare's sonnet 73. Lever considers, however, that the first new English sonnet by Surrey is 'Love that doth reign' but provides no historical evidence. See also his analysis of Spenser's *Amoretti* VII and Sidney's 'Leave me, O Love' as the only examples of use by either of the Surrey sonnet form. Both sonnets reveal a special subjectivity within an objective form: 'the pure Surrey form . . . gave admirable expression to a moment of objective self-examination' (Lever, 119 n. 1, 135). What Lever suggests is that both great poets had learned Surrey's new dynamic of a dialectical structure that in objective distanced form made possible deep personal feeling. *The Anchor Anthology of Sixteenth-Century Verse*, ed. Richard S. Silvester (1974), p.xxvi.

parents in purgatory. Her French hood and high collar in the effigy reflect early Tudor styling as much as the popular saints' names of the daughters, Elizabeth, Anne, Frances, and Ursula. Her father represented the highest levels of honour, 'a man of valour and authority,' wrote the Venetian ambassador, 'with a revenue of 25,000 ducats, and it is his custom always to cavalcade with 200 horse.' When the ancient de Vere title of Lord Great Chamberlain was given, less than a month after Oxford's death, to Thomas Cromwell, the newly created Earl of Essex, the event may have been particularly insulting to Oxford's 24-year-old son-in-law and to Oxford's son, who did not regain the title of Lord Great Chamberlain until the reign of Queen Mary (and then without any actual creation). In fact, four months after Surrey's beheading, the new Lord Protector Somerset told the Countess of Surrey's brother—the sixteenth earl and future father of the poet Earl of Oxford—to surrender his patent 'for the clere extinction of his pretenced clayme to the saide office' of Lord Great Chamberlain.[4]

Another visual record of the Countess of Surrey, the Holbein drawing at Windsor (Plate 2), is usually viewed in tandem with the two portraits of the Earl of Surrey, both appearing about the same age. In this portrait, her only one, the countess' dark brown eyes stare, unlike her young husband's, directly at the painter and seem to be watching for clues in a new terrain. Her pursed mouth, square face, and rather flattened nose recall her parents' effigies, notably in the determination of the jaw. With her sturdy body, if small shoulders, she holds her hands tightly together (in one of the few Holbein drawings of hands). Her large head-dress appears a burden; the tightly fitting English hood, its forehead roll yellow, fits firmly over her ears so that no hair shows and continues with an enormous black fall. She is also wearing a pendant of red and yellow jewels with a chain that drops into the upper part of her breast, the only part of her dress open. Her gown is pink velvet (in Holbein's direction *rosa felbet*) as are her large sleeves, their size in contrast to the closely fitted small shoulders edged by a red lining.

In 1532, probably the year of the Holbein drawings, there had been good reasons for the marriage of the Earl of Surrey to Frances de Vere. The ties between most of the de Veres and the Howards (and their Mowbray forebears) had been close for centuries. Even when the family leader had chosen a different master in the Wars of the Roses, the wives of each had been protected and supported financially by the other, as the Howard notebooks show. In this sense, the marriage of Frances and the young heir apparent to the dukedom of Norfolk simply extended the alliances and brought two fortunes closer together as well as fitting the wishes of Anne Boleyn in 1532. Three years later Surrey left Richmond and started to live with his wife at Kenninghall. There on 12 March 1536, Frances Surrey gave birth to their first son, Thomas, named for his grandfather and great-grandfather. The next year Norfolk increased Surrey's allowance by the considerable sum of £400 per annum, as he received new funds and estates from dissolved religious centres

[4] *LP*, vol. 6, ii, 732; *CSPVen*, vol. 4, 295; *APC 1547–50*, 93.

such as the ancient Franciscan friary at Norwich, whose surrender Surrey received on 20 September 1537. On 25 February 1538, the countess gave birth to her second child, another son. As the Duke of Norfolk wrote to Henry VIII on 14 March, 'My daughter of Surrey is brought to bed of a son and, notwithstanding she looked not to have been delivered unto after Palm Sunday, yet God be thanked, the child is as lusty a boy as needeth to be.' His name will be Henry, and the proud grandfather had intended, so Norfolk wrote to the king, if the countess 'had gone her full reckoning, and then had a son', he would have 'sent to the king's highness to have beseeched him to have had it christened in his name'. As probably happened with the baby's father, Norfolk wanted the king as godfather. But, because the mother 'was so long delivered before her reckoning', the women at Kenninghall will not allow the duke to 'let the child be so long unchristened'. Norfolk concluded this announcement with a boast that he rejoices that both his sons have heirs 'of age to await on my lord Prince', Prince Edward, and Norfolk also trusted these new male Howards will 'await' upon the King Henry himself.[5] The enormous crisis of begetting his own heir and the years Norfolk himself had waited for the birth of a son will not be repeated. The title could continue.

In fact, Surrey continued to produce, and his wife provided his seed, in the metaphor of the time, with the fertile ground that the strong body drawn by Holbein had promised. She delivered five children in eleven years, without any apparent difficulty (and, at over 40, she would deliver a sixth by her second husband). After her second son by Surrey, the young countess gave birth to three girls, Jane, Catherine, and Margaret, the latter born a few weeks after her father's execution. During his lifetime, their father may have had the older two girls educated with his sons under Hadrianus Junius, for certainly, as Nott notes, the poet earl paid care to his daughters' training. Probably both the young daughters as well as the young sons composed a letter in Latin, supervised by Hadrianus Junius, to their father in France as a leader of the army and a hero of the nation (N1: 171–2). The proof of the training of the daughters lay in their later achievements as women in the Tudor aristocracy. Jane Howard married into the Neville family, her kin both paternally and maternally, and became the Countess of Westmorland, a recusant and tragic figure in her cousin Queen Elizabeth's reign, as her poignant letters reveal. Her tutor after her father's death, John Foxe, had particular praise for her in the same era as Lady Jane Grey, the Cooke sisters, and Queen Elizabeth herself. Foxe found Jane Howard's Greek and Latin so superb 'that she might well stand in competition with the most learned men of that time, for the praise of elegancy in both' (N1: cix). Her character also revealed the strength of her mother and her father in the crises of her later life, as all the family reeled from the beheading of their cherished brother the fourth Duke of Norfolk, and then she from her own husband's exile in the 1570s as a young man (she never saw him again before her own death in June 1593) in a northern Catholic conspiracy. Even her

[5] *LP*, vol. 13, 1, 504. Cf. PRO, SP 1/130/43.

enemies learned to respect her, as a secret agent's letter to Sadler reveals: 'for rypeness of wytt, rydeness of memory, and playn and pythy utterans of hyr words, I have talked to many but never wyth her lyke.' In those final days, when she wrote despairing letters to Burghley, she cried out: 'We and our country [are] shamed for ever, that now in the ende we should seeke holes to creepe into.'

The second sister Catherine was probably named for Queen Catherine Howard, who may have been her godmother. She made an excellent and less politically disturbing marriage to Henry, Lord Berkeley, but, according to Stone, encouraged her husband's excesses which gradually destroyed the Berkeley inheritance, including hunting and hawking with 150 servants in 'tawny cloth coats in summer, with the badge of the white Lyon rampant imbroidered on the left sleeve' and in winter, in coats of 'white frize lined with crimsen taffety'. She was beloved by her brother Henry, later Earl of Northampton. From indications in her brother's manuscripts, Lady Berkeley was a woman interested in scholarship, an acquaintance of Sir Philip Sidney (although twice she rejected him as a son-in-law), and a ritualist in social protocol—so addicted to the Howard craze for falconry that her dresses were stained with bird-droppings. With 'hair yellowish' and splendid complexion, 'somewhat tall', she moved with a 'pace the most stately and upright' and was 'of stomach great and haughtie'. Like her sister, she was 'of speech passing eloquent and ready' with never a 'mistaken, misplaced, or mispronounced word or syllable' and also 'as ready and significant with her pen, her invention as quick as her first thoughts, and her words as ready as her invention'. Skilled in French and 'perfect' in Italian, she also played the lute with such 'ravishment' that her husband and servant 'secretly hearkened under her windows'. After the 1572 death of her brother, the fourth Duke of Norfolk, which recapitulated for all the children the shock of their father's beheading, she retreated to Berkeley House in Warwickshire, where she died in 1596. Elizabeth I had been right when she said: 'Noe, noe, Lady Berkeley, wee know you will never love us for the death of your brother.'

The third daughter, Margaret, the child Surrey never saw, married Lord Scrope of Bolton, Governor of Carlisle, Warden of the West Marches, another family connection, and remains a shadowy figure, dying in 1592. Her husband, of an ancient northern family, was briefly custodian to Mary Queen of Scots, with whom Lady Scrope developed a friendship. She may have acted as a go-between between her brother and the queen who lamented 'What has not the House of Howard suffered for my sake' and who on her death left her rosary to Philip Howard's countess. In a final letter from Margaret's sister Jane, the early world of the children is recalled. The baby of the family, Margaret had a happy nature and the family had given her the name of a character from Ariosto: 'farewell, good syster, and I trust to God yet for all, that we shall be as merry as wee were when you weare named Angelyca.'[6]

[6] Quotations here are from *Memorials of the Howard Family*, Bodleian Library 2182 (n.b.5) 24 and 38; Lawrence Stone, *Family and Fortune: Studies in Aristocratic Finance in the Sixteenth and*

The arrival of each of these grandchildren excited the third Duke of Norfolk, and by the summer of 1538 he began the most ancient of the Howard games, aggrandizement by marriage. The rising fortunes of the Seymours, the uncles and guardians of the future king, made them logical connections for the Howards. Also, at this time Edward Seymour, Earl of Hertford, disliked Cromwell or at least pretended to lean towards a political alliance with Norfolk and the conservatives. For the Howards, it was foolish not to move in the Seymour direction, whatever his relatively modest origins and previous service under Buckingham and Richmond. Although Henry VIII gave his consent as announced in a letter of 14 July 1538, written to Cromwell by the rising Sir Ralph Sadler, a Gentleman of the Privy Chamber, the proposal for a marriage between Sir Thomas Seymour and the widowed Duchess of Richmond collapsed after the first overtures. According to Bapst, the duchess herself, barely 20, abruptly left the court for Kenninghall, possibly to consult her older brother, who saw this proposal as a gross violation of the memory of Richmond and one more shock in a disappearing world.[7] For the young Countess of Surrey, it was one more crisis she was learning to cope with.

The Young Earl and Countess at Court

In England's own deepening crisis with Europe, Surrey, in his early twenties, found his position as the heir to the Duke of Norfolk more and more demanding. By March 1539 Surrey had been dispatched to Norfolk from London, where he and his young wife were residing with their children, to set up greater defences in East Anglia. The powers of the Holy Roman Empire—and Catholic France as well—possessed now not only the right but the sanctifying privilege of destroying Henry VIII, because his excommunication had been fully promulgated by the Roman pontiff. Not only did the English King engage in the greatest bulwark-building for centuries on the coasts of England, but he initiated a political strategy to unify England and his court, including conservatives and loyal blood nobility. In the first session of the Parliament of 1539, which opened on 28 April, Cromwell obtained an Act dissolving the remaining monasteries. This Parliament also authorized the king to issue proclamations in emergency conditions with the authority of statutes. Then Henry VIII prorogued the session for one final coup, the enactment of the Bill of Six Articles that reaffirmed certain doctrines and customs from the old Christianity, a conservative victory that ensured loyalty at a time of national emergency from certain nobility and clergy. Within a fortnight, 500 persons in London were indicted for heresy, but neither side could claim

Seventeenth Centuries (1973), 244–51; and Robinson, *Dukes of Norfolk*, 80. For more on Lady Berkeley, see *Complete Peerage*, vol. 2, 1238, and Duncan-Jones, *Sir Philip Sidney*, 74.

[7] For the proposal, *SP*, vol. 1,ii, 107; Bapst, *Deux gentilshommes-poètes*, 238.

victory. Both religious sides suffered losses and the king continued his destruction of the old White Rose nobility, finally beheading the old Countess of Salisbury (the niece of two Yorkist kings and the mother of the traitor Reginald Pole), in which process the old woman's shoulders were literally hacked before the new executioner could trim off the ancient head with its white hair. In June Surrey and his father were designated official mourners at a diplomatic ploy, a spectacular liturgy staged for the recently deceased wife of Charles V. Of course, as the influence of the Howards increased, so did the rewards, with Surrey gaining Ashdown Forest in Sussex in reward for his defence work in East Anglia and, early in 1540, the buildings and lands of Wymondham priory in Norfolk.

At the same time, from her silent perspective, the young countess could not miss the dexterity and even magnificence of her young husband in his duties. A particularly theatrical court occasion in which Surrey excelled occurred on May Day 1540 at Greenwich. In honour of the new Queen Anne of Cleves, herself part of the general strategy to bolster England against the Empire, a tournament, with its nostalgic recall and reinforcement of the old medieval codes, was led by the 24-year-old Surrey. He was the Queen's Chief Defender in the lists, his shield with its silver lion and Howard arms the foremost of all shields. Armed at all points, the poet earl rode behind an elaborate float of the Roman goddess of arms, his horse covered with the same Howard devices of gold and silver as his white velvet coat. A moment had come for him to display his honour as a stylish *vir armatus*. Sir John Dudley, soon to be Viscount Lisle and Lord Admiral, led the eight knight challengers (including Lord Clinton, recently widowed from his first wife). After the parading and then clearing of the field of the lists, Surrey in his pavilion allowed his squire, Thomas Clere, to close his visor and then exchange his steel-tipped spear for the tilting lance itself, wooden and hollow and tipped with a coronal of three or four spreading points that would unhorse, if not wound, his opponent. Clere then adjusted the crucial grand-guard that was hooked to the helmet and fixed to the breastplate by screws. This grand-guard covered the breast and left shoulder that would be, in the fight, most vulnerable at the moment when the one-eyed Surrey would race down the lists, lance lifted, to attack Dudley, who would aim, as all jousters did, at the breast and shoulder. Thus, fully armoured and locked in his steel harness, on this May Day, the poet Earl of Surrey guided his horse out to his end of the tilt or wooden barrier running the length of the field.

At the trumpet flourish, with knights spurring their horses, the joust began, lasting two days. In a triumph that must have appeared to his young wife a distinctive honour, Surrey ran eight courses successfully each day, never being unhorsed and shattering his lance only as Dudley remained in his saddle. Two more days followed, with swords this time instead of lances, but without thrusting blows, only attempts to unhorse the enemy. As the chief of the twenty-nine defenders, Surrey had the same success as on the two previous days. The younger Surrey had proved himself a match for the older Dudley, but the competition was a toss-up, with arms, expensive robes, and silver vessels given to both sides by the new Queen Anne. In her honour the whole event had been enacted, at the same time as Henry VIII was planning to annul the marriage. It was also a day of triumph for all the Howards.

This was the public Surrey, who now attracted attention not only at court but in the realm at large. He had proved himself at arms and no doubt could prove himself in that critical (and only) test of establishing honour for a young nobleman: leading a military command as a true *vir armatus*, a role to which Surrey would be drawn more and more in the next few years. For Frances Surrey, this prospect of an attractive young husband in a court where the king himself did not set a model of chastity gave their marriage a kind of vulnerability. Surrey's father had already set a standard of adultery in his own household, and although the king himself insisted on a code of fidelity for all others at his court, as Francis I did not, exceptions could be made, particularly in the case of the young Earl of Surrey, whose handsome body had now displayed itself before the whole court.

In one of Surrey's lyrics (modelled after Wyatt) such a slip from marital fidelity may be inscribed or at least conjectured. 'Though I regarded not' implies, once more, dialogue, a community of two. The speaker is addressing someone to whom he feels an obligation to explain the situation dramatized in the poem's lively series of antithetical images. In the song metre of iambic trimetre and in eight-line stanzas rhyming *ababcdcd*, the poem develops a series of analogies, proof in Scholastic logic. They offer a musical, if logical, argument leading to the moral stance of constancy that closes the poem.

Though I regarded not
The promise made by me,
Or passed not to spot
My faith and honesty,
Yet were my fancy strange,
And wilful will to wite,
If I sought now to change
A falcon for a kite.

The speaker develops in the next three stanzas a progressing argument of analogies, animal and geographical, to prove his fidelity, ending with 'No, no, I have no mind / To make exchanges so' before he inverts the Petrarchan cliché of fire burning the lover into fire as a sign of faith, making the sign the logical base for constancy.

The fire it cannot freeze.
For it is not his kind,
Nor true love cannot lose
The constancy of the mind,
Yet as soon shall the fire
Want heat to blaze and burn,
As I in such desire,
Have once a thought to turn.

In two other poems that define the act of fidelity, Surrey also develops this same sense of relationship, but more formally. In them, dialogue turns more on the lover's assertion of his constancy, using the cliches of *petrarchismo* more directly, so that Tottel gave the title 'The constant louer lamenteth' to the lyric 'Since fortune's wrath envieth the wealth'. This *frottola* transforms Petrarchan clichés amid a changing landscape of winter, summer, and sea. It ends in an epigram of total fidelity: 'Such as I was, such will I be, / Your own, what would you more of me.' In another song poem, 'Give place, you lovers,' praise of fidelity joins with an 'allusive correlative', in Panofsky's term, of Penelope from ancient Greece to shape one of Surrey's most musical and popular texts:

Give place, you lovers, here before
That spent your boasts and brags in vain:
My lady's beauty passeth more
The best of yours, I dare well sayn,
Than doth the sun, the candle light,
Or brightest day, the darkest night.

Probably adapted from a poem by his court acquaintance (and John Donne's grandfather), John Heywood, Surrey's text has a more precise rhetorical structure, set as a deliberative classical oration.[8] In the *narratio* of this oration as song, Surrey gives the emblematic clue to the woman he is describing by comparing her to Penelope, the classical model of the faithful wife.

And thereto hath a troth as just,
As had Penelope the fair,
For what she saith, you may it trust,
As it by writing sealed were,
And virtues hath she many more,
Than I with pen have skill to show.

In fact, as the oratorical argument of the whole poem demonstrates, what guarantees the poet's right language and even his sense of his own vocation is the enduring fact of his beloved's total 'troth', equal to Penelope's. Her fidelity makes the texts possible.

The Reign of Catherine Howard

Catherine Howard's span of less than 500 days as Queen of England marks the most serene and calm period of Surrey's later life. The teenaged queen consort appears to have turned to the younger Surrey and his wife for support and counsel,

[8] C. W. Jentoft, 'Surrey's Four "Orations" and the Influence of Rhetoric on Dramatic Effect', *Papers on Language and Literature*, 9 (1973), 256. See Puttenham, *English Poesie*, 192–3, on the figure of 'hiperbole' in this poem.

even though Norfolk was the official head of the family. Catherine had been brought up in the fairly isolated East Anglian countryside by her old step-grandmother, the dowager Duchess of Norfolk, that is, before her first visits to Norfolk House across the Thames from Whitehall, and then to the court where she served Anne of Cleves. At the Bishop of Winchester's house, she caught the king's eye, as no doubt she was intended to. Now as queen of the court, the teenaged Howard may have discovered her stylish first cousin and his wife as real protectors in her genuine bewilderment. Fear of her uncle and Gardiner, manipulators to whom obedience was expected, may have led the queen to Surrey, who now saw himself, once more, as protector of another royal figure. He could use his own influence, so he may have thought, for the best of ends. In March 1541, for example, with Henry VIII still hopelessly in love and dazzled by Catherine's small young body and countenance 'fort delie', as the French ambassador Marillac wrote to Francis I, the queen asked her husband a favour for which only Surrey could have been the intercessor. Choosing her time carefully, Queen Catherine waited until the royal barge from Whitehall to Greenwich was under way. Then she turned as they passed the Tower, reminding her husband of the service of Sir Thomas Wyatt through the years. She asked that he be released from the Tower, where he had been imprisoned for supposedly conspiring with Cardinal Pole. Henry VIII consented but on rather stringent terms (no doubt surmising that the request came from Surrey and therefore the Howards themselves). Wyatt must end his 15-year-old separation from his wife and resume his conjugal responsibilities. Henry VIII did not want the diplomat to continue his bad marital example at the court over which the king and his young Catherine presided in such nuptial bliss.[9]

In Catherine Howard's brief reign, the Countess of Surrey reached the zenith of a court career, as did her husband. In the inventory of the queen's jewels after her beheading—one of the few records surviving from Catherine Howard—the Countess of Surrey appears to have been a particular favourite. 'The lady Surre' was given a brooch studded with a series of minute diamonds and rubies, as one was also given to her little cousin, Princess Elizabeth, who alone was given two gifts, the second a rosary with 'crosses, pillars, and tassels attached'. The only other gifts by the young queen, among all the other women at court, were single rosaries to Lady Carew (her cousin), the Countess of Rutland, and Lady Margaret Douglas, and then an elaborate pomander of gold to her step-daughter older than she, the Princess Mary.[10] Strangely, after the reign of Queen Catherine Howard, no record exists of further attendance by the countess at court for the rest of her life. In the countess' last years, her marriage in 1553 (or perhaps earlier) to Thomas Steynings may have demeaned her in the eyes of her social equals, as Steynings was only a modest Suffolk gentleman. In any case, the last twenty-five years of her life were spent largely in undisturbed retirement at Steynings' home

[9] For Marillac, see *Memorials of the Howard Family*, 13. For the Wyatt episode, CSP*Span*, vol. 6,i, 155 (314).

[10] *LP*, vol. 16, 1389.

in the vicinity of Framlingham Castle at Earl Soham, with a new son named Henry and (in one record) a daughter, Maria. On 17 January 1563, she was the leading mourner at the funeral of her daughter-in-law, the wife of the young Duke of Norfolk. The countess then died in 1577, five years after her older son was beheaded, as his father had been, on Tower Hill.

But Catherine Howard's 500 days proved a glory for Frances Surrey because of the increasing honour given her husband and, through him, to her. Only a month after the young Howard queen was 'shewed openly as Quene at Hampton Court', on 8 September 1541, the Earl of Surrey became joint Steward of the University of Cambridge with his father, a role Surrey may have wanted. But the poet earl's highest ritualization of honour came on 23 April 1541. In the most splendid moment of Tudor nobility in his life, and with promise of greater honour, the Earl of Surrey was formally elected as a Knight of the Order of the Garter at the annual meeting of the Chapter of the Garter on St George's Day. As the poet earl knew, on the basis of this honouring Surrey could inscribe new texts redefining the meaning of all nobility. In the ceremony, when Henry VIII presented the garter after a long ritual, the heir apparent to the Duke of Norfolk then tied the garter about his leg and 'setting himself to exert his eloquence to the utmost, in the most humble manner possible,' thanked the king, 'afterwards saluting also the whole Society as became him.' The following 22 May 1541, Surrey was given possession of his stall in the medieval Chapel of St George at Windsor. In the three designations of the Order of the Garter—Princes (dukes and earls), Barons (lords), and Knights—Surrey was now listed as 'Prince'. Of the twenty-six elaborate stalls, one was for the king and twenty-five for the Knights Companion in Edward III's redesigning of the collectivity symbolized by King Arthur's Round Table. Surrey's was the fifth on the Sovereign's right, affixed to which was his banner, sword, and helmet, instruments that would remind any Knight of the Garter just how true honour was expected to be first won and then kept—in the labour and pain of battle.[11]

Thus, just between two decisive events in the poet earl's life—his initiation into the Order of the Garter and the writing of his elegy on Wyatt—occurred an episode that prefigured the role now expected of him at the level of the highest blood nobility. With Sir Thomas Seymour he was ordered to accompany Sir William Fitzwilliam and Lord Russell to Calais to observe the growing struggle on the continent between the Empire and France and 'set order there' in the Marches of Calais, as Holinshed noted. Although it was a hasty trip ('My lord of Surrey and Sir Thomas Seamour came only for their pastime [as] they have not brought in all over 24 persons with them'), Surrey himself examined in detail the defences and walls of the English city and continued on to the outlying Guisnes to study its fortifications in the spot where the adolescent Surrey and Richmond had once crossed into France.

11 Casady, *Henry Howard*, 82–3. *Garter: Register of the Most Noble Order of the Garter*, ed. John Anstis (1724), vol. 2, 421–3, 287.

Also between the two events of Surrey's initiation and his Wyatt elegy occurred the fall of Queen Catherine Howard. At Queen Catherine's trial in December 1541, Norfolk as Earl Marshal had to preside and give judgement on that which, according to the French ambassador Marillac, 'concerne le deshonneur de son sang' ('concerns the dishonour of his blood'). According to the ambassador, Norfolk laughed during his examination of the prisoners, as though he were rejoicing, and at the trial Surrey was also present. Marillac reported to Francis I that the Howard brothers of the young queen actually 'se promenoient a cheval par la ville' ('promenaded on horse back through the city') in the bizarre customs of this land ('Telle est la coustoume de ce pays').[12] On 13 February 1542, Surrey represented his father at the execution, Norfolk having—wisely—retired to East Anglia. The delegation of this family responsibility Surrey carried alone in the face of terrible shame. Like her first cousin Queen Anne Boleyn, Queen Catherine was buried immediately in the church of St Peter ad Vincula in the Tower, body and severed head tipped into a grave that is now as anonymous as that of the other Howard queen and all the other victims in that spot. Her shame went beyond death. No one knows which skeleton is hers.

Three Texts of Love: 'My heart's delight, my sorrow's leech'

Surrey and his wife witnessed the common breakdown of their Camelot world centred so briefly on the young queen. By 1542 this union of wife and husband functioned as Surrey's friendship with Richmond had earlier: the peace of two lovers holding each other in the eye of raging storm after storm. Their love did not 'rage' but turned into a steadily developing friendship surrounded by violence and history that could kill them. At least in Surrey's poetic texts of fidelity, the young countess became, in phrases from one of Surrey's most popular lyrics in the later Tudor world, 'my heart's delight, my sorrow's leech [healer], mine earthly goddess here.' Surrey's final three texts about his wife reveal this remarkable level of friendship and intimacy.

In fact, so strong is this figuration that in two of the poems Surrey inverts gender for his deeper penetration into the life of the beloved. He writes poems in his wife's voice, a ventriloquism of utter love. These poems from the war front in France during 1544–6 are among his most original and the first major lyrics in English in the voice of a woman (Wyatt's single poem in a woman's voice is satiric). Although all have roots in Chaucer and Ovid (the Latin *Heroides* that Chaucer translated), the rhetoric, the topicality, the realism—above all, the lyric genre for such a voice—are new. Once more, as in Surrey's two crucial images of English nobility and honour in the 1540s, Sir Thomas Wyatt and Thomas Clere,

[12] For the military trips, see *LP*, vol. 16, 808; Holinshed, *Chronicles*, vol. 4, 1581. *Correspondance politique de MM. de Castillon et de Marillac*, ed. Jean Kaulek (1885), 371.

the poet turns to the margins of power to inscribe an authentic model of sacrifice. The unusual popularity of both ventriloquized poems throughout the whole English Renaissance enhanced the reputation of Surrey as a progenitor of new voices and new models of fidelity. Even more singular is the fact that Surrey wrote these poems in a deliberate act of transvestism. He became a woman in the midst of the totally male environment of a Renaissance war, the exhausting campaigns around Boulogne in 1544–6. Assuming this role—and the consciousness of the poet in doing so—no doubt provided Surrey with relief from the never-ending strain of male brutalizing male. It certainly let him enter a sexual dialectic through which the poet earl could find his own free sense of eros, that is, penetration of an intimate life like his own in the midst of war—a life deeper than the constant violence he existed in. In her body, which had allowed the genealogy of his own body, and in her textualized voice, which allowed another genealogy, Surrey took on an unusual harmony with history and generation in which the two young persons had become one.

'O happy dames' was early set to music, appearing in a Bassus part-book dating from 1540–50 and later in an organist's anthology of musical settings compiled around 1560–5 (the Mulliner Book).[13] The Duchess of Richmond, who probably received the original text from her sister-in-law, wrote it into the Devonshire Manuscript, with Lady Margaret Douglas herself inscribing the crucial final line: 'Now he comes, will he come? alas, no, no!' The evidence that Lady Margaret had not left for Scotland to marry Darnley's father but was still at Kenninghall or Lambeth, and that the first stanza was written in Lord Mountjoy's anthology before his death in October 1544, gives substantial proof of its date. Surrey wrote the poem probably as he left for the front during the early part of that year. In fact, the speaker describes such a sea-crossing as Surrey may have had. Adapting *Troilus*' rhyme royal and the structure of Phyllis' Complaint in Ovid's *Heroides* (ii) (the latter made popular in Renaissance France by the ironic Petrarchist Seraphino), Surrey combined sources to invent a line of vocal flexibility that made the earl's poem popular for decades. It is precisely a singing or reciting voice that Surrey dramatizes. He makes 'O happy dames' an exercise in demonstrative oratory, imagining a real audience for the female speaker. The love lament thus objectifies the figure of *ethopoeia*, 'a certaine Oracion made by voice, and lamentable imitacion, vpon the state of any one'.[14] The opening stanza as *exordium* appeals as a ballad to be sung and sets the social scene: the female speaker is in a company of women, a bonding in misery (an obverse of male warriors in the misery of war). In this verse letter in reverse, all the women are invited to sing

[13] PRO SP 1/246 f. 28v; BL Add. MS 30513, f.107r. For theoretical problems raised by a male voice like Surrey's taking on a female's, see E. D. Harvey, *Ventriloquized Voices: Feminist Theory and English Renaissance Texts* (1992), esp. ch. 1. See also Heale, *Wyatt, Surrey and Early Tudor Poetry*, 62–3: 'A female voice may also have allowed Surrey to give expression to aspects of his own experience not easily articulated by a male voice in the cultural codes of his time. The woman's experience as represented in Surrey's female-voiced poems is one of marginality and passivity.'

[14] Peterson, *English Lyric*, 17.

together, as befits a Tudor part-song. In the second lyric, they will dance together—both poems by Surrey acting out a therapy for lonely women on the home front.

In the first poem, the first stanza sets the dilemma (and the sexual imagery heightens the physical absence): 'Oh happy dames,' the speaker cries out, 'that may embrace / The fruit of your delight, / Help to bewail the woeful case' and 'heavy plight / Of me' who once rejoiced in 'The fortune of my pleasant choice: / Good ladies, help to fill my mourning voice.' Seeing oneself as 'the fruit of your delight' and 'pleasant choice' may appear as more solipsistic inversions for the poet earl, but the dramatized terms reify, in contrast to the adulterous Tudor monarch or to Surrey's father (and mother), a fidelity and constancy so strong as to generate textual androgyny:

> In a ship, fraught with remembrance
> Of words and pleasures past,
> He sails, that hath in governance
> My life, while it may last,
> With scalding sighs, for want of gale,
> Furthering his hopes, that is his sail,
> Toward me, the sweet port of his avale [departing].

In the third stanza, the speaker sees in her dreams the male's eyes that 'sometime so delighted' her that even now 'they do me good' and their absence (the 'absent flame' that now makes her burn) is so painful she cries out in a figure of *mempsis* (a cry for help): 'But when I find the lack, Lord how I mourn!' The fourth stanza continues the strange prosody of octosyllabic and trisyllabic lines; then the final decasyllabic line (acting like a chorus) reverts to a familiar Virgilian text. The lonely female lover is looking across an empty sea during the night, another Dido: 'When other lovers in arms across / Rejoice their chief delight,' weeping, 'I stand the bitter night / In my window, where I may see' the clouds moving in a strong wind and, in the next stanza, 'green waves', 'salt flood', 'rage of wind', and 'a thousand fancies' that then 'assail my restless mind'. She imagines drowned her 'sweet foe' (Troilus' oxymoron for Crysede). In the final stanzas, even though the seas have calmed her mind, she is still in terror with that paradox of all lovers: 'mirth [is] mingled with woe / And of each thought a doubt doth grow' whether her lover husband will ever come back. Her final outburst Lady Margaret Douglas knew well how to inscribe: 'Alas, no, no!'

Surrey's second poem in a woman's voice—'Good ladies, you that have your pleasure in exile'—identifies directly his wife as the speaker (or singer) of this Poulter's Measure lyric. At one point, in a catalogue of dreams, the woman narrates 'Another time the same doth tell me he is come / And playing, where I shall him find, with T., his little son.' This latter refers to Surrey's elder son, Thomas, then about 8 years old; imagining this scene of father and son may have relieved Surrey at the front in besieged Boulogne. This poem also has the structure of a demonstrative oration[15] with an *exordium* that invites women whose husbands

[15] C. W. Jentoft, 'Surrey's Four "Orations" ', 250–62.

are away and for 'whom love hath bound, by order of desire, / To love your lords' to join with her in a dance: 'Step in your foot, come take a place and mourn with me awhile.' The *narratio* also recapitulates the sea-crossing and its dangers, after which the speaker (or dancer) recounts her fearful dreams, so lovingly detailed that the young countess may herself have had such dreams and written to her husband about them (Surrey's verse letter may in turn have been a way of comforting her).

And with a kiss methinks I say, 'Now welcome home my knight;
Welcome my sweet, alas, the stay of my welfare.
Thy presence bringeth forth a truce betwixt me and my care.'
Then lively doth he look and saluteth me again,
And saith, 'My dear, how is it now that you have all this pain?'

At his voice, the first and only response from the male in the poem, the speaker falls on her bed like Troilus and sobs, one more version of Surrey's alienation. When the woman wakes from her dream, and 'the anguish of my former woe beginneth more extreme,' she can find no place 'uneath'[16] to calm 'the grief of my unquiet mind'. At the end, the young wife has only one freedom left: she can speak her sorrow and sing and dance it to shape new history and hope.

The third poem honouring his wife, beginning 'If care do cause men cry, why do not I complain?' became Surrey's single most popular lyric, being set to music, among other versions, to the lute (one transcription dated 18 May 1558, when Surrey's wife and mother were still alive). The male speaker does not 'complain' because of her, of what the woman is for him. On the contrary, 'in my thought I roll her beauties to and fro: / Her laughing chere, her lovely look, my heart that pierced so.' Her faith renews his faith and obviates any complaint. In the full context of the long poem, Surrey dramatizes nothing less than the biography of a beloved: 'So sweet a wight, so sad and wise, that is so true and just.'

Written in Poulter's Measure, the long poem of sixty lines had numerous musical settings in manuscripts and texts continuing into the late seventeenth century. It therefore provides significant evidence that Surrey's audience thought of Poulter's Measure as a song measure in half-lines rather than expanded lines of twelve and fourteen syllables. Clearly a performance piece for audiences like those at Surrey House, 'If care do cause' also develops that other characteristic of Poulter's Measure, at least as Surrey uses it and as Wyatt invented it for 'in Spayne': the lyric as verse letter. In fact, precisely the absence of the lovers ('when I think how far this earth doth us divide') motivates the lover to write to assure the beloved of his own faith, the declaration that ends the poem—Surrey's 'all for love' motif with Troilus' chivalric oaths. If this part dramatizes the moral stance towards which all the other parts have led, that is, the closure therapy Renaissance audiences expected, it has a function in the long lyric. The woman's faith has

[16] This is one of several words from Chaucer that Surrey reinvested for the English Renaissance, as noted in the study by Vere Rubel, *Poetic Diction in the English Renaissance: From Skelton to Spenser* (1941), 57–82.

helped the lover, in his different landscape, survive. As transcendent and exalted as Arcite's Emyln in Chaucer's Knight's Tale, but in a lyric and dialogic context, this woman has become a continuous interior landscape for the male lover, greater than any actual distant landscape. Her life *within* him functions as the reason why no complaint is needed. The question in the first line can thus be answered as long as the text (and her life in his text) survives.

> And so determine I to serve until my breath,
> Yea, rather die a thousand times than once to false my faith.
> And if my feeble corpse through weight of woeful smart
> Do fail or faint, my will it is that still she keep my heart.
> And when this carcase here to earth shall be refared,
> I do bequeath my wearied ghost to serve her afterward.

This 'afterward' had its own metamorphosis in two events. The first came at her husband's beheading. From the crown, the Countess of Surrey received virtually nothing, neither clothes nor jewels nor any furnishings at all from Surrey House. From Kenninghall, she did receive a 'parcel' of a bag of gold and groats as ready cash and the barest minimum of eating utensils and bowls, as well as a few other scattered items and some consideration, in the official report to the king, of her condition. The pregnant young countess was allowed four horses for her carriage, and over ten riding horses, all once her husband's, with personal names, and one great sorrel gelding trotting horse 'of my lord of Surrey with his brand'. Her children were to be taken from her control and put under the supervision of her sister-in-law, the Duchess of Richmond, now fleeing to Reigate in Surrey with the precious Howard grandchildren to their new tutor John Foxe.

The second came nearly seventy years later when the couple's second son and only surviving child, Henry, Earl of Northampton, gained his own empowerment at the court of Lady Margaret Douglas' grandson after years of waiting under his cousin, Anne Boleyn's daughter. He soon turned to the proper burial of his father and mother. The cult of the Earl of Surrey no longer had to go underground or be inverted. Music, art, theatre, poetry, fiction: the image of Surrey and his inventions could be found everywhere. Although Thetford Priory had long been demolished by 1610, the Howard tombs at Framlingham, in the parish church of St Michael the Archangel, still stood in their early English Renaissance splendour, a promise of what might have been (or so Surrey's son believed). Then, just north of these, in the open space left of the nave, the Jacobean Northampton erected an ornate tomb (with brilliant traces of red) for his parents, at its front the smaller kneeling figures of himself and his older brother Thomas, the beheaded fourth Duke of Norfolk, and at the other end, the three daughters (the Countess of Westmorland with her coronet) kneeling in piety. On the slab of the tomb are the reclining effigies, hands folded in expectation, side by side, of Henry, the poet Earl of Surrey, and his wife, Frances.

8

Imprisonments

In the years following the execution of his cousin Queen Catherine, Surrey would need that 'leech' or healing power of his wife. In that time, a counter-reaction to Surrey's effort at 'politicization' set in at the Tudor court and forecast, however he might want to ignore it, his future. Surrey was imprisoned three times in the early 1540s, and his behaviour became increasingly reckless, not unusual for a young man of 25 (and not in the least had he been a nineteenth- or twentieth-century poet or artist), but careless for someone in his elevated position in 1543. Increasingly, given his historical dilemma, Surrey had little choice but to be ambitious and solipsistic if he wanted himself or his family to survive. Concentrating on self meant salvation for his family and their enormous network of clients throughout England. At the same time he was learning, with pain, that there could be no slip-ups in that strategy. This left little time for creating a new language for his poetry and his beloved 'Britain'.

Thus, although the normal temptations for a young ambitious nobleman of the highest rank were for Surrey a kind of continuous snare, the poet earl suffered another kind of imprisonment relatively new to his culture. The bad behaviour and fury exhibited on occasion by Surrey at court, the dangerous violent encounters, sprang, at least on one level, from the nature and inevitable sensitivity of Surrey as poet, whatever the slow entrapment of him by the court of Henry VIII. What might have been allowed and even expected of a Romantic or twentieth-century poet could not be tolerated in the reign of Henry VIII, especially from the heir of the Howards. His building of Surrey House may have resulted in part from a desire to alleviate this new kind of frustration and psychic enclosing. That is, by the 1540s, the poet Earl of Surrey may have desired to be free to seek what the nineteenth century specifically saw as the need of every artist: the silence to write or create out of the single self, to internalize out of that historical world Rilke called the 'wearisome Nowhere', the 'barren Too-Much' (5: 83, 86). Such deeper tensions increasingly took their toll on his character. The dichotomy of poet and earl allowed him less and less freedom and, like all such splits, opened him up to a violence within, as well as without, which he could not escape.

Kenninghall as Prison

From the heights of Surrey House and his seat of power, Surrey returned constantly to the flat plain of Kenninghall, which provided its own kind of incarceration in the 1540s. In fact, Kenninghall was the young man's proper address, as the bill of indictment of 1546 makes clear. Over 80 miles to the north-east of London or 'fifty leagues', as the French ambassador Marillac wrote to Francis I, Kenninghall as the main residence of the Howards had generated an enormous world that had probably increased since Surrey's mother was mistress. Its size and complexity are difficult to gauge today because, after the fury of its liberators in the English Revolution, what remains of Kenninghall is one part of one wing only, a country farmhouse, with the outside brickwork still quite vivid and a large number of bricked-up windows suggesting the grandeur of the Tudor house. Today, in the middle of fertile East Anglian wheat and vegetable fields, Kenninghall is the only land the Dukes of Norfolk still own in East Anglia. Located in the middle of a plain in western Norfolk but still swept (especially in winter) by winds from the North Sea, Kenninghall was probably inspired by the magnificence of Hampton Court and Wolsey's original design. Its brickwork and diaper ornamentation, its series of courtyards in an H shape, the north and south open, provide a design with the architectual flexibility Dr Andrew Boorde had called for in the first chapter of his 1542 *Dyetary of Health*, a text dedicated to Norfolk and probably alluding to the architecture of the new Kenninghall.[1] Although the spot had its own mythology as the ancient crowning place of Anglo-Saxon kings, the duke had deliberately cultivated its 700 acres, enclosing it with fences and stocking it with deer, for a strategic purpose: Kenninghall was located in Norfolk but near the border of Suffolk, the control of which the duke had never ceded to his long-time fellow duke, Charles Brandon. It was this strategy of location Surrey himself was following over fifteen years later when he chose Mount Surrey as his own base of operations. Like all Tudor nobility, the Howards were out to consolidate power through architecture.

If this surviving fragment of a wing could be multiplied by six times (or possibly eight), the size of this Howard hub of activity might be calculated. The inventories after the fall of the Howards in 1547 also help to suggest the size. They describe, for example, furnishings for a suite of apartments for the duke himself and another for the duchess, hers still intact despite the break-up of the marriage (her apparel at Kenninghall was returned to her only after her husband's attainder and her son's beheading); separate apartments for the earl himself; others for his wife, his children, and their 'master'; separate apartments for his sister, the widow Duchess of Richmond, and for his brother Lord Thomas Howard and, presumably, his family; and for Norfolk's mistress, Bess Holland, whose father, the duke's secretary, was lodged over the huge gate and entrance to the house. Hadrianus Junius, the Dutch humanist acting as physician to the household and also teaching the Howard children, had his separate quarters, probably nearby at Shelfanger

[1] Kaulek, *Correspondence*, 371. Andrew Boorde, *A compendyous regyment* (1542), ch. 1, esp. 19. For a local background to Kenninghall, cf. M. F. Serpell, *Kenninghall: History and St Mary's Church* (1982). I am grateful to Mrs Serpell for her help. I am also indebted to Mr and Mrs Brown, who welcomed me to the present Kenninghall and were farming there.

Hall. The Earl of Surrey had his lodgings, his master chamber and his bedchamber, on the second storey of the 'Ewery [a room for water pitchers, table linen, and towels] North'. There were also separate chambers for other household officers, the Almoner, the Auditor, the Master of the Horse, the Treasurer, the Hunter, and the Comptroller, as well as special quarters for the Children of the Chapel. There were more apartments in the indoor tennis court, as well as office areas and a single room for the 'lads' of the kitchen.

Just how enormous Kenninghall was can be calculated by proportioning three examples to the whole complex. The ducal chapel on 'the nether storye' or ground floor held a great wooden gilt retable, approximately 12 by 5 feet, depicting the Nativity, Crucifixion, and Resurrection of Christ 'wrought upon wainscot'. It needed a large space to give it proper perspective, and a large chapel needed a complementary large residence. In addition, the chapel contained expensive large tapestries of counterfeit arras, each depicting the story of the Passion and each 9 square yards. Some of the 'tablets' or wooden icons later delivered by Gates to the Protector Somerset were probably here, such as 'a tablet of gold' of the Blessed Virgin holding the head of Christ (the *Pietà* that ended the popular devotion of the Way of the Cross); a 'great tablet', with the Resurrection on one side and the Annunciation on the other; and another of St John at the Cross comforting the Virgin, a biblical subject also on the crystal cover of the great Gospel book kept especially by the Protector. Also taken for the Lord Protector were silver-plated boards for Psalters and three 'primer' or Mass books the Duchess of Norfolk had brought with her from Thornbury, each decorated with Stafford knots in silver gilt. Two organs and specially embroidered vestments, including forty-two copes, reveal the extent of the liturgical services carried out by a special choir, six domestic chaplains, and a full complement of 'clerks' and musicians. In the inventory after the Howard collapse, most of the chapel ornaments and vestments were assigned to the Princess Mary, except for the chapel plate which was to be melted down immediately for coins.

Princess Mary and the Lord Protector divided (equally) the livestock of 204 horses (the riding horses with personal names), 88 oxen, 115 steers, 407 sheep, and 420 hogs, with supplies in the salt store of 1617 codfish and other fish (eleven barrels of salmon). If the livestock give a proportionate idea of the whole estate in 1547, the size of the long gallery on the first floor shows the larger frame of Kenninghall. The long gallery had apartments above it and, below it, on the ground floor, was the great hall and formal presence chamber with six 'verdures' or tapestries, with Howard arms in their centre. In contrast to the great hall, in the upper long gallery were twenty-eight 'diverse other small tables of the vysenamies [physiognomies]' or portraits 'of sundry estates [that is, persons from various levels of society] being in diverse countries'. Such displays, emulating the royal collection, had become increasingly fashionable with the nobility, especially portraits of ancestors, but also 'hanging' in this Long Gallery was a 'faire table' showing the Siege of Pavia (where Francis I had been captured by Charles V) also later 'removed to the Lady Mary'. Here there may have been (out of over fifty in the inventories) large tapestries showing the Hercules myths and the Temptation of Paris. Surrey had other galleries to roam in: a short gallery on the top floor that led to a turret chamber and its view across the Norfolk plain, and then a press (or cupboard) gallery that contained items ranging from a yellow Bruges satin bed-canopy and valance to the harness of a horse and old armour.[2]

But in his roaming through Kenninghall, the poet earl could not escape the signs of his own power that imprisoned him there. Behind the statistics lay a world already making demands of both time and being on its heir apparent, slowly splitting the poet earl who must define, whatever the increasing discoveries of his talents and the perfections of his ear and single good eye, the collective 'affinity' of 'good lordship'. He was to be a future ruler 'deserving respect and "worship" '. It would be a mistake to think that the late medieval or early sixteenth-century house lacked privacy (at Kenninghall Surrey's special apartments were accessible only to his closest servants and separate from his family). Still the ducal seat at Kenninghall had its special social tensions no one could escape—tensions Hadrianus Junius described bitterly in one of his letters from Kenninghall. Two poems from this period indicate the need for a Stoic balancing of self amid such tensions. They show that what Surrey found increasingly hard to achieve, he could at least define for others. The first lyric, probably to his older son, became a popular song later in the century. This earliest attempt in English to reproduce the classical metre of sapphics (an experiment only Lord Herbert's brother George could handle successfully) translates Horace's ode on the Golden Mean. Surrey defines the fine art of balancing options: 'Of thy life, Thomas, this compass well mark: / Not aye with full sails the high seas to beat, / Nor by coward dread, in shunning storms dark' (43). A second such poem, a translation from Martial in powerful English phrasal units, is less experimental but continues, by the same direct address, the lessons in Stoic control, here catalogued as the aspects of the happy life, Horace's 'focus perennis' and 'toga rara' becoming in a figure of *hendiadys* (compression in which substantives act as adjectives) 'the household of continuance' and 'no charge of rule nor governance'. The ending reveals that Surrey could textualize at least the 'quiet mind' he would never have again: 'Contented with thine own estate, / Neither wish death nor fear his [its] might' (44: 15–16).[3]

[2] PRO LR 2/115 and 116. See also C. R. Manning, 'Kenninghall', *Norfolk Archaeology*, 7 (1892), 289–99; 15 (1904), 51–8.

[3] For the meaning of lordship, see Stone, *Family*, 85–90; Geoffrey Hindley, *England in the Age of Caxton* (1979), 176–7. For his life at Kenninghall, see Hadrianus' letter to Dorset where the eminent Dutch scholar is devastating in his account of the life at Kenninghall with Surrey gone ('when he is absent, I am once again beset with unpleasant and grim solitude' and 'a two-headed evil is upon me on both sides'). Seeking another position, Hardrianus writes: 'I am filled with the utmost distaste for that retreat where nothing can be gained for good character or good example, where corrupt ambition and shady alliances have shut off every path to integrity; taken away is the opportunity to confide in a sincere friend, everything is doubt and suspicion, no mention is made of letters [books] in illiterate conversation, and the brazen, headlong boldness of insolent youths (I refer to those darlings of fortune)'—presumably Surrey's children—who 'are turning everything upside-down'. In the Martial

Norfolk House in Lambeth and Two Satires

In London the moments of contemplation and silence would have been fewer. Surrey's daily schedule there ranged from morning conferences with stewards and other servants, midday dinners at Whitehall across the river or at some other palace or town house with influential courtiers, sittings for painters like Holbein and Scrots, afternoon and evening social events like dances and receptions, as well as the daily rituals of attending Mass and public functions (such as trials and executions). For such a schedule, Norfolk House in Lambeth, hardly larger than Surrey House, served as a base, although Surrey stayed elsewhere in London, most notoriously in the winter of 1543 at Mistress Milicent Arundell's tavern in St Lawrence (Jewry) Lane, and then in the same year at Hampton Court, voting with his father at the Chapter of the Order of the Garter on Christmas Eve. Over 150 years later, a drawing of Lambeth Palace, the official residence of the Archbishop of Canterbury, and of the church of St Mary beside the palace gates, shows a landscape still rural and wooded, and immense traffic on the Thames with a landing at one large house to the west of St Mary's. The river before Norfolk House was, in the eyes of the secretary to the Duke of Najera in 1544, so splendid that no 'more beautiful river should exist in the world, for the city stands on either side of it, and innumerable boats, vessels, and other craft are seen moving on the stream.'

Norfolk House appears to have been as commanding a residence for social events as the court of Henry VIII required. When Surrey's son, the fourth Duke of Norfolk, sold Norfolk House over two decades later, after converting the abandoned monastery of Charterhouse further downstream into a magnificent town residence for himself, the old mansion was described as a 'capital messuage', or major dwelling-place with outlying buildings and adjoining lands, including acres of pasture, meadow, and a marshland called 'the Hopes'. The original size

poem—BL Harleian MS 78, 29v–r—Surrey was probably addressing a friend, who may have been Sir Edward Warner, an accuser at his trial. The trochaic 'Warner' surfaces, in various versions, for the opening 'Martial' or 'Marshall' and for the iambic 'My friends' in the song versions. These latter reveal the popularity of Surrey's translation and were found in the Mulliner Songbook and Bassus partbook, the emphasis on 'friends' in its address giving the poem the sense of group participation or salon performances. These versions had, as Stevens has shown in his discussion of the musical transcription of this poem, a 'rare delicacy and feeling' and subtlety equal to the performances of later Elizabethan madrigal composers. By Surrey's beheading, the poem already possessed a wide manuscript audience, even in the universities, for in 1547 in William Baldwin's *A Treatise of Morall Phylosophie* there was published, unascribed, Surrey's long epigram from Martial, one of the three publications of a Surrey text before Tottel. At the beginning of the Jacobean period, Sir John Harington had copies of this popular translation in his autograph copy of his epigrams presented to Prince Henry in 1605, and headed it 'A translation of the Earl of Surreys out of Martiall directed by him to one Maister Warner'. For discussion of musical settings, see Stevens, *Music and Poetry*, 162–3, and Ivy Mumford, 'Musical Settings to the Poems of Surrey', *English Miscellany*, 16 (1957), 14–16. It should also be noted that earlier Harington had written an epigram to his friend Sir John Davies of Hereford defending his own trans-textualizing of Martial by citing, in order of importance: 'But Surrey did the same, and worthy Wyatt, / And they had praise and reputation by it' and then naming Donne's grandfather, John Heywood, among other epigrammists.

can be deduced by the fact that the Howards had been forced, through the years, to buy two inns (the 'George' and the 'Bell') on either side, adding them to east and west wings of the mansion. Indeed, with a frontage of 125 feet, the original Norfolk House had a great gate on the road that went from Lambeth in Surrey to the then St George's Fields. Through this gate, horses and carriages passed into the duke's large paved yard. To the west of the courtyard rose the duke's large chapel and, on the east, kitchens, and then on the first floor 'a greate chamber', a gallery (where in August 1546 the Garter King of Arms Barker confronted Surrey about his coat of arms). To its side was an oratory for private prayer and meditation or possibly for serious music or readings, and several private rooms or 'closets'. A central hall opened on an immense garden to the south, also 125 feet in width.[4]

Two poems reflect the backdrop of Norfolk House in the 1540s. Each has a satiric intensity not found in other Petrarchan texts by Surrey and they provide excellent examples, among the earliest, of Tudor *vers de société*. They also illustrate the sexual battle-grounds of that world. The first of these 'Too dearly had I bought my green and youthful years' reads like a verse letter. The shortest Poulter's Measure poem by Surrey, its twenty-two lines read like an elaborated epigram. With flourishes and acid satiric thrusts in a poem only waiting for heroic couplets to turn it into neoclassical bravado, the speaker consoles directly a younger male friend. The friend is having sexual difficulties that not only threaten the younger man's dignity but insult the whole structure of the blood nobility. On one level, the poem inscribes a relatively modest male chauvinism, with the deception of the woman as simply part of the courtly love game to be played. On another, the larger questions of deceit, especially of language, undercut the premises on which both noblemen base their lives, both the older one giving the advice and the younger one suffering 'secret smart'. Surrey's act of protection marks the narrative of the text, the loving gesture by an older male to a younger. Unlike the lover in earlier texts, the speaker here does not bewail his alienation but analyses another's. He can help, as he announces at the start through a kind of *litotes*, because he had bought his own 'green' years too expensively and recognizes 'when craft for love appears'. He has total and intense sympathy for the younger male:

> So stands it now with me for my beloved friend:
> This case is thine for whom I feel such torment of my mind;
> And for thy sake I burn so in my secret breast,
> That till thou know my whole disease my heart can have no rest.

In this figure of *anastrophe*, Surrey reverses expectation: the younger man is not asked to unburden himself immediately but to bear as delicately with the

[4] For the description of the Thames, see *LP*, vol. 19, 517 (273); *Archaeologia*, 23 (1831), 354 ff. For Norfolk House, London City Council, *Survey of London*, ed. Sir Howard Roberts and Walter H. Godfrey (1951), 23, South Bank and Vauxhall: The Parish of St. Mary Lambeth, 1, 137–40.

older male as the older does with the younger. So figured, the speaker's sympathy leads to his revealing to the younger male the depth of deception and the breakdown of their chivalric code: 'Where thou hast loved so long with heart and all thy power, / I see thee fed with feigned words, thy freedom to devour.' Punning once more on the word 'freedom' (as nobility), Surrey makes the word the point of the lyric. When the lover thought that 'in [the beloved's] grace' he 'held the most, she bore thee but in hand,' in the idiom of the day. She was abusing him with false promises. She has done even worse. 'Her pleasant cheer' is 'in chiefest of thy suit', that is, for one of his own servants: 'When thou art gone, I see him come, that gathers up the fruit' and, most dishonourable of all, 'I see the base degree / Of him to whom she gave the heart that promised was to thee.' This lowering of social rank is thus the ultimate crime of the woman. It leads to the final thrust of the epigram and aphoristic general indictment: 'I see, what would you more, stood never man so sure / On woman's word but wisdom would mistrust it to endure.'

This misogynist attack continues in the next satire that Surrey composed during this period. In one of his strangest texts, written in the long lines of Poulter's Measure out of an outrage almost cosmic, the poem goes well beyond the insult that precipitated it. 'Each beast can choose his fere according to his mind' illustrates, in fact, that the more an author raves about one subject, he is really addressing another. In this case, the breach of a code of male/female relations and of class status in which a young woman refused to dance with Surrey became an insult that usually only men gave to men. The violence and outburst can hardly be explained by the incident itself. The poet earl appears to have recognized from the start of the poem the dangers of his uncontrolled emotions. He plants immediately an objective structure—a beast fable, with Chaucerian overtones—for the progression of the narrative that should distance as formally as possible the painful incident (and its meaning) from himself.

Thus the first lines set, with bitter irony, the *propositio* that logically announces the governing theory or cause behind the whole series of effects making up the poem. Even a single beast can choose his mate as he will and also 'show a friendly cheer like to their beastly kind,' that is, not be so rude about it. In the third line, Surrey begins his fiction by inventing a third-person observer or narrator of the event on the dance floor that triggered the insult and narrative. 'A lion I saw there,' says the narrator, 'as white as any snow.' The narrator enjoys gazing on 'this gentle beast', whose face and body show him as a natural superior, 'Which seemed well to lead the race, his port the same did show' and 'seemed me of noble blood to be.' Building on the old badge emblem traditions of chivalry (the lion for the Howards), Surrey uses the double 'seemed' of the narrator to work towards greater objectivity. Objectivity works also in his use of *litotes*, where understatement not only establishes a narration for what the court might recognize as a *roman à clef* but so frames and objectifies the old chivalric fiction of the white lion (silver in the heraldic argent of any coat of arms) that it helps to deflect the enormous male conceit of the protagonist and, behind him, the poet inventing it all.

The whole poem builds on the image of Surrey dancing, and in this same period the young earl is described as dancing not only with the Princess Mary but with Lady Margaret Douglas. This was at the receptions in February 1544 for the Duke of Najera, whom Surrey had been specially chosen to greet at Dover and then escort with Queen Catherine Parr's brother, just created Earl of Essex, through London and Westminster to meet Henry VIII. At one such reception, more encompassing than any at Norfolk House, the queen herself had theatrically led the ladies in, at the moment 'musicians with violins' were introduced to the audience. The third Queen Catherine was as spectacularly dressed as in all her mannerist portraits, on this occasion in a robe of cloth of gold, a petticoat of brocade with sleeves lined with crimson satin and trimmed with three-ply crimson velvet, a train of two yards, a headdress studded with brilliant diamonds, a girdle of gold with enormous pendants, and two crosses around her neck. This fervent reformed Christian, who would call her heart 'stonie' in her *Lamentacion* of the next year, had led the dance with her brother, the new Earl of Essex, probably in a slow dance like a pavane. After it, Surrey also danced with both Princess Mary and Lady Margaret in the ceremonial pavane introduced from Spain by Henry VIII's first Catherine and suited for this reception. With its soft turns, hands touching, *vis-à-vis*, the pavane was often followed in this period by the dynamic galliard. That evening, because a Venetian in the king's (or more likely, the Princess Mary's) household danced galliards with 'wings in his feet', it is likely Surrey and both princesses (including 11-year-old Elizabeth) may also have danced galliards, leaping in the air together. Often without touching hands, dancers of the galliard would have hurled themselves in the same triple-time configuration of small and great jumps before the vigorous turns this dance from the court of Francis I called for.[5]

In Surrey's satiric text 'Each beast', such dancing becomes part of the narrative, as the third-person observer notes: 'And as he pranc'd before, still seeking for a mate,' the lion was one 'who would say there is none here I trow [believe] will me forsake.' Then the narrator perceives 'a wolf as white as whale's bone, / A fairer beast, a fresher hue, beheld I never none' but the she-wolf has one problem: 'her looks were fierce, and froward eke her grace.' Towards this beautiful young woman with the perfect complexion, 'this gentle beast gan him advance apace, / And with a beck full low he bowed at her feet' and, says the narrator, 'In humble wise as who would say I am too far unmeet.'

The reaction of the wolf-woman to the young lion's advance and invitation to dance is ferocious. The scorn in her face 'wherewith she him rewarded' had never had its equal, at least for one who deserved well (at least in this narrative) like the young lion. More insulting, the young woman pulls back in disgust 'near a foot or

[5] BL Harleian MS 8219, f. 114.

twain', then snaps back 'with spite and great disdain', saying ' "Lion," ' if you had known my mind beforehand, you could have saved yourself the trouble and ' "all thy pain forlorn." ' She is direct and sarcastic: ' "Do way, I let you weet [understand], thou shalt not play with me, / But range about" ' for someone more suitable for you. The young lion has obviously not been treated in this way before, especially in such a public forum as a court dance and by a female he, as a male, could not challenge. He immediately 'beat his tail, his eyes began to flame,' and, says the third-person audience, 'I might perceive his noble heart much moved by the same.' This further use of *litotes* and then the narrator's noting how 'saw I him refrain, and eke his rage assuage' attempt to distance Surrey himself from the poem he is crafting. In fact, it is in that distance from his own fury that the text is even possible. Thus, with this space established (or the attempt to do so), the poem moves to its second stage, its main argument.

In over fifty lines that now end the poem, the long monologue of the white lion 'when he was past his rage' inscribes the male's own worthiness and the honour and nobility of his family. The whole of this fiction leads, in fact, to one more version of Surrey's 'SAT SVPER EST.' The male white lion is clearly hurt by the ferocious denial of the wolf-woman: ' "Cruel, you do me wrong, to set me thus so light, / Without desert for my good will, to show me such despite." ' He comes to the point at once: ' "How can you thus entreat a lion of the race / That with his paws a crowned king devoured in the place?" ' This reference to the battle of Flodden and, indirectly, to the augmentation of the Scottish crown allowed on the Howard coat of arms sets the sequence. His nature is thus ' "to prey on no simple food / As long as he may suck the flesh, and drink of noble blood." ' Furthermore, the lion remarks, if you are young and beautiful, what about me? ' "Am I not of your hue?" ' His 'blood is not untrue' and to prove his genealogy, the speaker now gives what he considers to be an exemplum of the nobility of the white lion, Howard honour and love combined, as pure as in Chaucer's *Troilus*. This was an actual narrative the haughty young woman would know well, for it had been the great love-story of the Henrician court: ' "For you yourself doth know it is not long ago / Since that for love one of the race did end his life in woe" ' (27–37). The price for Lord Thomas Howard's loving so purely Lady Margaret Douglas had been the Tower and death. Now Surrey names such a sacrifice not only worthy of his family name but as the model for younger white lions.

After narrating this proof of noblest love, the young lion continues his sarcasm: ' "But well I may perceive that nought it moved you, / My good intent, my gentle heart, nor yet my kind so true." ' Surrey uses 'kind' for its ambiguity, its old and new meanings of nobility. Also, in this strange warfare with a woman, probably the first so violent in English and well beyond the malice of a Wyatt, the difference is finally not so much between the sexes or even between his attraction and her repulsion as, at least in the text, between the speaker's true nobility and the woman's lack of it: ' "My kind is to desire the honour of the field." ' A Howard must lead, even in dance.

With this keynote of 'honour', the poem begins to abandon its objective frame. More vitrolic in its attack, the text now focuses no longer on the woman but on what she represents. Whatever her ' "coy looks / I am no man that will be train'd, nor tangled by such hooks." ' Although some want to bow, ' "I will observe the law that nature gave to me," ' his inalienable right, in natural law, as a noble of the blood. As a true lion, the speaker of the monologue within the third-person narration will act like one. He will ' "conquer such as will resist and let the rest go free." ' Then, to dramatize his freedom, the lion-speaker invokes a frequent Surrey image, that of the falcon. It was a daring allusion, one to Anne Boleyn and, after the recent beheading of Catherine Howard, perhaps to her.

> And as a falcon free that soareth in the air,
> Which never fed on hand or lure, that for no stale doth care,
> While that I live and breathe such shall my custom be,
> In wildness of the woods to seek my prey where pleaseth me,
> Where many one shall rue, that never made offence.

The text is quite clear: the lion declares war on the wolf's kind. The revenge motif follows to the end with a kind of hysteria and loss of thematic control, hysteria that apparently Surrey recognizes enough to frame it in language. At the end, with ' "more despite and ire than I can now express," ' the young lion boasts that he ' "was author of this game",' asking her first and then setting up the whole action on the dance floor. As proof, he has created a poetic discourse and its fiction. Whatever his 'wrath', he has redeemed the honour of the Howards, his honour. Enough has survived, and he concludes his monologue with no apology for the uneven text: ' "It boots me not that by my wrath I should disturb the same." '

What triggered this outburst? Was it merely another example of a power-hungry aristocrat, with the deranged pride of his mother, furious because he was powerless to make an intervention during the collapse of his class? Or a male with sexual ambiguities and neuroses, all of which surfaced under female rejection into bad manners and hysteria? Or was he left angry at unfulfilment and deeply guilty at dreaming of affection from the beautiful young woman? Or did the woman simply tell the young Narcissus, the whining Howard brat, about the truth of what he was, and he could not take it? The resolutions against the woman, the images of Flodden and the lovers in the Tower, the image of the falcon, all suggest this rage moved to a larger issue, the definition of honour, on the noisy dance floor as in war, 'the honour of the field'. This shift in the battle-ground to sexes at war over a metaphysical issue such as honour signals a profound change. Not only is Surrey cracking under contradictory pressures but probably he is cracking up in the transformed culture of England as it tried to define its own new realities. Gender, sexuality—but not necessarily desire and certainly not male honour—became a battle-ground. The world of Flodden, at least its codes, was simply not surviving. On such a dance floor, then, possibly in 'the greate chambre' at Norfolk House in Lambeth, at a party Surrey may have hosted in August 1542, the young woman touched on the rawest of nerves by violating a ritual in a society ready to explode. This 'she-wolf' had forced the poet earl to acknowledge that his definition of honour was not inclusive enough to survive the new codes the Tudor world was bringing into being.

Who was the woman? An early tradition identifies her with Anne Seymour, the second wife of Edward Seymour, then the Earl of Hertford. The Stanhope badge of her family was the wolf, and Seymour himself came from Wulfhall in Savernake Forest (under Buckingham's patronage). Her identification had obviously existed before Drayton, who added in the later Renaissance, as a gloss to Surrey's 'heroicall epistle' to Geraldine, a note on 'beautious Stanhope': 'Of the Beautie of that Lady, he himselfe testifies, in an Elegie which he writ of her, refusing to dance with him, which he seemeth to allegorize under a Lion and a Wolfe.' For Drayton, Anne Seymour was probably a name or foil by which he could evoke for Elizabethan and Jacobean audiences that long-ago court of Henry VIII. In actuality, 'beautious' was not the best term for the Countess of Hertford in 1542 or the fiery Duchess of Somerset, who quarrelled bitterly in 1548 with her former reformed Christian friend Queen Catherine Parr on the rights of precedence (after the widowed queen's sudden marriage to the duchess's brother-in-law Sir Thomas) and then in the next year, in an emotional letter to Paget, defended her husband shortly before his arrest on 8 October 1549: 'Ah, good lord, what a miserable unnatural time is this? What hath my lord done to any of these noble men? or others? that they should thus rage and seek the extremity to him and his that never had thought in the like towards any of them?' and 'Oh, that I could bear this as I ought to do with patience and quietness, but it passeth all frail flesh to do.'[6] In the early 1540s, this loyal advocate of her husband may have had good reason to refuse to dance with Surrey. If it is true that Surrey had struck Seymour in 1537 and that in the next few years old Norfolk had tried to match the Howards with the Seymours but Surrey had violently objected, then this second wife of the Earl of Hertford may have been insulted by Surrey's daring to ask her to dance without first apologizing. Whether he was acting out of *noblesse oblige* (was he the host?) or simple attraction to her looks, she would not have taken his invitation to the dance, without apology, with 'patience and quietness'.

Fleet Prison and a Letter

Stoic patience and Plutarchan quietness of mind were more difficult for Surrey to attain in the last years of his life. Both in his increased inward sensitivity (the self he

[6] For the social occasion, Bapst, *Deux gentilshommes-poètes*, 370–6. Drayton, *Works*, 2:285. Starkey, *Rivals in Power*, 129.

could not deny, as his continuous writing showed him) and the external political pressures about him (over which he had no control), the poet earl was unwittingly making himself more and more vulnerable. In his excesses of spirit and sensitivity, and his obvious fights against depression and a temptation to violence, enemies could find opportunities. For such excess, Surrey was twice arrested and imprisoned in the Fleet Prison in 1542–3, his second and third imprisonments after the first at Windsor. From the fourth in 1546–7 Surrey never returned.

Previously, two altercations had involved Surrey. The first episode illustrates the tempers and male challenges seemingly natural to the period and, further, the kind of family infighting Surrey had to deal with at all times, even in the relative sanctuary of Mount Surrey. In April 1539, Norfolk's nephew Sir Edmund Knyvett caused a great disturbance in Norwich. At the election of the knights of the shire of Norfolk for Parliament, Sir Edmund, Surrey's hostile accuser in 1546, stood as candidate against the two nominees supported by the Duke of Norfolk. When he was rejected, he turned against the winner, Sir Richard Southwell, a Howard cousin and client, 'in such fume' that other parties broke them up, fearing a dreaded breach of the peace. When the bad blood persisted, the duke had to intervene, Norfolk finally binding them both over to Star Chamber with a bond of £2000 apiece. The nephew then turned on his uncle and 'used such marvelous words and fashion' that the duke had either to confine him or charge him on allegiance to keep peace. 'He is young,' wrote Norfolk to Cromwell on the occasion, 'and trusts too much to his wit' and his Welsh friends. Unfortunately the matter did not end. When Knyvett did come to court to answer the charge, he was accompanied by Surrey's young squire, Thomas Clere. At that point the emotional Knyvett lost control. On 10 June he was arraigned for 'striking of one Master Clere of Norfolke, servant with the Earle of Surrey, within the Kings house in the Tenice Court.' Closely connected to the Boleyns, Clere would soon be engaged to Mary Shelton, the sister-in-law of Knyvett; he would be, one would presume, someone solicitous of Knyvett. Within the environs of the court, that is, of Henry VIII's own person, on the tennis court at Greenwich, Knyvett became suddenly angered by some action or remark of Clere's (was he losing the game?) and struck him, the same crime allegedly committed by Surrey against Seymour in 1537. Knyvett was quickly seized, tried, and condemned to lose his right hand. At that time Norfolk had power enough to intervene and, when Knyvett himself made the chivalrous request that his left hand be removed but that his right remain to serve the king, he was saved. The other altercation involving Surrey is simply noted in the margins of a Privy Council meeting on 4 September 1540. A John Kynton is reprimanded for his 'naughty and ungracious words to my l of Surrey', phrasing that suggests the exalted level of Surrey's rank and the constant temptation of words in a society where tempers were nothing if not violent—especially for a direct descendant of Hotspur like Surrey.[7]

[7] John Stow, *Annales*, 581–2. *LP*, vol. 14, i, 800 (380–1); ii, 67–8.

Surrey's first imprisonment in 1542 may also have been a matter of family honour and may have involved no one less than Cardinal Pole, to whom in 1546 the same cousin Knyvett connected Surrey, saying under examination that 'he knew no untruth directly by the Earl of Surrey, but suspected him of dissimulation and vanity' and he did know 'a servant of [Surrey's] had been in Italy with Cardinal Poole, and was receiv'd again at his return.' Although the exact cause of Surrey's imprisonment is not clear, three documents date it. On 13 July 1542, the Privy Council sent an order: 'the Warden off the Fleete for to receyve therle off Surrey, to remayne there prisoner during the Kinges plesor, having twoo off his servantes to attende upon him, and to suffer none to resorte to bankett wyth him.' Then on 25 July Surrey wrote a letter to the Council asking for his release, a long inscription by an angry but contrite young man that exemplified Surrey's mastery of Tudor prose. The main strategy of Surrey's eloquent plea for freedom—the second document—invents a rhetorical ethos of misguided youth, innocent if self-willed. There is no attempt to ask forgiveness for the mysterious crime itself, other than to plead recklessness. That what he did was justified, if offensive to the king's presence, is the unspoken premise.

Thus, the letter begins with a strong sense of bravado, a device defining his worthy person, the proof being 'the quiet conversation of [Surrey's] passed life' and his current act of contrition. He also dared to remind the Privy Council that he has written before: a body servant with him in prison, Thomas Pickering, had brought before the Council several communications (Surrey had been writing constantly while in prison), but they were 'not sufficiently' pondered nor debated 'with myself', and so far the earl had 'received no other comfort than my passed folly hath deserved'—that is, no reply. So again he thinks it his 'duty' to write the council 'to renew my suit' and 'humbly to require you rather to impute this error to the fury of reckless youth, than to a will not conformable and contented, with the quiet learning of the just reward of my folly'. He now sees how 'a Prince offended' by such an act 'hath none redress upon his subject but condign punishment, without respect of person'.

Then Surrey dramatically counters to justify himself: 'Yet, let my youth unpractised in durance obtain pardon' because even the 'gentle chastisement' of a Prince may be too much. If it were lawful, Surrey reminds the council, 'the precedent of other young men reconciled' does exist and 'by so gentle a warning,' he would 'learn how to bridle my heady will: which in youth is rarely attained without adversity.' In fact, in a probable reference to his receiving the Garter only the spring before, he adds (with rhetorical brilliance): if he could 'without vaunt lay before you the quiet conversation of my passed life; which (unstained with any unhonest touch, unseeming in such a man as it hath pleased God and the King to make me),' all this past 'might perfectly promise new amendment of mine offence.' The young earl is perfectly aware of the dangers of 'mine affliction (in which time malice is most ready to slander the innocent)' and so at this point in his letter, he follows his survival tactic that the best defence is an offensive. He asks that they double his time in prison, a better fate than being condemned 'in your grave heads, without answer or further examination to be quickly delivered; this heinous offence always unexcused, whereupon I was committed to this noisome prison; whose pestilent airs are not unlike to bring some alteration of health.'

If he is indeed 'not a member rather to be clean cut away, than reformed', and must forbear the king's 'presence; (which unto every loving subject, specially unto me, from a Prince cannot be less counted than a living death),' then could he be commanded into the country like Windsor, 'to some place of open air, with like restraint of liberty, there to abide his Grace's pleasure'? Above all, the King's Majesty must 'think, that this simple body rashly adventured in the revenge of mine own quarrel, shall be without respect always ready to be employed in his service.' After all, the poet earl is not 'the first young man that, governed by fury, hath enterprised such things as he hath afterwards repented'. Most of all, he is not 'so wed to mine own will, that I had rather with favourable surmises obstinately to stand to the defence of my folly, than humbly to confess the same, infected with any such spot; as He knoweth, to whom there is nothing unknown: who preserve you to his pleasure. Amen' (N 167–9). Surrey's diction reveals the shift in the ideology now ruling England. The reformed Christian term 'infected' was suited for a court increasingly driven by older Lutheran and more recent Calvinist ideologies. His strategy also shows his need for a new kind of self-justifying ethos, in this case, the biblical prodigal son myth that Surrey manipulates with mature control at the same time that he suggests that his immaturity and bad behaviour were only a problem of bad timing.

A third dated document gives the details of his freedom: on 1 August 1542, less than three weeks after his letter, Surrey appeared before the Privy Council at Windsor. He was freed on bond of 10,000 marks, a hefty sum, with one important caveat that identifies the problem and the person: under the heading *Henricus, Comes de Surrey, recognoscit domino regi xm mercas*, 'The condition of this recognisance is suche as iff thabovedbownden Erle off Surrey do neyther by himselff, his servantes, or any other at his procurement, any bodily displesor ether by word or dede to Jhon a Legh, esquier, or to any of his, than, etc.' It is not clear just who this John à Leigh was, but Bapst identifies him, without giving sources, as a minor courtier who had returned from Italy, been interrogated by the Privy Council about his visit to Pole, and in his comments implicated either the Howards or Surrey. The earl may have responded with a verbal onslaught or possibly physical attack at such a serious challenge not only to his honour but his family.[8] Queen Catherine Howard had now been dead for well over a year. At 26, the poet must learn to control himself if he wanted not only to aim at the centre of power but to survive.

[8] *APC*, vol. 1, 17, 19. Bapst, *Deux gentilshommes-poètes*, 257–8. Cf. Susan Brigden, *London and the Reformation* (1989), 621.

The Second Imprisonment

The next episode, which landed him in the Fleet less than a year later, could not be so easily dismissed. Instead of a defensive letter this time, Surrey wrote his greatest satire, a carefully calculated poetic oration that allowed him again to distance his text from his offence and then translate his own fury at being so humiliated into a new prophetic role for himself—an ironic metamorphosis. The result was that the structure by which the poet resolved himself developed into a vehement verse letter to London itself and, by inference, to Surrey's synchronic world of the court and England itself in 1543. It obviously hit its target. The poem surfaced as evidence at his trial in 1546 in the Lord Chancellor Wriothesley's recorded notes.

The episode began with a series of events. Shortly after the beheading of the second Queen Catherine, the alliance between France and Spain, which Henry VIII had dreaded most of all, broke up. The excommunication of the English King could now sustain even less effect than it had before, so the English were delighted when open warfare broke out between France and the Empire. Although Henry VIII would take neither side, both wooed or threatened him, the French intimidating him through their Scottish ally. When in September 1542 the Scots banished two Lords Douglas, one the estranged husband of the king's sister Margaret, the father of Lady Margaret Douglas, this act and the Scots' tiresome raiding gave Henry VIII the excuse he needed and the Howards their chance to regain the spotlight. In August 1542 Surrey was released from the Fleet, as the king did indeed need his services, for which, as Surrey had just written in his July letter, he stood 'ready'. Norfolk was sent north in a pre-emptive strike against the Scots: by his side were both his sons and his brother, Lord William Howard, who had also been released from the Tower. Norfolk entered Scotland on 21 October 1542, at the head of an army of more than 20,000 men. The English army remained only nine days, pillaging and burning and meeting little opposition. Surrey and his squire Thomas Clere watched Kelso burn to the ground. It is likely that Surrey was then sent south (his father had left) conducting the Scottish prisoners, upper gentry and nobility, to Henry VIII so that at court they could swear fealty to the English Crown. On Friday, 19 January 1543—exactly four years before his beheading—Surrey and his group of Howard dependants, his squire Clere, Clere's brother Sir John, William Pickering, and then John Hussey, the treasurer to the duke, all ate meat in an inn belonging to a Mistress Millicent Arundell in St Lawrence Jewry, near St Paul's. According to evidence presented to the Privy Council on 28 March, this was not the only occasion they had eaten meat on a fast day and they continued to do so after the start of Lent. In fact, one maid of Mistress Arundell's complained to her butcher of his cheating her over a knuckle of veal for the earl. From now on, she wanted the best 'for peers of the realm should thereof eat and besides that of a prince'. What prince? asked the butcher. 'The Earl of Surrey,' she answered, to which the butcher replied: 'He was no prince, but a man of honour, and of more honour like to be.' To this the young woman retorted: 'Yes, and if oughts other than good should become of the King he is like to be king.' The butcher shot back: 'It is not so.' She returned: 'It is said so.'

Later, at the Westminster hearing on Surrey's riotous escapade, Mistress Millicent gave it a more sinister colouring. She confessed that 'once when my lord of Surrey was displeased about buying of cloth she told her maids in the kitchen how he fumed.' Then she added: 'I wonder they will thus mock a prince.' 'Why,' quoth her maid Alys, 'is he a prince?' 'Yea, Mary, is he,' answered Mistress Millicent, 'and if aught should come to the King but good, his father should stand for King.' Joan Whetnall, another maid, confessed that, talking with her fellows, she had noted how the arms on my lord of Surrey's bed 'were very like the King's', and also thought 'if aught came at the King and my lord Prince [Edward], he would be king after his father.'

Thus, if eating meat on Friday and in Lent, the violation in 1543 of a communal religious ritual, were merely a façade for deeper suspicions of Surrey, the Privy Council soon had better evidence. In an incident 'about Candlemas last' (the Feast of the Purification of the Virgin on 2 February and significantly, in that year, four days before Ash Wednesday), Surrey went out for a night of pre-Lenten revelry. After weeks of warfare in Scotland, Surrey and his male companions may have found the prospect of carnival too tempting. At around nine at night, comparatively late for a city that locked up early in winter, 'my lord of Surrey, Thos. Clere, young Wiat [the younger Thomas Wyatt], Shelley (my lord of Surrey's servant), and young Pickering, with their servants,' sallied out of Mistress Millicent's house on St Lawrence Lane, carrying four great stonebows (crossbows that shot only stones). For the next five hours they roamed the streets of London, firing at passers-by and breaking the glass windows of houses, especially the fancy windows of the new rich like Sir Richard Gresham on Milk Street, who had made great profits from the dissolution of the monasteries, and those of Alderman Birch nearby. They also shot at apprentices in Cheapside, and everywhere 'my Lord and his company', as the Council heard, disturbed the peace. Then at two o'clock in the morning, they jumped into boats on the Thames, probably at Paul's Wharf, and crossed over, in the cold January night (but warmer than Scotland), to the south shore or Bankside and there shot at the 'queanes' or whores. In all such adolescent bullying, of course, they were hardly different from those young Englishmen in 1519 who, with Francis I, aimed stones and missiles at innocent citizens along the streets of Paris. But it was a different time, and Surrey himself could never have the freedom of other young aristocrats in their twenties in 1543.

On the next night, Mistress Millicent heard the poet earl lamenting to his friend George Blagge. The reformed Christian Blagge was rebuking him harshly for such idiocy. According to the testimony of Mistress Millicent two months later, Surrey said 'that he had liever than all the good in the world it were undone, for he was sure it would come before the King and his Council' and adding 'we shall have a maddening time in our youth and therefore I am very sorry for it.' He was right to be sorry. Did Surrey in his rank of society think he could behave like any other soldier on leave? Or drop his guard and vent pent-up feelings at any moment, just as any other wealthy young man—or poet or artist—might do?

On 28 March 1543, Surrey was ordered to appear before the Privy Council on 1 April. On coming before the Council, Surrey alleged that he had permission to eat meat, although he had been indiscreet in doing so. As for the other charge of 'a lewde and unsemely manner' of acting, 'he cowlde nott denye butt he hadde verye evyll done therein, submitting himselff therefore to suche ponishement as sholde to them be thowght good.' He was committed to the Fleet. The same day Surrey's friends Wyatt and Pickering confessed to eating meat but denied the other charges until Clere admitted his guilt. Then they were all sent to the Tower. Chapuys was soon reporting on the episode to the Emperor: Surrey and his comrades were accused of 'breaking the glass windows of honest merchants of this city' and then he noted that they were all 'professing Lutheranism', supposedly by eating meat on Friday, to which the Imperial Ambassador added his special opprobrium, 'to which heretical sect the above-mentioned earl is said to belong, besides being a Frenchman at heart'.[9]

Surrey's second spell in the Fleet did not last more than a month. Although he did not attend the Chapter of the Garter on 28 April 1543, and was excused from the 6 May Feast of the order at Windsor Castle, he may have been out of prison before that date. By 27 May he was at Hampton Court, where the king asked him to witness an oath the monarch would recite. The king now had need of Surrey as a new *vir armatus*. In that May the English King and Charles V had just ratified a secret treaty for the invasion of France, and Henry VIII's oath was about this treaty. He wanted his trusted witness, the young Howard (admired by Charles V), to be one of his instruments to carry out this oath of invasion. This approach by the king to Surrey implies two facts: the episode had been forgiven by him, and the king still considered the young poet earl a player in the faction game at court. But, in the light of what was to happen three and four years later, was more made of this episode than needed to be? Did Seymour himself construct the whole episode as a preparation for a final assault? Or was the personality of Surrey just unstable enough to destroy itself without any factional strategy? Certain maxims in a text attributed to the Seymours disclose arguments the Earl of Hertford might have used in the Privy Council: 'The Earle of Surrey and other nobility were imprisoned for eating flesh in Lent' is followed by 'A secreat & unobserved contempt of ye law is a close undermining of authority; which must be either its selfe in indulging nothing, or be nothing in allowing all' (Angelo's justice in Shakespeare's *Measure For Measure*); this is followed by 'Liberty knows no restraint, no limit, when winked at.'[10]

[9] *LP*, vol. 18, i, 73(1), 237, 351, 127. Also cf. Casady's account, *Henry Howard*, 95–101.

[10] BL Add. MS 1523, ff.36v–37.

'London, hast thou accused me?'

Surrey may have written his invective 'London, hast thou accused me?' in the Fleet Prison during April 1543. Its rough texture indicates a lack of time for revision or mature editing. Wyatt had died only the October before, and Surrey's elegy had been published six weeks later. 'London, hast thou' renegotiates the sarcasm and irony of the older poet, using a stanzaic form of *terza rima* (*abcbcbcdc*, etc.) from Wyatt's own satires and, behind them, Alamanni's satires and, behind both, the serious moral use of the form by Petrarch and its progenitor, Dante. The other formal choice Surrey made for his text reveals his difference in satiric attack. He reduces Wyatt's pentameter line to a tetrameter, eight syllables, to accelerate his invective. The reason for the rhythmic shift becomes clear as the poem develops. Surrey does not want the meditative structure of ten syllables per line and the frequent enjambement of his other poem in *terza rima*, the Petrarch *capitolo*, 'The sun hath twice.' Rather, Juvenal is his model. Surrey's perception of the failure of social community needed a more direct vehement statement like Juvenal's broad attacks on Rome, not Horace's softer mocking cadences. As in his epic verse he needed a series of end-stopped lines to assert his new theme of prophetic liberation.

The result is an extremely formal text that shows cracks. The cosmic violence Surrey sees inscribed in the originating episode becomes hyperbolic narrative like Juvenal's satire. The poem vacillates between Juvenalian extravagance and precise Horatian control of syntax. Through its cracked texture, the meaning of the text can be most compelling, the outrage overflowing, and the poem may have hit its target. In Wrothesley's scribbled notes during the examination of Surrey in 1546, Surrey's 'exclamacion against Lundon', a text then three years old and distributed only in manuscript, entered the courtroom.[11] And probably by no accident: Surrey's satire is shaped like a formal judicial oration, defending his scandalous behaviour in a public arena. In this ironic fiction of the courtroom, of course, the actual facts do not matter so much as Surrey's truth of the representation, the lawyer's fiction. As in the Windsor poems, the earl's truth is the truth of the invention, of the poem itself and its fiction, not the truth of the originating episode nor even his own guilt or innocence. For Surrey, the poet, as Sidney says in his *Defense*, 'never affirmeth' (439). The poem could never justify him in the eyes of the law, as the earl knew, but it did give the young Howard another form by which to interpret his painful life, which no poetic form or text could now save, as he must also have known. The poem only gave him the gift of language to interpret his history.

Surrey had learned oratorical form from Cicero (and the oratorical as poetic text identified Juvenalian satire).[12] Surrey's strategy centred on a weird judicial

[11] *LP*, vol. 21, ii, 555 (18). For the poem as oration, see Jentoft, ' "Orations" ', 250–62.

[12] Gilbert Highet, *Juvenal the Satirist, A Study* (1954).

metamorphosis: legitimating the hell-raising night by turning it into a bold oracular sign. Cicero and the new English Bible, especially the sonorous rhythms of Tyndale, would be made particularly Surrey's. The young earl's text to justify adolescent behaviour would carry, in its transfiguration into poetry, the noble task of warning London of its wickedness. As Surrey cries out at the climax of his prophecy: 'Oh member of false Babylon! / The shop of craft, the den of ire. / Thy dreadful doom draws fast upon.' Thus, in a city that had seen, in Surrey's full memory, the deaths of More, Fisher, the Carthusians, Luther's beloved Barnes, Pilgrims of Grace like Darcy and Aske, Anabaptists, his uncle, the Howard queens, Wyatt, and would soon see the fiery death of Anne Askew, among hundreds of others, he reminds London of a greater law: 'Thy martyr's blood, by sword and fire, / In heav'n and earth for justice call.' In a new oratorical ethos, the poet now views himself as a grander protector than either the friend of Geraldine or the comrade at court or in the field, grander than either the *vir togatus* or *vir armatus*. As Jeremiah exhorted, so too he will use bows and missiles against the new Babylon and with the specific linguistic authority of a holy biblical prophet (AH 2: 89–91).

To characterize an outrageous ethos, Surrey uses established linguistic strategies. Not least is the scholastic (out of Aristotle) proof of an enthymeme or 'argument urbanely fallacious', as Tesauro later called this kind of reasoning by truncated syllogism.[13] Furthermore, all such syllogistic strategies develop in the text out of an oratorical set of 'places'. These constitute Surrey's mock-heroic defence of himself and his behaviour (a defence never made in actuality, either by letter or before an audience of peers). The poem's exordium or first 'place' of the oration immediately makes London the villain, with the first line's initial heavy trochee and then the strong accent on 'me'. London thus becomes, by inversion, a breacher of laws and breaker of all peace: 'London, hast thou accused me / Of breach of laws, the root of strife?' In a rhetorical figure of *exuscitatio* (building pathos to influence an audience), Surrey inverts the charge for which the speaker must apologize. Thus, Surrey's speaker in his 'breast did boil to see, / So fervent hot, thy dissolute life,' and his normal repression could no longer hold out against the 'sins, that grow / Within [London's] wicked walls so rife,' whatever the threat of 'terror' waiting for him if he did cry out. This structuring of the ethos of the orator comprises the *narratio*, the next 'place' of the judicial oration, with the irony continuing when Surrey turns his outrage into the basis for an act of humility. The heat of his blood can be excused because, in Renaissance physiological theory, anger (righteous, in Surrey's case), like love, raises the blood temperature and causes the blood to boil around an expanded heart, with strong, even violent effects. Thus, in Surrey's logic, this God-driven heat must find a means to express itself. If 'by words' the 'preachers know / What hope is left for to redress,' then in

[13] Aristotle *Rhetoric*, ed. and trans. John Henry Freese (1967), vol. 2, pp. xx–xxiii, esp. pp. xxii, 10–12. Cf. S. L. Bethell, 'The Nature of Metaphysical Wit', *Northern Miscellany of Literary Criticism*, 1 (1953), 19–40.

order for 'my hidden burden to express' itself, the speaker must find his own special 'means'.

Surrey is now at the place of his central thesis or *propositio*. Humility caused him to act as he did in order to find this means 'to express' his sensitivity to the justice of a God in Whose eyes 'no fault is free.' This poet/prophet is like 'all such as work unright / In most quiet'. In fact, the speaker equates the sleep of London citizens with *accedia*, the sleep of the soul in contrast to the georgic Virgilian labour of the poet-prophet. The speaker cannot rest until his moral call is fulfilled. Thus, in Surrey's outrageous narrative text, a new prophet is born:

> In secret silence of the night
> This made me, with a reckless breast
> To wake thy sluggards with my bow.
> A figure of the Lord's behest,
> Whose scourge for sin the Scriptures show.

And what Surrey's 'Scriptures' show is that, as in nature a 'fearful thunder clap' tells us 'sudden flame' or lightning is 'at hand', so 'the soundless rap' of Surrey's pebble-stones on corrupt aldermen's houses might make London see 'the dreadful plague . . . of God's wrath'. The propriety of such a fictional excuse for outrageous or even immoral behaviour has little to do, of course, with the fiction itself. For the poet, the greater point is that Surrey at 27 is a prophet unrecognized, an incarnation of a new kind of English nobility and honour. Having now stated his *propositio*, Surrey's orator proceeds to his *confirmatio*, and this 'place' works out of the earlier term 'sin'. The term 'sin' here becomes both a genus needing differentia and a cause seeking effects, with special results in the ensuing brilliant catalogue of the seven deadly sins. If the prophetic figure and the language describing it are distinctly reformed Christian, then the *amplificatio* of the seven deadly sins recaptitulates Surrey's medieval past, with its tendency towards personification, all an echo of what Surrey could have heard and seen in church homily and church window, in local morality play and in schoolboy catechism. By the *refutatio*, the language of the satire, with its awkward classical inversions, has become so zealous and intense that the effects can be unbearably self-righteous, if not comical and silly: 'Thy windows had done me no spite; / But proud people that dread no fall . . .' Before proud London, the orator has been 'wrested to wrath in fervent zeal'. God has implemented a 'secret call' in Surrey 'to strife'. But the hearts of London citizens are 'endured', like stones themselves and so, paraphrasing Petrarch on medieval Rome, the speaker cries out: 'Oh shameless whore! is dread then gone?'

London as the new Babylon dominates the last part of the poem. The sudden shift to a larger myth transforms the absurd gesture and childish rationalization into a finale echoing the Book of Revelation (the blood of prophets and saints in the city) and Ezekiel (the destruction of Jerusalem). Imprisoned in the Fleet for the second time, daring to write no excuse this time about madcap youth, Surrey trans-textualizes himself. The poem now leaps to a new level, greater even than the neuroses of the Howard poet. The speaker identifies with all the persecuted: 'The Lord shall hear their just desire.' This perception not only climaxes this poem but marks a major turning-point in Surrey's continuing definition of nobility. It continues the transformation of honour developed in the Wyatt elegy six months before.

The obvious arrogance of turning himself into a Hebrew prophet thus carries an odd dimension of humility for this scion of blood nobility. He finds honour now in all persecuted, whatever their social level. Such equality of suffering redefines honour and sets the meaning of his closure. The inscription of the evil society meant, as the Bible had taught, that the poet-prophet himself could no longer escape the wicked city. Indeed, such universal suffering as Surrey may have learned from the shame of his first Fleet imprisonment and certainly from the second was now shared by even the nobility of blood in the new Tudor state. In Surrey's uneven eyes, a new future for honour inscriptions was rising. From now on, in Surrey's logic, any definition of nobility will have to be revised. From Anabaptists to Anne Askew to Catherine Howard to underground monks and nuns to exhausted or beheaded poets, a common bond had emerged.

In his closure, the poet earl turns his speaking character into the ethos of humility the public courtroom demanded, and so processes his own canonization. In 'secret silence of the night' and the silence of language on a page has been born a new poet-prophet—a type of European artist who, outside religion and the Bible, challenges society. In Surrey's strategy, the London of Henry VIII is given a universal dimension in terms of the central text of Early Modern England: the Bible (in this case, the 1539 authorized Bible with the Holbein frontispiece). London is a new Babylon, only the latest. How trivial then is Surrey's own minor disturbance in the enormity of evil dramatized through rhetorical figures like *ominatio* (a prophesying of evil consequences). How liberating for its citizens is Surrey's inscription of the city's true meaning. Mock-heroic could now become heroic.

Unexpectedly, then, in this uneven text Surrey cannot fully control, a genuine prophecy does begin to emerge, with the kind of ironic reversal Surrey had read in the metamorphosis of Folly in Erasmus' *Praise of Folly*. That is, the hyperbole of the collapsing city, the hellish version of Aeneas' burning Troy, becomes, in this irony, almost operatic, like the ending of some masque Surrey might have seen at Fontainebleau. Here eschatological terror becomes redemptive for the reader (as later in the ending of Pope's *Dunciad*). Mock-heroic now allows its readers also to take on heroic tasks, the building of a new city after the burning of the old. In the middle of Surrey's London, set afire with wrath, all the lustful stricken, all the idols burnt, and towers falling in the new apocalypse, the elect that survive are rendering 'unto the righteous Lord', who judges all Babylons, 'immortal praise with one accord'. The elect are singing a true communal song in a new language. The surviving Surrey is himself singing, their new protector. With new poetic language and originating forms, he is leading the singing in fact with all those who embody this new kind of honour born of breakdown, both of his culture and himself.

The New Role of the Poet

One of Surrey's last sonnets embodies another prophetic attack. In his originating form of the discursive English sonnet, a superbly detailed representation of a tyrant reveals a total failure of honour and the moral breakdown of a royal court. The central figure of Sardanapalus (never named in the poem except through *antonomasia*, the figure of allusion) has long been identified with Henry VIII. Probably written after Queen Catherine Howard's beheading, the sonnet uses the popular Renaissance topos (begun by Boccaccio out of classical origins) of the degenerate Assyrian king. For Surrey, the Assyrian king whose control has failed and who succumbs to the lure of suicide as honour might just as powerfully reflect not only the English king but Surrey himself. In any case, the composite character of the degenerate male and the degenerate court haunted Surrey as images of breakdown that could kill him one way or another.

Th' Assyrians' king, in peace with foul desire
And filthy lusts that stained his regal heart,
In war that should set princely hearts afire
Vanquished did yield for want of martial art;
The dint of swords from kisses seemed strange,
And harder than his lady's side his targe,
From glutton feasts to soldier's fare a change,
His helmet far above a garland's charge;
Who scarce the name of manhood did retain,
Drenched in sloth and womanish delight,
Feeble of spirit, impatient of pain,
When he had lost his honour and his right,
Proud time of wealth, in storms appall'd with dread,
Murder'd himself to show some manful deed.

The option of suicide, the Roman option of Dido and Seneca, may have haunted Surrey in the 1540s, as at Windsor after the death of Richmond. Instead of suicide, however, Surrey wrote a poem—a bitter satire—about the degeneracy of a society from what he saw as its earlier ideals of honour. In this sense, besides Henry VIII and the young earl himself, there is a third figure to consider to interpret the prophetic sonnet: Surrey's new poet. Against the laziness of a degenerate king who can only achieve honour through suicide, Surrey projects a Virgilian georgic figure of life, a maker of poetic language whose whole life of building the right forms is radically contrasted with Sardanapalus'. A year before he wrote his satire on London, Surrey found such a new Virgilian hero, an archetype already operating in English society and working to redeem the city of London and the English court, Britain itself. Surrey's elegy on Wyatt, rising from this period of increasing imprisonment, reveals a positive model of Virgilian labour for himself and for England, away from Sardanapalus temptations of self. Nobility is defined by labour, the work and the blood of the poet, not necessarily by inherited blood.

The paradox is that, from his opulent heights on Mount Surrey, the Howard heir apparent exalted the role of the poet to a new level in English society. In 1542 he described a laureateship both Petrarch and Virgil, his masters, would have understood. As the highest representative of the nobility of blood (outside the royal family), he ironically enhanced another nobility. More remarkably and dangerously, he allowed his revolutionary elegy on a social inferior to be published. After such a text as a literary event, and after Tottel's publishing blitz in the 1550s, Surrey's own nobility helped to enfranchise English poet-makers and, by extension, artists, for the next centuries. In this sense, in the autumn of 1542, the new model of prophet-poet is born—Surrey's Wyatt and Surrey as Wyatt. This birth of renewed nobility was announced by a printing-press in London, the city the poet earl intended to redeem from 'desolate life' and 'dreadful doom' by prophetic powers of language. The role of the poet had changed forever.

9

A New Body of Honour: Sir Thomas Wyatt

Early in October 1542 Sir Thomas Wyatt died. He was 39 years old, and Holbein's 1541 portrait of his head, bare neck, bare shoulders, and upper chest with hair shows that, in his last years, the body had remained strong. But the effects of his final imprisonment may have been exhausting, and this rather staged portrait may not show the deeper consequences of his years as England's powerful diplomat and his delicate manoeuvring between European and English courts. In contrast to his genuine labour representing the turbulent Henrician court to Europe, Wyatt had always sought 'the quyet mind' he had named in his 1529 translation of Plutarch and described in a satire to his friend John Poins. Under that tension between the poet's need for self and contemplation and the demands of his nation, he laboured, having accepted the call of his time as clearly as Aeneas had.

In that labour, Wyatt's letters and communiqués and certain of his poems reveal not only his sensitivity to language in foreign courts but his almost animal alertness to survival tracks for his country and himself. His everyday duties required a vigilance that only a contemporary of Machiavelli could have understood. For Wyatt, such survival tactics had to be focused in his power of speech. 'His apt and handsome repartyes were rather naturall than affected: subtile and acute, prompt and easy, yet not carelesse: never rendering himself contemptible to please others,' wrote a contemporary.[1] His source of strength could also defeat him. On 3 February 1540, writing from Brussels, Wyatt reported to Henry VIII on his interview with Charles V, who, 'in all the processe, not ons or twise, but offten . . . clypped my tale with imperius and brave wordes ynow, wherby dryven to replie, to retorne to the matter, and to disgresse, other wise then euer with hym I have bene acustomid, skant my memory can containe the particular incidentes, wyche to me were as notable as the principall.' This kind of specific give and take could lead not only to vivid dialogue with the Holy Roman Emperor but, on many occasions, with Francis I, who did not like Wyatt, seeing him as a Lutheran. As reported in Wyatt's 1540 letter, both emperor and English poet debate like two Humanist pedants, speaking in Charles V's favourite language, French. They both demand the precise meaning of words and fight particularly over the politically charged 'ingrate'. In this precision, a poet's power of language could offend. The emperor later reported to Francis I that he thought, pointing to his head, Wyatt

[1] BL Sloane MS 26.

lived in fantasy, and, on the occasion of the linguistic debate, the emperor said, so Wyatt reported to Henry VIII, that 'I [Wyatt] offten prikkid hym with wordes.'[2] A poet's sensitivity to language could lead to imprisonment and worse, as the younger Surrey in his more vulnerable social position had learned.

The later Holbein portrait of Wyatt appears first as a roundel woodcut in John Leland's commemorative volume, which came out within weeks after Wyatt's death. The picture was part of the general canonization process Leland intended, and the bareness of Wyatt's body (and bald head) matches the stark almost possessed gaze of his upturned eyes. Earlier, in the time of Anne Boleyn, Holbein had drawn Wyatt in a different pose (Plate 17). That drawing gains its power from the same eyes, tawny against Holbein's pink paper. They focus an almost angry turn and twist of his head towards some figure offstage right, the poet's stark observation appearing to trap the figure and drain it of information before a word is spoken. In the 1530s, Holbein had played such fierceness of the eyes against a hat rakishly inclined over thinning hair combed forward and, in the midst of a massive beard and moustache, a tightly held mouth. Although the later portrait shows a Wyatt as stripped as the contrite David in the Penitential Psalms, the earlier Holbein shows an almost sullen figure accustomed to repression and to waiting on fools who could, he knew, kill him.

When Leland appropriated the second Holbein portrait of Wyatt for his book of elegies, he moved fast. The speed with which Leland, a close friend of both Wyatt and Surrey, composed his *Naeniae* or commemorative volume on Wyatt was remarkable. Even more exceptional was the fact that Surrey had written his elegy before then, as Leland refers to it in his *Naeniae*. Apparently from the war front in Scotland, Surrey honoured Wyatt in a special text. For the first time in his life, Surrey allowed a poem of his to be published (presumably with some difficulty because he was still in the north)—his only poem printed in his lifetime. Surrey had been in Scotland since his August release from prison and may have sent his poem back by his new friend and military comrade, the younger Sir Thomas Wyatt, when the son returned to clear up his father's affairs after the Sherborne Abbey funeral on 11 October 1542. The older poet's death had followed an exhausting ride to the port of Falmouth to greet the new Spanish Ambassador, Dr Corrierez, who had been Court Orator for the Emperor. Henry VIII had sent the elder Wyatt, whom the Imperial Court Orator admired and knew well. England's first great modern poet did not survive the trip.

Wyatt's Imprisonment and Humiliation

Wyatt's death ended a friendship with Surrey, which might have begun as early as 1532, when both were in Calais with Anne Boleyn, but appears to have flourished

[2] Kenneth Muir, *Life and Letters of Sir Thomas Wyatt* (Liverpool: Liverpool University Press, 1963) 134, hereafter noted in text as M.

after 1540, when Wyatt returned from his duties on the continent and Surrey was actively engaged at court. Despite almost fifteen years' difference in age and the looming disparity in their social rank, the friendship appears to have been constant and moved on to the generation of Wyatt's son, a little younger than Surrey. In March 1541 Surrey had a chance to rescue his fellow poet and, in subtle manoeuvring that took daring, interceded with his first cousin, Queen Catherine Howard. The whole act of rescue had been bold but successful. As a result, Wyatt did not die on Tower Hill but in honour as a free man.

His final imprisonment in the Tower produced considerable bitterness. When in January 1541 Sir Richard Southwell was sent to Wyatt's residence at Allington Castle to clear it not only of his mistress, Elizabeth Darrell, and his young daughter-in-law but of all servants, plate, and goods, the famous diplomat was arrested at Hampton Court. He had been tied by the hands, an unusual humiliation in England, especially for a person of honour who had represented the English king in Europe. Wyatt was then paraded with twenty-four archers to the Tower of London, his third imprisonment there. The French Ambassador Marillac was deeply shocked at the sudden fall and humiliation of one of Europe's leading diplomats, someone the English king had been so intimate with, especially in conversation. But Henry VIII had heard evidence hinting at a relationship with Cardinal Pole and, as only this combination of the White Rose and papal Rome could so anger the English king, he had become enraged. Marillac described the court panic after Wyatt's arrest: 'Although he is more regretted than any man arrested in England these three years, both by Englishmen and foreigners, no man is bold enough to say a word for him' (M 175–6).

As Wyatt's *Defence* would reveal, he was being defeated by a misunderstanding of his language, his use of metaphor and proverb (M 198, 202), and the misinterpretation of his actions while in Rome. In fact, except for Surrey's later intervention through his royal cousin, Wyatt might well have suffered beheading. The older poet had probably seen Surrey's first royal cousin beheaded, and only six months before his own arrest, on Tower Hill Wyatt had heard his friend Cromwell passionately call out to him from the scaffold, in a memorable scene in which Cromwell revealed not only a generous nature but extraordinary linguistic skill, just before the shamed Lord Privy Seal was beheaded.[3] Wyatt's fear of his own

[3] Roy Strong, *Tudor and Jacobean Portraits* (1969), vol. 1, 338–9. For general discussion of both portraits, see Roberts, *Drawings by Holbein*, 128. For a study of the relationships of Wyatt's poetic texts, political intrigue, and the personalities of Wyatt and Surrey's cousin Bryan, see Susan Brigden ' "The Shadow That You Know": Sir Thomas Wyatt and Sir Francis Bryan at Court and in Embassy', *Historical Journal*, 39/1 (1996), 1–31. For an idea of the depth of friendship Wyatt offered and his popularity at court, see the report on Cromwell's execution by a contemporary Spanish observer in *Chronicle of King Henry VIII of England Being a Contemporary Record of Some of the Principal Events of the Reigns of Henry VIII and Edward VI. Written in Spanish by an Unknown Hand*, trans. and ed. Martin A. Sharpe Hume (1889), 103–4. In this report, looking out on the crowd from the scaffold, Cromwell 'noticed Master Wyatt, the gentleman who had been imprisoned for the affair of Queen Anne' and called out to him: ' "Oh, gentle Wyatt, good-bye, and pray to God for me." ' The Spaniard then remarks: 'There was always great friendship between these two, and Wyatt could not

beheading may have dominated all his being in 1541, but the practical knowledge of what he had lost because of the indeterminacy of court justice became actual in the conditions of the Tower in 1541. In a *strambotto* from the Tower written to his close friend, Surrey's cousin Sir Francis Bryan, Wyatt closes with his favourite form of the proverb to dramatize his own enduring mental torment and his sense of total vulnerability.

> Syghes ar my foode, drynke are my teares;
> Clynkinge of fetters suche musycke wolde crave;
> Synke and close ayer away my lyf wears;
> Innocencie is all the hope I have.
> Rayne, wynde, or wether I iudge by myne ears.
> Mallice assaulted that [what] rightiousnes should have.
> Sure I am, Brian, this wounde shall heale agayne,
> But yet, alas, the scarre shall styll remayne. (MT 244)

'Myne earle'

For Wyatt, deep respect for the younger poet obviously grew over time. A mark of that respect is Wyatt's *strambotto* to Surrey, with its special theme of innocence. Possibly written after Surrey manoeuvred Wyatt's final release from the Tower, the text certainly originated after the 'blodye dayes' of 1536. Such violence at the court of Henry VIII dominates Wyatt's surprisingly personal lyric to Surrey, whom he singles out not only by name as noble in descent but by his subject-matter as nobility in desert:

answer him for tears,' at the sight of which the other courtiers 'marvelled greatly to see that Master Wyatt was in such grief' at the beheading of a condemned traitor. Then the Spaniard perceptively notes: 'Cromwell, who was a very clever man, noticing it [the outspoken grief and tears and the danger to his friend], said out loud, "Oh, Wyatt, do not weep, for if I were no more guilty than thou wert when they took thee, I should not be in this pass." ' It was a gesture of enormous love from the friend about to be beheaded. The Spaniard catches the meaning of the deflecting gesture: 'Everybody was very fond of Wyatt, so they pretended not to notice; but if it had been anyone else they might have arrested him, to see whether he knew of any other treason which Cromwell might have plotted.' Compare the accuracy of the Spaniard's reporting of this scene with the reports in Corpus Christi College library, Cambridge, MS CCCC 168 and BL Harleian MS 3362, f. 79r. Known as the Spanish Chronicle (and cited thus in this book), the authenticity of the historical account has been questioned. Hume's lengthy introduction about the possible Spanish observer at the Tudor court during this period and the provenance of the manuscript in the Spanish archives in Madrid suggest, however, that its prolific details cannot be totally dismissed. Despite Hume's rather Romantic diction, the editor does accurately indicate how the text builds on precise details towards a total effect: 'The barbarous sacrifice of the noble Surrey, the last effort of the dying despot, is told here with many small touches which reveal the eye-witness or deeply interested spectator.' As further evidence of its authenticity, the Victorian text had the full help and cooperation of the eminent historian James Gairdner in its preparation for press.

Somtyme the pryde of mye assured trothe
Contemned all helpp of god and eke of man:
But when I saw man blyndlye how he goi'the
In demyng hartes, whiche none but god there can,
And his [God's] domes hyd wheareby mans Malyce growth;
Myne Earle, this doute my hart did humble than,
FFor errour so might murder Innocence.
Then sang I thus in god my Confydence. (MT 239)

This conversational poem hinges, for all its tone of familiarity, on the word 'doute'. In meaning closer to Dame Julian of Norwich's 'for doubte of death' and Chaucer's 'doute of Jesus Christ', Wyatt's term carries not only fear but also a sense of profound awe—at both the vulnerability of human existence and the power of God, 'my Confidence'. In Wyatt's text, the word 'doute' follows the courteous recognition of Surrey as 'myne Earle'. It signifies the twofold act that is the performance of the poem: a doubting and then a singing in confidence. Wyatt's dual structure results, in fact, from two syllogisms, the conclusion of one being the major premise of the next, the sixth line doubling as both in the turning-point of the poem. This technical double effect defines the powerful role of Surrey as catalyst and mediator. Surrey has been witness to the same political and social violence as Wyatt; he is also witness to Wyatt's religious fervour which the poem describes.

The first syllogism arises from Wyatt's intensely held Christian vision of an inscrutable God with hidden judgements ('domes'). Such a God appears as the Other before the pride of human beings with their judging hearts, and the dichotomy resulting from human pride allows evil to flourish (at least in the logic of Wyatt's text). In such a fearful dilemma (the nature of all history), community (what the personal address to 'myne Earle' signifies) and humility are necessary for survival. Only then can the murderous potentiality of error not destroy the necessary condition for all life (again, in the logic of the text), that is, innocence. As Wyatt's own life-shattering imprisonment could attest, a world without innocence can only lead to terror and exhaustion (and, as Wyatt could not know, to Surrey's beheading a few years later). In such a world of terror and breakdown—the social actualization of Luther's and Calvin's basic human condition of original sin—Wyatt's solution is a community of language and humility. Wyatt simply recapitulates in his poetic text, then, what would become—and indeed already had—the humble Calvinist *ecclesia* with its emphasis on the Word. And so the poet's confidence springs from his double syllogism: in true noble community and humility—virtues of social dignity and honour 'Myne Earle' would understand—a poet may sing and praise the reality of genuine innocence. This the contrite David, Wyatt's recent subject, had sought and for it Wyatt could hope.

In the Arundel Harington manuscript, Wyatt's text to Surrey appears after his translation of Psalm 37, the kind of paraphrase Surrey himself would make in his last days in the Tower. The connection between Wyatt's Psalm 37 and the incidental lyric to Surrey, both with implicit calls for Stoic control at court, appears in Wyatt's first lines of the psalm that define the 'new erectyed men': 'Altho thow se th'owtragius clime aloft, / Envie not thowe his blinde prosperitye' and 'Move not thy hert by theyre felicity' (MT 94).

Why Surrey Wrote his Texts on Wyatt

Wyatt's sudden death at 39, ending a friendship that had become closer and closer, gave Surrey the occasion to reflect, at 26 and in his new military role, on the older poet's career. At this moment of death and loss—one more after so many—Surrey wrote five poems on Wyatt: four sonnets and one long elegy in his newly invented heroic quatrain, used before only for the Duke of Richmond, 'a king's son'. The writing of these poems may have been spread over time, but the central event in four poems, the unjust death of Wyatt, finds its most structured representation in Surrey's elegy in heroic quatrains. Wyatt's sudden death must have helped to focus what the poet earl had seen as latent in his culture. As Leland, England's first great antiquarian, suggests in his elegaic *Naeniae* on Wyatt (and later Cheke in his elegy on Surrey), such reflections on the poet's life at a time of national transformation were not singular among the court and university circles dominating the intellectual world of England. The fact that both Leland's and Surrey's responses to the death were so immediate in 1542 proves how much the ideology of the poet as a social force had already been worked out or at the least debated, however randomly, in Henrician society, especially since the Thynne edition of Chaucer. As Starkey, Elyot, and Berners were responding to Tudor transformations, so was the literary world. Such a debate was a natural consequence of the court's new emphasis on learning, illustrated by the young Prince Edward himself. In Surrey's last summer, the heir apparent to the throne sent a Latin letter to his stepmother Queen Catherine with the same classical phrase the printer William Caxton had put in his 1491 *Mirrour of the World*: 'Vox audita perit / littera scripta manet' ('The voice heard perishes; written words remain').[4] Thus, in a period of *renovatio* and 'new learning' that inevitably meant new terms for all communal life in England, and in language that held this society together, Surrey may well have considered the national role of a poet. Could it be established once more with the honour of a laureateship—one acknowledged by society and not by self to self, like the Howard poet John Skelton in his 'Garland of Laurel'? The poet could be, in this sense, a protector of the community, the guardian of language as Aeneas had

[4] Edited by Oliver H. Prior for the Early English Text Society (1913), 5. Edward VI's letter is from Hunsdon on 10 June 1546: 'Literae enim manet, caetera autem quae videntur pereunt. Literae etiam conducunt ad bonos mores, ignorantia autem ad malos ducit', in *Literary Remains of King Edward the Sixth*, ed. J. G. Nichols (1867), 22. *Ignorantia* had been the great enemy in his stepmother's recent religious treatise *Lamentacion* modelled on Marguerite of Navarre's *Miroir*.

guarded the household gods, as Virgil had glorified Augustus and the new empire, and as Petrarch, a diplomat like Wyatt, had worked to unify Europe and renew Rome, even receiving his laureate there. Troy—and its genetic offspring in the new city of Rome and the revived new Rome—now stood in the protection of poets, to paraphrase Anchises' farewell to Troy in Book II of Surrey's *Aeneid*: ' "O native gods, your family defend! / Preserve your line! This warning comes of you, / And Troy stands in your protection now" ' (2: 925–7). Like the household gods, the relics of language to be transmitted will be protected by poets. In Surrey's new classicism, Wyatt's death focused one of the poet earl's evolving solutions to the cultural crisis of his time.

Surrey's poems on Wyatt can thus be interpreted as special interventionist acts in two ways. First, in these texts Surrey wanted to, and in fact did help to, transform the conception of honour in Early Modern England. He identified the role of the poet, the maker of language as 'honourable', in Tottel's 1557 description of Surrey's style, and as 'noble', in Sidney's 1580 operative terms for both Surrey's life and his texts. Secondly, Surrey printed his poem. This startling act put the young earl in danger. That is, a Leland could write on a Wyatt, but the Earl of Surrey, the heir apparent to the duke of Norfolk, a probable Earl Marshal of the kingdom, could only write an elegy on a prince like Henry, Duke of Richmond, but hardly for someone of lower rank. At the Tudor court, protocol could determine survival. Even to write a poem on Richmond had been to run the risk of identifying Surrey for his father as someone as irrelevant (or even absurd) as Skelton or Barclay, a higher court jester. Also, in the Petrarchan fictions, Geraldine is not fully identified, and in composing love poems, someone of Surrey's exalted position also skirted humiliation and absurdity.

As a result of this publishing event in autumn 1542, the role of the poet in English society did change. All classes and audiences could now read the poem 'immediately' (in Cromwell's sense of urgent time) and learn that nobility was authorized in the newly emerging English language. The courtly fashioning of English was the task Sir Brian Tuke had called for in his nationalistic preface to Thynne's Chaucer in 1532, and by the time of Puttenham in 1589, the authority of the poet could reach high levels of political power. Indeed, in his *Arte of English Poesie*, Surrey and Wyatt ('betweene whom I finde very litle difference') had both become 'courtly makers'. If they formed a new Orphic model for England by 1590, the model had risen from the role of Surrey as originator and from the nobility of poets Tottel had deliberately played on when he wrote in his 'Printer to the Reader' in June 1557: 'That our tong is able in that kynde to do as praiseworthely as the rest'—what he calls 'the workes of diuers Latines, Italians, and other'—is due to 'the honourable stile of the noble earle of Surrey, and the weightinesse of the depewitted sir Thomas Wyat the elders verse, with seuerall graces in sondry good Englishe writers, [all of which] doe flow abundantly.' Tottel's plural poet synthesized as 'the ryght honourable Lorde Henry Haward late Earle of Surrey' thus represented, at least from later perspectives, transcendent values that could not only inform but cheer on new generations of language-makers, who might range socially from a bricklayer's stepson and a scrivener's son in London to a country boy from Warwickshire. It was a reinvesting of old genealogy with new birth and new forms, a new nobility, a new honour. Troy—the continuing city—now stood in the protection of poets.[5]

Three Sonnets on the Death of Wyatt

Within weeks of Wyatt's death in October 1542, John Leland published his elegaic *Naeniae*. At the same time, Surrey had already written and printed his elegy on Wyatt, although, as befitted a nobleman of his rank, he did so anonymously with a title obviously given by the printer: *An excellent Epitaffe of syr Thomas Wyat*. Beyond the overtly communal inscription of his printed elegy, Surrey added three more poems in manuscript that members of court and university circles, if not the general public, could read. They are written in the English sonnet form that Surrey invented for Richmond and used for his Petrarchan texts of love. Because these elegaic sonnets—the first series in English—suggest a destabilizing thesis, namely that mastery of language could reveal a source of true nobility in society, they must be read in conjunction with Surrey's longer elegy on Wyatt. In fact, the three sonnets share one implicit theme enlarged in the elegy: the loss of this poet and his language is a communal loss of the highest order. Such a poet-prophet as the translator of the Penitential Psalms purifies society. 'In Princes' hearts God's scourge yprinted deep,' writes Surrey in one of these sonnets, 'Might them awake out of their sinful sleep'—prophetic themes Surrey would use six months later to justify his wild behaviour in London.

The above couplet ends Surrey's sonnet 'The great Macedon that out of Persia' (31). Surrey may have written this sonnet for a living Wyatt, a token of admiration and friendship that also gave a special authorization to Wyatt's most famous text in his time, his seven Penitential Psalms. In an unusual secretary hand nowhere else in the Egerton manuscript, Surrey's sonnet is a preface, in a manuscript otherwise copied by Wyatt himself, with a special originality: the first commendatory sonnet in English. It was first printed by Sir John Harington as preface to his 1549 edition of Wyatt's Penitential Psalms. Nott is probably right to surmise

[5] The danger of lowering one's social position by writing poetry can be seen in the strictures by Sir Thomas Elyot against even a gentleman 'plainge or singing in a commune audience' in *Boke*, vol. 1, 42. *Tottel's Miscellany*, vol. 1, 2; Puttenham, *English Poesie*, 62, 60. Cf. William Kennedy, *Authorizing Petrarch* (1994), 234: 'To young Edmund Spenser the sonnet as cultivated by Wyatt and Howard, as well as by Petrarch and Du Bellay, might seem a preeminently moral genre and a forecast of life in high places. En route to Cambridge for a university education that would make him eligible for the gentleman's class, he could only construe the action depicted in Tottel's *Miscellany* as a portent of what might await him in a higher station. If the *Miscellany* offered its bourgeois readers a stereotype of the aristocratic world, it also implied the risks of entering that world.'

Surrey wrote the poem around 1541 as part of a campaign to honour Wyatt in prison (1: 334). This sonnet was certainly not written earlier, and certainly not before the Windsor sonnet and elegy, as Mason surmises,[6] for a simple reason (one many readers either miss or refuse to concede). Wyatt and Surrey were not only friends but admirers of each other's texts. As in any intellectual friendship, Wyatt himself may have borrowed from Surrey for his Penitential Psalms, not necessarily and certainly not only the other way around. In any case, as Muir and Thomson conclude (ix), it is improbable Wyatt wrote his Psalms (with their echoes of Surrey) so early and did not leave a more polished copy-text. Describing such friendship as theirs in his elegiac sonnets, Surrey borrows naturally his own recently developed Petrarchan techniques; he writes the language of love for Wyatt, the male relationship still within the ethic of the Tudor and Stuart courts.

'The great Macedon' begins with another device of *antonomasia*. 'The great Macedon' or Alexander may have won over Darius, 'of whose huge pow'r all Asia rang,' but, says Surrey, following a topos in Plutarch (recapitulated in the 1532 dedication to Henry VIII of Gower's *Confessio Amantis*), Alexander placed Homer's epics in a rich chest (or in Surrey's extreme example of Latinizing inversion, 'In the rich ark if Homer's rhymes he plac'd') because the great Macedonian longed for such texts as praise for himself. The first quatrain focuses on this exemplum of Alexander; the second then turns to a new model of hero, asking in a figure of *erotesis*: 'What holy grave, what worthy sepulchre / To Wyatt's Psalms should Christians then purchase?' Without a *volta*, the sonnet moves directly to describe the masterpiece of Wyatt. Surrey focuses his epideitic strategy with alliteration, *chiasmus*, and *asyndeton* (words or phrases in a series), building a 'place' of praise in the contrasting second exemplum of Wyatt's David, the true 'mirror'.

> Where [Wyatt] doth paint the lively faith and pure,
> The steadfast hope, the sweet return to grace
> Of just David by perfect penitence,
> Where rulers may see in a mirror clear
> The bitter fruit of false concupiscence,
> How Jewry bought Urias' death full dear. (31: 7–12)

Not only David but Wyatt himself, in his act of poetic invention ('paint') presents a 'mirror': Wyatt's reformed Christian beliefs so 'lively' and 'pure' and 'steadfast' are brought centre-stage, as is the whole conversion motif, 'perfect penitence' directly lifted from Wyatt's Psalm 51 (MT 108: 444). As Surrey's new poem suggests, if poets are thrust out of Sardanapalus courts, still they can inscribe the acts of princes and judge them. Poets as prophets can help to protect the moral life of the community: rulers, beware.

Surrey's sonnet 'In the rude age when science was not so rife' (34) continues the blame and praise dichotomy. It has a syllogistic structure, three 'If' clauses building on the logical topics of comparison and contrast. The major premise points

[6] H. A. Mason, *Humanism and Poetry in the Early Tudor Period* (1959), 238–42.

out, in a figure of *chronographia* (the invention of an era through words), that in earlier times, when knowledge was not so developed, Jove in Crete 'and other . . . taught / Arts to revert to profit of our life' so that, after their deaths, Jove and others had 'their temples sought'. The second 'if' clause, the minor premise, states that 'in no unthankful time' virtue now fails to blazon 'her endless fame' and so does not 'deter from crime' nor encourage youth, 'our sequel to inflame'. And so, argues Surrey in his sestet and conclusion, if 'Wyatt's friends' bemoan him, whose 'rare wit spent employed to our avail / Where Christ is taught,' do they deserve social blame? This simple argument appears in a complex syntax that follows classical inversion almost impossible for English (the poem gives evidence of being a hastily written epigram, badly needing revision).[7] Could the poem have been written in a furious answer to someone who had accused Surrey of writing a serious text on someone of considerably lower social rank? Although the mixed metaphors of the accusatory final couplet show haste, with a shift to the second person, their bitter invective works. In the dramatic situation of the poem, the spectator confronts an enemy of Wyatt's (Bishop Bonner?) who has come to mourn. He notes how this hypocrite is consumed with jealousy looking at Wyatt's noble body: Wyatt's 'lively face thy breast [Bonner's?] how did it fret' and Wyatt's ashes or 'cinders' (a classical synecdoche and the first use of the word in English) 'yet with envy do thee eat.'

'Divers thy death do diversely bemoan' (33) is perhaps the first example in English of a funeral sonnet, with the same blame and praise dichotomy.[8] It stands in relationship to the Wyatt elegy as Surrey's Windsor sonnet does to the Richmond elegy. Opening with strong alliteration, assonance, and *polyptoton* (repetition of the root word in various grammatical forms), the first line operates as a generalized cause generating topics that build, threefold, on the motif of tears. Each substructure, two in the octet and one in the sestet, ends with the differing effects of such tears. This bifurcating structure builds out of the kind of Agricola place-logic that Ramus would develop. The first line of the text locates the speaker (and reader) at a funeral, the one Surrey did not attend in Sherborne Abbey. As in the classical *epicedium* (funeral hymn), the corpse is spread out in front of mourners.

Addressing the dead body, the speaker points in the octet to 'some' who once 'lurked' in the living presence of Wyatt, 'whose breasts envy with hate had sown,' now shedding the false tears of Caesar on Pompey's head. He points to others 'that watched' the living Wyatt 'with eager thirst to drink [his] guiltless blood' but

[7] See the various commentaries on this poem in Jentoft, 'Surrey's Five Elegies: Rhetoric, Structure, and the Poetry of Praise', *PMLA*, 91 (1976), 28–30 and Anthony Low's answer in *PMLA*, 91 (1976), 914–15; Edgar F. Daniels, 'Surrey's "In the Rude Age" ', *Notes and Queries*, 201 (1956), 14–15; *Tottel's Miscellany*, vol. 2, 311; and G. W. Pigman III, *Grief and English Renaissance Elegy* (1985), 73–5.

[8] A. L. Bennett, 'The Principal Rhetorical Conventions of the Renaissance Personal Elegy', *Studies in Philology*, 51 (1943), 114. For a description of these sonnets (and the sonnet on Clere) that relates them to the Arundel portrait, see Heale, *Wyatt, Surrey and Early Tudor Poetry* and her analogy (89): 'Surrey's elegaic sonnets aspire to the inscriptional brevity of an epitaph, like the image of the broken column, surviving monuments against an eroding sea of time.'

now mourn with 'envious tears to hear thy fame so good'. In the sestet, the personal lament of the speaker as lover dominates, rising to the revelation of genuine 'tears'. Here Surrey borrows phrasing directly from his 1537 sonnet on Richmond, using the same ejaculatory imagery. This time tears 'avale' or fall down on the outstretched body of the beloved, the Wyatt/Thisbe female beneath the streaming ejaculations of the Pyramus/Surrey male. At the same time as this erotic release, the real centre of this sonnet reveals itself: Surrey will 'honour the place,' the exposed and public body, 'that such a jewel bred.' It is the gesture of honour in all the panegryric sonnets. As in Roman ritual, he will 'kiss the ground' on which Wyatt's body rests, then kiss the dead body itself, as if he had been at the actual funeral.[9] The popular myth of Pyramus and Thisbe universalizes this final kissing gesture and helps to structure an objective intimacy. In fact, in the sestet, like a Petrarchan lover, Surrey catalogues Wyatt's body. The naming acts like the hand of a lover, moving from the head to the breast that acts as synedoche for the whole body. Finally, the lover/weeper, transformed into the suicidal Pyramus, drops his tears on the beloved body, a combination of both clearly staged motif and, as Surrey's text develops it, utter love.

But I that knew what harboured in that head,
What virtues rare were tempered in that breast,
Honour the place that such a jewel bred,
And kiss the ground whereas thy corpse doth rest
With vapoured eyes from whence such streams avale
As Pyramus did on Thisbe's breast bewail.

The Occasion of Surrey's Epitaffe: Leland's Elegies

For Surrey's public elegy on Wyatt, Leland's elegies are as fitting a prologue as are Surrey's sonnets. Both the full Latin title Leland gives his texts—*NAENIAE in mortem Thomae Viati equitis incomparabilis. loanne Lelando Antiqvario Avtore. Londini Anno M.D. XLII*—and the Ciceronian origin of the genre he names in the title provide, for the reader of 1542, the depth of occasion. Furthermore, one of these *naeniae* will sing of another courtier still living, not only heir to the greatest aristocratic title in England but heir to the poetic mantle of Wyatt. The poet Earl of Surrey, who may have financed, in fact, the publication of Leland's elegies,

[9] Caesar's weeping refers to a Lucan episode Wyatt had once used as classical motif in a poem. In his closure here, Surrey echoes Chaucer at the end of *Troilus* (5, 1791–2), who discusses his own poetic genealogy at the moment he sends forth his 'litel bok': 'And kis the steppes, where as thow seest pace / Virgile, Ovide, Omer, Lucan, and Stace.' Here Surrey's sonnet concentration allows him to combine the high stylization of Roman funerary form, hyperbolic personal gestures, and even misreadings (Thisbe does the actual wailing in Ovid) with English genealogy. For further comment on Surrey's switch of gender, see Lever, *Courtly Letters*, 204–5 and Crewe, *Trials of Authorship*, 76.

is now England's premier poet. He is uniquely both patron and poet. In his elegies, Leland names no other member of court so eminent as Surrey, whom Leland calls, in his *Itinerary*, 'elegantis litteraturae plane studiossimus' ('clearly most devoted to elegant literature'). Thus, in his dedication of the whole *Naeniae*, Leland honours Surrey: 'The Song of John Leland, the Antiquary, dedicated to the most learned and most noble young Earl of Surrey.'[10] The dedication further spells out the relationship of these two poets with a realism that could only have come from first-hand knowledge and direct observation:

> Accept, illustrious Earl, this mournful song
> Wherein I praised your Wyatt, whom in brief space
> Death brought beneath the earth. He greatly loved
> Your name. You revered him while he was alive,
> And since his death, have given him due praise
> In such a song as Chaucer had approved
> As sweet, and worthy of his mother-tongue.
> Continue, Howard, his virtues to revive,
> And you'll confirm it by your honoured race. (M 262)

Surrey was not, of course, a close friend of Wyatt's. In the sixth *naenia* Sir Thomas Poynings, George Blagge, and John Mason are named as Wyatt's close friends: 'three, above all, he chose for himself' (263–4). In the eyes of Leland, however, Surrey was something more than a friend to the older Wyatt, as his *naenia* entitled 'The Sole Phoenix' points out:

> The world a single Phoenix can contain.
> And when one dies, another one is born.
> When Wyatt, that rare bird, was taken away
> By death, he gave us Howard as his heir. (265)

Wyatt as Beloved Body

Surrey's famous elegy on Wyatt proves how quickly the phoenix could be reborn. The poem was both composed and published within weeks after the October 1542 death of Wyatt. Although Surrey's gesture appears spontaneous, the oratorical strategy of the elegy shows self-conscious craft, the work of a master of English at the age of 26. Ideas that may have been gathering for some time now

[10] For the definition of Leland's form, see Cicero, *De legibus*, 2, 24: 'honouratorum virorum laudes cantu ad tibicinem prosequantur, cui nomen *naenia*' (the praises of honourable men to be sung to the accompaniment of a flute, to which (we give) the name *naenia*'). The reference to Surrey can be found in *The Itinerary of John Leland the Antiquary*, ed. Thomas Hearn (1768) 'Cygnea Cantio' 83. I use Muir's translation of Leland's *Naenia* but Leland's original Latin should be read in BL 1075 m. 16 (4) or in *Poems*, ed. Foxwell, Appendix B. The subtlety and nuance of Leland's Latin (especially about Surrey) reveal more of the relationship.

found the right form. For the poem, Surrey used, for the second and last time, his new invention of the heroic quatrain created for Richmond, the royal model for the nobility the earl would renew. His text thus recapitulates the strategy of an epideictic oration but one now more obviously designed for a public audience than the Windsor elegy. Topics of blame and praise, shame and honour, structure the elegy. The title sets up a generic inscription, stressing its public importance for the reader: the *Epitaffe of syr Thomas Wyat . . . wherein are touchyd, and set furth the state of mannes lyfe*. Wyatt himself becomes generic in the long poem as the embodiment of communal honour, beloved human being, and redeeming poet. Leland alluded to the poem immediately, and even in December 1543, Peter Bentham remarked, in his dedication of his translation of Jacopo di Porcia, *The Preceptes of Warre*, 'Wyate was a worthye floure of our tounge, as appereth by the mornefulle ballet made of hys death in Englysshe, whyche is mooste wyttye fyne and eloquent.' Bentham further recognized the new social role of the poet and commended 'the nobles and gentlemen of England who wrote in Chaucer's language' and, by chauvinistic implication, honoured himself because of his own English translation.[11] In fact, the strong influence of this first printed Renaissance 'personal elegy' lasted to the English Revolution and had specific lines and images imitated by major and minor poets. By June 1557, when the elegy was printed in *Tottel's Miscellany* as one of twenty such 'personal elegies' (outnumbered only by love lyrics), it had transfigured not only Wyatt and the relationship of Wyatt and Surrey but, for Tottel and Puttenham (and through them, for the next centuries), the plural English archetype of a poetic 'honourable stile'. It thus transfigured Surrey himself.[12]

Surrey's transfiguration of honour in the poem begins and ends paradoxically in the act of humility Wyatt called for in his *strambotto* to Surrey. If there is to be a moral stance and resolution at the end of this poem—in this case, making the textualized Wyatt into a guide for Tudor time—then the epiphany of honour at the end must evolve within the poem itself. So, in this process, Surrey fashions a dialectical text to expose the nature of the body before him—to set up the real presence of a corpse in the poem. Valorization of the heroic presence of Wyatt lies precisely in such a thesis being actualized in the text: a poet who was a communal (and, as a reformed Christian, universal) voice of honour has died, the worker victim of an idle Sardanapalus society. The substructure of blame in the poem exactly expresses bitterness at such loss of labour and a noble voice. As subtext, this

[11] The only original copy of Surrey's printed elegy is at the Huntington Library (STC 26054), sig. A1r–v. In this text there are no other poems or 'ditties'. The reference to Surrey's elegy in Leland's *Naenia* (STC 15446) is on sig. A2r (M 237). The dedication to the Bentham translation (STC 20116) is on sig. A7r.

[12] Bennett, 107–26. For the relationship of Wyatt and Surrey, see Thomson's remarks in *Wyatt*, 166 ff. where she surveys of Wyatt and his background, though she limits discussion to Surrey's imitations of Petrarch *vis-à-vis* Wyatt's own. A perceptive evaluation of the relationship is by Frederic B. Tromly, 'Surrey's Fidelity to Wyatt in "Wyatt Resteth Here"' in *SP* 77 (Fall 1980), vol. 4, 376–87. For a full discussion of this influence and of the influence of the Surrey texts on Wyatt, see W. A. Sessions, 'Surrey's Wyatt: Autumn 1542 and the New Poet', in *Rethinking the Henrician Era*, ed. Herman, 168–92.

blame finds its positive antithesis in the major motif of Wyatt as labourer, a worker in society, an embodiment of both Renaissance and Reformation concepts of social reform. Such labour had been the teaching of Virgil as he moved from the *Georgics* to the *Aeneid*. Thus, the English poet's Virgilian honour derives from Wyatt's labour in time, in his making of history by act and invented word. Quite significantly, then, on the first page of the printed 1542 text—the first appearance of the poem—the single engraved woodcut shows two labourers at work in a field (Plate 19).

In the text, the Virgilian georgic model outweighs the loss and bitterness. The archetypal poet worker Sir Thomas Wyatt laboured in society by personifying Castiglione's noble courtier for whom, as Signior Ottaviano had argued, virtue is action. Erasmus and other humanists had attacked sloth as a terrible sin in the early Renaissance, and sloth had been used as a good reason to destroy the idle monasteries. The attack was integral to emerging Protestant conceptions of social anthropology, and the irony is that the aristocratic Surrey would use this motif of laziness and its obverse, georgic labour, throughout all of his work. Thus, during the last months of 1542, when the elegy was printed and Surrey was writing as he did everywhere, even at the Scottish war front, the poet earl may have been translating Virgil and particularly Book IV. Two crucial passages in that book (the second repeating the first) recapitulate the georgic theme that Virgil had used from the *Eclogues* on.[13] Jupiter himself declares to Mercury that Aeneas must abandon Dido for the greater good of founding Rome. In this injunction, the Father of the Gods balances the dialectic of 'laude' and 'laborem' or in Surrey's translation (298, 352) 'honour' and 'pain' (when Mercury repeats Jove's injunction, Surrey uses 'travail'). Virgilian *labor* (one of the three key words in the *Aeneid* with *fatum* and *pietas*) thus valorizes the body of the 39-year-old Wyatt stretched out before Surrey, the opposite of the bloated body of the suicide Sardanapalus.

Surrey begins his catalogue of Wyatt's corpse with two figures, *paradox* and *polyptoton*. They set up a parody of the communal and liturgical *hic requiescit* formula by translating inversely, as Camden in Shakespeare's time noted, the old Roman burial formula the Renaissance had renewed: 'Hic mortvvs reqviescit semel / Qui vivvs reqvievit nvnqvam' ('Here rests the ever dead / Who living never rested').[14] In his fiction, Surrey is literally leaning over the dead body of Wyatt as, in his more suicidal Windsor sonnet, he leans over the castle parapet, imagining the beloved body of Richmond. In both dramatized scenes, the speaker-actor is distraught to the point of despair.

In the first line of his Wyatt elegy, the ironic structure for the whole poem is set: Wyatt's body may be resting here but, alive, it never rested. By implication, it never will after this georgic enactment that is the poem. Wyatt's synchronic body thus

[13] Castiglione, 329–30. For the influence of the Virgilian georgics theme in the Renaissance, see W. A. Sessions, 'Spenser's Georgics', *English Literary Renaissance*, 10 (1980), 202–38.

[14] Camden, *Remaines*, 39.

carries a diachronic honour that Surrey's text will continually (and literally) imprint through the heroic seriality of ongoing quatrains. The result is that Surrey begins his ritualizing of honour with the resolution and confidence that had ended Wyatt's earlier *strambotto* to Surrey:

> W. resteth here, that quick could never rest,
> Whose heavenly gifts increased by disdain,
> And virtue sank the deeper in his breast,
> Such profit he of envy could obtain.

The dichotomizing of the first line continues in the whole stanza. With 'gifts' from heaven by nature and 'virtue' and 'profit' intensified by envy, Wyatt transformed the court's scorn by his particular labour now set forth in the antithetical grammar: lines 1 and 3 have independent clauses with subordination in line 1 leading into line 2; line 4, although independent, appears subordinate with its inversion. The generic antithesis continues in a series as realistic as Erasmus could have desired—a catalogue, an inverted Petrarchan blazon of Wyatt's outstretched body, no similes but direct metaphors.

To those 'places' that classical rhetoricians had prescribed for epideitic orations, Surrey now adds a sensational modern device. Anatomy was a recent controversial scientific technique first introduced into Europe by Surrey's contemporary in Paris and a friend of Hadrianus Junius, the Flemish humanist Andreas Vesalius. Surrey may have had contact with this personal physician of Charles V during the poet earl's sojourn with the emperor in France in 1543. Surrey's new poetic structure thus provided the original groundwork for that Renaissance staple, the literary anatomy, which Shakespeare, Donne, Bacon, Burton, and countless other writers would use. So, dominating the central seven stanzas of the elegy will be the blazon catalogue of anatomy. Such dissection will reveal Wyatt's noble labour, and the praise of parts puts the whole body into dramatic focus (as Shakespeare's Mark Anthony's cataloguing praise does the bleeding body of Julius Caesar). Here before the poet/speaker (and reader) is the imagined *corpus delicti*, the necessary proof needed in order to prosecute the offenders, the legal proof and judicial gesture required by a law court.[15] Once so displayed, the accusation can be indirect: the body is praised so that the killers can be seen in heinous contrast to the noble visible evidence.

If this anatomy of a realistic *corpus delicti* proved as revolutionary as Bentham's 'worthye flame' had suggested, so did the 'wittye' reductive syntax. Anatomizing performs through a series of phrasal units, with their own appositive and subordinate clauses. Syntax cuts like a sharp knife, using *asyndeton*, *isocolon* (words or phrases parallel in structure or length), and *amplificatio* to display density and objectivity in the text, evidence to indict the killers of this body. No such concentrated elegy had appeared before in English and seldom, if ever, until the twentieth century, in stanzas with a single substantive (the name of the gift catalogued)

[15] *Black's Law Dictionary*, ed. Henry C. Black (1990), 344.

without a verb and simply modified by phrases and clauses. The poem also had a new modern sense of motion, even speed: the ironic first quatrain and the emotional ninth quatrain with its final couplet frame the anatomy itself as the centre of the poem. This steady progression between two points of stasis (the iconic opening and closing) structures the poem. It conveys in a real mimesis a living body 'where force and beauty met'. In the tension of labour and honour that marked Wyatt's body and life, now revealed to readers, the poet has become a martyred real presence spread out on a printed page. The heroic dead poet has become a new kind of eucharistic sacrifice on a new kind of altar transfigured from all the stripped altars.

By no accident, this catalogue of the beloved body adds one more ritual of performance. Surrey invokes the seven gifts of the Holy Spirit, a teaching of the old Christianity, as ways to focus the virtues of Wyatt's outstretched body. Thus in the *partitio*, the logical topic that subsumes this middle progressing structure of the elegy, Surrey starts with the beloved head: emblematic of prudence, a cardinal virtue for the Church, a gift of the Holy Spirit.

> A head, where wisdom mysteries did frame,
> Whose hammers beat still in that lively grain
> As on a stithy, where some work of fame
> Was daily wrought to turn to Britain's gain.

'Mysteries' carries its French meaning of the Christian sacraments here as well as the Roman *ministerium*, a georgic term for social service and activity that naturally leads to the blacksmith image of the next lines.[16] Surrey expands this meaning of poetic labour in the last lines of the stanza, directing such labour towards a Roman word for England in 1542 just being renewed: 'Britain's'. Thus the head embodies the humanist conception of labour at its highest, service to the realm, the highest point of human wisdom and prudence for most of Surrey's 1542 audience.

In the second stanza, justice, a special gift of the Holy Spirit for Surrey and his Tudor audience, appears in Wyatt's 'visage stern and mild', a new face of honour that shines as brightly for the poet earl as Molinet's Honor's face for the 'Flodden Duke' at Bruges in 1468. The face's paradox of being strict and yet generous serves well, 'Vice to contemn, in virtues to rejoice,' a balanced justice that will continue despite 'great storms'. As revealed in the Holbein drawings, Wyatt's face of justice, 'whom grace assured so', allowed him to sustain the blows of fortune. The older poet was thus not fortune's fool; rather, as the ideal Stoic, as Horatio to Hamlet, Wyatt could keep his composure, his Plutarchian 'quiet mind'. Wyatt can 'live upright and smile at fortune's choice.' Different from the ironic introspective Wyatt of most twentieth-century criticism, Surrey's Wyatt has a magisterial

[16] For another example of poetic genealogy, Surrey's image of a blacksmith (used also in Wyatt, MT 209) follows as Spenser describes the lover Scudamour in *The Faerie Queene* 4, Canto 8, and as Ben Jonson describes his own georgics of the poet in his ode to Shakespeare, the 'living line' that results from striking 'the second heat / Upon the muses' anvil' (58–63).

control of a society he elected to serve generously. Because he did not choose to be detached, the reformed Christian Wyatt now emerges as a model Renaissance courtier. He controls occasion, its justice, and thereby embodies a peculiarly updated courtly honour.

This honour was strongly evident in Wyatt's writing. The work of the poet's hand moved naturally from such control of occasion to the textualizing of his world. This is the third point of the anatomy blazon of love:

> A hand that taught what might be said in rhyme,
> That reft Chaucer the glory of his wit,
> A mark, the which, unperfected for time,
> Some may approach but never none shall hit.

Wyatt had taught his generation the possibilities of English poetry for the new British language being formed by elegant translations like Tyndale's and Elyot's and resounding communal texts like Cranmer's *Book of Common Prayer* being written in the same year of 1542. In his writing, Wyatt hit the 'mark'—Surrey's original and realistic archery image. Not only did Wyatt divert the 'glory' of the great Chaucer, but he set a standard for future poet/archers to approach though 'none shall hit.' This setting of a poetic standard was a great achievement, Surrey implies. Once more, Surrey builds on antithesis and dialectic, the hyperbole in the second and fourth line balanced by the literary critic's assessment in the third: Wyatt's work needed revision. His cruel early death, brought on by a vicious society, made his enormous gifts and potential talents 'unperfected' for lack of 'time'—the horror that now haunts Surrey himself.

Both hand and tongue are related to the Holy Spirit's gift of language, and so in the next stanza, the fourth point of the anatomy:

> A tongue that serv'd in foreign realms his king,
> Whose courteous talk to virtue did inflame
> Each noble heart, a worthy guide to bring
> Our English youth by travail unto fame.

Wyatt performed the highest function of the humanist courtier. He inflamed 'each noble heart' and especially guided 'our English youth' to 'travail' or labour if they wanted 'fame'. By his own immense labour in Madrid, Fontainebleau and Paris, Rome, and Vienna, Wyatt demonstrated to young male English courtiers the means for redeeming society. In his texts of 'courteous talk', as well as in his diplomatic example, honour and 'virtue' were restored.

In the next stage of his anatomy, Surrey turns to Wyatt's eyes, famous, as Holbein had graphically shown, for their 'piercing look' that 'did represent a mind / With virtue fraught, reposed, void of guile.' Behind their fierceness and sullen angry gaze, his mind could rest in innocence, in the kind of contemplation Wyatt had suggested for his friend John Poins. Such control rising from innocence thus allowed the judgements of the eyes to be blinded by no false affections or emotions. Was it any wonder then those beloved eyes had the power 'friends to allure, and foes to reconcile'? This motif of innocence continues in the next stanza where, in an elaborate figure of litotes, the power of Wyatt's heart reveals itself through a series of Stoic negatives: 'where dread yet never so impress'd / To hide the thought that might the truth advance' (the mark of the good Renaissance counsellor like Lear's Kent); and, whether lifted high or 'repress'd' in fortune, neither 'to swell in wealth, nor yield unto mischance'. Like the ideal of Seneca (from whose texts the diplomat could quote at ease), Wyatt could balance the temptations to power.

In the final stanza of his Petrarchan blazon, Surrey summarizes the 'heav'nly gifts', all as one in the body before him:

> A valiant corpse, where force and beauty met,
> Happy, alas, too happy but for foes,
> Lived, and ran the race that nature set
> Of manhood's shape, where she the mould did lose. (29–32)

Surrey ends his serious parody of the gifts of the Holy Spirit, the Petrarchan blazon, and the scientific anatomy with a grammatical shock. The emphatic past tense of 'met'—after a paucity of verbs—dramatically shifts the progress of the text. The grammar alone announces that Wyatt is truly dead. In this next stage of the poem, Surrey projects a death-defeating strategy, one based on genealogy, his own version of the classical apotheosis of the hero. His hyperbole in this stanza builds on an analogue of generations, reified in the text through Surrey's textual genealogy. That is, Surrey transcribes into the three last lines of his stanza a Virgilian passage in which the beautiful and noble Dido sums up her own life just before she commits suicide and disappears from the epic text, beginning: 'Vixi, et, quem dederat cursum fortuna, peregi' (653) and in Surrey's translation:

> I lived and ran the course fortune did grant
> And under earth my great ghost now shall wend,
> A goodly town I built, and saw my walls,
> Happy, alas too happy, if these coasts
> The Trojan ships had never touched aye. (59: 873–7)

To Dido's self-inscription, Surrey joins passages from St Paul's Letters to the Ephesians and the Corinthians on the strong athlete and the Christian's purposeful body, texts appropriate for the reformed Christian modern poet. Thus, directly through Virgil and St Paul—among the highest figurations for Tudor culture—Wyatt becomes as textualized and transfigured in honour as Molinet's Honour. He becomes an appropriate model, like a male classical statue, for all to view in the public forum of a printed elegy. Wyatt now embodies the paradigm of honour for future communities. He has been transformed into a martyr for the future honour of language-making. His (and Surrey's) precise self-conscious language as 'courtly makers' teaches what true nobility is and what roles of honour the future offers society in a radically displaced history.

So transfigured, Wyatt's body of honour is ready for another realm. In time to come, Wyatt will be a universal witness to honour. In Surrey's ideologizing, 'That simple soul is fled' and 'to the heav'ns' from whence his seven gifts had come; but he has left behind 'with such as covet Christ to know, / Witness of faith that never shall be dead.' For those who are elect and élite, those who 'covet', in the new Christian diction, to know the highest forms of honour, whatever social class and rank, Wyatt will be an archetype, a 'witness of faith'. As so many poets (and artists) would be, as earlier Christ himself was and his saints, so Wyatt was 'sent for our wealth, but not received so'. Wyatt has authenticated a language (and epitaph) that will flourish in a life of texts to follow, a new British inscription of immortality, a new even secular kind of Orphic poet. In fact, the Christian paradigm has been used to lead to a 'witness' beyond itself: the central paradigm of the redeemed and redeeming poet, the Orphic sole survivor, like Orpheus himself (as portrayed in an Ovidian tapestry Surrey may have seen in Boulogne in 1532). The Greek poet's severed head, still alive, floated across the sea from its dismembered body in Thrace to Lesbos and into an island cave, where in the myth it still sings.

As the heir to the Earl Marshal of the kingdom, Surrey might have become the dispenser of honour for the blood nobility. Now, in the Wyatt elegy, he inaugurates in effect his own new College of Arms by introducing into England and into the English language a clear archetype for the collectivity of noble language-makers of an 'honourable stile', in Tottel's phrase. And, in fact, this is the corporate body the later Renaissance and the neoclassical satirists recognized as authoritative 'legislators' for the political body of society at large, a role defined through Orpheus and Amphion in Sidney's *Defense* and renewed by both Shelley and Yeats in a phrase ('unacknowledged legislators') that directly validates all poets since the Romantics. For Surrey's corporate body, a 'Poets' Corner' in Westminster Abbey will stand as synecdoche and a visible sign to society at large. At the time of Tottel, Chaucer's body was entombed there by Queen Mary I in a deliberate political gesture. In such collectivity, Surrey's elegy on Wyatt will have the effect of an innovative holy relic, available through printing-presses now, but just as capable of continuous intercession through continuous reading by thousands of readers through centuries. If Surrey's grandson Philip Howard entered a universal religious litany in 1970 to be invoked as a martyr by the nations, so, in the same manner, would Surrey's Wyatt in 1542 and for generations. The relics of a modern poet survive and are invoked, consciously or unconsciously, as Surrey's idea of the modern poet survives.

The couplet that completes this dramatization of communal fidelity and 'witness' repeats the motif of a 'jewel'. It states the obvious, the third required stage of the traditional elegy: consolation after both public praise and sorrow. The body and the life of Wyatt have been actualized as a reminder to surviving Tudor society of its failure to create a proper system for true nobility and honour. Tudor society destroys its greatest heroes. 'Thus for our guilt this jewel have we lost; / The earth his bones, the heav'n possess his ghost.' The origin of this final couplet is Ecclesiastes (12: 7), a book from which Surrey himself would soon translate. Quite naturally, then, the final moral stance of Surrey's oration over the dead body is both prophetic and homiletic. The audience must change its perception of honour and remember the 'health' of Wyatt's life and language. It must transform its own life and communal body. Summed up and anatomized in the thirty-nine lines of the elegy (including the 'AMEN' published at the end of early printed editions), the dead body of the 39-year-old Wyatt functions, with the same message, as did Apollo's naked torso for Rilke in the early twentieth century. Resurrected by Surrey's language, Wyatt's prophetic body says directly to his Tudor audience: 'You must change.'[17]

[17] Line 14 of a Petrarchan sonnet in 'Archaïscher Torso Apollos' in *Neue Gedichte, Andere Teil*: 'Du muss dein Leben ändern' ('You must change your life'). This force of the speaking reforming body of Wyatt, the new poet's body, before his audience comes from Surrey's special diction, not least the word 'witness', which, as Heale, *Wyatt, Surrey and Early Tudor Poetry* (39) shows, derives from Tyndale's translation of the Christian Bible, especially the Epistle to the Hebrews 12: 1. Stephen Merriam Foley, *Thomas Wyatt* (1990), p. 38, makes the point that the physical presence of the writing subject displaces itself 'onto the social presences that authenticate his sign, among them the emergence of human letters as a cultural field in the elite culture of early Tudor England'.

10

The Origins of Blank Verse

What is remarkable about Surrey's blank verse is that it has no clear origin except within one personality and one life-story. Whatever conceptions and techniques Surrey developed from specific literary sources, whether Chaucer, the French, the Italians, or Gawain Douglas, finally and mysteriously blank verse originated out of a single person—Henry, Earl of Surrey. Before Surrey, in English, as an astute editor of Wyatt has observed, there had been 'nothing quite like it'. Blank verse with its flexibility, its 'readiness', in T. S. Eliot's term, surprised everyone. It had not evolved with time but was suddenly, 'immediately', invented—by a young man, not always mature, at a specific time and place terrible in their dislocations.

What accounts for the survival of blank verse for four centuries has been, in fact, its 'readiness', its dialectic of syllables and stresses so structured by Surrey as always to provide for voice and ear a controlled flexibility. Blank verse is 'The kind of sound our sentences would make / If only we could leave them to themselves,' Hollander writes.[1] The young earl's language was intended specifically as discourse for a Tudor court, a language of nobility with the heightened conversation one might hear flowing at Surrey House, at Windsor, at Whitehall. It was written, then, at least on one level, with a specific political goal in mind, a *renovatio* of English blood nobility. In this sense, although the final effect may have been natural and universal, blank verse began as personal stylization, as a calculated social effect of a metre that counterpointed syllables and stresses as never used before in English, a result of invention. The freedom and flexibility of a language for Tudor 'nobul hartys' had been consciously designed by the young earl. Technical interplay and linear tension were to turn ordinary language into poetry, all in an absence of rhyme never so absolute since 1066. In this absence, if Wright is correct, Surrey carried—to an even greater ritualization—Wyatt's own experiments in reproducing the human voice. As in Wyatt, Surrey's worked through a 'dual basis', a dialectic in which 'the metrical line and the natural rhythm of the language engage each other in a continuing struggle and, in order to abide harmoniously in each other's presence, submit to certain standard modifications.' From this engagement and harmony come the poetic line and, what is important for Surrey,

[1] Thomson, *Wyatt*, 35. See also O. B. Hardison, *Prosody and Purpose in the English Renaissance* (1989), 27 on the singularity of Surrey's 'self-conscious' invention. T. S. Eliot, 'What Is a Classic?' in *On Poetry and Poets* (1961), 73–4; cf. Kermode, *The Classic*, 15–16. John Hollander, *Rhyme's Reason* (1981), 12–13.

the verse paragraph. Surrey, like his offspring Milton, did intend that his heroic line express 'Things unattempted yet in verse or prose'.[2]

In fact, Surrey's radical discovery was to find just how far to bring the strength of prose into the epic verse line. Poulter's Measure was the long prose-like line Wyatt had invented in his translation of the *Aeneid*, 'Iopas Song', a passage just before Aeneas' retrospective narrative of Book II that Surrey himself translated. Yet, although Poulter's Measure—for the development of which Surrey would be famous—could be broken down into sing-song ballad metre, blank verse could not. The young earl wanted his English *Aeneid* to have the drive of a narrative that progressed, without a break, from strong phrasal units into lines into verse paragraphs into books. For that, he invented the sustaining interplay of ten syllables (and seldom more) and four or five stresses (seldom more or less) for narration, conversation, and soliloquy. Especially in the long monologues—the whole of Book II, for example—this balancing of stress and syllable built an objective structure for the most profound subjectivity. Virgil's own dialectic of objectivity and intimacy, especially in the two books Surrey translated (or the ones that have survived), was thus made English and local in the 1540s, one more encoding after 1500 years of the *Aeneid* now 'peculiar to a particular group, or generation, or social environment', in Lévi-Strauss' definition of kind.[3]

Nowhere is Surrey's translation of the Virgilian dialectic clearer than at a crucial moment in Book II of the *Aeneid*. Here the whole problem of expression, the poetic subjectivity that must find the right communal language for a waiting audience, comes centre-stage. Aeneas has suddenly stopped his retrospective narrative. He looks at his audience around Dido's banquet table and wonders aloud at the adequacy of any language or language-maker to represent indeterminate history and its horrors.

[2] George T. Wright, 'Wyatt's Decasyllabic Line', *Studies in Philology*, 822 (Spring 1985), 133. *Paradise Lost*, 1: 16. See Hardison's remark that Milton had to learn 'many of Surrey's discoveries about English heroic verse all over again' in *Prosody*, 146–7. For a more definitive statement on the two poets, see John Shawcross, 'Milton and Blank Verse Precedents', *ANQ: A Quarterly Journal of Short Articles, Notes, and Reviews*, NS 3/4 (Oct. 1990), 160–3. Of all Milton's works, the prosody of *Paradise Regained* most reflects that of Surrey's blank verse, with its special use of *aporia* and its emphasis on phrasal units and stress rhythms within a generally precise syllabic count.

[3] Claude Lévi-Strauss, *Structural Anthropology*, trans. Claire Jacobson and Brooke Grundfest Schoepf (1963), 198. For opinions on the nature of form in language relevant to the origins of blank verse, see also Georges Charbonnier, *Conversations with Claude Lévi-Strauss*, trans. John and Doreen Weightman (1969), 127–8, where Lévi-Strauss notes, 'in all language phenomena, there is more than just communication' and the language of poetry, like that of shamanism, may have a 'surplus of signifiers', with symbols and rituals offering more than specific cure, as had Orpheus' original *teletae* (see Ivan M. Linforth, *The Arts of Orpheus* (1941), 166). For Lévi-Strauss, the unexpressed may become expressed in the total gesture of ritual; the unconscious, especially in tightly constructed syntax, may disclose, paradoxically through controlled rhythms, previously inexpressible 'psychic states'. A theory of Aristotelian catharsis follows. Through 'an ordered and intelligible form' the sick audience may even undergo 'a real experience', a catharsis: ritualized continuous form 'induces the release of the physiological process, that is, the reorganization, in a favorable direction' of the sick patient or sick audience.

'Who can express the slaughter of that night?
Or tell the number of the corpses slain?
Or can in tears bewail them worthily?
The ancient famous city falleth down,
That many years did hold such seigniory;
With senseless bodies every street is spread,
Each palace, and sacred porch of the gods.'

In the last decade of his life, the young earl had found a specifically English heroic line—deep within himself—for the objective representation of a history he did not fully understand but must encounter and confront. His line of ten unrhymed syllables will inscribe a narrative of Virgilian destiny: uncontrolled eros before an equally uncontrolled thanatos, history's constant tendency 'ruere in peius' ('to sink into the worse'), in the phrase from the *Georgics* (1: 200), which Curtius sees as crucial to any interpretation of Virgil. Although only two books have survived the final ransacking of Surrey House, Kenninghall, and Norfolk House at Lambeth, Surrey had doubtless planned translations of the entire twelve books of Virgil's epic. In his eyes, he would recreate the Virgilian heroic dialectic in Tudor England, a new language in a new world, and thus to 'take the lost and past and rebuild it out of new substance on foreign soil [is] the will and the way of Virgilian wisdom.'[4]

With this dialectic built on the sorrows of Dido and the burning of old Troy, in the Renaissance the *Aeneid* was a communal work as exalted as the Bible. In fact, Virgil provided a tragic perspective for Martin Luther. For Luther, subjectivity (in whatever person or text) is the beginning and end of all knowledge of Jesus Christ. But Virgil gives the master expression for the self's painful discovery of its own nothingness that precedes the love of Christ. On his deathbed, a year before Surrey's beheading, Luther scribbled his last written words, showing his constant devotion to the experiential retelling of the Christian Gospel but, more emphatically, his devotion to Cicero, especially the Roman orator's letters, and then to all the works of Virgil, even the *Eclogues* and the *Georgics*. Most of all, in the scribbling, Luther paraphrased Statius: 'Do not lay hands on the divine *Aeneid*, but bow down and honour its tracks.' Luther then added his own response—the last words he ever wrote—affirming the bases of Virgilian history: 'We are beggars. That is true.'[5]

The vulnerability of both Dido weeping and Aeneas lamenting his lost city are the primary character inscriptions of Surrey's Virgil, but both books from the *Aeneid* stand at the same time as representations of a special hope and burden:

[4] E. R. Curtius, *Essays on European Literature*, trans. Michael Kowal (1973), 4–9. For various statements of the Virgilian dialectic, see C. M. Bowra, *From Virgil to Milton* (1963), 59–84; Friedrich Klinger, *Virgil: Bucolia, Georgica, Aeneis* (1967); Brooks Otis, *Virgil* (1963); J. Wright Duff, *A Literary History of Rome* (1967); David R. Slavitt, *Virgil* (1991), particularly 'Dido's Shadow', 100–18.

[5] *Works of Martin Luther*, ed. C. M. Jacobs (1931), vol. 5, 15. See W. A. Sessions, 'Mutations of "Pietas Litterata" ' in *Renaissance Papers 1976*, ed. Dennis G. Donovan and A. Leigh Deneef (1977), 1–10. For the Roman background here, see Gerhard Ebeling, *Luther*, trans. R. A. Wilson (1970), 241.

the action of identifying the right political community out of breakdown. They both express the first step of building any new community of nobility and its right language: the breakthrough out of breakdown. Because Virgil had always served that purpose of building community out of loss and death, the *Aeneid* early became a text for educating and defining local heroes in terms of Rome. As Bolgar remarks, in the Roman empire, 'Virgil was worth a legion' in the inculcation of provinces. From the beginning, Roman readers saw that Virgil had synthesized a text to hold the dialectic of both 'lacrima rerum' ('tears of things'), as Aeneas comments to Achates (1: 462), and the building of a new Rome ('dum conderet urbem') in the prologue (1: 5). Virgil's text could thus energize the founding of all human societies because it had defined the human dimensions of all labour: the love that drives and the death that limits, the 'boundary situations' from which no life escapes.[6]

Yet why was Surrey drawn to Virgil rather than Horace, for example, or the popular Seneca? Was it simply, as his detractors believed, the arrogant earl's conceited ambition to show off by translating the greatest of all literary works, the greatest text of the greatest genre (as Sidney calls it in his *Defense*)? Or had he discovered in Virgil a cultural transfer in which not only does old Troy become new Rome but, as Bellamy notes, 'the exile from Troy becomes the origin of the narcissistic self in history,' the isolated questing (questioning) self? In this narcissism and quest, did the Howard heir want an authority for his new discourse that would make the reformed Tudor court, with its humanist ambitions and dreams of style, listen and take note? What else then but the language of Aeneas (and Dido)—as Surrey heard it—for the 'nobul hartys' to speak as *amici principis*, friends of an emperor like Elyot's Alexander Severus or the *philoi* of an Alexander himself? A new blood nobility under Surrey's direction serving a king (young or old) could speak with linguistic dignity. They might rule together with their leader, in the manner illustrated in Surrey's uncle Berners' *Golden Boke of Marcus Aurelius*. This leader might open up for them a new Rome, a true Renaissance.

Thus, if there were to be an empire, it would be united by such power of a mother language as universal as Latin made accessible by the blank-verse voices of its heroes in the next centuries. But, to make all this possible, did the poet not want a communal document recapitulated out of himself but with the purpose Trissino had announced in his 1529 *Poetica*: 'The ancient poets contributed to the perfection of men in antiquity'?[7] Indeed ancient Rome had been built on Latin and Greek texts by poets who were themselves heroes of society. Thus, at a specific point in his campaign for 'politicization', the poet earl began his translation. Transferring the Roman epic into English would be one more way to bring order

[6] R. R. Bolgar, *The Classical Heritage and Its Beneficiaries* (1954), 61. For the best modern philosophical discussion of the concepts of *eros* and *thanatos* as 'boundary situations' ('Grenzsituation') see Karl Jaspers, *Philosophy*, trans. E. B. Ashton (1970–1), vol. 2 *passim* and vol. 3, 177–218.

[7] Elizabeth J. Bellamy, *Translations of Power: Narcissism and the Unconscious in Epic History* (1992), 81; Hardison, *Prosody*, 81.

to the dislocation of his own time, another Roman role to control the 'frencey in our commyn wele', in Thomas Starkey's phrase. Most important, by translating and creating a heroic language, Surrey would focus himself as the centre of a new nobility.

What is clear is that for the poet there was no question but that he alone must take on such a task. He was the sole survivor, like Aeneas, of a special genealogy—or so he thought. While the ultimate goal in the 1540s was community, noble *philoi*, Surrey was realizing that he was as alone in his political goals as Aeneas in Book II when the Trojan prince discovers he is the only survivor of the brave band with whom he has been fighting. 'Iamque adeo super unus eram,' says Aeneas recalling that moment of isolation, in Virgil's only use in his epic of the verb in Surrey's motto: 'SAT SVPER EST.' Whereas C. Day-Lewis's translation catches the meaning, 'Yes, I was now the one man left of my party,' Surrey's shorter, more awkward line, faithful to his ten syllables, catches in its *hyperbaton* (reshaping normal word order) the tragic concentration of the original: 'There was no moe but I left of them all.' In the young earl's uneven eyes, there was no one like him in England, and, as history would show, there were few in England or in Europe who ever attempted to bring together the two genealogies, blood and poetry, in a synthesis that, for a modern historian, 'burned like a meteor'.[8]

By taking the losses of his own life, his own history, and transforming them into a new language, the poet entered a future, as Heidegger comments about Rilke. That future may be given a voice before it arrives, in radically new language. The poet does not seek an ideologized abstract future but 'rather,' says Heidegger, 'he arrives out of the future [into the present], in such a way that the future is present only in the arrival of his words.' And the form of this 'arrival' is a poetic structuring out of a genealogy so powerful it becomes the probable future. It offers a special freedom and then recurs as freedom because of the energizing form. In this sense, the originating poet remains, in Heidegger's logic, *in* the recurring form, however represented in a new time and place: 'The more purely the arrival happens [originates], the more its remaining occurs as present.' 'Enough' might survive in the centuries ahead as no one expected.[9]

[8] *The Aeneid of Virgil* trans. C. Day-Lewis (1953), 52. It should be noted that in the Latin, Virgil uses the older broken grammatical form of *superesse* and the past tense, 'super . . . eram' for 'supersum'. This is the separated form Surrey will use. In Virgil's line the *super* is adverbial, and a Greek figure of *tmesis* or verbal separation is used in a deliberate archaizing and echoing of an older Greek text within the Roman modern text. For the quotation, see Starkey, *Reign*, 147.

[9] Martin Heidegger, *Poetry, Language, Thought*, trans. and introd. by Albert Hofstadter (1971), 141–2. For an intriguing theory on how a verse form can shape content, see the remarks on the alexandrine in Roland Barthes, *Mythologies*, trans. Annette Lavers (1972), 133. The French is from *Mythologies*, (1957). Cf. Louis Hjelmslev, *Prolegomena to a Theory of Language*, trans. Francis J. Whitfield (1961), 119. What appears to interest Barthes is the persistence through time of the alexandrine, a form that signals for him, in the flux of ongoing synchronic history, diachronic 'value' in itself 'both as meaning of a discourse and as signifier of a new whole, which is its poetic signification'. If Barthes means what he says here about a form contemporary with Surrey, alexandrines in themselves will generate a narrative of actual facts (denotation) through their recurring form which would tell a 'true' and universal story in the whole discourse, the alexandrine making the larger effect of life

Thus, in whatever paradox, the immature Surrey discovered a continuing form—blank verse—that made the deepest subjectivity objective, open, for all audiences. Even more than translations of the Bible in Tudor England and Cranmer's majestic writing of the English liturgy, Surrey's contemporary translation and language, as communal as theirs, would have to be generated from his own self, the paradoxes of his own life. In those terrible dilemmas, he had discovered the ironic structures for his translations and the dialectic of self and history that would make blank verse universal by the twentieth century, more typically over four centuries, as the 'language of suffering', in a modern critic's definition.[10] By no accident, great soliloquies have defined the form, bearing Surrey's originating mark of intense self-consciousness within the serial narrative frame of a history, whether Marlowe's Dido (directly modelled on Surrey's) or his Edward II or Doctor Faustus, Shakespeare's Hamlet or Othello or Lear, Webster's Duchess of Malfi, or Milton's Satan, Adam, and Samson, Wordsworth's self in the *Prelude*, Keats' reflective Hyperion, Browning's Andrea del Sarto (or any of his Italian self-doubters), Robert Frost's puzzled farmers, Wallace Stevens' speaker in 'Sunday Morning', defining self through the woman in the peignoir, or Robert Lowell's lost seamen, to name an obvious few.

possible in ways language without a repeating form cannot. By regularizing the discourse, no matter the subject-matter, into a 'new whole' with the 'signification' of myth generated by the repeating form, the alexandrine brings more life to the text, what Barthes call 'poetic signification'. In Barthes' linguistic paradox of the alexandrine as denotative myth-making, the value of specific linguistic forms for naturalizing or making denotative discourse of any subject-matter, for making subject-matter both synchronic and diachronic at the same time, comes from an observable phenomenon. The more actualizing the universalizing mimesis of the form at its inception, the more it is 'expressive' of life itself, the more form gives life to any content, no matter how revolutionary or different. In fact, for Barthes, 'Language is never anything but a system of forms, and the meaning is a form' ('La langue n'est jamais qu'un système de formes, le sens est une forme'). One may note that even for a Marxist like Anthony Easthope in 'Problematizing the Pentameter', *New Literary History*, 12/3 (Spring 1981), 481, 485, such originating effects linger, however negative (one presumes, like the radiation still around us, so we are told, from the cosmic 'big bang'). Easthope has demonstrated in his discussion of the English pentametre that ideological effects (such as individualism) 'persist in and with the meter' and 'most manifestly during its founding moment of the Renaissance.' If blank verse is then ideologically initiated metre (whether incipiently capitalistic or not), the poet-maker inventing it incorporates, in Easthope's terms, both historical 'process' and 'closure' at the same time into the very life and movement of the verse form. That is, the form keeps together both activity—history, process—*and* the closure of the lyric voice, the individual soliloquizing, actualizing her pain in language, in a counterpoint. For Easthope, the pentametre line inscribes the capitalist individualism of the modern world, an epoch with a peculiar 'British' inscription of 'a single voice self-possessed, self-controlled, impersonally self-expressive', in other words, a lyric voice.

[10] Howard Baker, *Induction to Tragedy* (Baton Rouge: Louisiana State University Press, 1939) 105. Cf. Wolfgang Clemen, *English Tragedy Before Shakespeare: The Development of Dramatic Speech* (New York: Barnes & Noble, Inc., 1961), Chapter Two, 'The Set Speech in Renaissance Drama,' for the rhetorical self-consciousness of the set dramatic speeches (in a style beloved and demanded by Tudor and Stuart audiences), for their ornamentation and the power of their being 'preeminently speech-drama' (40), and their emphasis on Aristotelian catharsis as a means of therapeutic Stoic healing (39).

Surrey's Theory of Translation

If Roman roles led Surrey to translate Virgil's epic, the actual process led him, by the nature of language itself, beyond that historical and political task. To translate, Surrey would have to go deeper into his own self and the language he heard there, whatever the violence around him or before him. One might argue, as Mason does with Wyatt, that Surrey's best work develops out of his humanist mode of translation, bringing two worlds together. In fact, of the three evolving stages of his *oeuvre*, Petrarchan, Virgilian, and biblical, each works out of a textual genealogy as powerful and commanding as that of either the Howards' or the Staffords'—at least for a poet who could no more escape his poetic vocation than his dynastic one. In this sense of vocation, Giamatti has understood the primal act of translation. Explicating the myth of the resurrected Hippolytus whose severed body is healed by Aesculapius, Giamatti defines the dialectic that leads poets from old texts to the 'immediately' new: 'The humanist's supreme reaction is finally his own sense of himself; his crucial composition is the reconstruction of self out of what the past has given him—a sense of self that is defined by the activity of making up the self. The humanist is Aesculapius to his own Hippolytus, restorer of himself out of the fragments old and new of his own humanity.'[11]

If the key word here is 'activity', it is restoring once more the Virgilian 'activity', a Roman dialectic—and finding the right compositional technique to express it 'on foreign soil'. In short, it means having a theory of how to translate Virgil. In a hitherto unnoticed text exactly contemporary, Surrey's theory of translation may be partially reconstructed. At the very time that Surrey was wrestling with problems of composition and technical invention as well as conceptualizing Virgil, John Clerke, secretary to the Duke of Norfolk, dedicated a translation of his own to the poet earl. In it Clerke, possibly Surrey's former tutor, describes what may have been, in fact, the young earl's theory of composition in a preface that is certainly one of the earliest pieces of coherent literary criticism in English.

Clerke's one purely literary work omitted from John Bale's Edwardian catalogue of his work is 'A certain treaty moste wyttely deuysed', a translation of a French version of the Spanish narrative *Tractado de Arnalte e Lucenda* that introduces, in fact, the sentimental novel into England. The translation is 'dedicat to the ryght honorable Henry Erle of Surrey, one of the knyghtes of the moste honorable ordre of the Garter, Sonne and heyre apparaunt to the ryght hygh and myghtie prynce Thomas duke of Norfolke, hygh Treasorus, and Erle mershall of Englande.' The place and date of this preface have considerable importance: 'wyrtten at Lambythe,' that is, at the Howard mansion on the River Thames, on 'the xvii. daye of Marche, 1543'. The preface thus dates, as closely as any

[11] For more discussion of Surrey as translator, see Sessions, *Surrey*, 20–39; Mason, *Humanism*, 179 ff. A. Bartlett Giamatti, 'Hippolytus among the Exiles: The Romance of Early Humanism', in *Poetic Traditions of the English Renaissance*, ed. Maynard Mack and George deForest Lord (1982), 17.

document, Surrey's translations of Virgil during the same period of time when the 26-year-old also printed his elegy on Wyatt. It is as good a date as any to mark the birth of blank verse.[12]

In his preface, Clerke confirms 'by longe experyence, not onely the great wysdom and synguler judgement wherewith God the dysposer of all thynges, hath most abundantly endowed you, but also the exceding great paynes and trauayles sustained by your selfe in traductions [translations] as well out of the Laten, Italien as the Spanishe, and French, wherby your Lordship surmounteth many others, not only in knowledge, but also in laude and commendation.' Now Clerke 'wyll rather prudently accordynge to your accustomed faschyon regarde' his own text of translation. He will, like Surrey, 'consyder the wytty deuyse of the thynge, the maner of the Locucyons, the wyse sentences and the subtyll and dyscret answeres made on bothe parties,' a kind of interplay that will more than follow 'the order of the wordes in the other tonges', the lack of which order has disgraced authors when they 'publysche theyr owne foly'. These bad translators 'in the place of lybertie' have enslaved themselves by not 'hauyng respect to thobseruacyon of that thyng whiche in this case is moste specyalie requisit'. That is, they do not see text as a whole so that 'the sence of the Aucthour is ofte depraued, and the grace ne perfection of thone ne other tonge dewly expressed.' Instead, a good writer understands 'that euery tonge hath his properties, maner of Locucyons perticuler vehemencies, dignyties, and rychesses'. In this perception, a good translator has 'arrested' himself 'only upon the sentences [thoughts] and maiesties therof so curyously [skillfully] as I fyrmely trust thintencion of thauthor is truely expressed'.

In his preface, therefore, Clerke's terms show Surrey's process of holistic form. It is a composite form such as Surrey may have learned first-hand at Fontainebleau from cinquecento Italy. What was new in England and sophisticated was the synthesis: the young earl's witty or intelligent division of the whole; the right arrangement of discourse; galvanizing and pithy thoughts set out in Roman aphoristic form ('wyse sentences'); the subtle interplay between the text to be translated and the poet's own text ('subtyll and dyscret answeres made on bothe parties'). Indeed, Clerke's precise analysis of Surrey's style of translating shows an English earl in 1542 as an artist consumed with problems of composition but hardly the arrogant playboy aristocrat. If anything, Henry of Surrey is obsessed not with his own personality but with detailed technical labour. In this sense of precise vocation, a woodcut entitled 'The Auctour' at the exact end of this preface is revealing. A writer in a flowing gown and with flowing hair sits on a low stool (or kneels), holding a quill before a long strip of paper extending across a knee. Behind the writer, a river flows and beside it a city with a bridge and a round tower, a view not unlike what Clerke himself could have seen from Lambeth in 1542. In this perspective of a poet in a city, the representation in the woodcut may be intended to signify Virgil, viewed as either writing by his native Mincius (as described in the

[12] All quotations are from the original Clerke text in the British Library.

Georgics) or by the Tiber in Rome. More typically for the history of this woodcut itself, however, the writer represents the prophetic St John the Divine on the Greek island of Patmos writing his Apocalypse—the poet as prophet.[13]

Surrey's Virgil in 1554: The First Text

In September 1554, in the second year of the reign of Mary I, John Day, the printer, published Surrey's fourth book from the *Aeneid*, announcing that Virgil was now 'translated into English, and drawn into a straunge metre' by the late heir to the greatest title in England outside the royal family. The honour of Rome had been made British, and a poet from the highest level of English society had turned such a Roman text into English as never before. Surrey's first son, Thomas, the new Duke of Norfolk, had succeeded to the title on 25 August 1554, a few weeks before. His ascendancy marked, in fact, the official occasion for this first appearance of blank verse. By an irony, Surrey's original intent in the 1540s for composing the form, that is, the enhancement of his own and the Howards' political and social ascendancy and the development of a new nobility, was now being fulfilled. To the new duke William Awen, an 'oratour' in the ducal household, dedicated the 1554 text, honouring the father in whom two genealogies of honour had converged.

In the dedication, Awen combines literary criticism and editorial sleuthing: 'When it chauced a copye of thys part of Virgill, traunslated by your graces father (right honorable Lord)' had come to Awen through a friend, he 'held ye [the] same as no smal treasure, because I had heard it, lyke as others the monumentes of that noble wyt of hys [Surrey's], whych was in thys doute incomparable, of al men to be commended.' The 'oratour'/editor had always been concerned that Surrey's 'noble' texts be available for all citizens and no longer 'kept as a priuate treasure

[13] Composite form as theory may have come to Surrey from Aristotle's *Poetics*, but it was a lesson already learned in England, at least according to Richard Pace (*De Fructu*, 104–5, 77). Sir Thomas More would arrive at words from sentences, not the laborious other way around—a mark of More's genius, Pace emphasizes in his treatise on a liberal education, published at the time of Surrey's birth. More could perceive from variety a true whole or, as the personification of Geometry describes it in Pace's same treatise, he understood that a striving for glory and its restoration frames a holistic search among variety. The particular device of Clerke's woodcut indicates a specific printer, John Wyer, who published Clerke's book in 1543. In his other printed texts, this device of Wyer's signifies St John on the Greek island of Patmos inspired by the Holy Spirit to write prophecy, the Book of the Apocalypse (Revelation). There is a significant difference here, however, from these other versions: in them an eagle soars above the writer and his city. Here there is none. Because in the Tudor period secular woodcuts in books frequently have movable iconography, Wyer or Clerke may have adapted the meaning of the printer's device, so significantly placed, for his own purpose of showing a figure to represent the more secular Virgil as a poet like Surrey. Cf. Ronald B. McKerrow, *Printers' & Publishers' Devices in England & Scotland 1485–1640* (London, 1913). I am indebted to Dr Ruth Samson Luborsky for her direction and advice and to her and Betty Ingram for their definitive text *A Guide to English Illustrated Books 1536–1603* (forthcoming).

in the handes of a fewe' but 'publyshed to the common profyt and delectation of many'. In this praise, Awen suggests a great deal about Surrey's actual composition: the poet earl must have written rapidly and, it would seem, almost anywhere, with little time for revision in the ten to fifteen years given to composing all his poems. Thus, 'the reding of the authors copy it selfe, by reason of speedye wrytyng thereof was somewhat doutful,' says Awen. Indeed, Awen appears quite certain of the fact Surrey 'had not tyme sufficient to the due examinacion thereof, after it was wrytten'. After comparing three texts, Awen has determined which text he considers 'most worthy to be alowed, whych was both to the latyn moste agreable, and also best standing with the dignity of that kynde of mytre'. Thus, argues Awen in his conclusion, 'this my doing I trust no honest man shall be able to reproue, but rather it shall be an occasion, to such as fauour the monimentes of so noble a wyt, if they haue a better copy to publyshe the same.' That is, the art and language of the poet Earl of Surrey should be available to serve the greater community. As Hardison notes, Awen is specifically 'claiming Surrey's verse is the English equivalent to ancient heroic meter', the highest language of any community, Awen's word 'dignity' or honour being the operative term. Because the young duke's 'oratour' feels confident of support—'(as I nothyn doute of your graces goodnesse),' he writes to Surrey's 18-year-old son: 'it shal no lytle encourage me hereafter to bring other hys workes to light, as they shal come to my hands,' a task he never fulfilled.[14]

This hope of greater profits from the one Englishman—Surrey—who could combine so stylishly two genealogies may also have appealed to John Day. Indeed, in 1554, in a court and university world off-balance after incessant Edwardian iconoclasm, this free flexible form—a new textualizing of honour—might become something quite marketable for a printer, a profitable, if ambiguous, instrument of nobility. A new generation seeking forms of honour (and this included almost all reformed Christians) might find blank verse suited to the new social desire of Queen Mary's *renovatio*: she would recover or restore the shapes of an

[14] Awen's dedication is reprinted in *Surrey's 'Fourth Boke of Virgill'*, ed. Henry Hartman (1933), 3–4; the title-page is on p. xv. All lines in the original spelling are from this edition. Cf. *Horati Epistolae*, II, 3, 396; see also 333–4 for the *prodesse* and *delectare* formula. By manipulating Horace in his dedication, Awen could spell out the problem of getting the right manuscripts in hand. He can also justify his solution. In fact, 'although it were taken of one [was compared with]' other copy also in Surrey's handwriting, Awen's copy of Surrey's translation of Virgil's Book IV was 'wrytten wyth the authors owne hande'. He thus possessed two holographs of Surrey's fourth book. But the young Duke's 'Oratour' did not feel 'so certaine' that his copy was 'selfe sufficient' enough 'to be publyshed'. Either the mutual friend who provided Awen with his holograph of Surrey's text or Awen himself had access to information about the beheaded Surrey's text which was later lost or suppressed. To be sure, Awen had the right connections, for he soon compared his copy, so he writes to the young duke, with 'two other copies also', not holographs like his, but 'written out by other men'. Awen's text of Surrey's translation of Book IV should be compared to Hargrave MS 205 in the British Library. Comparisons of all three texts from Awen-Day, Tottel, and Hargrave with those of Gawain Douglas' *Aeneados* can be found in *The Aeneid of Henry Howard, Earl of Surrey*, ed. Florence Ridley, University of California Publications, English Studies, no. 26 (1963). See also Hardison's remarks on the Awen text in *Prosody*, 130–1; 146–7.

older world within a burgeoning new society, denying neither. So Day, a reformed Christian friend of Chaucer's editor Thynne, sensed the financial advantages of making an icon of blood nobility and even the restoration of old nobility, before his own débâcle on 16 October 1554, the *terminus ad quem* for dating the appearance of Surrey's first text of blank verse. On that day, after 'rydyng owt of Northfoke', Day with his servant, 'a prest, and an-odur prynter' was sent to the Tower 'for pryntyng of noythy [naughty or heretical] bokes'. Day did not resume printing until 1557.[15]

Yet neither the new queen nor the adolescent duke had objected to the publication of this 'straunge metre' and so, after three years, Tottel could feel politically safe when, in 1557, he launched his own publishing blitz centred on Surrey. Indeed, in 1554 both queen and duke appeared to give tacit approval to a revolutionary (or at least non-evolutionary) text that both or, more probably, their advisers thought would garner greater social legitimacy for the regime and themselves as the highest nobility. Indeed, Virgil by a Howard would combine *redivivus*, in the new power of print, an honour of blood and of virtue. First named 'blank verse' in 1589 by Surrey's hagiographer Thomas Nashe,[16] Surrey's 'straunge metre' would provide in 1554—at least Marian advisers might have hoped—both a remythologizing of England's Troy origins (giving the new reign greater authenticity) and become another text for the old Tudor game of elegant British *Romanitas* and, as with Lord Berners, from one of their own blood.

At the beginning of her rule, shrewdly, Mary I wanted to be careful of any returning to her mother's world, even though she could, of course, settle old scores by stealth, even, in one legend, burning in the presence of her cousin Reginald, Cardinal Pole (the purest survivor of the White Rose and now the Archbishop of Canterbury), the disinterred body of her father on the Lady Chapel floor of St George's at Windsor and then dumping his ashes and bones, like Thomas à Becket's, into the rubbish.[17] More positively, the new Queen of England had her own agenda for the future. She had no intention of worsening by revenge the wreck that London had become by 1554, as the ambassadors were reporting, with its defaced churches, empty monasteries, and ruined structures, at least not yet. She had too much hope; she wanted to transform her world through a new *Romanitas* emerging now from the Council of Trent and the presence of her marriage with the possibility of a child. Nostalgia was a political luxury her sister

[15] Henry Machyn, *Diary*, ed. John Gough Nichols, Camden Society, 42 (1848) 72; cf. Strype *Ecclesiastical Memorials*, vol. 5, 201. E. Gordon Duff, *A Century of English Book Trade* (1905), 38; and A. W. Pollard, *Hand-Lists of English Printers, 1501–1556* (1913) 4.

[16] Thomas Nashe, *To Gentlemen Students of Both Universities* in *Works*, ed. Ronald B. McKerrow and F. P. Wilson (1958), vol. 3, 311–12. Attacking Shakespeare, Robert Greene in his *A Groatsworth of Wit* (1923) marks the stressed emotional outburst that he sees as paradigmatic in blank verse: Shakespeare 'supposes he is as well able to bombast out a blanke verse as the best of you' (45).

[17] Scarisbrick, *Henry VIII*, 497. Whatever the truth of a story that cannot be verified or denied, the screen and tomb ornaments for Henry VIII did remain intact (although eagerly dismantled and sold during the English Revolution) as was the empty sarcophagus and its base (later used for Nelson's tomb at St Paul's).

Elizabeth might play at, but not Mary Tudor. It was altogether natural, therefore, to tolerate any text, however 'straunge', that would honour such a recently ascended figure of blood nobility as the young Howard duke in a family with an unspoken martyr, a father who had invented a language for the future.

Most splendidly of all, a coup for Marian humanists, the occasion and text provided a totally original heroic line of unrhymed verse, borrowing from the latest continental fashions that the Seymours, the Hobys, the Dudleys, the Sidneys, and their survivors coveted. Surrey's odd language could exemplify conservative innovation; just as Queen Mary had appropriated the emblem of reformed Christians 'Veritas filia temporum' ('Truth is the daughter of time'), so might the new Marian Renaissance produce its own Virgil, a Howard whose poetry the queen had doubtless heard, as Awen claims he had. After all, had not Mary I opened her first Parliament with a specific reference to the poet Earl of Surrey and the horror of his death? The queen had recalled the cruelty of Henry VIII's laws and included Surrey's death brought on by 'words': 'And Henry Earl of Surrey . . . for such like words, and the poor crime of assuming somewhat into his coat of arms, was actually beheaded' and 'many honourable and noble persons, and others of good reputation' and 'for words only, suffered shameful deaths, not accustomed to nobles.'[18] So now 'words' by the earl will be honoured because they inscribed ancient Rome itself in an English that would make the queen's own time heroic. A public might believe the future did belong to the beneficent liberating forces of Queen Mary I, who had saved the realm from the thraldom of Queen Jane and the power of John Dudley, who had made himself Duke of Northumberland. She was the first ruling queen in England for centuries, a woman harbinger of a possible golden age.

In that hope, then, the Howards may have read this first acknowledged publication of any of the earl's poetry. They read in print the fourth book of Virgil's *Aeneid*—a communal work ranking with the Bible—translated by their beheaded son, father, and brother. After seven long years, the voice from the severed head had suddenly become alive. Its measured language they may have recognized from earlier afternoons and evenings at Kenninghall, Surrey House, and Lambeth—not the wild uncontrolled poems at the end or the sobbing outbursts on Surrey's forced march through Holborn in December 1546. What they could now read was control and mastery: the strange rhythms of ten syllables without rhyme, breaks and silences in the line, strong native alliteration and continental assonance, odd spondaic emphases, and lines flowing one into the other. Once more, the terrible story could be told:

> But nowe the wounded Quene wyth heuy care,
> Throughout the vaines she nourisheth the plai,
> Surprised with blynde flame: and to hyr mynde
> Gan eke resort the prowes of the man,
> And honour of hys race.

[18] Strype, *Ecclesiastical Memorials*, vol. 3, 1, 58.

Surrey may have originated these first lines in the 1540s, but they were suddenly alive a decade later. They open Book IV and reveal, as nowhere else, Virgil's perspective on the interplay between subjectivity—the broken self—and progressing history that permeates the entire Roman epic:

> whyles in her brest
> Imprinted stacke his wordes, and pyctures forme:
> Ne to her lyms care graunteth quyet rest.

What would have struck the audience at once in Surrey's text would have been what the printer uneasily prepares for, the novelty of the form. In this opening passage, the first in blank verse ever to be published, Surrey generates a pattern of English stresses in a system of exact decasyllabic lines. Surrey's first line with five firm accents renders the effect of the tragic subject and her suffering. These stresses also try to reproduce, with the exactitude of short and long syllables, the quantitative beats of Virgil's longer dactylic hexameter, a rhythm recognized by a second generation trained by the humanists of Sir Thomas More's generation. Surrey's pause after the sixth syllable moves the narrative forward by focusing on Dido and her high nobility. In the next line, however, the caesura comes after 'vaines'. Here stresses are reduced for the more sinister noun–verb–noun relationship to describe Dido's suffering. The third line becomes more experimental, hardly strict iambic, and once more, the caesura is put later. In this line, the first six syllables realistically enact the plague power and surprise of sexual love ('blynde flame' is an English metonymy for it). Then the text shifts to the first stage of a new representation. Virgil and now Surrey will give a psychological inscription—'and to hyr mynde'—to the historical dilemma Dido is suffering. To prepare for the enjambement effect, unaccented syllables slow down. They lead to Surrey's internal rhyme 'mind' (Virgil's 'animo'). That word directs the reader to the self caught in the paradox of love, a subjectivity brutalized by the necessary history of building new Rome.

That history becomes, in the next line and a half, a male figuration of honour. Surrey renders Virgil's 'gentis honos' in four simple stresses with a deliberate chiasmatic structure (centring 'resort'/'prowess' with auxiliaries on either side). Such a chiasmus climaxes in the opening phrase of the fifth line 'And honour of his race'. After this phrase, again with a shifting caesura to after the sixth syllable, Surrey moves into another key run-on structure to continue thematic emphases: if Dido's 'mind' can contemplate ('resort' to) the Trojan's erotic nobility, then, with that same sensitivity, her 'breast' is 'imprinted' and 'stuck' with the lover's language and male countenance ('picture's form' for Virgil's 'voltus', Surrey's abstract possessive unusual for its day and hinting at Dido's coming madness).

In such highly stylized translation, Surrey reveals not only Dido's trap but his own new language of nobility. Technically, he is rendering a consciously set metric, a counterpoint, to use Gerard Manley Hopkins' term,[19] between a nearly

[19] *The Poetical Works of Gerard Manley Hopkins*, ed. Norman H. Mackenzie (1990), 116. Hopkins' term means that 'two rhythms are in some manner running at once' and the pattern in

1. Hans Holbein the Younger, *Henry VIII and Henry VII*, cartoon for the mural at Whitehall Palace, National Portrait Gallery. By courtesy of the National Portrait Gallery, London.

2. Hans Holbein the Younger, *Frances, Countess of Surrey*, Windsor Castle. The Royal Collection © Her Majesty the Queen.

3. Hans Holbein the Younger, *Henry Howard*, *Earl of Surrey*, Windsor Castle. The Royal Collection © Her Majesty the Queen.

4. *Elizabeth, second Duchess of Norfolk*; painter unknown, Arundel Castle. Reproduced by kind permission of His Grace the Duke of Norfolk.

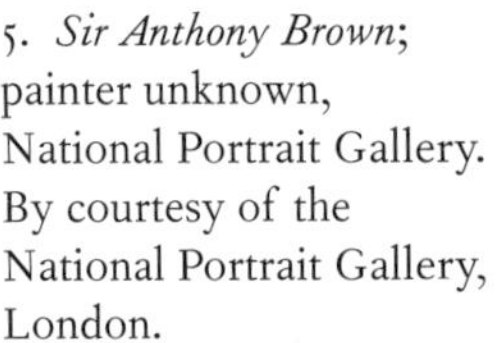

5. *Sir Anthony Brown*; painter unknown, National Portrait Gallery. By courtesy of the National Portrait Gallery, London.

6. Tomb of the Duke of Richmond, St Michael's church, Framlingham. Photographed by Mrs V. Runnacles.

7. Joos van Cleve, *Francis I, King of France*, Windsor Castle. The Royal Collection © Her Majesty the Queen.

8. Lucas Hornebolte, *Henry Fitzroy, Duke of Richmond*, Windsor Castle. The Royal Collection © Her Majesty the Queen.

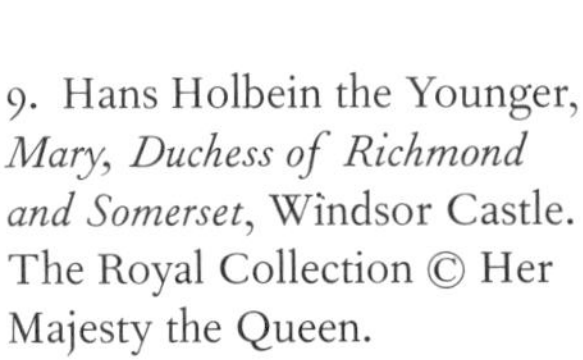

9. Hans Holbein the Younger, *Mary, Duchess of Richmond and Somerset*, Windsor Castle. The Royal Collection © Her Majesty the Queen.

The Lady of Richmond.

10. Hans Holbein the Younger, *Henry Howard, Earl of Surrey*, Windsor Castle. The Royal Collection © Her Majesty the Queen.

11. Hans Holbein the Younger, (?) *Mary (Shelton), Lady Heveningham*, Windsor Castle. The Royal Collection © Her Majesty the Queen.

12. Remains of Kenninghall, Norfolk. Photographed by Mrs V. Runnacles.

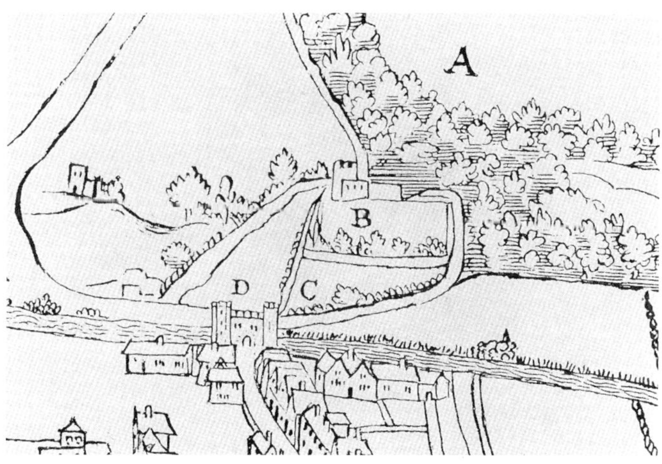

13. *Catherine Parr*; painter unknown, National Portrait Gallery. By courtesy of the National Portrait Gallery, London.

14. Mount Surrey and Surrey House (B), from Dr William Cunyngham, 'Cosmographical Glass, 1559' with a map entitled 'Nordovicum, Angliae civitas, anno 1558, I. B. F.', Norfolk Room, Norwich Public Library. Photographed by Terence J. Burchell, by courtesy of the Norwich Public Library.

The Byble in Englyshe, that is to saye the content of al the holy scrypture, both of ye olde, and newe testament, with a prologe therinto, made by the reuerende father in God, Thomas archbyschop of Cantorbury.
This is the Byble apoynted to the vse of the churches.
Prynted by Edward whytchurche
Cum priuilegio ad imprimendum solum.
M.D.xl.

15. Hans Holbein the Younger (or his school), title-page of the 1539 Great Bible. By courtesy of the Huntington Library, San Marino.

16. Hans Holbein the Younger, *Thomas Cromwell*, Frick Collection. By courtesy of the Frick Collection, New York.

17. Hans Holbein the Younger, *Sir Thomas Wyatt*, Windsor Castle. The Royal Collection © Her Majesty the Queen.

18. *Sir Anthony Denny*; painter unknown, Courtauld Institute of Art. By courtesy of the Courtauld Institute of Art, London.

19. The woodcut on the first page of the 1542 edition of the Earl of Surrey's elegy on Sir Thomas Wyatt. By courtesy of the Huntington Library, San Marino.

20. School of Holbein, *Henry Howard, Earl of Surrey*, Pierpont Morgan Library. By courtesy of the Pierpont Morgan Library, New York. I, 259.

21. Anthony van der Wyngaerde, drawing of Tower Hill, 1549, Ashmolean Museum. By courtesy of the Ashmolean Museum, Oxford.

22. Hans Holbein the Younger, *Sir Richard Southwell*, Windsor Castle. The Royal Collection © Her Majesty the Queen.

23. Tomb of the poet Earl and Countess of Surrey, St Michael's church, Framlingham. Photographed by Mrs V. Runnacles.

24. *Allegory of Edward VI's Reign*; painter unknown, National Portrait Gallery. By courtesy of the National Portrait Gallery, London.

25. *Edward Seymour, Earl of Hertford, later Duke of Somerset and Lord Protector*; painter unknown. By courtesy of Hulton Getty/Tony Stone Images.

absolute base structure of ten syllables and a varying pattern of strong stresses, usually four or five within the same line. Surrey's unrhymed contrapuntal structure of varying stresses and constant syllables will identify the signature of a new English master. The poet will give the new *boni amici* taking on Roman roles a language with which to build a Renaissance in England.

Surrey's Virgil in 1557: The Second Text

Tottel's great insight—or Harington's or the mastermind's behind the collection of the *Miscellany*—was to understand, with a merchant's cunning, a historical opportunity. In 1557 Tottel recognized what his audience wanted. In publishing Surrey's texts, he would literally capitalize on a progressive logic: icon and word—the old and the new—could now be blended as never before to generate something contemporary and attractive and profitable. Furthermore, Richard Tottel was shrewd enough in those summer days of 1557 when the Tudor queen was both burning new Christian martyrs in London, Oxford, and Canterbury and, in all churches, restoring altar stones (with saints' relics) to announce, on his title-page, that the entire *Miscellany* was 'written by the ryght honorable Lorde Henry Hawarde late Earle of Surrey, and other' (1: 2). Surrey's text and the person of Surrey will also do the work of Marian *renovatio*. In the midst of martyrdoms, Mary I brought joy to many, if not most, English Christians with the restored large roods and screens, new statues of the Blessed Virgin and St John in York Minster, for example, and in Kent, with Archdeacon Harpsfield's request that not just repainting but exceptional gilding be given to icons and religious objects.[20] Yet the hopelessness of Dido's city abandoned by history lingered in her reign. Even in Westminster Abbey, with so grand a superstructure of wood as the one Queen Mary I built around the holiest shrine left in England—now the only body of a saint acknowledged and left in its original place—the wood of the 41-year-old queen could not match the marble and mosaic base of St Edward's tomb built by Henry III in a sacramental age. The Confessor's tomb had been mutilated earlier in an act sanctioned by both Edward VI and Archbishop Cranmer. Now Mary Tudor's black and gilt wood over the broken mosaics on the shrine could only pretend to that earlier age. At her death, the wooden niches stood as empty as the

Surrey's blank verse does play a consistent ten syllables in a line against an unregulated number of stresses. This contrapuntal effect *is* the single rhythm itself or what Hopkins apparently finds in 'counterpoint in music, which is two or more strains of tune going on together'. On the impossibility of separating counterpoint but recognizing that it works as dialectic, see Steven Paul Sher, 'Literature and Music', in *Interrelations of Literature*, ed. Jean-Pierre Barricelli and Joseph Gibaldi (1982), 225–50.

20 Aston, *Iconoclasts*, vol. 1, 294: If 'the large size of the new roods was a grand affirmation of restated faith in the layman's painted book' and, once more in England's green and pleasant land, 'the ubiquity of the cross spoke Christ through picture instead of scripture,' still it was all 'a dogmatic response to the iconomach's belief in the sufficiency of the word'.

marble ones, with neither statues nor decoration of any kind; if feretories rarely bore sculpture and were more often left open for the use of pilgrims, these wooden structures, however temporary, were still destined to be abandoned spaces.

But, whether or not Mary I was a Dido *redivivus*, an up-and-coming Tottel saw only opportunity in her reign. In his preface to the 1557 *Miscellany*, Tottel follows Awen (and Horace) in arguing for the higher communal good of publishing the poems: 'And for this point (good reder) thine own profit and pleasure, in these presently, and in moe hereafter, shal answere for my defence.' He now addresses the general reader, no exalted aristocrat like a young duke. Of course, if the greedy readers hoarding Surrey's texts (or others') are aristocratic, Tottel has no intention of being identified with any other group but them. In fact, Tottel is careful to attack those who 'mislike the statelinesse of stile remoued from the rude skill of common eares'. He further establishes his bias; his aim is not to valorize his own bourgeois class and certainly not any proletariat, but to identify fully with the blood nobility, with the example of Surrey himself in the title. Not surprisingly, Tottel ends his short preface with that snobbery defining most English and European humanism until the English Revolution.[21] Tottel harshly concludes: 'I exhort the vnlearned, by reding to be more skilfull, and to purge that swinelike grossenesse, that maketh the swete maierome not to smell to their delight' (1: 2).

In June 1557, Tottel had sensed cunningly such a historical moment of change. His *Miscellany* according to Marotti, became the first of four crucial texts in the Renaissance that 'affected the literary institutionalization of the lyric and the functioning of authors, publishers, and consumers/readers within print culture'. In both his lyric and epic texts of June 1557, Tottel focused for the nobility two views of time in texts 'enhanced by association with a figure whose life held some special interest,' Marotti continues, and whose 'high rank and death by execution assured him a certain romantic notoriety.' The forces of the old icon and the new printed book (for some, the Eternal Word) could gather up the momentum of Marian political ferment and look immediately to the ideology of the reign to come. Tottel was right on target. In exactly seventeen months, after the appalling death of Queen Mary on 17 November 1558, the daughter of Anne Boleyn ascended the throne on the feast-day of the popular St Hugh of Lincoln, remaining queen for forty-five years. In this period (amid more aggressive, if totally different, inscriptions of honour and nobility), blank verse had its second triumph. In

[21] Vernon Hall Jr., *Renaissance Literary Criticism: A Study of its Social Content* (1959). For a clear example of how such class ideals remained, see the dialectic in Milton's prologue to Book IX of *Paradise Lost*. Also see Braudel 2, 725–33. For Tottel's manipulation of this basic social impulse of early England, see Wendy Wall, *The Imprint of Gender: Authorship and Publication in the Renaissance* (1993): Tottel (and his imitators) 'marketed exclusivity'. Books of lyrics (and also, one assumes, Surrey's two books of the *Aeneid*) 'functioned as conduct books' demonstrating 'to more common audiences the poetic practices entertained by graceful courtly readers and writers' (97). See Lerer, *Courtly Letters*: Tottel, 'for but the price of the volume, will present them with the secret sights of the coterie poets' (165).

Surrey's cousin's reign was the Orphean and Horatian advent for England which Awen's dedication had predicted and that blank verse texts will now fulfil.

Thus, on 21 June 1557, Richard Tottel brought out, between the first two editions of his *Miscellany* in the same month, his *Certain Bokes of Virgiles Aeneis*, Surrey's translations of Book II and Book IV. Listed in the same year in the *Stationers' Register*,[22] the editions presented a new Surrey poem, his translation of Book II of Virgil's epic—the monologue narrative of Aeneas at Dido's banquet. Tottel also presented a greatly edited Book IV, the love tragedy of Dido, with considerably smoother iambic pentametre than in the Day–Awen text three years earlier. Once more the surviving Howards could read the language of their son, brother, father, and husband. The erratic mother, the virgin sister soon to die, the always silent younger brother, the widow and adolescent children, all knew that the poet earl's actual body still lay dishonoured in the London church of All Hallows Barking, the parish church near the scaffold. There the bloody trunk of the young man had been deposited ten years earlier. Yet now, in the opening narrative of Aeneas, they read a heroic line in English that embodied him and their own world as nothing else had (or, as his survivors will learn, ever would).

They whisted all, with fixed face attent,
When prince Aeneas from the royal seat
Thus 'gan to speak: "O queen, it is thy will
I should renew a woe [that] cannot be told,
How that the Greeks did spoil and overthrow
The Phrygian wealth and wailful realm of Troy,
Those ruthful things that I myself beheld,
And whereof no small part fell to my share.
Which to express, who could refrain from tears?"

Hearing this new language, the Howards and other Marian audiences, including the 24-year-old Princess Elizabeth (who later, in the Sieve portrait, compared herself to Dido), 'whisted all'. In their silence before a narrative that retold Virgil's primal historical breakdown, Surrey may have had his poetic intention realized, what Trissino had prophesied for the Renaissance, 'Poetry can work its magic again on contemporary society.' The poet earl's magic came from a new technology, a breakthrough that all the audience heard. In a line of four stressed frontal vowels (the deeper 'all' barely making a fifth stress) Surrey reveals the immediate audience at Dido's banquet table. Thus, the first line stresses the same vowel-sounds in two strong verb forms, one—'whisted'—Anglo-Saxon and the other (a verbal)—'fixed'—consciously Latinate, especially when linked with 'face'. In this juxtaposition, designed also to set at once the sombre 'dignity' of his new metre, the earl inaugurates his textual interplay of native words, archaic diction, and continental word-choices, particularly neologisms (but significantly few 'ink-horn'

[22] Marotti, *Manuscript, Print*, xv, 216. The text is STC 24798 and is listed in *A Transcript of the Registers of the Company of Stationers of London, 1554–1640 A. D.*, ed. Edward Arber (1894).

terms). This counterpointing of syntax and diction marks Surrey's method of composition. Here it more than compensates for the absence of rhyme.[23]

The counterpoint leads to direct contact with an audience. These first nine lines of Surrey's first verse paragraph point, in a figure of *erotesis*, to the key rhetorical question: 'Which to express, who could refrain from tears?' If the answer to the question is obvious ('no one'), Aeneas' questioning sets up, by its form, immediate audience participation. The question will keep the question of expression—the writer's, the readers'—alive. The reader/listener must be open to enact what Book II as an overture to the epic will demand from its audience, an Aristotelian catharsis of 'tears'. The final question of the first verse paragraph of Surrey's epic thus becomes a key point of rhetorical engagement with the reader/auditor. It is the first step towards an appropriate pity and fear that will heal the 'whisted' audience caught in their own terrible history.

The earl's retrospective narrative will enact, therefore, the dialectic of a blood noble (Aeneas) as the sole survivor who can epitomize social and political ideals by pitting city-building against city-burning. So in his first lines, with epic directness, Surrey takes his narrative qua narrative centre stage. The key term in these lines—'express'—offers the reader the chance to see language as language: the distancing of the speaking self (and therefore the reading self) in relation to time and within a progressing history. In this sense of historical progression, and the progression in blank verse itself, Surrey will always follow T. S. Eliot's injunction that with society it is not so much that 'the maintenance of the standard is the price of our freedom,' as it is that 'the readiness' of a text, its ability to move in and through time, constitutes 'the defence of freedom against chaos'.[24] The right

[23] Trissino is quoted in Hardison, *Prosody* 81. It should be noted that Surrey's opening passage of nine lines sets up an immediate field of temporal 'echoes' that supports this texture. This field becomes solipsistic and self-inverted as it develops its narrative. Cf. Ants Oras, 'Surrey's Technique of Verbal Echoes: A Method and Its Background', *Journal of English and Germanic Philology*, 50 (1951), 305–6. Not only does this opening passage (textually to be linked with the questions that follow it) contain an echoing system of Anglo-Saxon 'wh' and 'w' intersecting the more Mediterranean 'r' sounds, whose repetition signals a virtual leitmotif; it also inscribes at least seven distinct assonantal units: the initial 'whisted'/'fixed'; 'seat'/'speak'; 'queen'/'Greeks'; 'woe'/'told'/'no'; 'spoil'/'Troy'; 'wealth'/'realm'/'myself'/'beheld'/'fell'; and 'share'/'tears', at least in the probable pronunciation of the 1540s, as Fausto Cercignani, *Shakespeare's Works and Elizabethan Pronunciation* (1981), 163, 171, 357 suggests for Shakespeare. If these are compounded with consonantal support and instances of slant rhyme or virtual open repetition (even at line-ends, as in 'told'/'overthrow'/'Troy'/'beheld'), the assonantal units tend to bracket whole ideas and themes. These seven units may occur, for example, before Surrey's frequent caesurae at the end of the fourth syllable or act as an end-stop for the whole line. Such a final effect becomes, of course, more articulate than any simple pattern of rhyme and more emphatic in setting the tone of the painful narrative. In other words, the system of analogies governing the composition more than compensates for the lack of rhyme. Rubel, *Poetic Diction* ch. 5. Surrey's is the first cited use of 'whisted' in English in the *OED*, an example among many such first uses by Surrey.

[24] For the greater Aristotelian effect, Surrey rearranges Virgil's syntax to emphasize 'tears' (in the Latin, Virgil's 'tears' image belongs after the proper nouns two lines after Surrey's initial question). Obviously Surrey wants the counterpoint or tension between 'express' and 'tears' to dominate the beginning of his story. It will itself renew 'a woe [that] can not be told'. But to emphasize the cathartic process going on within the hero himself, the poet makes a key mistranslation in line 2. He follows

expression in that space of time that is the text—its 'readiness'—in fact makes this self historical, objective, active in society—perhaps one of the *boni amici* at the centre of power because such a 'friend' can speak, 'express' meaning 'against chaos'.

Surrey uses the term 'express' again, in another Virgilian moment of distancing. Yet three events occur to Aeneas before he arrives at that moment Aristotle calls *anagnorisis* or self-recognition: first, Aeneas experiences his ghost dream of the Trojan 'father' Hector, with his demands of genealogy; then he hears Panthus' prophecy of annihilation; and finally he organizes his comrades in a hopeless but noble task ('Oh you young men, of courage stout in vain, / For nought you strive to save the burning town' 446–7). At that moment—the recognition of what has happened since Aeneas awoke to the fire and saw himself as sole survivor—Surrey repeats the counterpoint of 'tears' and 'express'. Aeneas, speaking directly to Dido and his audience, poses his and the poet's most central question: 'Who can express the slaughter of that night?'

Surrey's Blank Verse: Chaucer

In Surrey's world, the right expression for any artist demanded a genealogy. Surrey had three immediate sources to turn to in the late 1530s and 1540s when he was composing his *Aeneid*. The first was his English literary father and that of all early Renaissance poets in England. In fact, it would have come as no surprise for audiences in 1554 and 1557 that, for a modern critic, 'the nearest thing to [blank verse] rhythmically' turns out to be Chaucer's *Canterbury Tales*. Surrey's counterpointing progression resembled human speech but became, as Pearsall says about Chaucer, poetic language out of 'the speech rhythms of the highly cultivated audience for which he wrote'. In fact, both Surrey and Chaucer had followed the 'one law of nature more powerful than any of these varying currents, or influences from abroad or from the past'; as T. S. Eliot remarks on the music inherent in

Gawain Douglas's *Aeneid*, a mistranslation hardly by accident in this second book, where Surrey works for as much literalism as possible in order to be faithful to Virgil, often inverting and stretching English syntax into figures of *hyperbaton* and *anastrophe* (reversal of normal word order). In line 2, instead of following Virgil's 'Pater Aeneas', Surrey keeps the alliterative effect but translates 'Prince Aeneas'. See Eliot, *On Poetry*, 73–4. It should be noted that Cheke's pupil Ascham misses entirely the progressive dialectic in Surrey's blank verse. Although he hails Surrey as one of the masters of his age, Ascham attacks Surrey's blank verse as walking with wooden feet, in one of the most incisive critical images of the Renaissance (*Works*, 331). In his *Well-Weighed Syllables: Elizabethan Verse in Classical Metres* (1974), 98, Derek Attridge has demonstrated how Ascham's criticism stems from his hearing classroom Latin verse as the ideal musical model—so quick had been the success of the humanists!—with its absolute expectation of short and long syllables divorced from local speech rhythms, a formally recited Latin with consistent substructures impossible in a Germanic language. Ascham misses the principle of equivalence operating for Surrey, a perpetual adjustment or accommodation of syllabic count to stress, a principle quite consistent with native English that Ascham ignores but that Chaucer taught Surrey.

poetic form: 'poetry must not stray too far from the ordinary everyday language which we use and hear.'[25]

For that Erasmian realism of voice, Surrey took Chaucer's syllabic centring of the human voice that made poetry appear so conversational. Thus, Surrey's blank verse is, first and foremost, syllabic, voiced strongly as in the Mediterranean world. After Chaucer, the tightly held Germanic vowels (the tightness of English voices Milton complains about in *Of Education*) could be made expressive, imitating Romance language vowels, especially if syllables were held in a kind of tension with northern gutteral consonants surrounding them. Surrey accelerated this counterpointing syllabic revolution. After him, English verse affirmed fully the Chaucerian rhythm centring in 'syllables-as-events', to use Chatman's phrase, so that, in such base-line dynamics as Surrey's, 'the only important question for metrics is "How many syllables are there?" ' Surrey's answer in his heroic line would have been as emphatic as Chaucer's in the *Canterbury Tales*: ten. Although French contemporaries like Machaut influenced the invention of the English syllabic line and specifically the norm of the decasyllabic, the originality in a Germanic language like English sprang from Chaucer himself. Then, after Surrey, the ten-syllable line became the firm base for most English poetry. In non-dramatic verse, Surrey, Sidney, Shakespeare, among others, as Wright notes, 'avoid writing lines in which the number of syllables is problematical.'[26]

Surrey's Blank Verse: France and Italy

The experience of France strengthened Surrey's concept of a syllabic base. France also provided the most cogent of all social and political models for blank verse. Francis I wrote the first such unrhymed verse in French. In 1525, in prison in Madrid, the French king had translated into his native language unrhymed Italian

[25] Suzanne Woods, *Natural Emphasis: English Versification from Chaucer to Dryden* (1985), 13, 21. See her analysis of the first lines of the General Prologue to the *Canterbury Tales* that demonstrate the same kind of counterpointing prosody that Surrey invented for his blank verse. Derek Pearsall, *Old English and Middle English Poetry* (1977), 197. Cf. James G. Southworth, *The Prosody of Chaucer and His Followers: Supplementary Chapters to* 'Verses of Cadence' (1962; reprint 1978), 3–4. T. S. Eliot *On Poetry*, 21.

[26] Erasmus' realism is discussed in Sessions, 'Mutations', 1–10. Seymour Chatman, *A Theory of Meter* (1965), 39, notes the problematic of identifying just what a syllable consists of or of 'identifying [its] boundaries'. He does not see identification as serious in determining a metre for which the central question is the number of syllables. I am grateful to Professor Gilbert Youmans for his generous help with linguistics studies here to which I can only allude, especially his 'Iambic Pentameter: Statistics or Generative Grammar?', *Language and Style*, 19/4 (1986), 388–403. For the Machaut influence, see Woods, *Natural Emphasis*, 30–1. Cf. *Chaucer and His Contemporaries*, ed. R. Barton Palmer (1991); James I. Wimsatt, *Chaucer and His French Contemporaries: Natural Music in 1400* (1991), especially ch. 9 and the discussion of a court audience; and John Stevens, 'The "Music" of the Lyric: Machaut, Deschamps, Chaucer', in *Medieval and Pseudo-Medieval Lierature*, ed. Piero Boitani and Anna Torti (1984). George T. Wright, *Shakespeare's Metrical Art* (1988) 150, 158.

verse from the manuscript given him by his courtier, Luigi Alamanni, a text developed from Virgil's *Georgics* (and published in 1533 when Surrey was in France). For this reason, almost certainly among the earl's readings in France were both French and Italian poems in the newly discovered unrhymed hendecasyllabic lines (in Italy, *versi sciolti*), especially those reconstructing the most avant-garde *Aeneids* of the day. Surrey may also have known of Trissino's blank-verse epic in progress (or even read the 1524 preface to the tragedy *Sophonisba* with blank-verse dialogue).[27] The extent of Surrey's borrowing from the Italian texts he encountered in France is enough to demonstrate, first, the precision and depth of the young Howard heir apparent's reading and skill in languages and, secondly, the achievement of the poet earl's transfer of *versi sciolti* based on syllabication into a Germanic stress-language like English. In every case, they reveal that Surrey found in the Italians, as Ridley notes, 'a standard of accuracy'[28] and precision that valorized Surrey's syllabic experiments in his native tongue. The result was a relationship, a tension of north and south in Surrey's blank verse, that gave Chaucer's revolution a quantum leap into new speech and discourse.

This Italian influence from the world of Fontainebleau can be seen in Surrey's blank verse at three obvious points: its power of linguistic reduction; its system of verbal echoes or *concatenazione*, in Trissino's term; and its power of syntax. As a result of these Italian influences on the poet, Surrey's *Aeneid* is as succinct as any English translation of Virgil until the late twentieth century. Surrey's is, in fact, even more concise than those of the Italians: against the original 804 lines of Virgil's Book II, the Scottish poet Douglas has 1442, the Italian Ippolito's translation 1217, and Surrey 1070; against the original 705 lines of Virgil's Book IV, Douglas has 1374, the Italian Liburnio 1141, and Surrey 943. For this concision, Surrey had placed his system of stress rhythms and phrasal units within his own larger evolving system of rhythmic and aural analogies. Such analogizing of

[27] Trissino's 1524 dedication of *Sophonisba*, his blank-verse tragedy, to the Medici Pope Leo X justified the flexibility he found in his new medium of *versi sciolti*, the unrhymed dialogue of eleven-syllable lines (hendecasyllabic) he had incorporated in the tragedy. He showed how this form dramatized the nature of suffering and was superior for that reason. Thus, for Trissino, one of the first in Renaissance Italy to introduce the new editions of Aristotle's *Poetics* into critical analysis, new unrhymed verse not only helps the narrative, moving it forward and actualizing its speeches, but energizes the necessary moving of the audience to pity ('ma nel muovere compassione necessario'). *Versi sciolti*, the unrhymed language of deep subjectivity and suffering that rouses the pity necessary for catharsis, 'is born from sorrow' ('nasce dal dolore'). Its development is natural and flexible and continuous and cannot be hampered by rhyme: 'sorrow does not reveal itself in carefully thought-out words,' certainly not in rhyme. Cf. the more exact Italian text in Trissino's *Sophonisba* (1524), fol. iii, v. See also Hardison, *Purpose*, 81–6. Trissino had long been in the highest of Italian intellectual circles and had himself been patron to many artists, his most spectacular discovery being the Italian youth whom he led to study modern and ancient architecture and gave the name derived from the Greek goddess Pallas Athena, Palladius, who in turn gave his name to the style of revived classical architecture some scholars believe Surrey may have used at Surrey House.

[28] *Aeneid*, ed. Ridley, 32. Ridley and Hartman analyse many of the previous studies on Italian predecessors for Surrey's translation of Virgil, and Padelford in his edition of Surrey cites actual borrowings from the Italian texts. Cf. John M. Berdan, *Early Tudor Poetry 1485–1547* (1961), 536–8; Hardison, *Purpose*, 129–30.

rhythms and sounds Surrey had learned directly from the Latin verse of Virgil and Horace and also from the Italians, from Petrarch to Trissino. This system of analogies Oras calls Surrey's 'phonetic echoes', but neither Oras' term nor Wellek's more taxonomic 'orchestration'[29] is quite as accurate as Trissino's 1529 *concatenazione*.

In fact, rejecting both *terza rima* and *ottava rima* for his own heroic unrhymed hendecasyllabic (*versi sciolti*) line, Trissino believed that rhyme hindered what was necessary for the modern heroic epic, namely a new freedom and flexibility or 'the continuous development of the material and the interweaving [*concatenazione*] of the meanings and the constructions'. This kind of dialectical flowing among parts would produce a special epic *enargia*, notably revealed in the 'particularizing of descriptions', in Trissino's phrase. These resulted from the technical effects of holistic syntax (what Clerke had praised in Surrey) and its interplay of parts to whole, evident in the musical effect of phrasing. This is the natural poetic stylizing of human conversation; as Jones notes in Surrey, stylized phrasing is the key to his texts. Such natural English phrasing (focused by stresses and caesurae) thus helps to develop in Surrey the human situations out of which Virgil's great soliloquies grow: psychological turmoil revealed in rhetorical figures of aporia from Greek and Latin drama—the doubting or questioning within a speaker, either of self or of audience or of both.[30]

The first such Italianate 'particularized' speech in Surrey's translation is an oration—Laocoön's outcry ('Oh wretched citizens') against the credulous Trojans in Book II. Surrey reveals, in classical figures of oratory, a progression of stylized phrasing. A disjunctive syllogism, strong figures of *brachylogia* (a series of nouns without conjunctions), an overarching apostrophe, all rise through *auxesis* (increase in intensity) and *graditio* to the famous final line, appropriately a closure of six stresses like Virgil's hexameters—the 'yea' acting as a double caesura and dividing that last line into alliterative units as though in Anglo-Saxon phrases.

> "Either the Greeks are in this timber hid,
> Or this an engine is to annoy our walls,
> To view our towers, and overwhelm our town;
> Here lurks some craft. Good Trojans, give no trust
> Unto this horse; for whatsoever it be,
> I dread the Greeks, yea, when they offer gifts."

[29] The statistics are from Ridley, 36. Oras, 'Surrey's Technique', 305–6. Wellek is cited in Oras.

[30] Hardison, *Prosody*, 81. Jones, *Surrey*, xv. In Virgil, the Greek meaning of *aporia* (as the actual device is used in Euripides *Troas*, for example) is nearer to Dido's wavering rhetoric than the more ironic Ciceronian figures of *dubitatio* or *diaporesis*; there is less of the feigned in the *Aeneid* and more of genuine difficulty and loss. Puttenham appears to understand this larger meaning, the disjunctiveness of desire that marks Virgil's use of *aporia*. The figure '*Aporia*, or the Doubtfull' is like the figure just before it, in Puttenham's catalogue, '*Paradoxon* or the Wondrer'. Puttenham cites *aporia* 'because ofentimes we will seeme to cast perils, and make doubt of things when by a plaine manner of speech wee might affirme or deny him' and Puttenham illustrates the figure in a poem derived from the Medea story in Euripides, 'of a cruell mother who murdred her owne child'.

Surrey's Blank Verse: Britain

This metrical use of stress rhythm to develop phrasal units suggests a native source for Surrey's blank verse. The poet earl may have been revising, with the consciousness of a new antiquarian like Leland, an older English line marked by balanced alliteration and four stresses per line with any number of syllables. If Surrey did consciously revert to Anglo-Saxon prosody, did he see his new heroic metre for Tudor courtiers as a reconstructed language of genuine British heroes like Hereward the Wake, his putative Saxon ancestor, who had defied in the name of the nobility the Norman king? The old texts he could not read, but the signs of that ancient world he could—the nearby body of St Edmund, the hero king, and the abbey at Bury St Edmunds with its undecipherable manuscripts from the past; the windy plain of Kenninghall, where East Anglian kings had been crowned; the bodies of the Anglo-Saxon saints in the still towering Gothic structure of St Paul's overshadowing London and the Thames. Also, Surrey was translating Virgil in the year he composed his elegy on Wyatt in the north, with the English army where the Scottish dialect recalled the old Anglo-Saxon. In the same year his admirer Sir John Cheke, at Cambridge where Surrey was Steward of the University, was calling for new British diction and Leland was writing the first biography of Chaucer and rescuing manuscripts in monasteries (the Latin and Anglo-Saxon manuscripts, if not sold abroad, so said Leland's fervent admirer and disciple John Bale, were often used for scouring candlesticks or as toilet paper).[31]

In the earl's clarion call for new Roman roles for a renewed blood nobility, he naturally envisoned his translation of Virgil as another national epic. He wanted a language reflecting that earlier imitation of Roman nobility mirrored (at least for Early Modern Renaissance) in King Arthur and his Round Table of knights. After all, did not Surrey House appear to reflect, at least in its exterior, that Arthurian Roman world? Yet, unlike the poets of the century before, Surrey did not seek out the alliterative revival that still existed around him (Wyatt himself

[31] Sir John Cheke, who was teaching at Cambridge in the period after 1540 when Surrey became steward of the university, had specifically objected to foreign diction and sought a language more heroic and English. Leland also was discovering the old Anglo-Saxon and medieval manuscripts, as his follower John Bale admiringly noted, not least in that one monastery Surrey and his ancestors had known well, Bury St Edmunds in East Anglia. Cf. Jesse W. Harris, *John Bale: A Study in the Minor Literature of the Reformation* (1940), 111 and Bale's *Preface to Leland's New Year Gift* (1549). Although the Anglo-Saxon manuscripts may not have been considered verse at all in 1542, they did represent a mysterious native past still evident to the Henrician world (not all wayside crosses had been destroyed, for example). In theatrical performances and folksongs, Surrey heard these old rhythms and he had also read Chaucer's parodies of Alliterative Revival texts in his *Tale of Sir Thopas*. He had also seen the devices in the other old texts, their heavily marked four-stresses and their slash-mark or virgule indicating a mid-line pause (Wyatt used them). Surrey certainly knew the poetry of Lydgate, a monk at Bury St Edmunds, whose broken-backed lines strangely manipulated Chaucer's, as did those of other fifteenth-century poets. Their freedom of caesura followed more the older English liberty than the more rigid continental placing after the fourth syllable. See C. S. Lewis, 'The Fifteenth-Century Heroic Line', *Essays and Studies by Members of the English Association*, 24 (1938), 28–41, on the problems in the period just before Wyatt and Surrey.

marked lines with virgules). Rather, he reverted to that basic stress rhythm of the older world and specifically to that four-stress pattern Frye sees as 'inherent in the structure of the English language'.[32] Surrey's new English line of unrhymed iambic pentametre implicitly carried an older pattern where not only continental syllabication but marked stresses, four or five, formed the poetic unit.

Seeking a language for future English heroes out of the archaic and the more primitive, Surrey may have turned to Gawain Douglas' *Aeneid*, praised as a masterpiece in the twentieth century by Ezra Pound and C. S. Lewis. The Scottish text was used by Surrey both for specific borrowings of archaic diction, as Castiglione's Frederico had called for, and for Douglas' older inscriptions from Burgundy of *gloire* and honour. The borrowings of Surrey from Douglas in phrasing and diction are pervasive (40 per cent of the entire text), at crucial points in Surrey's translation, such as Dido's last speech, ' "Why then," quoth she, "unwroken shall we die?" '; in the macabre description of Fame's eyes under her wings, 'as many waker eyes lurk underneath'; or Virgil's comparison of Dido to a Bacchante, 'And whisketh through the town like Bacchus' nun.' Technically, Douglas' text still conveyed, despite its imitation of Chaucer's heroic couplets and loose iambic pentameter, old English stress rhythms, the phrasal units marked by caesurae. In a language closer to Surrey's English than any other modern European language and closer than anything else to the original Anglo-Saxon, Douglas had finished his Scottish translation in 1513, two months before the Battle of Flodden, in which his remaining brothers were slaughtered by the Howards. He himself embodied the twin honours of nobility and text-maker, as Henry VIII specifically described him when he wrote to Rome nominating the surviving Douglas son for a bishopric, 'nobility not only of birth but of mind'.[33]

Although Douglas' *Aeneid* remained unpublished until 1553, when its publication may have stirred Awen to publish Surrey's the next year, it had evidently circulated in manuscript in both Scotland and England. Remarkably, Surrey may have had access to a special manuscript of Douglas' translation held by the

[32] See Appendix I in Woods, *Natural Emphasis*; also, 'A Note on Wyatt's Metres' and 'A Note on Wyatt's Pronunciation' by R. A. Rebholz, ed. *Sir Thomas Wyatt: The Complete Poems* (1975), 44–58. Northrop Frye, *Anatomy of Criticism: Four Essays* (1967), 251–62 and 270 ff. In his introduction to *Sound and Poetry* (1957), Frye pointed out how the quicker the line is read, the more the four stresses appear, only the rhymes keeping more stresses (p. xviii). In 'The Native Rhythm of English Meters', *Texas Studies in Literature and Language*, 5/4 (Winter 1964), Joseph Malof discusses how the form of iambic pentametre 'gives a continuous sense of order and reference' against the freer four-stress tendency to pull away, the whole 'creating the tension between metre and rhythm' (588). Qualifying responses to Frye can be found in W. K. Wimsatt and Monroe C. Beardsley, 'The Concept of Meter: An Exercise in Abstraction', *PMLA*, 74 (1959), 585–98, and in Martin Halpern, 'On the Two Chief Metrical Modes in English', *PMLA*, 77/3 (June 1962), 177–86. For a lucid definition of Anglo-Saxon verse, see Derek Pearsall, *Old English and Middle English Poetry* (1977), 15.

[33] For Henry VIII's praise, see Ridley's edition, 14. For evidence on the Trinity College manuscript, 29. Surrey's Book II—the translation that uses Douglas most—has 143 passages from this Trinity manuscript of Douglas' *Aeneid*, unlike any other of the existing five manuscripts, a high percentage out of the 880 apparent borrowings from Douglas by Surrey in both books.

Scottish bishop's family, perhaps the one surviving today at Trinity College, Cambridge. Using it, Surrey and his audience appear to have interpreted the *Aeneid* as did Douglas himself (who substituted 'curtas Aeneas' for 'pius Aeneas'), that is, as a grander Knight's Tale, an Arthurian romance, the cosmic *chanson de geste* and close to Molinet and Douglas' own *Palice of Honour*. This is the *Aeneid* as represented on tapestries found today at Hampton Court, dating from the early sixteenth century and originating in Flanders (and possibly belonging to the famous collection of Cardinal Wolsey): a blonde stalwart Aeneas, with a large round burgherish hat, leads his men and encounters a blonde Dido as distraught as any heroine of Ovid or medieval romance or twentieth-century soap opera.[34] Such a large simplistic reading provides a popular frame for the old story, one both idealistic and melodramatic, the frame Surrey knew well, one suited for readings and performance. Thus, in the 1540s, a young woman as noble as Dido, a Princess Mary or her royal first cousin, Lady Margaret Douglas, might have recited, beneath the same tapestries at Hampton Court, not only the simple grand inscriptions of Douglas, which matched the world of the tapestries, but Surrey's own decasyllabic lines in succinct 'straunge metre' that made Dido alive as never before. Lady Margaret Douglas is, in fact, the critical link to Surrey's audience. To this grand-niece of Gawain Douglas, a family manuscript might naturally have come down, especially when, from girlhood on, she appears to have felt quite close to her male Scottish roots. This text of the *Aeneid* Lady Margaret might naturally lend to the friend who had written more intimately than anyone she knew about nobility, sacrificial love, and death.

Nowhere is this legacy from Douglas better seen than in Surrey's originality in turning Douglas' syntax and prosody to modern devices of fluid characterization. What emerges is a realistic effect implicit in the Latin but never before so intimately expressed, not unlike a novelistic stream of consciousness. In a passage from Book IV, the young Trojan prince debates within himself after he has heard the harsh rebuke of the god Mercury for living with Dido. In coming to his difficult choice to leave, Surrey's Aeneas modulates his flow of consciousness in alliterating phrases with varying caesurae and in lines tending to four dominant stresses. The result is virtually a portrait of the poet earl himself, certainly a vivid record of self-reflection and one of Surrey's most powerful examples of aporia or doubting of self. At a point of either breakdown or resolution, Aeneas uses phrases that show the historical crisis he cannot escape and the self talking to the self in the middle of it.

[34] Hampton Court Tapestries A 15362–18, listed in the inventories of the early Stuarts and also in the Inventory of Henry VIII (BL Harleian MS 1419A, f. 207v, item 11962—the latter at Hampton Court in 1547). For performance theories of blank verse, see Coburn Freer, *The Poetics of Jacobean Drama* (1981), ch. 2, 'Contexts of Blank Verse Drama', especially his discussion of Renaissance audience expectation and on 38: 'When the students read nondramatic poetry—Virgil, for example—they would have been expected to act out the verse in their manner of recitation.' Also, see Hardison, *Prosody*, 268–71; George T. Wright, *Shakespeare's Metrical Art*, 299.

Aeneas with that vision stricken down,
Well near bestraught, upstart his hair for dread;
Amid his throat his voice likewise gan stick.
For to depart by flight he longeth now,
And the sweet land to leave, astonished sore
With this advice and message of the gods.
What may he do, alas? Or by what words
Dare he persuade the raging queen in love?
Or in what sort may he his tale begin?
Now here, now there, his reckless mind gan run,
And diversely him draws, discoursing all.

Dido's Songs of Self as Public Catharsis

The speeches of Dido identify the point in Surrey's *Aeneid* where the tensions of self and violent history find expressions of the greatest human vulnerability. These speeches that influenced Marlowe's originating of his own blank verse in theatre become not only objective songs of a self in agony but acts of public cartharsis. Universal myth and probability become most intimate and alive in them by becoming personal. They evoke genuine pity and fear at the terrible power of history to destroy a helpless woman. In this exaggerated theatre, Surrey's antinomies of self and history, of syllable and stress, come centre-stage.

In fact, Virgil himself had already made his Latin text fiercely declamatory, even borrowing from Euripides' *Medea* a character device whereby Dido makes the present Aeneas absent by a third-person shift, as Medea with Jason. In Virgil's narrative, after Aeneas proclaims his total piety towards the call of the gods, given him first in Troy, to found the new city ('Against my will to Italy I go') Dido turns on him. On the contrary, she screams, you have been 'faithless', with no goddess for mother and no 'Dardanus beginner of thy race,' but rather 'of hard rocks mount Caucase monstrous / Bred thee, and teats of tiger gave thee suck.' Then the young queen turns on herself, her solipsistic rhetorical questions blotting out the lover's presence and, with him, objective existence of any kind:

But what should I dissemble now my chere [face],
Or me reserve to hope of greater things?
Minds he our tears? Or ever moved his eyen?
Wept he for ruth? Or pitied he our love?
What shall I set before? Or where begin?
Juno nor Jove with just eyes this beholds.
Faith is nowhere in surety to be found.

Amid irregular stresses and caesurae, calculated alliteration, figures of speech, slant rhyme, a bravura range of verb tenses and moods (more various than in Virgil's Latin), all to support effects of aporia, the syllabic base seldom varies. It is constant. Two lines may be hendecasyllabic, depending on Surrey's elided pronunciation ('eyen' pronounced as 'mine'), but the decasyllabic dominates. Indeed, the syllabic constancy helps give Surrey's diversely stressed lines a proverbial economy as though written for a Latin Senecan chorus, the effect the young poet probably wanted. Thus, as Virgil intended—an intention St Augustine understood when in his *Confessions* he chose Dido and not Aeneas as a childhood model[35]—the young woman in the pain of love sums up the vulnerability of all human nature (implied in Dido's *volnus* or 'wound' at the opening of Book IV). Surrey's realistic English underscores this vulnerability. However theatrical Dido's soliloquies in English, rising to virtual operatic arias of self, Surrey's dramatized realism deepens her choice and her character in them, especially her self-recognition at the point of death.

Not being able to sleep, or when she does, haunted by lurid dreams, Dido rises on her last morning to find Aeneas' fleet sailing away from Carthage. Tearing 'her golden tress', she vows revenge, then catches herself in a speech that ends with painful recognition of her powerlessness. Such overwhelming cosmic agency, and the young woman's failure to control it, Surrey translates from Virgil's 'fatia impia' and Douglas' strong Saxon 'frawart werdis': ' "What said I? But where am I? What frenzy / Alters thy mind? Unhappy Dido, now / Hath thee beset a froward destiny?" ' Chaucer probably underscored for Surrey the comparatively new English word 'destiny', operative both in his Knight's Tale and in his own Dido's lament in *The Legend of Good Women*. But nothing less than 'froward destiny' is at work here, for Dido recognizes her entrapment in a history Virgil is redefining for his world in an epic dedicated to Augustus Caesar. Isolated and no longer working for her kingdom, the young queen of highest blood nobility must face, without flinching, her own destruction in the progression of a world narrative the gods are writing. Indeed, this imminent disappearance of her individual voice gives Dido's soliloquies their edge and the sense of 'superest', as with Medea: enough still endures in her language at the point of death.

For the moment of Dido's actual dying, Surrey draws a new linguistic icon in English. This poetic icon contrasts to the old stripped ones of wood, mosaic, and stained glass. In 1554 and 1557 the death of Dido became, once more, Virgil's masterpiece of Aristotelian catharsis and 'tears', at least as Queen Mary's generation read the ancient process in new English. After the young queen falls on Aeneas' sword, the blade and her hands covered instantly with blood, a line describes a world all too familiar to the Tudor court: 'The clamour rang unto the palace top,' the sort of scream Queen Catherine Howard might have made, in a fabled incident, along a gallery of Hampton Court. 'The bruit' moves on 'throughout all th'astonished town,' and roofs and air 'resound . . . With wailing great and women's shrill yelling.' The final lines build, with three powerful instances of enjambement, a progressing inevitability. In these lines, Surrey exactly

[35] St Augustine, *Confessions*. trans. William Watts (1968) I:13:38–43.

imitates Virgil. Six stresses (with only ten syllables, however) give Surrey's line the sonority of the Roman hexameter. They reveal a grand linguistic icon that his audience not only would have expected but heard and seen as their own.

> But Dido striveth to lift up again
> Her heavy eyen, and hath no power thereto:
> Deep in her breast that fixed wound doth gape.
> Thrice leaning on her elbow gan she raise
> Herself upward, and thrice she overthrew
> Upon the bed, ranging with wand'ring eyes
> The skies for light, and wept when she it found.

A Roman Portrait

While translating Virgil, Surrey had his portrait painted by Holbein (Plate IV). Its significance is that it reveals in 1541 the self-conscious pose of a Romanizing aristocrat at the same time as, in its emblematic structure, it shows a portrait of the young man as a Virgilian poet. Dated to early 1541 because of its inscription 'HENRY HOWARD ERLE OF SVRRY / ANNO AETATIS SVA 25,' the portrait had a remarkable later history, being included as an inset in the grand family portrait Van Dyck painted for the Stuart 'Collector Earl' of Arundel.[36] Holbein's oil portrait of the young earl resides today in the Museo de São Paulo in Brazil in a uniquely displayed collection. Into his tropical world, the tawny-yellow eyes of the poet look out with deeper contemplation than in any other portrait of him, face turned in three-quarters profile, left eye more enlarged and projecting than the other. His gaze is as fixed as the gaze of Holbein's Thomas More, the portrait Surrey's most resembles. The right ear (the only one showing) is so modelled under the wide circular lines of the cap that its emphasis as an emblem—the ear of a poet—is evident. Surrounding a closed mouth and detailed light-rose lips and running down the recessive chin are light red hairs. The same red hair also shows underneath the earl's round Italian cap of shining black velvet with a huge black plume. The sweep and texture of the cap contrast with the bright flesh-tones of Surrey's face, the youth's lightness and white skin that intensify his gaze.

There is a peculiarly Roman gesture in Surrey's holding the massive black fur cloak drawn tight around him. His right hand (the only other part of his body

[36] Arundel would also inset the Holbein painting of the 3rd Duke of Norfolk (like the insets of heraldry) into the family portrait modelled after the family portrait of Charles I now at Wilton House. Arundel's family portrait came after he had been asked to head the army to invade Scotland in 1538. It exists today in a Fruytiers copy, the Van Dyck lost or destroyed. For Surrey's great-grandson, who wanted to be named another Duke of Norfolk but never was, this final family portrait before the English Revolution 'would have been', as Howarth notes (164), 'a *coup de théâtre* and the principals, actors in a ritual quite as solemn as any which Arundel presided over as Earl Marshal'.

revealed except for the face and ear) clutches the cloak as though it were a Roman toga in a Roman gesture of peace (hand on breast), like the Roman sculpture Arundel later collected. Even the fitting of this cloak up over Surrey's neck (almost to his ear) indicates a Roman model in an English winter garment, a ribbon around the neck barely visible. The picture has its own light counterpoint in the midst of the black cloak: the deliberate contrast of an intricately woven cream-coloured silk (or linen) shirt, with a collar of a Burgundian or Italian design of eagles, garlands, flowers, and birds and with extended cuffs over an exposed hand with knuckles bending white as they hold the massive black cloak.

On the right index finger of the hand is a gold ring (possibly painted later), with a cameo or metal-engraved design of some figure, possibly one of the Roman emperors, as on the scabbards in the Arundel portrait. This, the only ring in all of Surrey's portraits and the only decoration in the picture, betokens a gesture of fidelity. It indirectly dates the picture. A few months later, after being received into the Order of the Garter, Surrey would have worn, for such a formal portrait, the Garter collar and the George depending from it for such a formal portrait. Here the single gold ring of fidelity matches Surrey's light eyes in colouring. This right hand with its ring holding the toga so firmly was also originating in these same months a new heroic line of blank verse. The poet needs only to survive long enough to develop that original language he is hearing with Holbein's exquisitely modelled ear. He needs only enough time to give shape to the vision he is seeing in those uneven eyes that look well beyond the picture, a vision for which he alone has invented blank verse.

11

'Lieutenant General of the King'

By Royal Letters Patent issued on 3 September 1545, Henry VIII designated the 29-year-old poet Earl of Surrey, 'The King's Lieutenant' (a civil appointment) and 'Captain-General' (a military appointment for Boulogne-sur-Mer). In this special citation, Surrey's main task was to defend and command the key port of Boulogne on the Channel coast of northern France. The old Roman city of Boulogne (Julius Caesar had used it as a staging area for Britain) had fallen to the English only a year before. The defeat of the French and the fall of the city signalled the most spectacular military triumph of Henry VIII's career, with the Tudor monarch present in the front lines outside the city walls with young Surrey and most courtiers in attendance. The surrender of 1544 had been carefully dramatized to make the decaying Henry VIII appear like Henry V on the nearby field of Agincourt; to facilitate the surrender, at least according to some French records, Seymour may have pulled off one of the greatest coups of his career, reportedly bribing the young and easily intimidated French commandant, Jacques de Coucy, Sieur Vervin, with 150,000 rose nobles, for taking which he was beheaded by Francis I.[1] The seriousness of the Boulogne campaign (and Surrey now as leader of it) is evidenced by the fact that, on taking command in 1545, Surrey faced the Duc d'Orléans at the walls of Boulogne. The 23-year-old Charles, Duc d'Orléans, was the French king's favoured son and also the darling of the liberal faction of Madame d'Etampes and Marguerite of Navarre against the Dauphin Henry with his Medici wife and his older mistress, Diane de Poitiers. This fraternal rivalry might have had international repercussions if Boulogne under Surrey's command had not decided the next turn of history for the French royal family.

The French prince commanded the French fort of Outreau, on the opposite side of the estuary from Boulogne at the entrance to the Channel. The fort was small but had elaborate Italian bastions, the latest technology developed for the French siege. For Francis I, the loss of Boulogne in September 1544 had been particularly humiliating, and its recapture dominated the military strategy of his last years. In 1545 he had reason to see the whole situation tragic as well. Within a week of Surrey's taking command, on 9 September, Francis I's stylish son Charles collapsed suddenly while commanding the new French fort and 'while strutting and

[1] Thomas Rymer, *Foedera* (1728), vol. 15, 80. In the Latin, Surrey's title indicates a viceroy, and his military title is both Captain and General. The terms cannot be equated with modern terms: Surrey now commanded the English bastion of Boulogne. For the rather dubious surrender story, see Nott, vol. 1, p. lviii.

play-acting before the walls of the city'. He soon died, not in a heroic battle but in a nearby hunting lodge from one of those swift mysterious fevers the insanitary nature of war was always breeding. As Winchester was to comment from Bruges in the following November, in the midst of Surrey's successful defence, 'The French King hath so moch spoken of Bolen that he wyl have it, and it hath been soo noysed in the worlde that in Bolen consistith now al his reputacion, as he taketh it.'[2] Boulogne had become a bitter arena of honour for both English and French.

Surrey's appointment had not been anticipated. After Henry VIII returned to England from France in 1544, he had entrusted the task of defending the Boulonnais to his brother-in-law the Duke of Suffolk, but Suffolk had died unexpectedly *en route* for France on 22 August 1545. Suffolk's death, leaving as heir a mere 10-year old boy, meant that the Duke of Norfolk had no ducal rival in maturity and experience left. Surrey's own place in the hierarchy of English society therefore increased. His appointment may have reflected this unexpected ascendancy as much as his own military successes in the northern marches and in Scotland. The natural alternative to Surrey had been Edward Seymour, the Earl of Hertford, who had already served with distinction in the capture of Boulogne but from May 1545 had been commander of the English forces in the north, in September leading a successful raid into Scotland. Surrey's service in the Scottish campaign of 1542 and in the French campaign two years later indicated the distinct probability that Surrey would prove a formidable military commander. Thus, as Casady notes, the honour of the new appointment may have provided a clear signal of the Howard heir apparent's growing reputation as a superior military leader. In his own right, then, Surrey was achieving an authentic means of nobility through the Arthurian role of *vir armatus*. The fact that the Privy Council itself agreed to Surrey's appointment on 31 August—that is, three days before the public announcement—meant that, however needed and superior Seymour and Dudley were (and Dudley had already commanded Boulogne for a few months after its fall in 1544), Surrey had won a victory of prestige at court. He had impressed Henry VIII. On 25 August, three days after Brandon's sudden death, Paget assured Norfolk that Surrey's new honour was 'ment to hym for the best and in consideracion of the desyre he hath to se and serve'.[3]

This 'desyre' Surrey had shown to the whole court. Honour as *vir armatus* had come in increments, however. Just before his appointment as protector of Boulogne, Surrey had been commanding troops in the Pas de Calais, the area extending out from the English stronghold port on the French coast of the Channel. In fact, by August 1545, Surrey had departed for France with 5000 men and so at first, in Paget's congratulatory letter on 25 August, he was to be 'general of all the crews at Guines and the Marches, a goodly band of eight thousand men', nothing more.[4] This was a large number of men to command, but no sooner had Paget

[2] Smith, *Henry VIII*, 219. Gardiner, *Letters*, 183–4.

[3] Casady, *Henry Howard*, 131.

[4] *LP*, vol. 20, ii, 209.

written than five days later, Surrey was promoted to command Boulogne (and Lord Grey told to give up the command and take over Surrey's defence). What had happened? Perhaps it was only mixed communications between the king's court and the front lines, but in those few days in late August and early September 1545, Surrey's command at Guisnes had achieved some spectacular success. Attacking the French army at Ardres and encamping his men in the more exposed areas outside the walls of Guisnes (the Privy Council gave permission 'for encampeng nere Claeswood according to his owne devise'), Surrey skirmished on 2 September 1545, and during this period the commander of Ardres, the renowned Baron de Dampierre, was killed. A few days had produced a spectacularly fast and brilliant victory for the Earl of Surrey. It had come from his strategy of a solid support system played against a flexible free-attack force, another system of counterpoint.[5]

Military Glory in 1545

Surrey had been moving towards high military honour since he fought in the Pilgrimage of Grace. What did such honour mean for Surrey (or for Seymour or Dudley, England's leading warriors)? Did the poet earl accept Erasmus' and More's severe arguments against European wars and against the old Burgundian codes of chivalry that Erasmus particularly loathed? Would he have agreed with the Howard ally, Stephen Gardiner, the Bishop of Winchester, who wrote to Paget from Bruges on 13 November 1545, comparing to a theatre the Imperial court in its two weeks of ritual for the Order of the Golden Fleece? Here was a 'worlde where reason prevayleth not, lernyng prevaylith not, convenauntes be not soo regarded, but the lest pretense suffiseth to avoyde thobservation of them.' Such theatre the bishop, Paget, and Wriothesley had once acted in as undergraduates at Cambridge, specifically in Plautus' *Miles Gloriosus* ('The Swaggering Soldier'): 'If we thre shuld nowe sitte together and take counsayl what wer to be doon, as we did in the comedye, we shuld not be a litel troubled, and Palestrio [Wriothesley's role] fayne to muse longer for compassing of this matier and seding of it, as the poete callith it, thenne he did there.' Now indeed, 'our parties [are also] in this tragedie that nowe is in hand.' Winchester, who had grown up on humanist texts like *Utopia*, had seen first-hand that, of the three great rulers of Europe in the 1540s, the most nostalgic could be the most ruthless. Charles V's sack of Rome in 1527 and his degradation of Pope Clement VII had proved a shock to the civilized world. With his great-grandfather Charles the Bold as his namesake, Charles V as a boy and young man had neglected classical education and humanist studies to read the grand myths of Olivier and Roland (and also the romances of Troy and the cycles of Arthur). With riches now pouring in from Peru and Mexico, and the

[5] *APC*, vol. 1, 237. Although the question of just when Dampierre was killed is problematic, and Holinshed says Grey led the attack, Surrey's skirmish may have been the occasion.

destinies of the new peoples of the New World in his hands, this Arthurian native of Ghent ruled a world from the Andes to the Danube out of which a Don Quixote would naturally emerge. In fact, wrote Winchester back to England, the anachronism of the Golden Fleece is 'so far out of order as there is small cause to make any feast,' much less for two weeks in the midst of a brutal war with France.[6]

Yet, as rulers of Early Modern Europe knew, illusion was necessary in war, not only to stimulate the male eros to the initiative all military engagement still requires but to counter the constant fear in every war, personal annihilation. One such Elizabethan illustration of initiative and illusion, a direct advertisement for military honour, praises Surrey as the high English exemplar of nobility, a virtual mythic hero. Thomas Challoner, clerk to the Privy Council under Edward VI, wrote a Latin epic on Edward Shelley, who was killed in Surrey's disastrous skirmish at St Etienne in January 1546. In that epic, written early in Queen Elizabeth I's reign but published in the year of Spenser's Virgilian *Shepheardes Calender* (1579), Surrey's military subordinate Shelley becomes a new Roman hero, rising from English roots to universal definition in Tudor Virgilian hexameters. At least that is the intention of its author, a survivor of four monarchs. In his Latin text, Roman terms and a Roman setting define Challoner's locally encoded hero. At the same time as Shelley is honoured, Surrey, his general, is also named a hero. A major point thus emerges in this Latin text. Challoner is writing in a period when he could easily condemn Surrey's role in the fatal skirmish if he had thought him as inept as Henry VIII, the Privy Council, and the court had indirectly and directly iterated. For Challoner, Surrey is, in fact, the hero who has made possible the heroism of Shelley: 'Perceiving all these things entirely with his eyes, Surrey the Hero then bent the [French] empire under the power of the English.'

Challoner develops this praise of Surrey in an actual Latin borrowing from Virgil (Panthus' prophetic outcry in Book II). For Challoner's Surrey, there has been 'ineluctabile tempus' (time that cannot be called back).[7] Writing from the perspective of a courtier close to the centres of successive regimes, Edwardian, Marian, and Elizabethan (indeed as clerk to the Privy Council at Surrey's downfall), Challoner revises the history of Surrey's ordeal and beheading. In fact, Challoner is the first person from such a high political position to explain publicly in print that Surrey had been the victim of 'Livor' [Envy] and 'Calumnia' [False Accusation]. In Challoner's elegy, Surrey is transformed into a courtier martyr for all seasons. 'Many souls of the noble endure' through their 'illustrious acts' and not 'whether you look at the toga' representing rank and communal recognition or whether their 'laurels [are] brought forth by a wound.' For these 'whom the Fates have buried in a tomb, the most through envy . . . it will be worth it' that 'an emulous

[6] Gardiner, *Letters*, 86 (186–7), 90–102 (211–27). For analysis of Winchester's relationship to the Empire and his perceptions of the court there, see Glyn Redworth, *In Defence of the Church Catholic: The Life of Stephen Gardiner* (1990), esp. ch. 9.

[7] Panthus' phrase is later echoed in the *Aeneid* in Jupiter's 'inreparabile tempus' on the bitter death of the young man Pallas, both originating in the *Georgics* in a crucial definition of Virgilian labour. See the analysis of this phrase in Sessions, 'Spenser's Georgics', 206.

nation' learn about them, especially the recently lost who can still be remembered. 'Imitating' native heroes will lead the 'patria' (fatherland) to noble action.

Then Challoner epitomizes such nobility. 'The ancient family of Norfolk' (and this reference suggests the young fourth Duke of Norfolk as a possible dedicatory target for the Latin epic) has had 'many proofs' of such nobility pour from it: the Howards have been, in a figure of *auxesis*, 'great in books, greater in arms, and greatest in faithful counsel'. 'Yet one—alas!' says Challoner in a dramatic *anacoluthon* (a deliberate break or omission in a sentence), has suffered the most. 'Torn by blood-thirsty fate, the hero Surrey could have been set above the whole' family of high achievers, except that 'fierce Lachesis has cut off the rising honors, and heedless poisonous Envy' has destroyed the young man by means of 'oblique witchcraft'. Lachesis (one of the Fates) has submitted to Envy, 'that two-headed monster, sent from Erebos, already so many times fatal to the British court.' Because she is 'so closely tied to authority,' the 'treacherous' figure of Envy 'can pluck' with impunity 'the fruit hoped for by the nation,' can 'mutilate the heights of strong new growth.'

Thus, 'that one perished; a little while ago jealous Nemesis exacted [Surrey's] punishment by blood.' Yet the 'envious hand' still 'glowing in such a crime' is no 'rejoicing survivor'. In fact, 'the wound' of that beheading still 'appears to our weeping eyes', for the reason that 'too much the young man, unknowing, atoned for the ancient angers.' In fact, history itself has revolted against this crime. For this young man Surrey, the day so terrible ('ingrata dies') and the time that cannot be called back (Virgil's 'ineluctabile tempus') have already begun to inscribe a revision ('superaddere limam'), and it will not be the last revision of this 'fall quite shunned'. Indeed, says Challoner in his *peroratio*, 'I know not one greater' than Surrey whom 'the ages of our time have seen nor one more distinguished of bright acts.' The earl 'held under his burning breast such virtue, and his was such a spirit generous in language' that he possessed 'vigour', on the one hand, 'suited for horsemanship, for military preparations, for joining battle' and, on the other, 'at the same time, [for] singing.' His talents were quite 'suited to adorn the elegant hero's hair with a fresh cluster of flowers on the sacred peak of Parnassus'.[8] Challoner's myth of the heroic Surrey contrasts with the totally self-centred and irrational figure of the young poet with his 'treasonable follies' that the early Tudor courts had projected. On the contrary, it recapitulates earlier classical traditions of martyrdom and, at a crucial time, originates a new basis—the military as well as the 'singing'—for the next three decades of cult-building for the poet earl.

Earlier Military Success: The Praise of Charles V

Surrey's reputation as a military hero lasted well into the Restoration, with John Aubrey conflating the court gossip and memory of the poet earl into a mythic

[8] Thomas Challoner, *De Rep Anglorum Instauranda Libri Decem* (1579), 323–4 and 328.

figure, 'a man equally celebrated *tam Marti quam Mercum*' ('as much Mars as Mercury'), and even David Hume in the eighteenth century indicated military achievement as Surrey's main claim to glory. More spectacularly in his own time, no one less than Charles V honoured the young Howard heir apparent as both *vir armatus* and *vir togatus*. In autumn 1543 the poet earl received the praise of the Holy Roman Emperor in two letters. This social and political success at the highest level of European honour was all the more remarkable because, only six months before, Chapuys had reported on Surrey's escapade in London and Surrey's Lutheran and French tendencies. Fresh from his prison experience in 1543, Surrey was sent over to inspect the front lines, a second time now, to Landrecy in Picardy on the border of the Empire and France, the holding of which city had become a point of prestige for Francis I (in 1545 he was said to esteem it as much as Turin in Italy). Sir John Wallop was the English commander there with the Imperial forces; and when Surrey and other young members of the nobility visited Landrecy in November 1543, Wallop wrote to Henry VIII that never had there been such 'a war where there was so much for youth to learn'—and, in fact, a modern historian calls the time of Surrey's military years in France 'more decisive for the evolution of the art of war' than any other in the next 250 years.[9]

Because an invitation from the Emperor was a prerequisite for Surrey's visit to the Imperial army, Henry VIII wrote on 1 October 1543, to 'nostre tres chier et tres ame frere et cousin' that 'Our very dear and most beloved cousin, the earl of Surrey, knight of Our Order, has applied' to visit the Imperial camp. Henry VIII was anxious that 'We may through him have news of your successes' and Surrey 'may at the same time acquire that experience in military affairs that will make him the true heir and successor of his ancestors.' Nine days later, Surrey was involved in discussions with Wallop and Arschot, the Great Master and Wallop's Imperial counterpart. Exploring the trench fortifications as Wallop showed him about Landrecy, Surrey was 'somewhat saluted', Wallop reported, by French fire, his travelling companion George Blagge narrowly escaping a bullet. The encounter was more dramatic two weeks later when Surrey's fascination with new technology jeopardized his safety. Then he watched the German engineers attack the besieged city with new mining techniques against the French bulwarks. He saw the equally innovative artillery of the Germans, 'the mortar that shoots artificial bullets'. On that night of 25 October 'it was a strange and dreadful sight to see the bullet fly into the air spouting fire on every side; and at his [its] fall they might well perceive how he [it] leaped from place to place, casting out fire, and within a while after burst forth and shot off guns out of him [it] an hundred shot every one as loud to the hearing as a *hacquebut à crocq* [a supported portable matchlock gun] whereof they counted well four score [of such bullets].'

9 John Aubrey, *The Natural History and Antiquities of the Country of Surrey* (London, 1718–19), vol. 5, 246, 248. David Hume *History of England* (1873–7), vol. 4, 283. *LP*, vol. 11, 445. J. R. Hale, 'Armies, Navies and the Art of War' in *New Cambridge Modern History*, vol. 2 (The Reformation), ed. G. R. Elton (1990), 540.

Innovative technology and experimentation always drew Surrey to his most daring. Thus, in 1545, Norfolk's steward Hussey reminded Surrey defending Boulogne that 'His Majesty took it in very ill part that ye should adventure your presence in standing upon the bridge of the fortress for the better viewing' of the French fortifications, especially as one of two Italian military engineers with him, Tomaso, 'hath much advanced your hardiness [boldness] and not forgotten your negligence in adventuring your person so dangerously.' Not surprisingly, after only a few weeks in autumn 1543, Wallop could write to Paget to tell Norfolk: 'My lord of Surrey has lost no time.'[10]

On this trip, Surrey's tendency to logorrhoea merged with his outraged reaction to lassitude in Imperial command centres. Distressed by the unnecessary observation of courtly etiquette in the Imperial army, the poet earl felt, as had his ancestor Hotspur, formality obstructing practicality. Surrey's 'certain foolish letter' was leaked to the Imperial ambassador Chapuys. But, by late October, it was too late for the ambassador to attack Surrey. On 21/22 October 1543, the Emperor himself had written the first of two encomia of the poet earl such as few members of the Henrician court ever received. 'As for your recommendation of the son of our cousin the Duke of Norfolk that he may train himself in the things of war,' so Charles V wrote to Henry VIII, 'he already provides such a good example of your nation that he cannot fail to get instruction from us. All our men respect him as one who merits the valour of [his] father and [as one who has] the noble heart [le gentil coeur] of the son; and we thank you for your recommendation.'[11]

During this period, 'the noble heart' Surrey had been allowed to enter the Emperor's entourage to discuss military strategy (in fluent French) and display his technical knowledge and expertise. By 4 November Chapuys wrote to the Emperor and announced how Charles V's first letter and the news of Surrey's success has impressed the English court. 'The King has been exceedingly pleased at the good reception the Earl of Surrey has met with at the Imperial camp,' and Norfolk is 'so grateful at this show of kindness on Your Imperial Majesty's part' that he has said loudly at court how 'nothing would be so agreeable to him as to find an opportunity of risking his person, his family and his property for your Majesty's [Charles V's] service.' Norfolk thus played the letter for all it was worth. After the recent escapades and imprisonments, the Howards could finally claim a special prestige in their heir.

Surrey was also involved in fighting beside the Emperor who, according to Wallop, 'showed signs of a noble and valiant courage' in a particularly cold and windy Saturday skirmish. Then, on the next morning after that skirmish, Sunday, 4 November 1543, Surrey and his cousin Sir Francis Bryan attended a council in

[10] *LP* 18,ii:235,266,310;19:738.

[11] *CSPSpan*, vol. 6, ii, 250 (514). Surrey's letter may have been quite practical: according to Col. Peter Moore, Surrey may have been trying to recruit for England German mercenaries. For both comments by Charles V about Surrey, see the French texts in Bapst, *Deux gentilshommes-poètes*, 282 and 287, and also in *SP*, vol. 9, 920 (526–7), 938 (554).

the Emperor's tent, with the great powers of the Empire, from the Spanish Dukes of Alburquerque and Najera to the German Dukes of Brunswick and Saxony, 'le premier gentilhomme de sa chambre'. Thus, when Surrey prepared to return home, he came straight from Charles V, who himself wrote to Chapuys on 19 November: 'Lastly, when the earl of Sorey came to take leave to return home, We Ourselves told him verbally what the [French] Duke's errand had been and how We had answered his application.' When Surrey was called back to England, Bryan reported to Henry VIII that 'My Lord of Surrey' on a Sunday afternoon, after dinner, had come to the Emperor's 'lodgynge, ther takynge his leave' and Charles V had 'handelyd him aftir a veary gentil sort: ho [he] can reaport it better than I can whrit,' added Bryan.[12] In fact, on that Sunday two days earlier, Surrey had taken with him a private letter from the Emperor Charles V to Henry VIII. It was about the latest diplomatic moves of the Empire with the French. Carrying it emphasized the high place of honour Surrey now held in the Emperor's eyes. 'Our cousin the count of Sorey returning, We shall be relieved from having to write you a long letter because he will tell you the occurrences of this place,' observed the Emperor from Valenciennes to the English king, continuing that Surrey 'has provided good witness in our army of whose son he is and how he does not wish to falter in following his father and his ancestors. With so noble a heart and such dexterity [avec si gentil coeur et telle dexterité] there has been no need for him to learn anything. In fact, you cannot command him anything he does not know how to do.' Surrey had gained the esteem and confidence of Charles V.

Earlier Military Success: The Siege of Montreuil

By June 1544, Surrey took the next initiative towards the ultimate rank of 'the King's Lieutenant General'. It came in the campaign to capture Montreuil-sur-Mer, a seaport on the Channel until the late Middle Ages (and the sea is just visible today from its walls). In 1544 Montreuil was the French fortress town in the area surrounding Calais and Boulogne. Writing to the Privy Council on 26 June 1544, and with the Lord Privy Seal Russell to aid him, Norfolk announced that he would undertake the siege. Capture of Montreuil would mean a major step towards amassing an army to invade Paris. The whole English army had a battle force at Boulogne under Suffolk and then under Henry VIII himself of 3159 horsemen and 9688 foot-soldiers, and at Montreuil, a vanguard led by Norfolk of 372 horsemen and 9606 foot-soldiers and a rearguard led by Russell of 547 horsemen and 9017 foot-soldiers. Of these, about 500 would be pioneers (miners and explosive experts) and the Imperial leader de Bewers was to have ready 4400 horsemen and nearly 4000 foot-soldiers. All these soldiers, cavalry, and engineers

[12] For Chapuys, *CSPSpan*, vol. 6, ii, 254 (518). *LP*, vol. 18, ii, 345 (193–4). For the Emperor's letters, *CSPSpan*, vol. 6, ii, 260 (523). *SP*, vol. 9, 934 (356–7).

had, of course, their own army of servants and camp-followers and vast stores of equipment, all of which could turn into a logistical nightmare if a strong control system were not instituted. For that purpose, Henry VIII had already appointed the poet Earl of Surrey as the Lord Marshal of the new army. At Montreuil Surrey now took charge of supplies and ordnance for almost 20,000 men and the logistical systems surrounding them. It was hardly a task for an earl or any man who might be solipsistic or inflexibly arrogant. Surrey was not. Openness and sympathy to all possibilities were needed in order to keep the army going and surviving. In addition to his previous daring raids, Surrey now acted as Marshal of the Field, chosen specifically to transform this large force into one of the best attack units in Europe. The direction beyond Montreuil for the English drive beckoned towards Paris through the Somme. Then all could attend a singing of *Te Deum* for Henry VIII in Notre Dame, his hope in 1544 as earlier in 1513 and 1524. Indeed, if Montreuil could have been taken, the entire French defence system along the north-eastern channel would have cracked. Paris and Notre Dame would have received Henry VIII as they had his ancestor Henry V.

None of this was likely. Two negative factors immediately became apparent to Norfolk and Surrey. First, to prevent a triumphal entry, Francis I moved swiftly. To lift any English seige, so Norfolk heard, the French king was sending his two sons, the Dauphin and his brother the Duc d'Orléans, with an immense force, including almost 2000 horsemen. Second, the topography of Montreuil made it almost impossible for the English to conquer, 'a veritable porcupine of fortifications defended by 4000 French troops'. The walls of Montreuil rose on naturally high earth ramparts from the pastoral valley of the small River Canche. The stream turns out from the city towards the sea, runs just to the right and beneath the Abbeville Gate and empties into the Channel at nearby Etaples. Added to the natural heights, the man-made brick and earth bulwarks of the wall rose even higher in 1544 to thwart any incursions similar to the Imperial invasion of 1537. The result was that, when the English did finally find a good camp-site and begin their siege, it was always in range of French cannon-fire. 'The town stands so ungraciously,' wrote Norfolk to Suffolk, 'there is no place out of danger.' Also, their own cannon could not fire effectively to reach such walls (they 'would have to shoot so upright that it would be long ere a good breach was made').

Having chosen the Abbeville Gate as the most accessible point, Norfolk tried to set up a broad-based system of trenches and encampments in the valley and on the slopes that pointed towards the central target. He had seen that, with such intricate fortifications and walls before and above them, the English could never surround the entire city. Writing on 13 July 1544, Norfolk reported they 'have laid siege to Monstrell, but not like a siege, for two gates are left open [for the French] and a third may be used freely at night.' Furthermore, winds, rain, and storms in that summer and early autumn, pouring into the Channel from the Atlantic, made the soldiers feel their clothes always sodden and the tents damp. Disease was rampant among horses, other livestock, and the soldiers themselves; mud everywhere. Worst of all, as an experienced Welsh soldier in Norfolk's army, Ellis Gruffydd, a reformed Christian infantryman who loathed young officers, remarked, not even 60,000 men could surround such a fortress as Montreuil, especially when victuals and munitions had to be conveyed 20 miles to their camps every day, with over 1000 men escorting the victuallers—a constant dilemma for a Lord Marshal in charge of military logistics.[13]

To these near disasters, Surrey as a Marshal of the Field responded with efficiency and, in Charles V's word, dexterity. Norfolk's letters to king and council—no doubt drafted by Surrey—set out in detail requests for food and ordnance necessary to remedy the situation. But the Privy Council and the king were less interested in Montreuil than in Boulogne, the one French city Henry VIII had to win. Surrey and his father would have to fend for themselves. Without surprise, as revealed in the dispatches, in early June 1544, the army lacked beer (local water was dangerous), bread, and grain; the Flemish merchants had inflated the costs of all supplies; the wagons from the Empire were too few, too small, and too weak; the English horses 'so evill' that it took fourteen or fifteen to pull the portable 'ovynes' that keep falling apart during the forced marches; the men need bread and drink, and 'it is painful to send horsemen and footmen day by day to St. Omer's to convey victuals' when the French raiding parties are everywhere and 'there is not powder and munitions for more than eight or ten days' battery.' These were merely the start of a series of administrative nightmares for the 28-year-old Lord Marshal. First he had to find appropriate sites for encampments and for trenching, gunnery, and fortification.[14] Despite the lack of cooperation from the Imperial forces, when the actual siege began in July 1544 Surrey had already located his camp just below the Abbeville Gate, 'half a mile'. He had also begun his system of trenches, especially one for 'the great ordnance', slowly digging them with his pioneers towards the town.

Surrey's logistical strategy was clearly succeeding when Russell wrote with enthusiasm to Paget on 1 August that the English 'are now within little more the level

[13] Smith, *Henry VIII*, 207. *LP*, vol. 19, i, 786, 795. Gilbert John Miller, *Tudor Mercenaries and Auxiliaries 1485–1547* (1980) 99–101; also 156.

[14] The Imperial forces were no help in finding a camp site. On 4 July 1544, Surrey followed out the suggestions of the Imperial officers only to find the sites they named worthless. 'Might have been at Monstrell [Montreuil] three or four days past,' Norfolk wrote, 'but that their [Imperial] guides have taken them up and down the hills, through hedges, woods, and marshes, and all to lodge them on French ground and save their own friends.' A good part of the large army 'has only drunk water since yesterday sevennight' and it is midsummer in Picardy. No food is forthcoming from the Empire, and 'tomorrow night' they will start searching for a site nearer Montreuil. Already it is clear, Norfolk writes, they can only attack the town nearest the castle and its most fortified gate (Abbeville). They simply do not have enough cannon to make two 'batters' upon a place as fortified as Montreuil is. A recommended 'ground' that Surrey and the Lord Warden and Poynings were sent to investigate had 'neither grass nor forrage for horses and [did have] suche hills and passages' that no large army could manoeuvre in them. Added to this dispatch are details in Norfolk's own hand of the supplies held by the French themselves; Surrey's scouts had done their job well. PRO SP 1/189 ff. 151–4; *LP*, vol. 19, i, 836, 837. A description of the intricacies of duty for 'the high marshall', especially in finding and establishing a camp site can be found in Charles Cruickshank, *Henry VIII and the Invasion of France* (1991) 47.

of a half-hake of the town before Abdvylde gate, and have beaten down a round tower and begun a mount which will ere long beat over their great bulwark of earth, which is their chief defence on that part.' Indeed Norfolk could write to the Privy Council on 4 August: 'The English have gained a marvellous good name among all the strangers here.' That 'good name' came not only from a strong siege but from raids like the rescue party led by Surrey and his young uncle Lord William Howard with de Bewers and 'our best horsemen'. Leaving at midnight to save an Imperial force of 400 horsemen that the Bourbon Duc de Vendôme had surrounded, Surrey and his party had ridden only ten miles when they learned of Vendôme's retreat. Surrey and the new company of horsemen then rode out to capture what remained of the French, only returning the next night at eleven. If this dispatch reveals Surrey as bold warrior, the ending of the same dispatch shows Surrey's stabilizing of supplies without which no daring attack could have proceeded: through his father, he acknowledges they have 30,000 sheaf of livery arrows at 18d.; 18,200 bows at £1,853.13s. 4d.[15]

Surrey's duties as 'highe marshall', as Barnabas Rich called the position in 1587, was subordinate only to the general, in this case, his father; otherwise, he had a supreme command. In fact, the 'highe' Marshal's trumpet could sound first in the morning, and at Montreuil Surrey and his particular troop would be first to be mounted. If, as defined by Francis Markham in 1622, the Marshal must have an impeccable character at all times and be in control of the situation, then 'as his place is most honorable, where honour is, there should be his residence.' Such honour existed only in relationship to dexterity in commanding: orders for the scouts; planning with the sergeant-major for the guards, then with the victual-master, the wagon-master, and all other officers for proper lodgements and organizations of the batteries; viewing and upkeep of the camp itself; maintenance of uniforms (in Surrey's time, the proper red and bright yellow); above all, constant inspection of ditches, latrines, entrenchments, and assault weapons. At the same time, the Lord Marshal had to have a special relationship with 'his Cavalry, or Horse Army', both for attack and for defence, particularly in the case of sudden enemy assaults. There is clear evidence that Surrey met such crises with equanimity and tactical harmony so that, when the final retreat from Montreuil took place over four months later—the arrangement of the retreat or 'Remove' was one of the most critical of any Lord Marshal's tasks[16]—no major loss had occurred to Norfolk's army, either in supplies or in manpower. Any such loss would have been noted, especially in the trial evidence of 1546. Surrey's ability to manage time and limited resources had been exceptional. Not a single complaint was heard.

Surrey may have visualized the role of Lord Marshal as a definite stage towards higher honour, towards the military inscription he needed as a future leader of the realm. He may have posed in the dress of Lord Marshal or, more likely, in the pose

[15] *LP*, vol. 19, i, 907; ii, 4. G. Miller, *Tudor Mercenaries*, 156.

[16] Barnabas Rich, *Pathway to military practice* (1587); Francis Markham, *Five Decades of Epistles of Warre* (1622), 189 ff.

of the general commander of Boulogne. Today, in a workroom of the New Bodleian Library in Oxford, a rather crude painting (with heavy brush strokes darkened by four centuries) on a small panel reveals Surrey as though in a modern photograph sent from the war front. Surrey in quarter-length wears a flat black cap, and the head here is less turned than in other portraits so that one eye seems off-balance. Amid a rough unkempt beard and moustache the poet's full lips are tense, and only a left ear is carefully modelled. He wears an undistinguished fur cloak and dark doublet whose red *puffo* slashing in two rows provides the only colour in the entire portrait. This red sash is like the red commander's sash, the field sign worn by Charles V in his famous portrait on horseback in battle in 1549 by Titian.[17]

A Daring Raid and Two Young Comrades

Surrey's managerial skills would always be in context with his manoeuvring techniques, especially on raids where the two combined. On Tuesday evening, 2 September 1544, Norfolk reported to Henry VIII, now in France, that 'my son of Surrey, my lord of Sussex, my lord Mount Joye, my brother William, my lord Latymer, Mr. Treasurer and all the rest of the noblemen whom I sent forth upon Saturday at 10 at night' had returned, 'without loss of any man slayne' from a raiding party all the way to the northern suburbs of Abbeville, 'where the English horsemen had a hot skirmish.' Assisted by de Bewers's Imperial horsemen, the band of noblemen not only burnt two walled towns, frightening the inhabitants of a third into burning theirs, but also brought 'a verye grete boetye of all sortes of cattle' back to camp, 'and the noblemen and gentlemen kept their footmen in such order that they borrowed nothing of the Burgonians.' Most striking of all, they 'finally have made such an excourse, that the like hath not been made since these wars began.' Cardinal du Bellay, that conceited 'glorious' man, who is coming to visit the camp as an emissary from Francis I to the English king, 'might well see what was done, nothing to his contentation'.

In the war party, at least two of the young aristocrats appreciated Surrey's poetic powers as well as his military prowess. An exact contemporary of Surrey's, Charles Blount, 'my Lord Mount Joye', had been honoured by Erasmus' dedication to him of his 1529 *Adagia* and his 1535 *Livy*, and Leland had addressed two Latin eulogies to him. Mountjoy went to France in 1544 with a manuscript of Surrey's poems and considerably more enthusiasm than he had at 20, serving under Norfolk in the Pilgrimage of Grace. In his last will and testament made on

[17] I am grateful to Gary Hill for help in locating this portrait. The colour of the outer garments in the portrait may be dark blue and the sash simply part of a uniform. As John Stow noted in *Annales* 587, 'Those of the foreward under the Duke of Norfolk, were apparelled in blew coates garded with red, and had caps and hosen after the same sute, party blew, and partie red.'

30 April 1544, on the eve of his crossing the Channel, Mountjoy revealed his personal support for the ensuing campaign, instructing his executors, if he were killed in battle, to put an epitaph on his grave that will remind his children that they 'kepe themselfes wordye of so moche honour as to be called hereafter to dye for ther maister and countrey.'[18] This advice he followed himself, never swerving in his loyalty to Henry VIII, even when his brother-in-law, the Marquess of Exeter, was executed in 1539 and his young nephew, Edward Courtenay, imprisoned in the Tower. Only weeks after Boulogne fell, Mountjoy died on 10 October 1544, at his estate of Hook in Dorset. Either a wound lingering from the September skirmish or a disease picked up in the camps killed the young man; infection was always a greater threat than a more glorious death in a charge or raiding party.

Another member of this skirmishing party was the the 18-year-old Thomas Radcliffe, Surrey's first cousin, whose mother was a much younger half-sister of Norfolk and the fifth daughter of the 'Flodden Duke'. Radcliffe was the heir to his father Henry, the second Earl of Sussex (that earl's mother had been the sister of Surrey's grandfather, the Duke of Buckingham); in June 1536 this old earl had proposed that the Duke of Richmond be placed ahead of the Princess Mary in succession to the throne, possibly at the Howards' request. Young Thomas Radcliffe's older brother had recently been killed in Scotland with Surrey, and ties of strong friendship between the older Howard and his younger cousin (now the heir) are found in Surrey's six-line *strambotto* to him. Written at the war front, this epigram exhibits Surrey's own awareness of duty and the performance it requires in war. It also presents Surrey once more in his role as personal protector. The final couplet of this hastily written poem further demonstrates the recurring power in this period, whatever the landscape, of two sets of texts in Surrey's mind: the Bible and Wyatt. Beginning 'My Ratclif, when thy reckless youth offends,' the older cousin admonishes: 'Receive thy scourge by others' chastisement' because, without such self-recognition aided by friends, 'plagues are sent without advertisement.' Although 'Solomon said, the wronged shall recure' (regain health), 'Wyatt said true, the scar doth aye endure.' Surrey warns his cousin: better avoid any occasion of violence because, however it turns out, you—or your enemy—can never forget it.

It was a lesson the young man apparently learned, his deathbed words as the powerful third Earl of Sussex almost forty years later being a realistic allusion to Leicester and the court: 'You know not the beast so well as I do.' In his long life, Sussex became one of the major courtiers and military figures of the Marian and Elizabethan reigns, advising not only the Catholic Majesties Philip of Spain and Mary but also the Earl of Leceister (intervening in the struggle over Anjou). Sussex appears to have befriended the young Sir Philip Sidney, not only because

[18] PRO, SP 49/817. G. Miller, *Tudor Mercenaries*, 159. The quotation from Sussex is from the *DNB*. It should be noted that, as a boy, Sir Philip Sidney had another living contact with Surrey: the Howard steward Ralph Holditch, who kept the Latin household book of 1519 when Surrey was a child, became the steward of the Sidney household when Sidney was growing up. Cf. Head, *Ebbs*, 261.

his barren second wife Frances was such a devoted aunt to the poet, but also because Sussex himself supported Tudor drama and mid-century literary figures and activities. The powerful Earl of Sussex was, in fact, a living bridge between the two poets, the Earl of Surrey, his first cousin, and Sir Philip Sidney, his nephew. If he told Sidney many stories of Surrey, even passing manuscripts to him, then, from the highest blood nobility, Sidney knew a living Surrey.

The Death of Thomas Clere

Montreuil produced a personal tragedy for Surrey that resulted in one of his greatest lyrics. His squire Thomas Clere was either wounded before Abbeville Gate or, more likely, caught in the camps and trenches a disease that refused to heal. Clere died the following April and was buried in the Howard Chapel at St Mary's, Lambeth. Evidently an intimate friend as well as a long-standing servant, Clere may have understood Surrey better than anyone else: it was he who arranged Surrey's schedules for him, including the times the earl wanted for his own writing and reading, and it was this first cousin of Anne Boleyn and the fiancé of Margaret Shelton who watched over Surrey's body every day. Clere's death had come after the fall of Boulogne. On 11 September 1544, the poet earl, accompanied by his uncle Lord William Howard and Clere, answered Henry VIII's command to join him at Boulogne to witness its capture. That afternoon they saw 'the trayne of powder' set to the upper part of the city and the old citadel as well as to the castle and the famous pilgrimage church of the Virgin Mary (in whose crypt today, with the ruins of a Roman temple, are huge cannonballs from this 1544 attack). Henry VIII, Surrey (and Clere), and Lord William went up to the royal viewing place and watched the citadel blow apart, 'at which fall many of oure men were hurt with stones whiche flewe very farre off' (HB 692). The surrender of Boulogne was so stage-managed that, before and after the event, Henry VIII was the real focus of the occasion. The king, disabled by his excessive corpulence, had to be transported in a litter. At the same time, Channel storms wrecked many tents and festivities planned for the triumphal entry into Boulogne, but nothing could keep the English king from entering the city as a reborn Henry V. Once in the city, he supervised the new English fortifications, including the pulling down of what was left of the Marian shrine to build a new bastion and then the knighting of many who had distinguished themselves during the siege, including Sir Anthony Denny and young Radcliffe. Nothing could be allowed to spoil one of the few unalloyed victories for Henry VIII. He had crossed the Channel in a ship with golden sails and now, although he would leave 'incontinent' (swiftly), he had seen the French surrender—his dream realized. In the following January, at another downturn in his health, the English king remembered how physically alive he had felt during those weeks in France.

But on the very day Boulogne surrendered, Charles V and Francis I signed a peace treaty. Henry VIII and the English armies were left dangling. Because of this and the fact that the point about Henry VIII and his greater presence over France had been made, especially to the king himself, the Privy Council ordered the abandonment of the siege of Montreuil. On Friday, 26 September 1544, Norfolk and Surrey complied, taking their ordnance and baggage through the low tides of the Canche estuary to the port of Etaples. Surrey's influence is clear in Norfolk's final dispatch from Montreuil when it warns about '40 sails of Englishmen and Flemings at Estaples laden with victuals, &c., which, unless we get sufficient wafting to bring them to Boleyne on Sunday or Monday morning, will be lost every one.'[19] Some time in those last days, in that pulling out, Thomas Clere became ill. He was to linger exactly six months.

Surrey's sonnet epitaph for Clere originates in a series of *metonymies* (subjects defined by parts or traits). Places and names act as concentrated signs for a male life moving towards a final sacrifice. Not surprisingly, the lyric becomes another English inscription of both Dido and Aeneas—and of Surrey's own prophetic view of himself. With the same dramatic situation and genre as the Wyatt elegy and the earlier Windsor sonnet on Richmond, the lyric acts as an *epicedium*, this time with an implied display (the poem was to be inscribed on a metal tablet over the actual tomb and effigy). To focus his poem, Surrey enlarges on the epitaph ascribed to Virgil by Suetonius: 'Mantua me genuit. Calabri rapuere, tenet nunc / Parthenope; cecini pascua rura duces' ('Mantua gave birth to me; Calabria killed me; now Parthenope [Naples] holds me: I sang of fields, landscapes, and leaders'). Unlike the extravagant *hyperbole* of earlier Tudor elegies, Surrey's understated fourteen end-stopped lines echo the precision of his *Aeneid* translations. With military beat, the lyric builds on the *asyndeton*, *litotes*, and *zeugma* (one word applied to two or more) in Virgil's Latin epitaph. These astringent figures of speech operate within an overall antithesis, a structure of irony and distancing through which the reader (pausing along a crowded church aisle) can view the martyred life as narrated through places and relationships.

In the first quatrains, Surrey immediately shores up the cultural ties of the dead young man to justify the interment of Clere's corpse in the Howard chapel at St Mary's Lambeth. With an 'opening like the military clang of steel', the first line gives the whole life. Familial bulwarks are shored up to reach into the highest levels of society (even to that of a queen, Anne Boleyn, whose name still cannot be mentioned). Then, from blood nobility to nobility of act, Surrey continues to follow the rhetorical instructions for an epideictic oration. He 'places' in context a model *vir armatus* and 'gentle heart', whose life as a series of places and names counterpointed Surrey's own. The poet has inverted the more typically English allegorical inscription of sacrifice in which the higher dies for the lower by making a socially higher male the object of Clere's loving sacrifice and the lower male

[19] *Diarium super viagio Regis, obsidione et captione Bononiae* in Rymer, *Foedera*, vol. 15, 52. *SP*, vol. 10, 1039 (69–70).

really the nobler by his act of sacrifice and death. The result of such inversion is that Surrey's elegy on Clere is 'one of the few poems before the Elizabethan era that offers a sense of an authentic life',[20] not the heaven or apotheosis more common in Tudor elegies. By equating the two lives, Clere becomes, in the topography of the poem, another sign for Surrey in the places of England.

> Norfolk sprang thee, Lambeth holds thee dead,
> Clere of the county of Cleremont though hight;
> Within the womb of Ormond's race thou bred,
> And saw'st thy cousin crowned in thy sight;
> Shelton for love, Surrey for lord thou chose;
> Aye me, while life did last that league was tender,
> Tracing whose steps thou sawest Kelsal blaze,
> Landrecy burnt, and battered Boulogne 'render;
> At Muttrell [Montreuil] gates, hopeless of all recure,
> Thine Earl half dead gave in thy hand his will.
> Which cause did thee this pining death procure,
> Ere summers four times seven thou couldst fulfil;
> Ah, Clere, if love had booted care or cost,
> Heaven had not won, nor earth so timely lost.

The key term in Surrey's logic is 'league', ending an alliterative pattern with 'love', 'lord', and 'life' and dominating not only the second half of the octet but the logic of the sestet and even the couplet, where the final effect of the 'league' is joined and lamented at the same time. The word thus acts as a hinge, originating a progression in which objective collectivity (social and historical inscription) becomes increasingly personal, dramatizing the bond of three lovers, Mary Shelton, Thomas Clere, and Surrey himself.

The catalogue of war places—not distant battle landscapes like those of Chaucer's Knight, but immediate places that identify intimate and dependent moments—climaxes in the odd exchange of death 'at Muttrell Gate', a synecdoche for the whole experience of the 'league'. The exchange suggests, rather unambiguously, that Clere's fatal wounds had been received either in preserving Surrey's own life or obeying his instructions. Through expansion and connection, the exchange, the actual moment of the wounding or loss, becomes itself a legacy of the 'league'. Focusing on Surrey's grammar here reveals just how crucial the earl's concept of 'league' is in the paradigm of the sonnet. The subordinate relative clause 'which cause did thee this pining death procure,' which Zitner calls 'gelatinous', actually stresses the final expression of this 'league' for which Clere gave his life. The exact relationship of Surrey's will in hand and Clere's death appears ambiguous, but the narrative behind the reference may be simple. Surrey, quite sick from dysentery or in any case collapsing, writes his will, gives it to

[20] Virgil's epitaph can be found in *Suetonius*, ed. J. C. Rolfe (1914), vol. 2, 476–7. Leonard Nathan, 'The Course of the Particular: Surrey's Epitaph on Thomas Clere and the Fifteenth-Century Lyric Tradition', *SEL*, 17/1 (Winter 1977) 3–12.

Clere; he then recovers in time for the September retreat as Clere's wound or illness (aggravated by Surrey's illness?) worsens. The exchange between the two, whatever its actual nature (including disease), is made in the poem to focus the relationship. Surrey may be socially superior and more powerful—the poem had to be clear on this—but, as Zitner notes, 'to possess is also to be possessed.'[21]

Once more with calculated objective intimacy, Surrey has graduated his emotional effects of subjectivity, first in the ejaculative 'aye me' and then with the tactful *zeugma* of 'care or cost' in the ironic *anagnorisis* of the couplet, the moral recognition Tudor readers demanded: love tried to save (and did inscribe) but Clere is sacrificed, 'timely lost'. Time and earth (and text) are now the centre of this history, not heaven and apotheosis. The living 'league' and its memory have been transformed into a text, a poem. As long as the text is read by audiences in church or elsewhere, the 'league' of the two young men lasts.

In the reign of Lady Margaret Douglas' grandson, James I, William Camden first published this sonnet, which followed into anthologies, taking the text directly from the actual epitaph he had seen at St Mary's, Lambeth. Surrey's antiquarian grandson Lord William Howard (the brother of Philip) saw the tablet, perceptively calling the sonnet 'faelicis ingenii specimen, et singularis facundiae argumentum' ('a specimen of felicitous wit and an argument of special eloquence'). By the time of Shakespeare (who may also have seen it), Surrey's English sonnet on Clere had become what the poet earl wanted. Looking at that figure in the brass, readers would find above it Surrey's announcement of an utterly new honour and nobility. Without the poem, the memorial brass effigy exists today (and is popular as a rubbing) in a church that is now the Museum of Garden History, the former Howard chapel serving as a tea and coffee shop. The effigy, with its coat of arms at the top, indicates armour and battle-gear of the kind (allowing for rank differences) Surrey would have worn from a cuirass superbly fitted over chest and waist to chain-mail extending over the hips, loins, and upper thighs to knee-guards and carefully constructed greaves, the whole metallic enclosure seemingly unsuited either to summer heat or violent storms or the speed of charging horses. In the outstretched body, Thomas Clere's ungloved hands with long fingers are clasped in a final prayer. Twenty months after his death, the name of 'Clere' appeared strangely in the notes and memoranda the Lord Chancellor Wriothesley was making during Surrey's trial.[22]

Earlier Military Success: The Campaign at Sea

A series of events demonstrates Surrey's immersion by April 1545 in the life of his society, his acceptance of the changes in England. The war had helped him to

[21] Lever, *The Elizabethan Love Sonnet*, 50. S. P. Zitner, 'Truth and Mourning in a Sonnet by Surrey,' *ELH*, 50 (1983), 515 but see the entire essay (509–29). As Zitner demonstrates, Nott originated the romanticizing of the episode (lxvii) and he based it on inaccurate facts.

[22] Brenan and Statham, *House of Howard*, 391. *LP*, vol. 21, 2, 555 (18).

accept his dangerous rank and its demands on his life and time. The aggression that had marked his early behaviour had now been subsumed in warfare, the all-demanding Roman role of *vir armatus*.[23] A new aspect of this role appeared during the summer of 1545. Surrey was called to attend Henry VIII as his aide during the king's visit to the Solent on the south coast of England. He had already known he would leave soon for France and had begun to recruit his army in East Anglia, when a threatened French invasion with 200 ships, in retaliation for Boulogne, turned the attention of the king to the south coast. Henry VIII assumed personal responsibility for the defence of England, and so in mid-July 1545, the king inspected the readiness of south coast ports and harbours against a possible French landing. On Saturday afternoon, 18 July, the Lord Admiral Lisle, John Dudley, was entertaining the king, the young earl, and others at dinner aboard his flagship, the 1000-ton *Harry Grace á Dieu* or *Great Harry* anchored in the Solent, the large body of water between the Isle of Wight and the mainland of England, with Portsmouth and other coastal defences nearby. The entourage of the king had been considerable, including the Imperial ambassador who advised the monarch to surrender Boulogne for peace and was promptly given a lecture on honour. Whatever his corpulence and bad legs, Henry VIII was in charge as ever, his gesturing hand, directives, and intellect far from failing.

In fact, it was the English king on board *The Great Harry* who insisted that a lookout be sent to the maintop and thus saved the day. What that lookout first thought he saw was a merchant fleet; a second look showed him a vast armada, as powerful as any ever seen in English waters. Immediately the 53-year-old king dispatched all admirals and captains to their ships. He and Surrey took a longboat for the shore to Southsea Castle near Portsmouth. From there in the next thirty-six hours, Surrey watched the ensuing naval engagement and one of the most spectacular disasters of the century. First, on that Saturday night, a system of warning fires woke England to the news that she had been invaded. Then on the next day, as the great ships lined up for battle in the Solent, to the horror of the

[23] Surrey did, in fact, order a new set of armour and harness on 21 April 1545, in the month of Clere's funeral, from the King's Armourer, to whom he paid £10. Two days later, on St George's Day, he and his father attended the the Chapter of the Order of the Garter at 'the Mannour called St. James's, near the Palace of Westminster,' and on 17 May Surrey as Knight of the Garter celebrated the Order's feast-day (transferred from 23 April because of Holy Week that year). During this same period both father and son were named to the commissions 'to arrange and collect the Benevolence which the King by advice of his Council has decreed towards defence against the French King'. However unpopular the benevolence as a tax, Surrey's work as its commissioner in Norfolk, as in his other public duties, brought him no complaint or accusation of indecorum (certainly no charge of being a spoiled aristocrat persecuting the innocent proletariat). Inhabitants not only paid the benevolence, as Surrey and the other commissioners had asked, but sent the forty soldiers he requested. During this same period the king also granted Surrey the abbot's manor at Windham Reginae and further gifts like licences to alienate manors and sites in East Anglia as some compensation (but not enough) for the immense amounts of cash the Howards had already expended for their own troops and supplies during the French war. Christmas 1544 was spent with the king, Queen Catherine Parr, and the three royal children at Hampton Court, where on Christmas Day the king himself attended a meeting of the Chapter of the Order of the Garter that Surrey attended. Blomefield, *History of Norfolk*, vol. 3, 214; vol. 2, 504; *LP*, vol. 20,i, 558, 623, 1237.

spectators on land, Vice-Admiral Carew's flagship, the recently christened *Mary Rose*, a 600-ton man-of-war, keeled over and sank, with 700 men on board. Water poured through cannon ports that had not been closed. Despairing cries could be heard across the Solent on the hot windless day, and Lady Mary Carew, watching her husband drown before her eyes, fainted at the feet of the king. As she was lifted, the king comforted the young woman by remarking that another male Carew will soon carry on the line. Then answering the Imperial ambassador, who had wondered out loud how the English could ever survive now, Henry VIII retorted: 'From such a hard beginning there can only be a better ending.' A change of wind prevented a battle. The French could hardly feel any satisfaction. Just before their own invasion, the French flagship, the 800-ton *Carraquon*, had burned at Le Havre as a result of a kitchen fire during Francis I's send-off dinner. As Scarisbrick has noted, the whole Franco-English war of the 1540s proved that strange humours and accidents could dominate any large plans, poorly supported as all these strategies were by inadequate maps, insufficient lines of supply and communication, and sudden desertions by all sides, especially by mercenaries. The only salvation in most cases came from the sheer will of military leaders.[24]

In this case too, the king wanted decisive action. On the following Tuesday Surrey was back on board *The Great Harry*. The king wanted a plan from the Lord Admiral Dudley—there had to be a firm response at once—and Surrey represented the king to Dudley, who replied immediately to Henry VIII that his 'Pourpus' or best strategy is to 'follo' some French on land: 'So thought I, and sayde then to my Lorde of *Surrey*, that thes *French* Men which be here, if they Lande, they may happen fynde soche a Blaste that they shall never see theyr owne Contrey agayne.' Of course, the future Duke of Northumberland and virtual ruler of England seven years later is willing 'to shede the beste Bloude in my Body to remove theym out of your Sight; but have your Grace no doubt in any hasty or unadvised or presumptyous Enterpris that I shall mak.' Indeed, concluded 'Your Majestie's most humble and obedient Subject and Servant, John Lisle': 'yf I have any knowledge how to serve you in any Kinde of Thing, I have received the same frome your silffe; and being so nere the Fontayne, and wold dye for Thirste, yt were little Joye of my Liffe.'[25]

Commander and Protector of Boulogne

While the French navy distracted the English fleet in the Channel, Francis I intensified his forces to recapture Boulogne, the continuing sign of dishonour for him in the eyes of Europe. The French army began to block the city off from out-

[24] Alexander McKee, 'Henry VIII as Military Commander', *History Today*, 41 (June 1991), 22–37. Scarisbrick, *Henry VIII*, 450.

[25] *A Collection of State Papers*, ed. Samuel Haynes (1740), 51–2.

siders in June 1545 and lay siege to it. To break this tightening noose and relieve the English forces defending the city, Henry VIII sent his brother-in-law, the Duke of Suffolk, but significantly not Norfolk. Surrey was appointed leader of the vanguard of the new army to defend Boulogne. Surrey's work mustering soldiers in East Anglia had been disrupted by the July invasion scare, but by 9 August 1545, he had 5000 men ready to embark, with Surrey's own allowance of five marks a day. On the 15th, Surrey sailed to Calais, where another 3000 men awaited him. The poet earl now had 8000 soldiers to command; he had the experience, the vigour of youth, and the desire to prove himself as superior a *vir armatus* as Nennius' Arthur and as Surrey's ancestors Edward I and Edward III. Then came the sudden deaths in late August, first of Thomas Lord Poynings, the commander of Boulogne, and then of the Duke of Suffolk himself. The poet Earl of Surrey succeeded as general of the king's forces in France.

In the autumn of 1545 (as today) the Channel port of Boulogne had three main geographical centres: the upper town with its old citadel, fortress, and cathedral of the Virgin Mary; the lower town or 'base Bullain', as Surrey calls it in a verse letter, with its waterfront on the east bank of the River Liane, its businesses, and the old church of St Nicholas; and the promontory to the north overlooking the estuary and the sea. This promontory marked the site of the ancient Roman *pharos* with its beacon tower (the original Latin name 'turrei ardens' corrupted into the French 'Tour d'Ordre' in Surrey's time). Lasting until the bombing raids of World War II, this structure dated from the time of Caligula and possibly earlier when, in 43 BC, Caesar launched his invasion of Britain from Bononia or Boulogne. This Roman tower Surrey had first seen thirteen years before in totally different circumstances, as a backdrop for musical and visual ceremonies dominated by Francis I. In the same spot now, Surrey stood alone, ruling in a city of ruins.

To defend the crippled city, the new general had to keep a line of defence running among all three parts of Boulogne. That line had to descend from the high citadel to the low riverside with its single earthwork bastion that the surveyor and royal engineer John Rogers was completing during Surrey's command. Then the line of defence had to ascend up steep densely populated streets. Outside the walls, Surrey's defence had to become a trenching line to a temporary English fortification called 'the Young Man' before it linked up with the old Roman beacon tower and lighthouse called 'the Old Man' on the promontory. In that high spot, English engineers had constructed an elaborate system of earthworks with a battery of cannon. The ruins of this brick fort of 1545 are visible today.

Among these points, Surrey had to keep communications and lines of supplies and men circulating. He had also to consult with master engineers like John Rogers about the logistics of space. Roger's work was remarkable and illustrated, as Shelby notes, the 'transformation of the medieval master masons into the architects and engineers of modern buildings'. It was also expensive, and his master military projects at Boulogne cost the sum of £122,696. What Surrey realized quite soon was that only in this continuous movement and defensive building such as Rogers' could a commander of Boulogne establish a basic matrix of operations. That settled, he could get to the real work. One French fort was finished, Fort Outreau across the Liane River, which ran in front of Lower Boulogne; but its artillery could not reach the English harbour with any degree of accuracy. Surrey's main strategy was therefore to keep another fort from being built closer to the sea and capable of hitting the estuary and harbour and so interrupt all supplies that came and went by sea. To accomplish this, he frequently sent out skirmishes and raids and even occupied a system of trenches on the bank opposite the city. They led out from an older abandoned French fort and converged a few miles from Boulogne at the church of St Etienne. The strongest French encampment lay on Mount Lambert, the highest point of the area, from which the French could shoot into Surrey's citadel itself (and the English fire back), but it could present no serious offensive because of its distance.

Surrey's primary tactic that the best defence is an offence meant that only attacks on these forts could keep open his supply lines down the Liane River and estuary to the sea, his connection to the English port of Calais (as all land routes were blocked by the French). Surrey's men would also range wider into the Boullonnais towards Hardelot with its sand dunes and pines and, because these strategies worked well, they conquered various links to Calais. Indeed, the irony for Surrey was that, as a military historian comments, 'by the spring of 1546 the English defensive system at Boulogne was beginning to take shape.' It was at that moment Surrey was recalled. In six months, Surrey had found a disaster area and turned Henry VIII's 'Enterprise of Boulogne' into a functioning defensive system that could support an offence, or at least lay the foundation for the great strides of Lord Grey in the following summer. Thus, Surrey had in no sense lost the 'Enterprise of Boulogne' but had helped to build a fortress whose technology the new French king Henry II (Surrey's adolescent friend) greatly admired when, through negotiation, he took Boulogne back.[26]

Of course, success had meant less and less money from London. Increasingly, there was the prospect of no money at all. As Hoyle indicates, funding a war on the scale the English king wanted was possible 'only because of the most breathtaking acts of will by the king and by the subordination of every aspect of government finance to the imperative of war'. In November, at the height of Surrey's tenure as general, Wriothesley could barely scrape together £20,000 when the cost of garrisoning, fortifying, and feeding Boulogne from September 1544 to October 1545 had been over £133,000. 'I assure you master Secretary,' he wrote to Paget, 'I am at my wits' end how we shall possibly shift for three months following, and especially for the two next,' with the bulk of his money, £15,000, from the mint—'our holy anchor'—and its increasingly debased coinage, and from the Court of Augmentations, through whom all the monastic wealth and spoils had

[26] L. R. Shelby, *John Rogers: Tudor Military Engineer* (1967), 1, 55–7, 68, 76, and 83. Cf. 92 where Rogers' brutal 'impressing and transporting workers from England' is described.

once flowed, now reduced to a trickle of £3000. However Henry VIII may have used these sources and the 'benevolences' or forced gifts provided by all those who could pay in 1542 and 1544, and the forced loans and subsidies demanded from both lay and clerical estates in 1543 and 1545, the Tudor king was near bankruptcy. He had inherited enormous wealth from his father in 1509 and more from the boom of the 1530s. But, as Dietz shows, the monastic land bonanza had soon collapsed, not to mention the wealth in lead, for example, from the outside of the churches and the spoils of gold and silver inside. The French wars alone had eaten up almost all the profits from the Tudor destruction of the 1000-year-old monastic system. In fact, as Surrey struggled to keep Henry VIII's dream alive, the English monarch had begun to plot how he might 'borrow' church plate. Seymour applauded the idea with good reformed Christian logic that would soon serve a state increasingly his to control as Protector, writing: 'God's service, which consisteth not in jewels, plate or ornaments of gold and silver, cannot thereby be anything diminished, and those things better employed for the weal and defence of the realm.' A scribbled note in an early copy of Lord Herbert's seventeenth-century history of the reign of Henry VIII is clear: 'Our kings charges in winninge and keepinge Boulogne was 1,342,552 [pounds], 3 [shillings], 7 [pence].' As Hoyle notes, the actual figures were much higher. Of the £2.1 million spent on all Henry's military adventures, excluding the costs of fortification and garrisons, 'the costs of war 1542–7 fall to around £1.6 million, say four times the cost of the campaigns of 1522–4,' and with all costs included, closer to £2 million. Like all such military adventures of this kind in history, the more Henry VIII spent and the more lives wasted and lost, the more he felt he must hold on—at least until he could find the proper victim whose destruction might justify the disaster.[27]

With a basic dilemma between the old king's atavistic sense of honour and the Privy Council's recognition of disaster but fear of offending the king, Surrey's situation took on, in the six months of his tenure as general, a special temptation. The desires that had led Surrey now met the equally solipsistic desires of a king and culture for whom the peace-dove humanists had prophesied such doom as that befalling the English army in France in 1545 and the English economy. As Norfolk knew better than most, the new French war could only be more hopeless than the first in 1513. That war his friend More had satirized in his *Utopia* and Erasmus lamented. Even naming Surrey as 'Lieutenant General' hinted at desperation. Edward Seymour, the Earl of Hertford, was in Scotland; Lisle was Lord Admiral; Russell and Arundel in the west of the realm; and Norfolk guarded the eastern coasts. As no other available military figure in England had shown the

[27] Richard Hoyle, 'War and Public Finance' in *The Reign of Henry VIII*, ed. MacCulloch, 91 (also see Table 4.3 on 90). F. Dietz, *English Public Finance 1485–1558*, University of Illinois Studies in the Social Sciences, ix (1920) 149, reprinted as *English Public Finance 1485–1641* (1964), vol. I. For the whole question of the monastic wealth and the Court of Augmentations (over which Norfolk had presided as steward in the late 1530s) see W. C. Richardson, *The History of the Court of Augumentation* (1961). *LP*, vol. 20, i, 984, 986, 1145. For the scribbled note, see Bodleian Library, Delta 624, 443.

level of power and energy needed, who else but the young Howard heir apparent, the latest version of a family of generals?

A commandant was thus needed who had the hope and logistical sense to build morale and fortifications and to fight. A vision of self and experience in logistics were both needed to set up defences for supplies that had to come by sea, up the river, then be unloaded and distributed to the three vital areas of the city from the harbour, often in the midst of traffic jams of wagons and carriages that hindered all flow of supplies, as the former Lord Marshal complained to Calais (N1: 219). At the same time, the poet earl had continually to be on the offensive. Indeed, after the September death of the Duc d'Orléans, the grand Maréchal du Biez turned the whole French army (with young French aristocrats who flocked from Paris and Fontainebleau to fight after Orléans' death) to entrap Surrey and his forces.[28] Against the Maréchal's superior numbers (the French always outnumbered the English garrison), Surrey's flexible horsemen attacked French workers and slowly chipped away at the rising Fort Châtillon while never seeking a direct engagement with the formidable French army. Surrey also sent out larger reconnaissance parties to attack French wagon-trains full of supplies and food. The position of a commandant thus required just the kind of young warrior the poet earl had become, one who operated in an interplay of offensive manoeuvres from a solid base, attacks from a constant matrix, all within a continuously flexible system—not unlike a system of prosody. Even if outnumbered, Surrey's army was holding its own and keeping the French from building. He was thus bringing hope to a despairing king in a dying body.

Henry VIII, Surrey, and the Dream of Honour

As the king's body was telling him, Boulogne might represent his final act as a reincarnated Henry V. In any case, for a few months in late 1545 and early 1546, the poet who invented blank verse and the English sonnet was in charge of a war, certainly its most crucial campaign, and he and his master lived in a series of metaphors that were ruining the realm. As Surrey's extant letters to Henry VIII reveal, the two Henrys were held in a kind of triangular desire by the dream of honour both held and Surrey could articulate. For a while, as general, Surrey could control the triangle by the language of his letters from a besieged city. He was acting out one more successful role, inventing another kind of splendid fiction, 'une tableau tout imaginaire', but this time within the violence of war.

This relationship was perceived by the Privy Council and court as dangerous, not least by Surrey's own father. Thus, hardly had Surrey taken over as general and commander of Boulgne than Norfolk wrote from Windsor on 27 September

[28] Bapst, *Deux gentilshommes-poètes*, 316–17.

1545. He was answering Surrey who had just written that he was 'grieved' that his father had carelessly revealed to the court what Surrey's messenger, Richard Cavendish, had told the father in secret. Norfolk was direct: 'Have yourself in await, that ye animate not the King too much for the keeping of Boulogne; for who so doth, at length shall get small thanks.' Norfolk's words of warning went unheeded. From the moment of his arrival at Boulogne, Surrey was determined, whatever the cost, to prevent its recapture by the French. He would defy his father. He was planning to stay, despite the request of his father and the admonitions of the Privy Council. One of his first tasks had been 'to rid all harlots and common women out of Boulogne and enquire whether any head officers had received money above their entertainment and appointed their servants to certain charges whereby the King was ill served.' In a war as uncontrolled as this one, the new army would have to live in as spartan a way as their general in order to keep a firm base of operations. At the same time, Surrey began his command with a flexibility of contact and support for all members of his military community. On 14 September, a letter to the Privy Council set the tone of his leadership: he wrote to intercede for two Englishmen whose 'pinnaces' (small ships) had safely delivered supplies of muttons, barrels of butter and of beer, only on their return to be captured by the French. As a former Lord Marshal, Surrey understood the value of right supply lines and the meaning of such financial loss. He also shrewdly knew the need to build a reputation for sustaining the human beings involved in such systemic flow to the front lines. Thus he gave a special recommendation to Paget for one of his men, a T. Shelley that Nott equates with the Edward Shelley whom Challoner made the hero of his Latin epic. This is the Shelley who had been Surrey's servant and was now a captain at Boulogne, 'whose rare virtues I could write more at large, but that I know virtue for the self, is to you sufficiently recommended' and 'I dare promise more of that man, his truth and honesty, than of any man that I know alive.' In granting this favour to Shelley, Paget is to 'think the pleasure done to myself [Surrey], praying to pardon my earnest writing: for the worthiness of the man bears it.' This letter demonstrates a pattern of commendation or concern that continued throughout Surrey's command, especially for the younger Thomas Wyatt, who attacked nearby Hardelot castle by racing through the turnpike and, at a gate on the first bridge, breaking open the door, killing one of the watchmen, and then capturing another two watchmen before setting 'his hackbutters in the brage about the castle'—the whole episode Arthurian, quite distant from the ironic realism of his diplomat father. Such a life of bravura would end, while Wyatt was still a young man, in an almost successful overthrow of the first Tudor queen before his own bloody head would be set on London Bridge.[29]

[29] Surrey would ask, among many other examples, for the local Water Bailiff Croft to be appointed as lieutenant or for help for 'poor Sir Andrew Flammock, whose service, as I observed in the town and field, hath been always of such sort, as me thinketh he hath well deserved to be defended from poverty in his old days' (both were rewarded even after Surrey's departure). Surrey would also resolve differences

It was clear within a month that Surrey had defied his father. At the end of October 1545, Norfolk had his treasurer, Thomas Hussey, an old friend to the younger Howard, write with enough innuendoes to force the chivalric Surrey to consider abandoning Boulogne. Early in this letter, Hussey refers to a request Surrey probably made from the moment of his overseas assignment: 'This present Thursday my lord's Grace, your father, told me of your request for the access of your wife and children to Boulogne and what answers the King him therein.' As a rule, the Howards had taken their wives with them when they went on special assignments. The fact that Surrey as general (in that position he had the right) had called so early for his family reveals how deeply intertwined the lives of his family were, especially as the 29-year-old Surrey had just become a father for the fourth time. A besieged city was quite another thing, however, and Surrey's request shows how deeply he took his whole command, if he would risk his family, especially the baby daughter. The request demonstrates once more how much he needed that other self, his wife, his 'sorrow's leech', for whom he had already composed verse letters from France. As Norfolk probably had Hussey write, the answer from the king and council was negative. His family could not come. Surrey had one more reason to abandon Boulogne.

Another was money. Surrey owed large sums. Hussey quoted a conversation with Norfolk. ' "What way," he [Norfolk] asked, "taketh my son for payment of his debts?" I [Hussey] answered, "I know not." "Well," ' says Norfolk, he owes his client Richard Fulmerston ' "an honest sum. And what oweth he you?" ' to which Hussey answers: ' "So much as I can be content to forbear in respect to his necessity." ' If this was Hussey's gentle way of reminding Surrey of just how much the young man owed him, it was also humiliating. Further, the Howard household treasurer told Surrey that his father would stop a land deal going through that would have paid all of Surrey's debts. For Norfolk, Surrey must not only find another way to settle his debts but 'handle Fulmerston discreetly and send [his] resolute answer.' Surrey must learn, says the father, to keep money in his hands, 'for you can not both pay your whole debts and furnish your present necessities.' Norfolk was worried about the continued expenditure on Surrey House, 'committed to [Sir Richard] Southwell's charge' to oversee its completion. It will not have the underwriting of Norfolk. The result is, says Hussey, 'we shall make shift

between the Albanians and Spaniards (Boulogne was filled with mercenaries). He would ask special consideration for Sir Richard Wingfield recently ransomed after seventeen months; he petitioned the king whose 'gracious favour' in this case will 'encourage all others your Highness's subjects,' adding with characteristic dash, 'to adventure their lives in the service of so noble and thankful a Prince, as never yet left acceptable service unrewarded.' For those closest to him, he gives special praise, always writing directly to the king. Both Sir Thomas Palmer and young Wyatt 'whom your Majesty of ignorant men hath framed to such towardness and knowledge in the war, that . . . your Majesty hath not of their behavior and youth many the like within your realm, both for their hardiness [boldness], painfulness, circumspection, and natural disposition to the war.' They are to be given 'credit for the declaration of such conferences and discourses as we have had together concerning the order of your Majesty's wars on this side the sea.' BL Harleian MS ff. 283, 329. For the military references, see N1: 185, 188–9, 223–4, 229, 205, 213.

for them [creditors] upon my credit in this town [Norwich].' His father is putting the greatest pressure on Surrey: 'My lord of Norfolk is determined that your revenues at Lady Day [Annunciation] last [March 25, 1545], shall be received by the steward, and the overplus paid to your ministers.' Hussey acknowledges the enormous success and fame Surrey had already gained in England by reminding him of his father's: 'Your Lordship remains in as good fame on this side the seas as your lucky succeedings have prospered happily on that side.' Hussey's conclusions come to the point: 'Handle the matter wisely for the sale of your lands, for my lord of Norfolk said he would see your debts paid.' Hussey literally underlines his point: '*And by these means and others ye may be made weary of your will of Boulogne*.' Then he adds cautiously: 'As my trust is in you, burn this letter.'

In Hussey's letter, Surrey had been threatened by every loved thing, from family to Surrey House, and even by his carefully chosen furnishings. Two weeks later, on 6 November, Hussey wrote again. This time he was more blunt. Surrey had been writing letters personally to the King, and Norfolk had seen them. The father was incensed: 'My Lord, to be plain with you, I see my lord's Grace, the Duke of Norfolk, somewhat offended in seeing your letters to the King's Majesty of such vehemence as touching the animating of the King's Majesty for the keeping of Boulogne.' The old duke was especially angry that to his own 'divers letters addressed to your lordship', Surrey had 'given simple credence or little belief'. In one of these letters to Henry VIII, Surrey had referred to Boulogne as 'the chiefest jewel in his crown'. With language like this, Norfolk rails, Surrey's reports 'set back in six hours' the work of six days of the Privy Council to influence the king to halt the war, 'such importance be your letters in the King's opinion at this time.' The duke recognized that 'ye may by your practices sustain Boulogne for two or three months, yet he thinketh it impossible that it may continue six months, for as much as he certainly knoweth the realm of England can not possibly bear the charges of defending Boulogne.'

Hussey then cited the duke's statistics on the expenditure of the war and the lack of revenue and then added: 'Moreover, I have heard the Duke say that he would rather bury you and the rest of his children before he should give his consent to the ruin of this realm.' Then Hussey added ominously and prophetically: 'and that he has no doubt but that ye should be removed in spite of your head, work what ye could.' There can be no hope of gaining any recompense 'owte of the Kyng's coffers' and Surrey could always be helped by his father to the captainship at Guisnes or the deputyship of Calais 'if Bowlleyne is rendride [surrendered]'. And so Hussey summed up: 'To have my judgment for Boulogne, as I can learn, every Councilor sayeth: "Away with it." And the King and your Lordship sayth, "We will keep it." ' No council member (including Norfolk 'who will bark in it [council] to his dying day') will move for the surrender but they do 'stay the King from sending over 1500 pioneers and 3000 men of war for the better accomplishing of the French fortress according to your late devise.' And another thing: the king has been quite upset ('in very ill part') that 'ye should adventure your presence in standing upon the bridge of the fortress,' showing 'negligence in adventuring your person so dangerously'. In a period when losses in an army were calculated by how many nobility and officers were killed and little else, the price of losing one Surrey would be great humiliation for Henry VIII. Once more, Surrey is to be very careful with this letter. He is to burn it, for letters written by friend to friend are now being brought to the king. 'If ye shall write any in secrecy, send it by a sure person.'[30]

Letters to Henry VIII

Of the surviving letters to Henry VIII written in December 1545 and January 1546, most end with Surrey's 'sincere' placing of himself in reverence to the king, not only his probable godfather but, through the Woodvilles, his fourth cousin. In one, having praised young Wyatt and Palmer and the 'wars on this side of the sea', Surrey added: his own service 'hath proceeded, I take God to witness, rather of a care beyond all other affections to your Majesty's service, than to any presumption of knowledge'. The earl hoped 'your Majesty will at least take in good part upon the sight of things, the humble advertisement from time to time of him, whom most unworthy, your Majesty hath placed here.' Further, Surrey did not think it his 'duty to use any other means for the declaration of the discourse of any service to be done here, than to [use direct discourse] to your Majesty' as though to a real soul mate. To this structured 'sincere' discourse to the king, in diction and in narrated incidents, Surrey would bring all the male camaraderie (including memories of the king's great friend of his youth, the Lord Admiral Edward Howard) and such high chivalric adventure as the ageing king could still remember with joy. In his language, the poet will present to the king a true type of the old Burgundian *gloire* and presence. For these few months, Surrey was thus leading the old king, as had for seven years his cousin Anne Boleyn, to some immense hope. If it was the hope of a transcendent self, of some freedom from his dying body, it was also the hope of another Agincourt, the heroic battlefield of his childhood, a first hope too strong for illusion.

Another letter reads like a battle narrative from an earlier century. Surrey describes his raiding party on 'sixteen carts laden with thirty pieces of wine' that had retreated to Montreuil, now the nearest stronghold of the French army. Then, with Surrey's spies telling their general that 700 horsemen will come with new carts and that the German mercenaries hired by the French are bringing supplies from Dieppe and Etaples, Surrey sends forth, three hours before dawn, in the dead of a freezing night, the younger Wyatt and Palmer with 1000 footmen 'to embush themselves under the hill side where the church of St. Etienne stood'. This church,

[30] For Hussey's first letter, *LP* 20,ii: 658 (301). For the second, PRO, SP, BB/351; also, *LP* 20,ii: 738.

named for the young first Christian martyr Stephen, had been occupied by the French; around it they had built a trench system in a perimetre fashion to keep the English from coming across the bridge. Abandoned, it was taken over by Surrey's forces. One of the purposes of such a reconnaissance, says Surrey in a special ploy to the king, was 'to seek out the ground of most advantage of your Majesty's camp, if it should be your pleasure to come to the field the next year'. In fact, Surrey's recurrent teaser to the king in these letters is that the king will return in triumph. From this, it appears that, in his own plans and timetable, Surrey was planning to conquer all the French outposts within a year. Then the king could return to Boulogne to see the triumph of another Howard hero. The Tudor monarch would then have another royal apotheosis now joined to Surrey's.

Surrey continued his letter: he set his men 'upon the skantling of the hill as nigh as we could', where they were soon engaged in combat. Surrey's next descriptions sound as though they came from the medieval Romance *Lancelot du Lac*: 'At the which charge Mr. Marshall very honestly and hardily brake his mace upon a Frenchman; Mr. Shelly brake his staff upon a tall young gentlemen . . . and took him prisoner: and in effect, all the men at arms of this town [Boulogne] brake their staves.' Soon Surrey's cavalry 'drove them from place to place' among the sand dunes and 'so from hill to hill to Hardelot'. The poet's men also drove away all supply-wagons that day and stopped other troop movements. When the horses of the enemy had been 'well dagged with arrows' and 'for one day right well affrayed,' Surrey called his men to return.

The earl now wished—in a direct appeal to Henry VIII—'to God that your Majesty, with the surety of the same, had seen the willing hearts as well of the gentlemen and strangers [mercenaries] of this town, as also of the poor soldiers.' The young general ended his letter with another teaser to the old king: 'Not doubting but when your pleasure shall be such to keep the field,' the English king will see himself how the French king tries to save his fortress, and how the earl and his men performed in the field 'and how easy it is to keep the strait.' The latter refers to a crucial part of Surrey's military strategy. He will keep the low ground down from the high point of the French fort Outreau, to the left of Mont St Etienne, and between these high points and the shoreline (or what is today Equihen-Plage). Through this 'strait' would pass not only supplies for Fort Outreau but any materials for the building of a new fort (Fort Châtillon was built on the shore, in fact, after Surrey had been recalled). Before he sends his letter, Surrey commends various of his men as usual and, in giving a chivalric ascription to one, reveals a special narrative: 'Francis Aslebyc, that hurt Mons. d'Aumale, break [broke] his staff very honestly.' The latter alludes to one of the most graphic incidents on the French side of the war. Surrey names the actual assailant (Surrey's letter is the only known source) and then describes how the later powerful Duc de Guise, the uncle of Mary Queen of Scots, received the permanent scar and deformation of his nose (a lance pierced him between the nose and eye and entered the head) which earned him the surname 'Le Balafré'—in revenge for which he of the mangled face led the French forces to capture Calais from the English forces of Mary I and return it permanently to France.

The next letter is three days later, 7 December 1545. After a 'right painful' arrival of Sir George Pollard 'in the bitterness of the weather' and 'lack of meat [fodder] for his horses here' and Vice-Admiral George Cotton's forcing of French supply ships into the Somme (both men deserving the king's thanks), Surrey sent out before dawn 'our whole ambush of horsemen and footmen at St. Etienne'. He even put field pieces in the trenches to keep the pressure up and let his horsemen attack any French wagon-trains so that they are driving them back to Montreuil, and here Surrey puns: 'chafed for choler, and yet I think right well a-cold'. Again Surrey invites the king to come to France: the young man thinks 'it [would be] not unmeet that your Majesty saw' those ships he is describing, for the king would himself perceive just how difficult it is for the French to be supplied.

Surrey's next surviving letter to the king on 5 January 1546, just two days before the St Etienne disaster, is less personal. Surrey is concerned with his own plans for making Boulogne a permanent part of England. The young Howard general has fully surveyed the whole of Boulogne and is sending back by the engineer Rogers a plat (a map and diagram) of where the earl sees new fortifications are needed. Fort Outreau now lies in misery, in Surrey's judgement, and if the 'great revictualment now prepared' can be stopped as Surrey was planning to do by skirmishing soon at St Etienne, 'your Majesty should never need to besiege the same.' Of course, 'if the enemy have commodity the next year to finish the same, the difficulty to win it will increase.' Surrey is already planning his own next year as commander at Boulogne. The besieging needs to be sustained, and the summer of 1546 will be a good time because men can 'lie in the field'. The only problem is keeping the wagon-trains away, but the basic strategy is clear: 'Your Majesty's only mean to win the fort, as me seemeth, is to prevent the enemy in the field' and so encamp in the marshes and on the banks of the Liane and elsewhere 'with trenches and a mount in every camp'. In that way, no supplies can reach the French fort. 'I think,' says Surrey, if French horsemen are controlled and the English control the sea, 'the [French] fortress would be starved before the season of the year would serve the enemy to put his gallies to the sea.' Surrey is already caculating the numbers of men needed for the new English camp he will build in summer 1546, especially pioneers. He is totally confident. For 'the surety of the whole enterprise, there is no doubt but every soldier will set his hands thereto.' With an English camp on the French side of the river, and the river to the sea in English hands, and with new English cannon, Fort Outreau will be quite besieged 'and more desperate of succour'. Then the French army, no matter how large, cannot dislodge the English and their strong trenches around the hill of St Etienne. Surrey's army can then take 'advantage of the highest grounds, enterlacing [the Strait] with trenches, the one hill to the other, and receive our victuals always in surety'.

At no point does the poet earl break from the intoxication of presenting his plan. Boldly the poet general asks the king 'to return your resolution' to listen to

Surrey: reduce the number of foot-soldiers and take the captains who no longer have men to use them, still with a captain's pay, in other capacities or 'service'. The result of Surrey's reformation of personnel will be a more efficient fighting force, costing comparatively little and boosting morale: 'The charge whereof shall not be great, and the comfort to your subjects here much, when they shall see that your Majesty will entertain them still for their passed service.' What Surrey was obviously trying to build among his men was a force in which each soldier perceived his own part, his destiny, in the whole picture, what Aeneas had consciously tried, in the last six books of Virgil's epic, to instil in his own men as the best battle strategy. Thus Surrey exhorts the king: 'Beseeching the same to remember [his men] generally with some letter of comfort, which shall afresh encourage them most willingly to adventure their lives, according to their most bounden duty, in your Majesty's service.' And the poet general once more waxes: 'Assuring your Majesty, upon my most bounden duty to the same, that as I cannot speak but sith my coming hither, I dare say at this present there was never Prince more truly served in that behalf.' But the ships still need to come; one of his garrisons has lived on biscuit and water for six days, with no wood or coal in January; and for ten days, his own army has had no hay for horses. Two days later, Surrey would be defeated in a skirmish that essentially ended his military career (N1: 181–96).

A Sonnet from Boulogne

Surrey's capacity to write poetry, whatever the prevalent conditions of his life, appears in a sonnet (probably his last) composed at Boulogne. With a rhyme scheme neither English nor Petrarchan but a variation on the old medieval practice of *equivocatio* or through-rhyme (perhaps evidence of hasty writing), the lyric discloses how Surrey was coming to terms with his own inner aggression. Ironically, in the midst of war, he was reconciling the contradictions in his life and within himself. The voice in the lyric locates itself in Lower Boulogne and alludes to the steep terrain of the city and, in a text adumbrating the place sonnets of Sidney, Donne, Milton, and the Romantics, geography is used to dramatize an abstract moral stance. Some profound experience, personified in the opening lines 'fancy, which that I have served long' and 'That hath always been enemy to mine ease', has caused the speaker to want to flee himself. He would 'press out of the throng' and 'by flight my painful heart to please', seeking 'faith more strong'. The whole experience of the narrative leads towards more, however, than just a love affair or Petrarchan loneliness. In the sestet, with a direct address to self, time used improperly 'to run this race so long' is denounced and the speaker makes an overt act of contrition and confession in Boulogne. His history 'Brought me amidst the hills in base Bullain: / Where I am now, as restless to remain, / Against my will, full pleased with my pain.' Closure operates here as a kind of catharsis that prepares the speaker to re-enter history. This process of conversion in Surrey's poem operates in terms not just of the final couplet but of the last three lines, all rhyming. The speaker can now endure the paradox of his place and history (Lower Boulogne amid its steep hills); he can accept the terrible ambiguities and strains of violence on his inner self. The poet general can even write a sonnet in Boulogne. He is ready where he is and now, wherever he will be, 'full pleased with my pain'. He would need that assurance in the last twelve months of his life.

12

The Shame of St Etienne

The battle of St Etienne occurred on Thursday, 7 January 1546. A disastrous encounter between the English and French forces turned into an episode of total dishonour for the young earl, marking the first stage of Surrey's downfall. Three contemporary documents detail this episode. Despite their variants, all three documents show Surrey had been quite accurate when he had written that the French garrison and labourers at Fort Outreau suffered from want of food and other supplies. He had also been right to speak up for his men; as one of the documents (hardly friendly to Surrey) notes: 'not a penny in the pockets of the common soldiers, because the English had not been paid for nine months.'[1] Without money, the English army had to eat what had been kept in the king's storehouse, much of it spoiled or rotten: 'The bread was hard and baked with corn and meal which lost its taste and savour, and the salt beef stank when it was lifted out of the brine,' butter 'of many colours and the cheese dry and hard' (G 340). Nevertheless, although the Privy Council sent little and Calais could not send supplies except by ship, Surrey had managed to avoid the starvation that threatened the French. In fact, to save Fort Outreau, Maréchal du Biez decided to direct a relief operation himself. He was to take a huge wagon-train along the coast from Montreuil with the protection on either side of 500 French horsemen and 4000 mercenaries.

In the first of the three accounts about the fatal encounter at St Etienne—the report by du Bellay—the Maréchal left the camp before Montreuil and 'prit le chemin du Mont St. Etienne' ('took the road towards Mount St Etienne'). Here he found 'le Milord Sorel' with 6000 English soldiers waiting for him, whereas the Maréchal had 'cinquante homes d'armes' ('fifty men at arms'), each of whom individually would typically have had about five cavalry of his own. To that great number the French had added a mercenary force under a German count of 4000 Landsknechten (infantry) and then, led by a Breton captain, 200 Harquebusiers (carrying the latest and most powerful types of shoulder guns). With the advice of these military aides, the French leader decided to attack when Surrey had trapped him; with a limited force and retiring, du Biez would lose the wagons and supplies if he did not. The French thus marched straight out against Surrey's force, and 'le combat fut longue et furieux' ('the fight was long and furious'), in fact, so much

[1] This is from the account by Elis Gruffydd in National Library of Wales, Mostyn MS 158 ff. 642–5, as translated by M. Bryn Davies, 'Surrey at Boulogne', *HLQ*, 23 (1960), 339–48. All citations from this translation listed as G. I am indebted to Col. Peter R. Moore for interpretation of the episode at St Etienne and for his help in general in understanding Surrey's military strategies.

so that only 'enfin' (finally) were the English forced to retreat from where they had stopped 'en un petit fort' or in a bastion-trench they did not know how to guard. Although 700 to 800 English died, 'Le Milord Sorel, fils du Duc de Northfolk, leur General' escaped with the rest in the flight and 140 or 160 English were captured as prisoners.[2] Du Bellay's account of the length of the battle varies from all the other accounts. It does not emphasize the single event of the day that turned the course of the battle, namely the sudden retreat of the English foot-soldiers in the second line. According to the other accounts, the French were on the point of being routed when this retreat occurred. Surrey's horsemen had already burned the wagons and turned the supplies back, the objective of the encounter having been achieved. But the French had counter-attacked to save what remained.

Surrey's personal anguish became a special focus of disdain in a second contemporary account. Written in Welsh by Ellis Gruffydd, a member of the garrison of Calais from 1527 to 1552, the chronicle exhibits the same ideological frame as do the other parts of his chronicle that deal with the war. Thus, in the Welsh narrative, Surrey becomes an enemy to the true reformed Christian religion and the new Edwardian Tudor state for which audience Gruffydd is writing in 1552. In one of the first modern inscriptions of the proletarian common soldier, Surrey becomes an enemy to the worthy lower-class citizen. Class anger and religious prejudice determine the categories of moral action for Gruffydd. Although the Welsh account gives full details, some no doubt based on original accurate reports (Gruffydd was not a member of the Boulogne garrison and knew nothing first-hand), its errors, as in its first statement, show the author's ideological cast: 'News of this [impending supply train to Fort Outreau] came to the Earl of Surrey, who could have sent for the soldiers in Calais and Guines [Surrey did, in fact, have horsemen from the latter], who were doing nothing [these were foot-soldiers and, as one, Gruffydd should know], but this his pride would not allow him to do, for he wanted the glory for himself alone.'

Whatever the truth of Surrey's 'pride', the poet general surely knew his 'glory' could never be 'for himself alone' for the simple reason that a failure of men could only mean a general's failure. Living in a community defined by terms not his own, Surrey could have nothing for himself alone, not even for the comfort of his family. Such a general was less free, in fact, than anyone on the Welshman's social level of a common soldier. Also, as a good general, Surrey 'called the soldiers suddenly, without warning, and without giving any reason' for going into battle. Spies were everywhere, and as in any war, knowledge of an impending attack by an enemy could mean failure. Further, the English had been skirmishing for weeks. His letters show that the poet earl did recognize just what Gruffydd complained about, how such fighting soldiers needed to 'have raised their hearts which had fallen from sadness and pity at their great poverty'. Surrey's letters also

[2] Martin du Bellay, *Mémoires* in *General Collection of French Memoirs*, vol. 21, 269 cited in N1: 202. According to the English accounts in *LP*, vol. 21, i, 19, the English killed at Saint Etienne were 205, still a large number.

demonstrate that he would never have condoned what Gruffydd says brought 'much hatred and envy' and class warfare between the officers 'and the common soldiers': namely the lechery of 'the captains and those who were getting double pay [foreigners]'. After all, it was the young general who had dismissed the whores and sought to bring his family over. Whatever the reality, Surrey becomes, in such reporting, one more ideological abstraction in the Welshman's view of triumphant history.

In the Welsh account, the skirmish started early that Thursday morning. The English horsemen charged immediately. Then the infantry climbed slowly up the hill towards St Etienne, 'like geese in single file following the gander' so that, when the head of the column was on the field, the tail was just leaving Boulogne two miles away. Surrey's Marshal, Sir Ralph Ellerker, told the general 'to keep to the trench which the French had dug the year before' because of their inferior numbers. 'But the Earl would not listen to him' writes Gruffydd. Surrey wanted to fight 'not like a saintly godly soldier, who would put his trust and hope in God and look to victory more from the intervention of God than from the strength of brutish men, as testified by John and Judas Maccabaeus, and many other devout soldiers as recorded in the Holy Scriptures.' Gruffydd gives a preacher's condemnation: 'No, the Earl paid no heed either to the hand of God and his favours, nor to the unwillingness and lassitude of his soldiers.' In actuality, Surrey's supposedly bad strategy turned out to be correct: 'in the pride of his folly [Surrey] gave orders to destroy the stores which were going to the bailey [Outreau] near by.' Surrey did not prepare his men to meet the enemy ('veterans from Germany') properly 'like a kindly well-intentioned captain, who kept God in his mind, to comfort the soldiers with kindly, tender, godly words'. Surrey did not call 'on God to strengthen the hearts and hand of his soldiers so as to get the upper hand more through the grace of God than his own efforts'. In fact, 'this was very far from the Earl's mind, who, though he was a good scholar, had never followed such [Christian] teachings' and so used harsh language for his soldiers and ordered his captains forward.

Then comes the strange episode that brought the dishonour of St Etienne. In the Welsh chronicle, after the first 'shock [of encounter] the handgunners on either side [of the front line] fired together and after firing' were followed by officers with only swords, as the 'handgunners' retreated behind the second line to load their guns to fire again. 'The ignorant cowardly soldiers saw this as [did] those [other common soldiers] who had never before seen two armies in the course of joining battle, so they turned and began to flee.' The French then became 'as cruel as wolves among sheep' and 'killed 22 of the best and bravest captains of Boulogne [who formed the front lines] in a mass at the same place'. When the English footsoldiers straggled back across the river to Boulogne, the tide came up the Liane from the sea and so the survivors made for the single bridge, the Pont de Bricques, where many were pushed off and drowned. At this point, racing among his troops, 'the Earl cried loudly on the people to turn and fight in order to face the attack, but they would not listen and only retreated faster.' Although the poet was neither trying to escape himself nor encouraging escape, he was horrified at the panic. In the narrative, Surrey is dismayed enough to 'cry out and lament like a man in a frenzy, and he begged Sir John Bridges and some of the gentlemen who were with him to stick their swords through his guts and make him forget the day.' According to Gruffydd, a common English soldier told Surrey to quit all his moaning, just go ahead and kill himself, or let the French do him in.

Not until nine o'clock at night did the English army arrive back, in the Welsh narrative. As soon as 'the Earl and his Council' reached the citadel 'and had taken off their arms and armour', they began to write to the king (it should be noted that, although his is a prejudiced version, the Welshman indicates that Surrey did at once try to inform the king, without delay—a critical point in the later evidence). 'Most sensible men,' says Gruffydd, 'thought it [the defeat] happened because of the lack of any sense of the virtue in praying to God and trusting in him for the victory, but chiefly because of the Earl their leader, whose head and heart were swollen with pride, arrogance, and empty confidence in his own unreasoning bravery.' In his report for the regime of the Lord Protector, the Welshman now tries to blame Surrey and his 'unreasoning bravery' even more. Everyone knew the defeat came from Surrey's 'lack of patience' but the Boulogne Council wanted to absolve him and so found one captain who had first turned back and fled as a scapegoat. 'The Earl caused him to be hung the next morning with two or three of the poor soldiers, more for telling the truth about their captains than for anything they had done against the king.' There is no official record of such hangings, but just before his death, Lord Poynings had hanged one soldier who had complained because the pay was late, and in May 1545, Seymour himself hanged six German mercenaries for mutiny.

Surrey's Letter to the King

The third contemporary account is that by Surrey himself. On the very next morning, a Friday, the poet earl wrote to the king directly to explain—in more chivalric terms—what actually happened. Surrey begins with a calm narration of how his spies told him du Biez was heading towards the new fort, and so 'we took yesterday before day [Thursday, 7 January 1546] the trenches at St. Etienne, with six hundred footmen, and sent out Mr. Ellerkar with all the horsemen of this town; and Mr. Pollard with two hundred that he brought the night before from Guisnes, to discover whither their [French] camp marched.' Just as Pollard and his horsemen were passing by the sand dunes and small pines of Hardelot, Pollard 'was hurt with a culverin in the knee, and died thereof the night following; of whom your Majesty had a notable loss.' It was a good way to begin a letter that could describe nothing but a disaster. This first loss was no one's fault, certainly not Surrey's.

So, as soon as the earl heard of the approach of the French, he issued out from the gates of Boulogne with Bridges, Palmer, Wyatt, and 2000 foot-soldiers, 'and by that time that we had set our horsemen and footmen in order of battle without the trench of St. Etienne,' the French were also ready for battle. Both du Bellay and Surrey narrate how both leaders waited and then made conscious decisions to attack. After Surrey saw the enemy fewer in number than his spies had said and 'the courage and good will that seemed in our men (the surety of your Majesty's pieces being provided for),' the poet general decided to give the order to charge. In a spirit of chivalric 'courage', the English went out 'with a squadre of pikes and bills', sixty in file, and then 'two wings of harquebussiers, and one of bows' and horsemen on the right wing. Surrey now remarks with special emphasis: 'Many of the Captains and Gentlemen were in the first rank by their desire; for because they were well armed in corselets.' Against the advancing German mercenaries allied to the French, with their two wings of deadly harquebussiers and two troops of armed horsemen looming on the horizon, charged the English Lord Marshal Sir Ralph Ellerker; Sir Edward Bellingham, whom Henry VIII had sent over; Sir Thomas Shelley (probably Challoner's hero); and other officers 'with all the horsemen of this town'. Quickly they 'brake their [enemies'] harquebussiers'. The joined forces were now immense; this battle was no longer a skirmish. The enemy horsemen began to flee, and Surrey's horsemen pursued them, killing on every side until they drove the French south, destroying ninety wagons. On the field the English footmen with pikes and bills now met the mercenaries 'with a cry of as great courage, and in as good order as we could wish'.

Then at the trenches, after the first row had shot and the nobility and officers had fought, the second row of common soldiers following them 'were come to the push of the pike'. At the sight of a possibly fierce encounter between themselves and the French pikes, the common support-soldiers (many of them new levies) panicked. 'There grew a disorder in our men, and without cause fled; at which time many of our gentlemen were slain,' announced Surrey flatly. These gentlemen had begun with 'as hardy an onset as hath been seen, and could but have had good success, if they had been followed'. Surrey's army soon retreated to lower trenches but did not stay there and 'took the river', their flight giving the enemy courage to pursue them even though the early winter night had come on. Only in one section of his eloquent letter to Henry VIII did the poet earl suggest the emotion and passion at which Gruffydd had sneered and found so unmanly: 'Assuring your Majesty that the fury of their flight was such, that it booted little the travail that was taken upon every strait to stay them. And so seeing it not possible to stop them, we suffered them to retire to the town.'

Surrey now came to the exacting part of his letter. He must admit the shame but show it in the best possible light. 'Thus was there loss and victory on both sides,' and on that Friday morning he was writing his letter, Surrey and his council had numbered the dead, 205 in all, ten captains dead, among them Edward Poynings, and four missing, Crayford, Palmer, Shelley, and Cobham. 'All these,' said Surrey, 'were slain in the first rank.' Among those on this front line who escaped was the young Wyatt, the earl adding with a special poignance: 'Assuring your Majesty that there were never gentlemen served more hardily, if it had chanced and saving the disorder of our footmen that fled without cause, when all things almost seemed won.' As this aside suggests, from now on, Surrey would find it hard to forgive himself for the first loss of his military career and for the men who were killed in it. As he did here, he would start one subject but his sorrow ends it: 'The enemy took more loss than we, but for the gentlemen; whose loss was much to be lamented.' Surrey keeps justifying the whole adventure and its real success: 'we have kept the field from the break of day'; the enemy, with their large arrays of men and weapons, had pulled out immediately to Montreuil, leaving their carriages behind them. Only twenty carts entered Fort Chatillion and these only with biscuit. Surrey beseeches the king, 'though the success hath not been such as we wished, to accept the good intent of us all; considering,' says Surrey with guileful *litotes*, 'that it seemed to us, in a matter of such importance, a necessary thing to present the fight.' Even at just such a critical moment of humiliation, Surrey remembered his men. The king is to remember the 'good service' of his Lord Marshal Ellerker, 'which was such, as if all the rest had answered to the same, the enemy had been utterly discomforted,' and he recommends Henry Dudley, 'a man for his knowledge, heart, and of good service,' for the vacant position now, with Poynings dead, of Captain of his Majesty's guard in Boulogne.

In the final part of his letter, the young earl reflects on this loss whose effect will soon be much greater than he could imagine. First, 'th'enemies enterprise [was] disappointed.' More French were slain than English and the new French fort 'in as great misery as before' and then a bitter reminder with the rhythms of verse: 'and a sudden flight the let [hindrance] of a full victory.' At this point in his dispatch, Surrey theorizes that the real problem may lie in the English common soldier. Assigning no fault to himself or his advisers (as might be expected in any Tudor officer), Surrey does add one final surmise: the fault may be inherent in the mercurial nature not only of war and its fortunes but in the independence of the English national character: 'And if any disorder there were,' wrote Surrey, 'we assure your Majesty there was no default in the rulers, nor lack of courage to be given them, but a humor that sometime reigneth in Englishmen.' Thinking of these common soldiers leads to the evidence that Gruffydd had it right: the English foot-soldiers, many raw recruits, were not being paid. Surrey is tactful but firm: 'humbly thanking your Majesty that it hath pleased the same to consider their payment,' Surrey knows such payment 'shall much revive their hearts to adventure most willingly their lives, according to their most bounden duty, in your Majesty's service, to make recompence for the disorder that now they have made.' In a postscript, Surrey asks, as if indirectly, the real question: 'It may please your Majesty to resolve what is further to be done by us' (N1: 198–202).

Court Reaction

Lord Herbert of Cherbury's account of the episode ends with a paraphrase of du Bellay: 'the earl himself also being constrain'd to save himself as he could' (HB 602). It was a description that would characterize the rest of Surrey's life. Immediately, so Lord Herbert dramatically noted, Surrey's letter of 8 January to Henry VIII 'yet did so little satisfy our king (who lov'd no noise but of victory), that he ever after disaffected him [Surrey]: for which cause also he was shortly remov'd, and the Earl of Hertford appointed to succeed' (714–15). After Surrey's débâcle, the English court feared the loss of national reputation on the continent. The Privy Council soon wrote to Winchester at Bruges and to other diplomats: 'The Frenchmen will doubtless report it as a great victory, because in the misorder they got one or two of the captains' ensigns. Our men, however, gained their object.' The court's fear was justified: the encounter at St Etienne was considered a military disaster for Henry VIII and was viewed as such throughout Europe. Hardly more than a week after the disaster of St Etienne, the new Imperial ambassador, van der Delft, was writing to the Emperor that the English had lost at St Etienne 'about 1,200 foot-soldiers, with 8 English and 4 Italian captains' and then added what he considered so important that Charles V needed to know: 'The Earl of Surrey has consequently lost greatly in reputation, and there is considerable discontent at these heavy losses.'[3]

In the weeks and months ahead, the disgrace that grew and the slackening of interest in Surrey's military strategies may have been part of a process of entrapment, but biographers like Nott and Casady are wrong to assume that Surrey had greater gifts than his enemies who were supposedly setting a trap to destroy the poet. There was hardly any comparison in 1545 between the position of the Earl of Hertford, Edward Seymour, both as *vir armatus* and *vir togatus* at this time, and Surrey, and far less as the year wore on. Seymour had not only distinguished himself as the leading military figure of England, both in Scotland and in France, but had also represented the king in almost every major diplomatic initiative. Whatever the immense promise of Surrey, both Seymour and Dudley, the Lord Admiral, more than matched the poet earl in their greater experience, as Hertford was already around 50 and the Lord Admiral about 43. Not only their achievements but their genealogy was superior to that of most of the court. Seymour and Surrey were, in fact, cousins as the descendants of Edward III. Imperial and French ambassadors were right to note that Seymour and Dudley were the most competent leaders of the Tudor court and, in any dispensation in the succession, they would have power. Norfolk was quite correct by late spring 1546 to want, once more, to form a family alliance between Hertford's children and those of either Surrey or his younger son Lord Thomas. Even Dudley now had wider experience than Surrey, both as Lord Admiral and as military strategist, and as a clever

[3] *LP*, vol. 21, i, 65. *CSPSpan*, vol. 8, 184, 186, 226.

courtier who had played cards with the ageing king, for example, through most of the winter of 1545–6. Most of all, for whatever reasons (Surrey's lack of independence from his father did not help), the poet earl had not built substantial networks for himself within the court itself, nor did he have any faction of his own to join in or gain any support. Whatever texts of self he would put forth in the next months could only be his alone. Politically, the Howard heir was already dead.

Thus, the court letters that followed the débâcle at St Etienne show how isolated Surrey was becoming. On 11 January 1546, the Privy Council sent a letter to Surrey, curiously dated (11 December): they have heard of the encounter and of the death of Sir George Pollard and 'cannot but marvel very much that in so many days you have advertised hither no part of that matter'. If Surrey had been successful in his encounter, the 'great wisdom' of the king 'might have tended to your further success and comfort' but 'if your chance at this time have not been even so good as you would have wished [an echo of Surrey's own phrasing] yet his Majesty . . . of his great clemency considereth the uncertainty and unstable chance of the wars, knowing the truth might and would perchance have resolved upon such order for the redubbe, and supply of this loss.' In fact, 'his Majesty hath specially commanded us to require you t'advertise without further delay, the very truth and whole circumstances of this chance.' Furthermore, in any other situation or anything else the king should know about, Surrey is 'to fail not' to inform the king 'of the full truth thereof accordingly' (N1: 196–7).

Surrey could not miss what had happened: his close relationship with Henry VIII had ended. The failure at St Etienne had ignited the series of explosive disasters that had been waiting for months for just such an event. Surrey became vulnerable all at once. From France, Surrey had guessed what might happen. He dispatched on 10 January the one figure as close to him in 1545 as Clere had been, a virtual *alter ego*, the younger Thomas Wyatt, to explain what has really happened. The disaster at St Etienne haunts all his work now so that, in a later letter to the king (13 February), when asking for special recognition 'of your princely liberality' for horsemen, Surrey added with a kind of melancholy: 'Assuring your Highness that the service here is more accident to losses, than in any other place where your Majesty is served' (N1: 206).

Paget, the king's secretary, now became the stern voice of the king and the council. A letter from Paget in this period shows the devastating effect of Surrey's dishonour at St Etienne, or at least its interpretation at court and the dramatic change in Surrey's reputation everywhere. After acknowledging various plans the earl has put forth, Paget takes the 'occasion to write unto you frankly my poor opinion; trusting your Lordship will take the same in no worse part than I mean it.' First, Edward Seymour, the Earl of Hertford, is not only coming over; he is be the new King's Lieutenant General in France and 'I fear your authority of Lieutenant shall be touched, for I believe that the later ordering of a Lieutenant taketh away the commission of him that was there before.' Paget proceeds to lecture Surrey on honour. 'Now, my Lord, because you have been pleased I should write mine advice to your Lordship in things concerning your honour and benefit, I could no less do than put you in remembrance how much in mine opinion this shall touch your honour' if you do not act properly and do not remain 'in silence' until Hertford comes over. Surrey could lose not only his 'authority' at Boulogne but 'also it should fortune ye to come abroad without any place of estimation in the field; which the world would much muse at, and, though there be no such matter, [the world would] think you were rejected upon occasion of some either negligence, inexperience, or such other fault; for so many heads[,] so many judgments.' Paget, of lowly birth, advises further the Howard heir, the grandson of the 'Flodden Duke' and the Duke of Buckingham, the close friend of the king's first son. The poet earl should demote himself to a commander of the vanguard or the rear 'or to such other place of honour as should be meet for you; for so should you be where knowledge and experience may be gotten'. Indeed, perhaps, he will find an occasion 'to do some notable service in revenge of your men, at the last encounter with the enemies, which should be to your reputation in the world'. Paget could now ignore all Surrey had achieved; he became patronizing: 'Whereas, being hitherto noted as you are a man of a noble courage, and of a desire to shew the same to the face of your enemies, if you should now tarry at home within a wall, having I doubt [fear] a shew of your authority touched, it would be thought abroad either you were desirous to tarry in a sure place of rest, or else that the credit of your courage and forwardness to serve were diminished; and that you were taken here for a man of [little] activity or service.' Paget hopes that Surrey will 'use' him 'as a mean to his Majesty' to find 'such a place as may best stand with your honour'. When Seymour comes over, said Paget on 25 February 1546, 'the Earl of Hertford shall be the King's Lieutenant of the army,' with Dorset as 'Captain of the Foreward, and the Earl of Surrey, who is yet Captain of Boulogne, shall lead the rearward.'[4] By 8 March, whatever the poet earl's control, Seymour will make the appointments. Surrey's men are no longer his. Henry VIII also wants Rogers' plans for the fortifications to be used, because of 'the uncertainty of your opinions touching that matter', a fact that must have surprised Surrey who two months before had submitted a precise plan. Rogers is 'plain and blunt', but the king wants his plans followed (N 216–17).

In response to Paget's March letter and the others, Surrey wrote his last long dispatch from Boulogne on 15 March 1545. He outlined what he had already done to fortify the city and recalled the plat he had earlier sent, one devised with Southwell. The poet earl is quite detailed and complains that Rogers has not been cooperative, to the distress of his men. 'And now, Mr. Secretary, as one that neither

[4] At the same time, Surrey became vulnerable at the front in France. Lord Gray at Calais wanted more of the Boulogne men, and Surrey was angry at him for such a demand, to which fight Paget added the aside that describes the new atmosphere: '(whatsoever untrue reports which any man, which travaileth by sinister means to set your two Lordships at variance, to the continual torment, if it so be, of yourselves and the dangerous hinderance of his Majesty's affairs doth tell your Lordship).' Even the Italians now wanted to serve under Seymour. *Historical Manuscripts Commission*, vol. 3, 212; LP vol. 21,i, 272.

dare keep silence [as Paget had wanted], nor meddle in those things that are excluded out of my charge, I can do yet no less in discharge of my duty but revoke my consent from the plat of this garrison devised by me.' In fact, Surrey continued, 'beseeching you to think that if the zeal that I bear to his Majesty's service did not touch me, I would be loth to speak like an ignorant fool in things that are before weighed and considered by men of more experience.' But the 'zeal' does 'touch' him. Surrey intended that the king should know his own royal role in supplying Boulogne: 'Mistrusting not but his Highness most prudently considereth that it were not meet the state of this jewel should depend upon the success of any other enterprize; but to be furnished of men and victuals of himself [itself]: which, how time, th'enemy, and the visitation of God may waste, the year past may serve you for a precedent.' Finally Surrey had not only been fortifying Boulogne but making his own skirmishes; in the latest around Outreau, 'I see that the Frenchmen can run as fast away up the hill, as the Englishmen not long ago ran down,' a reference to St Etienne. He commends the two leaders of the foot-soldiers to Paget and hopes he will thank them, and says that, if Paget had come over to see a skirmish, he wishes the King's Secretary had seen this one (N 220–3).

The answer from the Privy Council on 21 March is clear: by 'mouth' (whose?) the king has heard that Surrey considers some danger 'in works appointed to be done there' and since Surrey 'cannot be so well able in writing to express [his] mind' than if he were at court himself, he is required to return to England. In fact, 'for as much as his Majesty hath now of fresh advertisements again of treasons that are conspired, specially touching the victuals, and munition of these pieces; his Majesty prayeth you all to have a marvellous diligent regard thereto.' Each man is 'to look to his particular charge as no traiterous enterprise be unforeseen, whereby should ensue any danger to any his Highness's said pieces.' For the first time, the association of Surrey and treason has been made. Within ten days the young earl was in England. In his last letter about Boulogne, dated 14 July 1546, almost five months to the day before his beheading, Surrey lashed out with that 'frankness' that he says Paget will know 'is my natural, to use' with friends, to say 'upon my honour' the king's funds were not squandered on foreigners (in fact, at Boulogne Surrey spent 'an hundred ducats of mine own purse, and somewhat else'). In unjustly dismissing Surrey's servants, Lord Gray had said these servants and Surrey himself used certain funds to Surrey's 'gain', a point designed, Surrey felt, to insult him. The earl demands the restitution of these funds to his servants, funds the servants 'hath lost, and purchased so dearly with so many dangers of life'. As for Gray, who was his subordinate when Surrey was in charge of all the king's forces in France and had resented the Howard general, in his accusation of Surrey, 'he can have none honour.' Although for the Howard heir to receive this accusation was tantamount to a challenge, the former general wants the record straight in what is his own challenge: 'For there be in Boulogne too many witnesses that Henry of Surrey was never for singular profect [profit] corrupted; nor never yet bribe closed his hand: which lesson I learned of my Father; and wish to succeed him therein as in the rest' (N 227–31).

On 28 March, the special Imperial emissary Scepperus reported back: 'The Earl of Surrey, formerly captain of Boulogne, arrived at Court yesterday, but was coldly received and did not have access to the king.' He also noted Norfolk's absence from the court. If Surrey did intend to go back to Boulogne after March 1546, and Paget had suggested he would go back 'for the ordering of his things there', the poet earl must also have known that, once at court, he could never leave it until the battle for the Protectorate was decided. At home the poet earl was receiving gifts from the king that did not appear to represent disfavour. Early in April, Surrey acquired, in recognition of 'his services' in France, Wymondham Priory in Norfolk, the conventual buildings and estates, their 'reversion and rent', with the single exception of the rectory and advowson of the parish church. In May he was named to the commission to collect further benevolences in Norfolk because the legacy of Boulogne had dramatically affected the whole economic network of England. In early June Surrey quarrelled with his sister about the Seymour marriage proposals, a quarrel that was widely interpreted as saying that Surrey had invited his sister to become Henry VIII's whore. Once again that summer, Surrey's words betrayed him. The Lord Admiral Dudley received a letter from him. He promptly turned it into evidence against the poet earl, writing to Paget on 12 July: 'I send a letter which my Lord of Surrey sent unto my lodgings this morning, wherein is contained so many parables that I do not perfectly understand it. This letter (if you think it meet) I require you to show it to the King's Majesty.'[5] Surrey's letter to the Lord Admiral does not survive, but another does. In August, Surrey wrote to Mary Shelton, once one of a 'league' of three. By then, every sign by the poet earl may have been carefully and secretly watched. The letter was later seized as evidence for the Privy Council, as Southwell's own inscription on the letter attests. In the increasing breakdown of the king's body, the prize of the Protectorate was now too great to be ignored. As Challoner's elegy suggests, his enemies may have known there was only one solution for their own progressing history: such a poet Earl of Surrey, the body in his last portrait with its obvious aspirations, had to be annihilated. Surrey was providing them with the ripe moment—if in no other way, just by remaining himself. Whatever he did, the enough that would now survive—especially his texts of grandeur, like his portrait—provided enough to kill him.

[5] *LP* vol. 21,i, 488, 1263. Cf. Casady, *Henry Howard*, 178.

PART III

'Enough survives'

13

Surrey's Last Portrait

Time was running out. The race for the succession, in which the winner would take all, was coming to an end. In these last months, Surrey had his portrait painted with the symbolic theme of time and its uses (Frontispiece). In the portrait, the poet represents himself at his most glorious, the redeemer of fleeting time—Virgil's 'irreparabile tempus'. His own detailed body reveals, under an almost theatrical Italian arch with the inscription 'ANNO DNI 1546 AETATIS SVE 29,' a special symbolic message in the motto of the portrait: 'Enough Survives.' Unlike all the other bodies that had disappeared one after another in the reign of Henry VIII, this glorious male body rises out of the canvas towards the future of a new Renaissance—if only his audience will seize the message on the canvas.

In the summer of 1546, the earl sent instructions to the painter of his final portrait with a letter to Mary Shelton, later seized by his betrayer, Sir Richard Southwell. It is probable therefore in that summer and autumn the painter Gwillem Scrots (William Stretes) was finishing a grand portrait of the poet earl that a recent discovery has shown to have been begun at least a year, if not two, before. In an increasingly hopeless political situation, Surrey could project few texts. His biblical translations were gaining favour in the reformed court, but only when he had finished the first six books of the *Aeneid* could he introduce his epic language to the audience that would decide his political fate. Now he needed a bolder statement than translations, a grander text. Whether the version now at Arundel Castle in the south of England is the original or not, grandeur did exist in the 1546 original, as a series of documents from the later Renaissance shows. This iconic grandeur was thus part of Surrey's political strategy during his last months. Emblematic evidence, intricately structured into the portrait, showed that the poet Earl Henry of Surrey possessed a right to be Protector to the young Prince Edward, soon to be king.

Of all the Roman roles, the Protectorate in 1546 epitomized the greatest for the *boni amici*, the *amici principis*. By the symbolic logic of his portrait, Surrey thus demonstrates a presence for that role, a *corpus delicti* with promise of a future, a body whose genealogy of honour, in text-making and blood, no one else could claim. So intended and so viewed, the result was predictable. The picture was seized for trial evidence and Surrey deemed a threat to carefully worked-out plans for the succession. He was, in Wriothesley's own terms, 'an unmeet man to live in a commonwealth,' certainly of the kind the future Lord Protector and Duke of Northumberland envisioned.

Thus, on 5 March 1551, a record of a payment was made to 'gwillm [Guillim or William] Strete [Stretes or Scrots]', the Flemish court painter, for three 'tables', two of the young king and one of the then attainted and beheaded Surrey: 'To gwillm Strete the k. painter the som of L [50] marke for recompense of iij great tables [full-length] made by the sayd Gwillm whereof ij were the pictures of his highness sent to Sr Phillip hobby and Sr John Mason [royal ambassadors abroad]. The third was a picture of the late earle of Surrey attainted and by the counsailes comaundement fetched from the said Gwillms howse.' Was Scrots working on the portrait at the time of the poet earl's arrest when it was 'fetched' from the artist's studio and confiscated for signs of treason? Indeed, a year earlier in the autumn of 1545, when Surrey was at the front in France, his father's steward Hussey had written to him that his portrait had been delayed because the painter was busy working on a portrait of Queen Catherine Parr (Plate 13). Textual evidence in this letter, recently discovered, thus dates the inception of this last portrait. Given the sensitivity of the queen to the latest continental styles (as witnessed by her elaborate costume and protocol during the visit of the Imperial Duke of Najera early in her marriage), and her frequent exchange of portraits with the royal family, including portraits by Scrots, it is entirely possible the delay continued.

Scrots may indeed have been working on Surrey's last portrait in summer, autumn, and December 1546. Yet, whether Surrey's last portrait was finished or not, his audience clearly saw enough. Surrey's intent was soon transformed from offence into treason, a point William Thomas, Clerk of Edward VI's Privy Council, would make about a picture of Surrey. Henry, Earl of Surrey, says Thomas in 1552, had not only arrogated to himself royal arms but in 'one picture especially', he 'had painted himself with the crown on his right hand and the King on his left hand'.[1] No such picture appears to have existed (and Thomas probably never saw any picture of Surrey); Thomas was referring to documents about the trial, including the allusion to a portrait that had a picture of a child in it, whom Thomas identified as the young Prince Edward. In his defence of Henry VIII, Thomas had known that it was probably Surrey's last portrait that had been a part of the evidence against the attainted earl. Of course, it was natural for Seymour, Dudley, and Paget to take quite seriously any picture by the official court painter, but especially one of the Howard heir who had had himself sketched, drawn, and painted more times, as Strong notes, than anyone else at the court of Henry VIII, except for the king. Even in an age when portraits had social and political uses, documenting events as a modern photograph might, the number of surviving representations is exceptional. The portrait at Arundel Castle today shows why. With the calculated intimacy almost all Surrey's portraits have, the Arundel portrait

[1] BL MS Royal 18 CXXIV, f. 69v. Cf. also John Strype, *Ecclesiastical Memorials*, vol. 2,ii, 217. Strype incorrectly names Thomas Hoby, not his brother Philip. For a recent discovery about the painter, see W. A. Sessions, 'The Earl of Surrey and Catherine Parr: A Letter and Two Portraits' *ANQ: A Quarterly Journal of Short Articles, Notes, and Reviews*, MS 5/2–3 (April–July 1992), 128–30. William Thomas, *The Pilgrim: A Dialogue on the Life and Actions of King Henry VIII*, edited J. A. Froude (1861), 72–4.

displays the entire body of Henry Howard as no other body of the English blood nobility had quite been portrayed before. In fact, as Waterhouse suggests, the original by Guillem (William) Scrots (Stretes) in 1546 may have been the first full-length individualized portrait of a nobleman in England in the latest continental fashion of mannerism, even in Italianate dress.[2] For all Tudor and Stuart audiences, the elaborate full-length could not but contrast with the Holbein Henry VIII looming over the court at Whitehall. Surrey may have wanted such a daring public analogy (as he had dared to break codes with the printed Wyatt elegy and the Clere sonnet), but it is just as probable the young poet earl had in mind, as an analogy to his portrait, those elegant models of charisma and personality in the northern Italian and Imperial full-length studies of young men in black. Scrots, the king's official artist after the death of Holbein, had already painted a number of full-lengths for the Imperial family, all quite public and viewed by the Habsburg courts. They were more avant-garde than anything in England and, for the reason of stylish originality, he had been brought to England with a large salary.

Surrey was an early subject for Scrots. (Was the Howard friend the Bishop of Winchester the intermediary who brought Scrots over, suggesting Surrey as subject?) In the succession crisis of 1546, Surrey's portrait was to focus a point in time so that a displayed body of Aristotelian magnanimity (as described in the *Ethics* and rendered by mannerist wizardry) enacts all the possibilities Surrey's life had brought him to. The symbolic argument of his right to the Protectorate would be there for all to see in an emblematic frame an audience knew how to read, only twenty years away from reading stained-glass windows, icons, and statues. It was better than any shouting argument, which could only lead to more violence. Above all, the portrait justifies the humanist Latin motto inscribed on the dark plinth of the golden column on which the central figure is leaning: 'SAT SVPER EST.' Time has been fulfilled in the young earl pausing under that arch of time and directing by look and gesture the way to the new city. With that look (in a slightly turned face, uneven eyes, tense lines between the eyebrows) and an open mouth probably speaking, Surrey's body poses the question of the right faction. He asks nothing less than conversion of the spectator to his cause of greater nobility, all within the overwhelming reality of himself that could not be denied.

Such an effect of subjectivity could only come from manipulated structure. In this sense, Surrey's instructions to the painter must have focused on a detailed

[2] Strong, *Tudor Portraits*, vol. 1, 370. Ellis Waterhouse, *Painting in Britain 1530 to 1790* (1953), 25–6. For the importance of these portraits, see Catherine MacLeod, 'Guillim Scrots in England', unpublished MA report (Courtauld Institute, University of London, May 1990), ch. 2. The portraits of Edward VI differ from the Surrey portrait whose face is, according to MacLeod, 'more three-dimensional than Edward's'. Both faces are long with schematic eyes set apart (as also in Scrots' portrait of the Archduke Ferdinand) and with rather thick eyelids. In the portrait of Edward VI at the Los Angeles County Museum, the relationship of the full-length stance to the Surrey portrait is more striking because of the son's deliberate spread-eagled imitation of his father and the direct gaze. The Italianate style might have included an opening down the doublet but for Surrey this is avoided in order to give the highest effect to his Great George, one of the focal points of the power portrait.

logic of emblems within a holistic symbolic frame—precisely the relationship of total effect and detailed interpretation Gombrich sees as the mark of the true *icones symbolicae*. Gombrich finds 'symbolism which gains new importance in the Renaissance with the revival of Neo-Platonism' not in generalized figures but in precisely detailed and historical 'revelation'. For him, 'antithesis between aesthetic and literary interpretation, between sensuality and symbol, may be largely imported' by later generations. Immense details in a picture may portray, in fact, signs as well as authentic realism. Conversely, a simple design (whether a Japanese drawing or a Mondrian) does not necessarily convey symbolic meaning. 'A moment's reflection will show,' Gombrich argues, 'that the most schematic or rudimentary image can be intended as a [realistic] representation of an individual while the most detailed portrait can stand for the concept or type,' that is, appear as symbolic or emblematic argument.[3] In 1546, at hand for Surrey and Scrots was the Renaissance emblematic tradition that had accelerated with Alciati fifteen years before in Italy (and Hadrianus Junius wrote a letter to Alciati in the 1540s from Kenninghall on their common interests). In this tradition of exact representation between verbal text and picture, which influenced mannerism at its inception, the signs in Surrey's last portrait (especially if coupled with a text like 'SAT SVPER EST') could provide 'events'. These were equal to those in any written humanist text and even hold a superior relationship to that printed text.

In fact, as Kipling demonstrates about Burgundian origins for such perception in England,[4] any strict dichotomy of texts, political, visual, literary, would probably not have occurred to early Tudor courtiers. Habits of perception were still substantially unaffected by the increasingly stark emphasis on letter and printed text that reformed Christians and humanists were bringing in the place of performative religious icons from their own recent present, such as the cultic wooden statue of Our Lady of Walshingham, publicly burned only nine years before by Cromwell. In portraits, as Early Modern English courts knew well, the details often indulged in idealized fantasy and even lies, as in the visualizations of religious cults. But at their centre was, more often than not, a genuine historicity. Because of this basis in actual history, the symbolic and the probable—'tout imaginaire'—could always lead not only to social reality but political interpretation and even a programme of conversion.

The Portrait at Arundel Castle

This logic of emblems, the evolution of symbol into the probability of an act, appears most clearly in the elaborate portrait at Arundel Castle (Frontispiece).

[3] E. H. Gombrich, '*Icones Symbolicae*: The Visual Image in Neo-Platonic Thought', *Journal of the Warburg and Courtauld Institutes*, 11 (1948), 167, 185, 187. For the effect of such a symbolic argument, see Starkey, *Reign*, 146.

[4] Gordon Kipling, *The Triumph of Honour*, ch. 3 and 4.

Plainer full-lengths at Parham Park and at Knole, both dating from the Renaissance, or a nineteenth-century imitation at Castle Howard express the essential gestures of pausing and leaning on a broken column.[5] With a more mercurial body, Surrey stares as candidly at the viewer as Holbein's Henry VIII, his feet apart like the king's but, instead of thick calves calmly balancing immense weight, Surrey's legs are bent, a sprinter's body slightly coiled as though ready to break through the coarse canvas—the physical embodiment of the Latin motto. As it exists today on the east wall of the Barons Hall at Arundel Castle, the portrait is a large single-canvas painting of approximately 87 inches by 86, rather unfinished on its left side and at its bottom. The young man rests his right arm momentarily on the broken shaft of a golden column, his other hand nonchalantly on his hip. Behind him a flowing cape suggests motion in the middle of which the young man has paused. The broad massive centring of the dark-brown fur cape gives it the effect of a Roman toga adapted to Surrey's place and time and, most important, to Surrey's formal style as renewed *vir comitatus*, worthy to be called in the future as all Dukes of Norfolk were, 'Right High and Mighty Prince'. With his right arm leaning, Surrey's left arm is akimbo against the thick cape so that the wide dark surface seems to spring from him. If Surrey is not quite 'Wrapped in my careless cloak', in the words of his popular Petrarchan lyric, the cape does highlight his elongated torso and fitted black doublet. Silver filigree covers that doublet and extends to his short breeches so that Surrey's body has the tight shape of an adapted Roman warrior framed against the flowing cape. In fact, the cape does not seem to have caught up with the driving momentum of the young man, but it will—so the narrative in the portrait seems to say—because in the next moment this man of action, his left arm akimbo, will be hurrying on.

The poet earl appears to have just emerged through the arch with his age on it. His whole body in the centre-piece is bathed in a light that comes off-stage from left of the viewer, the place on the canvas where conventionally the reading of Renaissance portraits begins. Waiting impatiently before his audience, the figure of 'fastidious elegance' with an open mouth beneath a red tufted moustache and an untrimmed beard speaks. On either side of him, in a kind of purgatorial grey (with the exception of two brightly coloured shields) are two statues, close-mouthed, male and female, and with them, as Auerbach notes, an 'Italianate accessory decoration of columns, garlands, reliefs, cherubs, masks, and arches'. In contrast to Surrey's light-filled three-quarter stare at the spectator are the blind or downcast eyes of the draped pallid figures in the frame outside the brightly lit body. The frame is crucial to interpretation of the picture. Thus, ascending to the architrave from the young nude ancestors with their shields are swags of elongated fruit, eight motion-filled but blind *putti* amid vases and goat-heads, all

[5] For a full discussion of the differences among these portraits, recently examined by X-rays, see MacLeod, 'Guillim Scrots', 36–7. There may be one more variant of the Surrey portrait recently auctioned in New York.

figures *en grisaille*, silver-grey and melancholy and set against a reddish-gold ground, simulating porphyry. These frame designs, with their possible origin in what Surrey saw at Fontainebleau,[6] operate amid crowned grotesque Silenus heads with mouths wide open and bucrania or decorated animal skulls, all decidedly Bacchic. The frame has the effect of a masque setting.

What they project is the life of the imagination and the past outside present time, an unconscious (even bestial) world of art and history. The emblematic function of the frame is thus the same as that of its centre: the ghost-like male and female figures identified only by their heraldic shields and a naked sexuality (more symbolic before Victorian draperies were added) represent the force of time. Thus the shields, the only touch of full colour in the frame and the richest colour in the entire picture, depict the earl's direct descent from two kings. In the male hand is a detailed shield from the Howard father: the arms of the son of Edward I, Thomas of Brotherton, the Earl of Norfolk, the arms of England but significantly with an argent label of three points for difference (a label that was later used for Edward III's heir, the Black Prince, and became the sign of an heir apparent). In the female hand is a shield from the Stafford mother: the arms of the son of Edward III, Thomas of Woodstock, quarterly within a bordure argent, that mark, without the Woodstock border, the standard arms used by English monarchs from about 1406 to 1603. It is the inclusion of these latter arms deriving from the Staffords that offers possible evidence that the Arundel portrait could not have been painted during the time of Henry VIII when, after the attainder of Surrey's grandfather, the Duke of Buckingham, such arms no longer existed and certainly could not have been displayed in public. Even in the Arundel portrait, one specialist has argued that the marks of cadency in each are painted 'as unobtrusive as possible' with the Brotherton white label 'almost invisible' and the argent bordure on the Woodstock shield of Surrey's mother a grey that blends into the background. Surrey's links to royalty, his claims to the throne, are heightened and the distinctions muted.[7] Thus, leaning on columns as does the hero of the portrait, the naked pair direct the viewer to focus on the present fertility of the hero in living colour, his genealogy worthy to make him a possible king, certainly a rightful protector for a king. By such technical discrimination and grey shading, the glowing white of Surrey's youthful face and his bright uneven eyes above an orange-tawny beard are allowed to focus directly, even emotionally, upon the spectator, to demonstrate that fertile life of possibilities.

Elaborately dressed, the young man bears across his broad chest the chain collar of the Order of the Garter, England's highest mark of nobility, and, depending

[6] The first quotation is from William Graunt, *Court Painting in England from Tudor to Victorian Times* (1980), 28. Erna Auerbach, *Tudor Artists* (1954), 91. Cf. her 'Holbein's followers in England', *Burlington Magazine*, 93 (1951), 49. For theories about the influence of Fontainebleau on this portrait, see the entry on the Arundel Castle portrait of Surrey in *Dynasties: Painting in Tudor and Jacobean England 1530–1630*, ed. Karen Hearn (1995), 49–52. While this entry has some factual errors and an unproven theory about the provenance of the portrait, it introduces quite well the mystery of this last picture of the poet earl.

from it, the Great George or magnificently encased jewel of St George, the patron saint of the nation. Strongly lit are Surrey's hands, both without rings, the right one clasping, casually but firmly, finely detailed off-white gloves that he may soon put on again. Such handling of gloves, an expensive item in Renaissance dress, indicated superiority (Surrey's holding them attracts attention just as Castiglione wanted a woman handling gloves to do). If the position of the hands—and the fact that he is ungloved—imply a readiness to draw his rapier if necessary, the rather stiff glove-fingers themselves support Surrey's own index finger. That finger points directly to the rounded codpiece nestled between supple thighs. This latter effect of fertility is reinforced by the spectral nude male statue that begins the picture on Surrey's left. The message of full-seeded genealogy is thus rendered in Surrey's last portrait as in Holbein's Henry VIII at Whitehall. In fact, at the base of the erection of the golden-red column, its cornice and plinth, the universal Latin text announces Surrey's own force of genealogy: 'SAT SVPER EST.'

It is clear, then, that this light-filled body is intimately tied to a special genealogy centred in the three bodies (as in the four bodies of Holbein's Whitehall mural). In the portrait, therefore, such genealogy operates as 'conceptual metaphor not marginal cartoon', as Spiegel suggests, a process of enough 'surviving' to project a 'narrative *mythos*' that 'governs the very shape and significance of the past'. Serial genealogy can become, in this sense, ironic freedom, as Foucault notes, a 'singularity of events [in an individual descended body] outside of any monotonous finality'. Basic to all such achievement in genealogy, then, is the freedom, however painful, of a singularity that can dissipate, in Foucault's term, its own life-force—what in fact Auerbach has catalogued about the Renaissance Howard heir, who 'encouraged the introduction of classic architecture' and 'the Italian style of music' and, as his last portrait signifies, 'the beginning of the Italo-Flemish Renaissance style in England, a style which was already generally accepted everywhere on the Continent during that period' and one among several styles that made Surrey's 'influence on the visual arts (as well as on poetry) . . . still noticeable in the second half of the century'.[8] However accurate this account, Surrey did emerge as a legend of new charisma but with a difference that can only be recognized at first (or always) in its singular ambiguity.

Such ambivalence does hardly more than confirm what Lee Patterson remarks about Troilus, Surrey's prototypical hero (as for Henry V, who carried Chaucer's text with him, possibly to Agincourt): the Trojan prince is 'an inextricable compound of deep feeling and play acting, the authentic and the theatrical'. Ambivalence also marks an aphorism on Surrey by a contemporary: 'All greatnesse is subject to envy; but none more than that which is insolent and affected,

[7] Brian Abel Ragan, 'Semiotics and Heraldry', *Semiotica*, 100/1 (1994), 32.

[8] Gabrielle M. Spiegel, 'Genealogy: Form and Function in Medieval Historical Narrative', *History and Theory*, 22/1 (1983), 48–50. Foucault, *Language*, 148, also 153, 155, 157. At that moment of renewal and origination of new form for Foucault, the individual in history becomes, in a special phallic image, 'the vertical projection of its [own] position'. In Foucault's metaphor, It links up. Auerbach, *Tudor Portraits*, 73.

being never its selfe without its pomp and shew.' But the point of such 'shew' is what Nietschze understood about the nature of genealogy and its singular 'resistance' to a seemingly inevitable progression of a history that always calls itself modern. Genealogy must be rewritten in blood, as Nietschze suggests, made a new text either of body or mind (or both), if any new direction for nobility is to be given. This canon of genealogy both Henry VIII and Surrey lived by, for in their world, as Duby comments, 'to be noble is to be able to refer to a genealogy,'[9] roots that lead to greater life even at the price of self-annihilation or that of others. In such a world, at least for Surrey, only textualized ambivalence—seen as violence by his enemies—could provide the proper 'resistance' of the singular self to overwhelming history and offer any hope of building, in the midst of actual violence, a new city of 'nobul hartys'.

To resist is therefore to be bold and even reckless, a point Sir Thomas Hoby may have meant when he translated Castiglione's crucial term of *sprezzatura* as 'recklessnesse'. By twentieth-century standards, Hoby's early Tudor translation of the word hardly seems appropriate to describe the art of avoiding affectation and the true art that does not pretend to be art. It is, however, to miss what Surrey's younger contemporary understood in the English courtier and in Castiglione's text, which the poet earl knew well: all such 'resistance' or *sprezzatura* requires that an encounter with history be taking place, not Platonic detachment. Any real encounter with time must be made performance—art hiding art—and, as theatre, be dialogic enough (that is, hold to a serial, not unitive sequence in performance) in order to balance options for a real future. If, as Rebhorn comments,[10]

[9] Patterson, *Chaucer*, 151. Cf. Michael André Bernstein's opening of his review of Ralph Freedman's *Life of a Poet: Rainer Maria Rilke* in the *New Republic* (23 May 1996): 'An incessant self-mythologizing and an unmistakable authenticity collided in Rilke's writing virtually from the beginning.' BL Sloane MS 34. Georges Duby, 'Structures de parente et noblesse dans la France du nord aux Xle et Xlle siecles', in *Hommes et structures du moyen age* (1973), 283. Cf. E. Le Roy Ladurie, 'Family Structures and Inheritance Customs in Sixteenth Century France', in *Family and Inheritance, Rural Society in Western Europe 1200–1800*, ed. J. Goody, J. Thirsk, and E. P. Thompson (1976), 56. Le Roy Ladurie explains the semiotics of noble genealogy as operating as a downward drive, as 'sap Flowing downward, according to some mysterious force, to nourish the lower limits and offshoots of a tall tree'.

[10] Wayne A. Rebhorn, *Courtly Performances: Masking and Festivity in Castiglione's Book of the Courtier* (1978), 180, 41, 18. For an interpretation of Castiglione's term that reflects Surrey's own strategy in his last portrait, see Frank Whigham, *Ambition and Privilege: The Social Tropes of Elizabethan Courtesy Theory* (1994), esp. 93–5: 'Theoretically speaking, then, if rank cannot be grasped voluntarily, its fundamental manifestations will be seen as unchosen, simply self-expressive, not aimed to transmit information or to persuade a witness: in short, as not rhetorical.' See also the broader social perceptions of Castiglione's terms in Daniel Javitch, *Poetry and Courtliness in Renaissance England* (1978). In this connection of the right representation for the right social moment, see M. T. Crane, *Framing Authority: Sayings, Self and Society in Sixteenth-Century England* (1993). In all this, it should be remembered that what Surrey is primarily doing is constructing a blazon of himself. His own displayed body is now the beloved's being anatomized, in this case by the court, for the patriotic purpose, like his blank verse for new English heroes, of redeeming a nation through a renewed nobility and a new language. If the Arundel portrait was created for the Jacobean earl of Arundel, the fact of its being a blazon, an inversion of the Petrarchan anatomizing, takes on even greater significance.

Castiglione's courtiers are masked actors, then the men and women in Urbino evenings must get the courtly show, in a real sense, on the road. They must perform. They must dare everything with a certain 'recklessnesse' or lightness, without affectation, in order to achieve noble purposes before specific audiences. This was the boldness of Anne Boleyn and of her and Surrey's uncle Lord Berners' Huon of Bordeaux: 'bold, honourable, and heroycall resolution which enflames the soule with a continuall thirsting desire'. *Sprezzatura* means, in this sense, a self-willed call to action and history, a 'resistance' within history itself both to its indeterminancy and to determined external choice by showing nothing more than the 'sincerity' of the dramatized self. *Sprezzatura* indicates the lightness, the reckless wit and daring to create a new text, including a new portrait of self with specific emblems calling 'immediately' (in Cromwell's term) for interpretation and action.

But is the portrait of Surrey at Arundel Castle the original Scrots of 1546 or a later re-creation? The answer is not certain, and it does not matter as far as Surrey's motivation is concerned. A portrait with his intentions did exist from the 1540s; both the Earl of Northampton and Camden refer to the last portrait and its motto. The only other early allusion is a 1637 French source that describes the portrait in the collection at Arundel House in London. If the single painting on coarsely woven canvas at Arundel is the same as that observed in 1637, it may have been a 1540s painting re-created by Inigo Jones around 1610 for Surrey's great-grandson Thomas Howard, the Earl of Arundel, with the possible assistance of some unknown Italian artist. In such a process of restoration and re-creation that was deliberately anachronistic (including a Jacobean conception of shields), Jones, only recently returned from Italy, took an old 'table'—generally but not always a gesso-covered wooden panel—of the poet Earl of Surrey painted by Scrots in 1546. This may have been either from the collection of Lord Lumley, who may have left it in the 1590s to his kinsman, the Earl of Arundel, or from the family treasures that had survived the beheading in 1572 of the fourth Duke of Norfolk, Surrey's son, and watched over by the duke's brother and Surrey's second son, Henry, Earl of Northampton, Privy Councillor in 1610 under James I. Whoever the Jacobean artist was in this scenario, he kept the basic ideology of the original Scrots portrait. He included the original motto and leaning gesture, and transferred the whole performance into the precarious political situation of Arundel himself.[11]

[11] For the question of the shields, see R. Dennys, *Heraldry and Heralds* (1982), 129, 201–2. The two nude figures are holding not the flat-topped shields that had existed in England from the first years after the Norman Conquest and through the Tudors (what Surrey and his 1546 portrait would have used), but the pointed shields considered by Jacobean antiquarians like William Camden to have been earlier, either from the Battle of Hastings, or more antique, at least probably for Inigo Jones and Arundel, from origins Arthurian or early Anglo-Saxon, ultimately Roman. For a counter-argument, see MacLeod, 'Guillim Scrots', 199. In a recent discovery, in a letter to me dated 10 August 1992, John Brooke-Little, Clarenceux King of Arms, finds the shields, their shape and content, to be decidedly later than the 1540s, either 17th-century or even Victorian in construction but not genuinely early

So the point would have been the same for the poet Earl of Surrey. If this scenario is true, Surrey's political intention would have been realized over sixty years later by his great-grandson. As courtiers passed by in the Great Hall of Arundel House with its series of Howard portraits (the absent ones, like Arundel's saint father, all the more significant), this portrait would press on the spectator its special genealogy through Jones' meticulous reconstruction of Surrey's earlier costume and dress, down to doublet and hose. Looking at this image from a reinvented past, Jacobean and Caroline courtiers would have meditated on Surrey's power of generation and then on that of the living host before them, Surrey's great-grandson, Thomas, Earl of Arundel, quite suited himself to become a new Caroline Duke of Norfolk. In those years from the time when the young Earl of Arundel finally regained his house until the English Revolution, it was in the Great Hall that courtiers and the two Stuart kings would receive hospitality at Arundel's table. So, across the top of Surrey's Arundel portrait, where the background of reddish-gold is richest, and against which blind cupids play, just above the inscription of Surrey's age, a pair of the amorini hold the large gold 'H'. And just underneath the 'H' Stuart courtiers would have viewed one of the most spectacular bodies of honour the Renaissance would textualize. As Arundel's secretary, Henry Peacham, comments in his 1634 *The Compleat Gentleman*: 'Honours and titles externally conferred are but attendant upon desert, and are as apparell and the drapery to a beautiful body' and so, if that body is 'nobly borne, and a scholer withall', it 'deserveth double Honour'.[12]

Tudor. For the French source, see Roy Strong, *English Icon* (1969), 72. For the definition of 'table', see Susan Foister, 'Paintings and Other Works of Art in Sixteenth-Century English Inventories', *Burlington Magazine*, 123 (1981), 273–82. For a discussion of the provenance of this portrait, see the correspondence in the archives of the National Portrait Gallery (London) between Dr John Robinson, archivist at Arundel Castle, and Dr Malcolm Rogers of the National Portrait Gallery. I am grateful to Dr Rogers and the staff of the NPG for the privilege of reading this material as well as the reports on the X-raying of the Arundel portrait, and other information relating to the portrait. I am also indebted to Dr Rogers for early support and interest in my study of the Earl of Surrey. The argument for Inigo Jones as painter of the Arundel portrait can be found in Roy Strong, 'Some Early Portraits at Arundel Castle', *Connoisseur*, 197 (1978), 198–200, a thesis he later confirmed to me in a letter dated 11 September 1984: 'The Surrey at Arundel is certainly early seventeenth-century.' David Howarth, *Lord Arundel and His Circle* (1985) sees the portrait 'in a consciously Elizabethan revivalist style' and contextualizes the painting within Jones' work at the time. For a counter-argument, see MacLeod, 38–44. The X-ray photographs of the portrait do not appear to offer any conclusive evidence either way. My recent discovery about the Hellenistic/Roman figuration in Surrey's Great George appears to date the portrait as more Jacobean than early Tudor. Although the recent Fontainebleau evidence for earlier dating in Hearn, *Dynasties* (52) can be explained as a part of what was copied from an original into a deliberately archaized Jacobean portrait, the question of provenance is still open. The origins of the portrait at Arundel Castle are still a mystery. There is no mystery, however, that there *was* some earlier portrait with a Latin motto and a broken column and that Scrots probably painted it.

[12] Howarth, *Arundel*, 102. Henry Peacham, *The Compleat Gentleman, Fashioning him absolute, in the most necessary and commendable Qualities concerning Minde or Body, that may be requited in a Noble Gentleman* (1634), 18.

Hermeneutical Frames: Five Emblems of Time

The central symbolic argument of Surrey's last portrait (as it exists today at Arundel Castle)—the power of time and the young poet earl's ability to control it—can be especially seen in five visualizations so focused as to have the power of emblems: (1) the motion of the extended cape Surrey is wearing; (2) the chain collar and the Great George that hold cape to body (the chain is draped over the cape); (3) the hand on the hip; (4) the golden column on which Surrey leans; and (5) the Latin motto in the dark space of the base of the broken column.

The motion of the cape

Under the arch of time, the young Surrey waits in his white-plumed, dark crimson cap, its silver and gold aglets on satin and velvet. Below the inscription of age, Surrey's cape appears to be flowing or catching up as the young man is pausing. That is, if time or history is literally inscribed from above, the heroic figure beneath, the chivalric 'champion' and Protector of England, centres the motion of the cape as the motion of time. This body of honour pauses in the middle of its history, centring the whole picture through the pause (and implied speech) and his stare at the spectator. In look or voice, the message is the same: only he can control time and bring it to fulfilment. In this portrait without nostalgia, Surrey displays the kind of energizing power acknowledged in his bill of indictment as threatening, a 'peril'.

The cape's flow is further heightened by its silhouette against the other area of light in the picture: the brightening horizon and the spreading landscape between Surrey's legs. This concentrated light in the lower part of the centre-piece is above the dark broken wall that appears to represent a Gothic structure. The time of the picture thus appears to be dawn, the light of a morning cloudy and grey but promising. Although the use of such perspective may be Italian, what may be unique—and, if the Arundel portrait is the original, anticipates a great deal on the continent—is such a horizon and landscape as background for the full-length figure.[13] Thus, behind this silhouetted cape, suspended in its outward flow, is the design of horizontal clouds and the *trompe-l'oeil* of the Italian perspective (its technique reminiscent of Vasari, del Piombo, and Salviati in the latest Italian Imperial mode). Its realistic difference from most continental portraiture extends even to single weeds or plants on the ruined wall, which appear to be moving as if in some wind. This is clearly not a picture like those full-length Allori and Moroni portraits that show other contemplations on the uses of time, a deliberate Platonic stasis in their young men in black. Rather, in Surrey's portrait, emblematic forms are manipulated not to extend meditation but to invite action, an Aristotelian

[13] Waterhouse, *Painting in Britain*, 27. See also *Dynasties*, ed. Hearn, 49.

process. Through simulated motion, the cape's flowing dramatizes a moment that will pass soon and so must be seized by spectators. The ruined wall and dawning light inscribe time as a moment of readiness and promise, if a 'peril' to the Howard heir's enemies.

The Great George and the Garter

Whereas the spread-out fur cape focuses the motion of time, the wide-spreading collar across Surrey's chest appears to hold the toga-cape to the body of honour. The collar authorizes and anchors the motion of this body in time and history. The original for this collar may have been the gold collar described in the inventory of items seized from Surrey House in early 1547. That collar with 54 knots weighed 36 ounces and appears to have ended up in the crown jewels of Edward VI. The ponderous chain collar thus shows off a precisely etched gold design of knots and Tudor roses, from which the Great George depends. The chain collar in the portrait is more stylized and elegant than most (compared to that of Holbein's Thomas More, for example). In its interspersed series of Tudor roses (only allowed on such a Garter collar) with gold knot bows between, each rose has a pearl in its centre and is encircled by the Old French motto 'Honi soyt, qui mal y pense' which Surrey's ancestor Edward III originated as a motto for the Order of the Garter at Windsor Castle. The George hanging from the chain collar in Surrey's portrait at Arundel Castle is not so traditional.

In it, the figures of the Roman warrior saint and his horse over the fallen dragon are magnificently encased in gold and are 'represented on a heater-shaped shield surrounded by jewels'—in contrast, for example, to Holbein's undecorated George in his portrait of Sir Henry Guildford. More strikingly, this figure within Surrey's George in the Arundel portrait has no armour. He wears only a shirt or blouse that frees the neck and arms themselves as bare as the legs beneath the classical tunic (no greaves at all). His young head covered with thick hair, this Roman warrior is holding a spear or trident in a backward pose, his horse rising with the same figuration as numerous Greek statues of a nude young male and horse. Here, in fact, is the most profound and unusual inscription of *Romanitas* in the entire portrait. Surrey's St George is not dressed in full medieval armour as in Thynne's 1532 icon for his edition of Chaucer's Knight's Tale—the traditional imaging of the George and what Scrots was painting, for example, in the same years for the George of Edward VI. Extraordinarily original, if painted in 1546, this ancient Roman warrior saint, almost a Greek athlete, looks as a warrior in the eastern Roman army AD 305, the real St George, might have looked. Such a version of St George as a Greek warrior (and not as a medieval knight) does not appear in other Georges until later Elizabethan portraits, its most powerful representation in the Great George of the 1597 full-length portrait of the Earl of Essex by Marcus Gheeraerts the Younger. Here St George is a Greek warrior in a different figuration (a raised sword like a scimitar) but, like Surrey's, Essex's bears no resemblance to the medieval knights of the Georges in the Henrician period. In fact, the Great George of Surrey's portrait remains one of the strongest proofs for the Jacobean provenance of the Arundel portrait.[14]

This collar and its dependency—and the actual garter just below Surrey's left knee—comprise the most significant decorations of the poet's costume. The collar and the George literally hold in place the flowing cape—the flowing of time. True honour controls time and history. Worn in all official court portraits by those who could display such honour, as Surrey could since the spring of 1541, the heavy collar gestures towards antiquarianism (that is, chain collars, with their echoes of Rome, as believed to have been worn in the heroic world of Beowulf and Surrey's putative ancestor, Hereward the Wake). Henry VIII had made the feast-day of the Roman St George, 23 April 1509, his accession day, as earlier Henry V had made, immediately after the Battle of Agincourt in 1415, the feast-day of the Roman warrior a universal holy day of the highest rank for England. As Surrey knew well from his reading of his uncle Lord Berners' stylish translations of Froissart's realistic histories of knighthood (as opposed to Malory's mythic re-inventions or Chaucer's Knight's Tale) English heroes needed constantly to actualize the figure of the young Roman saint in real history in order to keep the idea of a national 'champion' alive. In the Arundel portrait, at the centre of Surrey's chest, the George thus implicitly juxtaposes the Howard heir with earlier heroes, especially the warrior saint whose youth and myth of salvation and deliverance—a full redeeming of time—link themselves to the young male body in the portrait.

One more aspect of Surrey's last portrait was radically new for English portraiture in 1546 and quite innovative in 1610. This is the predominance of Surrey's

[14] The quotation is from the Catalogue of Burlington Fine Arts Club Exhibition of Early English Portraiture (London, 1909) 95. Although it is quite possible that Surrey's originality of design in 1546 would have included such figuration, the Great George in the Arundel portrait offers stronger proof that Inigo Jones (or some Jacobean painter) painted this central figure anew in 1610 (or supervised its painting). Indeed, a survey of the portraits with the Great George in the National Portrait Gallery suggests that the old medieval figuration of a knight in armour (as exemplified for Surrey's generation in Thynne's original woodcut for his Chaucer edition of 1532) continues throughout most of the Tudor period earlier exemplified in that of the Duke of Suffolk. There are later exceptions, however, and these suggest that the newer, more antique figuration may have carried political overtones. The earliest example in the NPG is the George of the Earl of Arundel painted in 1565; he bought Nonesuch from the queen and his collection formed the basis of his son-in-law Lord Lumley's famous collection. The 1569 portrait by Hans Eworth of the stepson of Surrey's 'Geraldine', Anthony Browne, Lord Montague, a strong Catholic of the period, shows the same Roman figuration, not least the more open classical helmet, short tunic, greaves, and a rising horse. The more dramatic 1597 portrait of Essex by another Flemish painter, Marcus Gheeraerts the Younger, keeps the same Roman figuration, and here above a charging white horse, St George, the full embodiment of *Romanitas*, holds a raised sword. In the earliest Great and Lesser George owned by the British Museum, that of William Compton, the Earl of Northampton newly created in 1628 (Surrey's son Henry had held the title under James I), the figurations of both are, underneath heavy encrusting of jewels and enamel, Roman and Hellenistic, more like Surrey's and Essex's (the raised sword here is like a Turkish scimitar). The same hermeneutical principle thus works in the Caroline reign, before the breakdown of the revolution, as with Surrey eighty years before: the most avant-garde future can be revealed in new inscriptions of the antique. This had been the whole point of Bacon's *De sapientia veterum*, published in 1609 at the same time the Arundel portrait may have been painted.

legs, loose and informal, and the Garter below his left knee, which dominates the lower part of the picture, almost its centre. A full white pearl hangs from the side fold of the tie on the Garter and shines out against the ruined Gothic wall and single plants blowing in the imagined wind. The large pearl on the Garter accents the rubies and diamonds encrusted on its surface, no longer blue but gold (at least the gold shines forth). All that is fully visible from the Garter motto on the surface is the one word 'pense' with each letter alternating in gold and white (as on Henry VIII's in the Whitehall mural). As with the contrast of the flowing cape and the heavy chain, so the Garter and its encrusted weight are countered by the impatience of Surrey's legs in their off-white hose. Surrey's long legs end in open slashed shoes (the most unfinished part of the Arundel Castle portrait, possibly because of the framing of the whole at the Stuart Arundel House). The shoes and legs are posed, as though only for an instant, before the young man sprints forth again, full codpiece hanging loose in its nest of counterpointing diagonals and stud-heads of sword and dagger. The Romanizing continues in the detailed stud-heads of ancient emperors amid grisaille enamels, 'the height of fashion for 1546,' according to Norman. Both weapons may have been at Surrey House and confiscated directly for the newly entitled Duke of Somerset: 'two rapiers, all gilt, grave antique' and 'a gilt dagger, with a sheath of black velvet' (N1: cxiv–xv). As the future Protector knew, however archaic they may be in origin, these visible forms of Rome in England spelled immense power at a time of succession like that of January 1547, although one of Edward VI's first acts was to try to eradicate the Order of the Garter and destroy its matrix of honour at Windsor.[15]

The hand on the hip

A physical gesture extends the authorizing force of the gold chain, the George, and the Garter. Surrey's left hand on his hip, also in the Parham Park and Knole portraits, invokes and then renegotiates an old tradition. In fact, if original in 1546, this gesture may have encouraged, if not authorized, a whole series of English courtier portraits, from the Earl of Leicester, the Earl of Oxford, Sidney, Raleigh, Lord Herbert of Cherbury, and Van Dyck's Charles I, to name the obvious ones, all with hand on hip. The Flemish painter Scrots had worked from his own Imperial and Burgundian precedents (themselves from Imperial Rome) to gain this effect in Surrey's portrait—he had already used the gesture in his portrayal of Habsburg princes—and in this gesture Surrey may have desired to imitate contemporary European figurations, from Seisenegger's Georg Fugger to Pontormo's Cosimo dei Medici. Although in Europe the flamboyant sign of elbow

[15] For the importance of collars, see F. M. Stenton, *Anglo-Saxon England* (1971), 605–6. For A. V. B. Norman, see *Dynasties*, ed. Hearn, 52. For Edward VI and Garter, see John King, *Tudor Royal Iconography*, 99–100. See also Aston, *Iconoclasts*, 274–5. This attack may have been on St George as a Catholic hangover and not on the order itself.

and hip appears continually from Imperial Roman sculpture to Mick Jagger, the miniatures of the Burgundian grand dukes (familiar to both Yorkist and Tudor courts) particularly use it to identify a royal nonchalance as a *sprezzatura* only possible in the total ease of genuine authority and commanding presence.[16] In 1546 the gesture had never been used before for any nobility in England.

The golden column

With one hand on the hip, the other hand and arm are also emblematically placed. Surrey leans on the broken column with an inscribed plinth. The gesture marks, first of all, the seriousness of the figure's pausing in the moment of time that is the portrait. Waiting to hear the question or give his own answer, Scrots' figure leans the weight of his new body of honour on the broken shaft of the golden column. It is another gesture of reckless nonchalance, an Italian *sprezzatura* to match the Italian design of Surrey's costume. For the Renaissance viewer, the broken column had its own intricate iconography. In fact, three cultural emblems are working here. A broken column could textualize the classical myths of Hercules and

[16] See Joaneath Spicer, 'The Renaissance Elbow', in *The Cultural History of Gesture*, ed. Jan Bremmer and Herman Roodenburg (1991), 84–128. Scrots had already made the gesture, for example, a crucial point in his portraits of Imperial princes in Vienna. Seisenegger's stylish 1541 portrait of Georg Fugger shows a young man (exactly the same age as Surrey) in totally black attire with white-plumed hat, sword in right hand like the Emperor in Seisenegger's famous portrait, but Fugger's left hand on his hip. Cf. Kurt Löcher, *Jakob Seisenegger: Hofmaler Kaiser Ferdinands I* (1962), 87. Also in Italy, ten years before, Pontormo had painted his sexually ambiguous portrait of the young Duke Cosimo I de' Medici as a halberdier, the left hand firmly on the hip (and the right holding his upright pike). Late in the 15th century, the gesture of hand on hip had been copied from Roman medals of the emperors and inscribed for the Magi in *The Book of the Hours*, the three riding together and the gesture of one with a hand on hip that also holds the reins of his horse, as in Erwin Panofsky, *Early Netherlandish Painting* (1953), 64. Cf. *Les très riches heures du duc de Berry*, ed. Edmond Pognon and trans. David Macrae (n.d.), 60–1. The Constantine medal is striking in its use of the gesture. This medal was modelled on the widely imitated statue of Marcus Aurelius (thought to be Constantine) on the Capitol in Rome. For the most spectacular of all the Burgundian inscriptions of this gesture, see the miniature, certainly from the 1450s, of the father of Charles the Bold, the Grand Duke Philip the Good (the great-great-grandfather of the Holy Roman Emperor Charles V), in whose reign the Burgundian realm reached its apogee. He receives a heavily illuminated volume of the *Chroniques de Hainhault* from a kneeling courtier, over whose head he stares. His small son beside him, the duke is wearing the jewelled collar draped across his shoulder from which the Golden Fleece depends. The Grand Duke's feet are elongated in quite pointed slippers and on his head is an elaborately swirled flat black hat, with chin-strap (not more ornate, however, than another black hat and ostrich feather of his that cost an enormous 110,000 crowns, literally enough to feed a small army). For a duke whose *valet de chambre* was Jan van Eyck, the calculation of the hat-effect in the miniature works as an inscription of authority. In his right hand (with his modishly long fingernails) Duke Philip holds a small sword, but his left arm is akimbo, in a virtual curve to give weight (and height) to his stature, the whole meriting Chastellain's description of this body of honour in the mid-fifteenth century: Philip the Good 'deserved a crown on the strength of his physical appearance alone', quoted in Richard Vaughan, *Charles the Bold: the Last Valois Duke of Burgundy* (1974), 151. See another Burgundian text in the Bodleian Library, MS Douce 278 f. 21v, where the son of the Holy Roman Emperor, a prince identified by his crown, holds his hand on the hip with a special *hauteur*—a gesture found nowhere else in the text.

his heroic fortitude and, just as emphatically, the story of Samson from the Book of Judges in the Bible, especially his noble suicide for God and His chosen people. Both emblems of endurance and patience Surrey may have seen first-hand in France in the 1540s when he rode and served with Charles V (and such figuration was obviously accessible to Scrots at the Imperial courts). In armour forged for the horse of the emperor in Augsburg in 1517–18, there are only two heroic motifs for the entire armour, those of Samson and Hercules, and both with images of broken columns.[17] The third symbolic figuration for the broken column is Rome itself. In dialogue with the ruined overgrown wall in the horizon, Surrey's broken golden column could also enact the Renaissance motif of the ruins of Rome, soon to be found in Ronsard and Spenser.

Another text or emblem is working here. The broken column had appeared as an emblem in two lyrics each by Surrey's masters, Petrarch—a poet increasingly identified in England with the reform of court and religion—and Wyatt. Thus, for the literate Tudor spectator who in the fiction of the portrait has interrupted Surrey with a question, the young earl presents himself emblematically with the broken column and recalls two sonnets and Surrey's genealogy as a poet. Writing on the deaths of Laura and his patron, Cardinal Colonna, in *Rime* 269, Petrarch had lamented: 'Rotto e l'alta colonna, e'l verde lauro / che facean ombra al mio stanco pensero' ('Broken is the high column, and the green laurel that made shade for my tired thought'). Wyatt had adapted the sophisticated Italian text. He transformed it to lament the beheading of his powerful patron Cromwell, from whose demise Wyatt never recovered politically.

The piller pearisht is whearto I Lent [leaned],
  The strongest staye of myne vnquyet mynde;
The lyke of it no man agayne can fynde,
Ffrom East to west, still seking though he went. (MTCCXXXVI)

The missing face of honour

There was one more hermeneutic signal for the golden column on which Surrey leans. Interpreting this emblem and Surrey's leaning gesture on it involves another 'staye' of Surrey's brief life, Henry Fitzroy, the Duke of Richmond. On the plinth of the broken column, in what is now blank space except for the Latin motto, Surrey intended to paint the portrait of his beloved friend and brother-in-law, as

[17] See *Resplendence of the Spanish Monarchy: Renaissance Tapestries and Armor from the Patrimonio Nacional*, ed. Antonio Domínguez Ortiz, Concha Herrero Carretero, and José A. Godoy (New York: Metropolitan Museum of Art, 1992), 123, 130–7. For the tradition of fortitude, see Cesare Ripa, *Iconologia* (1611), 16 and 17. For the relation to the Columns of Hercules (i.e., the Straits of Gibraltar) and Charles V's motto 'Plus Ultra' see Guy de Tervarent, *Attributs et symboles dans l'art profane 1450–1600* (1958), 108. For Samson and the whole Christian iconography of the broken column, see Monsignor X. Barbier de Montault, *Traité d'iconographie chrétienne* (1890), vol. 1, 218–19; vol. 3, 147, 231, 267, 315.

revealed in a letter sent by Surrey to his steward Hugh Ellis at Lambeth in the first week of August 1546. Writing from Kenninghall, and promising to send Ellis some badly needed money, Surrey also enclosed a letter to be speedily delivered by hand: 'I pray delyver this letter wt all spede to Mrs. Heuvingham [the recently married Mary Shelton], whom yew shall fynde at heromes Cheltons [Jerome Shelton's] howse in London, or els will be ther wth in iij days.' Then he adds instructions for a portrait painter: 'Comawnd the paynter to leve owt the tablet wher my Lord off Richemondes picture shuld stand, ffor I will have nothyng ther, nor yet the tablet, but all dowbet.' This inset portrait would probably have been in the space beneath the pedestal supporting the broken column, blank now except for the motto 'SAT SVPER EST.'[18] According to the letter, the space was to contain a portrait of Richmond, perhaps copied from the miniature that has survived and that Surrey or his sister may have kept for their own.

Signing 'ffrom Kenyngale this Wednesday, H. Surrey,' the poet then wrote across the enclosed letter 'Delyver this letter to none but her own handes.' Mary Shelton was the daughter of an old East Anglian family with strong ties to the Howard dynasty. The family had powerful court connections, Mary's father a steward of the household of the royal princesses and her mother, a cousin of Anne Boleyn, at one time governess to the Princess Mary. Mary Shelton's sister Margaret had been, in fact, a lady-in-waiting to Anne Boleyn and was rumoured in 1536 to be Henry VIII's mistress. The female member of the 'league' with Surrey and Clere, after whose death she had married into another East Anglian family (probably through Surrey's influence), she became a major figure in the transmission of the Devonshire Manuscript, a doubtless frequent visitor at Surrey's musical and literary gatherings. The drawing of Mary Shelton by Holbein from the mid-1530s (Plate 11) shows a sharp watchful face, lips tight, beneath a gabled headdress. Her eyes are quite focused (even if one is slightly cast), with a tapering nose and drooping chin but with shoulders that hold a tense animal pose of watching. Mary Shelton may have become more of a confidante by 1546, as the secrecy of the letter suggests;[19] she could come and go at court, not least into the pivotal household of the Christian humanist queen. She could report on a world where the role of the Howards was becoming more tenuous and Surrey's place more perilous. Others recognized her possible role in a Surrey network. On the back of this same letter, intercepted at some point, Sir Richard Southwell wrote a note to the Privy Council: 'Yt maye please your good Lordshippez to examyn Mes Henygham, late Marye Shelton, of theffect of th'earle of Surrey his lettre sent unto her; for yt ys thowght that menye secrettes hathe passed betwen them before her maryage and sethens.'

This emblem of the young Richmond within his last portrait was to make a simple point: the poet earl had once been the closest friend and *incitateur* of the

[18] For the influence of Petrarch, see Yates, *Astrea*, 77. For the letter, PRO SP 1/223, f. 36. For the place of the portrait, see Casady, *Henry Howard*, 23.

[19] Remley, 'Shelton', 40.

young Prince Edward's own half-brother. This earlier role had been preparation for a new role of Protector that Surrey's living body of honour should now be given. Identifying the 'dowbet' emblem also explains two strange references in documents from the period. On 23 January 1547, just after Surrey's beheading, the new Imperial ambassador van der Delft wrote to Charles V about the shocking event: 'Last Wednesday the earl of Surrey was executed' and 'the principal charges against him were that he had usurped the royal arms of England, and had also used certain ancient pictures representing him[self], suspected to have been inspired by evil thoughts.' The ambassador refers to only one picture: 'As to the picture, which represented a broken pillar against which he was leaning with a young child beneath the pillar, he excused himself by saying that he had done nothing to the prejudice of anyone, nor had he acted maliciously.'[20] The second reference is in the Spanish Chronicle, supposedly compiled by a Spanish merchant in this period. Here the 'dowbet' picture originates an episode. Surrey's sister does not listen to her brother but gives 'herself up to her pleasures'. Before that change of character in Richmond's widow, Surrey 'always visited her, and showed great affection for her, telling her all his affairs'. The hermeneutics of his last portrait was one such affair Surrey told his sister. In his secret picture within the picture, he explained, 'the arms of his father were joined to those of the King, and surrounded by the garter,' but, instead of 'Honi soit qui mal y pense,' Surrey had 'put in English "Till then thus" [or in the Spaniard's broken English, 'tel dandus' or 'tel (till) Dan (then) dus (thus)'] and then ordered the painter to put another painted canvas over it, so that it looked as if no other painting was there.' When warned by his father (whom the sister informed) of the danger, Surrey answered that 'our ancestors bore those arms, and I am much better than any of them, so do not grieve about it.' But the father did worry, telling Surrey not to 'tell thy brother Thomas, who is too young to be trusted' and asked to see the picture within the picture. Surrey told him another canvas with another painting had been put over it.

The Spanish Chronicle then elaborates the episode. Because Surrey had threatened her in 'her mode of life', the sister went to Henry VIII and told him about the painting. He called Paget and Seymour, who advised the king to arrest Surrey, and so the king set the trap with the Captain of the Guard and his halberdiers for the next day at Whitehall when the young earl was to come into the palace in early afternoon after dinner. On the day after the arrest, in the Tower, as the old duke was with Seymour 'and other nobles' to ask Surrey 'what he meant by having the painting done, the painting itself having been taken before the King,' the old duke was arrested. Surrey's sister had told the king the duke knew about the painting. When Surrey was finally interrogated, away from his father, and asked his intention in the painting, the poet earl replied: 'My lords, you know that all my ancestors have borne these arms, and King Henry VII took them away from the Duke, my father.' 'But,' said Seymour and the others anxiously, 'what does the

[20] *CSPSpan*, vol. 9, 3.

inscription mean?' 'It means, my lords,' answered Surrey directly, ' "that so it will remain until it comes to light." ' The king, on hearing this prophetic meaning, ordered the the whole painting broken into pieces (143–4).[21]

The inscription appears to have the same general meaning as the motto that did finally appear on the column: 'SAT SVPER EST.' Enough survives. Thus, however garbled the mottoes in the memory of the Spanish businessman, Surrey's intention is the same in both: the picture of Richmond and then the motto substituted for it represent Surrey's own nobility and the continuity of honour. If politically it would be inept to juxtapose the picture of the young prince's bastard brother at the moment the strictly reformed Christian Edward VI is about to ascend the throne, a motto can mean and say the same. Richmond, the Other Henry, still remains. He survives in that Latin motto now substituted for his body. In a world where language—a Latin motto—will achieve great effect, certainly for the young humanist Prince of Wales, already a master of Latin and Greek, the motto as the most literal statement in the entire portrait can reveal 'immediately' the meaning of the whole performance in the portrait: 'SAT SVPER EST.' If then, in the detailed portrait and its emblematic logic, enough nobility does survive, the consequence is for the spectator to join the young poet earl in the Virgilian labour of building a new society, a Renaissance in England. The spectator is invited to break through the disappearances of fleeing time—Virgil's 'irreparabile tempus'—but only in terms of that historic individual in whose presence and detailed visible body 'Enough Survives.'

[21] A text that provides an interesting parallel to the Spanish Chronicle is BL MS Stowe 396, f. 8. Here too, in the midst of obvious exaggeration, is a body of facts, in this case circulating around some visual artefact of Surrey's, 'sundry devises made in arras Cloath', especially 'a Pillar broken in the middest with an H on one side and an R on the other on the Topp whereof stood the Kinges Armes, and on the Pedestall his own; which being seen by divers' was interpreted to mean that the king 'should come to ruine by his owne Armes' and Surrey succeed him. In this account, Surrey at his trial gave another interpretation, the pillar as himself broken by the king represented by the king's arms, and the letters H and R standing for 'Hereditas restas. because he [Surrey] had now nothing to trust to but his inheritance', that is, the letters as another version of 'SAT SUPER EST'.

14

The Final Days

At the end of his long chronicle, the early Tudor historian Edward Hall allows himself one last burst of Burgundian *gloire*. Although briefer than other extravagant renditions of honour that mark his history, his account of the August 1546 reception for the French Admiral subtly completes his text (the historian himself would die in seven months) that otherwise ends abruptly with the burning alive of Anne Askew and her companions in July, the beheading of Surrey in January, and the death of Henry VIII a week later. Arriving in the Thames off Greenwich with twelve great ships, the Admiral of France Claude d'Annebault, the governor of Normandy, was first greeted and escorted to London by the queen's brother, the Earl of Essex, with the Earl of Derby. On St Bartholomew's eve, 23 August, d'Annebault sailed by barge up the Thames towards Hampton Court with his entourage of 200 nobility and clergy. On the way, at the river-bank at Hounslow, the young Prince Edward rode to meet him, the boy's horsemanship giving to all who looked an impression of serene control intensified by his dress, especially his crimson and white satin doublet sewn with jewels.

In fact, for this performance, the future king had been carefully preparing himself, even writing to his stepmother, Queen Catherine Parr, about the problem of the Lord Admiral's Latin and their ability to converse in that language (taught him by Cheke) in which the 8-year-old knew he could exhibit not only control but force: 'quod si calleat, vellem plus discere quod illi loquar, cum ei obviam venero' ('But if he is proficient [in Latin], I should like to learn more of what to say to him when I do meet him').[1] Meeting the admiral with the prince were his uncle Edward Seymour, the Earl of Hertford, the young Earls of Huntingdon and Shrewsbury, the prince's gentlemen, and 200 yeomen of the guard dressed in cloth of gold (100 attendants for the prince, 40 for his uncle Hertford, 30 for Shrewsbury, 20 for Huntingdon, and, an interesting addition, 20 attendants for Sir Richard Southwell, listed in the riding party). When the French admiral met the boy, the pair embraced 'in such lowly and honorable maner', the admiral kissing the boy's hands and the boy kissing the bearded man on both cheeks—'that all the beholders gretely reioysed'. Then, in the welcoming speeches, the prince spoke for the first time before so large an audience and out of doors. All the crowd 'much marueyled at [his] wyt and audacitie' of discourse. The profile portrait of Prince Edward

[1] *Literary Remains of King Edward the Sixth*, ed. J. G. Nichols, FSA, printed for the Roxburghe Club (1867), 22 (Letter 23).

painted at this time reveals him as he may have looked that August afternoon: delicate white skin, even pale features with auburn-gold hair, grey eyes with long lashes and a deliberate gaze ahead.

The next day, a Thursday, marked the climax of the visit: 'On Barthelemew daye, the kyng rychly appareled, welcomed in great triumph went to the chapel, where the league was sworne and signed.' Just recovered from a serious physical collapse, the king had summoned considerable energies to make this appearance, although from the time Seymour had led the negotiations with the French in June, Henry VIII had followed every step carefully. On this Thursday Surrey became prominent for the first time. The poet earl was called upon, in a special order of precedence, to greet the French entourage in a series of ceremonies that brings Hall to his most ecstastic: 'To tel you of the costlye banquet houses, that were built, & of the great banquettes, the costly Maskes, the liberal huntynges that were shewed to hym, you woulde much maruel, and skant beleue' (867–8). In fact, for that day and evening, the poet earl became the living image of his own last portrait. Surrey's nobility of blood and his reputation as scholar and poet gave a precedence neither Seymour nor Dudley could ever honorably gain. As one of fifteen who were to prepare horses for the admiral 'with footcloths', he also had special duties as royal cup-bearer in serving the admiral to be performed only with the king, the Archbishop of Canterbury, and his father. More important, in the order of the receiving line, the arrangement of the nobility of the entire realm, Surrey was to be ranked immediately after the Princesses Mary and Elizabeth, and above all other earls, whatever their function (even Hertford as the Lord Great Chamberlain), because he was the son of a duke.[2] His sister, the widow of a duke, the king's other son, outranked all the other women (including 'Geraldine' in the queen's privy chamber entourage), the Duchess of Richmond only after the royal ladies, Anne of Cleves and Lady Margaret Douglas. With this precedence, Surrey projected his own body of honour that August evening at Hampton Court, where even the torch-bearers wore cloth of gold.

Anne Askew: A Body on Fire

But another kind of witness and inscription of honour had taken place just the month before in that final summer of 1546. In this martyrdom, Surrey's presence had strangely figured. This time the influence sprang not from Surrey's blood

[2] *Complete Peerage*, vol. 9, 616 (g). When the second Duke of Norfolk, the 'Flodden Duke', dropped the earldom of Surrey to provide his heir with the title, the future third duke, Henry Howard's father, was thereafter treated as a junior marquess holding precedence over all the earls. Although the poet earl was only a courtesy peer (who could sit in the House of Commons), he enjoyed the same rank of junior marquess as his father had. Thus, at the Hampton Court peace conference in August 1546, he was placed above the earls of Hertford (Seymour) and Shrewsbury (the title that still designates the premier earl).

nobility but from his poetry, from a text that a young Lincolnshire gentlewoman incorporated into her own self-validating ballad before she was burned alive. If anything, the borrowing by Anne Askew of a passage from Surrey's paraphrase of Ecclesiastes confirmed the new prestige of Surrey as text-maker generated by the 1542 Wyatt elegy and his recent Bible translations. It also confirmed Surrey's revolution in language and social inscription. Whether the reformed Christian hero that July had read the elegy on Wyatt or not, she obviously knew the last phase of Surrey's poetic career, his religious verse. Here language and ideology joined, the one like the other, as she obviously recognized. Thus, in her own poetic inscription of self before her martyrdom (her Dido soliloquy before her own burning pyre), she took one Surrey passage as her own. Askew put lines from the poet earl's paraphrase of the third chapter of Ecclesiastes into her famous ballad of death. In these lines, Surrey had given Anne Askew terms to identify the killer of them both, Henry VIII.

The young woman had challenged Henry VIII directly on the specific dogma of the Real Presence, which was held not only by the old king but fervently by the young Edward (who later defended it, in spite of Cranmer, even writing his only poem proclaiming its truth). For Anne Askew, there was no Real Presence on the altar, and what she expressed quietly, with patience and fervour, Surrey's friend Blagge had announced in the midst of St Paul's: the Host was a lie. He was immediately arrested. As his pardon, dated 17 July 1546, states, Blagge had declared on the previous 9 May within the congested crowds of St Paul's Cathedral that 'the Sacrament of the Altar did not good, neither to the quick nor dead' and that 'the good Lord's body could not in any means be minished ne impaired.' With sarcasm, Blagge went further in this special public place in the Tudor world: if Christ's body in the Host were 'laid up there' so that 'a mouse might come' to the consecrated bread, 'the mouse would eat it every whit' and so 'in his opinion it were well done that the mouse were taken and put in the pix' (the container for the Host). The mouse was as good as any consecrated Host that falsely pretended to represent the actual body of Jesus Christ. For Surrey's friend, the world of metaphor and analogy was fast becoming, however literalized, no way to define reality. God could no longer be confined to human metaphor, with its lies and illusions. For Anne Askew, what presence of Jesus Christ there was on any Christian altar could be understood only as Zwinglian memorialism, not even Calvinist actualization through faith nor the more old-fashioned Lutheran consubstantiation.

Luther's first attack had made the essential point against this central dogma of the old religion: no place or materiality was sacred in itself. Erasmus had told a despairing young German courtier the same thing in 1501: in subjectivity Christ could be found, not in any external sign. Internalizing in the name of Jesus Christ—the self in Christ—determined concrete reality and everything else—not the other way around. No dialectic existed between the sacred and the profane except through interiorizing faith: 'Sola Fides' in the Pauline phrase embellished in Luther's Bible by adding his 'sola' or 'allein' to Paul's original passage in Romans

3: 28. For Anne Askew, Christ's internalizing ubiquity meant real presence within each soul, and therefore presence and honour could happen everywhere, as simple as that. Even a woman could become a knight for Jesus Christ or an armed warrior, in her updating of St Paul's Ephesian imagery. Thus, the young British woman announces at the opening of her ballad: 'L/yke as the armed knyght / Appointed to the fielde / With thys world wyll I fyght / And fayth shall be my shielde.' The questing figure of Lancelot du Lac was having a strange British metamorphosis.

John Bale had 'The Balade whych Anne Askewe made and sange whan she was in Newgate' first printed in Germany immediately after the young woman's being burnt alive. The ballad had appeared in Bale's authorial canonization of her—the first making of a saint from a book in England and probably in Europe. Foxe develops the cult of the righteous woman more completely in his martyrology, and indeed Foxe records how he and Bale met each other, after Bale's return from exile, in the reformed Christian household of the Duchess of Richmond, presumably at Reigate in Surrey. It was precisely Bale's works like this account of Anne Askew that laid the basis for the grand revisionist martyrology of John Foxe.[3]

In order to save the history of this first woman martyr, Bale printed immediately not only her life-story but appended the ballad she had written in prison. Here was a figuration that signalled a new social type, as he determined correctly. Anne Askew represented a new progression in the history of God's chosen people. Her life typified the true Christian martyr's history made modern, especially in her updated and quite self-conscious suffering before her death by fire. In the first woodblock of Bale's text, the figure of Anne Askew emerges from the threat of a dragon, holding the lily of a virgin martyr (like St Agnes) in another variation of the popular woodcut *Veritas filia temporis* ('truth is the daughter of time'). In Anne Askew can be seen, Bale argues, a model of early 'Christen contancye' as once existed in 'the Brytayne churche, or the prymatyve church of thys realme, whych neuer had autoryte of the Romysh pope'. The British woman had not reverted to 'lyenge legendes, popish fables, nor yet old wyves parables' but to the realism of truth, genuine texts and models: 'the most lyvelye autoryees and examples of the sacred Bible'. Her authenticity is marked by the fact that in the 'anguysh and payne of her broken ioyntes and broused armes and eyes' she saw 'most pacyent Job, for example of godly sufferaunce'. She never doubted her calling, despite 'the stinke of Newgate [prison], nor yet the burning fyer of Smithfeld', where she became a human torch. For this prophetic witness, Bale concludes with mottoes from the Hebrew prophets Ezekiel and Daniel and then defines his new hero: 'Thus is she a gyant canonysed in Christes bloude, though she never have other canonysacyon of pope, prrest, nor Byshopp.' By 1546 it is not merely that an underground saint had been immediately born, but 'a gyant' who is a woman confirmed as a body of heroic nobility by her authenticity of sacrifice, her burning body of honour.

[3] Harris, *Bale*, 119, 111.

Most of all, Anne Askew's lyric poem (printed) authenticated this martyrdom: a soliloquy of her suffering before death—textualized by herself about herself—in the popular form of the ballad, a reduction of the Poulter's Measure line that Surrey used for his Biblical paraphrases. Anne Askew's ballad written in jail and appended to Bale's hagiographic text thus confirms a heroic self-election. In her lyric, the woman begins by declaring both her allegiance to the honour of Jesus Christ at the price of the world and her androgynous knight identity. The ballad ends with articulated acceptance of suffering and the coming death in fire. Both as woman and as Christian who must die, Askew contrasts her own act of sacrifice for Christ with the evil of the totalizing enemy who is killing her. Thus, at a key point in her ballad, Askew turns to the poetry of the Earl of Surrey for the portrayal of such a Satanic figure. The importance of this borrowing from Surrey lies in more than the remarkable fact of Surrey's lines as inspiration for a Protestant martyr. In her act of self-justification, Anne Askew borrows from the avant-garde poet earl to authenticate herself as poet as well as martyr. That is, in the text, just before her paraphrase of Surrey's paraphrase, the Lincolnshire gentlewoman gives herself the strongest self-inscription. As she writes, it has always been a question for Askew of finding the right language for what she actually felt and saw. Surrey's is the right language. Now she 'internalizes' her own act of writing, as Luther desired, and at that moment Surrey gives her the right poetic genealogy—himself—to express, like Aeneas, her own 'slaughter'.

> I am not she that lyst
> My anker to lete fall
> For euerye dryslynge myst
> My shyppe substanciall.
> Not oft use I to wryght
> In prose nor yet in ryme
> Yet wyll I shewe one syght
> That I saw in my time.

That 'syght' the young woman has seen has been so genuine, so deeply and radically primitive a phenomenon, that she is compelled to 'express' it in her own 'tears', to use Virgil's terms. She has no practice as a poet, but the horror of the 'syght' is her equivalent of burning Troy or Surrey's London. Whatever her personal will, she must act. She must write her own poem and so, after her authorial digression, Askew borrows directly from Surrey for the climax of her ballad. It is an indictment of Henry VIII, for her neither Supreme Head nor Sardanapalus but 'Sathan' himself:

> I saw a ryall trone
> Where Jutcye shuld haue sytt
> But in her stede was one
> Of modye cruell wytt.
> Absorpt was ryghtwysnesse

As of the raging floude
Sathan in hys excesse.
Sucke up the gyltelesse bloude
  Then thought I Jesus lorde
Whan thu shalt iudge us all
Harde is it to recorde
On these men what wyll fall.[4]

Surrey's text, probably written in the previous spring after his ignominious return from France, is more elaborate, its paraphrase revising the Book of Revelation source:

I saw a royal throne whereas that Justice should have sit;
  Instead of whom I saw, with fierce and cruel mode,
Where Wrong was set, that bloody beast, that drunk the guiltless blood.
  Then thought I thus: One day the Lord shall sit in dome [judgement],
To view his flock and choose the pure: the spotted have no room.

Askew's borrowing from Surrey recognizes Surrey's originality in 1546 and his transformation in the early modern coding of both honour and nobility. For both of them, what became finally clear was that, in the perspective of a final judgement and the horror of 'that bloody beast' who drinks innocent blood, the old structures of blood nobility would not necessarily be wrong, just not sufficient. They may not be enough for a new moral being, poet or martyr or nobleman. Before the nightmare of history, as both the male severed head of Surrey and the female burning body of Askew would witness, nothing could be guaranteed, except that honour—the sense of self both entering and transcending history—would always seek new forms for the deepest self who survives the violence of history. Survival was sure, the Lincolnshire woman was asserting in her new ballad; she herself had written about her own 'resistance' to death and Satan. For this sense of 'resistance' of a higher genealogy (blood, poetic text, prophecy) to breakdown and violence, honour and its forms served not only to encode but to assert any special self surviving history. As Albert Camus affirmed 400 years later, 'honour, like pity, is the irrational virtue that carries on after justice and reason have become powerless.'[5]

4 *The first examination of Anne Askew, lately martyred in Smithfelde, by the Romysh popes upholders, with the elucydacyon of Johan Bale* (1546) STC 848, 3, 49, 62 3. Other references to this work are given in the text. See also *The Examinations of Anne Askew*, ed. Elaine V. Beilin (1996) for a comprehensive introduction and textual history. Cf. also the full discussion of the Anne Askew episode in Brigden, *London*, 370–6. See also Derek A. Wilson, *A Tudor Tapestry: Men, Women, and Society in Reformation England* (1972).

5 'In the conflicts of this century, I have felt close to all obstinate men, particularly to those who have never been able to abandon their faith in honour. I have shared and I continue to share many contemporary hysterias. But . . . honour, like pity, is the irrational virtue that carries on after justice and reason have become powerless.' Camus' definition was given just before his accidental death in Jean Bloch-Michel, 'The Obstinate Confidence of a Pessimistic Man,' *Reporter*, 17 (28 November 1957), 37.

Arrest and Forced March

No act dramatized Surrey's loss of honour at the English court more than his forced march on 12 December 1546. Alone, but under guard, the poet earl had to walk from the Lord Chancellor Wriothesley's house in Ely Place to the Tower of London—a mile and a half of shame. It was a Roman humiliation, the opposite of the imperial triumph through the streets the heir to the Duke of Norfolk might have expected a year earlier in France, and greater than Wyatt's humiliation, when arrested, at being tied by the hands. Arrested ten days earlier at Whitehall Palace, Surrey had been deceived, at least as narrated in the Spanish Chronicle, into his final capture by the explicit order of Henry VIII to his halberdier guards in yellow and red (144). In consultation with the Privy Council, who had orchestrated the steps of the arrest, especially its surprise, Henry VIII 'ordered the captain of the guard very secretly to take the Earl' and swiftly. Early Thursday afternoon, 2 December, entering the palace 'after dinner', Surrey saw the captain of the halberdiers walking towards him down the stairs in the hall of the Tudor palace. 'Welcome, my lord,' said the captain, Sir Anthony Wingfield (Surrey's cousin by marriage), who had already, at the king's direct command, a dozen halberdiers waiting in an adjoining corridor. The captain then began to lead the young earl towards the corridor away from his entourage, remarking, 'I wish to ask you to intercede for me with the Duke, your father, in a matter in which I need his favour, if you will deign to listen to me.' Surrey graciously consented. Known for his approachability, Surrey had acted as protector for both men and women at Henry VIII's court. The two had hardly disappeared from the crowded hall before the other halberdiers ran out, seized the young man, and, in the carefully planned kidnapping, hustled him, 'without attracting notice', to the river-landing of the Renaissance palace of honour that Henry VIII had built for Anne Boleyn. A boat was waiting on the Thames and the young poet was whisked away so fast that not until that night was Surrey's arrest first known. The Howard heir apparent had been forced to submit, without word to friend or family, to an arrest and capture he had known, for years, was always possible.

Surrey's anger rose at the audacity and deceit of his capture. His enemies had used a menial—the captain's request had brought out the generosity evident in all of Surrey's recent letters and military dispatches from France—to trap him. An outright chivalric encounter he might have expected, but his life at court had ended not in heroic struggle but in banality. From Whitehall his boat travelled probably to the Blackfriars landing and from there, the mile up to Ely Place, the former palace of the East Anglian bishop used by the Lord Chancellor as headquarters, and next to it, the church of the Anglo-Saxon saint from Ely, St Etheldreda. There Surrey remained under strict guard for ten days of interrogation and deposition. Then came the Sunday march from Ely Place to the Tower, on foot through Holborn, an act of specific shame and dishonour.

The Windsor Herald Charles Wriothesley, first cousin of the Lord Chancellor, recorded this Sunday march on 12 December. On this vigil day before St Lucy's, the winter solstice in the old calendar and a popular saint's day celebrated with lights and candles, the young Surrey had been forced, surrounded by guards and himself on foot, through the streets of Holborn—a humiliation for any nobleman but multiplied for Surrey. Before lively Sunday (pre-Puritan) shopping crowds on a holiday eve, he walked completely alone, with no servant or aide (even in the Tower he always had a servant). Most disgraceful of all, not only did he lack a horse to ride like his own bay jennet, and the accoutrements such a horse required, but he wore no proper dress for his rank, especially in public. Gone were trumpets with silken banners showing the Howard arms that preceded him and the large entourage of thirty to fifty horsemen about which the Lord Chancellor had scribbled during Surrey's interrogation: 'Ryding wt many men in the streetes' of London. It was a specially calculated insult to the young man about whom the Lord Chancellor had also jotted down: 'My lord of Surrey's pride and his gown of gold' and 'My lord of S. dissembling.' All signs and images of power were gone. Even his father had been arrested on that Sunday and sent to the Tower. The most powerful nobleman in the kingdom, Norfolk had rushed back to London from Kenninghall in East Anglia at the news of his son's arrest. Then, after a few days, he was seized himself (his letters to the Bishop of Winchester had been intercepted). The Lord Chancellor and the rest of the Privy Council must have realized it would have been pointless to make the old man walk in shame, strong though he was. A dramatic spectacle of terror was necessary, however, to threaten any other older nobility of the blood (or new nobility) who dared to challenge the new dispensation of the realm. Surrey's forced march made the point. All his splendour and glamour could be seen as the lie it really was. As the Windsor Herald details: 'The 12th daie of December the Duke of Norfolke and the Earle of Surrey, his sonne, were sent to the Towre of London prisonners, the duke going by water, but the Erle of Surrey was lead openlie from my Lord Chauncelor's in Holborne throwe London by Sir Anthonie Wyngfield, Capteine of the gard, and the lieutenante of the Towre [Sir Walter Stonor]' (1: 176). The march to the Tower had sealed Surrey's fate. Once in the Tower he was lost, as no one less than Henry VIII had explained to the naïve Cranmer only a few years before: 'O Lorde God! What fonde [foolish] symplicitie have you: so to permitt yourself to be ymprisoned, that every enemy of yours may take vantage againste you,' for once in prison three or four 'false knaves' (much more than the required two or one) could make witness and condemn you, 'whiche els now being at your libertie dare not ones open thair lipps or appere before your face'.[6]

Descended from heralds, the Lord Chancellor Thomas Wriothesley had himself arranged this humiliation of the walk, as he probably stage-managed the

[6] *LP*, vol. 21,ii, 555 (18); PRO *SP* 1/227, f. 129. 'Anecdotes and Character of Archbishop Cranmer, by Ralph Morice, his Secretary', in *Narratives of the Days of the Reformation*, ed. J. G. Nichols, Camden First Series, 77 (1849), 255.

depositions and the trial. Wriothesley had been one of numerous ambitious lower gentry who had risen to power under Henry VIII, a 'new erected man'. Because of his close connection with heraldry, Wriothesley probably devised the single charge against Surrey that stuck: the Howard heir had fabricated a coat of arms that spelled treason. He had been active at first on the side of Cromwell and the reformers. The 1538 Holbein miniature of Wriothesley, with his upward look and bright, almost ecstatic blue eyes, discloses a young man on the rise, soon to marry the niece of Stephen Gardiner, Bishop of Winchester. In fact, he had been particularly useful to Cromwell in acts of iconoclasm against the ancient centres of Canterbury and Winchester. At the latter cathedral, in his desire to loot ecclesiastical wealth for the Crown, he had smashed ancient statues and stained glass and then, at his most useful, in the middle of the night, demolished the ancient pilgrimage tomb of St Swithin (such a cultural artefact that on St Swithin's July feast-day, all English weather had been forecast). Also during that fatal night, to his uncle's further dismay, Wriothesley had eradicated the 700-year-old tomb and shrine of Alfred the Great at nearby Hyde Abbey, the body of the Anglo-Saxon king lost forever. He would break all forms of transcendence, the old myths and the old forms of honour. The Bishop of Winchester, who influenced his life, later defined for Cranmer the connection of the two iconoclasms: 'The destruction of images conteineth an enterprise to subvert religion and the state of the worlde with it; and specially the nobilitie, who, by images, set forth and spread abrode, to be red of all people, their linage and parentage, with remembrance of their state and acts.'[7] Later, with the same obedience but on a different side, Wriothesley had dutifully twisted the rack to break the reformed Christian Anne Askew's body, although he could not be counted on by the Howard conservatives. Before her beheading he had interrogated ruthlessly Queen Catherine Howard, as well as the aged widow of the 'Flodden Duke' and all the family involved. Then, as Seymour and Dudley returned to the court in late summer and Norfolk realized, as Bess Holland said in her trial evidence, that he was being excluded from, as she called it, 'The Privy Privy Council' (HB 737), the Lord Chancellor quietly switched sides. He soon orchestrated the single charge—the misuse of heraldic forms—against Surrey in the bill of indictment, after the initial charges of striking a gentleman and fomenting a *coup d'état* were discarded. The Lord Chancellor understood best of the Privy Council the intricacies of such a conspicuous heraldic display.

Yet, on that festival Sunday, Surrey's forced march to the Tower may have had an unexpected effect. The crowd was neither hostile nor indifferent to the young man, who had been, just a year before, a general at Boulogne and whose daring and bravery recalled the legendary 'Flodden Duke' still praised in ballads. An anonymous figure wrote down a single entry for the day in the strangely continuous *Chronicle of Grey Friars* of this period. Just who this observer was—a former

[7] Gardiner, *Letters*, 308. The tomb of Alfred the Great was not the only royal tomb destroyed in the Dissolution. The tombs of Henry I at Reading and Stephen at Faversham were destroyed and the bodies lost.

Franciscan gray-robed monk (their great centre had been near Ely House) operating underground, as were certain formerly cloistered men and women, or someone keeping a record—is not clear. 'This yere the XIIth day of December,' the observer wrote, 'the dewke of Norffoke and the yearle of Sorre hys sonne were comyttyd unto the tower of London: and the dewke went be watter from the Lorde chaunseler's place in Holborne, and soo downe unto the wattersyde and so be [by] watter unto the tower; and hys sonne the yerle of Sorre went thorrow the cytte of London makynge grete lamentacion.'[8] The grammar of the terse final phrase, with its ambiguous participle, underscores the intensity of the event. If Surrey were himself lamenting, was it with violence, an un-Puritan hero like Achilles bellowing on the beaches before Troy? Or was it the cry of 'the most proud foolish boy in England', as the evangelical Dean of Westbury told George Constantine in 1538, a Surrey finally confronted with the results of his immature dangerous game-playing? It was certainly not Victorian silent manly suffering. Words and sounds poured out loud enough to still a holiday crowd or at least be heard above it. Or does the participle 'making', as in a French or Latin position, refer to 'the cytte of London' and its crowds? Were they captured, as the romantic Bapst believes, by the sight of this descendant of Plantagenet kings so reduced? Antony Antony, another mysterious observer of Henry VIII's last days,[9] is less ambiguous: both Surrey and his father were locked up in the Tower by four o'clock that Sunday afternoon, that is, by nightfall in the northern European winter.

'That conjured league'

According to most accounts, correct or incorrect, Surrey's cousin Sir Richard Southwell betrayed the poet in a single act, accusing him of displaying a false coat of arms. Southwell did not act alone, as his accusation shows. He had switched sides. Surrey refers, in his paraphrase of Psalm 55 written in the Tower, to a conspiracy against him. In two vivid examples of apostrophe, the violence of which does not exist in the Latin Vulgate from which he is translating, Surrey's speaker cries out: 'Rayne those unbrydled tungs! breake that conjured league!' The 'league' (a word of love in the Clere sonnet) pursues him like wild animals: 'My foes they bray so loud, and eke threpe on so fast, / Buckled to do me scathe, so is their malice bent.' Was this 'league' Surrey's paranoid delusion, or did it exist as the natural reaction of a healthy realm in defending itself against so totally disruptive and neurotic a force or simply as a political faction that did not support Surrey or the Howards but only had to sit still and let the young heir destroy himself? In any case, conspiracy is certainly what the later Renaissance saw. Conspiracy destroyed the poet earl—so testify voices from Mary I and Hadrianus Junius to

[8] *Chronicle of Grey Friars*, ed. J. G. Nichols, Camden Society, 53 (1852), 52.

[9] Bapst, *Deux gentilshommes-poètes* 352; Bodleian Library Delta MS 624, handwritten notes in margin of 565 based on the original diary of Antony Antony.

Challoner (and implicit in the myths of Nashe and Drayton) to Sir Walter Raleigh to the Jacobean Earl of Arundel and Lord Herbert of Cherbury, who wrote: 'Divers at the king's council disaffected [Surrey], and particularly the Earl of [Hertford (Seymour)], as knowing that after the king's death (now thought to be imminent) none was so capable to oppose him in the place he aspir'd to of protector. All which circumstances concurring, and being voiced abroad, encouraged divers of [Surrey's] adversaries to declare themselves' (737). And 'declare' they did, whether telling the truth or not, Wriothesley announcing, to the resident and foreign ambassadors in London, immediately after Surrey's arrest the charge (never in the actual bill of indictment but implicit in the trial) that both Howards had intended to seize the king and his son, murder most of the council, and take over the kingdom. Ironically, the scenario of taking over the realm was already taking place in another quarter, the accusers themselves.

Lord Herbert had singled out from the 'divers of his adversaries' Edward Seymour, the Earl of Hertford (Plate 25), through his mother's descent of royal lineage. Surrey had a special animosity towards Seymour, according to his sister (HB 737), but the soon-to-be Duke of Somerset had always been a leader of considerable sophistication who may have held a profound admiration for the poet earl. They had been visiting friends, in fact, in the late 1530s when Surrey was beginning his *Aeneid*. When, by the end of January 1547, Seymour became the Lord Protector and virtual ruler of the realm for the next two years before his own beheading, he had gained exactly what the poet earl had desired and sought in the last years of his life: the Lord Protectorate of the new young king, who was to describe the new Roman role of his uncle in a proclamation issued on 4 June 1550: 'by the Advise and Consent of our most dearely beloved Uncle Edward Duke of Somerset Governor of our Person, and Protector of all our Realmes, Dominions, and Subjects . . .' As the new Protector, Seymour quickly took over both of the imprisoned Norfolk's offices, Lord Treasurer and Earl Marshal, leaving for Dudley the office he had earlier taken from Surrey's wife's family (the de Veres), that of Lord Great Chamberlain. Most of all, Seymour assumed, within two months of Surrey's death, the venerated title of Duke of Somerset, previously associated with the family of Henry VIII's grandmother, Margaret Beaufort and the Lancastarians, and given in 1525 to Henry Fitzroy. With these titles, Seymour was soon using the royal 'we'.[10]

As the Duke of Somerset, Seymour was to follow a judicious policy towards ultimate reformation of the kingdom, always keeping, as Bush notes, 'the classical principle of measure as the touchstone of conduct'. This measure might include considerable iconoclasm, the vivid process of which can be viewed in one of its few visualizations in an allegorical picture Aston has analysed (Plate 24): Henry VIII in bed points to his son and the new Somerset beside him and then the other

[10] *LP*, vol. 21,ii, 697, 555 (18). *Garter Register*, vol. 1, p. xxv. For the range of Edward Seymour's extraordinary executive ability, see *Report*, ed. Blatcher (HMC), x–xi, 12 ff., 16, 23, 29, 35, 45, 55 and, for his first letter as Somerset using the royal 'we', 108.

new succession of power, behind which men is an inset picture showing two statues (one a tall pillar with the Virgin Mary and Child) being efficiently toppled. In this newly organized society based on reformed Christianity and on the new élite meant to rule it, Seymour kept 'the consideration of how man should conduct himself' as a central focus, a good humanist principle. This focus could also mean that the purest Christian principles and the amassing of enormous wealth from the ruin of others could resolve themselves into a matter of formal governance and urbane styling (what Somerset seized from Surrey House illustrates the Protector's excellent taste). Elegance performed as a kind of ultimate truth as it literally tore down the old world for the purer.[11] Almost four years to the day after Surrey's execution, on 22 January 1552, Edward Seymour, the Duke of Somerset, was beheaded on Tower Hill. This time he had been trapped by John Dudley, then the Duke of Northumberland and, after Somerset's annihilation, the only duke except for the boy Suffolk left in the kingdom. So, even in 1546, within Surrey's 'conjured league', new hatreds were rising. In another of his scribbled notes at Surrey's trial, Wriothesley had perceived a force that did not include him: 'Things in common. Paget, Hertford [Seymour], Admiral [Dudley], Denney.'

The Lord Admiral in 1546, John Dudley, the future grandfather of Sir Philip Sidney, became virtual ruler of the realm after 1552 and reigned with even more power than Somerset (although he deliberately eschewed the dangerous title of Protector) until his own capture and beheading by the new Queen Mary I. As an indication of what lay ahead, already in the first months of Edward VI's reign, Dudley had appeared at court with an entourage of a hundred, forty gentleman in black velvet with white and black sleeves, sixty in simpler cloth.[12] The third of Surrey's 'adversaries', like Lepidus in the old Roman triumvirate, represented the new kind of strategist who arranges everything but does not pull the trigger himself. Sir William Paget also personified the superb civil service Cromwell had transformed out of the offices of Wolsey and the efficient late Yorkist and early Tudor bureaucracies into a universal model for centuries of government service. After his arrest, Surrey recognized his own deception by this ambiguous if thoroughly competent hatchet man, who had always expressed friendship, though less so as the earl's power waned. Behind this loose triumvirate stood, of course, the greater practical power of the Privy Chamber and the absolute guardian of the king in his last months, Sir Anthony Denny. To this power, the only one Surrey might reach, Surrey dedicated a poem from the Tower.

Denny may earlier have distributed Surrey's poems to Anne Askew. Whether Anne Askew read the Wyatt elegy and Surrey's new heroic conception of the poet or not, her court supporters probably had, including Denny. These friends at court had come under considerable political pressure because of their sympathy for the helpless gentlewoman from Lincolnshire in Newgate prison, and the

[11] M. L. Bush, *The Government Policy of Protector Somerset* (1975), 112. For a discussion of the iconoclastic signs in this picture, see Aston, *The King's Bedpost*, esp. 89–96, 108–12.

[12] Wilbur Kitchener Jordan, *Edward VI* (1968–70), vol. 1, 94.

women, particularly the beautiful Lady Denny, as well as Lady Hoby, the Countess of Hertford, the fiery young Duchess of Suffolk, all under the patronage of the third Queen Catherine, exemplified for Bale the holy women around Christ, who followed him from Galilee and gave of their own substance. To the queen's weekly devotional readings and instructive sermons by Bishop Hugh Latimer and other reformed humanist Christian intellectuals, these women (with their husbands and relatives like the future translator of Castiglione, Sir Thomas Hoby) brought stylish religious texts they could commend. It is possible that to these readings Surrey's own brother brought manuscripts of the earl's biblical paraphrases, copied as they were in a collection and seldom separately (the earl could not himself attend, for obvious reasons). In fact, in the last Lent of 1546 Lord Thomas Howard argued indiscreetly in his reformed fervour about scripture with other young gentlemen of the court; in the queen's chamber he vented his rage against conservative Christians and ranted elsewhere at court, to the extent that he had been arrested. The Howard presence, brother and sister, was thus not unknown to élite reformed Christianity. Indeed, in these groups Surrey may have found one last audience. What would have been more natural for Queen Catherine's circle than to read together (or even sing) an elegant recent 'Englishing' of the Bible's wisdom literature by England's greatest living poet? Who better could have admired not only Surrey's choice of reformed diction but experimental rhythms that promised a language of the future—the vernacular Luther wanted—for their religion of the future?

To a powerful member of this circle, Sir Anthony Denny, 'the courtier *par excellence* of the last years of the reign' of Henry VIII (Plate 18), Surrey dedicated one of his Psalm translations in the Tower in December 1546. He added a prefatory lyric. The poet earl knew Denny synthesized in his person both the humanism and the religion that drove the late Henrician and Edwardian courts. Surrey's Davidic text, with its careful Erasmian equivalence of translation, thus served as a medium for his real message. Denny had been trained at St Paul's under Lely, the greatest Latinist in England, and then at St John's, Cambridge, during the ascendancy of Bishop Fisher. In this same year as Surrey's arrest, the printer to the young Prince Edward had declared Denny 'a favourable supporter of all good learning and a very *Maecenas* of all towards wits'. The powerful courtier had already shown patronage to both the older Sir Thomas Elyot and the younger Roger Ascham and had been praised by Sir John Cheke for his 'desire of knowledge of antiquities'.[13] Although this early courtly model of Puritan humanism appears to lack Burgundian chivalry or Castiglione's *sprezzatura*, in his painting by Holbein he certainly possesses the *gravitas* Castiglione in the first book of *The Courtier* required, the intensity stemming as much from Denny's humanism and Roman modelling as from his religious commitments. For Surrey, he may have appeared as an updated Roman *amicus principis*.

[13] Starkey, *Reign*, 142, 133–6. Cf. King, *Tudor Royal Iconography*, 54–6 and *passim*.

But he also had charge of all access to the private apartments of the king. In a period when the king was increasingly sedentary although as politically alert as ever, Denny acted as conduit for both monarch and court. On call twenty-four hours a day, he provided a sounding-board for the king after, or before, discussions and debates with Paget or Seymour or the jester Will Somer or anyone else at court. In 1546 Denny also controlled, with his brother-in-law, John Gates, the dying king's 'dry stamp' for the royal signature. He could conceivably control executions. Most of all, as Surrey knew, Denny's power would hold until the last day of Henry VIII's reign, as it did, in fact. When the king was dying on the afternoon of 27 January 1547, Denny had the courage and objectivity (after all, he had been Groom of the Stool for a long time) to tell the monarch that not even the Supreme Head could escape death. The king must prepare himself, soul and body. After hearing this from Denny, Henry VIII replied, assured of his own real presence as ever: 'Yet is the mercy of Christ able to pardon me all my sins, though they were greater than they be.'[14]

If Denny might determine the use of the 'dry stamp', then Surrey's poem to him acts, by no surprise, as an apologia (but with no outright confession). In Surrey's eyes, fashionable Davidic contrition might lead to official forgiveness, especially if expressed in the kind of stylish syllogism Denny and the humanist court would appreciate. The one-sentence prefatory lyric, in the musical form of a *strambotto*, begins with a long subordinate clause of self-justification, with familiar themes ('reckless youth') bordering on whining in a series of abstract nouns. Then they rise to what might have been a genuine act of contrition; but the subjective act is arrived at by rigorous logic. Thus, in its form as enthymeme, the minor premise suppressed, the poem heads immediately, after the introductory major premise, to an accusation of self—'My Denny, then mine error, deep impressed, / Began to work despair of liberty'—and then to the conclusion of sudden grace, the leap from 'despair' to the one figure of 'David, the perfect warrior', who alone, it seems, will teach this earl humility.

It is a question if Surrey achieves the announced intention of penitence in the paraphrased text of Psalm 88 that followed in long lines of Poulter's Measure. The speaker does ask the Lord to 'Grant that the just request of this repentant mind / So pierce thine eares that in thy sight some favor it may find.' But the real centre of Surrey's paraphrase emerges angrily with the question: 'Within this careful mind, burdened with care and grief, / Why dost thou not appear, Oh Lord, that shouldst be his relief?' Surrey directly catalogues the consequences of 'blind endured [hardened] hearts' who cannot see a poet prophet in their midst. A poet alone can give God the right kind of honour and praise.

[14] Scarisbrick, *Henry VIII*, 495. Because Denny was made an executor of Henry's last controversial will, he was also involved in the crucial takeover of the new Edwardian state. But ultimately he received no position of high rank. In a final twist in his relationship with Surrey, Denny was named one of King Edward's leaders against Kett's rebellion in 1549 and fought in Norwich against the rebels in Surrey House.

Nor blasted [blazoned] may thy name be by the mouth of those
Whom death hath shut in silence so as they may not disclose.
The lively voice of them that in thy word delight
Must be the trump that must resound the glory of thy might.

Of all the 'conjured league', only Denny could understand the value of that 'trump' in English culture in 1546. Surrey tried in the Tower to reach one of the few hopes left him by using his greatest asset now, not his power of blood but language. It would not be enough.

Sir Richard Southwell

Although each of Surrey's 'adversaries' had the will to survive and win the spoils in the breakdown of the Henrician state, Sir Richard Southwell had a greater motive and greater fear: his own extinction with his Howard cousin benefactors. Sir Richard Southwell must have acceded to the temptation of betrayal by summer or early autumn of 1546. Whatever role he actually played, Southwell remained in the later Howard family cult as the evil genius of the young father's tragic death. The effect appeared to them all the more Judas-like because Southwell, orphaned in 1515, had been brought up with Surrey, thirteen years his junior, remaining close at hand for all of Surrey's short life. In the 1590s, seemingly quite consciously, the betrayal was redeemed, in another twist of genealogy, by Richard Southwell's grandson (through illegitimacy). The poet and Jesuit martyr Robert Southwell (also canonized by Pope Paul VI in 1970) acted as chaplain to the Countess of Arundel, the wife of the imprisoned future saint Philip Howard. In Arundel House, Southwell wrote not only his famous Christmas lyric 'The Burning Babe' (with its influence on Donne and Crashaw) but the devotional tracts that reveal the steadfastness the East Anglian saint would have under the rack and torture of Topcliffe and other pursuivants. Southwell was also tutor to the future 'Collector Earl', Surrey's great-grandson, who years later exchanged, from his room in Arundel House that held over thirty Holbeins in oils, Holbein's portrait (Plate 22) of 'the man who had brought his ancestor the poet Earl of Surrey to his knees'.[15] With no sorrow, except to lose such a work of art, Arundel gave the portrait to Cosimo II of Florence so that today, watching the crowds in the Uffizi, is the long face, slightly receding chin (with scars Holbein adroitly marks), and the eyes (Holbein calls them 'yellow') of the man whose career began with committing murder for his kinsman Norfolk and ended as a true servant of Queen Mary.

The betrayal came quickly. In the first days of December 1546, after a conversation with the poet earl, Southwell supposedly received an insulting letter from

[15] Howarth, *Arundel*, 71. For the place of Southwell and the whole *métier* of the Howard household, see Susan Vokes, 'The Early Career of Thomas, Lord Howard, Earl of Surrey and Third Duke of Norfolk, 1474–*c*.1525', esp. ch. 4 and Part III.

Surrey. He took the insulting letter to the council and through them to the king, a replay of the summer and Surrey's letter to Dudley. As a result of writing this letter with insults and threats—far worse than voicing them—Surrey was arrested. On 2 December, Southwell came forth, saying 'he knew certain things of the earl, that touched fidelity to the king.' Although no witnesses were actually needed for crimes condemned by the Succession Act of 1536 and only one witness was needed for conviction in other crimes if the judges deemed that witness of good character,[16] Southwell was especially needed because soon in December the first two charges against Surrey were deemed too weak for proof. A charge that would stick had to be found. Wriothesley, the son of heralds, found one that could be manipulated by himself and the heralds, and be made believable to the dying king. In the indictment, whether Southwell or not, someone reported that on last 7 October he had seen at Kenninghall Palace, the greatest of the Howard mansions, a treasonably designed coat of arms. He had probably seen this coat of arms also at Surrey House since, as Surrey's letter from Hussey specifically mentions, Southwell had been commissioned to buy glass for the many windows of a new mansion that required the display of such arms. According to the accusation, Surrey had displayed a coat of arms that showed in the first quarter of the design the royal arms of the Anglo-Saxon king St Edward the Confessor, who ruled England from 1042 to 1066 (roughly the same time as Surrey's putative ancestor, Hereward the Wake, a coincidence of much interest to the examining Wriothesley in his fourth, sixth, ninth, and tenth interrogatories to Surrey). Even though he had the silver labels in this quarter to show its difference from the royal arms, these could also indicate the arms of the Prince of Wales, so the young earl was considered by the realm to have identified himself with the heir to the throne and to have made a claim to royal power.

Surrey was astounded at this first in a series of betrayals by friends and family. In the 2 December confrontation, just after his arrest, before the Lord Chancellor, Seymour, Dudley, Paget, and others at Ely House, the poet earl had been almost speechless, then turned 'vehemently' and 'affirmed himself a true man, desiring to be try'd by justice, or else offering himself to fight in his shirt with Southwel' (HB 737). The strange request of a challenge confirmed the Romance world of Lancelot du Lac, in which fantasy, his sister said, he always lived. Although as late as the 1520s Charles V had offered trial by single combat, 'in his shirt', and Surrey himself had offered this challenge in France in 1545, this form of fighting, like trial by ordeal, had virtually disappeared. Proving his innocence in this type of single combat was to give Southwell the advantage of wearing armour while Surrey wore only the linen shirt beneath such armour—in short, as designed in the highest codes of chivalry, the poet earl would allow God to justify his innocence. Hearing this request, the Privy Council, meeting that December in Seymour's

[16] Richard Marius, *Thomas More: A Biography* (1984), 508. But for proof of the validity of the two-witness rule (and Wriothesley's use of it to condemn Surrey), see Peter R. Moore, 'Hamlet and the Two Witness Rule', *Notes and Queries*, 242 (new series, 44) (1997), 498–503.

house, may have been inwardly delighted at this pathetic gesture of the Howard heir so out of political reality and now so vulnerable. For the moment, the Privy Council committed both Surrey and Southwell—the equation an insult—to confinement. In a few days they forced Surrey to march through London to the Tower. Southwell was freed.

Henry VIII

But there was one sole power behind all the 'divers' forces attacking Surrey. Neither the triumvirate, Denny, nor Southwell could dare act if the king himself were not implicitly giving the sign that the young poet must be killed. If the men in control of the government saw theirs as a God-given future without limit, an inevitable progression of a reformed Christianity and a new Roman *renovatio* that had come to birth through the power and genealogy of the grand figure straddling the wall of the Privy Chamber at Whitehall, the absolute king gave them the power to dream their future. The future itself regarded the king and the Privy Council and Surrey's last days rather differently.

For that future (at least before the English Revolution) neither the king nor the Edwardian makers of a newly elected kingdom were considered either absolute or particularly just. Raleigh gave language to the new attitude towards the first Supreme Head: 'If all the pictures and Patternes of a mercilesse Prince were lost in the World, they might all againe be painted to the life, out of the story of this King.' Sir Walter Raleigh saw Surrey, for example, as a victim who had embodied the highest nobility at the same time that Surrey's grandfather Buckingham became a special martyr of honour for James I. In the same Jacobean world, the Jesuit Robert Parsons tallied up the executions by Henry VIII of two queens, three chancellors, three cardinals, two dukes, two earls, one marquis, two countesses, and five peers. Although the underground Jesuit and friend of Surrey's martyred grandson Philip Howard does not count Lutheran martyrs like Robert Barnes or the Anabaptists or Sacramentarians like Anne Askew, or his fellow Catholics (strangely silent on the execution of commons and nobles in the Pilgrimage of Grace or the disappearance and execution of resisting monks in the 1530s), the inaccurate tally nevertheless makes its point. In Parsons's eyes, Henry VIII set out to destroy the old nobility of England and thereby the basis of an ancient civilization that neither demanded nor needed a violent change of social order, certainly not one ending in a Dudley as tyrant ruler.[17]

But the Elizabethan Jesuit misses a finer point, as does Raleigh. When the 18-year-old Henry had ascended the throne in 1509, he had inherited a nobility of

[17] Sir Walter Raleigh, *The History of the World*, ed. C. A. Patrides (1971), 56. Philip Hughes, SJ, *The Reformation in England* (1954), vol. 2, 101. For a carefully documented analysis of just what was being lost in terms of social and communal inscription, see Eamon Duffy, *The Stripping of the Altars*, especially the concluding chapter on Elizabeth I.

twelve high noblemen and thirty barons. In the early years of his reign he had added four barons by the restoration or revival of titles. By the end of Henry VIII's reign, not only was the old blood nobility reduced by 33 per cent from natural and artificial causes, but 41 per cent of the new nobility created by Henry VIII were also reduced.[18] Thus, if any philosophical conception of blood nobility appears seriously in doubt after Erasmus' attacks in his 1501 *Handbook of a Christian Soldier*, so was the presence of any nobility in jeopardy, in the new Henrician realm of the one and the many, unless sanctioned by the state in the person of the Supreme Head. Whether a White Rose noblewoman like the aged mother of Reginald Pole, the Countess of Salisbury, or a new Christian martyr like Anne Askew, no man or woman, young or old, was to be spared. This was the new equality of justice.

The irony was that finally not even the Supreme Head could control either the order or definitions in the progression of history he had unleashed. He could not assure the succession beyond the reign of his son to his daughters or to his sister's great-grandson and the Stuarts and, least of all, avoid the English Revolution and its consequences for the next centuries that would deny ideologically any validity of total royal presence. In his last days, the dying king clearly brooded over the indeterminacy before him. Immediately he had to secure the succession and life of his young son, remembering all too well the horrors of the Wars of the Roses, caused by the boy King Henry VI and into which indeterminacy Edward V with another Protector Uncle had disappeared. As long as he was alive, the old king may have determined that no one, not even Surrey's 'conjured league', could act without his direction. That Christmas of 1546 Henry VIII was so caught up in directing history, in saving his son by condemning the Howards, that he never left London at all after he dashed back from Oatlands. Unusually he sent the queen and most of the court on to the palace at Greenwich for Christmas without him. He had spotted in the Howards a threat to his genealogy, especially the poet earl, as one who aspired to be not only a stylish Protector but a Renaissance monarch. When Henry VIII found evidence of such aspiration in Surrey and was deliberately lied to by Wriothesley and the Garter King of Arms, his leading herald, about Surrey's coat of arms, he felt justified in destroying the Howards, especially the son who threatened his own.

Bill of Indictment and Judgement

The bill of indictment and judgement finally given against Henry Howard, Earl of Surrey, spells out the exact terms, in the eyes of the English realm, of his dishonour and the reason for his execution. The bill was based on an Act passed hurriedly ten years before, in July 1536, part of which (C. 7) was designed as an Act of

18 H. Miller, *Henry VIII*, 38–41.

Succession and part of which (C. 4) specifically to declare as a traitor to the Crown Surrey's uncle, Lord Thomas Howard, who had secretly married Lady Margaret Douglas. Updated and rephrased for Surrey's situation in 1547, the act's three traditional parts correspond to a syllogism: the act itself, the facts of the particular case, and then the judgement based on the conjunction of the major and minor premises; or whoever does A should die, Surrey did A, therefore Surrey should die. The major premise of Surrey's Latin bill of indictment stipulated that no person or persons may 'maliciously or wilfully' cause 'through words spoken, written, or printed, or through any external deed or act' not just harm but 'danger' to 'the royal bodily presence [*celsitudo* in the Latin text] of the said Lord now King' or to 'those persons of his blood or of his succession having to do with the state of this realm of England'. Thus 'if any person or persons by art have imaged, invented, or attempted through the colour of any pretext to deprive the said Lord King, the Queen, or the heir legitimately procreated from the body of the said Lord King' of any of their 'titles, names, ranks, or royal state or royal power'—no matter who this person or persons be—'let them be adjudged High Traitors' and their offence 'High Treason'. Once convicted, such traitors are to suffer the death penalty.

Surrey's treason was egregious. It was a matter of falsely 'imaged' honour that threatened 'to deprive' the king's 'heir' of his 'titles' and all the other marks of his royal honour. Since 'the most excellent Illustrious and Mighty our Lord Henry VIII by grace of God king of England, France, and Ireland, Defender of the Faith, and on earth Supreme Head of the Church of England and Ireland is the true and indubitable king of this realm of England,' he has 'carried, borne, displayed and used certain arms and insignia of the highest nobility', that is, the arms of St Edward the Confessor as described by heralds: ' "viz. Azure, a cross fleury, between five martlets [birds] gold." ' This 'aforesaid present Lord King and his ancestors of the highest nobility, one and all, kings of this realm of England, from the time beyond the memory of man' had displayed such arms that 'uniquely belong to and appertain to the present Lord King and his said ancestor-kings and throne of this kingdom of England' and are 'not for any other persons whatsoever in the same manner and form' as the king and his ancestors have displayed them. Furthermore, 'since also the most excellent Lord Edward now prince of this kingdom of England and Son and Heir-Apparent of the said excellent most mighty Lord present King' can also hold, bear, and use 'by pure and absolute right [*de mero jure*]' the 'said arms and insignia' but designated by ' "three labels silver" ' to indicate he is the true heir apparent, it is treason that the young Earl of Surrey should display a coat of arms with the arms of Edward the Confessor in the first quarter, even if they are differenced from the king's by three silver labels. This difference belongs only to an heir apparent, in this case, to the throne of England. Did Surrey see himself as a prince who was an heir to the throne? Did he plan an insurrection? Would he be king?

The terrible act, therefore, of 'Henry Howard recently of Kenninghall in County Norfolk, holding the highly noble Order of the Garter otherwise called

Henry Earl of Surrey, not having God before his eyes but seduced by diabolical incitement and not at all weighing his owed loyalty' but acting 'as a false and malicious traitor and public enemy to the said most mighty and most serene Lord present King' occurred 'on the 7th day of October in the 38th year of the reign of the said Lord King [1546], at Kenninghall in the said County of Norfolk.' On that day Henry Surrey 'falsely, maliciously, and treasonably and indeed openly and publicly held, displayed, and bore, and used' the arms of St Edward the Confessor. He was thereby 'willing, wishing, and desiring, and, with all his nefarious art and talent, imaging, inventing, practicing, and attempting to deprive the aforementioned most illustrious and serene our King of the rights, dignity, titles, and names of his royal state.'

For that painted display at Kenninghall, possibly on a glass window, Surrey 'no less treasonably then and there did cause to be made and painted together and joined with his own proper arms and insignia of Henry Howard himself the said arms and insignia of the said Lord now King with three labels called "Three labels silver" '. It should be noted that no such coat of arms, not even that listed in the inventory of the ransacked Surrey House, was ever brought forward as evidence. Yet the indictment assumed that Surrey committed this act for nothing less than 'the purpose of undermining, destroying, annihilating, and scandalizing the true and indubitable title of the said Lord King now on the throne of his kingdom England'. Although he had used the labels of difference, he had a diabolic intention in doing so: 'no less treasonably for the purpose of disinheriting and cutting off the same most excellent Lord Prince Edward from his true and indubitable title and from the throne of this kingdom England.'

In his October display Surrey had given enough 'occasion by which the same Lord King could now be shaken and cut off' and led 'into scandal, peril, derogation, and contempt' of his reign and 'his said legitimate title to his said throne of England' threatened. There was yet a larger offence. By these signs, Surrey intended rebellion. In a age when, as Anglo notes, even more than a prince's or nobleman's own person, his coat of arms was known everywhere,[19] the bill intimates that use of such arms had threatened the 'peril' of a future rebellion like the recent Pilgrimage of Grace. In the language of the text—stated even before the offence against king and prince—Surrey had 'falsely, maliciously, and treasonably' schemed 'to extinguish utterly and annihilate the heart-felt love and obedience which the true and faithful subjects of the said Lord King of this his realm of England bear to the same Lord King and by right are held to bear.' In this desire, the young earl intended to break up the bond between king and people rendered on the title-page of the 1539 Bible. He would 'stir up sedition between the said Lord King and all the faithful subjects of the King and cause the same Lord King to be deprived and disinherited from the throne of this his kingdom of England and his other honor, his preminences and power.' In this scheming, Surrey had offended not only

[19] Sidney Anglo, *Images of Tudor Kingship* (1992), 28–38.

'against the form and effect of the aforementioned statute and diverse other statutes of this kind by chance recently published and passed but also against the peace of the said Lord King, his throne and his dignity', his real presence.

The poet was condemned to die. Although finally commuted to beheading, the immediate judgement of the indictment was that the body of the poet earl was to be drawn and quartered at inglorious Tyburn, the details spelled out in the text of, first, his hanging, after which, still breathing, head to be severed and the body of the young man to be split into four parts, and then head and split body to be placed where 'the said Lord King would want to assign them.'[20]

Ransacking of Kenninghall and Surrey House

Everything was now taken away from the still living Henry, Earl of Surrey. By the time he began writing Psalms in the Tower, the young poet had doubtless heard (probably through his single servant) of the terror that had come to his family, especially his pregnant wife, and the almost total ransacking of Kenninghall and Surrey House in Norwich and the general destruction of all that the Howards had held in honour for generations. The comprehensive report on this ransacking disappeared as have almost all documents in this matter in which Southwell was concerned.[21] The records that do remain tell a great deal, not least the report of a commission to discover evidence of treason that set out immediately for East Anglia on the vigil of St Lucy's 'betwixt three and foure of the clock in the afternone', the northern European sky already dark. The authority for this commission—Southwell, another Howard cousin Wymond Carew, and Sir John Gates, Denny's brother-in-law and keeper of the king's stamp—came from the highest level in the king's palace. They rode steadily and 'arrived at your highnes Towne of Thetforde seven Miles from Kennynghall the mondaie at night following and were at the Duke of Nofffolk his house this tuesdaie the fourteneth of this instant by the breke of the daie so that the first newes of the Duke of Norffolk and his Soone cam thether by us.' The shock was, of course, extreme for the retinue of over 200 servants and the Howard women left behind in the palace on the plain of western Norfolk. After first locking the gates and back doors of the great house

[20] I have translated the Latin in Nott, vol. 1, pp. lxxvii–xxx, following also the transcription in *The Third Report of the Deputy Keeper of the Public Records* (1842), 267 from PRO KB8/14. This report also includes records of the oyer and terminer hearings at Norwich Castle on 31 December 1546, 1, 7, 10, and 11 January 1547. The Writ of Certiorari 'commanding' the indictment to be returned to the Chancery and the Justices' Precept was addressed to the Constable of the Tower. He was to 'bring up the Earl of Surrey at Guildhall on Thursday the 13th of January' at which time 'The Lord Chancellor, pursuant to the Writ of Certiorari ad the Precept of the Justices, brings [would bring] the Indictment into Court.' At his trial Surrey pleaded not Guilty and the 'Venire of Jury from the county of Norfolk awarded instanter' then gave their verdict of GUILTY 'but as to what goods or chattels, lands or tenements the said Sir Henry Howard possessed, the Jury know not.' The 'Judgment, as is usual of High Treason' was 'execution to be had at Tyburn.'

[21] Casady, *Henry Howard*, 195.

so no one could escape in the first light, they 'dyd declare our desire to speak with the Duchesse of Richmond and Elizabeth Holland', the old duke's young mistress for over fifteen years. Although the women were 'newlie risan and not redie', after learning who the men were, 'they cam unto us without delaie.' In the dining chamber, the men 'imparted unto them the case and condicion wherin the said Duke and his Soon without your great mercy dyd stonde'. The young Duchess of Richmond was 'sore prelexed' and began 'trimbleng' and in her shock 'like to fall downe'. But 'commyng unto herself agayne,' the letter continues, 'she was not we assure your maieste forgetfull of her dewtie and did most humblie and Reverentlie upon her knees humble herself in all unto your highness,' that is, the Duchess of Richmond, Henry VIII's only daughter-in-law, knelt down before the three male agents, two of whom were either cousins or former family friends, and blurted out: 'althoughe nature constrained her soore to loove her father whom she hathe ever thought to be a trewe and faithfull Subject and alsoo to desire the well doeng of his Soon her naturall brother whom she noteth to be a rasshe man yeat for her part she woolde nor will hide or conceill any thing from your maiestes knowledge speciallie if it be of weight or otherwise as it shall fall in her remembraunce.' She preferred to write down any information to help the investigation. The interrogators were touched by 'her humble conformity' and her 'trothe and franknesse', but desired to see her 'chambers and coofers'. Not only did they find no writings worth sending but found in her private world 'her coofers and chambers soo bare, as Your Maiestie woold hardlie think her Juelles suche as she hadde solde or laide to gage to paie her debtes as she her maydens and the Almoner doe saie.' It was a different situation with the old duke's mistress Elizabeth Holland, in whose chamber they found 'gerdelles, beades buttons of golde pearle and Ringes sett stones of diverse sortes', so much that the three began to make their first of many inventories.

'And as we have begonne here at this hedde house,' the three would send out their 'most discreat and trustie Servauntes' to the other Howard houses in Norfolk and Suffolk 'to staie that nothing shalbe embeaseled' until they could get there. Already the Almoner has promised to send the gold and silver plate along. There was no immediate cash on that morning of 14 December but the Steward may, the commissioners thought, have some 'upon this last accompt' and in the next dispatch the three promise the king they will let him know all about the jewels found here or elsewhere and of 'the clere yerelie valewe of his [Norfolk's] possessions and all other his yerelie Revenue'. Robert Holditch, Norfolk's controller who had written the Latin household book in 1519, now turned over £1480 in cash (and was to pay sums of ready cash until January 1549). In a few months, another Howard steward, Richard Fulmerston, to whom Surrey owed money, bought the ancient Thetford Priory from the new Protector who, with Dudley, made quick sale after quick sale of Howard estates throughout the realm.[22]

[22] PRO LR. 2/113/129; 2/115/1. CPR 1547–8 33; 126; 171; 201; 211 detail these sales. For the background, see H. Miller, 'Henry VIII's Unwritten Will', 84–105. For a full account of what happened to the Howard estates after 1547, see Head, *Ebbs*, ch. 10 and 11. Some of Surrey's best horses went to Sir

There was now the question of what to do about 'therle of Surrey his wief and children with certen women in the Norsery attending upon them'. Close up the house? Or keep part open as 'shall seme meat tattend upon the said Earle his wief lookeng her tyme to lye inne at this next Candelmasse [2 February]'? With Surrey's wife, the young countess, ready to have her child in six weeks, at the Feast of the Purification of the Virgin, what should they do? The men beseech 'your highnis to signify unto us where and in what place your pleasour is to bestowe her for the tyme and also whom it pleaseth your grace to appoint for the defraieng of the chardges of thousehold'. The three men knew they could not take Surrey's wife with them because, even if she could travel, the young woman would become, by her swollen body, a witness particularly unwanted by the Privy Council. It was decided to move her—at least a revealing item about Surrey's wife in a later inventory indicates that. From the apparel of the old Duke of Norfolk, there had been taken 'a night gown of black satin much worn, and furred with coney and lamb, which was delivered to the Lady of Surrey to put about her in her chariot.' The expectant Frances de Vere Howard, who was obviously being moved from Kenninghall, had been waiting in her 'chariot', and had become chilled and weakened in the roar and collapse of the December morning. After her departure and that of the Duchess of Richmond and Bess Holland the next day, the central Howard estate was closed and handed over to Southwell until the Princess Mary arrived there to live out the Edwardian years.

Finally 'All the said Duke his writenges and bookes wee have taken unto our chardge and shall withall diligence peruse them and further doo as the waight of them shall requere.' Surrey's holograph manuscripts both at Kenninghall and Surrey House and in London at Lambeth were also seized (some or most forever lost or, if Sir John Harington was in the search party, held by him). With that, the three agents pray that God will 'preserve your roiall Maiestie in longe and hartie helthe', and signed off 'ffrom Kennynghall betwixt the houres of vi and vii in the evening this tuesdaie' 14 December 1546, 'in the xxxviiith of your most victorious and happie Reigne.' They added an immediate postscript: the Duchess of Richmond and Elizabeth Holland 'take their iourney towardes London in the morneng or the next daie at the furthest' for interrogation. The agents wrote across their letter 'hast hast post hast for thy lif.'[23]

Anger as Transcendence

Once in the Tower of London, his whole world on fire like Aeneas', Surrey began to write. New poems expressed an ancient mode of survival: anger, Surrey's fury

Anthony Browne, who was Master of the King's Horses: 'Coursers of the late Erle of Surrey iiij' in the Inventory of Henry VIII in Society of Antiquaries MS 129, f. 444r.

[23] The entire letter is found in PRO SP 1/227, ff. 82–83v. Cf. *LP* vol. 21,ii, 548; also *SP*, vol. 1,ii, 264 (888–90).

at his fate, Seneca's 'Medea superest'. Even now Surrey had not surrendered but was following Medea's and Seneca's 'sense of reality', as Braden remarks, which arrives 'not from the unchangeable truth of past history but from the turmoil of affective experience, where history is taken up and remade'. Writing itself was the 'affective' instinct of the young man who had invented for a decade most of the original literary forms of his time and whose power of representation would have its own genealogy. Even now, accelerating towards death in the most terrible location in his world, Surrey could write new poems, probably in Beauchamp Tower, today near the Queen's House but in Henry VIII's time a place for imprisoned noblemen of the highest rank and the official residence of the Lieutenant of the Tower, Sir Walter Stonor. Consisting of three storeys (of which the middle one—where Surrey probably resided—is almost the height of the ramparts), Surrey's father was probably here for the next six years. In a greater irony, both Surrey's heir and then his heir's heir, those offspring of his blood for whom he had been retextualizing concepts of nobility, were imprisoned in the Beauchamp Tower for conspiracy against their Howard cousin Elizabeth I.

Denounced by her for his putative role in the Mary Stuart conspiracy (the Scottish queen might have become his fourth wife), Thomas, fourth Duke of Norfolk, was beheaded at 37 on the same scaffold as his father after spending three years in the Tower. Surrey's son declared on his scaffold his innocence and his allegiance as a reformed Christian, his tutor and lifelong friend John Foxe by his side. Surrey's grandson, Philip, Earl of Arundel and Surrey, became the most famous recusant of his day, spending over twelve years in the Tower and never seeing his only son Thomas, the future 'Collector Earl', before he languished in 1595, the victim at 38 of the last Tudor monarch. All three—Surrey, son, grandson—had a view from their cell, clearer on the rampart, of what Foucault calls the 'spectacle of the scaffold', the ever-visible 'zero-degree of torture'. St Philip's own handwriting above a fireplace in the Beauchamp Tower survives to relate his transcendent terms for escaping that 'zero-degree'. 'Quanto plus afflictionis pro Christo in saeculo, tanto plus gloriae cum Christo in futuro' ('The more suffering for Christ in time, so much more glory with Christ to come'). His grandfather had another kind of transcendence, however, for his last days and the 'zero-degree': anger, writing in anger.[24]

Psalm 55

All the biblical paraphrases written in the Tower carry the wildness of the laments along Holborn streets, but Surrey's paraphrase of Psalm 55 goes further. Horrible

[24] Gordon Braden, *Renaissance Tragedy and the Senecan Tradition: Anger's Privilege* (1985), 40. *APC*, vol. 2, 381. Michel Foucault, *Discipline and Punishment: The Birth of the Prison*, trans. Alan Sheridan (1977), 43.

animal images focus on the traitor who had accused him of displaying a false coat of arms. This last of the complete Bible paraphrases was written after both his paraphrases of Psalm 88, with its prologue to Denny, and of Psalm 73, with its prologue to George Blagge. Although Surrey's last major poem may lack the relative contrition of earlier paraphrases, its anger only David's anguished voice could convey. The result is a jagged totally solipsistic text—the collapsing personality and violence of a modern twentieth-century post-structuralist text like the sonnets (based on Surrey's form) of the later Robert Lowell or John Berryman. In breakdown, the imprisoned Howard heir confronts his steady progress into annihilation. In drumming end-stopped lines that also typify his epic verse, Surrey combines alliterative Anglo-Saxon diction, strong verbs, and a terrifying combination of abstract subjects with concrete modifiers: he has become so trapped an animal that 'Care pierceth my entrails and travaileth my spirit' and a 'grisly fear of death environeth my breast; / A trembling cold of dread clean overwhelmeth my heart.'

For this translation, Surrey abandons the melody of Poulter's Measure used for the other paraphrases. He invents a blank verse of hexameters—certainly the first lyric use in English of a consciously imitated classical line like the alexandrine he may have heard at Fontainebleau. Thus, the poem that soon passed through court circles to Sir John Cheke reveals a special terror: he is being reduced not just at court but in the scale of being, to the 'zero-degree' of annihilation. Driven by this recognition and the sight of the scaffold, the speaker's mounting fury is almost breathless until the disjunction of the last lines and their final breakdown into the original Latin that Surrey adapts from the Vulgate. Towards this breakdown, Surrey's alexandrines help to control the rising fury but do not reduce it. Early in the poem the speaker attacks the source of the violence against him: 'For I deciphered have amid our towne the strife' where 'Guile and wrong' keep 'the walls' of London 'both day and night', and 'mischief with care' keeps 'the market stead' and 'wickedness with craft in heaps swarm through the street.' In this terrible city, adding to the Vulgate, Surrey writes that it was not his 'declared foe'—was this Seymour or Henry VIII himself?—that 'wrought' him 'all this reproach'. All this 'harm so looked for, it weigheth half the less.' Surrey had become cunning; he knew how to fight such a 'foe' as Seymour. 'For though mine enemies hap had been for to prevail, / I could have hid my face from venom of his eye.' Rather, his betrayal came from a beloved friend, in Surrey's Chaucerian oxymoron, 'a friendly foe', traditionally identified as Sir Richard Southwell, who had been sent by Cromwell in the year that Holbein had painted him to the Tower to take away all his books from Sir Thomas More. A biblical certainty follows in the speaker's curse operating like Dido's final malediction on Aeneas and his descendants: 'Such sudden surprise quick may them whole devour.' The speaker's certainty of history supports his hope that 'It was the Lord'—not the 'our Lord' of the old Christianity used earlier in Surrey's Psalm 8 translation—'that broke the bloody compacts of those / That prelooked on with ire to slaughter me and mine.'

'Prelooked' is a neologism that combines Latin and basic English, and its syncretic effect of diction and imagery continues in domestic figures such as the transferred simile from Coverdale: 'Butter falls not so soft' as does the patience of God. From this point in the text, Surrey writes his own poem. He abandons any biblical source. A 'Friowr whose harme and tongue presents the wicked sort / Of those false wolves' intensifies the speaker's rage. In fact, the fury cannot contain itself in English. The final line is in Latin and in 'th'other Psalm of David find I ease,' says the speaker. Jones identifies this 'Psalm' as an untranslated line from the original Vulgate source.[25] In fact, the Latin from this line ends his poem: 'lacta curam tuam super dominum et ipse te enutriet' ('Throw yourself upon the Lord, and He will nourish you'). Although the ending in Latin hardly resolves the anger of the poem into contrition, it does offer solace—trust as much in the Latin that had marked his life as in God.

'The seed of kings'

Within hours of arriving in the Tower on the afternoon of 12 December, Surrey had met one more victim, in fact, a cousin who was more of a Plantagenet than himself, the nephew of Cardinal Pole. Within days he had written a text about the young man who, in the poet's eyes, needed a protector—a role the earl had been playing since his entry into court in 1529. Now he denounced a victimization as terrible as his own. The reference to Edward Courtenay, a descendant of the Yorkist White Rose, appears in a biblical translation. During his final five weeks in the Tower, Surrey composed paraphrases not only of Psalms but also of chapters from Ecclesiastes. The sixteenth-century musical term 'paraphrase' implies an interweaving of texts rather than a strict translation, as Erasmus had shown in his new Latin Ecclesiastes in 1536. Surrey is the first man of letters in England, at least the first practising poet with a popular secular audience, to translate into English the Hebrew wisdom book. In such stylish weaving of the original Vulgate Latin, his main source, and the Latin commentary of the Lutheran Campensis, Surrey introduces a story that oddly paralleled his own. In 1538 Edward Courtenay, aged 12, had been sent to the Tower with his father, the Marquess of Exeter, who had

[25] *Poems*, ed. Jones, 153–4. See Brigden's interpretation of 'Friowr' in 'Henry Howard', 511. For a fuller analysis of Surrey's religious paraphrases, especially in their context as a 16th-century tradition, see Rivka Zim, *English Metrical Psalms: Poetry as Praise and Prayer 1535–1601* (1987). See also the perceptive contextualizing of these poems in Heale, *Wyatt, Surrey and Early Tudor Poetry*, ch. 5, and my own setting for them in 'Surrey's Psalms in the Tower', in *Sacred and Profane: Secular and Devotional Interplay in Early Modern British Literature*, ed. H. Wilcox, R. Todd, and A. MacDonald (1996), 16–31. For the shift in Surrey's performances here, see Lerer, *Courtly Letters*, 65, on the definition of the word 'sad' in this period and 'the veracity of word and deed that counteracts the glib performativity of courtliness'.

been promptly beheaded in a 'logical sequel to the defeat of the Pilgrimage of Grace' and the terror it brought. Eight years later, in the last weeks of Henry VIII's life, the new political order still could not endure another Plantagenet, especially in the interval between kings. But at least in one way young Edward Courtenay could be grateful he was still in the Tower; Montague's child, arrested at the same time and the last male heir of the Poles, had simply disappeared there, probably in 1542 after the demise of Catherine Howard and her faction. At 20 in December 1546, Courtenay remained imprisoned long after Surrey's beheading, one of three still in prison throughout the entire reign of Edward VI (in fact, on the scaffold, Sir John Gates specifically apologized for his hatred in having kept the young man so needlessly in prison). Courtenay only found freedom, as one of many, on the accession of Mary I in 1553, then to reveal a mental deterioration 'simply intoxicated by unaccustomed freedom' that led to death in Venice, perhaps by Spanish poisoning, of this 'last sprig of the White Rose'.[26]

Surrey's biblical text for his cousin turns on the threatening figure of Henry VIII. The paraphrase moves from biblical wisdom literature to one of Surrey's original prophetic outbursts.

In better far estate stand children, poor and wise,
Than aged kings wedded to will that work without advice.
In prison have I seen, ere this, a woeful wight
That never knew what freedom meant, nor tasted of delight;
With such unhoped hap in most despair hath met,
Within the hands that erst wore gyves [shackles] to have a sceptre set.
And by conjures the seed of kings is thrust from state,
Whereon aggrieved people work oft-times their hidden hate.[27]

A Psalm from the Tower: George Blagge

Hardly had this translation been dispatched than Surrey wrote another. It involved another betrayal, probably stemming from a fight in the late spring before. In fact, the acceleration of what the later Renaissance called a 'conspiracy' to kill Surrey may have begun in an argument between Surrey and his old acquaintance George Blagge. Mentioned by Leland in his *Naeniae* as one of Wyatt's three closest friends, Blagge had also been with Surrey in early trips to France, if not as his servant, as Casady claims, and Blagge had rebuked the Howard heir after

[26] For details and sources of the Courtenay story, see Miller, *Nobility*, 68, 65. Cf. *Reports of the Deputy Keeper of the Public Records* 3, Appendix ii: 255–7; also, David M. Loades, *Mary Tudor: A Life* (1989), 200; and for the Venetian events, see Emma Gurney-Salter, *Tudor England Through Venetian Eyes* (1930), 59–60. Also King, *Tudor Royal Iconography*, 215.

[27] The new language is so caustic and vehement that, for Hughey (*AH*, vol. 2, 118), the lines with 'septre' and 'seade of kyngs' give the unmistakable hint of a possible conspiracy.

Surrey's night on the town in 1543. The close friendship also involved the reading and appreciation of Surrey's poems and linguistic experiments, as the Surrey texts in Blagge's manuscript illustrate. Even the violent response of each young man to the other in the summer of 1546 shows the level of friendship that may have existed before Blagge joined, quite actively, the forces that would now kill the poet. Where betrayal of Surrey by Southwell had come from fear of not surviving after the succession, Blagge's betrayal (if it can be called that) came from genuine ideological difference. Only weeks before, Blagge had been tried and convicted in three quick days in Newgate prison, condemned, like Anne Askew, to be burned alive. When his male connections to the Privy Chamber had rescued him, the king had cried out to the square-bodied young man, 'Ah! my *Pig*!' Blagge had replied: 'Yea, if your Majesty had not been better to me than your bishops were, your *Pig* had been roasted ere this time!' The degree to which Blagge, who would die in three years at 39, was radicalized by this arrest and near-death can be seen in his famous epitaph two years later on the death of the politically disgraced Wriothesley, who killed himself in a mental breakdown 'by giving himself a dose'.[28] Blagge called him 'picture of pryde, of papistrye the platt, / in whome treason, as in a Throne did sytt' his blue eyes 'glearing lyke a Catt' (*AH* 1: 344; 2: 442).

Yet, as Surrey's dedicatory lyric and the diction in his Psalm 73 demonstrate, the earl's general sympathies were with the religious position of Wyatt and Blagge. Now, in 1546, the difference between Surrey and a Blagge or a Sir Anthony Browne (the old Christian opposite in the political spectrum from Blagge) lay in an ideology more immediate than religion: a differing view of how to construct the Tudor state after the succession—the question of the Protectorate. Who should have the enormous power waiting just ahead? The reported conversation of Blagge and Surrey echoes like the conversations reported about Surrey's grandfather Buckingham. What are the rights of true blood nobility in a period of breakdown? Is Blagge, in refusing to accept the Howards' role, telling Surrey that the Tyndalian concept of the state as absolutized in a king is the only way of personal and social salvation for its citizens, including the blood nobility?

What is significant is that Blagge himself did not testify to the summer fight. There is no deposition of any kind from him. Another courtier, Edward Rogers, a member of the queen's household, had, however, a precise recollection of Blagge 'speaking of the matter'.[29] The fact of the fight and its language turned out to be pivotal and formed, in many ways, the foundation for all other depositions in

[28] Casady, *Henry Howard*, 186. Casady writes an elaborate fictional scene based on the trial evidence concerning both Blagge and Southwell. The Blagge manuscript was discovered in this century and recorded in Kenneth Muir, 'Surrey Poems in the Blagge Manuscript', *Notes and Queries*, 205, NS 7, 10 (Oct. 1960) 368–70. For Blagge's pardon, see *LP*, vol. 21,i, 1383, and for the response to the king, see Patrick F. Tytler, *England under the Reigns of Edward VI and Mary* (1839), vol. 1, 146. Also cf. Starkey, *Reign*, 140, 149–50. For the demise of Wriothesley, see Strype, *Ecclesiastical Memorials*, vol. 3, 430.

[29] For Rogers' testimony and that of Carew, see *LP*, vol. 21,ii, 555(4). Also, for all the depositions, see Casady, *Henry Howard*, 194–200.

December 1546. Blagge's narrative led to Rogers' juicier revelation (reinforced by details about Blagge by Sir Gawain Carew when, from the sidelines at the Hampton Court reception in August 1546, Carew and Rogers had gossiped as they watched Surrey and his sister take precedence 'when the Admiral of France was here'). In Rogers' retelling of Blagge's retelling of his conversation with Surrey, Blagge appears noble and direct, declaring outright to the young earl, once his friend, that the king should 'specially appoint thereto' those courtiers 'meetest to rule the Prince in the event of the King's death'. Hearing this, Surrey must have recognized at once that Blagge was assuming the new Henrician code of honour as a premise for such an act: the king, not the honoured estates of the kingdom, determined all. Those 'meetest to rule' in this scenario could only mean the currently active Privy Council and 'new erectyed men', to whom Henry VIII was increasingly passing on his total authority in his realm. Surrey's answer was immediate and, for him, perfectly logical. He replied with calm—Rogers' evidence does not suggest otherwise—that 'his father was meetest [to be Protector], both for good services done and for estate.' As a friend who had observed Surrey's portraits and read closely the texts of his last years, what had Blagge expected the earl to say? It should be noted that Surrey names his father as 'meetest' and nowhere names himself as a possible Protector.

In the next sequence of Rogers' testimony, Blagge becomes immediately aggressive, even insolent. He attacks the poet's father whose conservative position he had no doubt grown to fear and loathe. If the Duke of Norfolk should become Protector, and by implication, the friend before him, Blagge resounds, then 'the Prince should be but evil taught.' Here was a full attack not from enemies but from a friend, one even closer to Wyatt. The shock to Surrey must have come now not only from the recognition that their friendship had failed but that even a friend so close to Wyatt had not accepted his political strategies of the last years. At that moment of recognition and shocked silence for the poet earl (isolated as Aeneas in Troy), Blagge's aggression escalated. Without waiting for an answer to 'evil taught', Blagge plunged into another violent personal insult almost as if he were baiting his friend: 'Rather than it should come to pass that the Prince should be under the government of your father or you, I would bide the adventure to thrust this dagger.' It is Blagge who brings in Surrey's name for the first time as a possible Protector.

The calm Surrey of this dialogue, at least as Rogers gives it in his deposition, could hardly be characterized as hysterical or 'folish'. Instead, as Rogers explicitly notes, Surrey merely replied that Blagge was 'very hasty' and then used a proverb that generalized the violence but did express Surrey's growing hurt: 'God sent a shrewd cow short horns'—the same proverb Norfolk had written to Cromwell at a critical juncture, Norfolk adding '*veritas liberabit*' ('the truth shall set free').[30] Had Surrey's laconic phrasing hinted at Blagge's short thick body with

[30] *LP*, vol. 11, 1138.

a phallic insult as well? The limited control that describes the tempers of most Renaissance aristocrats began to break. Rogers is clear about Blagge's answer: 'Yea, my lord (quod Blage), and I trust your horns also shall be so short as ye shall not be able to do any hurt with them.' Rogers ends the argument here, but his narrative continues. The poet earl, left to himself, began to brood: 'Afterwards the Earl, who at the time had no weapon, took sword and dagger and went to Blage's house and said unto him that of late he [Blagge] had been very hasty with him.' Then Rogers stops his testimony abruptly, with no more facts.

What actually happened? For one thing, at Blagge's house, whether Surrey banged on the door or not (as Casady fictionalizes), no physical attack was made, despite what Rogers hints, or how the whole court repeated and used the episode at his trial. Of course, whatever its truth, the episode could be used to frame Surrey. He was now totally vulnerable. The reported violence and display of temper on Surrey's part could be used to augment the young Howard's reputation as violent. Most of all, the story would divulge to the court Surrey's horrifying and illegal ambitions, the 'diabolical' pretensions named in Surrey's bill of indictment. What is unspoken in Roger's December testimony is, of course, the singular fact that now, in Blagge, Surrey saw vividly—and probably for the first time—the total failure of all his political strategies. Not only did enough not survive. With Blagge, Surrey's enough could never survive in the inevitable future of the Protectorate. Surrey was being perceived, even by his friends, even by a surrogate for his beloved Wyatt, as a figure who could bring no true social order to his world, his Roman roles and language utterly meaningless for such a new state. This was the terrifying subject of Surrey's Psalm 73 dedicated to George Blagge: an approaching total annihilation is already at work. He is losing everything.

All the various witnesses who follow Rogers accelerate the theme of Surrey's wicked, illegal ambition aiming towards the Protectorate, at least in evidence that survives. Sir Gawain Carew not only added that Surrey had told him personally (but 'place and time now out of my remembrance') that 'those men which are made by the King's Majesty of vile birth hath been the distraction of all the nobility of this realm' but he repeated the testimony of Rogers who had, so Carew said, 'told me of the Earl's saying "If God should call the King's Majesty unto His mercy" (whose life and health the Lord long preserve) that he thought no man so meet to have the governance of the Prince as my lord his father.' The roundabout evidence continued. From the queen's household, Sir Edward Warner came forth. Another friend from East Anglia (his mother's Blennerhasset family had been in service to the Howards), Warner had recently married the widow of the poet Sir Thomas Wyatt, probably with the help of Surrey who had dedicated, at least in one manuscript, a poem to his friend. Although Warner himself had heard Surrey say nothing 'that was ony prejudys to the kinges majesty or his posteryte', he did recall an incriminating conversation 'last summer' with one of the lively young men in Queen Catherine Parr's pious entourage, 'Master [Richard] Devereux', the heir apparent to Lord Ferrers. Warner's friend was told of 'serteyne commounycaciones off the pryde and vayne glory of the seyd erll' and particularly in one, Devereux had 'sayd what yff he [Surrey] be accusyd to the Kyng that he [Surrey] shold say yff god shold call the kyng to this mercy who was so meete to governe the prynse as my lord hys father'. When Warner asked if such an eventuality of Norfolk as Protector were possible, the young Devereux, the ancestor of the Elizabethan Earl of Essex, answered: 'yt may be so.' Warner then fully 'lookyd every day to see hyme [Surrey] In the cass that he ys nowe'.[31] Surrey had condemned himself with his own words—at least as Devereux reported it to Warner, who was reporting it, of course, in turn to Paget, who in turn was taking the information back to Seymour and Dudley and the Privy Council. In this sequence building from the initial Blagge episode, Surrey's first cousin Knyvet's testimony would act as a kind of climax: the court would not forget the phrase 'new erectyd men' nor Surrey's aggressive 'I malice not so low. My malice is higher. My malice climbs higher.' For such a sequence of witnesses, the attack on Surrey's coat of arms and Southwell's evidence simply provided the trigger. That false and idolatrous sign exhibited in October 1546 at Kenninghall marked the visible manifestation of an enormous 'diabolical' pride almost equal to the Pope's in Rome.

In this context of evidence-building being orchestrated, especially by Wriothesley, to kill him, Surrey wrote, a few weeks before his death, his poem to Blagge. The former friend was now in a position of political connection that could control Surrey's life or death. Introducing his paraphrase of Psalm 73, Surrey's lyric to Blagge delivers a calculated exercise in sincerity, perhaps genuine. At least it keeps a traditional threefold performance of contrition, if not humiliation, to dramatize the moral righteousness of his life. Blagge himself (and all the court readers) would have observed in this shortened sonnet (a totally new form)[32] more, however, than a modern reader: from its opening ship image to its final allusion to King David, Surrey's text to Blagge evokes Wyatt without a mention of the name, reminding 'Tom Thumb' of another world where they had shared a beloved friend. 'The sudden storms that heave me to and fro / Had well near pierced faith, my guiding sail,' says Surrey's speaker, setting up the same syllogistic frame as in his poem to Denny: eleven lines announce the crisis in a major premise and suppressed minor only to leap in a couplet to the conclusion and the redeeming figure of David (now significantly not a warrior but a king succouring the poet): 'But now, my Blagge, mine error well I see' because of the 'goodly light King David giveth me'. Admitting only 'error', the poet earl is set straight, so the logic suggests, by an act in which grace comes from his self-advertised ability not only to read a holy Davidic text but to write one.

The Psalm paraphrase that follows is in Poulter's Measure and dramatizes the annihilation settling into the poet earl's consciousness for the first time. Its 'many

[31] PRO, *SP* 1/227, ff. 99–99v, 101–102v.

[32] H. A. Mason, 'Wyatt and the Psalms—II', *Times Literary Supplement* (6 Mar. 1953), 160. See

interpolations of the poet's thoughts, and so many departures from the strict sense of the Latin' demonstrate the terror of this discovery (AH2: 106). Within the general order of the Vulgate Latin, with interpretations from commentaries and translations of reformed Christians like Coverdale and Campensis, Surrey builds a more dichotomous structure than those of any of his sources. Logically, he pits the wicked against the suffering 'elect' with their gifts of language. The penitence built into the basic poetic structure in the original Hebrew and Latin is dramatically shifted here into a long discourse in which self-justification is the tenor of the Psalm and its vehicle, the Psalm's Davidic argument (transferred to Surrey) that enough survives within the poet. In the first part of his paraphrase, Surrey's line 'Whose glutton cheeks sloth feeds so fat as scant their eyes be seen' evokes the engraving in 1544 of Henry VIII by the Flemish Cornelis Matsys, the monarch's last portrait. Surrey indicts, however, the whole court: 'Unto whose cruel power most men for dread are fain / To bend and bow with lofty looks, whilst they vaunt in their reign.' With 'bloody hands' and 'cruelty' they 'scourge the poor' and 'To tempt the living God they think it no offence, / And pierce the simple with their tongues, that can make no defence.'

In such indeterminacy, bewailing 'the woeful state wherein thy chosen stand', the speaker finds in the second section 'no wit could pierce so far' God's 'holy dooms', the hidden reasons for all this pain and seeming chaos of history. Once more, Surrey uses reformed Christian diction for his own purposes: the Vulgate 'filiorum tuorum' and Campensis' 'thyne owne chyldren' become Surrey's 'thy chosen'. So the poet's final vision of the just and unjust builds on a fantasy where wicked men shall see 'their glory fade, thy sword of vengeance shall / Unto their drunken eyes in blood disclose their errors all.' Here the judgement scene of sheep and goats from St Matthew's Gospel is transposed by Surrey into a bitter quite original key: 'And when their golden fleece is from their back yshorn, / The spots that underneath were hid, thy chosen sheep shall scorn.' But 'till that happy day', in another original line (emphasized by rare internal rhyme), 'My eyes yield tears, my years consume between hope and despair.' All this defeat could have led the speaker to suicide. 'But when I stood in dread to drench, thy hands still did me stay' and have been 'my guide' with 'grace to comfort me therein' even as 'withered skin unto my bones did cleave'—one of the earliest Renaissance poetic figurations of melancholy. In this self-described 'internalized' state of grace, the speaker/poet now sees his role in history. In his closure, the voice of God in the poet prophet will triumph.

> Where I that in thy word have set my trust and joy,
> The high reward that 'longs thereto shall quietly enjoy.
> And my unworthy lips, inspired with thy grace,
> Shall thus forespeak thy secret works in sight of Adam's race.

also his 'The First Two Printed Texts of Surrey's Poems', *Times Literary Supplement* (4 June 1971), 656. Also, see Eckert, 'Poetry of Henry Howard', 56.

Surrey's Last Letter

A few days after his forced march, Surrey wrote his final letter. In it, the poet earl submits himself to that tribunal that will make judgement, not at the end of Christian time on the spotted and unspotted goats and sheep, but in England 1547. It shows how out of touch with the shifts at court he had become. His autograph letter to the Privy Council proposes a daring solution for his forthcoming trial, the daring alone demonstrating that Surrey had yet fully to understand Tudor judgement and that death will not escape him. The poet earl sets the stage for this 'bold' request by developing an ethos of youth used before in oration letters, but now youth is collapsing in body and horrified that he has entrapped his aged father.

> yt may leke your honorable Lordships that sythe the begynnyng off my durance the dysplease [displeasure] off my master [the king] / myche losse off blood with other dystemperance off nature / with my sorow to see the long aprovyd trewght off myne old father browght in questyon by auny stuere [stir] betwene Southwell and me / hath sore feblyd me as is to be sene / wherof lest sycknes myght folow by meane wheroff my wittes shuld not be so ffreshe to unburden my conscyence off suche matter / as I have replyd in expectation off som off your Lordships to have bene sent from the kynges Maiestie to have takyn my examynacyon I have resolved most humbly to make thys sute.

This long Ciceronian sentence, with its balancing of subordinate clauses and effects of *gradatio*, reveals a sharp humanist intelligence still at work in the Tower. After such an exordium and *narratio*, Surrey comes directly to his proposition. He would name his own judges: Wriothesley, Russell, Winchester, and Browne. They had examined him 'iiij yeres past' in 'the examynacyon of matteres touchyng alegeance that layd to my charge wherin God knowyth with what daunger I eskapyd norwithstanding my inocency.' But three of these—Surrey could not know—will not help him at all, the Bishop of Winchester now exiled from the presence of the king, Wriothesley now his active enemy, and Russell, who would shift with the winds of power. Surrey is almost childish in his hope. Not only will he reveal to them 'suche matter off importans as depend'—and in the manuscript the rest of this line is torn away—but he trusts 'his Maieste shall hold him contentyd the with [therewith] when I am hard'—a recall to Surrey's power of language. In particular, he is furious at the lawyer Sir John Baker, a 'new erectyed man' in the Privy Council who would be 'present at the formall examyncyon' and had already interrogated him relentlessly about his rights of inheritance. Although he does not want him at his trial, the Howard heir is gracious to all in his *peroratio*: 'neverthe lesse my matter is preiudycyall to no creatur onlesse to my selfe and that the almyghty preserve you / your Lordships myserable humbly to commaund,' signed 'henry Surrey'.[33]

[33] PRO SP 1/224, f. 76.

If this letter reveals a serious misreading of court politics, the text's practical concerns, realism, and suffering contrast with the romantic description of Surrey's attempted escape in the Spanish Chronicle, as dashing and swashbuckling as anything Nashe invented fifty years later. In this narrative, immediately after the arrest of Surrey's father and the stripping of the painting that had caused his arrest (and the revealing of the secret motto 'Till then thus'), Surrey turns to his servant (in the chronicle named 'Martin') and tells him to bring a dagger. The Chronicler places Surrey at St Thomas' Tower, better known as the Watergate giving access to the Tower from the river—for Surrey an impossibility in 1546 as St Thomas' formed part of the Tudor royal apartments—and from there Surrey planned to escape through his latrine that emptied directly into the river. Having chosen a midnight to escape, Surrey announced he was unwell to the two guards and then later 'took the lid off the closet and saw that there was only about two feet of water' and so proceeded to drop himself into the Thames. But 'at that instant' the guards did not find him in bed and soon seized him before he dropped into the river. Although Surrey was unable to resist, he was, says the Chronicler, 'so courageous that he would have killed them both before anyone knew of it'. To prevent more escapes, in this version of Surrey's last days, the trial was set immediately (146–8).

The Last Poem

Surrey's very last poem—a fragment that resembles a Petrarchan sonnet—projects the same prophetic theme as in his coat of arms and last portrait: the poet earl is the noble self (with generations within that self) who acts as a prophetic sign against a violent history. The chaotic lyric, the angriest of all, is consumed with righteous fury, far from the patience that Surrey as Davidic poet had described for himself to Blagge and Denny. The actual lyric text reads, however, less like prophecy, less like the noble first Duke of Norfolk on Bosworth Field sacrificing himself for an exalted body of honour, but more like an incoherent scream. Even so, Surrey can textualize the scream. The poet earl attempts to frame this reflection on the absurdity of his death with an objective context. He gives a solipsistic Latin title, 'Bonum est mihi quod humiliasti me' to the lyric, taken almost verbatim from the Vulgate Psalm 118: 71–2 ('It is good for me that you have humiliated me'), its next line in the Psalm continuing with 'because I may learn your justifications.' Surrey's attempt at objectivity and distancing obviously made its point. His poem had a texture his second son, the long-surviving Henry, the Jacobean Earl of Northampton, remembered. Drawing on his father's fame in dedicating a 1580s text 'A dutifull defence of the lawfull regiment of weomen,' to his second cousin Elizabeth I (his father's first cousin once removed), the son tells, at a climactic part of his text, what the queen may have remembered about her elegant poet cousin, that this poem was the last Surrey wrote: 'Therefore I confesse that David in his thankfull sonet after long experience . . . made his understanding ripe, and my father in his last thing that he wrote before his end "Domin [sic] est michi [sic] quod humiliasti me." '[34]

The son was more perceptive than the centuries have presumed. The poem does portray an 'understanding ripe' of life and history. It is not the result of serenity, however. At first the earl may announce 'The storms are past, these clouds are overblown, / And humble cheer great rigor hath repressed' or that Surrey has 'patience graft in a determined brest'. This way of patience may even lead in the text to Cicero's famous description of the noble Scipio Africanus in *De officiis* (III, i) as never less alone than when alone: 'And in the heart where heaps of griefs were grown' revenge 'hath planted mirth and rest' so that 'No company so pleasant as mine own.' The poet may remark how 'Thraldom at large hath made this prison free' echoing his Windsor elegy and the cultural image originated by the imprisoned Boethius. Surrey may even echo Aeneas' cry of encouragement to his desperate survivors 'forsan et haec olim meminisse iuvabit' (I: 203) in 'Danger well past remembered works delight.'

But such serenity makes it barely through ten lines. As Surrey closes his poem and ends a life of writing, he reverses the earlier strategy with a gesture of outrage. 'Understanding ripe' was not serene. In this absolute last moment of any Surrey text, the poet earl looks, not surprisingly, into a mirror. Obsessed with the historical roles subjectivity must play, he recognizes his loss in that mirror of self, 'the cureless wound that bleedeth night and day'. An image from Boethius and Michaut, recapitulated in Chaucer's 'Thus gan he [Troilus] make a mirrour of his mind' (1: 365), the mirror becomes more immediate and historical in Surrey. Surrey sets the topos, in fact, for Shakespeare and the later Renaissance, with Sackville's transforming the genealogy for his *Induction* to the *Mirrour for Magistrates*: 'the glas / of brittell state of cares' (164–5).[35] For Surrey, the mirror

[34] Bodleian Library MS 903 (Arch. A 170) (2953) ff. 6r–v. Humiliation would be a lesson this long-surviving son would learn. In his 1594 portrait, the son Henry stands gaunt, holding a globe of knowledge; in his background is a flower covered by a cloud, as his hopes and family fortunes and honour had been darkened; so suggests Linda Levy Peck, *Northampton: Patronage and Policy at the Court of James I* (1982), 12. Reduced to the slight income his sister Lady Berkeley gave him, the future Jacobean Earl of Northampton became the only nobleman of the Elizabethan era to teach at a university. Although 'obsessed with his family heritage', he was 'frequently forced to abase himself before men of lesser lineage'. But the reversal of his affluent childhood did produce one clear result: 'a strong will to survive' and, towards that end, an almost fatal attraction to young courtiers like Essex and James' Scottish favorite Robert Carr, the Earl of Somerset, 'who were much like his father, his hope perhaps to regain the golden days of his childhood'.

[35] *Poems*, ed. Jones, 131. Sackville praised Surrey in a poem even before he had adapted Surrey's blank verse for the theatre in 1561, in the Roman drama *Gorboduc*, written with the Calvinist Thomas Norton. Later, as the powerful Earl of Dorset, Sackville had married his heir to Surrey's granddaughter (the loving sister of Philip Howard, who may have brought her grandfather's portrait to Knole). At James I's court, Sackville was therefore part of a specially interested audience for the theatre with his fellow Privy Councillor, Surrey's surviving son, the Earl of Northampton. There, in court performances of plays like *King Lear*, as Professor Jones has remarked to me, he and the surviving Henry would have heard once more the blank verse invented by the elderly Howard's father over sixty-five

reveals nothing less than the continually bleeding wound of his intimate self. Subjectivity will not disappear but only intensify as it reaches death. In his closure, Surrey desires the mirror to reflect both the Howard loss and the possible extinction of the Howard line in himself, a metonymic disappearance for blood nobility itself. For Surrey, that loss of blood signals the death of any hope for renewed English culture and nobility or for a higher new civilization, the Renaissance he had hoped to bring: 'To spill that blood that hath so oft been shed / For Britain's sake, alas, and now is dead.'

Instead of despairing or smashing the mirror as Shakespeare's Richard II does, Surrey is angered by what he sees. Looking, Surrey compares himself to another courtier, probably his betrayer Southwell, whom he had challenged, 'a wretch that hath no heart to fight,' as the Howards had fought with 'heart' and honour for over two centuries. He still cannot comprehend why such abandonment should be happening to him: 'To think, alas, such hap [success] should granted be' to the 'wretch' and to the new society he exists in, the 'thraldom at large'. Surrey may appear as absurd as Seneca's Medea in her failure to understand her actual situation, but his anger before oblivion—of self, dynasty, cultural vision—never retreats to nostalgia or resignation. Above all, it is no leap to transcendence. Blood anchors him to reality. His own 'blood'—the blood of the poet as well as of the Howards—had prepared him for a triumphant role as leader of a new Renaissance civilization like the promised one he had viewed unfolding at Fontainebleau. If only he could not disappear but live, he could renew genealogies, first, as the new fourth Duke of Norfolk, the possible Protector of the new young King Edward, the new Earl Marshal, head of the College of Arms, and then as master of a new complex language, the maker of the completed Virgilian epic for the English Renaissance in British heroic metre. It was poetry others could use in a mastery that might make his beloved English language universal. What Surrey does not hide is the fact of the blood that will soon pour from his severed head 'that bleedeth day and night'. It is the blood of the poet as well as of the trapped young earl.

years before and adapted to theatre by Sackville himself over forty years earlier. In Shakespeare, they would have heard the mirror topos used once more in a living setting.

15

'Retailed to posterity': A Conclusion

Whatever Surrey's actions, Henry VIII ordered the killing of the Howard heir. However deceived by Wriothesley, the Garter King of Arms, or the Privy Council about Surrey's legal right to bear the arms of Edward the Confessor, he had determined that Surrey could not survive. All that was needed was the right case, the best narrative by which the young poet earl could be seen to have committed treason. No approval or consent from the masses on holiday streets or from nobility, old or new, was needed. For the Tudor monarch at the end, Surrey with his pretensions towards magnificence presented a special kind of 'peril', as the bill of indictment indicates, especially as he had exhibited these pretensions 'openly and publicly', without the Supreme Head's approval. No one was free to make such representations, not even a Howard with ancient liberties. The Howard blood had given Henry VIII two wives, without question his most satisfying sexually, but also the most devastating. Each had promised, in her own destructive way, a special glory and honour, one a transcendence of spirit and the other of body, and both had failed him. Now, with that memory of intimate failures, from the Howards rose another demonic ghost. Their poet first cousin threatened, in the king's aged eyes, the kingship of his young son, the Edward who would follow the Edward lost in the Tower at the time of the first Howard duke. Edward VI must not meet the fate of Edward V, the boy destroyed by older men in the Tower where Surrey now waited, the massive structure whose origin in the time of Julius Caesar, 'reported / Successively from age to age,' Shakespeare's Edward V questions and then, before his Protector uncle Richard can reply completely, finds his own answer. 'Methinks,' says the boy-king in Surrey's blank verse, 'the truth should live from age to age / As 'twere retailed to all posterity, / Even to the general all-ending day.' Now facing death, the king wanted, at any price, to save his own special generational 'truth', his son.

In fact, in their last days, the body of Surrey must have recalled for the sick king one generational 'truth' he could not forget—one of evil. It was no lie. He had himself been part of a 'truth' in all its retailing, justified in reality by his own body. With Surrey's young male body pretending before him, Henry VIII could recall the panic surrounding his childhood and the fears of his own father when such Burgundian figuration had threatened. What had terrorized Henry VII had been the shifting roles and disguises of handsome young male imposters like the 'bewitching' Perkin Warbeck, in Francis Bacon's phrase, tricksters 'with their stage-like greatness'.[1] Such imposture had only been settled dynastically when at the age of 3 the young Prince Henry himself was carried in the arms of the old Earl of Shrewsbury to his father on the throne. Surrey's grandfather Buckingham had placed a spur on the child's right heel, and the boy had been admitted to the Order of the Bath and the next day proclaimed the genuine Duke of York. Thus had the child Henry in the presence of his father eliminated all the spectres surrounding his father. The attractive Perkin Warbeck would no longer pretend to be the Duke of York. Whatever else, the little boy could now believe that, from that moment on, his real presence was a fortress his father could hold against chaos.

Now, a month before his death, the king's memories were everywhere aggravated by acute daily knowledge of breakdown of that body, once mighty and as exceptionally handsome as any imposter's. Disintegration turned his surviving will all the angrier and more vindictive. At the same time as the king's never-ending pain, the factions of Seymour, Dudley, and the queen had themselves been evolving. The dying Henry VIII probably knew quite well their enormous ambitions at a time of succession, but they were now the best means to dynastic survival and the cutting off of a civil war in which his only son would be as lost as the boy kings Henry VI and Edward V. In order to keep any hope alive, to 'retail' anything to 'posterity', the king must act. The pretending Surrey must be condemned and then eliminated, head severed from that body of honour. A legal reason for his execution must be found.

Henry VIII's Annotations

In almost the last document Henry VIII himself inscribed, the king took a set of charges against the poet, handwritten by the Lord Chancellor Wriothesley, and, in the king's own trembling hand, underlined and amended certain phrases. These charges were nine, and Wriothesley had, in addition, a list of eighteen interrogatories for Surrey in the hand of some clerk but with the Lord Chancellor's own corrections, as well as seventeen notes or jottings from the examinations in Wriothesley's own hand. The range of topics in these three groups of documents shows the full case for the destruction of Surrey, although there was only one charge finally in the bill of indictment, the illegal bearing of a coat of arms. Henry VIII saw the full importance of the document of the nine charges, for, despite the 55-year-old's extreme illness, he even appended (in the margins of the manuscript) notations of his own. For a monarch who had disliked, for almost thirty-eight years of ruling, any writing out of documents, this was a surprising feat to undertake within a month of his death. If nothing else, the gesture demonstrated Henry VIII's determination to destroy Surrey, 'his hatred inexorable', in Anglo's phrase.

[1] *Richard III*, III,i, 75–78. *Francis Bacon*, ed. James Spedding, 6:133 and 187.

What the king's notations also suggest is that it may not have been the arrested father, the old duke, who was the real target, but the son. The future belonged to the Tudors; it was they who must be 'retailed to posterity'. This sense of a progressive social order from which Surrey must be excluded appears to have pervaded all strategies to entrap Surrey. Wriothesley, in fact, said so. Almost forty years later, in 1585, Surrey's grandson Philip Howard, the Earl of Arundel and Surrey, recalled, in a crucial letter to his cousin, Elizabeth I, how 'my Grandfather was brought to his tryal, and condempned for such trifles as it amazed the standers by at that time, and it is ridiculous at this daye to all that hear the same. Naye he was so faultless in all respects' that Wriothesley, 'being one of his greatest enimyes, fearinge least his innocency would be a meane to save his life' told one of the jury, Sir Christopher Heydon, that 'though they saw noe other matter weightie inough to condemne him, yet it were sufficient reason to make him saie guiltie, for that he was an unmeet man to live in a Commonwealth.'

In the last decade of his life, Henry VIII wanted to command all projections of the future. In 1542, the year of Surrey's elegy on Wyatt, the king had issued an order to control all prophecies and, above all, their interpretation. The Crown made it a felony for any person to 'prynte or wryte, or elles speake sing or declare' prophecies relating not just to the king but to any persons, especially if they involved an interpretation the king could not control. No prediction for the future could be based on interpreting 'Armes feldes beastes fowles or other suche lyke thinges accustomed in armes cognisaunces badeges or signetes, or by reasone of lettres of the name of the King or of any other persone'.[2] Thus, the signs of a coat of arms—the legal sanction for Surrey's indictment—could prophesy the future by summarizing the past as a basis to control the future or at least give it meaning.

The first two of the nine charges with Henry VIII's underlining and editorial remarks (here in italics) turn on the question of the coat of arms and assume as truth the misinformation given him by Wriothesley and the Garter King of Arms. But, whether the Howard heir had a right to bear them or not, the coat of arms signified for the king his larger implications and pretensions: 'If a man comming *of the colateral lyne to the heyre* [the word is shakily written over] *off* the Crown, who ought *not* to beare tharmes of England *but on* the second quarter, with the difference of *theyre* [substituted by Henry VIII for the original *his*] auncestre, doo *presume* to chaunge his right place, and beare them in the first quarter, leaving out the true difference of thauncestre, and, in the lieu thereof, use *the very place* [here, in quite shaky lettering, Henry VIII has marked through the original 'use only the difference' and added his own phrase] only of the heire masle [male] apparant; *how this mans intent is to be iuggyd; and whether thys* importe any daunger, peril, or slaunder to the title of the Prince, or very Heire Apparant; and howe it wayeth in our lawes.' In the second charge, the emphasis is again on the proper forms and Surrey's presumption. 'If a man *presume to* take in his armes an olde

[2] *Images of Tudor Kingship*, 39. For the Philip Howard letter, see BL Sloane MS 2172 ff. 41–3. *Statutes of the Realm*, vol. 3, 850.

cote of the Crown, *whyche hys Auncester never bare, nor he of ryght owght to bear* and use it without difference; whither it may be to the peril or slaundre of the very heire of the Crown, or be taken to tende to his disturbaunce in the same; and in what peril they be, that consent that he shuld soo doo.'

Henry VIII continued annotating other charges. One sprang from the quarrel supposedly overheard at Whitehall the previous June between Surrey and his sister: 'If a man cumpassing *to hymself to governe the realm do actually goo abowght to rile the Kynge* and shuld for that purpose advise his daughter or suster to becom his harlot *thynkyng therby to bryng it to passe and so wolde rule bothe fader and soon, as by thys nexte artycle dothe more appere; whatt thys importyth.*' Here the king is responding to the evidence brought forth by Edward Rogers, who had said that Surrey had a specific strategy ready if the king should call the young duchess to him (to advise her to marry Sir Thomas Seymour): she should delay and visit the king again 'and so possibly . . . his Majesty might cast some love unto her; whereby in process she should bear as great a stroke about him as Madam Destampz doth about the French king.' The next article is even more threatening. 'If a Man saye thies wordes If the King dye who shuld have the rule of the prince but my father or I what it importeth.' Although the king's annotations end here, what he continued to read included a reference to the episode with Southwell that triggered Surrey's arrest: 'If a Man provoked and compelled by his dieutie of allegeaunce that shall declare Matier as he hereth touching the king and shall after be contynually threatened by the per[son] accused, to be killed or hurte for it W[hat] it importeth.' Surrey's arrogance is underscored, especially his verbal attacks: 'If a man shal saye thies wordes of a [man] or woman of the Realme, "If the King were dede, I shuld shortely shit him upp" What it importheth.' There is a reference to Surrey House and its pavilions and an echo of charges against his grandfather Buckingham: 'If a man take uppon him to use [tear in manuscript] in his Lordshipp, or to kepe plees [tear] himself free warren in his groun[ds, without] lycence What it importeth.' Finally there is a reference to Surrey's connection with foreigners: 'If a subiecte presume without ly[cence to] gyve armes to straungers What it imp[orteth].'[3]

Surrey's Coat of Arms

As Henry VIII's annotations reveal, the charge of treason focused on the validity of Surrey's coat of arms. Such insignia represented no small matter at a time of succession, especially as the king himself had established in 1530 that all such freedom of the College of Heralds began and ended with Henry VIII. At that time the Garter King of Arms Wriothesley was accused of acting *virtute officii* (by power of his office). The king ruled that 'all such authorities and privileges . . .

[3] PRO *SP* 1/227, ff. 121–4v. Cf. ff. 125–6v without the king's annotations to see the full power of Henry VIII's fury against Surrey. Rogers' testimony can be found in *LP*, vol. 21,ii, 555(4).

belongeth to his prerogative.' As Mervyn James notes, 'after 1530 the outlines of a more definitively state-controlled system of honour can be traced in the different emphasis given the herald's role; and in the more precise way in which heraldic jurisdiction was referred to the crown as its source.'[4] As the king knew, in the transformations of his realm in 1530, interpretation of a coat of arms could be, in a society that lived by a semiotics of honour, a very serious act. Even in days before the College of Arms, misreading of a coat of arms could be disastrous, as in the Battle of Barnet, when the arms of the Earl of Oxford were misread in the morning mist and Surrey's grandfather and great-grandfather could watch their enemy Warwick destroy his own ally. Death was not too serious a punishment for misusing the language of honour that determined the functioning of a society. For this reason, experimentation with this language could be a serious threat.

A manuscript exists, possibly seized from Surrey himself (it is believed to have belonged to the Garter King of Arms in the time of Elizabeth and James, whose father, Sir Gilbert Dethick, had been the Richmond Herald who summoned Barker to his meeting with Surrey in 1545 and was himself Garter King of Arms under Edward VI). It is entitled 'a drawing of arms Henry Howard Earl of surrey, for which he was attainted'. Although it shows considerably more quarterings (twelve) than usual in the Howard coat of arms, the whole is regularly marshalled. It begins in the first quarter with the Howard arms (although the Flodden augmentation is drawn incorrectly) and then the Brotherton (the three lions with no label) and then the Warenne, the Mowbray, and then the arms of Edward the Confessor (with a white label of three points). The seven that follow the arms of St Edward, from the next of Hamlin Plantegenet to the final Segrave are, in 1546, an acknowledged prerogative of the Mowbray—Howard inheritance (nothing in this coat of arms reflects Surrey's mother's family line of the Staffords). As Woodcock and Robinson point out, the event of a 'heraldic heiress' could dominate family lines as happened, in fact, in the Howard descent from the Mowbrays. Thus, if this drawing does indeed represent Surrey's arms, the seeming excess is quite legitimate and proves the poet's power of lineage in a form not unlike that devised by or for Surrey's dead friend, Henry Fitzroy, the Duke of Richmond. Furthermore, whether or not the manuscript shows an experiment in semiotics, in a twentieth-century herald's term, 'amateur heraldic doodling'—nothing like the coat of arms Surrey actually received on his creation as Knight of the Garter—the fact remains that, given the life-or-death issues in such arms, Surrey was neither frivolous nor fantastical. If an exercise, the drawing represents the kind of tentative fiction and invention a poet understood as necessary for experimentation in an art begun by heralds who in the thirteenth and fourteenth centuries had first been minstrels and poets.[5] As always with such experiments, the

[4] A. R. Wagner, *Heralds and Heraldry in the Middle Ages: An Inquiry into the Growth of the Armorial Functions of Heralds* (1956), 97; James, *English Politics*, 24–5.

[5] For the coat of arms, BL Harleian MS 1453. Thomas Woodcock and John Martin Robinson, *The Oxford Guide to Heraldry* (1990), 128–9. Cf. James William Edmund Doyle, *The Official Baronage of*

next step was the completed text which, as the poet earl knew, held legitimate claims on political and social reality.

Evidence about such experimentation became major trial evidence. Thus, both as text-maker and as earl Surrey would be on trial. But, as Neville Williams points out, if it were for heraldic offences Surrey would be tried, the trial did not take place before the Court of Chivalry, seemingly a legitimate venue. Instead, under the orchestration of Wriothesley, heraldry would be used not as an end in itself but as a means to focus the charge of treason more clearly. In fact, the heraldic charge became the capital offence and, in order to show the treasonable intent behind Surrey's supposed change in his coat of arms (for which change there was never any prima facie evidence, even in the trial, except by word of mouth), his experimentation with legitimacy had to be demonstrated. So, at once, in the mid-December 1546 gathering of depositions against him, Surrey's sister Mary complained that in such drawings of a coat of arms she had seen 'more than seven rolls; and that [in] some, . . . he had added more of Anjou, and of Lancelott Dulac' (HB 738). This strange reference to Lancelot's arms alluded to one of the most notoriously chivalric of Burgundian and French romances (partially recapitulated in a more realistic form by Malory). As Bloch notes, this narrative of the fatherless and disinherited young man (this aspect of his life far more focused in the narrative than his sexual affair with Guinevere) portrays a peculiar genealogical twist. It focuses on etymology, that is, on the words of a stone tablet at the grave where the questing Lancelot learns both the name of the father and of his own death.

In her same December evidence, the Duchess of Richmond alleged to her interrogators that 'her brother had reassum'd' the arms of his grandfather 'the Duke of Buckingham (who bare the king's arms) where the arms of her mother (daughter to the said duke) were rayned in his coat'. The mention of the beheaded duke and Surrey's controversial mother could only cause prejudice. Also in this drawing, she had seen her brother put in the place 'of the duke's coronet'—the crown Surrey would wear when he would become the fourth Duke of Norfolk—'a cap of maintenance purple, with powdred furr [ermine]'. It is probable that the young duchess had confused such a royal emblem as this 'cap' with the simple cap trimmed with ermine fur that the Howards had long used as a crest. She may also have read another sign wrong when she complained about the crown in the crest of Surrey's design for his coat of arms, that was 'to her judgment, much like to a close crown' (HB 738). It is possible that this was only the Crown of Scotland, the design of which had been granted for the crest of Surrey's grandfather after his great victory over the Scots at Flodden.[6] But if the Duchess of Richmond did in

England Showing the Succession, Dignities, and Offices of Every Peer from 1066 to 1885, Dukes–Viscounts (1886). Rodney Dennys, *Heraldry and the Heralds* (1982), 127. N. Denholm-Young, *History and Heraldry, 1254–1310: A Study of the Historical Value of the Rolls of Arms* (1965), 54–7.

[6] Neville Williams, *Henry VIII and His Court* (1971), 256. Bloch, *Etymologies and Genealogies*, 208. For the Howard 'cap', see the crest in 1513 of Lord Edmund Howard, Surrey's uncle and father of Queen Catherine Howard, in BM Cotton MS Claudius C III. Also, cf. Bapst, *Deux gentilshommes poètes*, 355 ff. For the confusion, see Ragan 18.

fact see what she vows she saw, if it were a closed crown that Surrey actually put into his redesigned coat of arms, this provides quite a different perspective on Surrey's 'doodling' during his last days.

Entering the closed crown, the imperial crown, into trial evidence solidified the poet earl's indictment, especially as it came from the mouth of his sister. After this, although she never mentioned her brother's supposed pandering of her to the king in her deposition, Surrey's sister could elaborate her trial evidence by accusing Surrey of a greater desire. The duchess added that she had spied 'underneath the arms . . . a cipher, which she took to be the king's cipher, HR'. This may have been the king's cipher in Surrey's drawing, as she claimed, or it may also have been simply Surrey's own initials HH. But, if it were HR, the fact suggests another configuration that did indeed haunt all of Surrey's icons of self in 1546, including his last portrait—Henry Fitzroy, Duke of Richmond. Here was a point of intimacy for both brother and sister, the sign of husband for the one and, for the other, the noble friend who might have become king.

But what the sister probably knew quite well she was not telling in December 1546. The Earl of Surrey had the hereditary right to bear in his own coat of arms the arms of St Edward the Confessor, the sign of the English monarch. Even in one of the trial interrogatories, the right had been unconsciously assumed. Wriothesley momentarily slipped when, in his seventh and eighth interrogatories to Surrey, he asked: 'To what intent you put the arms of St. Edward in your coat?' and 'Why you bear them at this time more than you or your father at other times before?' Although Surrey's maternal grandfather Buckingham could bear the arms of his direct ancestor, Thomas of Woodstock, the son of Edward III, and 'alone without any other Armes to be quartered therewith', Surrey had a stronger right to royal arms from his father's side. In January 1393, Richard II had ruled that Surrey's paternal ancestor Thomas Mowbray, the Duke of Norfolk, the grandfather of John Howard, the first Howard duke, could bear the arms themselves of Thomas of Brotherton, the son of Edward I, from whom Mowbray was descended. To this grant, one of the oldest surviving grants of arms by a king of England, Richard II gave Mowbray the right also to use for his crest 'unum leopardum de auro cum uno labello albo qui de jure fuit Cresta filii nostri primogeniti si quem procreassemus' ('a gold leopard—a lion passant guardant—with a white label that by right would have been the Crest of our first-born son if we had begotten him'), and then, in place of the label, the difference of 'unam Coronam de argento' ('a silver crown'). He could also bear the arms of St Edward the Confessor, who appears with King Richard in the Wilton triptych praying to the Virgin Mary. It was a remarkable grant by Shakespeare's 'mockery king of snow', Richard II, to Surrey's ancestor the Mowbray Duke of Norfolk (who died in exile in Venice), through whose daughter the Howards inherited not only the title of Duke of Norfolk in 1483 but the office of Earl Marshal.[7]

[7] *LP* 21, 2: 555 (8). For the Howard grants, see Robinson, *Dukes of Norfolk*, 50. CPR 1391–6, 350; Patent Roll 20 Richard II (4). Cf. Wagner 66–7 and Dennys 126 for Surrey's right to such a coat of arms.

For Surrey, St Edward's arms could be borne by the Howards everywhere, impaled, in dexter, with the arms of the younger son of Edward I, Surrey's ancestor Brotherton—the three golden lions passant with label (as seen in the Arundel portrait)—whose descendants led through the Mowbrays to the first Howard Duke of Norfolk. This was their 'freedom', in the ancient meaning of the word. Furthermore, these arms had been confirmed by Henry VIII's patent in 1514. That patent recovered the title of Duke of Norfolk for the older Thomas Howard after his victory at Flodden and deemed that the new Duke of Norfolk had precedence from 1397, the time of Richard II. The Howard duke could include as his predecessors the Mowbray dukes, not just his father—despite the fact that he was receiving such precedence through a woman, his grandmother. The right so granted in 1514 therefore gave Surrey in 1546 certain privileges. All such rights were be spelled out in an elaborately illustrated 1638 manuscript, Henry Lilly's 'The Genealogie of the Princelie Familie of the Howards,' prepared for Surrey's great-grandson Thomas, the Earl of Arundel, on the eve of the English Revolution.[8] Then, once more as in 1546, Howard arms projected genealogy at a time of breakdown and just before the total loss of Arundel's own ducal hopes, the destruction of Arundel Castle and Kenninghall and all Howard centres branded by the ruling council (including its Latin secretary Milton) as counter-revolutionary.

Thus, a clear right to bear the arms of St Edward as his ancestor was never the problem. But, as Anglo notes, 'whether or not Surrey had a serious entitlement to the arms was irrelevant.' It was enough that 'the heralds had declared against him' or, in actuality, appeared to. Most deadly, 'the King felt threatened and malevolent.' It is important to stress how symbolic in the Henrician world the image (and place) of the Confessor had become, at least for Henry VIII's concept of genealogy, if not for Cromwell's or Cranmer's. In a violently dislocated world, driven by indeterminate forces Henry Tudor had originated, the name of the Confessor marked continuity for the king, authenticity, presence, 'retailed to posterity' and metonymized in the name of his only living son. It was for St Edward the Confessor that Edward I and all the other Edwards were named, and his Westminster Abbey tomb was the only religious shrine left by Henry VIII in 1546, the Confessor's body still intact. For Henry VIII, it was the holiest spot in the entire kingdom, and so for the king, Surrey's 'heraldic indictment was deemed, and proved, sufficient.' It did not matter for the dying monarch that the arms for St Edward had themselves been invented from confusions over a Romanizing coin or that 'systematic heraldic display' barely existed before the twelfth century,

The Latin grant has an error: the indicative *fuit* should be the subjunctive *fuisset*. For the ambiguous role of Mowbray in the court of Richard II, see Donald R. Howard, *Chaucer: His Life, His Works, His World* (1987), 469–74.

[8] Robinson, *Dukes of Norfolk*, 242. The patent of restoration was given later by Charles II in 1661. For the genealogy, see Arundel Castle Manuscript 1638. Cf. Henry Howard of Corby, *Memorials of the Howard Family* (1834), 68 for a fuller justification and more evidence of Surrey's intrinsic right to bear the arms he used, both of Brotherton and of St Edward, naming four places where the Howards had always displayed these arms (a fifth, Thetford Priory, is named by LP).

certainly with 'no necessary "totemic" link between a particular figure and his heraldic sign, much less between his coat of arms and family'. In 1546, Henry VIII, like the Tudor court, believed heraldry had originated in Troy itself, as any representation of Hector as one of the Nine Worthies carrying his coat of arms could demonstrate, and as could be seen in a Burgundian manuscript dated 1450–60, 'Traitte du blason ou Armoiries', in the arms of Alexander the Great and Julius Caesar.[9] Surrey's heretical inscribing thus went to the roots of his society and how it organized itself, especially since 1530. It was for this reason that Wriothesley had shifted his attack on Surrey and found the surest way to kill him was one he knew well. He could draw on all the fears a deadly serious matter in a time of succession could provoke and then manipulate the forms which the Lord Chancellor knew from birth. The Lord Chancellor turned to his heraldic allies.

The deposition of the Garter King of Arms, Herald Christopher Barker, gave Wriothesley the evidence he needed to close his case and focus on the single charge in the bill of indictment, the charge that for four centuries has constituted the basis for Surrey's 'treasonable follies'. Although given in December 1546, the central evidence is dated back to 7 August 1545. The Garter King of Arms begins by stating that 'a little before' Surrey 'went to Boulogne, Richmond Herald [Sir Gilbert Dethick] wrote a letter to me to come with all speed to speak to the said Earl in a morning. And thither I ran,' only to wait an hour before being received. 'And at the last he sent for me into a gallery at his house in Lambeth, and there shewed me a scutcheon of the arms of Brotherton, and St. Edward, and Amory, and Mowbray quartered; and [said] he would bear it.' By what title can you bear this 'scutcheon'? asked the Garter King of Arms, to which Surrey answered, from his ancestor Brotherton, the son of Edward I. He had borne such a 'scutcheon'—so Barker reports the conversation. Either the Garter Herald is mistaken in his deposition or is falsifying Surrey's response (or Surrey himself is confused). Brotherton could not have borne such arms, because (1) he would have borne the arms of his descendant Mowbray, a physical impossibility, and (2) Brotherton's arms would not have included the arms of St Edward the Confessor. These arms had come into the Howard family crest by virtue of their descent from the Mowbrays, who had been given the right to bear the arms of St Edward the Confessor by Richard II himself. They had not existed in the Mowbray coat of arms before, nor were they ever in Brotherton's arms.

Barker interpolates in his evidence to the Privy Council that he had shown Surrey at once that this line was not properly in his pedigree, but Barker refers to only one quarter as wrong, and since this could not be that of Edward the

[9] Anglo, *Images*, 39. Bloch, *Etymologies and Genealogies*, 76; see the discussion of 1065 coins of Edward the Confessor in Strong, *Tudor Portraits*, vol. 1, 81. For the ancient heroes as confirming heraldry, see Bodleian Library MS Douce 278, ff. 1–3. Its full title is 'Traitte du blason ou Armoiries et des ordres de bataille en champs clos en plusieurs extraits des Livres du Songe du Vergier et de l'arbre des battailes'. I am indebted for this information to Dr J. F. R. Day and his forthcoming study *The Iconography of Honour: Chivalric Theory, Heraldry Treatises, and English Literature in the Age of Shakespeare*.

Confessor's arms, it would have to be another, most likely that of 'Amory' or Anjou (although Surrey's direct ancestor, Anjou in his coat of arms was questioned by both his sister Mary and the witness Warner). In fact, Surrey may have followed the advice of the Garter King. Anjou does not appear in any of the quarters in the existing manuscript of the shield. But in his testimony Barker makes no such distinction as to which quarter he objected to. The king and Privy Council could assume Surrey had been told sixteen months before that he could not bear the arms of St Edward the Confessor. This silence or suppression of a crucial distinction could then do its work. The result is that Surrey appears defiant and rebellious, dangerously so in 1546, when he replied, according to Barker's last account of Surrey's words, that he had found such a design 'in an house in Norfolk, in stone graven so and he would bear it. And I told him it was not in his honour [as an Howard] so to do.'[10] Thus the Garter King of Arms and Wriothesley, seeing how determined the king and council were to kill Surrey and how possibly threatened their own eminence and careers, could tell the king with perfect honesty that Surrey had been mistaken about who originally bore the old quartered crest with the arms of St Edward the Confessor in the first quarter. What they did not tell the king was that Surrey had a legal right in 1546 to bear those arms. It was not Brotherton, as Barker says Surrey says it was, who bore these arms but the Mowbrays who in turn 'retailed' the arms to the Howards. Indeed, Wriothesley and the Garter King of Arms, possibly, as Moore remarks, with old seals and drawings, could show Henry VIII that Brotherton never used the arms of the Confessor. Surrey's claim to derive his arms from the son of Edward I was false. In their own suppression of evidence and lying, they could prove the poet earl was lying and therefore, by such a pretension, threatening the throne and the king's genealogy. In all justice, he would have to be killed.

Further evidence from Barker, Garter King of Arms, in his December deposition demonstrates just how deeply involved the whole Henrician court had become in the fall of the Howards. When Surrey had persisted 'that he might lawfully bear' the arms of Brotherton and St Edward the Confessor, 'and after that I saw him so wilful,' Barker had gone to Warner, Surrey's friend in the household of Queen Catherine Parr (she had sent him in 1544 to plead for a reformed Christian schoolmaster before the Court of Aldermen). 'I spake to Mr. Warner, in Paul's,' the Garter King of Arms says to the Privy Council, 'to tell him that he [Surrey] might not do it [bear the disputed arms].'[11] For the Privy Council Warner had his own narrative that went beyond Barker's. In the summer and autumn of 1546, so said Surrey's friend, 'therll of Surre hathe had at dyvers tymes dyvers conferens

[10] *LP*, vol. 18, 315, 351. Although Anglo, *Images*, 38, amends the date to 1545, the evidence is still given in December 1546. I am indebted to Col. Peter R. Moore and his forthcoming ' "Gentlemen, Of What Have You Found Me Guilty?": The Charges Against the Earl of Surrey' for interpretation of the trial evidence, especially the silence and misinformation of the Garter King of Arms and, behind him, Wriothesley.

[11] Brigden, *London*, 359, 418. *LP*, vol. 21,ii, 568 and 547. See the Moore essay above. See the comments on this evidence in Casady, *Henry Howard* 196; in Nott 1, p. ci; and *LP*, vol. 21, i, 1425.

wythe me off his pedegre,' showing his friend 'sondry cotes' in which 'he myght bere the armys of Kyng Edward the seynt.' Now in December, after Surrey's arrest, having been 'comaundyd by Sir Wylliam padget,' the king's secretary, to write down what 'I cane remember' of any discourse between himself and Surrey 'consernyng hys pedegre & suche armis he tooke upone hyme to bere & also off any other matter that may In any wys apperteyne to the kynges most royall majesty or to hys posteryte,' Warner declares that 'I have not well agred that he myght so dare' to use the arms Surrey showed him. Further, Queen Catherine's servant had checked with Master Garter (in St Paul's) and discussed the 'dyvers scotchyns that he [Surrey] hathe causyd to be drawyne & set forthe,' including 'therll of angeoys armys whych was the ffyrst plantagynet of thys Realme'. Both agreed that 'he [Surrey] myght not ber the syd armys lawfully' (here the reference to the Anjou quartering as the wrong one is clear). Above all, says Warner to Paget, Surrey had himself checked with Master Garter and had been told such display was illegal, and it is probable Christopher Barker did not tell, once more, which quarter made the display illegal. The silence had its own reward. It was quite evident to the new regime just how valuable the Garter King of Arms had been. Exactly a month and a day after Surrey's beheading (on Edward VI's coronation day), Barker was made Knight of the Bath. Such an honour was highly unusual for a herald, as the *Dictionary of National Biography* notes, but only one in a pattern of rewards that followed the fortunes of almost all who gave witness against Surrey.[12] In the seventeenth century Lord Herbert of Cherbury found in contemporary sources that have since disappeared how 'notorious' it was that 'the king had not only withdrawn much of his wonted favour [from the Howards], but promised impunity to such as could discover any thing' (737).

Yet, in a London rife with gossip of treason and conspiracy (at least according to a November dispatch from the French ambassador) Surrey's own father had warned the young Howard, at least according to the deposition of the old duke's young mistress, Bess Holland. By 1546, for all Norfolk could understand, his heir seemed to be almost possessed, listening to no one. Or so both Surrey's sister and Bess Holland reported. Norfolk, the mistress said, had told her that Surrey 'had gathered them [coats of arms], himself knew not from whence' and placed the Norfolk arms (Brotherton in the first quarter) improperly. The old father had further told her she 'should take no pattern of his son's arms to work them with her needle in his house, but as he [Norfolk] gave them'. She certainly would not, said Bess Holland, because 'the Earl of Surrey lov'd her not, nor the Duchess of Richmond him; and that she addicted herself much to the said Duchess' (HB 738).

In all this reporting on Surrey's images and signs, however, a crucial point had not been lost. The Howard earl had not been passive since his return in dishonour from France in March 1546. Here the one positive testimony for the poet earl in the December depositions is revealing. Brought before the Privy Council and

[12] Bapst, *Deux gentilshommes-poètes*, 343. See the *DNB* entry under 'Christopher Barker'.

given a series of questions, Hugh Ellis, Surrey's servant, who had replaced Thomas Clere, remained loyal. At least he spoke a simple truth at the end of his deposition: 'Most humble beseching your honourable lordships for godes sake and the perfect knowledge of the Truth and consent that personally I may aunswer myn accuser in the premisses and then shall it be seene whither I be faultie in any of the same or not.' The deposition, and the bravery it took to express it against a hostile court, defines, as strongly as any document, Surrey's character as a young lord worthy to be served.

For the first question about the earl's encouragement of his sister to be the king's mistress, Ellis's reply is curt and ironic. He had obviously been a family servant who had observed a great deal: 'I never knew them so grete to gether to wisshe her so good a turn.' Next, Ellis had never heard Surrey either wish the king's death or indicate who should have 'the rule and government of the prince'. Indeed Ellis added vehemently 'by my faythe as I can remember I never hard him taulk of any such thing.' The only discord that he knew between the Privy Council and Surrey was that with the Lord Admiral Dudley, to whom Surrey 'dyd wryte his mynde in a lettre' in the previous July. Surrey also once told 'a pece of a taale' about 'master Ryche' all dressed up (absurdly?) at the battle front at Hardilot Castle near Boulogne. Sir Richard Rich was a leading courtier involved in the fall of Sir Thomas More and the persecution of Anne Askew, and was probably the king's solicitor against the poet earl at his January trial.

As for the crucial matter of 'thaunciant Armes of Englande', Ellis had heard Surrey say 'tht Kyng Edward dyd geve them to his predecessors and at bulloigne [Boulogne] in the presence of the Kinges highnes counsaile ther he [Surrey] divised the same to be payncted amonges other his cootes in skutchynnes which were sent from thense to norwich and are yett,' specified Ellis, in the house of Surrey's servant John Spence. 'And syns at Lambeth he drew out other Armes also for wyndowes which a glazier at Norwich hath to work in glasse for his newe house,' that is, for the windows of Surrey House, and also 'a Stampe of the same cootes [coats] for vessailes' at Surrey House. If Surrey wrote anything on matters of state, Ellis had not seen them, and the letters Surrey wrote from Lambeth to his father when the king was sick were all in his own hand. As to the young earl secretly yielding up Boulogne to the French, 'as god shalbe my iudge I dyd never in hym [find] a spot of any likelehode therof.' But Surrey had been disturbed by the January 1546 débâcle of his forces at St Etienne: 'If ever I hard hym saye he had the kinges maiestes dyspleasur or disfavour it was then for the which ever syns he hath taken great thought.' The defeat had been the great sorrow of Surrey's last year, to which was added a overwhelming financial drain that now included not only the earl's French war expenses but the heavy debts incurred in building his new house on Mount Surrey.

For Ellis, the Earl of Surrey was neither ambitious nor did he desire to flee the realm as other accused traitors had done. Rather, Ellis had heard Surrey clearly say 'if he survived his father he shulde have enoughe and that he wold never covet more.' Ellis provides here one more inscription of the motto Surrey had put on his last portrait 'SAT SVPER EST'—'Enough Survives.' Wriothesley himself made a precise note of this during the deposition, quoting Surrey: 'They will lett me aloon as long as my father lives, and after, I shall do well ynough.' Given such assertion as the motto and Ellis' testimony, it is no surprise that the court immediately sent special agents to examine heraldic designs at the unused but still undemolished Benedictine priory at Thetford, where the lords of Norfolk, Howard, and Mowbray, and, before them, the Bigods, had been buried for almost five centuries.[13]

The Father's Betrayal: Three Letters and a Confession

Four texts by the third Duke of Norfolk reveal, in their language, the actuality from which Surrey now had no escape. At last the old man was caught in the trap he had spent most of his life since Edward IV avoiding, awaiting at 74 what he knew could be the same fate that, as their judge, Norfolk had given his two royal nieces. Beneath the artifice of Norfolk's initial emotional letter to the king, then of his more formal letter to the Privy Council in mid-December, and then of his January confession lies the old father's genuine suffering. In Norfolk's astonishment at this turn in history, at the probable loss not only of 'Merry England' forever but of his heir and the whole Howard 'livelode', horror and pain moved quickly into realistic attempts at escape for them both. The texts show the strategies of the old duke at his most calculating, the last his final effort to save his son and heir just before Surrey's trial and, his father knew, the son's beheading.

In his first letter to the king from the Tower, recorded only by Lord Herbert (740–1), Norfolk wrote a passionate defence immediately on being imprisoned on St Lucy's eve. The letter demonstrates an intensity of role-playing and cunning Surrey could not manage: 'I your most humble subject prostitute at your foot, do most humbly beseech your highness to be my good and gracious lord. I am sure some great enemy of mine hath informed your majesty of some untrue matter against me.' Here Norfolk introduces the motif that distinguishes the oratorical ethos he now gives himself in all these texts: 'Sir, God doth know, in all my life, I never thought one untrue thought against you, or your succession, nor can no more judge or cast in my mind what should be laid to my charge, than the child that was born this night.' To be sure, if he knew that he had offended the king 'in any point of untruth', he would declare directly to king's person such a falsehood. In honour of 'all the old service I have done you in my life', Norfolk wants to be brought before the king to face his accusers, or at least before the council. If then he cannot 'make it apparent that I am wrongfully accus'd, let me, without any respite, have punishment according to my deserts'. In mid-discourse of this text,

[13] For the details of this evidence, PRO *SP* 1/227 ff.105, 129, 128r–v and *LP*, vol. 21,ii, 555 [18].

as though to accentuate his sudden shock at arrest and being in the Tower, Norfolk bursts out in an *anacoluthon*, 'Alas! most merciful prince, I have no refuge but only at your hands, and therefore at the reverence of Christ's passion have pity of me, and let me not be cast away by false enemies' informations.' What men could be offended by him unless it be those who 'are angry with me for being quick against such as have been accused for sacramentaries', like Anne Askew, who had denied the Real Presence?

This allusion leads the old duke to the now powerful margins of the English court, where a law of identity was developing that would lead directly to the English Revolution: theology and politics were becoming the same, as never before. Sensing the political shift and the victory of the margins, Norfolk wants to set his record straight: 'As for all causes of religion, I say now, and have said to your majesty and many others, I do know you to be a prince of such virtue and knowledge, that whatsoever laws you have in times past made, or hereafter shall make, I shall to the extremity of my power stick unto them as long as my life shall last.' This grand declaration is followed by the more pragmatic: 'so that if any men be angry with me for these causes, they do me wrong.' Norfolk will not accept the charge of being a papist and, as for other charges, he can only guess at their 'ill-will' and the 'casting of libels' he has heard. Finally, in asking pity of the king, he offers the king all his lands and goods (a shrewd move because otherwise Seymour and Dudley, Southwell and Gates, would, as he knew, grab up even more than they did).

In a separate letter to the Privy Council, Norfolk asks for 'some of the books that are at Lambeth; for unless I may have books to read e're I fall on sleep, and after I wake again, I cannot sleep, nor did not this dozen years.' Then he asks for a 'ghostly father', a confessor so 'that I may receive my Maker' and he also asks to hear Mass, promising not to speak 'to him that shall say mass'. He also asks for permission 'in the day-time to walk in the chamber without, and in the night to be lock'd in'. Finally he wants to send to the city to buy a book of St Augustine, *De Civitate Dei*, also Josephus, *De Antiquitatibus*, and then 'another of Sabellicus; who doth declare most of any book that I have read, how the Bishop of Rome from time to time hath usurp'd his power against all princes, by their unwise sufferance.' The old man has now identified himself as a new Christian humanist. His last request was simply for sheets. But when the king's 'most sorrowful subject' signed his first letter from the Tower—the only one directly to the king—what he asked most of all was for an opportunity to know the charges against him and then to 'hear some comfortable word from your majesty', his first wife's nephew.

The silence from the king must have been overwhelming. In the next weeks Norfolk heard stories, rumours of circumstance after circumstance, entangling him and his family and the dismantling of his world. In another letter, now directly to the Privy Council, which he knew by mid-December was orchestrating all events surrounding him, Norfolk repeated key motifs from his first letter (which the king may never have seen). Here the motifs were less emotional and more controlled within a Ciceronian form the duke could manipulate. Unlike Priam, brave but hopeless before a Pyrrhus in the fires of Troy, Norfolk turned cunning again. He begins directly by answering specific points. He recapitulates his recent examination by Seymour and Paget ('my Lord Great Chamberlain and Mr. Secretary'). First, 'there was never cypher between me and any man, save only such as I have had for the King's Majesty' and if he wrote in cipher, others like Paulet and Browne were involved in it and thus knew it could not bring harm to the king. Because the case against the Howards may have been building for months, with all texts and reports being checked out for any possible incrimination, the next accusations he had to answer derive, first, from a letter from the time of the Pilgrimage of Grace concerning 'the lewd speaking of the northern men', possibly about the power the rebels would give Norfolk if he joined them, and then, second, from a statement that appeared to favour the Pope. To this latter accusation Norfolk is characteristically direct. He knows what is at stake. 'To that purpose, as God help me now at my most need,' he remembers no such remark supporting the Pope either by himself or anyone else. Further, 'as for my implications, that the Bishop of Rome should have authority to do such things, if I had twenty lives, I would rather have spent them against him, than ever he should have any power in this realm; for no man knoweth better than I, by reading of stories, how his usurped power hath increased from time to time' and since 'the King's Majesty hath found him his enemy, no living man hath, both in his heart and with his tongue,' both in England and France and Scotland, 'spoken more sore against his said usurped power than I have done.' He has witnesses to prove it. Had he also been privy to a letter calling for 'overtures' between the Pope and Henry VIII, supposedly written from France to the Bishop of Winchester and given to the king at Dover with Norfolk at hand? Norfolk is precise (and, if the king or Seymour reads his letter, he reminds each of another life he and Surrey shared): he had not been with the king at Dover 'sith my Lord of Richmond died', when word of Richmond's death 'came to Sittingbourne'.

Having answered these questions, Norfolk asks to meet his accusers 'face to face, what they can say against me.' He is only asking what Cromwell asked, he says, and remembering Seymour's dislike of Cromwell, adds: 'My Lords, I trust ye think Cromwell and myself not to be like' for 'he was a false man, and surely I am a true poor gentleman.' The rest of the letter reveals the considerable sophistication of the old man's framing of arguments. They all build on the basic structure of an oratorical ethos: Norfolk is the good man who wants only to meet his accusers. 'My Lords,' the old duke cries out with calculated passion, 'there was never gold tried better by fire and water, than I have been; nor hath had greater enemies about my Sovereign Lord, than I have had: and yet, God be thanked, my truth hath ever tried me, as I doubt not it shall do in this cause.' The placing of 'truth' here echoes a recurring motif in his daughter's evidence and in his own texts. For Norfolk the word meant 'troth' as well (in 1546 both were pronounced almost the same), that is, fidelity and service. This devotion to 'truth'/'troth' leads to his declaration of innocence ('Surely, if I knew any thought I had offended his Majesty, I would surely have declared it to his person') before the body of the English king, his devotion to which Francis I had once praised.

Then Norfolk turns to the oratorical device of cataloguing, a place-logic. He names those events and acts that show his dedication to the person and body of the king and, indirectly, as in the first example, his enemies: 'Upon the Tuesday in Whitsun week [15 June 1546] last past, I brake unto his Majesty most humbly beseeching him to help that a marriage might be had between my daughter and Sir Thomas Seymour' and furthermore, 'whereas my son of Surrey hath a son, and divers daughters, that with his favour, a cross marriage might have be made between my Lord Great Chamberlain and them' and also his son Lord Thomas has a son that, from his Marney mother, will have 1000 marks a year and he too might marry one of Edward Seymour's daughters. 'I report me to your Lordships, whether my intent was such in this motion, or not.' In showing his openness to the king, he can also remind Seymour of the nobility the Howards could still give the future Protector. He also shows his son's 'favour'—whether true or not, a good ploy. But both Wolsey and Cromwell had intrigued to destroy him, Cromwell recalling once 'My Lord, ye are an happy man that your wife knoweth no hurt by you, for if she did she would undo you.' As for Buckingham, 'that of all men living he hated me most, thinking I was the man that had hurt him most to the King's Majesty' and his Welsh rebellious brother-in-law Sir Rhys ap Griffith 'wished many times how he might find the means to thrust his dagger in me'. The council should also recall as a sign of his loyalty to the king 'what malice both my nieces, that it pleased the King's Highness to marry, did bear unto me.' Further, 'who tried out the falsehood of the Lord Darcy' and the other leaders of the Pilgrimage of Grace, 'for which they suffered for, but only I!' and 'who shewed his Majesty of the words of my mother-in-law [stepmother], for which she was attained of misprision of treason [in Queen Catherine Howard's trial] but only I!'

These sycophantic acts of devotion, in which even close family members were betrayed and for which sycophancy his son would never have the performance skills, are transformed into strong emotional statements. In the *peroratio* of this oration, the central motif of 'truth'/'troth' comes centre-stage. Norfolk now recognizes the actuality of his own destruction but, more important, that of his son and heir. They are only days away from execution. Any price, any humiliation, can and must be paid for survival. Norfolk could pay more and better than his poet son with his strange figurations. The father must therefore emphasize, by a kind of *diaphora* or device of repetition, his essential ethos or character. From the truth motif ('in all times past unto this time I have shewed myself a most true man to my Sovereign Lord'), he logically moves into an emotional outburst. It is suited at this point in a Ciceronian oration to repeat the central motif, so: 'Alas! who can think that I, having been so long a true man, should now be false to his Majesty?' From this king, the old duke has 'received more of profit' than the Howard head deserves, but, 'poor man as I am,' he is still the king's 'son his [Richmond's] near kinsman'. Thus 'for whose sake shall I be an untrue man to [the king]? Alas! alas! my Lords, that ever it should be thought any untruth to be in me.' With that outburst, Norfolk concludes by asking the Privy Council to show this performance, 'this scribble letter', to the king and beseech him 'to remit out of his most noble, gentle heart, such displeasure as he hath conceived against me'. He shall always pray, during his life, 'for the continuance of his most Royal estate long to endure'. Once the greatest man in the kingdom after the king, Norfolk now signs his letter as 'his Highness poor prisoner, T. Norfolk.'[14]

By mid-January 1547 the silence from the king finally drove Norfolk to the act he loathed most. He admitted dishonour. He will make the act of confession necessary for any successful Tudor trial and conviction. His son had not made it, and this fact alone may have driven the father to make the terrible decision. Thus, on the day before his son's trial, Norfolk signed his statement of confession. The act signalled to his son, who would certainly be told of the confession, that he too must confess if he did not want to lose his head and destroy not only himself but his entire family. It also signalled to the council that, however foolishly his son would act at the trial (and Norfolk now had no confidence in the codes of honour his son might expound in public), the family had officially confessed. The whole episode could be concluded. His heir need not be killed, no matter how absurd and arrogant he appeared. His son should not be annihilated and lost forever.

The price Norfolk was willing to pay to save his son was abject submission and shame, a confession of what he had, in fact, not done: 'I Thomas, Duke of Norfolk, do confess and acknowledge my self most untruly, and contrary to my oath and allegiance, to have offended the king's most excellent majesty' by 'the disclosing and the opening of his privy and secret counsels at divers and sundry times to divers and sundry persons.' The generality fitted the whole occasion and was as much as Seymour and Dudley and the others could hope to get at this point. What they needed was evidence to nail down their immediate (and probably main) target—certainly if the trial the next day did not work out to the young earl's total shame. They got it: 'Also, I likewise confess, that I have concealed high treason, in keeping secret the false and traitorous act, most presumptuously committed by my son Henry Howard Earl of Surrey, against the king's majesty and his laws, in the putting and using the arms of St. Edward the Confessor'—an act of misprision—in his coat of arms that 'appertain only to the king of this realm' and 'whereunto the said earl by no means or way could make any claim or title by me, or any of mine or his ancestors.' Norfolk went a step further. He condemned himself 'likewise' confessing that since the death of his father, he had borne in the first quarter of his own coat of arms 'the arms of England, with a difference of three labels of silver', arms that properly belong to the Prince of Wales, the future Edward VI. This amounted to treason—and this was enough. By such neglect, he

[14] BL Cotton Titus B 1, 94. Also, Nott, vol. 1, Appendix 38. The *LP* reference vol. 21,ii, 554 has some errors, for example, the examiner with Paget being Seymour, not 'My lord Great Master'.

has 'not only done prejudice to the king's majesty, and the said lord the prince, but also given occasion that his highness might be disturb'd or interrupted of the crown of this realm, and my said lord prince might be destroy'd, disturb'd, and interrupted in fame, body, and title of the inheritance to the crown of this realm.' And then the admission: 'Which I know and confess, by the laws of the realm to be high treason.' His closure recognizes that he deserves to be attainted for such treason and 'to suffer the punishment, losses and forfeitures' that treason brings. Although he is 'not worthy to have or enjoy any part of the king's majesty's clemency or mercy,' he beseeches it and shall pray daily 'for the preservation of his most noble succession, as long as life and breath shall continue in me' (HB 745).

Not surprisingly, on that 12 January, for the signing of Norfolk's confession, the eight major members of the Privy Council were on the scene, and, with them, the two chief justices of the kingdom. It was a gala performance. This was the kill they had all been waiting for. Now they could take this victory as one more prelude to the supreme power for them from the Supreme Head that lay just ahead, especially after they had manipulated the terms of the king's will. With the Howards out of the way, they were home free.

Surrey's Trial: 13 January 1547

By 13 January 1547, the poet earl had surely recognized how hopeless his whole situation had become. The remarkable fact is that he still continued to fight. 'The 13th daie of Januarie was arraigned at the Guildhall Henrie Haward, knight of the noble Order of the Garter, Earle of Surrey, and sonne and heire of Thomas Duke of Norfolke, and that daie was condemned of highe treason,' writes the Windsor Herald Wriothesley (177). He also names some of the Comissioners: Thomas Wriothesley, Edward Seymour, John Dudley, William Paget, and the aged Anthony Browne (Plate 5), the husband of Surrey's 'Geraldine'. There was also the Lord Mayor of London, Henry Hoberthorn, who was knighted a few days after Surrey's trial. Besides these familiar courtiers there was Surrey's jury: commoners, the 'knightes and squires of Norfolke' required for the trial of a nobleman with a courtesy title only (Surrey was never made a peer). Because Surrey's alleged offence, the drawing of a false coat of arms at Kenninghall on the previous 7 October, had occurred in Norfolk, a grand jury at Norwich Castle had declared the indictment a true bill on 7 January 1547. Immediately thereafter a special commission of oyer and terminer, establishing the need for a trial, was appointed. A jury of Norfolk men were to assemble at Guildhall in London to try the indicted Earl of Surrey. The jury from Norfolk included some old and familiar names, Sir William Paston, Sir Francis Lovell, Sir John Gresham, Sir John Clere, among others.[15]

[15] H. Miller, *Henry VIII*, 26. *LP*, vol. 21,ii, 697 (365–6); see also Casady, *Henry Howard*, 214–16, for the trial and beheading.

Before this audience, for whom Paget and the others had rehearsed so much, Surrey spoke defending himself. There are no verbatim transcripts of what he said, although there is a record that for the arraignment he wore a coat of black satin furred with black coney (rabbit) that the Lieutenant-Warden of the Tower, Sir Walter Stoner, had purchased for him just for the event, so destitute was the young earl. All official records of the trial were deposited in the *baga de secretis* by Sir Robert Southwell, brother of Surrey's betrayer and Master of Rolls, and then 'bestowed in the Studie at Westminster Palys where other recordes do lye'. There within six months they were lost, although other records remained. The disappearance took place shortly after 5 July 1547, when Sir Robert Southwell 'deliverede uppe a bag of bokes sealed with his seal, wherein were conteigned writinges concerning the attaindre of the Duke of Norfolk and therle of Surrey his sonne'. These had been given to Southwell 'and other lerned men . . . to peruse' presumably after Surrey's trial and quick execution. It is possible that the whole process was now considered, if not illegal, certainly hasty; or the review of the evidence may have been for the purpose of removing or adjusting all questionable evidence, anything illegal or irregular. In any case, all official records of the trial vanished, as did the final reports on the mid-December ransacking of Kenninghall and Surrey House.[16]

Thus, the only extended narrative of this event comes from the Spanish Chronicle. According to this personal account, Surrey was tried at the Guildhall of London in a kind of special insult, 'this being the first time that ever such a thing was seen of a gentleman being tried there, but always at Westminster'. The young poet earl walked from the Tower in a spectacular display with 300 halberdiers, and, adds the Spanish businessman describing what he must have seen himself, 'it was fearful to see the enormous number of people in the streets.' When Surrey entered the vast Guildhall, with the blade of the executioner's axe still turned away from him, he was directly accused by the prosecution led by Sir Richard Rich for offences deserving death (his display of arms and his putative attempt to escape). But 'the Earl, with manly courage, said, "You are false, and to earn a piece of gold would condemn your own father."' The poet added he '"never sought to usurp the King's arms"'; everybody knew the Howards had a right to them: ' "Go to the church in Norfolk and you will see them there, for they have been ours for five hundred years." ' Surrey also defended the prophetic inscription of 'Tel Dandus' on his painting of the Garter, and when he is interrupted, in the Spanish account, by Paget who calls out 'Hold your peace, my lord; your idea was to commit treason, and as the King is old you thought to become

[16] PRO E159/341, m.22. *APC* 2:106. Casady, *Henry Howard*, 212. For the Act of Attainder, see House of Lords RO, Original Acts 37 Henry VIII, no. 23. The original Latin commission has the Great Seal appended and sewn on the original Act to which it assents. Under the flap through which the tag bearing the Great Seal passes, the king's sign manual 'Henry R' made with the dry stamp appears, not on the Act itself, although at the top of the Act are written the words of royal assent, 'Soit Fait'. See the rather strange history of this document in *Statutes of the Realm* (1810), introduction, Appendix F, p. lxxv.

king,' Surrey responds fiercely: 'And thou Catchpole [a reference to Paget's lowly birth as the son of a Sergeant of Mace of the City of London], what hast thou to do with it? Thou hadst better hold thy tongue, for the kingdom has never been well since the King put mean creatures like thee into the government.' The Lord Admiral Dudley then asked Surrey if he were so innocent and meant no harm, why had he covered over his painting and attempted to escape from the Tower? Surrey's answer to the grandfather of Sir Philip Sidney is interesting and appears to recall the imprisonment and execution of Dudley's own father, Edmund, the first of Henry VIII's victims. ' "I tried to get out," said the Earl, "to prevent myself from coming to the pass in which I am now; and you, my lord, know well that however right a man may be they always find the fallen one guilty" ' (146–8). For the third time, Surrey refers to a genealogy, to the father of an accuser.

Only Lord Herbert records Surrey's response to another witness (Southwell? Blagge?): 'And finally, when a witness was brought against him *viva voce*, who pretended to repeat some high words of the earl's by way of discourse,' to which this 'said witness should return a braving answer; the earl reply'd no otherwise to the jury, than that he left it to them to judge, whether it were probable that this man should speak thus to the Earl of Surrey, and he not strike him again' (739).

All records that do survive, however brief, suggest an astonishing feat: Surrey held his own for eight hours. With his life at stake, the poet earl reacted with his truest weapon, his gifts of language. In the strategy of the Privy Council, acting as the instrument of the king's honour, such discourse really did not matter, of course, even if Surrey's powers of language, Erasmus' 'treasure' of rhetorical devices that Surrey brought from a lifetime of humanist study, exploded. It did not matter if Surrey were now so absurd as to take on his own defence and talk and talk. It simply proved their case about his arrogant character. It was one more proof of the nearly deranged, almost Italianate nature of this would-be Protector, who kept giving them opportunity after opportunity to destroy him.

The day left its mark, however. Lord Herbert of Cherbury concluded his discussion of Surrey with just this emphasis on a master of language: 'And thus ended the earl: a man learned, and of an excellent wit, as his compositions shew.' Herbert had also heard of the miraculous talking-trial. He details the humanist resources, techniques, and strategies Surrey drew on for eight hours. 'Upon the thirteenth (the king being now dangerously sick) the Earl of Surrey was arraign'd in Guild-hall in London, before the lord chancellor, the lord mayor, and other commissioners,' and 'the earl, as he was of a deep understanding, sharp wit, and deep courage, defended himself many ways.' He manoeuvred, as though composing a special prosody or going on a military foray, 'sometimes denying their accusations as false, and together weakening the credit of his adversaries; sometimes interpreting the words he said, in a far other sense than that in which they were represented' (739). The Windsor Herald Wriothesley concluded his own entry on the trial with a whiff of amazement: 'He had such pleading for himself that he kept the Commissioners from nyne of the clock in the forenoune till five of the clocke at night or [before] he had [was given] judgment' (177). In a later Tudor document, thirty years detached from the scene, when Elizabeth I's cousin's reputation had risen, Holinshed was positively dismayed: 'Had he tempered his answers with such modesty as he shewed token of a right perfect, and ready wit, his praise had been the greater' (861).

There is no record of exactly what rhetoric rose and fell in the Guildhall, where as a commoner Surrey was being tried that January day, but Joseph Warton in the eighteenth century praised Surrey as 'the first English classical poet' whose 'streame' of language, in Cheke's phrase, had already impressed, if not captivated, generations—at least eighteenth-century poets believed that. In his last performance Surrey held his last audience for eight hours until five o'clock, using all the resources of his humanism. In the total dark of an English winter afternoon, the jury departed for deliberation. Although the rhetorical tropes, figures, and modulations of rhythm Surrey used that day are lost, one fact emerges. At no time in the entire day did Surrey perform the critical gesture, as Foucault notes, for this kind of legal theatre: confession. Nowhere in the long diatribe or violent tirade or Ciceronian eloquence (or whatever) came submission of any kind. The record would have noted even the slightest confession of guilt.[17]

Surrey's enemies at the trial had probably hoped, in letting the young Howard talk for hours, that he would either confess or slip up, in his posturing so like his grandfather Buckingham's over twenty-five years before. The real trial had been the examination of evidence in the middle of December, of course, and the outcome had already been decided during that Christmas the king did not spend at Greenwich. The point now was to give this kind of legal theatre the embellishment of confession or linguistic slip-up. What came slowly to bother Surrey's enemies was that the poet earl was not giving his audience either. Instead, he was offering the representation of a survivor, one whose image, if not his being, will not be defeated because his 'streame' of language will not be defeated. It was not a model or representation they wanted any public audience to see at this (for them) turning-point in history.

A curious fact appears in the surviving evidence of that day. Surrey's sustained performance appears to have worked. At least one part of his audience was impressed. The 'knightes and squires' from his native East Anglia did not follow the production cues set by Seymour, Dudley, and Paget. They deliberated well into the night, obviously so impressed by what they had heard that day that their consciences could let them defy the most powerful men in the kingdom, for, says the Spanish narrative, 'there was great difference of opinion amongst them' (148). The whole legal establishment outside the jury waited for the rehearsed ending to

[17] Thomas Warton, *The History of English Poetry, from the Close of the Eleventh to the Commencement of the Eighteenth Century* (1824), 645. Here Warton is emphasizing Surrey's continuity and his addition to the genealogy not merely in the invention of new specific forms out of old texts but in the outstanding achievements of Surrey's own total form: 'his justness of thought, correctness of style, and purity of expression'. Foucault, *Discipline*, 42. Cf. also Lacey Baldwin Smith, *Treason in Tudor England: Politics and Paranoia* (1986), for background for this trial.

this farce. It finally became too much. Signals may have been exchanged. Sir William Paget, who was stage-managing the production, slipped out.

In a short time, Paget was back from Whitehall Palace with the king's firm instructions. No Englishman, noble or commons, could miss, by 1547, the clear roar of Henry VIII. The old king was not yet so comatose that his powerful will could be frustrated in its desire. The poet Earl of Surrey must die. As a young man, Henry VIII had told the Venetian ambassador Giustiniani that he did 'not choose any one to have it in his power to command me, nor will I ever suffer it.' In 1533, the king had declared to Chapuys in a Maundy Thursday conference God and his conscience were on very good terms. In the last days of his life then, the Tudor king had the same total confidence as in 1494 when he became his father's genuine duke, a real presence. In the autumn of 1546 Henry VIII insisted on ordering, for autumn planting, French trees and grafts that could not bear fruit for another ten years. With such certainty, amid the daily court functioning around him of a Paget or a Denny or Herbert, the exact daily routine so beloved by the aged and by children, what else for his own hope of continuing life and fruit-trees but to protect his 9-year-old son from a brilliant menace like the young Earl of Surrey, so like the stylish male pretenders from whom as a boy he had saved his own father?[18]

The simple jurymen heard that bellow from Whitehall Palace. Paget went straight to their chamber. Within an hour the verdict was returned or rather, in the Spanish narrative, when called by name, each replied that Seymour would speak for them, and so Seymour did, declaring in the face of Surrey: 'Guilty, and he should die.' But, continues the narrative, Seymour 'had hardly said the words when the people made a great tumult, and it was a long while before they could be silenced, although they cried out to them to be quiet, but silence was at last restored.' In that silence, according to the Spanish businessman, the Earl of Surrey spoke out: 'Of what have you found me guilty? Surely you will find no law that justifies you; but I know the King wants to get rid of the noble blood around him, and to employ none but low people.' The poet Earl of Surrey was then pronounced a traitor for false images. For the wrong forms, he was condemned to die. The blade of the executioner's axe was turned towards the young man, and 'it was shocking to hear the things that he kept saying, and to see the grief of the people' (147–8).

The First Reports: Truth and Myth

The news of Surrey's execution was generally met abroad with disbelief. Once the act of beheading was viewed in some perspective, the English ambassadors were

[18] Giustinian, *Four Years*, vol. 1, 237. For the later declarations by Henry of his will, see *CSPSpan*, vol. 8, 367 (531); *LP* 6, 164; Smith, *Henry VIII*, 325.

instructed to blur the effects as, later in the Edwardian regime, Henry VIII was himself framed, ever so subtly, as barbaric in his systematic destruction of blood nobility. Already two days after Surrey's forced march to the Tower, the Imperial ambassador van der Delft was writing to the emperor. The Privy Council has been secretive but now 'the principal subject of their deliberations' can be seen. On Sunday 12 December the Duke of Norfolk, having arrived in London from Kenninghall on the same day, was taken to the Tower, and his son 'had been detained for five or six days previously in the house of the Lord Chancellor'. Although the reason for the arrests is not known, those who appear to know say that the two 'held secretly some ambiguous discourse against the King, while the latter was ill at Windsor six weeks ago; the object being to obtain the government of the Prince.' The 'hope of their liberation is very small,' the duke being 'deprived of his staff of office and of his Garter before he was taken to the Tower by water,' and 'the son being led thither publicly through the streets.' Three days later, van der Delft writes that Wriothesley has informed him of the reason for the arrests. 'It was,' so Wriothesley said, 'pitiable that persons of such high and noble lineage should have undertaken so shameful a business as to plan the seizure of the government of the King by sinister means.' Officially the son had not been under arrest for any plot to murder the council and seize the prince 'but in consequence of a letter of his, full of threats, written to a gentleman.' In fact, says the French original of this text sent to the Holy Roman Emperor himself, two other gentlemen—the two needed to make a serious case—'gentil sieurs'—came forward and accused him of conspiracy. And, adds the Imperial ambassador, 'though [the son] has always been so generous to his countrymen, there is not one of them, however devoted to him, but regards him as suspect; and the earl appeared much downcast on his way to the house [Tower? Ely House?].' When van der Delft wrote again to Charles V on Christmas Eve, he reported how power is passing from the king. It is now widely accepted, says the Imperial ambassador, that the Earl of Hertford, Edward Seymour, and the Lord Admiral, John Dudley, 'are in favour of the sects' and 'they have obtained such influence over the King as to lead him according to their fancy.' When at earlier times the other members of the Privy Council had referred the ambassador directly to the king, they are 'now of a different aspect, and much inclined to please and entertain the Earl and the Admiral'. In fact, 'it may now be assumed that these two have entirely obtained the favour and authority of the King,' for 'nothing is now done at court without their intervention, and the meetings of the Council are mostly held in the Earl of Hertford's house,' contrary to law. The ambassador even hears 'that the custody of the prince and the government of the realm will be entrusted to them; and the misfortunes that have befallen the house of Norfolk may well have come from the same quarter.' Van der Delft recapitulates as precisely and succinctly as anywhere the polarities of Surrey's last days: 'Last Wednesday the earl of Surrey was executed. Four or five days previously he had defended himself at his public trial from nine in the morning until five o'clock in the afternoon' against 'the principal charges' including 'that he had maintained that his father was the most qualified person, both on account of his services and his lineage, to be entrusted with the government of the Prince,' setting forth 'his merits and services in comparison with those of those who had been preferred to him.' At his trial, answering charges about his sister, the coat of arms, and the final portrait, the young earl 'did not spare any of the Lords of the King's Council, who were all present, and he addressed words to them that could not have been pleasant for them to hear.'

On the day before the Imperial ambassador's report, the French ambassador de Selve was already writing back to France the events of the day before: he had heard on Monday morning 13 December that 'my lord of Surrey' is imprisoned in the Tower 'on two principal charges, one that he had the means of attempting the castle of Hardelot, when he was at Boulogne, and neglected it, the other that he said there were some who made no great account of him but he trusted one day to make them very small.' At this same time three Englishmen overseas were overjoyed at the arrests of Surrey and his father. All three writing separately to the Lutheran theologian Heinrich Bullinger, these reformed Christians had followed the political events in their native land. One of them, John Hooper, was happy to report that 'our King has now confined in the Tower of London the duke of Norfolk and his eldest son, both of whom, if report be true, had conspired the death of the King and prince.' The second reformed Christian, John Burcher, on 31 December reported that 'the news from England is as agreeable' as that from Germany is depressing (Charles V was defeating German Protestants). 'The Duke of Norfolk whose authority extended to the North of England—a most bitter enemy of the word of God—has been imprisoned, with his son, with whom he made a secret attempt to restore the Pope and the monks; but their design was discovered.' John Hilles wrote on 26 January that Surrey and Norfolk were both executed and the Bishop of Winchester in the Tower. The future was becoming theirs.[19]

For their part, the Privy Council used, in their explanation of the arrest of the Howards, the same psychological strategy as these Protestants of divine intervention, a disaster God has prevented. The ambassador in the Low Countries, Edward Carne, wrote to the Privy Council on receiving the news on 15 December, 'signifying the detestable practice of the Duke of Norfolk and his son of Surrey, with their devilish intents now (thank God!) revealed'. On Christmas Day 1546, the Imperial Secretary Joyse received the English ambassador Thirlby, and Joyse too was glad the English king had discovered the treason in time, so that 'the mal ice coulde be brought to execution.' Promising to 'advertise thEmperour herof accordingly', he talked a little more of 'the haultenes of the Erle of Surrey', a point even the Imperial court knew, at least as Thirlby expressed it, and then bade the English ambassador farewell. Otherwise, the Imperial court was generally cool to

[19] *CSPSpan*, vol. 8, 364 (526), 365 (527), 367 (531), 370 (533–4); vol. 9, 3–4. *LP*, vol. 21,ii, 533, 608, 621, 652. Cf. the French original manuscript text in Österreichische Hof-, Haus-, England Hofs- und Staatsarchiv, Wien, Kart. 13, Berichte an Karl V. 1546–47.

any explanation from London. In January, Chapuys wrote to the Regent Mary herself that the imprisoned Surrey 'is considered a man of great courage' (in the official French of his report, the word is 'honneur'). Imperial coolness made the new Edwardian court uneasy, for the English ambassador in Paris, Nicholas Wotton, sought out the Imperial ambassador there, Saint-Mauris, in March to tell him 'that God had shown mercy to the late King and to his people in that the Earl of Surrey died before him, for otherwise he would have given the government trouble, though of course he would have been unable to allege anything against the young King Edward.' Wotton's remark reveals the fear of the new Tudor court and a primary reason for killing the Howard heir. In the eyes of Europe, the poet earl held not only a style worthy of a prince and even a monarch but the legitimacy, however far away in lineage. This was more than could be said of 'the young King Edward', born of an excommunicated father who had contracted an illegal marriage in the eyes of the Church, so any child from his marriage could never be a true Christian monarch. The fact of the excommunication made any new establishment in England, even the succession, quite shaky in its pretensions. And so, continued Saint-Mauris in his dispatch, the English ambassador cannot stop attacking Surrey, 'greatly' censuring 'the late Earl's insolence' and hinting 'that he had been put out of the way because it had been feared he might stir up some commotion'.[20]

In France, the same Wotton, the first Dean of Canterbury Cathedral, met no one less than Francis I on Christmas Eve 1546. The meeting was at the request of the French court itself. The French had already heard 'that thErle of Surrey was yn warde,' and so, wrote the new dean, 'they requyrid me to send theym worde what the mater was, if I knewe it.' It is noteworthy that it was the arrest of Surrey and not of Norfolk that first engaged the attention of the French court. Wotton used this great interest of the French to manipulate an interview with none other than the king himself, who also wondered about Surrey. Hearing the facts of the Howard betrayal from the English ambassador, Francis I expatiated cautiously and philosophically on 'thoffice and parte of Kynges and Princes' to govern and rule by 'ministringe justice indifferentlye to all sorte of menne' and 'so likewise the parte and dutye of subjectes is to be obedient and faithfull unto theyr Kinges and Princes.' Otherwise, the commonalty of a kingdom is affected, the French king concludes, not merely the monarchy itself. The French king is cautious, of course, in his language as he probes for the facts, for, 'yf the duke of Norffolke, and his sonne thErle of Surrey, have gone abowte' and done such things as 'I [Wotton] had declarid to Hym,' they deserve punishment. After all, said Francis I, he knew Henry VIII 'to be a Prince wyse juste and vertuouse' and he was 'well assurid that no private affection or passion shulde leade' Henry VIII 'to cause enye thinge to be done against theym [Norfolk and Surrey], otherwyse then right and justice requyrith.'

[20] *LP*, vol. 21,ii, 702, 645, 644. Cf. the French manuscript text of Chapuys' letter in Österreichische Hof-. Haus-, England Hofs- und Staatsarchiv, Wien, Kart. 13, Berichte an Maria von Ungarn, 1546–47.

It was a rather long response by the French king, who was naturally grateful the English king had communicated with him. In almost an aside—but crucial to Francis I's subtle interrogation, a point not altogether missed by Wotton—the French king asked 'whether this mater were all redye sufficientlye provid [proved]; whereunto,' the English ambassador says he told the monarch that it was 'by the confession of his sonne [Surrey], both agaynst hym self and his father to.' Then Wotton made the mistake of adding 'and yet I sayd the mater was yn examinacion stylle.' Francis I immediately caught the contradiction—a full confession by Surrey and yet the whole 'mater' still being examined? The French king must have guessed the lie that the Dean of Canterbury was telling (if the Privy Council had not lied, in fact, to Wotton about the confession). After his last statement, Wotton remarked that the French king 'wonderid moche, and sayed that He knewe the Duke of Norffolke, for He had been with Hym' and 'founde hym verye earnest yn' the cause of Henry VIII. 'He sayd He wolde never have thoughte enye suche thinge yn hym.' Then the French king added carefully: of course, if the duke 'had enye suche thinge yn his brest, it was no merveylle' that he did not disclose it to Francis I because of 'the great amitye that was betwixte Your two Majesties'. The interview was then concluded.[21]

By the time of Holinshed and the early Elizabethan period of Challoner's elegy, the beheading of the poet earl had begun to be transformed into a legend. The execution of the Howard heir apparent was based, in Holinshed's revision of an Edwardian revision, on 'certeine surmises of treason' that the historian did not even name (avoiding altogether the question of the coat of arms). This vagueness carries its own revisionist proof. Holinshed accuses Surrey of a lack of modesty in his answers at his trial; his close analysis of Surrey's rhetoric that day shows a special concern for an acknowledged (at least by Holinshed's time) master of the English language (the passages on Surrey are original, not incorporated from Hall, as was his frequent bent). Equally Holinshed's comments on the father and son do not indict them as traitors but simply define their situation in a terrible fate that overwhelmed two noble historical figures, the son lacking the virtue of reformed Christian humility: 'The evil hap as well of the father, as of the sonne, was greatlie lamented of manie, not onlie for the good seruice which the duke had doone in his daies in defense of this realme, but also for that the earle was a gentleman well learned, and knowne to haue an excellent wit, if he had beene thankefull to God for the same, and other such good gifts as he had indued him withall' (861). At the same time as this revisionist process, inscriptions of Surrey appeared with the ambiguity that made them material for a legend with the widest variance, the poet's death becoming very soon, in Walter Benjamin's phrase, 'the sanction of everything the story teller can tell'. That is, from the world of Henry VIII, 'the only true subject of chronicles', as the Elizabethan Nashe says in his romance on Surrey (254), Henry Howard, the poet earl, had already taken into the

[21] *SP*, vol. 11, 1463 (391–3). *CSPSpan*, vol. 8, 386 (556). I am indebted to Col. Peter R. Moore for his interpretation and re-examination of the original dispatch from Saint-Mauris.

future for Cheke and others to follow the cultural 'authority', as Benjamin notes, of 'the unforgettable'. Surrey was one of the originals for the later Renaissance of an originating narrative the early Tudor world became. Out of that world had come the 'unforgettable' mother of Elizabeth I and also Margaret Douglas, the grandmother of James I—one a first cousin to the poet, and the other an intimate friend.

Cavendish's elegy, hardly more than a year after Surrey's beheading, posed a strange figuration that added to the legend: a soliloquy by Surrey himself in a series from the history-makers of early Tudor England, all proving the truth of fortune's wheel. Like Cheke, Cavendish is fascinated by the poet's body of honour, the young 'Erle' asking at once 'What advauntage' before death did 'a dukes heyer' have, even with a body 'Endowed with suche qualities / as fewe in my tyme' that is also 'Lakkyng nothyng / that nature myght repayer' because 'In dewe proporcyon / [nature] wrought hathe euery lyme.' In his 'Verse in Prayse of Lorde Henrye Howarde Earle of Surrey,' Turbeville praises Surrey's extraordinary linguistic precision ('Eche worde in place with such a sleight is coucht' so that everything 'he treates so firmely toucht, / As Pallas [Athena] seemde within his Noble breast') but most of all Surrey is 'A Mirror' by which nobility of blood is redefined ('By him the Nobles had their vertues blazde') and, more powerfully, his totally original concept of nobility and honour is taken beyond any one estate or class through gifts of language: 'Eche that in life had well deserved aught, / By *Surreys* means an endles fame hath caught.'[22]

It was Sidney, however, the grandson of Surrey's great enemy Dudley, who gave him the inscription that made him an archetype for the later Renaissance. Sidney had been intimately acquainted with members of Surrey's family, from his uncle Sussex to his youthful friend Philip Howard (with their common godfather, Philip of Spain) to Lady Berkeley to Surrey's wife's nephew, Edward de Vere, the Earl of Oxford, who quarrelled with Sidney about precedence and honour on the tennis court (the queen decided in favour of the higher-ranked Oxford). In his *Defense*, Sidney had stressed Surrey's lyrics as contemporary models for young poets, but there was also a political analogy at work in his text. A beheaded young poet in 1547 or an unrewarded one in 1580 could thus re-inscribe language, as an aged

[22] Walter Benjamin, *Illuminations*, ed. Hannah Arendt and trans. Harry Zohn (1969), 94. Cavendish, 78–82. Turbeville, *Works*, B8v–C1. A letter copied and probably composed in Restoration England (although referring to earlier records) discusses the characters of Mary I and her father, especially lamenting his destruction of Surrey (BL Harleian MS 1579, 5v and 6r): 'But ye. last & one of the worst acts he ev[er] did was the uniust p[ro]ceeding, & takeing away the life of that miror of nobility therle of Surrey. . . . A man so worthy in himselfe, his p[ro]ginito.s soe loyall & faithfull to prince & country . . . & onely out of Suspicon which is noe proofe, God put ye Sword into this kings hands to make him the executioner of his revenge, & like an ignorant fencer, that whilst hee warded his head, he was hitt in the harte when hee suspected it not. // Thearle had to great a blood to haue so foule a thought hee was knowne to bee thankfull to god, & too pittifull to man to imbrace soe wilde an act' but 'God stird vp a house of meane discent,' the Dudleys, and the future Duke of Northumberland, set out to kill Surrey, whether 'out of malice to his [Surrey's] house, out of feare of his popularetie, out of a canckered envy to his vertue, or out of a diobollical divinacon it is unknowne.'

Tudor monarch, male or female, could not. Surrey would thus play the authorizing role for Sidney he later played for Southampton (to whom Nashe dedicated his romance) and Essex, the close friend of Surrey's son Henry. As Norbrook has shown, Sidney's own epic *Arcadia* 'demonstrates the distrust of the monarchy' reflecting 'the view of these aristocratic radicals (the monarchmachs) that only a strong nobility could safeguard liberty.' As the Countess of Pembroke suggests in her elegy on her brother, not only was Sidney safeguarding liberty at Zutphen and redefining the role of the nobility, but poets alone can inscribe such honour and understand both its function and transcendence in history. Society was primarily a matter of work for such safeguarding and inscribing, and poets, so Sidney wrote in his *Defense*, make societies work through music and language: 'Amphion was said to move stones with his poetry to build Thebes, and Orpheus to be listened to by beasts—indeed stony and beastly people.' In fact, says Sidney, ending his oration, poets perform a labour no monarch or historian has ever been able to deny: they affirm life 'retailed to posterity', a genealogy. They 'will make you immortal by their verses' (408, 458).

It was only natural then that by the 1590s, as Crewe has demonstrated, 'Surrey rather than Wyatt or Sidney epitomized for Elizabethans the phase of English Petrarchan sonneteering' (especially Surrey's sonnet form that Shakespeare used) and, with the sonnet form, there came the greater 'phase' of the blank verse dominating poetic texts from *Doctor Faustus* to *Volpone* and, during the Revolution, *Paradise Lost*.[23] In late Elizabethan and early Stuart reigns, Surrey as both poet and earl strengthened the political capital of the Howards, once more in power. By 1600, poetic texts and new literary forms would not allow the memory of the Earl of Surrey to be lost or eradicated. At the time of *Hamlet*, the severed head of Surrey was singing for all to hear.

The Scaffold: 19 January 1547

Of the few contemporary records of Surrey's beheading, the most direct is by the Windsor Herald Charles Wriothesley, the Lord Chancellor's first cousin, who wrote in his single *Chronicle* entry for that day: 'The nynetenth daie of Januarie

[23] For the originating role of the time of Henry VIII for the later Renaissance, see Peter C. Herman, 'Introduction' in *Rethinking the Henrician Era*, 1–6. David Norbrook, *Poetry and Politics in the English Renaissance* (1984) 94. Margaret P. Hannay, *Philip's Phoenix: Mary Sidney, Countess of Pembroke* (1990), 69. Jonathan Crewe, *Trials of Authorship: Anterior Forms and Poetic Reconstruction from Wyatt to Shakespeare* (1990), 79. For the intertexuality of Surrey and later generations, see Steven W. May, *The Elizabethan Courtier Poets: The Poems and Their Context* (1991). I am indebted to Professor May for his pointing to sources for Surrey (and his family), especially the uncollected material both printed and unprinted and needing investigation. A final proof for the persistence of the legend of Surrey can be found the text of the 1590s play *The Booke of Sir Thomas Moore*, part of it attributed to Shakespeare. Here the character of Norfolk is clearly drawn from his poet son (with some hints of the earlier Duke of Buckingham), especially in reference to Norfolk's poems.

the Erle of Surrey was lead out of the Towre to the skaffolde at the Towre Hill and their he was beheaded' (1: 177). The Exchequer record simply states that Surrey's board at the Tower was charged only to the nineteenth. In the accounts of the money to be paid to Sir Walter Stonor, Lieutenant of the Tower, the record gives a vivid description of the material surroundings of Surrey's last days, including not only Surrey's board but that of two 'persons that kept hem duryng the sayd vj weekes', the price of seacoals for fire 'in his chambre', five dozen candles, the four yards of 'ryght Sattyn for to make the sayd Erle a soote ayenst his arraynement' and the black coney fur used to trim the suit, and a pair of furred 'boskens' or shoes. Tapestries had also been brought in (for warmth in the freezing Tower as well as decoration), a feather bed, one bolster and two pillows, blankets, quilts, and sheets, as well as special utensils, including a flagon and salt shaker 'of Sylver, not gelt'. In such a world Surrey ended his days and wrote his last poems.

A contemporary wall-painting of Edward VI's coronation procession, exactly a month and a day after Surrey's beheading, reveals the route Surrey and his guards might have taken up to Tower Hill. Surviving today only in an eighteenth-century engraving, the lost mural (from Cowdray House of Surrey's 'Geraldine') depicts the royal procession winding from the Tower across the drawbridge and up an incline still surprisingly steep. Unlike the slow resplendent movement of the Cowdray House procession, the pace of the few men up the hill, most in black, on that January morning, was probably rapid. It was essential in the king's feeble condition that the Privy Council despatch the execution of Surrey promptly, with as few involved as possible. According to handwritten marginal notes on an early text of Lord Herbert's seventeenth-century text, Surrey was handed over at the drawbridge, like the common property he had become, from the hands of the Lieutenant of the Tower to 'ye sherrifs of London named Richard Cernas and Thomas Gurlyn'. To the Venetian emissaries and tradesmen watching the London scene during these years, such a formal gesture as the requirement of two sheriffs marked a ritual of justice and territory peculiarly English. The law of the City of London, the territory of the scaffold outside the walls of the Tower, controlled the protocol of the beheading. Even Surrey's grandfather, the Duke of Buckingham, had been led up Tower Hill by two sheriffs to his execution (HB 191).

A space vast for Tudor London, Tower Hill was sketched in 1549 by Surrey's Flemish contemporary Anthony van den Wyngaerde (Plate 21). If it had been sketched on that January morning, the men around the scaffold would have appeared diminutive, with little protection from January winds coming up the Thames from the North Sea across the odd empty space van den Wyngaerde depicts in the crowded city. Crossing this enclosed space between river, Tower, and city, the poet earl in his black satin coat would have stood before the single point of convergence in all the emptiness Wyngaerde drew: the scaffold. This 'spectacle of the scaffold' rose only four feet high. On this morning its wooden platform would be draped in black, and at the top of the nine steps of the scaffold—as drawn by van den Wyngaerde—stood the masked executioner. On this day the blade of his huge axe was turned, in traditional form, towards Surrey. Nine days later (on the eve of Norfolk's execution) the old king, who had personally directed almost every stage of Surrey's trial and arraignment, would himself be dead. Norfolk was to be spared. Surrey was to give, as Henry VIII's last victim, a special imprint to all the procession of the king's dead that had come before simply by ending it.

According to marginal notes in an early edition of Lord Herbert's *Henry VIII*, Henry Howard, the poet Earl of Surrey, ascended the scaffold, admitted offending the king, and dutifully asked pardon: 'Vpon Tower hill . . . ye sayd Harry Hauward submittinge himself to ye Law, sayinge yt he was iustly condemned by ye Lawe & was come to dye vnder ye Lawe' asking forgiveness of both God and 'ye kings Mats.,' finally making 'his petition to God & so he was behedded, on whose soule have mercy. Amen.'[24] This was the expected and state-approved form of recording deaths, especially of traitors, and the emphasis on the law (but not necessarily one's own culpability) can be found in the recorded last speeches of Queen Anne Boleyn and Edward Seymour, the Duke of Somerset, among others. Another tradition about Surrey's beheading appears more probable. According to the Spanish Chronicle, Surrey continued to talk and talk on the scaffold until the last moment, an outburst like his trial's, either hysterical, violent, or magnificent—or in all styles at once, with that ambiguity so irritating to those who prefer political contrition and neat closure as marks of civilization.

Whatever the final moments, the poet had to follow another form and ritual a prisoner could no more escape than the presence of the two sheriffs. Climbing the nine steps of the scaffold, a wooden bar to his left, the poet earl would have glanced at a man on a horse, sketched also by van den Wyngaerde, and, beside the horseman, the wagon already shrouded and ready to take away, in just a few moments, Surrey's severed head and bleeding body. The other ritual involved looking directly ahead at the last sight for any victim on Tower Hill. Especially when the body of the victim was stretched out on the block, the flat of the stomach against the cold wood and the eyes staring ahead, the sight could not be missed—authorities had seen to that. The image ahead was directly in line with the scaffold and block. Clear in the van den Wyngaerde drawing is what Surrey saw: the large raised crucifix and twisted body of Jesus Christ, which was in 1546 the highest cultural inscription of the Tudor world and of Renaissance Europe.

But whatever happened in that first light of 19 January 1547, it was over in a few moments. Another day had begun, with the first signs of life no doubt from the river and also from the roars of the four hungry lions and two leopards behind the wooden railings of the Tower (the Spanish Duke of Najera and his entourage had commented on them three years before). At Whitehall Palace, the day was being

[24] For the description of Surrey's last moments, see Bodleian Library, MS Delta 624 in the margins of 570; Gurney-Salter, *Venetian Eyes*, 110. This drawing of Tower Hill is in the Ashmolean Museum. In the drawing the crucifix has over it, as in Austrian and Swiss wayside crosses even today, a small cover or roof protecting it. Bodleian Library Delta 624, p. 570.

readied for new exact plans for the ceremonial installation of young Edward as the Prince of Wales and then for discussions of Henry VIII's preparations for yet another war with Scotland, the king 'taking the Scottish war very much to heart', reported the ambassadors. Two days before, the English king had told the French, Scotland's protector, he sought 'closer amity' and 'league defensive' with his rival Francis I (who was himself to die in two months of urinary and genital infection), but the French ambassador Odet de Selve suspected the English of having 'some evil fantasy of surprising us somewhere'. He was right. The English king had already borrowed on the Antwerp money market and was hiring foreign mercenaries and mustering an army of between 40,000 and 60,000 men. On this very day the English king was plotting and giving his last military order: destroy the French bastions around Boulogne, where Surrey the military hero had served and saved Henry VIII's last conquest, the last England ever made in France. With breath still in his massive body, Henry VIII had not given up his dream of honour in France.

But in that first thin light, the city whose space held Surrey's scaffold did not belong only to Henry VIII. Gulls and seabirds also rose, and the ubiquitous swans. 'Never,' the secretary to the Duke of Najera had written back to Spain, 'did I see a river so thickly covered with swans as this.'[25] Already with them, as Surrey bent his head with cropped red hair and thrust himself forward, stretching out his arms and slender neck and looking ahead at the only image he could see, there sprang up small clouds of kites and tame carrion birds. Generation into generation, as sixteenth-century chroniclers kept recording, the birds survived, loud and noisy and circling the scaffold space, the river, and the city that had been Surrey's London.

[25] Foucault, *Discipline*, 32. Delta 624, p. 570. Smith, *Henry VIII*, 261–2. *Archaeologia*, 23 (1831) 354 ff.

Bibliography

MANUSCRIPTS

Arundel Castle, Sussex

MS A 1047: record of costs for the tomb of the second Duke of Norfolk.

MS 1638: contains genealogy of the Howards until the English Revolution.

Bancroft Library, University of California, Berkeley

MS HF 5616 E5 NE: contains household book of the Duke of Norfolk (1524).

Bodleian Library, Oxford

MS 903 (Arch. A 170): contains the Earl of Northampton's letter to Elizabeth I.

MS Don C. 42: contains William Latymer's A Brief Treatise or Chronicle of the Most Virtuous Lady Anne Boleyn late Queene of Englande.

MS Douce 278: contains treatise on heraldry and the Burgundian court.

MS Laud Misc. 597: Eltham Ordinances.

Folio Delta 624: Edward, Lord Herbert of Chirbury, *The Life and Raigne of King Henry the Eighth* (London, 1549), interleaved with handwritten extracts from the Chronicle of Anthony Anthony.

British Library, London

Additional MS

1419A: Inventory of Henry VIII.

1523: contains Seymour maxims.

24493: contains letter of Surrey to the Prior of Bury St Edmunds.

6113: contains description of the investiture of the Marchioness of Pembroke.

17492: the Devonshire manuscript of poetry from the Surrey circle.

19193: contains description of the opening of the third Duke of Norfolk's tomb in the nineteenth century.

30513: contains the Mulliner Book of musical settings.

48976: contains drawing of Queen Anne, consort of Richard III, her only surviving image.

Arundel MS 318: contains poem of [Eleanor], Duchess of Buckingham, Surrey's grandmother.

Cotton MS

Caligula E II: contains letter to Cromwell about Surrey in France.

Claudius C III: contains copy of the crest of Lord Edmund Howard.

Cleopatra E VI: contains definitions of the Supreme Head.

Galba B VI: contains Wolsey's letter using grammatical terms for political events.

Titus B I: contains letters of the third Duke and Duchess of Norfolk.

Vespasian C XIV: contains household records at Hunsdon of the Princesses Mary and Elizabeth.

Vespasian F XIII: contains letter of Duchess of Richmond to Norfolk about getting her marriage settlement from Henry VIII.

Hargrave MS 205: contains Surrey's translation of Book IV of the *Aeneid*.

Harleian MS

78: contains papers of Charles Blount, fifth Lord Mountjoy.

1453: contains drawing of a coat of arms reputedly for Surrey.

1579: contains Marian response to Surrey's execution.

3362: contains report on Cromwell's execution.

8219: contains description of visit of the Duke of Najera.

Royal MS 18: contains manuscript of *La toison d'or* and record of payment to the painter Gwilm Strete (William Scrots).

Sloane MS

26: contains comments on Sir Thomas Wyatt.

34: contains comments on the third Duke of Buckingham and the Earl of Surrey.

2172: contains the letter of Philip Howard, Earl of Arundel, to Elizabeth I.

Stowe MS 396: contains records of trial of the Earl of Surrey, a description of one of Surrey's devices, and his arraignment.

College of Arms, London, MS 1:16: contains description of the Countess of Sussex's funeral.

Corpus Christi College, Cambridge, MS CCCC 168: contains report on Cromwell's execution.

Hatfield House, Hertfordshire, MS 4: contains treatise on church councils.

House of Lords Record Office, London, MS Original Acts 37 Henry VIII 32: text of the Act of Attainder of the third Duke of Norfolk and the Earl of Surrey.

Lambeth Palace Library, London

MS 711: contains Northampton's letter to Elizabeth I.

MS 265: contains the one surviving picture of Anthony Woodville, Lord Scales.

MS 1107 and MS 1163: details the relationship of Archbishop Cranmer and a general council of the Church.

National Library of Wales, Aberystwyth, MS Mostyn 158: contains account by Welsh soldier of the English forces in France, 1544–47.

Norfolk Record Office, Norwich

MS DCN 115/9 (3), 1542, 1544; and MS DCN 47/1, 1544–5: contains agreements with Surrey for the lease of St Leonard's Priory

MS NRS 27260, 361: documents on Bess Holland's death and her will.

MS NRS 2378 11: Latin household book 1519 of the Earl of Surrey.

Pembroke College Library, Cambridge, MS 300: Household book of the third Duke of Norfolk (1528).

Public Record Office, London (Kew) MS

C 1/1379/24: contains documents on Bess Holland's death and will.

C 66/613: contains licence to build Thornbury.

C 82/660: contains document of the creation of of the title of Marchioness of Pembroke.

E 101/60/22: contains account of money due for Surrey's upkeep in the Tower.

E 159/341: contains record of disposition of materials from Surrey's trial.

KB 8/14: contains the bill of indictment against Surrey and the records of Surrey's trial.

LR 1/115/1 and 2/113/129: contains description of sales of Howard property after 1546.

LR 2/115–6: contains 1546 inventory of Kenninghall and Surrey House and disposal of Surrey's property.

OB8 1/1419: contains itinerary of Henry VIII.

Prob 11/37/14: contains will of third Duke of Norfolk.

Prob 11/42A: contains will of third Duchess of Norfolk.

SP 1/105: contains letter from Norfolk to Cromwell about burial of the Duke of Richmond and Cromwell's son.

SP 1/46 95424: contains letters of the Duke of Richmond to Wolsey and Henry VIII.

SP 1/111: contains letter from Norfolk to Cromwell about settlement for the Duchess of Richmond and the state of the rebellion in the north.

SP 1/115 and SP 1/118: contain Norfolk's letter to Henry VIII on the Pilgrimage of Grace.

SP 1/122: contains Norfolk's letter to Cromwell from the North of England about the conditions there, Surrey's bad health, and the non-stop house party at Kenninghall.

SP 1/130/43: contains Norfolk's letter to Henry VIII on the birth of Surrey's second son, the future Earl of Northampton.

SP 1/131: contains letters of Duchess of Richmond to Cromwell about marriage settlement.

SP 1/143: contains letter from Thomas Eynns, late secretary to the Duke of Richmond, to Cromwell about Surrey.

SP 1/156: contains Norfolk's petition to Henry VIII and Cromwell for Thetford Priory as parish church.

SP 1/175–176: contains depositions about Surrey's 1543 Lenten escapades.

SP 1/182: contains letter from Sir John Wallop to Henry VIII, describing the arrival of Surrey and Blage in Landrecy.

SP 1/189–190: contains dispatches from Norfolk in France in 1544.

SP 1/209–210: contains letters from Thomas Hussey to Surrey in France.

SP 1/213: contains letter of Surrey to Henry VIII about his defeat at St Etienne, a draft of a letter from the Privy Council to Surrey, and a letter from the Privy Council to Gardiner and Thirlby in Bruges about Surrey's defeat.

SP 1/214: contains letter from Paget to Surrey in France.

SP 1/223: contains Surrey's letter to Thomas Hussey.

SP 1/224: contains Surrey's final letter to the Privy Council.

SP 1/227: contains all the key records of Surrey's last days.

SP 1/246: contains Bassus part-book for songs.

SP 2/L: contains drafts of parliamentary Acts.

SP 49/817: contains will of Charles Blount, fifth Lord Mountjoy.

Society of Antiquaries, Burlington House, London, MS 129: Inventory of Henry VIII.

Österreicherische Hof-, Haus-, und Staatsarchiv, Wien, England Korrespondenz MS

Kart. 4, Berichte an Karl V, 1529: contains Chapuys' letter to Charles V on meeting with the Duke of Norfolk.

Kart. 5, Berichte an Karl V, 1532: contains Chapuys' letter on Surrey's marriage.

Kart. 13, Berichte an Karl V, 1546–7: contains report of Imperial Ambassador on Surrey's last days.

Kart. 13, Berichte an Maria von Ungarn, 1546–7: contains report of Chapuys on the death of Surrey.

PRIMARY SOURCES

ASKEW, ANNE. *The Examinations of Anne Askew*, ed. Elaine V. Beilin. New York and Oxford, 1996.

—— *The First Examination of Anne Askew Lately Martyred in Smithfelde by the Romysh Popes Upholders with the Elucydacyon of Johan Bale*. Marburg, 1546.

ARISTOTLE. *The Generation of Animals*, trans. A. L. Peck. Cambridge, Mass., 1953.

—— *Poetics; Longinus on the Sublime; Demetrius on Style*, ed. and trans. W. Hamilton Fyfe and W. Rhys Roberts. Cambridge, Mass., 1965.

—— *Rhetoric*, ed. and trans. John Henry Freese. Cambridge, Mass., 1967.

The Arundel Harington Manuscript of Tudor Poetry, ed. Ruth Hughey. 2 vols. Columbus, Ohio, 1960.

ASCHAM, SIR ROGER. *The Whole Works*, ed. Dr. Giles. London, 1865.

AUBREY, JOHN. *The Natural History and Antiquities of the Country of Surrey*. 5 vols. London, 1718–19.

BALDWIN, WILLIAM. *The Canticles or Balades of Salomon Phraselyke Declared in English Metres*. London, 1549.

—— *A Treatise of Morall Phylosophie*. London, 1547.

BALE, JOHN. 'Preface' to John Leland's *The Laboryose Journey & Serche for England's Antiquitees*. London, 1549.

BARCLAY, ALEXANDER. *The Eclogues*. Early English Text Society Original Series 175, London, 1928, reprint 1960.

—— *The Famous Cronycle of the Warre which the Romans Had Against Jugurth Usurper of the Kyngdome of Numidy: Which Cronycle is Compyled in Latyn by the Renowened Romayn Salust. And Translated into Englysshe by Sir Alexander Barclay, Preest, at Commandement of the Righyt Hye and Mighty Prince: Thomas Duke of Norfolke*. London, 1520.

BARNES, ROBERT. *The Reformation Essays of Dr. Robert Barnes*, ed. N. S. Tjernagel. London, 1963.

BATES, CADWALLADER JOHN. *Flodden Field: A Collection of Some of the Earliest Evidence Concerning the Battle of Branxton Moor, 9th September 1513*. Newcastle upon Tyne, 1894.

BINDOFF, S. T. (ed.), *The House of Commons*. London, 1982.

BLOMEFIELD, FRANCIS, and PARKIN, C. *A Topographical History of Norfolk*. 11 vols. Fersfield, Norwich, and Lynn, 1739–75.

BLUNDEVILLE, THOMAS. *The Arte of Ryding and Breakinge Greate Horses, 1560*. Amsterdam, 1969.

BOORDE, ANDREW. *A Compendyous Regyment*. London, 1542.

CAMDEN, WILLIAM. *Remains Concerning Britain*. Toronto, 1984.

CASTIGLIONE, BALDESAR. *The Book of the Courtier*. trans. Charles S. Singleton. Garden City, NY 1959.

CASTILLON, —— DE. *Correspondance Politique de MM. de Castillon et de Marillac 1537–1542*, ed. Jean Kaulek. Paris, 1885.

CAVENDISH, GEORGE. *Metrical Visions*. ed. A. S. G. Edwards. Columbia, 1980.

CHALLONER, THOMAS. *De Rep Anglorum Instauranda Libri Decem*. London, 1579.

CHAUCER, GEOFFREY. *The Riverside Chaucer*, ed. Larry D. Benson. Boston, 1987.

COLVIN, HOWARD M. (ed.). *The History of the King's Works 1485–1660*. Vol. 3. London, 1975.

The Chronicle of Calais In the Reigns of Henry VII and Henry VIII to the Year 1540, ed. John Gough Nichols. Camden Society, First Series 53. London, 1846.

Chronicle of the Grey Friars of London, ed. John Gough Nichols. Camden Society, Old Series 53. London, 1852.

Chronicle of King Henry VIII of England Being a Contemporary Record of Some of the Principal Events of the Reigns of Henry VIII and Edward VI Written in Spanish by an Unknown Hand, ed. and trans. Martin A. Sharpe Hume. London, 1889.

CHURCHYARDE, THOMAS. *A Discourse of the Queenes Majesties Entertainement in Suffolk and Norfolk: With a Description of Many Things then presently Seene*. London, 1578.

COMMYNES, PHILIPPE DE. *Memoirs*, ed. Samuel Kinser, trans. Isabelle Cazeaux. 2 vols. Columbia, SC 1969–73.

DRAYTON, MICHAEL. *Poems*, ed E. J. M. Buxton. 2 vols. London, 1953.

EDWARD VI. *Literary Remains of King Edward the Sixth*, ed. John Gough Nichols. London, 1867.

ELLIS, HENRY (ed.). *Original Letters illustrative of English History from autographs in the British Museum and other collections*. 11 vols in 3 series. London, 1824, 1827, 1846.

ELTON, G. R. *The Tudor Constitution: Documents and Commentary*. Cambridge, 1960.

ELYOT, SIR THOMAS. *The Boke Named the Gouernour*, ed. H. H. S. Croft. 2 vols. London, 1880.

—— *Four Political Treatises: The Doctrinal of Princes (1533); Pasquil the Playne (1533); The Banquette of Sapience (1534); and the Image of Governance (1541)*, ed. Lillian Gottesman. Gainesville, Flag, 1967.

ERASMUS, DESIDERIUS. *Pilgrimages to Saint Mary of Walsingham and Saint Thomas of Canterbury*, trans. John Gough Nichols. Westminster: 1849.

—— *Opus epistolarum*, ed. P. S. and H. M. Allen. 12 vols. Oxford, 1906–58.

'Biographical Memoir of Henry Fitzroy, Duke of Richmond', ed. John Gough Nichols. Camden Society, Old Series 61. London, 1855.

FITZROY, HENRY, Duke of Richmond. 'Inventories of the Wardrobes, Plate, Chapel Stuff, etc., of Henry Fitzroy, Duke of Richmond and of the Wardrobe Stuff at Baynard's Castle of Katherine, Princess Dowager', ed. John Gough Nichols. Camden Society, Old Series 61. London, 1855.

Fontainebleau. *The School of Fontainebleau: An Exhibition of Paintings, Drawings, Engravings, Etchings, and Sculpture 1530–1619*. Fort Worth and Austin, Tex., 1965.

FOXE, JOHN. *Acts and Monuments of these latter and perilous days* . . . London, 1563. STC 11222.

—— *The Acts and Monuments of John Foxe*, ed. G. Townsend and S. R. Cattley. 8 vols. London, 1837–41.

France. *Catalogue des Actes de François ler*. Vol. 8. Paris, 1905.

FRANÇOIS I. *Oeuvres poetiques: Edition critique*, ed. J. E. Kane. Geneva, 1984.

FRANÇOIS I, *Entrevue de François premier avec Henry VIII à Boulogne-sur-Mer, en 1532*, ed. P. A. Hamy. Paris, 1898.

FROISSART, JEAN. *The Chronicles of Froissart*, trans. John, Lord Berners. New York, 1967.

GANZ, PAUL. *The Paintings of Hans Holbein*. London, 1950.

—— 'A Portrait by Hans Holbein the Younger', *Burlington Magazine*. 38 (1921), 210–20.

GARDINER, STEPHEN. *Letters*, ed. J. A. Muller. Cambridge: Cambridge UP, 1933.

GIUSTINIAN, SEBASTIAN. *Four Years at the Court of Henry VIII: Selection of Dispatches 1515–1519*. trans. Rawdon Brown. London, 1854.

GRAFTON, RICHARD. *Chronicle*, ed. J. Johnson et al. 2 vols. London, 1809.

HALL, EDWARD. *Chronicle Containing the History of England During the Reign of Henry the Eighth*, ed. J. Johnson et al. London, 1809; reprint, New York, Press, 1965.

HENRY VIII. *The Letters of King Henry VIII: A Selection, With a Few Other Documents*, ed. Muriel St. Clare Byrne. New York, 1936.

Herbert of Cherbury, Edward, Lord. *Autobiography*. London, 1870.

—— *The History of England under Henry VIII*. London, 1870.

—— *The Life and Raigne of King Henry the Eighth*. London, 1649.

Great Britain. Historical Manuscripts Commission. *Report on the Manuscripts of the Most Honorable the Marquess of Bath Preserved at Longleat*. Vol. 4: *Seymour Papers 1532–1686*, ed. Marjorie Blatcher. London, 1968.

—— Privy Council. *Acts of the Privy Council of England 1542–1547*, ed. J. R. Dasent. London, 1890–1907.

—— Privy Council. *Proceedings and Ordinances of the Privy Council of England VII*: 32 Henry VIII MDXL to 33 Henry VIII MDXLII, ed. H. Nicolas. London, 1837.

—— *Calendar Patent Rolls* 1391–1396; 1547–1548; 1548–1549. London, 1905; 1924.

—— *Calendar of State Papers Domestic, Edward VI, Philip and Mary, Elizabeth*. 9 vols. London, 1856–72. A supplementary volume ed. by C. S. Knighton, 1992, replaces the older Calendar for Edward VI 1547–53.

—— *Calendar of State Papers Foreign*. 23 vols. London, 1863–1950.

—— *Calendar of State Papers Spanish*, ed. P. de Gayangos, G. Mattingly, M. A. S. Hume, and R. Tyler. 15 vols in 20. London, 1862–1954.

—— *Calendar of State Papers Venetian*. Ed. R. Brown, C. Bentinck, and H. Brown. 9 vols. London, 1864–98.

—— House of Lords. *Journal* 1509–1577. Vol. 1. London, 1808.

—— *Letters and Papers, Foreign and Domestic, of the Reign of Henry VIII*. Ed. J. S. Brewer, J. Gairdner, and R. H. Brodie. 21 vols. and 2 vols. addenda. London, 1862–1932.

—— Public Record Office. *Third Report of the Deputy Keeper*. London, 1842.

—— *State Papers*, ed. Samuel Haynes. London, 1740.

—— *State Papers Published under the Authority of His Majesty's Commission, King Henry VIII*. 11 vols. London, 1830–52.

—— *State Trials*. Vol. 1, ed. T. B. Howell. London, 1816.

—— *Statutes of the Realm 1509–1547*. Vol. 3. London, 1817.

GUEVARA, ANTONIO DE. *The Golden Boke of Marcus Aurelius*, trans. John, Lord Berners. London, 1535. STC 12436.

HOLINSHED, RAPHAEL. *Chronicles*, ed. J. Johnson and H. Ellis. 6 vols. London, 1807–8.

Honor Military and Civill. London, 1602.

HOWARD, HENRY, Earl of Surrey. *The Aeneid of Henry Howard, Earl of Surrey*, ed. Florence Ridley. Berkeley, Cali. 1963.

—— *Epigrames &c by the Earle of Surrey*. London, 1574. Catalogued in the Sidney library as MS KAO U1475/2.

—— *Surrey's 'Fourth Boke of Virgill'*, ed. Henry Hartman. Purchase, NY, 1933.

—— *The Poems of Henry Howard Earl of Surrey*, ed. Frederick Morgan Padelford. Seattle: U of Washington P, 1920.

—— *Poems*, ed. Emrys Jones. Oxford, 1964.

—— *The Works of Henry Howard, Earl of Surrey and of Sir Thomas Wyatt the Elder*, ed. George Frederick Nott. 2 vols. New York, 1965.

HOWARD, HENRY. *Memorials of the Howard Family*. 1834.

HOWARD, JOHN. *The Household Books of John Howard, Duke of Norfolk 1462–1471; 1481–1483*, ed. and introd. Anne Crawford. Sroud 1992.

—— *The Household Books of John, Duke of Norfolk*, ed. J. Payne Collier. London, 1844.

HUTTON, W. *The Battle of Bosworth Field*, ed. J. G. Nichols. London, 1813.

JENTOFT, CLYDE W. (ed.). *Wyatt, Sir Thomas, and Henry Howard, Earl of Surrey: A Reference Guide*. Boston, 1980.

The Joyfull Receyving of the Queenes Most Excellent Majestie into hir Departure. London, 1578.

Julian of Norwich. *Revelations of Divine Love*, trans. M. L. Del Mastro. Garden City, NY, 1977.

JUNIUS, HADRIANUS. *Epistolae, Quibus accedit Eiusdem Vita et Oratio Artium Liberalium Dignitate: Nunquam Antea Edita. Cum Indice*. Dordrecht, 1570.

—— *Itinerary in England and Wales*, ed. L. T. Smith. 5 vols. 1906–8; reprint, London, 1964.

LELAND, JOHN. *Collectanea*, ed. Thomas Hearn. London, 1770.

Letters of Royal and Illustrious Ladies of Great Britain, ed. Mary Anne Everette Wood. London, 1846.

The Lisle Letters, ed. Muriel St Clare Byrne. Chicago and London, 1981.

London County Council. *Survey of London*, ed. Sir Howard Roberts and Walter H. Godfrey. London, 1951.

LUTHER, MARTIN. *Works*, ed. C. M. Jacobs. Philadelphia, 1931.

MACHYN, HENRY. *The Diary of a Citizen and Merchant Taylor of London 1550–63*, ed. John Gough Nichols. Camden Society, Old Series 42. London, 1848.

Manuale ad Vsum Perecelebris Ecclesiae Sarisburiensis, ed. A. Jefferies Collins. London, 1860.

MARKHAM, FRANCIS. *Five Decades of Epistles of Warre*. London, 1622.

MILTON, JOHN. *Complete Prose Works*, ed. Don M. Wolfe. New Haven: 1959.

—— *Poems*, ed. John Carey and Alastair Fowler. London: 1968.

The Mirror for Magistrates, ed. Lily B. Campbell. New York, 1938.

MOLINET, JEAN. *Chroniques*. Brussels, 1935.

MOLINET, JEAN. *Les Faict et Dictz de Jean Molinet*, ed. Noel Dupine. Paris, 1936.

MORE, THOMAS. *The English Works*, ed. W. E. Campbell. London, 1931.

—— *The History of King Richard III*, ed. Arthur Noel Kincaid. Gloucester, 1979.

—— *Utopia*, ed. Edward Surtz and J. H. Hexter. New Haven, 1964.

MORICE, RALPH. 'Anecdotes and Character of Archbishop Cranmer, by Ralph Morice, his Secretary', ed. John Gough Nichols. *Narratives of the Days of the Reformation.* Camden Society, First Series, 77, London, 1859.

MUIR, KENNETH. 'Unpublished Poems in the Devonshire Manuscript.' *Proceedings of the Leeds Philosophical and Literary Society*, 6/4 (1947), 253–82.

MYERS, A. R. (ed.). *The Household of Edward IV: The Black Book and the Ordinance of 1475*. Manchester, 1959.

NASHE, THOMAS. *The Unfortunate Traveller and Other Works*, ed. J. B. Steane. Baltimore, 1972.

—— *Works*, ed. Ronald B. McKerrow and F. P. Wilson. Oxford, 1958.

NEVILLE, ALEXANDER. *Alexandrii Nevylli Angli, De Furioribus Norfulciensium Ketto Duce, Liber Unus, Eiusdem Norwich and London, 1575.*

Order of the Garter. *The Register of the Most Noble Order of the Garter from its Cover in Black Velvet usually Called the Black Book with Notes and an Introduction.* 2 vols. London, 1724.

PACE, RICHARD. *De Fructu qui ex Doctrina Percipitur (The Benefit of a Liberal Education)*, ed. and trans. Frank Manley and Richard S. Sylvester. New York, 1967.

Paston Letters and Papers of the Fifteenth Century, ed. Norman Davis. 2 vols. Oxford, 1971.

PEACHAM, HENRY. *The Compleat Gentleman, Fashioning Him Absolute, In The Most Necessary and Commendable Qualities Concerning Minde or Body, That May be Requited in a Noble Gentleman.* London, 1636.

PERCY, THOMAS. *Bishop Percy's Folio Manuscript*, ed. J. W. Hales and F. J. Furnivall. London, 1868.

PUTTENHAM, GEORGE. *The Arte of English Poesie*, ed. G. D. Willcock and A. Walker. Cambridge, 1970.

RICH, BARNABAS. *Pathway to Military Practice*. London, 1587.

RICHARD III. *The Coronation of Richard III: The Extant Documents*, ed. Anne F. Sutton and P. W. Hammond. New York, 1983.

RIPA, CESARE. *Iconologia*. Padua, 1611.

ROBERTS, JANE. *Drawings by Holbein from the Court of Henry VIII*. London, 1987.

RYMER, THOMAS. *Foedera, Conventiones, Litterae, etc.* 15 vols. London, 1728.

SANUTO, MARINO. *I Diarii*. 58 vols. Venice, 1879–1903.

SIDNEY, SIR PHILIP. 'The Defense of Poesie', in *Literary Criticism: Plato to Dryden*. Detroit, 1962.

SILVESTER, RICHARD S. (ed.). *The Anchor Anthology of Sixteenth Century Verse*. New York, 1974.

SKELTON, JOHN. *The Complete English Poems*, ed. John Scattergood. New Haven and London, 1983.

SPELMAN, JOHN. *Reports*, ed. J. H. Baker. Selden Society, 2. London, 1977.

STAFFORD, EDWARD, Duke of Buckingham. 'Extracts from the Household Book of Edward Stafford, Duke of Buckingham'. ed. John Gage. *Archaeologia*, 25 (1834), 321–5.

STARKEY, THOMAS. *Dialogue Between Reginald Pole and Thomas Lupset*, ed. T. F. Mayer, Camden Society, Fourth Series 37. London, 1989.

Stationers' Company. *A Transcript of the Registers of the Company of Stationers of London, 1554–1640 A. D.* Ed. Edward E. Arber. Birmingham, 1894. STC 24798.

STOW, JOHN. *The Annales of England*. London, 1631.

STRONG, ROY. *Tudor and Jacobean Portraits*. 2 vols. London, 1969.

STRYPE, JOHN. *Annals of the Reformation*. Oxford, 1824.

—— *Ecclesiastical Memorials*. 3 vols. Oxford, 1810–28.

—— *The Life of the Learned Sir John Cheke*. Oxford, 1881.

TANNER, J. R. *Tudor Constitutional Documents A.D. 1485–1603 With An Historical Commentary*. Cambridge, 1951.

Thetford Priory, ed. F. J. E. Raby et al. Edinburgh, 1984.

THOMAS, WILLIAM. *The Pilgrim: A Dialogue on the Life and Actions of King Henry VIII*, ed. J. A. Froude. London, 1861.

TOTTEL, RICHARD. *Tottel's Miscellany (1557–1587)*, ed. Hyder Edward Rollins. Cambridge, Mass., 1929–30.

TURBEVILLE, GEORGE. *Epitaphes, Epigrams, Songs, and Sonnets*. London, 1567.

Tudor Royal Proclamations, ed. P. L. Hughes and J. F. Larkin. 2 vols. New Haven and London, 1964–9.

TYNDALE, WILLIAM. *An Answer to Sir Thomas More's Dialogue*, ed. Henry Walter. Cambridge, 1850.

—— *Doctrinal Treatises and Introductions to Different Portions of the Holy Scriptures, by William Tyndale, Martyr, 1536*, ed. Henry Walter. Cambridge, 1848.

VERGIL, POLYDORE. *Anglica Histori 1485–1537*, ed. and trans. Denys Hay. Camden Society, Third Series 74. London, 1950.

Wills from Doctors' Commons: A Selection from the Wills of Eminent Persons, 1495–1695, ed. John Gough Nichols and John Bruce. Camden Society, Old Series 83. London, 1863.

WEEVER, JOHN. *Ancient Funeral Monuments*. Amsterdam, 1631; reprint 1979.

WHITNEY, GEOFFREY. *A Choice of Emblemes*, ed. Henry Green and intro. Frank Fieler. New York, 1967.

WRIOTHESLEY, CHARLES. *A Chronicle of England During the Reign of the Tudors, from A.D. 1485–1559*, ed. William Douglas Hamilton. 2 vols. Camden Society, New Series 11. London, 1875; reprint, 1965.

WYATT, SIR THOMAS, *The Complete Poems*, ed. R. A. Rebholz. New Haven and London, 1975.

—— *Life and Letters of Sir Thomas Wyatt*, ed. Kenneth Muir. Liverpool, 1963.

—— *The Poetry of Sir Thomas Wyatt*, ed. Kenneth Muir and Patricia Thomson. Liverpool, 1969.

SECONDARY SOURCES

ALSOP, J. D. 'The Structure of Early Tudor Finance', in *Revolution Reassessed: Revisions in the History of the Tudor Government and Administrations*, ed. Christopher Coleman and David Starkey. Oxford, 1986, 137–55.

ANGLO, SIDNEY. *Images of Tudor Kingship*. London, 1992.

—— *Spectacle, Pageantry and Early Tudor Policy*. Oxford, 1969.

ASHE, GEOFFREY. *The Discovery of King Arthur*. Garden City, NY 1985.

ASTON, MARGARET. *England's Iconoclasts*. Vol. I, *Laws Against Images*. Oxford, 1988.

—— *The King's Bedpost: Reformation and Iconography in a Tudor Group Portrait*. Cambridge, 1988.

ATTRIDGE, DEREK. *Well-Weighted Syllables: Elizabethan Verse in Classical Metres*. Cambridge, 1974.

AUERBACH, ERNA. 'Holbein's Followers in England.' *Burlington Magazine*. 93 (1951), 44–51.

—— *Tudor Artists*. London, 1954.

AUGUSTINE, ST. *Confessions*, trans. William Watts. Cambridge, Mass. 1968.

BACON, SIR FRANCIS. *Works*, ed. James Spedding, Douglas Denon, Heath, and Robert Leslie Ellis. London, 1857–74; reprint Stuttgart-Bad Cannstatt, 1963.

BAKER, HOWARD. *Introduction to Tragedy*. Baton Rouge, La., 1939.

BALDI, SERGIO. 'The Secretary of the Duke of Norfolk and the First Italian Grammar in England', in *Studies in English Language and Literature Presented to Professor Dr. Karl Brunner on the Occasion of His Seventieth Birthday*, ed. Siegfried Korninger. Vienna, 1957, 1–27.

—— *Sir Thomas Wyatt*. London, 1961.

BAPST, EDMOND. *Deux gentilshommes-poètes de la cour de Henry VIII*. Paris, 1891.

BARNARD, FRANCIS PIERREPONT. *Edward IV's French Expedition of 1475: The Leaders and Their Badges*. 1925; reprint, Gloucester, 1975.

BARON, H. 'Mary (Howard) Fitzroy's Hand in the Devonshire Manuscript', *Review of English Studies*, 45 (1994), 318–45.

BARRINGTON, ROBERT. 'Philosophy and the Court in the Literature of the Early English Renaissance.' Ph.D. dissertation European University Institute, Florence, 1993.

BARTHES, ROLAND. *Mythologies*, trans. Annette Lavers. New York, 1972.

BEGUIN, SYLVIE, BINENBAUM, ORESTE, et al. *La Galerie François ler au Château de Fontainebleau*. Paris, 1972.

BEER, B. L. *Northumberland: The Political Career of John Dudley, Earl of Warwick and Duke of Northumberland*, Kent, Ohio, 1973.

BELLAMY, ELIZABETH J. *Translations of Power: Narcissism, and the Unconscious in Epic History*. Ithaca and London, 1992.

BELLAMY, JOHN G. *The Law of Treason in England in the Later Middle Ages*. Cambridge, 1970.

—— *The Tudor Law of Treason: An Introduction*. London: Routledge and Kegan Paul, 1979.

BENJAMIN, WALTER. *Illuminations*, ed. Hannah Arendt, trans. Harry Zohn. New York, 1969.

BENNETT, A. L. 'The Principal Rhetorical Conventions of the Renaissance Personal Elegy.' *Studies in Philology*. 51 (1943), 107–26.

BENSLY, W. T. 'St. Leonard's Priory, Norwich.' *Norfolk Archaeology*. 12 (1901), 190.

BERDAN, JOHN M. *Early Tudor Poetry 1485–1574*. New York, 1961.

BERNARD, G. W. 'The Fall of Anne Boleyn', *EHR*, 106 (1991), 584–610.

—— 'Anne Boleyn's Religion', *Historical Journal*, 36 (1993), 1–20.

BERNARD, G. W. (ed.). *The Tudor Nobility*. Manchester, 1992.

BETHELL, S. L. 'The Nature of Metaphysical Wit.' *Northern Miscellany of Literary Criticism*, 1 (1953), 19–40.

BLACK, HENRY C. (ed.). *Black's Law Dictionary*. Ed. Henry C. Black. Saint Paul, 1990.

BLAKE, N. F. 'Lord Berners: A Survey.' *Medievalia Et Humanistica*. NS 2 (1971), 118–30.

BLOCH, R. HOWARD. *Etymologies and Genealogies: A Literary Anthropology of the French Middle Ages*. Chicago and London, 1983.

BLOCH-MICHEL, JEAN. 'The Obstinate Confidence of a PessimisticMan.' *The Reporter*. 17 (28 Nov. 1957), 36–40.

BLUNT, ANTHONY. *Art and Architecture in France 1500 to 1700*. Baltimore, 1953.

—— 'L'Influence française sur l'architecture et la sculpture décorative en Angleterre pendant la première moitié du XVIe siècle.' *Revue de l'Art*, 4 (1969), 23.

BOFFEY, JULIA. *Manuscripts of English Courtly Love Lyrics in the Later Middle Ages*. Woodbridge, 1985.

BOLGAR, R. R. *The Classical Heritage and Its Beneficiaries*. Cambridge, 1954.

BORNKAMM, HEINRICH. *Luther's Doctrine of the Two Kingdoms in the Context of his Theology*, trans. Karl H. Hertz. Philadelphia, 1966.

BOURRILLY, V. L. *Jacques Colin, abbé de Saint-Ambroise*. 1905, reprint, Geneva, 1970.

BOUTELL, CHARLES. *Boutell's Heraldry*, ed. John Brooke-Little. London and New York, 1970.

BOWRA, C. M. *From Virgil to Milton*. London, 1963.

BRADEN, GORDON. *Renaissance Tragedy and the Senecan Tradition: Anger's Privilege*. New Haven, 1985.

BRAEKMAN, MARTINE. 'A Chaucerian "Courtly Love Aunter" by Henry Howard, Earl of Surrey', *Neophilologus* 79 (1995), 675–87.

BRANDI, KARL. *The Emperor Charles V*, trans. C. V. Wedgwood. London, 1939; reprint 1965.

BRAUDEL, FERNAND. *The Mediterranean and the Mediterranean World in the Age of Philip II*, trans. Sian Reynolds. New York, 1973.

BRENAN, GERALD, and STATHAM EDWARD PHILIPS. *The House of Howard*. London, 1907.

BRIDBURY, A. R. *Economic Growth: England in the Later Middle Ages*. London, 1962.

BRIGDEN, SUSAN. 'Henry Howard, Earl of Surrey, and the "Conjured League" ' *Historical Journal*, 37/3 (1994), 507–37.

—— *London and the Reformation*. Oxford, 1989.

—— ' "The Shadow That You Know": Sir Thomas Wyatt and Sir Francis Bryan at Court and in Embassy.' *Historical Journal*. 39/1 (1996), 1–31.

BROWN, PETER. *The Cult of the Saints: Its Rise and Function in Latin Christianity*. Chicago, 1982.

BUSH, MICHAEL. *The Government Policy of Protector Somerset*. London, 1975.

—— *The Pilgrimage of Grace. A Study of the Rebel Armies of October 1536*. Manchester, 1996.

BUTLER, J. *The Quest for Becket's Bones: The Mystery of the Relics of St Thomas of Canterbury*. New Haven and London, 1995.

CAMPBELL, JAMES. *Norwich*. London, 1975.

CAMPBELL, LORNE. *Renaissance Portraits: European Portrait-Painting in the 14th, 15th, and 16th Centuries*. New Haven and London, 1990.

CARLEY, JAMES. ' "Her moost lovyng and fryndely brother sendeth gretyng": Anne Boleyn's Manuscripts and their Sources', in *Illuminating the Book: Makers and Interpreters, Essays in Honour of Janet Backhouse*, ed. Michelle D. Brown and Scot McKendrick. London and Toronto, 1998, 261–80.

CASADY, EDWIN. *Henry Howard, Earl of Surrey*. New York, 1938.

CASSIRER, ERNST. *The Individual and the Cosmos in Renaissance Philosophy*, trans. Mario Domandi. New York and Evanston, 1963.

CERCIGNANI, FAUSTO. *Shakespeare's Works and Elizabethan Pronunciation*. Oxford, 1981.

CHASTEL, ANDRÉ. *The Age of Humanism: Europe 1480–1530*, trans. Katherine M. Delavenay and E. M. Gwyer. London, 1963.

CHATMAN, SEYMOUR. *A Theory of Meter*. The Hague, 1965.

CHERRY, BRIDGET, and PEVSNER, NIKOLAUS. *Buildings of England: Devon*. London, 1989.

CHILDE-PEMBERTON, W. S. *Elizabeth Blount and Henry the Eighth*. London, 1913.

CHRIMES, S. B. *Henry VII*. Berkeley, 1972.

CLEMENT, WOLFGANG. *English Tragedy Before Shakespeare: The Development of Dramatic Speech*. New York, 1961.

CLOUGH, CECIL H. 'Francis I and the Courtiers of Castiglione's *Courtier*.' *European Studies Review*, 8/1 (Jan. 1978), 23–70.

COKAYNE, GEORGE E. (ed.). *The Complete Peerage, or a History of the House of Lords and all its Members from the Earliest Times*. 12 vols. London, 1910–40.

COLLINSON, PATRICK. *Godly People: Essays in English Puritanism and Protestantism*. London, Hambledon Press, 1983.

CONDON, M. M. 'Ruling Elites in the Reign of Henry VII', in *Patronage, Pedigree, and Power in Later Medieval England*, ed. Charles Ross. Gloucester and Totowa, NJ, 1979.

CONRAD, FREDERICK WILLIAM. 'A Preservative Against Tyranny: The Political Theology of Sir Thomas Elyot.' Ph.D. dissertation, Johns Hopkins University, 1988.

CORTI, MARIA. *An Introduction to Literary Semiotics*, trans. Margherita Bogat and Allen Mandelbaum. Bloomington, 1978.

COUNCIL, NORMAN. *When Honour's At Stake*. London, 1973.

Counties and Communities: Essays on East Anglian History Presented to Hassel Smith, ed. Carole Rawcliffe, Roger Virgoe, and Richard Wilson. Norwich, 1996.

COURTHOPE, W. J. *A History of English Poetry*. New York, 1897.

COX-REARICK, JANET. *The Collection of Francis I: Royal Treasures*. New York, 1996.

CRAWFORD, ANNE. 'The Career of John Howard, Duke of Norfolk, 1420–1485.' MA (Phil.) thesis, University of London, 1975.

—— 'Victims of Attainder: The Howard and de Vere Women in the Late Fifteenth Century', in *Medieval Women in Southern England*. Reading Medieval Studies, 1989, 1–25.

CREWE, JONATHAN. *Unredeemed Rhetoric: Thomas Nashe and the Scandal of Authorship*. Baltimore and London, 1982.

—— *Trials of Authorship: Anterior Forms and Poetic Reconstruction from Wyatt to Shakespeare*. Berkeley, 1990.

CROOK, J. A. *Consilium Principis: Imperial Councils and Counsellors from Augustus to Diocletian*. Cambridge, 1955.

CURTIUS, E. R. *Essays on European Literature*, trans. Michael Kowal. Princeton, 1973.

DAVIES, EDGAR. 'Surrey's "In the Rude Age" ', *Notes and Queries*, 201 (1956), 14–15.

DAVIES, C. S. L. 'Popular Religion and the Pilgrimage of Grace', in *Order and Disorder in Early Modern England*, ed. A. Fletcher and J. Stevenson. Cambridge, 1985.

DAVIES, M. BRYN. 'Boulogne and Calais from 1545 to 1550.' *Bulletin of the Faculty of Arts, Fouad I University, Cairo*, 7 (1944), 1–90.

—— 'Surrey at Boulogne.' *Huntington Library Quarterly*. 23 (1960).

DAVIS, WALTER R. 'Contexts in Surrey's Poetry.' *English Literary Renaissance*. 4 (1974), 47.

DENHOLM-YOUNG, N. *History and Heraldry, 1254–1310: A Study of the Historical Value of the Rolls of Arms*. Oxford, 1965.

DICKENS, A. G. *The English Reformation*. London, 1964.

DIETZ, F. *English Public Finance 1485–1641*. 2 vols. Urbana, 1964.

DODDS, M. H. and DODDS, RUTH. *The Pilgrimage of Grace 1536–7, and the Exeter Conspiracy, 1539*. Cambridge, 1915.

DOWLING, MARIA. *Humanism in the Age of Henry VIII*. London, 1986.

DUBY, GEORGES. *The Chivalrous Society*, trans. Cynthia Postan. Berkeley and Los Angeles, 1977.

—— 'Structures de parente et noblesse dans la France de nord aux XIe et XIIe siècles', in *Hommes et Structures du Moyen Age*. Paris, 1973.

DUFF, J. WRIGHT. *A Literary History of Rome*. New York, 1967.

DUFFY, EAMON. *The Stripping of the Altars: Traditional Religion in England 1400–1580*. New Haven and London, 1992.

DUNCAN-JONES, KATHERINE. *Sir Philip Sidney, Courtier Poet*. New Haven and London, 1991.

EASTHOPE, ANTHONY. 'Problematizing the Pentametre.' *New Literary History*, 12/3 (Spring 1981), 481–5.

EBELING, GERHARD. *Luther*, trans. R. A. Wilson. Philadelphia: Fortress Press, 1970.

ECKERT, CHARLES W. 'The Poetry of Henry Howard, Earl of Surrey.' Ph.D. dissertation. Washington University, 1960.

EINSTEIN, ALFRED. *The Italian Madrigal*. 3 vols. Princeton, 1949.

ELIOT, T. S. *On Poetry and Poets*. New York, 1961.

ELTON, G. R. *England Under the Tudors*. London, 1955.

—— *Policy and Police: The Enforcement of the Reformation in the Age of Thomas Cromwell*. Cambridge, 1972.

—— *Reform and Reformation*. London, 1977.

—— *Reform and Renewal: Thomas Cromwell and the Commonweal*. Cambridge, 1973.

—— *The Tudor Revolution in Government: Administrative Changes in the Reign of Henry VIII*. Cambridge, 1959.

EVANS, MAURICE. *English Poetry in the Sixteenth Century*. New York, 1967.

FALCO, RAPHAEL. *Conceived Presences: Literary Genealogy in Renaissance England*. Amherst, Mass., 1994.

FIDELER, PAUL A. and MAYER, T. F. (eds.). *Political Thought and the Tudor Commonwealth: Deep Structure, Discourse, and Disguise*. London and New York, 1992.

FLETCHER, A. and STEPHENSON, J. (eds.). *Order and Disorder in Early Modern England*. Cambridge, 1975.

FLUGEL, J. C. 'On the Character and Married Live of Henry VIII', in *Psychoanalysis and History*, ed. Bruce Mazlish. New York, 1971.

FOLEY, STEPHEN MERRIAM. 'The Honorable Style of Henry Howard, Earl of Surrey: A Critical Reading of Surrey's Poetry.' Ph.D. dissertation, Yale University, 1979.

FOUCAULT, MICHEL. *Discipline and Punishment: The Birth of the Prison*, trans. Alan Sheridan. New York, 1977.

—— *Language, Counter-Memory, Practice: Selected Essays and Interviews*, ed. D. F. Bouchard, trans. D. F. Bouchard and S. Simon. Ithaca, NY, 1977.

FOXWELL, A. K. *A Study of Sir Thomas Wyatt's Poetry*. London, 1911.

FREER, COBURN. *The Poetics of Jacobean Drama*. Baltimore and London, 1981.

French Humanism 1470–1600, Ed. Werner L. Gundersheimer. London, 1969.

FRYE, NORTHROP. *Anatomy of Criticism: Four Essays*. New York, 1967.

GADAMER, HANS-GEORG. 'The Hermeneutics of Suspicion', in *Hermeneutics: Question and Prospects*, ed. Gary Shapiro and Alan Siod. Amherst, Mass., 1984.

GARDNER, HELEN. *A Reading of Paradise Lost*. Oxford, 1965.

GAUNT, WILLIAM. *Court Painting in England from Tudor to Victorian Times*. London, 1980.

GIAMATTI, A. BARTLETT. 'Hippolytus Among the Exiles: The Romance of Early Humanism', in *Poetic Traditions of the English Renaissance*, ed. Maynard Mack and George deForest Lord. New Haven and London, 1982.

GIROUARD, MARK. *Life in the English Country House: A Social and Architectural History*. New Haven and London, 1978.

GOLDBERG, JONATHAN. *Writing Matter: From the Hands of the Renaissance*. Stanford, 1990.

—— *Sodometries: Renaissance Texts. Modern Sexualities*. Stanford, 1992.

—— 'Introduction' *Queering the Renaissance*, ed. Jonathan Goldberg. Durham and London, 1994.

GOMBRICH, E. H. '*Icones Symbolicae*: The Visual Image in Neo-Platonic Thought.' *Journal of the Warburg and Courtauld Institutes*, 11 (1948), 166–90.

GRACE, F. R. 'The Life and Career of Thomas Howard, Third Duke of Norfolk 1473–1554.' MA thesis, University of Nottingham, 1961.

GREENBLATT, STEPHEN. *Renaissance Self-Fashioning*. Chicago and London, 1980.

—— 'Psychoanalysis and Renaissance Culture', in *Literary Theory/Renaissance Texts*, ed. Patricia Parker and David Quint. Baltimore, 1986.

GUNN, S. J. *Charles Brandon, Duke of Suffolk c. 1484–1545*. Oxford, 1994.

—— *Early Tudor Government 1485–1558*. New York, 1995.

—— 'Henry VIII's Foreign Policy and the Tudor Cult of Chivalry', in *Francois ler et Henri VIII: Deux Princes de la Renaissance*, ed. C. Criny-Deloison. Lille, 1996.

—— 'The Structures of Politics in Early Tudor England.' *Transactions of the Royal Historical Society*, ser. 6, 5 (1995), 59–90.

GURNEY-SALTER, EMMA. *Tudor England Through Venetian Eyes*. London, 1930.

GUY, JOHN. *Tudor England*. Oxford, 1988.

—— 'The Rhetoric of Counsel in Early Modern England.' *Tudor Political Culture*, ed. Dale Hoak. Cambridge, 1995.

GUY, JOHN, and FOX, ALISTAIR. 'The Henrician Age', in *The Varieties of British Political Thought 1500–1800*, ed. J. G. A. Pocock, Gordon J. Schochet, and Lois G. Schwoerer. Cambridge, 1993.

—— *Reassessing the Henrician Age: Humanism, Politics, and Reform*. Oxford: Oxford UP, 1986.

GUY-BRAY, STEPHEN. 'We Two Boys Together Clinging: The England of Surrey and the Duke of Richmond.' *English Studies in Canada*, 21 (1995), 138–50.

HAIGH, CHRISTOPHER. *English Reformation*. Oxford, 1993.

—— *Reformation and Resistance in Tudor Lancashire*. Cambridge, 1975.

HALE, J. R. 'Armies, Navies, and the Art of War', in *New Cambridge Modern History*, ed. G. R. Elton. Vol. 2. Cambridge, 1990, 540–69.

HALL, VERNON. *Renaissance Literary Criticism: A Study of its Social Content*, Gloucester, Mass., 1959.

HALPERN, MARTIN. 'On the Two Chief Metrical Modes in English.' *PMLA*, 77/3 (June 1962), 177–86.

HANHAM, ALISON. *Richard III and His Early Historians 1483–1535*. Oxford, Clarendon Press, 1975.

HANNAY, MARGARET P. *Philip's Phoenix: Mary Sidney, Countess of Pembroke*. New York and Oxford, 1990.

HARDISON, O. B. *Prosody and Purpose in the English Renaissance*. Baltimore and London, 1989.

HARRIER, RICHARD. *The Canon of Sir Thomas Wyatt's Poetry*. Cambridge, 1975.

HARRIS, BARBARA. *Edward Stafford, Third Duke of Buckingham, 1478–1521*. Stanford, Cal. 1986.

HARRIS, JESSE W. *John Bale: A Study in the Minor Literature of the Reformation*. Urbana, 1940.

HAUGAARD, W. J. 'Katherine Parr: The Religious Convictions of a Renaissance Queen.' *Renaissance Quarterly*, 22 (1969), 346–59.

HAUVETTE, HENRI. *Luigi Alamanni, un exile florentin à la cour de France au XVe siècle (1495–1556): Sa vie et son oeuvre*. Paris, 1903.

HAWKYARD, A. D. K. "Thornbury Castle." *Transactions of the Bristol and Gloucestershire Archaeological Society*, 95(1978), 51–8.

—— 'Uncles to the King and Protectors of the Throne: The Seymours' and ' "The Alcibiades of England": John Dudley, Duke of Northumberland', in *Rivals in Power: Lives and Letters of the Great Tudor Dynasties*, ed. David Starkey. London, 1990.

HEAD, DAVID. ' "Beyng Ledde and Seduced by the Devyll": The Attainder of Lord Thomas Howard and the Tudor Law of Treason.' *Sixteenth Century Journal*, 13/4 (Winter 1982), 3–16.

—— *The Ebbs and Flows of Fortune: The Life of Thomas Howard, Third Duke of Norfolk*. Athens, Ga., and London, 1995.

HEALE, ELIZABETH. 'Women and the Courtly Love Lyric: The Devonshire MS (BL Additional 17492).' *Modern Language Review*, 90/2 (April 1995), 296–313.

—— *Wyatt, Surrey and Early Tudor Court Poetry*. London and New York, 1998.

HEARN, KAREN (ed.). *Dynasties: Painting in Tudor and Jacobean England 1530–1630*. New York, 1995.

HEIDEGGER, MARTIN. *Poetry, Language, Thought*, trans. Albert Hofstadter. New York and London, 1971.

HIGHET, GILBERT. *Juvenal the Satirist: A Study*. Oxford, 1954.

HINDLEY, GEOFFREY. *England in the Age of Caxton*. London, 1979.

HJELMSLEV, LOUIS. *Prolegomena to a Theory of Language*, trans. Francis J. Whitfield. Madison, Wis., 1961.

HOLLANDER, JOHN. *Rhyme's Reason*. New York and London, 1981.

HOLLINGSWORTH, T. H. 'A Demographic Study of British Ducal Families', in *Population in History*, ed D. E. C. Everseley. Chicago, 1965.

HOOKER, J. R. 'Some Cautionary Notes on Henry VII: Household and Chamber System.' *Speculum*, 33 (1958), 75.

HOPKINS, GERARD MANLEY. *The Poetical Works*, ed. Norman H. Mackenzie. Oxford, 1990.

HOWARD, DONALD R. *Chaucer: His Life, His Work, His World*. New York, 1987.

HOWARD, MAURICE. *The Early Tudor Country House: Architecture and Politics 1490–1550*. London, 1987.

HOWARTH, DAVID. *Lord Arundel and His Circle*. New Haven and London, 1985.

HOWLETT, RICHARD. 'The Household Accounts of Kenninghall Palace in the Year 1515.' *Norfolk Archaeology*, 15 (1904), 51–60.

HUME, DAVID. *History of England*. London, 1873–77.

IVES, E. W. *Anne Boleyn*. Oxford, 1986.

—— 'Anne Boleyn and the early Reformation in England: The Contemporary Evidence', *Historical Journal*, 37 (1994), 389–400.

—— 'Henry VIII's Will: A Forensic Conundrum', *Historical Journal*, 35 (1992), 779–804.

—— 'The Queen and the Painters: Anne Boleyn, Holbein and Tudor Royal Portraits', *Apollo* (July, 1994), 36–45.

—— 'Stress, Faction and Ideology in Early Tudor England', *Historical Journal*, 34 (1991), 193–202.

JÄGER, WERNER. *Paideia*. New York, 1945.

JAMES, HENRY. *Art of Criticism: Henry James on the Theory and Practice of Fiction*. Ed. William Veeder and Susan M. Griffin. Chicago: U of Chicago P, 1986.

JAMES, MERVYN. *English Politics and Culture: Studies in Early Modern England*. Cambridge, 1986.

JARDINE, LISA. *Erasmus, Man of Letters: The Construction of Charisma in Print*. Princeton, 1993.

JAVITCH, DANIEL. *Poetry and Courtliness in Renaissance England*. Princeton, 1978.

JENTOFT, C. W. 'Surrey's Four "Orations" and the Influence of Rhetoric on Dramatic Effect.' *Papers on Language and Literature*, 9 (1973), 256.

JONES, MICHAEL K. and UNDERWOOD, MALCOLM G. *The King's Mother: Lady Margaret Beaufort, Countess of Richmond and Derby*. Cambridge, 1974.

JORDAN, WILBUR KITCHENER. *Edward IV*. Cambridge, 1968–70.

KANTOROWICZ, ERNST H. *The King's Two Bodies: A Study in Medieval Political Theology*. Princeton, 1957.

KELLEY, DONALD R. *The Beginning of Ideology: Consciousness and Society in the French Reformation*. Cambridge, 1981.

KENDALL, PAUL MURRAY. *Richard The Third*. New York, 1956.

KENNEDY, WILLIAM. *Authorizing Petrarch*. Ithaca and London, 1994.

KENT, ERNEST. 'The Houses of the Dukes of Norfolk in Norwich.' *Norfolk Archaeology*, 24/2 (1930), 73–87.

KERMODE, FRANK. *The Classic*. London, 1975.

KING, JOHN. *English Reformation Literature: The Tudor Origins of the Protestant Tradition*. Princeton, 1982.

—— *Tudor Royal Iconography: Literature and Art in an Age of Religious Crisis*. Princeton, 1982.

KIPLING, GORDON. *The Triumph of Honour: Burgundian Origins of the Elizabethan Renaissance*. Leiden, 1977.

KLINGER, FRIEDRICH. *Virgil: Bucolia, Georgica, Aeneis*. Zurich and Stuttgart, 1963.

KNECHT, ROBERT J. 'The Episcopate and the War of the Roses.' *University of Birmingham Historical Journal*, 6 (1958), 108–31.

—— *Francis I*. Cambridge, 1982.

—— *Renaissance Warrior and Patron: The Reign of Francis I*. Cambridge, 1994.

KNOWLES, DAVID. *Religious Orders in England*. Cambridge, 1959.

LADURIE, EMANUEL LE ROY. 'Family Structures and Inheritance Customs in Sixteenth Century France', in *Family and Inheritance, Rural Society in Western Europe 1200–1800*, ed. J. Goody, J. Thirsk, and E. P. Thompson. Cambridge, 1976.

LANDER, J. R. *Government and Community: England, 1450–1509*. Cambridge, 1980.

LATHROP, H. B. 'The Sonnet Forms of Wyatt and Surrey.' *Modern Philology*, 2 (1905), 463–70.

LEE, SIDNEY. *The French Renaissance in England*. Oxford, 1910.

LEHMBERG, STANFORD E. *The Later Parliaments of Henry VIII, 1536–1547*. Cambridge, 1977.

—— *The Reformation Parliament 1529–1536*. Cambridge, 1970.

LERER, SETH. *Chaucer and His Readers: Imagining the Author in Late-Medieval England*. Princeton, 1993.

—— *Courtly Letters in the Age of Henry VIII: Literary Culture and the Arts of Deceit*. Cambridge, 1997.

LEVER, J. W. *The Elizabethan Love Sonnet*. London, 1956.

LÉVI-STRAUSS, CLAUDE. *Conversations with Claude Lévi-Strauss*, ed. Georges Charbonnier and trans. John and Doreen Weightman. London, 1969.

—— *Structural Anthropology*, trans. Claire Jacobson and Brooke Grundfest Schoepf. New York and London, 1963.

LEWIS, C. S. *English Literature in the Sixteenth Century Excluding Drama*. Oxford, 1962.

—— 'The Fifteenth-Century Heroic Line.' *Essays and Studies by Members of the English Association*, 24 (1938), 28–41.

LINFORTH, IVAN M. *The Arts of Orpheus*. Berkeley, 1941.

LOADES, DAVID M. *John Dudley, Duke of Northumberland, 1504–1553*. Oxford, 1996.

—— *Mary Tudor: A Life*. Oxford, 1989.

MAC CULLOCH, DIARMUID. 'Introduction.' *The Reign of Henry VIII: Politics, Policy, and Piety*, ed. Diarmuid MacCulloch. London, 1995.

—— *Thomas Cranmer: A Life*. New Haven and London, 1996.

—— 'War and Glory Under a Young King: The Howards'; ' "Vain, Proud, Foolish Boy": The Earl of Surrey and the Fall of the Howards'; and ' "Beware of High Degree": The Howards under Elizabeth I', in *Rivals in Power: Lives and Letters of the Great Tudor Dynasties*, ed. David Starkey. London, 1990.

MACLEOD, CATHERINE. 'Guillim Scrots in England.' MA Thesis. University of London, 1990.

MALOF, JOSEPH. 'The Native Rhythm of English Meters.' *Texas Studies in Literature and Language*, 5/4 (Winter 1964), 580–94.

MANNING, C. R. 'Kenninghall.' *Norfolk Archaeology*, 7 (1982), 289–99.

MARCUSE, HERBERT. *Eros and Civilization: A Philosophical Inquiry into Freud*. Boston, 1966.

—— *Negations: Essays in Critical Theory*, trans. Jeremy J. Shapiro. Boston, 1968.

MARIUS, RICHARD. *Thomas More: A Biography*. New York, 1984.

MARKS, RICHARD. 'The Howard Tombs at Thetford and Framlingham: New Discoveries.' *Archaeological Journal*, 141 (1984), 252–68.

MAROTTI, ARTHUR F. *Manuscript, Print, and the English Renaissance Lyric*. Ithaca and London, 1995.

MASON, H. A. 'Wyatt and the Psalms—II.' *Times Literary Supplement* (6 March 1953), 160.

—— *Humanism and Poetry in the Early Tudor Period*. London, 1959.

MASON, H. A. 'The First Two Printed Texts of Surrey's Poems', *Times Literary Supplement* (4 June 1971), 656.

MATTINGLY, GARRET. *Catherine of Aragon*. Boston, 1941.

MAY, STEVEN W. *The Elizabethan Courtier Poets: The Poems and Their Context*. Columbia, 1991.

MCCONICA, J. K. *English Humanists and Reformation Politics Under Henry VIII*. Oxford, 1965.

MCEWEN, JOHN. 'The Battle of Flodden, September 9th 1513.' *History Today*, 8 (1958), 138–47.

MCFARLANE, K. B. 'Calender of Close Rolls, Henry VII.' *English Historical Review*, 81 (1966), 149–50.

—— *England in the Fifteenth Century: Collected Essays*. London, 1981.

—— *The Nobility of Later Medieval England*. Oxford, 1973.

MCKEE, ALEXANDER. 'Henry VIII as Military Commander.' *History Today*. 41 (June 1991), 22–37.

MCKERROW, RONALD B. *Printers' and Publishers' Devices in England and Scotland 1485–1640*. London, 1913.

MCNALTY, SIR ARTHUR. *Henry VIII: A Difficult Patient*. London, 1952.

MERCER, ERIC. *English Art, 1553–1625*. Vol. 7, Oxford History of English Art, ed. T. S. R. Boase. Oxford, 1962.

MILLER, GILBERT JOHN. *Tudor Mercenaries and Auxiliaries 1485–1547*. Charlottesville, Va, 1980.

MILLER, HELEN. *Henry VIII and the English Nobility*. Oxford, 1986.

—— 'Henry VIII's Unwritten Will; Grants of Lands and Honours in 1547', in *Wealth and Power in Tudor England: Essays Presented to S. T. Bindoff*, ed. E. W. Ives, R. J. Knecht, and J. J. Scarisbrick. London, 1978.

MITCHELL, JOSHUA. 'Luther: The Dialectic of Supersession and the Politics of Righteousness' in *Not by Reason Alone: Religion, History, and Identity in Early Modern Political Thought*. Chicago and London, 1993.

MONTAULT, X. BARBIERE DE. *Traité d'iconographie chrétienne*. Paris, 1890.

MOORE, KEITH L. *Clinically Oriented Anatomy*. 2nd ed. Baltimore, 1985.

MOORE, PETER R. 'Hamlet and the Two Witness Rule.' *Notes and Queries*, 242 NS 44/4 (December 1997), 498–503.

MUELLER, JANEL. *The Native Tongue and the Word: Developments in English Prose Style, 1380–1580*. Chicago and London, 1984.

MULLER, J. A. *Stephen Gardiner and the Tudor Reaction*. London, 1926.

MUMFORD, IVY. 'Musical Settings to the Poems of Surrey.' *English Miscellany* 16 (1957), 14–16.

MURPHY, VIRGINIA. 'Introduction' to *The Divorce Tracts of Henry VIII*, eds. Virginia Murphy and Edward Surtz, SJ. Angers, 1988.

NATHAN, LEONARD. 'The Course of the Particular: Surrey's Epitaph on Thomas Clere and the Fifteenth-Century Lyric Tradition.' *SEL*. 17/1 (Winter), 3–12.

NICHOLSON, GRAHAM. 'The Act of Appeals and the English Reformation', in *Law and Government Under the Tudors*, ed. Claire Cross, David Loades, and J. J. Scarisbrick. Cambridge, 1988.

—— 'The Nature and Function of Historical Argument in the Henrician Reformation.' Ph.D. thesis, University of Cambridge, 1977.

NICHOLSON, MARJORIE HOPE. *Mountain Gloom and Mountain Glory: The Development of the Aesthetics of the Infinite*. New York, 1963.

NIETZSCHE, FRIEDRICH. *The Genealogy of Morals*, trans. Francis Golffing. Garden City, NY, 1956.

NORBROOK, DAVID. *Poetry and Politics in the English Renaissance*. London, 1984.

Norwich Cathedral Church, City, and Diocese 1096–1996, ed. Atherton E. Fernie, C. Harper-Bill, and Hassel Smith. London and Rio Grande, 1996.

ORAS, ANTS. 'Surrey's Technique of Verbal Echoes: A Method and Its Background.' *Journal of English and Germanic Philology*. 50 (1951), 289–308.

OTIS, BROOKS. *Virgil*. Oxford, 1963.

PANOFSKY, DORA and PANOFSKY, ERWIN. 'The Iconography of the Galerie Francois ler at Fountainebleau.' *Gazette des Beaux-Arts*, 42 (1958), 172.

PANOFSKY, ERWIN. *Early Netherlandish Painting*. Cambridge, Mass., 1953.

PALMER, BARTON (ed.). *Chaucer and His Contemporaries*. New York, 1991.

PATTISON, BRUCE. *Music and Poetry of the English Renaissance*. London, 1948.

PATTERSON, LEE. *Chaucer and the Subject of History*. Madison, 1991.

PEARSALL, DEREK. *Old English and Middle English Poetry*. London, 1977.

PECK, LINDA LEVY. *Northampton: Patronage and Policy at the Court of James I*. London, 1982.

PICKTHORN, KENNETH. *Early Tudor Government*. Cambridge, 1951.

PIGMAN, G. W. III. *Grief and English Renaissance Elegy*. Cambridge, 1985.

POCOCK, J. G. A. 'Texts as Events: Reflections on the History of Political Thought', in *Politics of Discourse: The Literature and History of Seventeenth-Century England*, ed. Kevin Sharpe and Steven N. Zwicker. Berkeley, Cal., 1987.

POLLARD, A. F. 'Council, Star Chamber, and Privy Council Under the Tudors.' *English Historical Review*. 37 (1922), 337–60.

—— *Henry VIII*. London, 1968.

POUND, JOHN. 'The Social and Trade Structure of Norwich, 1525–1575', *Past and Present*, 34 (1966), 49–69.

—— *Tudor and Stuart Norwich*. Shopbryke Hall, 1988.

POWELL, J. ENOCH and WALLIS, KEITH. *The House of Lords in the Middle Ages: A History of the English House of Lords to 1540*, London, 1968.

PRESCOTT, ANNE LAKE. *French Poets and the English Renaissance: Studies in Fame and Transformation*. New Haven and London, 1978.

QUENTIN-BAUCHART, ERNEST. *La bibliothèque de Fontainebleau et les livres des derniers Valois à la Bibliothèque Nationale (1515–1589)*. Geneva, 1971.

QUINONES, RICARDO J. *The Renaissance Discovery of Time*. Cambridge, 1972.

RACKIN, PHYLLIS. 'Anti-Historians: Women's Roles in Shakespeare's Histories'. in *In Another Country: Feminist Perspectives on Renaissance Drama*, ed. Dorothea Kehler and Susan Baker. Metuchen and London, 1991.

—— 'Engendering the Tragic Audience: The Case of Richard III.' *Studies in the Literary Imagination*, 26/1 (Spring 1993), 47–66.

RAGAN, BRIAN ABLE. 'Semiotics and Heraldry.' *Semiotica*, 100/1 (1994), 5–31.

RAWCLIFFE, CAROLE. *The Staffords, Earls of Stafford and Dukes of Buckingham 1394–1521*. Cambridge, 1978.

REBHORN, WAYNE A. *Courtly Performances: Masking and Festivity in Castiglione's Book of the Courtier*. Detroit, 1978.

REDWORTH, GLYN. *In Defence of the Catholic Church: The Life of Stephen Gardiner*. Oxford, 1990.

RENAUDET, A. *Humanisme et Renaissance*. Geneva, 1958.

Resplendence of the Spanish Monarchy: Renaissance Tapestries and Armor from the Patrimonio Nacional, eds. Antonio Domínguez Ortiz, Concha Herrero Carreto, and José A. Godoy. New York, Metropolitan Museum of Art, 1992.

Rethinking the Henrician Era: Essays on Early Tudor Texts and Contexts, ed. Peter C. Herman. Chicago and Urbana, 1994.

RICHARDSON, W. C. *The History of the Court of Augumentation*. Baton Rouge, La, 1961.

RILKE, RAINER MARIA. *Duineser Elegien*. Frankfurt, 1958.

ROBINSON, JOHN MARTIN. *The Dukes of Norfolk: A Quincentennial History*. Oxford, 1982.

ROSS, CHARLES. *Richard III*. Berkeley, 1981.

ROWLANDS, JOHN. *Holbein: The Paintings of Hans Holbein the Younger*. Oxford, 1985.

RUBEL, VERE. *Poetic Diction in the English Renaissance: From Skelton to Spenser*. New York, 1941.

RUSSELL, C. *The Causes of the English Civil War*. Oxford, 1990.

RYE, WALTER. 'Surrey House and St. Leonard's Priory, Norwich.' *Norfolk Archaeology*, 15 (1904), 194.

SCARISBRICK, J. J. *Henry VIII*. Berkeley and Los Angeles, 1968.

SCHOLES, P. A. *The Puritans and Music*. London, 1934.

SCHRAMM, PERCY ERNST. *A History of the English Coronation*. Oxford, 1937.

SCOFIELD, C. L. *Life and Reign of Edward IV*. London, 1923.

SERPELL, M. F. *Kenninghall: History and St Mary's Church*. Norwich, 1982.

SESSIONS, W. A. 'The Earl of Surrey and Catherine Parr: A Letter and Two Portraits.' *ANQ: A Quarterly Journal of Short Articles, Notes, and Reviews*, NS 5/2–3 (April-July 1992), 128–30.

—— ' "Enough Survives": The Earl of Surrey and European Court Culture.' *History Today*, 41 (June 1991), 48–54.

—— *Henry Howard, Earl of Surrey*. Boston, 1986.

—— 'Mutations of "Pietas Litterata," ' in *Renaissance Papers 1976*, ed. Dennis G. Donovan and Leigh Deneef. Durham, NC, 1977.

—— 'Spenser's Georgics.' *English Literary Renaissance*, 10 (1980), 202–38.

—— 'Surrey's Wyatt: Autumn 1542 and the New Poet' in *Rethinking the Henrician Era*, ed. Peter Herman. Chicago and Urbana, 1994.

—— 'Surrey's Psalms in the Tower', in *Sacred and Profane: Secular and Devotional Interplay in Early Modern British Literature*, ed. Helen Wilcox, Richard Todd, and Alasdair MacDonald. Amsterdam, 1995, 142–50.

SHAWCROSS, JOHN. 'Milton and Blank Verse Precedents.' *ANQ: A Quarterly Journal of Short Articles, Notes, and Reviews*, NS 3/4 (Oct. 1990), 160–3.

SHELBY, L. R. *John Rogers: Tudor Military Engineer*. Oxford, 1967.

SHER, STEVEN PAUL. 'Literature and Music', in *Interrelations of Literature*, ed. Jean-Pierre Barricelli and Joseph Gibaldi. New York, 1982.

SIEVEKING, A. FORBES. 'Games', in *Shakespeare's England: An Account of the Life & Manners of his Age*. Oxford, 1916.

SKINNER, QUENTIN. *The Foundations of Modern Political Thought*. 2 vols. Cambridge, 1978.

SLAVIN, A. J. *Politics and Profit: A Study of Sir Ralph Sadler 1507–1547*. Cambridge, 1966.

SLAVITT, DAVID R. *Virgil*. New Haven and London, 1991.

SMITH, LACEY BALDWIN. 'English Treason Trials and Confessions in the Sixteenth Century'. in *Treason in Tudor England: Politics and Paranoia*. Princeton, 1986.

—— *Henry VIII: The Mask of Royalty*. London, 1971.

SOUTHALL, R. *The Courtly Maker: An Essay on the Poetry of Wyatt and his Contemporaries*. Oxford, 1964.

—— 'The Devonshire Manuscript Collection of Early Tudor Poetry, 1532–1541.' *Review of English Studies*, NS 15 (1964), 142–50.

—— 'Mary Fitzroy and "O Happy Dames" in the Devonshire Manuscript', *Review of English Studies*, 45 (1994), 313.

SOUTHWORTH, JAMES G. *The Prosody of Chaucer and His Followers: Supplementary Chapters to* 'Verses of Cadence.' 1962; reprint, Westport, Conn., 1978.

SPEARING, A. C. *Medieval to Renaissance in English Poetry*. Cambridge, 1985.

SPICER, JOANEATH. 'The Renaissance Elbow', in *The Cultural History of Gesture*, ed. Jan Bremmer and Herman Roodenburg. Ithaca, NY, 1991.

SPIEGEL, GABRIELLE M. 'Genealogy: Form and Function in Medieval Historical Narrative.' *History and Theory*, 22 (1983), 45–53.

STARKEY, DAVID. 'After the "Revolution" ' and 'Court and Government', in *Revolution Reassessed: Revisions in the History of the Tudor Government and Administrations*, eds. Christopher Coleman and David Starkey. Oxford, 1986.

—— 'The Court: Castiglione's Ideal and Tudor Reality'. *Journal of the Warburg and Courtauld Institutes* 45 (1982) 232–239.

—— 'Preface', in *The English Court: From the Wars of the Roses to the Civil War*, ed. David Starkey. London and New York, 1987.

—— 'Introduction', in *Henry VIII: A European Court in England*, ed. David Starkey. London, 1991.

—— 'Preface' and 'Intimacy and Innovation: The Rise of the Privy Chamber, 1485–1547'. *The English Court: From the Wars of the Roses to the Civil War*. London, 1987.

—— *The Reign of Henry VIII: Personalities and Politics*. London, 1985.

—— 'Representation through Intimacy'. *Symbols and Sentiments*, ed. Ioan Lewis. London, 1977.

—— 'Rivals in Power, The Tudors and the Nobility'. in *Rivals in Power: Lives and Letters of the Great Tudor Dynasties*, ed. David Starkey. London, 1990.

STENTON, F. M. *Anglo-Saxon England*. Oxford, 1971.

STEVENS, JOHN. *Music and Poetry in the Early Tudor Court*. Lincoln, Neb., 1961.

—— 'The "Music" of the Lyric: Machaut, Deschamps, Chaucer', in *Medieval and Pseudo-Medieval Literature*, ed. Piero Boitani and Anna Torti. Cambridge, 1984.

STEWART, ALAN. *Close Readers: Humanism and Sodomy in Early Modern England*. Princeton, 1997.

STONE, LAWRENCE. *The Crisis of the Aristocracy, 1558–1641*. Oxford, 1965.

—— *Families and Fortune: Studies in Aristocratic Finance in the Sixteenth and Seventeenth Centuries*. Oxford, 1973.

STONE, LAWRENCE, and COLVIN, HOWARD. 'The Howard Tombs at Framlingham, Suffolk.' *Archaeological Journal*, 82 (1965), 159–71.

STRONG, ROY. 'Edward VI and the Pope.' *Journal of the Warburg and Courtauld Institute*, 23 (1960) 311–13.

—— *The English Icon*. New York, 1969.

—— *The English Renaissance Miniature*. London, 1984.

—— *Holbein and Henry VIII*. London, 1967.

—— 'Some Early Portraits at Arundel Castle.' *Connoisseur*, 12 (1978), 198–200.

TAVARD, GEORGE HENRI. *Holy Writ or Holy Church: The Crisis of the Protestant Reformation*. New York, 1959.

TERVARENT, GUY DE. *Attributs et symboles dans l'art profane 1450–1600*. Geneva, 1958.

THOMPSON, W. D. J. CARGIL. *The Political Thought of Martin Luther*. Brighton, 1984.

THOMSON, PATRICIA. 'Wyatt and Surrey'. in *English Poetry and Prose, 1540 to 1674*, ed. Christopher Ricks. London, 1975.

THURLEY, SIMON. *The Royal Palaces of Tudor England: Architecture and Court Life 1460–1547*. New Haven and London, 1993.

TOBIN, PATRICIA DRECHSEL. *Time and the Novel*. Princeton, 1978.

TROMLY, FREDERIC B. 'Surrey's Fidelity to Wyatt in "Wyatt Resteth Here" '. *Studies in Philology*, 77 (Fall 1980), 4.

TRUEMAN, C. *Luther's Legacy: Salvation and English Reformers 1525–1556*. Oxford, 1994.

TUCKER, MELVILLE J. *The Life of Thomas Howard, 1443–1525*. London, 1964.

—— 'California MS AC 523, Formerly Philipps MS 3841', *Notes and Queries*, 11 (Oct. 1964), 375–6.

TUDOR-CRAIG, PAMELA. 'Henry VIII and King David'. in *Early Tudor England: Proceedings of the 1987 Harlaxton Symposium*, ed. Daniel Williams. Woodbridge, 1989.

—— *Richard III*. Ipswich, 1977.

TYTLER, PATRICK F. *England Under the Reigns of Edward VI and Mary*. London, 1839.

VAUGHAN, RICHARD. *Charles the Bold: The Last Valois Duke of Burgundy*. London, 1973.

VIRGOE, ROGER. 'The Recovery of the Howards in East Anglia 1485–1529', in *Wealth and Power in Tudor England: Essays Presented to S. T. Bindhoff*, ed. E. W. Ives, R. J. Knecht, and J. J. Scarisbrick. London, 1978.

VOKES, SUSAN. 'The Early Career of Thomas, Lord Howard, Earl of Surrey and Third Duke of Norfolk, 1474–1525.' Ph.D. Thesis, University of Hull, 1988.

WADDINGTON, RAYMOND B. 'The Bisexual Portrait of Francis I: Fontainebleau, Castiglione, and the Tone of Courtly Mythology', in *Playing With Gender: A Renaissance Pursuit*, ed. Jean R. Brink, Maryanne C. Horowitz, and Allison P. Coudert. Urbana and Chicago, 1991.

WAGNER, A. R. *Heralds and Heraldry in the Middle Ages: An Inquiry into the Growth of the Armorial Functions of Heralds*. London, 1956.

WALKER, GREG. *John Skelton and the Politics of the 1520s*. Cambridge and New York, 1988.

—— *Persuasive Fictions: Faction, Literature and Political Culture in the Reign of Henry VIII*. Aldershot, 1996.

—— *Plays of Persuasion: Drama and Politics*. New York and Cambridge, 1991.

WALL, WENDY. *The Imprint of Gender: Authorship and Publication in the English Renaissance*. Ithaca, 1993.

WALZER, MICHAEL. *The Revolution of the Saints: A Study in the Origins of Radical Politics*. Cambridge, Mass., 1965.

WARNICKE, RETHA M. *The Rise and Fall of Anne Boleyn: Family Politics and the Court of Henry VIII*. Cambridge, 1989.

WARTON, THOMAS. *The History of English Poetry, from the Close of the Eleventh to the Commencement of the Eighteenth Century*. London, 1824.

WATERHOUSE, ELLIS. *Painting in Britain 1530 to 1790*. London, 1953.

WEBER, MAX. 'Social Psychology of the World Religions'. in *From Max Weber*, eds. H. H. Gerth and C. Wright Mills. New York, 1958.

—— *Theory of Social and Economic Organization*, trans. A. M. Henderson and Talcott Parsons. New York, 1947.

WEIGHTMAN, CHRISTINE. *Margaret of York: Duchess of Burgundy 1446–1503*. New York, 1989.

WEINBURG, BERNARD. *A History of Literary Criticism in the Italian Renaissance*. Chicago, 1961.

WHINNEY, MARGARET. *Sculpture in Britain, 1530–1830*. Baltimore, 1964.

WILLEN, DIANE. *John Russell, First Earl of Bedford: One of the King's Men*. Royal Historical Society Studies in History 32, London, 1981.

—— 'Women and Religion in Early Modern England', in *Women in Reformation and Counter-Reformation Europe: Public and Private Worlds*, ed. Serrin Marshall. Bloomington and Indianapolis, 1989.

WILLIAMS, NEVILLE. *Henry VIII and His Court*. New York, 1971.

—— *Thomas Howard, the Fourth Duke of Norfolk*. London, 1964.

WILSON, DEREK A. *A Tudor Tapestry: Men, Women, and Society in Reformation England*. Pittsburgh, 1972.

WIMSATT, JAMES I. *Chaucer and His French Contemporaries: Natural Music in 1400*. Toronto, 1991.

WIMSATT, W. K. and BEARDSLEY, MONROE C. 'The Concept of Meter: An Exercise in Abstraction'. *PMLA*, 74 (1959).

WIND, EDGAR. *Pagan Mysteries in the Renaissance*. New York, 1968.

WOLFF, MAX J. 'Die Theorie der Italienischen Tragödie im 16 Jahrhundert.' *Archiv*, 66 (1912), 351–68.

WOLFFE, B. P. 'Henry VII's Land Revenues and Chamber Finance.' *English Historical Review*, 79 (1964), 225–54.

WOODS, SUZANNE. *Natural Emphasis: English Versification from Chaucer to Dryden*. San Marino, Cal., 1985.

WRIGHT, GEORGE. *Shakespeare's Metrical Art*. Berkeley, 1988.

—— 'Wyatt's Decasyllabic Line.' *Studies in Philology* 82/2 (Spring 1985), 129–59.

YATES, FRANCES A. *The French Academies in the 16th Century*. London, 1947.

YOUINGS, JOYCE. *The Dissolution of the Monasteries*. London, 1971.

YOUMANS, GILBERT. 'Iambic Pentametre: Statistics or Generative Grammar?' *Language and Style*, 19/4 (1986), 388–403.

ZAGORIN, PEREZ. 'Sir Thomas Wyatt and the Court of Henry VIII: The Courtier's Ambivalence', *Journal of Medieval and Renaissance Studies* 23 (1993), 113–41.

ZERNER, HENRI. *The School of Fontainebleau: Etchings and Engravings*. London, 1969.

ZIM, RIVKA. *English Metrical Psalms: Poetry as Praise and Prayer 1535–1601*. Cambridge, 1987.

ZITNER, S. P. 'Truth and Mourning in a Sonnet by Surrey.' *English Literary History*, 50 (Fall 1983), 509–29.

Index